Integrated Advertising, Promotion, and Marketing Communications

Canadian Edition

Integrated Advertising, Promotion, and Marketing Communications
Canadian Edition

Kenneth E. Clow
University of Louisiana at Monroe

Donald Baack
Pittsburg State University

John Peloza
Simon Fraser University

PEARSON

Toronto

Vice-President, Editorial Director: Gary Bennett
Editor-in-Chief: Nicole Lukach
Acquisitions Editor: Nick Durie
Marketing Manager: Leigh-Anne Graham
Developmental Editor: Catherine Belshaw
Project Manager: Ioana Gagea
Manufacturing Manager: Susan Johnson
Production Editor: Katie Wilbur, Element-Thomson North America
Copy Editor: Nancy Carroll
Proofreader: Suzanne Needs, Strong Finish
Compositor: Element-Thomson North America
Photo and Permissions Researcher: Terri Rothman
Art Director: Julia Hall
Interior and Cover Designer: Miguel Acevedo

Library and Archives Canada Cataloguing in Publication

Clow, Kenneth E.
    Integrated advertising, promotion, and marketing communications / Kenneth E. Clow, Donald Baack, John Peloza.—1st Canadian ed.

Includes index.
ISBN 978-0-13-802317-1
    1. Communication in marketing.   2. Advertising.   I. Baack, Donald   II. Peloza, John   III. Title.

HF5415.123.C56 2012   658.8'02   C2011-906025-6

ISBN 978-0-13-802317-1

To my sons, Dallas, Wes, Tim, and Roy, who provided encouragement, and especially to my wife, Susan, whose sacrifice and love made this textbook possible.

—Kenneth E. Clow

I would like to dedicate my efforts and contributions to the book to my wife, Pam; children, Jessica, Daniel, and David; and grandchildren, Danielle, Rile, Andy, Emilee, Jason, Damon, and Tatum.

—Donald Baack

To my parents, for teaching me to love learning; to my children, who give me the reason to pass it on; and to Elinor, who supports me always.

—John Peloza

Brief Contents

Contents

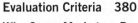

Preface

Marketing communications are an integral, and often the most visible, component of marketing. If you are a marketing major, understanding how companies can effectively communicate with customers and other stakeholders is the foundation you will need in order to develop effective marketing initiatives. This textbook will help you succeed in your marketing career.

If you are not a marketing major, consider all of the marketing communications around you. Any organization you work for will be involved in marketing its products or services. It is important to understand how the communications component of marketing is developed and why. Not only will this knowledge provide you with a better understanding of those involved in marketing in the organization where you will work, it will also provide you with better information to function as a consumer.

This textbook was created, in part, to help students like you understand the importance of integrated marketing communications (IMC), how they are produced and transmitted. The scope of the book is broad to encompass the many facets of marketing communications that organizations use to create dialogue with stakeholders. This includes not only traditional forms of advertising such as television and sales promotions (for example, contests), but also the incorporation of the elements of marketing communications into the Internet. Marketing communications today can be difficult to pin down to any one approach. Think of a television ad that encourages consumers to take part in a contest on Facebook and is supported by promotions at local retail stores. Most campaigns include a range of elements, each with its own role to play. This book takes a broad approach to help you understand how, when, and why each of these elements are an important part of an overall marketing communications initiative.

NEW TO THE CANADIAN EDITION

With any Canadian edition, one of the most obvious changes is the focus on Canadian brands to serve as examples for the concepts in a book. But there is more to being Canadian than just substituting Tim Hortons in place of Dunkin Donuts, eh? This book has been redesigned from the ground up for Canadian students. These changes include:

- **Industry Profiles** Each chapter opens with a profile featuring people working in marketing communications across Canada. These allow students to get a "flavour" for the industry and an idea of where they might fit in when embarking on their own careers. Importantly, these profiles are not just of people working in the major

centres in Canada known for marketing communications. They feature people in a range of cities across the country and working on a wide variety of marketing challenges, including small and large organizations, consumer and business audiences, and for-profit and not-for-profit organizations, just to name a few. The profiles include the following marketing communications employees:

- Kimberly Jang, Account Coordinator, Identica (a division of Cossette)
- Sushant Trivedi, Assistant Brand Manager, Gillette (Procter & Gamble)
- Erin Leigh, Client Services Coordinator, Impact Communications
- Marc Belcourt, Brand Communications Manager, BMW Canada
- Brent Mykyte, Creative Lead, City of Calgary
- Lisagh King, Director of Creative Services, McKim Cringan George
- Carmen Hunt, Media Director, TBWA
- Brigitte St-Germain, Director of Corporate Relations, Canadian Red Cross, Quebec Division
- Roman Hatashita, Founder and President, Hatashita International
- Paul Joliat, Vice President, Lang Marketing Network
- Nicole Armstrong, Associate Planner, Critical Mass
- Anthea Rowe, Communications Manager, Network for Business Sustainability
- Anita Kapadia, Marketing Manager, ResponseTek

- **IMC in Practice** The TELUS brand is featured throughout this book as an ongoing example. It appears in every chapter and highlights how each component of marketing communications—and indeed each chapter of this book—applies to one overall objective for a major Canadian brand. This example enables students to see how the concepts in each chapter are applied in the same context and the same organization, which makes the overall picture much clearer. These examples serve as a template for students to create their own marketing communications plan.

- **Fully integrated approach to IMC** The organization of the text is truly an integrated marketing communications approach, with no one element of IMC taking a central role. This better reflects the Canadian marketing communications landscape, where big-budget television campaigns are less common and marketers often rely on more innovative and local initiatives, such as retail sales promotions, digital marketing online, or direct marketing. The overall design of the book follows the general communication model behind all marketing communications: development of the message (objectives/strategy), followed by the coding of the message (creative development), delivery of the message through various media, and finally the feedback that comes from either measuring marketing objectives or the legal and ethical environment in which marketing communications are evaluated.

- **An equal blend of theory and practice** Students often lament that textbooks are too theory-rich and lack the real-world application they feel they will need when they go into the workforce. Yet theory is needed to make sense of the marketing communications world and to help students become managers who will be able to understand and manage marketing communications effectively. The "On the Job" feature in many chapters, for example, provides students with an application of the material in a very tangible, applied manner. This textbook seeks to create a happy medium between those that focus too heavily on marketing communications theory and those that focus more on examples without the theoretical underpinning needed to grasp and explain the concepts.

- **Up-to-date Canadian content** The content has been updated to reflect the Canadian environment that most Canadian students will work in when they graduate. Chapter 12, for example, which examines the regulatory landscape, covers the Canadian regulatory context exclusively. Similarly, material throughout all the chapters has been updated to reflect state of the art information in areas such as digital marketing. This not only reflects the specific interests of Canadian students, but also reflects an important trend of more marketing communications investment being directed to online environments, such as Facebook.

- **Current Canadian and global examples** The examples used to illustrate the concepts in this book are largely Canadian. The use of familiar local brands will help students understand how the concepts come alive in the marketplace. However, where it makes sense, global brands have been used to illustrate concepts. This mix of both local and global brands recognizes the media landscape in which students live. They are exposed not only to marketing communications from their local Canadian brands but also to messages from global firms such as Pepsi, Procter & Gamble, Kraft, and Coca-Cola, just to name a few. Canada is a country that competes in a global market, and the inclusion of these brands reflects the environment in which students—and indeed all Canadians—live.

INTEGRATED LEARNING PACKAGE

This first Canadian edition features a number of elements that are designed to help students get the most out of the content in each and every chapter.

- **Industry Profiles** Anybody who has spent a semester with students knows that they perk up when they listen to guest speakers or otherwise have exposure to people they feel can teach the "real world." That's why each chapter begins with a profile of someone working in the industry, with a focus on matching the industry professional with the chapter content. These profiles include the broad range of marketing communications professions students might enter. Importantly, the content of the profiles includes advice for students who seek to work in marketing communications, along with guidance for how to succeed in the workplace once they get there.

- **On the Job boxed feature** The "On the Job" feature found in many chapters provides students with an application of the material in a very tangible, applied manner. This feature supplies students with practical information about the industry that they can take with them into the workplace.

- **Cross-Cultural Discussions** Canada is a diverse country. And Canadian brands compete not only within Canada, but also in countries around the world. In some cases, students will work for foreign brands and be tasked with localizing them for a Canadian market. This feature at the end of each chapter explores the special challenges associated with communicating across cultures. These include a discussion of each unique area of Canada, the importance of cultural sensitivity to differences within the Canadian market, and how the Canadian market differs from other markets around the world.

- **Critical Thinking Exercises embedded throughout the chapters** The best way to know that you have truly learned a concept or theory is to apply it to a different situation. These critical thinking exercises require students to apply what they have learned in the chapter to a wide array of marketing situations.

- **Review Questions** To better grasp the materials in the text, the end-of-chapter materials are a must. They include a variety of exercises designed to help students comprehend and apply the chapter concepts. These questions are designed not only to review the chapter materials, but also to challenge and encourage students to dig deeper.

- **Integrated Learning Exercises** These exercises rely heavily on students' ability to research firms, industries, or other aspects of the marketing communications landscape in order to apply the concepts in the book. For example, in Chapter 4 the questions range from asking students to visit the *Marketing Magazine* website to investigate current campaigns in the market, to research how Canada Post can help marketers target consumers, and to search for campaigns that may have audiences beyond consumers. These exercises will encourage students to actively monitor the Canadian marketing communications landscape as well as fuel in-class discussions.

- **Creative Corner Exercises** The creative corner exercise is designed to accomplish three things. First, it allows students the ability to exercise their creative abilities. Most students come to marketing communications with the false assumption that it is largely about coming up with creative ideas for campaigns. These exercises allow students to feel like they are able to include creativity with the other material in most IMC courses that examine strategies and project management. The second way these exercises are useful is that they provide opportunities to let students see just how difficult it is to come up with great creative, especially without a focused creative brief. Third, and similar to the second point, these exercises allow students to gain empathy for the creative process and learn how they can add value to that process.

- **Ethics in Action** While Chapter 12 specifically examines the ethical landscape for marketing communications, many argue that an examination of ethics is best done when integrated into specific discussions rather than presented as a standalone topic. To facilitate both approaches, each chapter features an "Ethics in Action" section that provides a short example to illustrate an ethical issue specific to the chapter content. This gives instructors the freedom to introduce ethics throughout the course or as a standalone topic. It also enables students to consider issues on their own and consider how their own morals may impact on their perception of the material.

- **Case Study** One case is provided at the end of each chapter. These cases were written to help students learn by providing plausible scenarios that require thought and a review of chapter materials. The cases are designed to be detailed enough to allow for a strong examination of at least one issue from the relevant chapter, but short enough that they are focused and can be analyzed within the scope of a classroom discussion or as assigned work outside of class.

COMPANION WEBSITE

By visiting **www.pearsoncanada.ca/clow,** you can take online quizzes to help you determine whether you understand the key concepts in the chapters. You can also link to an eText and access the Building an IMC Campaign Workbook.

INSTRUCTOR RESOURCES

The following instructor supplements are available for downloading from a password-protected section of Pearson Education Canada's online catalogue (**www.pearsoned.ca/ highered**). Navigate to your book's catalogue page to view a list of those supplements that are available. See your local sales representative for details and access.

Instructor's Manual

The *Instructor's Manual* includes a chapter overview, chapter objectives, a detailed chapter outline that includes teaching tips, weblinks, and suggested answers to the Critical Thinking Exercises. The *Instructor's Manual* also comes with support for end-of-chapter material and bonus Case Studies.

Test Item File

Available in Microsoft Word format, this test bank includes more than 1500 questions. Questions range from multiple choice and true/false to short-answer and application. All questions are coded by level of difficulty and are linked to the textbook's learning objectives. These questions are also available in MyTest format.

MyTest

MyTest from Pearson Education Canada is a powerful assessment generation program that helps instructors easily create and print quizzes, tests, and exams, as well as homework or practice handouts. Questions and tests can all be authored online, allowing instructors ultimate flexibility and the ability to efficiently manage assessments at any time, from anywhere. MyTest for the first Canadian edition of *Integrated Advertising, Promotion, and Marketing Communications* includes more than 1,500 multiple-choice, true/false, and short answer questions. These questions are also available in Microsoft Word format on the Instructor's Resource Centre.

PowerPoint Presentation

The PowerPoint Presentation includes outlines and key points from each chapter. These slides provide instructors with visual talking points designed to engage students and stimulate classroom discussion. These slides were designed for instructors who like to customize their PowerPoint presentations using their own materials or the image library featured on the Instructor's Resource Centre.

Digital Image Library

The Image Library consists of many of the figures and exhibits featured in the text. These are ideal for PowerPoint customization.

Study on the Go

At the end of each chapter, you will find a unique QR code providing access to Study on the Go, an unprecedented mobile integration between text and online content. Students link to Pearson's unique Study on the Go content directly from their smartphones, allowing them to study whenever and wherever they wish! Go to one of the sites below to see how you can download an app to your smartphone for free. Once the app is installed, your phone will scan the code and link to a website containing Pearson's Study on the Go content, including the popular study tools Glossary Flashcards, Audio Summaries, and Quizzes, which can be accessed anytime.

ScanLife
http://get.scanlife.com/

NeoReader
http://get.neoreader.com/

QuickMark
http://www.quickmark.com.tw/

CourseSmart

CourseSmart is a new way for instructors and students to access textbooks online anytime from anywhere. With thousands of titles across hundreds of courses, CourseSmart helps instructors choose the best textbook for their class and give their students a new option for buying the assigned textbook as a lower cost eTextbook. For more information visit **www.coursesmart.com**.

Technology Specialists

Pearson's Technology Specialists work with faculty and campus course designers to ensure that Pearson technology products, assessment tools, and online course materials are tailored to meet your specific needs. This highly qualified team is dedicated to helping schools take full advantage of a wide range of educational resources, by assisting in the integration of a variety of instructional materials and media formats. Your local Pearson Education sales representative can provide you with more details on this service program.

Pearson Custom Library

For enrolments of at least 25 students, you can create your own textbook by choosing the chapters that best suit your own course needs. To begin building your custom text, visit **www.pearsoncustomlibrary.com**. You may also work with a dedicated Pearson Custom editor to create your ideal text—publishing your own original content or mixing and matching Pearson content. Contact your local Pearson Representative to get started.

ACKNOWLEDGMENTS

I would like to thank the following individuals who assisted in the development of the Canadian edition through their careful and thoughtful reviews:

Denton Anthony, St. Francis Xavier University

Brad Davis, Wilfrid Laurier University

Mary S. Dellar, McGill University

Sameer Deshpande, University of Lethbridge

Linda Clara Jay, North Island College

Stephanie Koonar, Langara College

Monica LaBarge, Queen's University

Luc Lagrandeur, Laurentian University

Ed J. McHugh, Nova Scotia Community College/Saint Mary's University

Judith Nash, Southern Alberta Institute of Technology

Robert J. Palmer, Bishop's University

Robin Ritchie, Carleton University

Suzanne Ross, Humber College

Shankar Seetharam, Centennial College

Harold J. Simpkins, Concordia University

I would like to thank the many individuals (too numerous to list here) who helped with this textbook. I appreciate the time and energy of everyone featured in the industry profiles that open each chapter. Exposure to industry experience and the "real" world is typically one of the most valuable aspects of any marketing communications course, and your contribution adds real value. I also want to thank Kate Baillie and her team at TELUS for agreeing to be part of this textbook. Their example illustrates the application of the content of each individual chapter and helps us understand how all the chapters contribute to one unified IMC perspective.

On a personal note, I would like to thank Nick Durie, Acquisitions Editor, who signed me for this first Canadian edition. And a big thank you to Catherine Belshaw, Developmental Editor, for countless hours of guidance, review, and support. I would also like to thank the entire Pearson Canada production group and the team of individuals who made this happen including: Terri Rothman, Ioana Gagea, Ashley Patterson, Miguel Acevedo, and Julia Hall.

Introduction

IMC COMPONENTS AND THE DESIGN OF THIS BOOK

This book provides insight that will allow aspiring marketing communications professionals to develop and deliver successful and integrated marketing campaigns. In order to accomplish this, the book is organized around the four major components of communications: Message Development, Message Design, Message Delivery, and Feedback. Each of these sections are discussed below and summarized in the figure below.

Part 1: Message Development

Part 1 builds the foundation for an IMC program. In Chapter 1, you will read about the players in the marketing communications industry and how the process is managed. Chapter 2 further describes the corporate image and brand management elements and integrates the IMC plan into the overall corporate strategy. An outline for developing an IMC plan is also presented.

Chapter 3 describes buyer behaviours. The steps of the consumer purchasing process explain how individuals make choices. Marketers identify the motives leading to purchases and factors affecting those purchase decisions. Then, the IMC program can be designed to influence these consumer choices. Understanding how audiences make decisions, and how marketing communications can support that process, is essential.

Chapter 4 describes the promotions opportunity analysis element of an IMC program. This includes identifying all target audiences. In the context of the target audience, the objective-setting process is discussed, along with the budgeting process to fund marketing communications.

Part 2: Message Design

Part 2 is devoted to message design and the steps in which the audience insight and key message are turned into a tangible marketing communications message. Several theories, which are explored in Chapter 5, are available to help the creative team design advertisements. The various advertising appeals that can be used, including those oriented toward fear, humour, sex, music, and logic, are explained in the chapter.

Chapter 6 reveals the ingredients involved in creating effective message strategies. The messages are delivered via various executional frameworks, which offer diverse ways to construct the actual commercial or advertisement. Issues related to the development and production of marketing communications are also discussed.

Part 3: Message Delivery

Part 3 contains analyses of a range of options available to marketers to place their messages in front of an audience.

Chapter 7 examines advertising media, such as television, radio, magazines, newspapers, and outdoor campaigns, and their respective advantages.

Direct marketing is discussed in Chapter 8. This includes the use of both direct-to-audience communications, such as mail, email, and telephone, and direct-response media designed to encourage customers to respond directly to a company.

Consumer and trade promotions are described in Chapter 9. These include marketing tools, such as coupons, contests, premiums, refunds, rebates, free samples, and price-off offers.

Chapter 10 focuses on public relations programs that connect with consumers in positive ways. These include emphasizing positive events and dealing with negative publicity.

Digital marketing (Chapter 11) includes a range of online tactics used by marketers, including social networks, blogs, banner ads, and websites.

Part 4: Message Feedback

Part 4 examines feedback the company receives from marketing communications plans. This feedback should be used to develop future campaigns. First, marketers must ensure that they are compliant with regulatory frameworks and ethical norms in their markets. Each of these issues is discussed in Chapter 12.

Chapter 13, the final chapter, explains how to evaluate an integrated marketing program. Evaluations can begin prior to any promotional campaign and continue during the campaign to post-campaign evaluations. Fully integrated marketing requires a careful linkage between planning and evaluation processes; one cannot occur without the other.

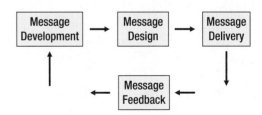

PART

1

Message Development

In this first of four parts to this book, we examine the development of message strategies for marketing communications. In Chapter 1, we examine the concept of integrated marketing communications (IMC) and the roles of various key players in the IMC industry. Chapter 2 includes an examination of brand positioning, as well as the planning template for IMC. Chapter 3 then examines how audiences receive and process marketing communications messages; insights which help marketers create more effective plans. Finally, Chapter 4 outlines the promotions opportunity analysis, which includes identification of audience segments, objectives, and budgets.

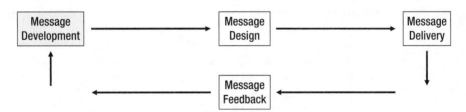

Step 1 in the Communications Process

1

CHAPTER OBJECTIVES

After reading this chapter, you should be able to answer the following questions:

- **What** role does communication play in marketing programs?
- **What** is the nature of the communication process?
- **How** should the communications model be applied to marketing issues?
- **What** isan integrated approach to marketing communications and **why** is it important?
- **Who** are the players in the marketing communications industry?
- **How** are marketing communications agencies selected?
- **How** does the concept of integrated marketing communications pertain to international operations?

INDUSTRY PROFILE
So You Want to Work in Marketing Communications?

Kimberly Jang, Account Coordinator, Identica (division of Cossette)
Vancouver, British Columbia

Ever since Kimberly was in grade 6 she knew she wanted to work in marketing communications. "We did a class exercise where we had to pretend to live the lives of different working people, and I was assigned the job of advertising professional. I took it as a sign," says Kimberly. "I always liked to be creative with drawing and painting, but when I got into high school I found that I also enjoyed taking a leadership role. I was always working to organize a sports team or serve on the student council. So the field of marketing communications seemed like a great way for me to merge those two interests into one career."

Kimberly's impression of the business was formed, in part, by popular culture through things like television and movies. "The impression most people have is that the process involves wearing flip flops and sitting around in brainstorm sessions. There is some of that, for sure. But when you start in the business most business school graduates like me go into an account coordinator job." This position involves working with people with various roles within the agency—*coordinating* the process—and often entails duties that do not live up to the stereotype.

"I spend lots of time using Excel," says Kimberly. "I do things like budget tracking, sending out billing, tracking agency revenues and timelines, and managing costs. One of the things that best prepared me for this work is the broad scope of business content in my undergraduate degree, courses like accounting and finance. Even the material we covered in HR classes is valuable because a big part of my job is working with other people on the team and I need to be able figure out how to work with them effectively in order to do my job. Having a grasp of marketing is just the starting point."

Although Kimberly's background in business education has no doubt helped her in the account coordinator position, she also brou ght to the job some expertise in graphic design. "While I'm not a designer per se, I do understand some of

1

Integrated Marketing Communications

the basics behind the design principles that professional designers use, and even understand some of the software that they use. That helps me work with designers more effectively because I understand their abilities and limitations. I know why it might take 10 hours to get a project done, whereas someone without my background might think it can be done in 30 minutes. So that lets me be a better manager of the whole process because I have a better idea of what to expect."

The opportunity to work as part of a team is the best part of the job for Kimberly. "Marketing communications attracts lots of different people. I work with people from around the world, and with people who perform lots of specialized tasks. So no two days—or even two hours—are the same. During a single morning I can work with a designer or creative director to set in motion the design of a new campaign, work with a production manager to get some-

Kimberly Jang, Account Coordinator, Identica (division of Cossette)
Source: John Peloza

thing printed and shipped out to a client, talk to a different client about starting a new project, and maybe a researcher who has some new data on a campaign that is being tracked in the market."

Marketing communications agency professionals typically work on many different clients at the same time. So one day Kimberly might be working in the banking business and the next day reading research reports for a client in the high-tech business. But her favourite clients are those in the nonprofit category. "Probably my favourite campaign so far is one I worked on for the David Suzuki Foundation. I liked it because I was able to see how marketing communications can make a positive difference for our society. It is sometimes criticized for being a bad thing, but marketing communications can and does make a positive impact all around us."

Kimberly got her start with an internship at Identica prior to be being hired full time. "It's a common way for people to break into the business because it gives you the best opportunity to learn multiple aspects of the business from the ground up." But be careful, she says, because most internships are not paid positions. "Mine was a two-month internship that was on a volunteer basis. I was lucky to get hired at the end of it because not everyone does." On top of that, competition for these positions can be fierce. In Kimberly's case there were over 30 people invited to the information session that included only six positions. "That's about a 20 percent chance at getting a *volunteer* position. It's tough. But well worth it in the end."

OVERVIEW

The global marketplace consists of a complex set of competitors battling for customers in a rapidly changing environment. New companies are formed on a daily basis. Companies that once operated in highly defined product categories now face competitive threats from every direction. Google, for instance, is a company that rose to prominence in the Internet search category but subsequently entered a variety of new markets, including telecommunications and GPS. Companies are feeling the pressure from this turbulent environment. Competitors used to be defined as companies across town, or across the country. But now firms compete with firms based anywhere in the world.

At the same time, the ways in which companies can communicate messages have also grown. Gone is the era of three television networks that dominate marketing communications spending. Today, firms can employ a wide variety of tactics, from social media and highly fragmented television media to sophisticated data analysis techniques, in order to focus their message.

In the face of these sophisticated and cluttered market conditions, firms try to be heard. Competitive pressure has made it critical that marketers find messages that resonate with audiences. Cluttered and diverse communication channels have made it imperative that marketers deliver those messages in a clear voice. This chapter examines the processes and challenges faced by marketers in the communication process. It includes an examination of the marketing communications industry as well as processes and techniques used by marketers to communicate in today's cluttered and fragmented landscape. But first, we will examine the communication process and introduce the concept of integrated marketing communications as a means of overcoming some of the challenges faced by marketers.

COMMUNICATION AND IMC PROGRAMS

Communication can be defined as transmitting, receiving, and processing information. When a person, group, or organization attempts to transfer an idea or message, communication occurs when the receiver (another person or group) is able to comprehend the information. The model of communication shown in Figure 1.1 shows how communication takes place as the message that was sent reaches its destination in a form that is understood by the intended audience.[1]

Although this model of communication can be applied to virtually any form of communication, it is particularly useful for examining the challenges faced when developing marketing communications. Consider the challenge of a marketing manager at Audi who is looking to generate interest (and ideally, ultimately, purchases) of the R8 model. Using the communications model (Figure 1.1), the **sender**, or the company behind the message, is Audi. Inherent in the sender is the marketing strategy employed by the firm. Here, Audi chooses an aspirational message to create desire for the vehicle, and create an overall halo for the complete Audi line of vehicles.

Encoding the message is the second step. This step involves taking the central message from the marketing strategy and turning it into some form of communication (a television commercial, a banner ad, a billboard, etc.).

Messages travel to audiences through various **transmission devices**. This third stage of the marketing communications process occurs when a channel or medium delivers the message. The channel may be a television carrying an advertisement, a Sunday paper with a coupon placed in it, a letter to the purchasing agent of a company, or a blog on a company's website. This ad for Audi was delivered through a billboard.

Marketing communications from Audi are among the most successful of all automotive brands.

Source: Courtesy of Audi Canada/Lowe Roche Advertising.

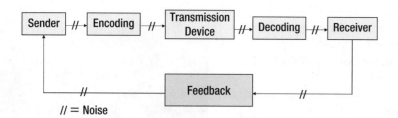

FIGURE 1.1
The Communication Process

Decoding occurs when the message reaches one or more of the receiver's senses. Consumers both hear and see television ads. Others consumers handle (touch) and read (see) a coupon offer. It is even possible to "smell" a message. A well-placed perfume sample might entice a buyer to purchase both the magazine containing the sample and the perfume being advertised. This process is obviously achieved more easily when it is placed in front of people who are in the market for a new vehicle, since they will naturally pay more attention than those who are not. Consider the Audi example in this section and then answer the following questions:

1. Would the advertisement dramatically attract your attention if you saw it on the street? Why?
2. What is the major message of the advertisement?
3. What makes the advertisement effective or ineffective?

It is possible that the same advertisement will be interpreted differently by different people. In other words, the message may not be received. Quality marketing communications occurs when customers (the **receivers**) decode or understand the message as it was intended by the sender. In the case of Audi, effective marketing communications depends on receivers getting the right message and responding in the desired fashion (i.e., shopping, buying, discussing the ad with their friends, etc.). This ad was very successful in generating buzz about the brand, and was crafted based on the insight that Audi drivers tend to be more concerned about the quality and engineering of the car than they are about using a vehicle to show off to other people.[2]

The final step of the communication process is **feedback**. It occurs when the sender of the marketing message receives feedback such as purchases, inquiries, questions, visits to the store, blogs, and website hits. Each action indicates that the message has reached the receiver and that the receiver is responding.

Throughout the entire model, marketing communications professionals must ensure that messages and feedback do not lose efficiency or effectiveness from noise. **Noise** is anything that distorts or disrupts a message. It can occur at any stage in the communication process, as shown in Figure 1.2. Examples of noise that affect television advertising are provided in Figure 1.2.

The most common form of noise affecting marketing communications is **clutter**. Modern consumers are exposed to hundreds of marketing messages each day. Most are tuned out. Clutter includes:

- Dozens of commercials per half-hour of television and radio programs
- Websites packed with banner ads and pop-ups
- A Sunday newspaper jammed with advertising supplements
- Multiple billboards on a city block
- The inside of a bus or subway car lined with ads

Communications from The Bay can result in feedback in a number of forms, including retail store visits, website visits, attitude change, or intention to shop.

Source: Copyright Hudson's Bay Company, used with their permission.

- The viewer is texting during a television commercial.
- The reader is having a conversation while reading a paper on a bus.
- An advertisement is placed next to an ad by a competitor.
- The encoding used humour that the audience does not find funny.
- The spokesperson in the ad overpowers the message.

Critical Thinking Exercise

The communications model presented in Figure 1.1 only works when the proper message is selected, the coding of the message is done properly, and it is delivered through the appropriate transmission devices. But in order to do this, marketers must understand how the audience will decode the messages. One of the most common differences among audiences, which impacts how they decode messages, is whether they are a consumer audience or a business audience. Suppose you are the marketing director for a company that makes office furniture. You sell to consumers who want a space in their homes to be productive, and you also sell to companies that want to furnish offices for their employees. How would your key messages differ for each audience? How would your coding and transmission devices be different for each audience?

In order to ensure that the right message is created and placed before the right audience at the right time, we use the concept of integrated marketing communications (IMC).

Integrated Marketing Communications

While examining the IMC concept, it is useful to consider the traditional framework of marketing. **The marketing mix** is the starting point. As shown in Figure 1.3, promotion is one of the four components of the mix. It is essential that the elements within the marketing communications component of the marketing mix work in concert with the other elements of the plan. For example, messages should be targeted to locations where distribution is established, and if a premium pricing strategy is pursued, this can be reinforced in marketing communications through placement in upscale media outlets and messages that reinforce quality and prestige over price.

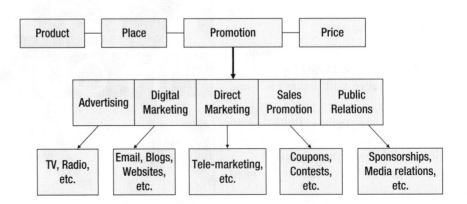

Although IMC programs may be described in several ways, the consensus is to define them as follows: **Integrated marketing communications (IMC)** is the coordination and integration of all marketing communications tools, avenues, and sources within a company into a seamless program that maximizes the impact on customers and other stakeholders at a minimal cost. This integration affects all of a firm's business-to-business, marketing channel, customer-focused, and internally directed communications.[3]

Two problems have typically plagued the execution of traditional marketing communications plans. The first was a focus on advertising as the core of any program, with additional activities such as promotion or direct marketing being developed as an "add on" to this core. In an IMC plan, each of the channels is assessed for its potential to deliver the message to the target audiences. This may mean that advertising plays a minimal role, while other elements, such as direct marketing or public relations, comprise the greater part of the plan.

The second problem was that the various pieces of marketing communications were often managed by different people who didn't work to one master plan. For example, the manager in charge of direct marketing did not effectively communicate with the person who was in charge of the television advertising or retail promotions. The result was messages that were unfocused, or in some cases even competed with each other. Before brokerage company Charles Schwab adopted an IMC perspective, they would have multiple direct marketing campaigns, each with its own message, running simultaneously.[4] It is conceivable that the consumer could get several different messages from the same company, all within the same week, with each saying something different. Through IMC planning, every piece of communication received by the audience is consistent on a single message. This includes more than just obvious consumer contact points, such as advertising or sales promotion. Tim Hortons integrates promotions onto the outside of every cup of coffee it serves, and even integrates the cups themselves into its most famous annual promotion. An IMC perspective includes an almost limitless number of contact points with the audience, with new ones emerging each year as technology opens up new means of communication.

Further, the data and insight developed through IMC campaigns is more likely to be shared with others and used in the development of future campaigns than would have been possible in traditional campaigns. For example, firms such as Dow Chemical, FedEx, and Hewlett-Packard take databases and use them to calculate and establish a customer value for each buyer. All customers are not equally valuable. Dow Chemical, FedEx, and Hewlett-Packard allocate sales and marketing communications resources to those customers with the greatest potential for return, based on calculations of customer values. This helps company leaders understand each customer's worth and treat each one individually, resulting in the highest possible return on investment for marketing expenditures.

THE RISE OF IMC

As discussed elsewhere in this chapter, marketing communications campaigns have not always been as integrated as those of today. The rise of the importance and widespread use of IMC can be attributed to a number of factors. See Figure 1.4.

Increased Accountability

Along with a general trend toward accountability in business, marketing communications must show its value to the firm. The push for accountability is being driven by chief executive officers (CEOs), chief financial officers (CFOs), and boards of directors who seek visible, measurable results from marketing

Campaigns now use multiple means of communicating with audiences, such as this print ad that includes a QR code which readers can use to access online material about the organization.

WE'VE GOT CANCER RUNNING SCARED

GENOMICS is pinpointing disease-causing DNA sequences in a single cell. Armed with new technology that spots cancer right at its source, we can now identify the disease early, so it can be treated faster. Soon, cancer will have no place left to hide.

Fighting the world's worst enemies. Find out how @ **WhyGenomics.ca**

OntarioGenomicsInstitute

FIGURE 1.4
Factors Contributing to the Growth of IMC

- ◆ Increased accountability
- ◆ Audience adoption of new media
- ◆ Information technology
- ◆ Increased competition

Source: Courtesy of vWrapz Inc. and 3M

Because of limited budgets, marketing communications investment by small businesses must be highly accountable and show clear results.

expenditures. According to Martyn Straw, chief strategy officer of the advertising agency BBDO Worldwide, corporate executives and business owners are tired of "funneling cash into TV commercials and glossy ads" that keep increasing in cost and seem to do less and less. As a result, a brand such as Pepsi is less likely to rely on 30-second television spots. Instead, alternative communication venues are combined with special events where names, profiles, and addresses of prospective Pepsi drinkers can be collected and tracked. Straw believes that marketing has gone from being a cost or expense to an investment. Marketing communications dollars must add value to generate new sales and higher profits.[5] An integrated perspective means that each investment in marketing communications is increasingly expected to perform a specific function. Further, by coordinating all of the marketing communications under one overall plan, there is less chance of duplication between different campaigns. Indeed, there are often synergies that are discovered when a campaign is planned and purchased as one initiative.

Audience Adoption of New Media

Technology has spawned literally millions of new media that have been enthusiastically embraced by consumers; for example, top YouTube videos receive millions of views within days of going viral. New handheld technologies such as iPhones and text-messaging systems have created an entirely new landscape and, in some cases, a new language. As a result, companies are adding expenditures, or shifting them from more traditional media to these increasingly popular outlets. For many products, including Neutrogena, Aveeno, and the flagship baby products company, Johnson & Johnson shifted approximately 20 percent of its marketing budget to non-traditional media, including social media outlets like Facebook and other communications tools like Twitter.[6]

This shift will continue to accelerate as more and more consumers who have grown up with these media enter the market. Younger consumers are more likely to engage in technologically based interactions with friends around the world. The challenge becomes finding ways to reach consumers who are increasingly sophisticated at blocking out traditional advertising messages but who can be reached through new technologies. Current thinking in marketing suggests that you cannot assume that the best approach is to capture someone's attention. Instead, marketing communications now means finding ways to engage with and interact with consumers and take advantage of the strengths of these new media.

Connect Hearing integrated a website into a national campaign that let consumers ask questions from audiology experts.

Source: Courtesy of Connect Hearing.

AskMJ

MJ DeSousa answers your questions on hearing

Meet MJ DeSousa

MJ DeSousa is Director of Professional Practice at Connect Hearing. She leads our team of hearing professionals working across the country.

Use the interactive video at right and get answers to your questions about hearing from MJ herself!

Visit the Ask MJ video library

Audiologist MJ DeSousa Answers Your Hearing Questions
Click on one of the questions in the video screen to play MJ's answer.

Your most recent questions and answers

Your question	MJ's answer	Your question	MJ's answer

Connect Hearing
YOUR HEARING PROFESSIONALS

Information Technology

Technology enables instant communications among business executives, employees, channel

Critical Thinking Exercise

Brand parity is a major problem for most marketers. Think of a product category where you consider brand parity to exist. Now, put yourself in the position of the marketing communications manager for one of those brands. What would you do differently in your marketing communications to help overcome the problem of brand parity?

members, and others around the world. It also creates opportunities for marketing communications. For example, in the past, predictions of consumer purchasing behaviours were based on the results of test markets, attitudinal research, and intention-to-buy surveys. Although these are excellent means of obtaining information about consumers, they are slow, costly, and potentially unreliable.

Today, purchase-behaviour predictions are more precise due to the development of the UPC (universal product code) bar-code system. The technology was originally used to manage inventories. Scanning every sale meant retailers were better able to develop efficient inventory-control systems.

At the same time, UPC codes combined with other technology programs allow large amounts of data and information about customers to be gathered. Advanced statistical software helps company leaders analyze these data. Connections between financial (e.g., credit card and banking) and business firms make it possible to collect purchasing data. This demographic and psychographic information about consumers can be correlated with the items they buy, as well as with information on when and where they make purchases. Consequently, marketers can determine who is buying a company's products and the best communications channels to reach them.

Increased Competition

Information technology and communications advances have dramatically changed the marketplace in other ways. Consumers can purchase goods and services from anywhere in the world. Competition no longer comes from the company just down the street—it can come from a firm 16,000 kilometres away that can supply a product faster and cheaper. Consumers want quality, but they also want a low price.

In this competitive environment, tangible differences between brands have become smaller over time. When a firm introduces a new innovation, it can be copied in days. Many competing brands in the market have nearly identical benefits. When consumers believe that most brands offer the same set of attributes, the result is **brand parity**. From the consumer's perspective, this means that shoppers will purchase from a *group* of accepted brands rather than one specific brand. When brand parity is present, quality is often not a major concern because consumers believe that only minor quality differences exist. Consumers routinely view quality levels of products as being nearly equal. As a result, they often base purchase decisions on other criteria, such as price, availability, or a specific promotional deal. The net effect is that brand loyalty has experienced a steady decline.[7] Consequently, integrated marketing communications becomes extremely important because purchase decisions are often made with the help of specific, targeted promotions or tailored messages that are based on customer behaviours and preferences, such as those found in many Facebook campaigns. Advertising alone, or advertising that is disconnected with other elements, such as sales promotion, are much less effective.

THE IMC INDUSTRY

The marketing communications industry in Canada employs tens of thousands of people, across a broad range of careers: from those who work in the planning of marketing objectives or creative development to those who develop the many vehicles used

FIGURE 1.5 The IMC Industry
Most marketers use a marketing communications agency to help them create and deliver messages to a target audience.

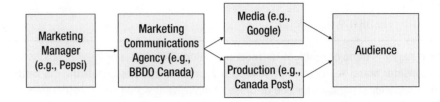

to deliver messages to audiences. Although most people can name hundreds of well-known brands in Canada, the names of many of the companies operating behind the scenes developing and delivering the marketing communications for those brands are unknown to them. This can create high anxiety for those wishing for a career in marketing communications. Before you can pursue a career in the industry, you must first understand the players in the industry and their roles. This section contains an overview of the IMC industry and, more importantly, the types of positions readers of this book can expect to fill.

Although not every marketing communications campaign is developed the same way, most follow a series of steps between the sender (typically a marketing manager) and receiver (the audience), as outlined in Figure 1.5. Through understanding the process and the players in the marketing communications industry you can better identify where you see yourself being successful in a career in marketing communications. You could find yourself working in many different roles for any of the industry players depicted here.

Marketing Managers

A marketing manager is a person who works directly for the company that will invest in the marketing communications. Marketing managers work for companies that we see every day, such as Tim Hortons, Labatt, United Way, BlackBerry, Bell, The Bay, RBC, and the Canadian Cancer Society. Some are large and some are small; some have consumer customers and some sell to businesses; some are for-profit and some are not-for-profit. Even governments are sources of marketing communications in Canada (in fact, the federal government is the single largest buyer of advertising media in the country). Despite the fact that all of these organizations are as diverse as Canada itself, the roles and responsibilities of the marketing managers working within them are relatively similar and include the following.

Setting Objectives

The first task of the marketing manager is to determine what role marketing communications can play within the broader context of the marketing plan. For example, if the marketing plan calls for increasing the market share of a firm by 15 percent over the next 12 months, how should marketing communications support that goal? Examples of potential objectives could be to generate specific levels of awareness within the population, or to drive a specific number of visitors to a website or retail store. The marketing manager must understand how marketing communications can create outcomes for the organization, and align those outcomes with the overall objectives.

Setting Budgets

Along with the objective, the marketing manager should be responsible for allocating a budget for the campaign. This may include negotiation with other managers within the firm to shift marketing dollars either toward or away from marketing communications relative to other activities (e.g., research and development, distribution capacity, etc.).

Coordinating Marketing Communications with Other Firm Activities

It is critical that the marketing communications campaign be executed in concert with the rest of the marketing functions performed elsewhere in the firm. For example, if the marketing communications plan calls for increased promotional activity in Ontario, it is important that the production and distribution functions are prepared to meet increased demand in that market.

Coordinating Agencies

Often the execution of marketing communications campaigns is done by other members of the same organization. More typically, the marketing manager hires external companies to develop or execute any number of elements of the marketing communications campaign. One of the most important decisions is whether to hire a marketing communications agency to perform this work or whether to do it in house.

Marketing Communications Agencies

There are a wide variety of marketing communications agencies in Canada. The largest are so-called **full-service agencies** that perform a broad range of marketing communications functions, such as brand development, creative development, advertising media, public relations, direct marketing, and so on. An example is Canada's largest marketing communications agency, Cossette. The company refers to its approach to IMC as Convergent Communications.™ By this they mean that they harness the specialized knowledge of people working in a range of marketing communications vehicles to deliver one overall objective. The company has offices across the country and offers services in virtually every area of marketing communications:

- Strategic Planning and Research
- Media Planning and Buying
- Search Engine Optimization
- Sales Promotion
- Direct Marketing
- Online/Interactive Marketing
- Website Design
- Public Relations
- Graphic Design

There are also co-called **niche agencies** that are defined by their strategy to specialize in one specific area of marketing communications. Agencies can specialize in one of three ways. The first way in which an agency can specialize is by communications tactic. For example, a company in Vancouver called PropStar works only in the area of product placement (**www.propstar.com**). Agencies specialize by many other marketing communications tools as well:

- PHD Canada (**www.pioneeringphd.com**) specializes in only the planning and purchasing of advertising media.
- Argyle Communications (**www.argylerowland.com**) specializes in only public relations campaigns for clients.
- Calgary-based Critical Mass (**www.criticalmass.com**) works for clients all around the world, but only in online environments.

The second way an agency can establish itself as niche is to specialize in a certain market. An example of a Canadian agency that has niched itself very successfully in the agricultural market is Calgary's AdFarm (**www.adfarmonline.com**).

A third way that agencies can be niche is by their target audience. Canada's Youthography (**www.youthography.com**) focuses on delivering marketing communications for clients interested in connecting with the youth market.

Of course, some niche agencies deliver a full range of marketing communications vehicles for their clients, so these two categories are not mutually

Noise Digital is an agency that specializes in communicating in the digital medium for a wide variety of brands, including Tic Tac.

Source: Courtesy of Noise Digital.

exclusive. Listings for marketing communications agencies in Canada are available from a number of sources. The Institute of Communications Agencies offers a member directory containing most major agencies in the country. Other resources include Marketing Magazine (**www.marketingmag.ca**) and Strategy Magazine (**www.strategyonline .ca**). These two magazines also offer career search support with job postings online. There are also specialized networks that organize in more focused areas. For example, in Canada many PR firms belong to the Canadian Council of Public Relations Firms (**http:// ccprf.ca**) which specializes in this one aspect of marketing communications. Many agencies also belong to associations based in regions, such as the Advertising Association of British Columbia (**www.aaabc.ca**). Most of these more specialized associations also offer job listings.

Critical Thinking Exercise

What are the benefits of hiring a niche agency? What are the drawbacks? What are the benefits of working for a niche agency? What are the drawbacks? Which niche model (marketing communications tool, market, or audience) do you think has the most potential for implementing effective IMC campaigns?

Most marketing communications agencies, particularly full-service agencies, house a range of professionals that each play a unique and complementary role in helping the client meet its objectives. Graduates from most college and university programs in marketing communications (the readers of this text) can expect to find opportunity in virtually all of these roles. Each of them is discussed in this section.

Account Services

This is the most common place for graduates of business programs to find work within the marketing communications agencies. The role usually begins with the title of Account Coordinator, with subsequent roles of Account Manager/Account Executive and Account Director as the employee gains experience and rises through the department. The account services role can be split into two components: strategy development and project management. Junior positions focus more on project management, while senior account positions focus more on strategy development.

At its heart, the account services function is the link between the client and the resources of the agency. Account services determines what needs to be accomplished within the agency and marshals the resources to get it done. This can include activities that range from the exciting (jetting off to an international locale to observe a shoot for a TV commercial), to the novel (sitting behind the glass watching a focus group discuss your client's brand), to the mundane (filling out budget control spreadsheets to report agency expenditures to your client). The skills most prized by employers for these positions are organizational skills and verbal/written communication skills.

Account Planning

Although less common in Canada, the account planning function began in the UK to supplement what some viewed as a shift by account services away from a customer perspective to a preoccupation with client relations. At its heart, the account planning role is one of research. Many account planners have research backgrounds, which is essential in helping them gain insight into a target audience and understand appropriate marketing opportunities for that audience. Account planners can be invaluable at assisting with the development of the strategic direction pursued by the agency. The role involves both formal research (e.g., facilitating focus groups or commissioning more quantitative data) and informal research (e.g., scanning pop culture outlets for emerging trends and market opportunities). The skills most valued by employers for account planners are strong market research and communication skills.

Creative

The role of the creative department is often the role visualized by outsiders. It is glamorized by television and movies to be about "eureka" moments where brilliant ideas are developed out of thin air. Although eureka moments do happen, the role is actually grounded in much hard work and research. Working from the strategy and objectives set by the account team, the creative team (consisting of a copywriter and art director) works to turn the message into action through a range of communication vehicles. This involves the oversight of any elements required for the communication, including photography, filming, graphic design, and illustration. The skill most valued by employers in this department is, quite simply, creativity. Most graduates of business programs will not find success in applying for these positions. Their competition comes from students in dedicated graphic design programs or writing-based programs, such as journalism, who will likely have a well-developed portfolio of examples prior to completing their education.

Source: Courtesy of Noise Digital. Used with permission of Nature's Path Foods, Inc. and Facebook.

The job of media planners is now more complex as online media provide many more flexible options. This campaign for Nature's Path invited consumers to submit photos of their 3 p.m. snack break.

Media Managers

If the agency develops advertising (online or traditional) as part of its offerings, it will likely have a media department. These are the people who help achieve clients' objectives by planning and buying the media that will place the message in front of the right audience at the right time. The role involves the ability to determine the right mix of media from a range of options to deliver the best return on investment overall. For example, even though advertising during the Stanley Cup finals might be expensive on a per-second basis, its ability to deliver large numbers of targeted viewers can still make it a good media investment. These people work closely with media companies (newspapers, TV networks, etc.) to determine the best options for their clients. The role is highly quantitative due to the reliance on both media costs and outcomes (e.g., number of views, hits, etc.) being measured. The skills most valued by employers for these positions are organizational skills, comfort with numbers, and communication skills.

Production Managers

The final element in the process of marketing communications agencies involves the production department. These are the people who have a hands-on role in bringing the ideas from the creative and media departments to life. Their roles include everything from graphic design, where a web programmer codes a message onto a mobile marketing platform for cell phones, to a producer who coordinates vendors for a television commercial, to a print manager who manages the production schedule of a company printing millions of pieces of direct mail. Production managers manage a broad range of outside production companies (printers, sound studios, etc.) that ultimately deliver the clients' message to the target audience. The role involves a deep understanding of the technical aspects of production in the related field, and helping the creative and account services team meet their objectives on time and on budget. The skills most highly valued are organizational skills and any knowledge specific to the position's area of expertise (e.g., print, web, etc.).

The agency process begins with the account services function, which is the client liaison. From there the account executive may access the account planning role for additional support in strategy and research. Once the strategy is determined, the account team briefs the creative department and media department on the particulars of the campaign. The final step in the process is the production of the various marketing communications elements, such as web design, television production, and so forth. The process is depicted in Figure 1.6.

FIGURE 1.6
Communications Agency Process

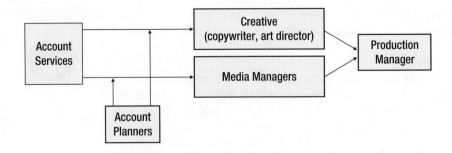

Should You Hire an External Marketing Communications Agency?

Many organizations hire external agencies to develop and execute their marketing communications campaigns. If you are a marketing manager and need to determine whether you should hire an external agency, you might consider the following:

Do you need objective expertise? When you hire an external agency, you are buying the collective expertise of a team of professionals. Often their collective experience covers decades. And because many agencies are selected because they have relevant expertise in a product category, they could know more about your audience and competitors than you do. They are also more likely to be objective when assessing your product or service compared with those of your competitors within the market category.

Do you have a complicated message? If your product or service is highly complex, hiring an external agency can create problems because you will need to spend the early portion of the relationship simply bringing the agency up to speed. When people work on marketing communications in-house, they typically already have a deep understanding of the product or service and can be more efficient from the outset.

Can you afford it? Hiring external agencies is typically more expensive than hiring employees in-house. If the average hourly rate for an agency employee (i.e., the rate at which the client is billed) is $125, you can see that hiring an employee directly can be much less expensive. However, the collective expertise and skill will be lower when hiring a single employee versus an agency with a broad range of professionals.

Do you need flexibility? Hiring employees internally provides the marketer with much less flexibility overall. For example, if you are unhappy with the performance of an agency, you can usually sever the relationship more easily than you could an employment contract. Also, if your business is highly cyclical (e.g., many companies sell the majority of their products in the weeks preceding Christmas) it may be more effective to hire an external agency for a short period rather than hire employees who will be busy for only a few months a year.

Do you have a need for coordination with other marketing activities? When hiring an external agency, it becomes more difficult to coordinate the marketing communications with other marketing activities of the firm. For example, many grocery stores produce weekly flyers that are developed in conjunction with the manufacturers of the products featured in those flyers. The content of weekly flyers is highly unstable, with changes being made as a result of sales force negotiations. As these changes come in, it is easier to administer them in-house, with graphic designers laying out the flyer right up to the last minute, than it is to hand them off to an external agency who might not be equipped to have someone standing by.

Choosing a Marketing Communications Agency

The process of selecting an agency is difficult. Choosing an agency that best suits a company requires careful planning. The industry association the Institute of Communication Agencies (**www.icacanada.ca**) provides a service called agency search that provides an unbiased consultancy based on best practices. However, most clients undertake the search internally. Figure 1.7 lists the steps involved in this process.

◆ Set goals.

◆ Define selection criteria.

◆ Request references.

◆ Consider the "pitch."

◆ Select agency.

Source: Fordimages.com.

FIGURE 1.7
Steps in Selecting a Marketing Communications Agency

Set Goals

Before making any contact with a marketing communications agency, company leaders identify and prioritize corporate goals. Goals provide a sense of direction for the marketing team, for the agency account team, and for the rest of the agency personnel. With clearly understood goals, each is more likely to be "on the same page" as preparation of the campaign unfolds. Without such goals, it becomes more difficult to know which agency to choose because company leaders do not have a clear idea of what they want to accomplish. Unambiguous goals help ensure a good fit between the company and the agency.

Define Selection Criteria

The second step in selecting an agency is stating the selection criteria that will be used to prioritize one agency over another. Even firms with experience in selecting agencies should set selection criteria in advance. The objective is to reduce bias that may enter into the decision. Emotions and other feelings can lead to decisions that are not in the company's best interests. Although good chemistry between the agency and the firm is important, this aspect of the choice comes later in the process, after the list has been narrowed down to two or three agencies. Figure 1.8 lists some of the criteria typically considered as part of the selection process. This list is especially useful in the initial screening process, when the task is to narrow the field to the top five (or fewer) agencies.

The *size* of the agency is important, especially as it compares to the size of the company hiring the agency. If a large firm were to hire a small agency, the small agency might be overwhelmed by the account. A small firm hiring a large agency might find that the company's account could be lost or could be treated as being insignificant. A good rule of thumb to follow regarding the size of the agency is that the account should be large enough for the agency so it is important to the agency but small enough that, if lost, the agency would not be badly affected.

One of the criteria for national advertisers such as Ford Canada may be representation in every region across Canada to ensure campaigns are implemented effectively at a local level.

Critical Thinking Exercise

How should you compensate your agency? There are many ways in which you can pay your agency. These include: a percentage of the amount they spend on your behalf (i.e., a commission), a flat rate based on an upfront quote, an hourly rate paid for each hour someone spends on your account, or payment based on achieving some metric or outcome.

What are the pros and cons of each of these payment types? Why do you think all four exist in the market today?

Sometimes an agency decides to reject an account because it is too small. For example, when Kathrin Brockmann at Truffini Chocolates in Vancouver (**www.truffini.com**)

FIGURE 1.8
Potential Evaluation Criteria in Choosing a
Marketing Communications Agency

- ◆ Size of the agency
- ◆ Relevant experience of the agency
- ◆ Conflicts of interest
- ◆ Creative reputation and capabilities
- ◆ Production capabilities
- ◆ Media purchasing capabilities
- ◆ Client retention rates
- ◆ Personal chemistry

decided to invest in a campaign to help build her brand across western Canada, some larger agencies turned down her offer to meet because her budget was too small. For large agencies, it just doesn't make financial sense to work with clients who cannot pay for their sophisticated services and processes.

Relevant experience in an industry is a second evaluation criterion. When an agency has experience in a given industry, the agency's employees are better able to understand the client firm, its customers, and the structure of the marketing channel. At the same time, it is important to be certain the agency does not have any *conflicts of interest.* An agency that has been hired by one manufacturer of automobile tires experiences a conflict of interest if the ad agency is hired by another tire manufacturer. This is a major issue for firms that niche by industry, or even by audience. AdFarm co-founder Ian Fitzgerald summarized the problem as follows: "If we are going to continue to offer truly specialized service we need to grow. And in order to grow we're going to have to have multiple clients within the various categories of agriculture—otherwise there just aren't enough clients. We'll take steps to ensure confidentiality like separate teams handling different clients and we ask that you trust us to never jeopardize the relationship by taking advantage of whatever insider knowledge we might have."[8]AdFarm's success demonstrates that, for the most part, clients value the specialized skill over the risks of conflicts.

An agency can also have relevant experience without representing a competitor. Such experience can be gained when an agency works for a similar company that operates in a different industry. For example, if an agency has a manufacturer of automobile batteries as a client, this experience may be relevant to selling automobile tires. The agency may also have recently lost an account, and their experience could be valuable to a competitor who can now hire them without conflicts.

The initial screening process includes an investigation into each agency's *creative reputation and capabilities.* One method of judging an agency's creativity is to ask for a list of awards the company has received. Although awards do not always indicate effective advertisements, in most cases there is a positive relationship between winning awards and writing effective ads. Most creative awards are given by peers. As a result, they are good indicators of what others think of the agency's creative efforts. Assessing creative capabilities is very important when preparing advertising campaigns for a different country in which the firm has limited experience.

Production capabilities and *media purchasing capabilities* of the agencies should be examined if these services are needed. A firm that needs an agency to produce a television commercial and also buy media time should check on these activities as part of the initial screening process. It should also be kept in mind that many agencies either have subsidiary companies perform the media work or subcontract it to a media firm. What is important is not whether the agency does the media buys itself, but that it has the capability of making sure it is done and that it fits with the ads being designed.

The final two selection criteria—*client retention rates* and *personal chemistry*—are revealed as the final steps of selection take place. Client retention rates are important because agencies that can keep clients satisfied for long periods of time are more likely to provide satisfaction for any new clients. Finally, the importance

AdFarm creates marketing communications that focus on the agriculture market.

There is a future out here.

of personal chemistry cannot be overstated. In most client–agency relationships, there is daily contact, often under very stressful deadlines. The ability to work well with an agency partner is essential.

These criteria lead to a focused subset of agencies that are pre-screened to meet the objectives of the client.

Request References

Once the initial screening is complete, the company requests references from the agencies still in the running for the contract. Most agencies willingly provide lists of their best customers to serve as references. A good strategy the company can use is to obtain references of current clients that have similar needs. Also, when possible, it helps to obtain names of former clients of the agency. Finding out why they switched can provide valuable information. Often changes are made for legitimate reasons. Discovering an agency's *client retention rate* helps reveal how effective the firm has been in working with various clients. Note that poor service is not the only reason a firm switches advertising agencies.

Background checks also provide useful information. Background checks start with finding firms that have dealt with each agency. Also, talking to media agents who sell media time provides insights into how an agency buys time and deals with customers. Companies that have formed contracts with individual agencies for production facilities or other services are excellent sources of information. Background checks help the client company make sure the agency can provide quality professional services.

From here, there should be only two or maybe three agencies left in contention. Now the process becomes more intimate, and the agencies present their detailed plans for the account. This is commonly known as "the pitch."

The Pitch

Preparing a pitch is time-consuming and costly for agencies; therefore, agencies only want to spend time on preparing pitches with a decent chance of being accepted. It is very upsetting to spend time preparing a pitch only to find out later the company had no desire to switch agencies but was told by upper management to solicit pitches.

Often the pitch includes a formal presentation addressing a specific problem, situation, or set of questions. This is called a *shootout*. The presentations reveal how each agency would deal with specific issues that arise as a campaign is prepared. This may even include creative development done for the client. This helps a client company decide which agency best understands the issues at stake and has developed an advertising or integrated communications approach that will solve the problem or issue. When ESPA, a luxury spa treatment and beauty-product retailer in the UK, decided to move the company's direct marketing activities from in-house to a direct marketing agency, the management team asked the agencies involved in the pitch to produce a direct mail campaign for ESPA that would boost awareness of its range of spa-inspired products, treatments, and services.[9]

Select an Agency

During the presentation phase, the opportunity exists to meet with creatives, media buyers, account executives, and other people who will work on the account. *Chemistry* between employees of the two different firms is critical. The client company's leaders must be convinced that they will work well together and that they will feel comfortable with each other. Chemistry can break or make the final decision.[10]

When Coca-Cola put its UK business up for a pitch, the shortlist included the incumbent agency, Universal McCann, plus three other agencies. ZenithOptimedia was on the original list of possible agencies, but had to withdraw because of conflict of interests (the company represented a competing brand). The account was to cover the Coke products of Diet Coke, Coke Zero, Sprite, Fanta, and Minute Maid. The bid went to Vizeum, because the team demonstrated during the pitch renewed thinking in key areas, particularly shopper marketing, environmental sustainability, and connecting with younger consumers in a digital age.[11]

FIGURE 1.9
Both Agencies and Clients Are Responsible to Make Their Relationship Work

Agencies should:

◆ Be process-driven. Develop processes to shift the focus away from reliance on personal relationships. A good process is more durable than a good relationship.

◆ Be committed. Commit to metrics to better understand the ROI from campaigns.

◆ Be more selective in pitching. Pitches are time-consuming, and agencies rarely apply learning from one pitch to another.

◆ Be understanding. Profile clients to ensure you communicate with them in the way they prefer. For example, some clients can spend hours talking about research, while others want to get involved in the creative process.

◆ Be engaged. Ensure senior management is engaged in the relationship.

Clients should:

◆ Be stable. Be sure your agency knows your expectations.

◆ Be motivating. This is not only about paying the agency fairly (which is important), but trying to get the people working for you excited about your product or service.

◆ Be evaluative. Be sure to give feedback, not only when things go badly, but when things go well.

◆ Be realistic. When setting budgets and objectives, be sure that the task is not too large for the resources available.

Source: *Adapted from David Wethey (2007), "Client-Agency Relationships" in* The Sage Handbook of Advertising, *edited by Gerard Tellis and Tim Ambler. Sage: Los Angeles.*

Bell Media sells radio media through more than 33 stations in cities across the country. Can you spot the stations in your city?

Whenever possible, a client company's leaders should visit the agency's office as part of the evaluation process. Agencies often use top company executives to win contracts, but then turn the account over to other individuals in the agency after signing the deal. Visiting the agency's office provides an opportunity to meet personnel who might work on the account. Talking with these individuals generates quality information about how the account will be handled. The visit also can be used to hammer out specific details, such as identifying the actual person(s) who will work on the advertisements and either agreeing to the use of freelancers (independent contractors who provide various services) to work on the project or prohibiting the agency from using such individuals.

After the selection process has been completed, the agency and the company work together to prepare the marketing communications campaign. As shown in Figure 1.9, each partner in this relationship must ensure they perform a number of tasks to make sure the relationship is successful.

Media Companies

If the marketing communications plan involves some aspect of media, a media company is involved. The media company is the group behind the vehicle itself. For example, Google is a media company in that it sells space based on its search function. Advertisers can purchase keywords to ensure their listing appears first in any relevant search. Other more traditional examples are producers of television or print content, such as CTV or Maclean's. These companies are essential in helping marketers reach targeted audiences with their messages.

Recently, consolidation in the media industry resulted in fewer companies that can offer more complete media options to potential advertisers. For example, Bell Media is a multimedia company with leading assets in television, radio and digital, selling media in television (CTV, Canada's #1 television network and lead broadcaster of the London 2012

Olympic Games, MuchMusic, BNN, TSN, and many other conventional and specialty stations), radio (through local stations across the country), and every online opportunity associated with each of these media properties (e.g., www.ctv.ca, www.muchmusic.com). Such coverage makes it very efficient for buyers of media, who get one-stop shopping when looking for audiences.

Production Companies

Related to the production department found in agencies mentioned earlier, many companies in Canada sell production services that help create and deliver marketing communications to Canadians. These include production companies offering services for broadcast marketing communications (e.g., sound studios, animators, editing companies), print production companies (printers, letter shops to process direct mail, Canada Post to deliver), and promotion companies to manage sales promotion (sweepstakes oversight, coupon processing, etc.).

COMMUNICATING ACROSS CULTURES

One of the realities of Canadian marketing is that many goods and services sold here are delivered through a subsidiary of a foreign company, most often an American company. Although there are many Canadian brands that are world leaders (e.g., BlackBerry, Tim Hortons, Roots, etc.) many of the most popular brands in Canada are American-based. These include brands from such firms as Nike, Kraft, Coca-Cola, Apple, Microsoft, Disney, and McDonald's, to name a few. This creates a challenge for the Canadian marketers working for these firms. On the one hand, there are pressures to ensure that marketing communications are relevant to the local Canadian market. This is the argument against simply replicating American marketing communications campaigns in the Canadian market. On the other hand, many argue that Canada is similar enough to the United States that the cost efficiencies of developing only one campaign outweigh any benefits to developing Canadian campaigns from scratch.

Virtually all non-Canadian companies that work with marketing communications agencies hire a local Canadian agency. The question is whether these agencies will simply execute the campaign in the Canadian market (e.g., buy local airtime) or develop messages and tactics that are designed specifically for the Canadian market. In some cases, such as McDonald's, the firm takes a hybrid approach, keeping some of the elements of the campaign from the home market while tailoring others to the Canadian market. For example, although the annual Monopoly game promotion is consistent across both the United States and Canada, the firm works with the local Canadian agency Cossette to develop some new campaign elements that are specific to the Canadian market.

Perhaps the two most important things to keep in mind when considering whether to work with a local Canadian agency to either execute a campaign developed elsewhere or build a Canadian campaign from the ground up are the degrees of similarity in both the consumer culture and the competitive landscape. If, for example, the consumer is highly similar and the competitors are, for the most part, identical, then merely executing an idea developed elsewhere might be the most cost-effective approach. The Canadian consumers who purchase Kraft salad dressings, for instance, are probably very similar to their American counterparts. Also, the competitors on the Canadian grocery store shelf are highly similar to those found in U.S. grocery stores. In this case, Kraft might consider merely hiring a Canadian agency to execute the U.S. campaign.

Another issue facing marketers is the vastness of the Canadian market and regional differences in both consumer behaviour and media across the country. This necessitates either that companies hire agencies unique to each region or, more likely, that individual agencies open offices in several Canadian cities to service local markets. For example, the large agency Grey Canada has offices in three Canadian cities. For most clients, campaigns are developed out of one office (usually located in the same city as the client organization), with the other offices providing local support for things like events or local media buys. People working in the Vancouver office, for instance, would be better able to spot opportunities in the local market than those working in the Toronto office.

At the end of each chapter of this book, an example will be given to illustrate how one company applies the concepts discussed in the chapter. The purpose of these examples is to show, within one marketing organization, how the concepts fit together. Although not meant to be a template for a marketing communications plan, each chapter illustration will offer you insight into how each concept fits the overall marketing communications function of the firm.

The firm that will serve as this chapter's illustration is TELUS. This firm, the TELUS brand, and the products it represents rely heavily on marketing communications for success.

Source: Courtesy of TELUS.

TELUS works with a number of different agencies, each with its own specific competencies.

Like many people in the marketing communications field, Kate Baillie, Director of Marketing for Broadband and Core Services for TELUS, doesn't have a very traditional background. "My undergraduate degree is in fashion design," says Kate. "I spent the first two years of my career on the creative end of the fashion business. But I was most interested in how the business worked so I went back to school to complete an MBA. My move into marketing and telecommunications happened over a number of years, and I officially joined TELUS when they bought a small start-up I was working for, building Wi-Fi hotspots."

On the other hand, Director of Marketing Communications Lara Johnson had marketing communications in her sights all along. "It all started with the TV show Melrose Place. It was the best pitch for a career in marketing communications. So unrealistic, of course, but it led me to pursue a degree in sociology, which gave me insight into why people do the things they do. And after graduating I cold-called every agency in town, eventually landing an internship position as my starting point."

Managing a brand with the scope of TELUS is a daunting task. The brand is supported by one of the largest marketing communications budgets in Canada. However, even with all of their resources, they still find value in working with external agencies to create and execute marketing communications. Kate justifies this approach with three advantages. "First, we could never attract the type of talent that specialized marketing communications agencies can. The people who tend to excel in the development of campaigns are often people who want exposure to lots of different types of clients in various industries that pose different challenges. Second, because of this diversity, we benefit because the people who work on our business at these agencies also work on other businesses. So when someone works on our account, they can apply any learning they have from other accounts—anything from a retailer to an insurance company to a car company—good ideas come from lots of different places, and we get access to a wide variety of ideas."

The third benefit again relates to the experience of agency personnel working outside the TELUS culture. "They bring an element of objectivity that we sometimes can't. When you work all day on something, there is a tendency to lose sight of how others outside the organization see it. Using agencies gives us perspective because they bring the voice of the customer to the table."

The TELUS brand can be seen in almost every form of marketing communications across the country. For Kate, this requires not one but a stable of agencies to make sure those with true understanding of any one type of marketing communications are on the agency roster. "Our Agency of Record [AOR] is Taxi who develops what we call 'big picture' ideas for the brand, and of course do a lot of the execution in media vehicles geared toward advertising. They are complemented with a host of other specialized agencies that work on other parts of our communications plan. So there is a direct marketing agency, a media-buying agency, a PR agency, an agency that does experiential marketing (street teams, events, etc.) for us when we do certain type of promotions, and other partners that we bring in when the need arises."

This brings both a challenge and an opportunity for Kate. The challenge is to ensure that each agency is working with the others to deliver a consistent brand message across all aspects of the marketing communications mix. But by ensuring that agencies across the communications mix can contribute to idea development, it's more likely that campaign ideas will be executed across as many channels as possible. "We use almost every type of marketing communications, and it helps to have ideas that we can take into whatever channel makes sense for us," says Kate.

Source: Used with permission of Kate Baillie, TELUS Communications.

For help developing your IMC Plan, go to **www.pearsoncanada.ca/clow**.

SUMMARY

Effective marketing communications are difficult to create. Competitive pressures, demands for accountability, developments in technology, a cluttered media landscape, and changing media consumption habits of audiences all create the need to be strategic when developing marketing communications. As a result, most companies now practise integrated marketing communications (IMC) to help them achieve their business goals with marketing communications.

Marketing communications takes place in the same context as any form of communication. The components of the communication process include the sender, an encoding process, the transmission device, the decoding process, and the receiver. Noise is anything that distorts or disrupts the flow of information from the sender to the receiver.

In the marketing arena, senders are companies seeking to transmit ideas to consumers, employees, other companies, retail outlets, and others. Encoding is the process of combining the key message with an audience insight and creating a tangible message. Transmission devices are the means of transmitting information and include advertisements, public relations efforts, press releases, sales activities, promotions, and a wide variety of additional verbal and nonverbal cues sent to receivers. Decoding occurs when the receivers (such as customers or retailers) encounter the message. Noise takes many forms in marketing, most notably the clutter of an overabundance of messages in every available channel.

Integrated marketing communications (IMC) takes advantage of the effective management of the communications channel. It seeks to target the right audience with the right message and deliver that message with the appropriate transmission device at the right time. Within the marketing mix of products, prices, distribution systems, and promotions, firms that speak with one clear voice are able to coordinate and integrate all marketing tools.

An entire industry exists to create and deliver these messages. It involves the manufacturers of goods and services and a host of media outlets and other companies, such as printers, that can help companies communicate with their target audiences. Most often, this communication is facilitated by a marketing communications agency that will help clients to code and convey their message in the most appropriate communication device. The roles within each area of the marketing industry vary, and many career opportunities are open to those with a business or marketing education, such as the readers of this text.

This text takes a strategic approach to the management of the marketing communications process. It will take aspiring marketing communications professionals through the process of developing and delivering effective IMC campaigns. Regardless of where people work within the process, it is critical that they understand the overall process so they can understand how their role can add value.

KEY TERMS

brand parity Occurs when there are few tangible distinctions between competing brands in mature markets.

clutter Exists when consumers are exposed to hundreds of marketing messages per day, and most are tuned out.

communication Transmitting, receiving, and processing information.

decoding Occurs when the receiver employs any of his or her senses (hearing, seeing, feeling) in an attempt to capture a message.

encoding The verbal (words, sounds) and nonverbal (gestures, facial expressions, posture) cues that the sender utilizes in dispatching a message.

feedback Information the sender obtains from the receiver regarding the receiver's perception or interpretation of a message.

full-service agencies Marketing communications agencies that offer a client a complete one-stop service across all aspects of an integrated marketing communications plan (e.g., advertising, public relations, interactive, etc.). These agencies also provide services from strategy to the execution/production of a campaign across a broad range of industries and product categories.

integrated marketing communications (IMC)   The coordination and integration of all marketing communications tools, avenues, and sources within a company into a seamless program that maximizes the impact on customers and other end users at a minimal cost. This affects all of a firm's business-to-business, marketing channel, customer-focused, and internally oriented communications.

marketing mix   Consists of products, prices, places (the distribution system), and promotions.

niche agencies   Marketing communications agencies that specialize in one of three ways: by IMC tool (e.g., public relations, product placement), by industry (e.g., agriculture) or by audience (e.g., young demographics).

noise   Anything that distorts or disrupts a message.

receivers   The intended audience for a message.

senders   The person(s) attempting to deliver a message or idea.

transmission devices   All of the items that carry a message from the sender to the receiver.

REVIEW QUESTIONS

1. Define communication. Why does it play such a crucial role in marketing and business?
2. What are the parts of an individual communications model?
3. Who are the typical senders in marketing communications? Who are the receivers?
4. Name the transmission devices, both human and non-human, that carry marketing messages. How can the human element become a problem?
5. Define clutter. Name some of the forms of clutter in marketing communications.
6. Define integrated marketing communications (IMC).
7. What reasons were given to explain the growth in importance of IMC plans in this chapter?
8. What is brand parity? How is it related to successful marketing efforts?
9. Who are the four main players in the overall marketing communications process?
10. What specific tasks do marketing managers perform?
11. What's the difference between a full-service agency and a niche agency?
12. What are the four main areas within full-service agencies and how do they work together to create marketing communications campaigns for clients?
13. What are the five steps involved in selecting a marketing communications agency?

INTEGRATED LEARNING EXERCISES

1. The Institute of Communication Agencies (ICA) counts most of the national advertisers in the country among its members. Visit their website (**http://www.icacanada.ca/members/index.cfm**) and link through to the websites of some of their member agencies. Do you think these agencies are doing a good job of communicating how they are different from their competitors? Do you think there is brand parity in the marketing communications market? If you were hired as the CEO of one of these agencies, what would you do to your website to differentiate yourself?

2. Find each of the following brands on the web. For each brand, discuss how effective its website is in communicating an overall message. Also discuss how well the website integrates the brand's communications through other vehicles such as advertising or sales promotion. Do you think this channel has the ability to reach their primary target markets?

   a. Tim Hortons (**www.timhortons.com**)
   b. TD Canada Trust (**www.tdcanadatrust.com**)
   c. Air Canada (**www.aircanada.com**)
   d. Canadian Tire (**www.canadiantire.ca**)
   e. A&W (**www.aw.ca**)
   f. Rona (**www.rona.ca**)

3. Information is one key to developing a successful integrated marketing communications program. But not all information needs to be expensive, primary research. Good insight can come from publicly available sources. Two of the leading marketing communications industry publications in Canada are Marketing Magazine (**www.marketingmag.ca**) and Strategy (**www.strategyonline.ca**). Access the websites of each magazine and examine the information and news available on each site. How could a manager use this information to aid in the development of an integrated marketing campaign?

STUDENT PROJECT

Creative Corner

One of Procter & Gamble's fastest growing products is Febreze. It is aimed at individuals who do not like washing laundry and has been positioned by P&G as an alternative method of completing this chore. An ideal target market is the almost 20 million college students in the United States and Canada. With busy class schedules, work, and social events, who has time to do laundry? For jeans and other clothes that are not quite dirty yet, Febreze offers the chance to "refresh" the clothes and eliminate any possible odours. John Paquin, Executive

Vice-President at the advertising agency WPP Grey Worldwide, which handles the Febreze product, states that "washing is not a convenient part of the lifestyle at college." He also recognizes that "mainstream media buys [such as television] are not effective for the 18- to 22-year-olds.[12] For more information about Febreze, access the Febreze website at **www.febreze.com.**

1. Identify media you would use to reach 18- to 22-year-old college students.

2. Design an advertisement for Febreze aimed at the college demographic. Where would you place your ad? Why?

→ ETHICS IN ACTION

Marketing managers hire agencies to provide them with expertise on developing, coding, and transmitting messages to a target audience. But sometimes agencies are pressured to engage in activities that they do not feel comfortable performing. For example, a client may ask an agency to develop an advertisement that specifically appeals to younger children because they are less able to discriminate between advertising and other content, such as television programming. Or an agency may be hired to promote a product that has the potential to harm consumers, such as cigarettes.

1. Do you think that marketing agencies are merely carrying out the wishes of a client who is operating within the bounds of the law, or do you think agencies have an ethical duty to try to dissuade clients from these types of activities? Develop three arguments that support the view that agencies carry responsibility and three arguments that support the view that agencies bear no responsibility.

2. If you do think there is an ethical duty, how far would you take it? Would you risk losing the client to take an ethical stance? Assume you have fired a client in the cola business because they asked you to develop a media strategy that would be placed in areas known to be frequented by children as young as eight years old. Write a one-page letter to your shareholders justifying this loss of revenue. ●

CASE STUDY | Brockmann's Chocolates

"It's different when it's your own money that you are spending," says Kathrin Brockmann. Her family business, Brockmann's Chocolates (**www.truffini.com**), was eyeing expansion into Ontario from its base in British Columbia and Kathrin was in charge of making the expansion work. She was anxious about the right way to approach things: "If this is done right it could literally triple our business, but if we get it wrong we could easily waste hundreds of thousands of dollars or even put the whole business in jeopardy."

After Kathrin graduated with a business degree from Simon Fraser University, she went to work buying media for an Internet dating company. During those two years she worked with budgets in the hundreds of thousands of dollars. "But Brockmann's Chocolates is a relatively small family business. We are profitable, but we'd be lucky to find $50,000 to fund a marketing communications campaign to support our expansion into Eastern Canada," explains Kathrin. And that's just the budget she set. "When we approached some agencies they simply turned us away because we didn't have a big enough budget. I know it takes money to make money, but now that I'm spending my own money I have a much more personal reason to make sure the campaign will deliver results."

Brockmann's Chocolates was started by Kathrin's father, Norbert Brockmann. Norbert is a master confectioner trained in Munich, Germany. He and his wife, Marianne, came to Canada in the summer of 1985. His lifelong dream was to create a line of fine chocolates that would be the very best a chocolate lover could enjoy. In the spring of 1999, the Truffini line was launched: a high-quality chocolate truffle line with the flair that reflected the Brockmann's European background.

The chocolate is manufactured using only the finest imported European chocolate and the freshest local ingredients available. Truffini truffles are all natural, with no artificial colours or flavours, no preservatives, no hydrogenated oils, and no trans fats.

Over the years the company has built up a considerable retail presence in western Canada, mainly British Columbia. Their products are found in many large grocery and retail chains, such as Safeway (**www.safeway.ca**), Save-On Foods (**www.saveonfoods.com**), and London Drugs (**www.londondrugs.com**). They are also found in more specialty retailers like Urban Fare (**www.urbanfare.com**), Nesters Food Market (**www.nestersmarket.com**), and Capers Community Market (**www.wholefoodsmarket.com/capers**). "The specialty retailers are a particularly good fit

Brockmann's has tried various tactics, including in-store sampling.

for us," says Kathrin. "They attract a higher end customer who is looking for something that is a little fresher, looking for a local product, and quite frankly is comfortable with paying more for a higher quality product."

The company offers a wide variety of flavours of chocolate across two main formats: bulk and packaged. "Our bulk business gives customers an easy way to sample our products," explains Kathrin. "Our chocolates in this section of the retailer let the customer buy only as much as they want. Bulk customers also tend to be a little more price conscious too." Gift giving, as with much of the chocolate business, drives the packaged side of the business. "In Safeway, for instance, our chocolates are placed in the floral section. The idea is that if someone is buying flowers for his wife, chocolates are a nice complement. If we make him walk all the way over to the confectionary aisle, we are likely to lose him. But right there next to the flowers it's an easier sale." On top of this, the business is highly seasonal. "The focus on chocolate as gifts means we do about 60 percent of our business over the last quarter, through Christmas. There is some buying for personal consumption on the packaged side of the business (as opposed to bulk), but it's sporadic. "Ferrero Rocher, for example, sells a three-pack that is likely driven by personal consumption, but for the most part people give packaged chocolates as gifts."

"Virtually all of our western Canadian retailers—even the ones that don't position themselves as being local—like the fact that we are based in British Columbia," says Kathrin. "We have good relationships with our retailers, and generally get great positioning in the stores. First, few other chocolates are found in the bulk section. Lindt is about the only other one. Second, like the Safeway example, we are generally placed outside the regular confectionary aisle, so it helps us differentiate. London Drugs, for example, places our products in the Carlton section with their greeting cards."

The company has achieved its success steadily over the years, winning over customers one at a time. Their investment in marketing communications was based on a few key initiatives. The first was in-store sampling. During peak purchasing periods, especially, the company would hand out free samples of its products to major retailers. External companies that specialize in this activity always did the sampling.

The second major pillar of the marketing communications effort was flyer advertising. The company would advertise its products in the flyers produced by major retailers. This type of advertising—known as co-op advertising—is also a way for the company to support the retailers. "It's great to be able to give some support back to the people that have been instrumental to our growth."

The company has also invested in some local radio ads in the Vancouver market and some outdoor advertising on transit. Although these forms of advertising have been sporadic, and certainly not at the weights that would give full coverage of the market, Kathrin recalls one particular story told by one of her salespeople. "He was standing outside a London Drugs store talking to the manager about our products. Right at that moment, two separate buses—each carrying our ad—drove by. It helped our salesperson reassure the manager that we have a popular product," says Kathrin. Although Brockmann's retailers don't demand that the company invest in its own advertising, Kathrin knows that they do appreciate any effort to help stimulate demand.

Finally, Brockmann's had also used sales promotions, using mainly price discounts. "We've done promo, especially in the first quarter when the whole category is really slow," explains Kathrin. "Valentine's Day notwithstanding, the first quarter is very slow because people tend to indulge at Christmas and spend the next three months making up for it."

Measurement of these activities has been light. Kathrin explains: "A company our size just doesn't have the budget to invest in a lot of market research. We know the in-store sampling works well because of the feedback we get from the people working the booths. And we've done some tracking of hits to our website, but generally we can't pinpoint our success to any one particular form of marketing communications. It's a combination of a good product, the packaging, the pricing, the retail location—so many things need to line up for us to be successful."

The company has indeed been successful. But after a long history of steady growth in Western Canada, with so many satisfied customers in British Columbia and Alberta, the company decided to enter the Ontario market.

"We are going back to basics with the Ontario launch," says Kathrin. "We see the Ontario market as the key to our future growth." The company will initially choose smaller retailers to sell its products. "The decision to stay small was about risk management as much as anything else," explains Kathrin. "Going into a Walmart or Loblaw's would be great, and the volumes are huge. But if the product doesn't sell, we're on the hook for all that product. People don't realize that the big stores don't buy the product and take responsibility until it's sold. If it doesn't sell, we pay for the price mark downs. Maybe larger companies like Nestlé can absorb those types of costs, but we can't."

The good news is that the Ontario market is rich with what smaller specialty retailers and Kathrin refer to as "mom and pop" stores. "Urban Fare only has a few locations in Vancouver, but that type of store is much more popular in Ontario. It lets us work with people who are more connected to our product."

Related to the choice of retail strategy, the firm needs to find distributors who can commit to the firm's success in the market. There are literally hundreds of possible distributors that the firm can choose from. These range from large operations that sell virtually any product to retailers, to those that specialize in niches, such as all natural or organic products, or that focus on certain areas within grocery retailers. "But the reality is," says Kathrin, "these companies have catalogues that might have thousands of products in them. I don't think we can rely solely on the distributor to do the job for us. We also need to build demand from consumers that will drive traffic and have retailers asking to stock our products."

"This is where marketing communications comes in," Kathrin states. "We need an integrated plan that will help us create that demand. And we need to do it on a shoestring budget, so we need to be smart. We need to do things that will help consumers appreciate our quality and build our brand over the long term, but also generate sales today."

Assume you are hired by Kathrin as a marketing coordinator as your first job. Help her tackle this challenge and answer the following questions:

1. What elements would your IMC plan include and why? What would each of them bring to the table in both (a) brand building over the long term and (b) sales in the short term.

2. Do you recommend that Brockmann's focus their marketing communications effort on finding distributors (i.e., a "push" campaign) or consumers (i.e., a "pull" campaign)? Develop a list of three pros and three cons for your recommendation.

3. Would you recommend hiring an external marketing communications agency or doing the campaign internally? Why or why not? Develop a 10-minute presentation to outline your recommendation.

4. Prepare a list of the kinds of questions you would want to ask about their customers in the British Columbia market in order to help the company penetrate the Ontario market.

5. How would you propose measuring the success of the campaign? How would you propose measuring the success of each aspect of the IMC campaign?

ENDNOTES

1. Donald Baack, "Communication Processes," *Organizational Behavior.* Houston: Dame Publications, Inc. (1998), pp. 313–37.

2. Hollie Shaw, "Getting It Right," *National Post*, December 17, 2010, p. FP12.

3. James G. Hutton, "Integrated Marketing Communications and the Evolution of Marketing Thought," *Journal of Business Research* 37 (November 1996), pp. 155–62.

4. John A. Quelch and Laura Winig, "Charles Schwab & Co., Inc.: The 'Talk To Chuck' Advertising Campaign," *Harvard Business School Case 9-507-005*, January 16, 2007.

5. Diane Brady, "Making Marketing Measure Up," *Businessweek* (December 13, 2004),

pp. 112–13; "Top 10: Issues Facing Senior Marketers in 2007," *Advertising Age* 78, no. 17 (April 23, 2007), p. 23.

6. Jack Neff, "J&J Jolts 'Old' Media with $250M Spend Shift," *Advertising Age* 78, no. 12 (March 19, 2007), pp. 1, 29.

7. Jean-Noel Kapferer, "The Roots of Brand Loyalty Decline: An International Comparison," *Ivey Business Journal* 69, no. 4 (March–April 2005), pp. 1–6.

8. Ian Fitzgerald, *Horse of a Different Wheelbase*, Fitzgerald Creative Corporation, 2005, p. 22.

9. "Spa Company ESPA in DM Agency Hunt," *Campaign* (UK), November 2, 2007, p. 3.

10. Heather Jacobs, "How to Make Sure Your Pitch Is Heard," *B&T Weekly* 57, no. 2597 (February 8, 2007), pp. 14–16.

11. Jemima Bokaie, "Coca-Cola Appoints Vizeum," *Marketing*, November 7, 2007, p. 6.

12. Parekh Rupal, "Febreze Sniffs Out New Target: Dorm Dwellers," *Advertising Age* (April, 2004), pp. 34–35.

2

After reading this chapter, you should be able to answer the following questions:

- **Why** is a strong brand vitally important to the success of many firms?
- **What** are family brands, brand extensions, flanker brands, co-brands, private brands, brand equity, and brand recognition?
- **How** can brands use different positioning strategies to succeed?
- **What** are contact points with customers that impact brand equity?
- **How** can marketing communications impact brand equity, and vice versa?
- **What** are the elements included in an integrated marketing communications plan?

INDUSTRY PROFILE
So You Want to Work in Marketing Communications?

Sushant Trivedi, Assistant Brand Manager, Gillette,
Procter & Gamble, Toronto

If you ask Sushant if he has his dream job, he says, "Not only do I have my dream job, but I also work on my dream brand. I've been a 'Gillette guy' for years, and have been very brand loyal to this brand. Getting to work on a brand that I identify with so strongly is a great experience. I also get to see the fruits of my labour in the market every day. If I go into a supermarket I see my brands on the shelf, or maybe I see an end of aisle display, I know that I was part of making that happen."

And because Procter & Gamble is world-renowned for its many brands, rigorous training, and emphasis on quantitative analysis, positions with the firm are highly sought after. Sushant explains, "My first introduction was through on campus recruiting, as it is for most people finishing school and looking for their first job. But before the interview there were a series of tests for things like personality, communications skills, as well as a logic and reasoning test. Just getting through the testing was difficult; they were as hard as any tests I wrote while in school." Only after these tests does the company interview potential candidates, and the first interview is with the regional managers in the local area. "In my case I met with the people from British Columbia and had my first interview with them. There were only a few people from my school that made it to this stage, and I was the only one that made it to the final stage, which is the interview at the Canadian head office in Toronto."

Sushant says that one of the reasons the company is so well respected as an employer is their approach to showing their managers many different aspects of the business. "It helps us get a much better view of the overall company, and lets us learn things on one brand and apply them to another. In fact, my position was supposed to be on the Charmin brand but at the last minute someone else was put into that position. Then my position with Gillette opened up because someone who was there went to work on the Pantene brand."

But the benefit of getting different experiences goes further than just brand management. "We also get a chance to work more in a sales role, or even work on

Branding, Positioning, and the Integrated Marketing Communications Plan

one of the major accounts like Loblaw's." The benefit of this for Sushant is that it gets the managers as close as possible to the customers. "You need to know the customer. One thing I didn't get much of in university was a sense of the importance of merchandising and relationships with the channel partners. When you work in a consumer goods company, having a strong channel drives revenues. Of course, consumer demand is still an integral part of our business, but a strong sales fundamental drives the brand and that's true in any category."

As part of the brand team for Gillette, Sushant needs to have a wide basket of skills because he and his team are responsible for virtually every aspect of the brand, from adding channels, to

Sushant Trivedi, Assistant Brand Manager, Procter & Gamble.

pricing, to product innovation—and of course marketing communications. "We are more like entrepreneurs than brand managers," says Sushant. "This is our business, and we run it the way we think it should be run. We are simply asked to grow the revenues and it's up to us to decide how best to do that. So we are responsible for everything from budget management to public relations. We have resources at P&G that can provide us with market research if we need it. If we see the competition doing something we can decide the best way to respond. If a new product is introduced, we work with the American team to develop the overall plan, and also as the Canadian representative to make sure it works for us. This means we need to be sensitive to cultural issues across Canada and understand how to ensure our retailers will support the product."

Being part of such a large effort, it's not surprising that Sushant lists his ability to work as part of a team as his most valuable skill. "The team includes lots of members, and we all need each other to make our brand successful. So if I talk to someone in demand planning or market research, I need to know how to work with them in order for them to give me what I need. But it also works the other way," says Sushant. "When people need something from me, I need to understand what their needs are so I can give them the support they are looking for. At the end of the day, everything we do should benefit the overall team working toward brand success."

Teamwork is one area where Sushant felt lucky to get lots of exposure in his education. "Although team projects in classes were sometimes a pain at the time, they taught me so much about working as part of a team. I'm using all of those lessons I learned in my job now because here, as in school, I don't get to choose who I work with. I need to be able to work with a wide variety of people who have a wide variety of skills and opinions and focus everyone on one goal."

"The other thing that really helped me develop teamwork skills was participating in case competitions during school." Sushant was an active participant in several competition teams, usually consisting of about four or five people. "During those competitions the team would be given a challenge to solve, and in some cases only a few hours to analyze the situation and recommend a solution. It forces you to develop the ability to work with others under some extreme conditions."

Another valuable skill for Sushant is his analytical ability. "We make all of our decisions based on data. So, for example, if we see that market share is decreasing we use data to try and find the cause, and also to figure out a way to solve the problem." Here again Sushant credits his education for preparing him for the challenge. "Case competitions especially were a great way to focus on how data and numbers dirty decisions. If I'm going to recommend that we launch a new channel, or run a promotion in Atlantic Canada, for example, I need to be able to show how that will deliver a return on investment to the company."

The third skill that Sushant credits for his success is his ability to effectively communicate. "This is true for both written and oral communication," explains Sushant. "At P&G we like to get things down to one page. If forces you to be focused and succinct in your writing. Being brief and succinct is far more difficult than most people imagine. Although I received some of these skills through my education, it's been something I've had to work on since starting here." Sushant does credit his education with helping him in his oral communication skills. "All those class presentations are proving very helpful now when I meet with vendors or channel partners, or if I'm briefing one of our agencies or internal teams."

One piece of advice Sushant would give any aspiring marketer is to not be afraid of asking questions or asking for help, especially in the very first few weeks of starting a job. "When I started at P&G there was an unbelievably steep learning curve. I love the fact that I'm always learning at my job, but early on it sometimes felt like I was swimming against the tide. But I found that when I asked for help people were eager to give it because we've all been there. We've all been the new person that needs a little extra help. The trick," says Sushant, "is to not be afraid to ask for help when you need it."

OVERVIEW

For many firms, their **brand** is one of their most valuable assets. Although a brand can be described as a name, logo, or other symbol used by firms to differentiate themselves from competitors, the value of a strong brand goes to the very heart of the marketing concept. It represents the value that a product or service offers to the customer, and includes aspects of every element of the marketing mix, including pricing; product features and attributes; distribution channels; and, of course, marketing communications. Advertising, consumer promotions, trade promotions, personal selling, the company's website, and other marketing activities all affect customer perceptions of the firm.

Marketing communications can be considered the promise made by the brand, while the actual product or service and related customer experience is the delivery of that promise. For example, some marketers wish to establish their brands as "luxury" brands. Although the products sold by these companies typically feature high quality, their marketing communications also communicate this quality, and attempt to create an image of quality in the mind of the customer. Therefore, brand managers and marketing communications professionals are responsible for developing and maintaining the brand. A company's image has a "bottom line" that can even be assigned a value on accounting statements.

When the marketing team is able to clearly understand the brand, it is easier to make solid connections with customers. A strong IMC plan begins with an understanding of the brand and the overall marketing objectives for the firm. This is then used to segment the potential population and define a target audience. Based on the knowledge of the brand and the target audience, an IMC plan can be crafted to ensure that the right message is placed in front of the right audience at the right time.

The first part of this chapter examines the activities involved in managing a brand. The second part addresses ways in which brands can position themselves relative to their competitors to gain an advantage. Next, the chapter examines ways that brands touch customers, and the importance of a coherent, overall brand message. The last part of the chapter introduces the IMC plan format.

BRANDS

Effective marketing communications starts with a clearly defined brand. The **brand identity** summarizes what the company stands for and the position the company has established. Whether it is the "good hands" of Allstate Insurance or the "good neighbours" at State Farm, the goal of brand management is to create a specific impression in the minds of clients and customers. In the case of insurance companies, helpfulness, safety, and security are common and favourable elements of their strong image.

A State Farm ad stressing security.

One major problem many established companies encounter is brand parity. Brand parity occurs when there are few tangible distinctions between competing brands in mature markets. Brand parity means customers see only minor product differences. In many product categories, even minor variations are hard to find.

What customers believe about a firm is far more important than how company officials view the image. Corporate names such as Tim Hortons, Toyota, Nike, and Petro-Canada all conjure images in the minds of customers. This is referred to as **brand equity**, and occurs when the customer is familiar with the brand and holds a positive opinion about it. Brand equity is most often conceptualized as the reactions a customer has to a brand versus their reactions to a fictitious or generic product within the same category. For example, the brand equity of Tide laundry detergent is based on the price premium customers are willing to pay for Tide versus other brands of detergent, especially a generic brand.

The value of a brand can be considerable. For many firms, the value in their brand is the majority of the value in their company. Which are the most valuable brands? Interbrand produces a list of the top 100 corporate brands. Companies such as Procter & Gamble, which have a portfolio of products and brands, were not included in the evaluation. In addition, companies that operate under different names in different countries, such as Wal-Mart, were not included. The list only notes corporations that provide products under one name. Using these criteria, Interbrand ranked Coca-Cola as the top global corporate brand. Microsoft was second. In Canada, Thomson Reuters was ranked as the most valuable brand. See Figure 2.1 for a complete listing.

TABLE 2.1 Top 10 Global Corporate Brands

Rank	Company	Brand Value (billions)	Country of Ownership
1	Coca-Cola	$70.5	United States
2	IBM	$64.7	United States
3	Microsoft	$60.9	United States
4	Google	$43.6	United States
5	General Electric	$42.8	United States
6	McDonald's	$33.6	United States
7	Intel	$32.0	United States
8	Nokia	$29.5	Finland
9	Disney	$28.7	United States
10	Hewlitt Packard	$26.9	United States

Source: "Best Global Brands 2010," Interbrand.com © 2011 Interbrand. All rights reserved.

Top 10 Canadian Brands

Rank	Company	Brand Value (billions)
1	Thomson Reuters	$9.41
2	TD	$6.67
3	RBC	$6.17
4	BlackBerry	$6.0
5	Shoppers Drug Mart	$3.43
6	Tim Hortons	$2.65
7	Bell	$2.45
8	Rogers	$2.28
9	Scotiabank	$2.16
10	BMO	$1.97

Source: "Best Canadian Brands 2010," Interbrand.com © 2011 Interbrand. All rights reserved.

HOW DOES A BRAND CREATE VALUE?

A strong brand creates value by providing benefits for both customers and the company. Each of these is discussed next.

Brand Value—The Customer Perspective

From a customer's perspective, the brand serves several useful functions. These include:

- Providing assurance regarding purchase decisions of familiar products in unfamiliar settings
- Giving assurance about the purchase when the buyer has little or no previous experience with the good or service
- Reducing search time in purchase decisions
- Providing psychological reinforcement and social acceptance of purchases

A strong brand provides customers with positive assurance about what to expect from a firm. A can of Coke or Pepsi purchased in Anchorage, Alaska, has a comparable taste to one purchased in Liverpool, UK, or Kuala Lumpur, Malaysia. KFC serves the same or similar meals in San Francisco as it does in Minneapolis or Paris. A woman on vacation knows that if she makes a purchase from a Wal-Mart in Texas, a defective item can be returned to a local Walmart store in Toronto.

This assurance has even greater value when customers seek to purchase goods or services with which they have little experience. Consider families on vacation. Many travellers look for names or logos of companies from their native areas. Purchasing from a familiar corporation is viewed as being a "safer" strategy than buying something from an unknown company. Taking a room at a hotel that the customer has never heard of seems riskier than utilizing a familiar chain. Thus, a family visiting Brazil might normally not stay at the Holiday Inn, but because it is a recognizable name they believe it is a lower-risk option than an unknown hotel.

Another significant role brands play for customers is reducing search time. Purchasing a product from a familiar firm saves time and effort. An individual loyal to Ford spends fewer hours searching for a new car than does someone with no loyalty to any automobile manufacturer. The same holds in purchasing low-cost items such as groceries. Search time is saved when a consumer purchases items from the same organization, such as Campbell's or Nabisco.

For many individuals, purchasing from a highly recognized company provides psychological reinforcement and social acceptance. Psychological reinforcement comes from feeling that a wise choice was made and the belief that the good or service will perform well. Social acceptance is derived from knowing that many other individuals also have purchased from the same firm. More importantly, other people, such as family and friends, are likely to accept the choice.

Source: Courtesy of TD Canada Trust.

TD Canada Trust has built its brand, in part, on the customer service it provides.

Critical Thinking Exercise

Think about the last purchase you made that cost over $100. How important was the brand in your decision? Do you agree with the idea that consumers benefit from brands? Write a one-page memo outlining how you feel the brand provided you with benefits in this purchase.

The same benefits are provided to both consumer and business-to-business audiences. A strong corporate image creates a major competitive advantage in the business-to-business marketplace since many of the processes that affect individual consumers also affect business buyers. Purchasing from a well-known company reduces the feelings of risk. A firm with a strong brand makes the choice easier for business customers seeking to reduce search time. Psychological reinforcement and social acceptance may also be present. Company buyers who make quality purchases might receive praise from organizational leaders and others involved in the process. A strong brand is especially valuable to a company expanding internationally. Members of foreign businesses are likely to feel more comfortable making transactions with a firm that has a strong brand. Risk and uncertainty are reduced when the buyer knows something about the seller. Therefore, a company such as IBM can expand into a new country and more quickly gain the confidence of consumers and businesses than a company with an unknown brand.

Measuring Brand Equity

Trying to determine whether brand equity exists is difficult. One method marketing experts use is **brand metrics**. Brand metrics measure returns on branding investments. Attitudinal measures associated with branding can be used to track awareness, recall, and recognition. To increase their power, these factors can be tied with other variables (e.g., brand awareness coupled with intent to buy). Brand awareness can also be connected to use of either the product class (mustard) or the brand (Kraft, Grey Poupon). Remember that when measuring awareness, recall, and recognition, a brand can be recalled for negative as well as positive reasons.[1]

Recognizing that popular brands are not always powerful brands, Reader's Digest commissioned a survey to understand which of Canada's brand garner the most trust from consumers. Figure 2.2 shows the most trusted brands in a range of categories.

Critical Thinking Exercise

The results in Figure 2.2 are from a national survey of conducted online with 1,500 Canadians. Do you agree with the results? Are there categories where you feel the brand listed is not the most trusted brand? Write a one-page memo to the brand manager of the brand you feel should be in the most trusted position, and outline how you feel he or she should use marketing communications to help get the top spot.

Brand Value—The Company Perspective

From the viewpoint of the firm itself, a strong brand generates many benefits.

- Extension of positive customer feelings to new products
- The ability to charge a higher price or fee
- Consumer loyalty leading to more frequent purchases

FIGURE 2.2
Canada's Most Trusted Brands

- **Claritin/Benadryl/Reactin** (Allergy Relief)
- **Febreeze/Glade** (Air Freshener)
- **Kellogg's** (Breakfast Cereal)
- **Tylenol** (Cough/Cold Remedy)
- **Tropicana** (Fruit Juice)
- **L'Oreal** (Hair Colouring)
- **Sony** (HD LCD/Plasma TV Manufacturer)
- **Toyota** (Hybrid Car Manufacturer)
- **Mr. Clean** (Household Cleaner)
- **Bell** (Internet Service Provider)
- **Splenda** (Low Calorie Sweetener)
- **Sun Life** (Life Insurance Company)
- **Becel** (Margarine)
- **Tylenol** (Pain Reliever)
- **Toyota** (Passenger Car Manufacturer)
- **Kraft** (Peanut Butter)
- **Crest** (Regular Toothpaste)
- **Iams** (Pet Food)
- **Dempsters/Wonder** (Sandwich Bread)
- **Sensodyne** (Sensitive Toothpaste)
- **Dove** (Skin Care – Body)
- **Oil of Olay/Nivea** (Skin Care – Face)
- **Quaker** (Snack Bars)
- **Gatorade** (Sport/Energy Drink)
- **Coppertone** (Sunscreen Skin Protection Product)
- **Michelin** (Tires)
- **Dyson/Hoover** (Vacuum Cleaner)
- **Jamieson** (Vitamins)
- **Yoplait** (Yogurt)

Source: *Trusted Brand 2011: Canada's Most Trusted Brands*, http://www.readersdigest.ca/trusted-brand-2011. © 1996–2011, Reader's Digest Magazines Canada Limited—© 1996–2011, The Reader's Digest Association (Canada) ULC — All rights reserved.

- Positive word-of-mouth endorsements
- Higher level of channel power
- The ability to attract quality employees
- More favourable ratings by financial observers and analysts

A strong brand provides the basis for the development of new goods and services. When consumers are already familiar with the corporate name and image, the introduction of a new product becomes much easier, because long-term customers are willing to give something new a try. Customers normally transfer their trust in and beliefs about the corporation to a new product. For example, when Tim Hortons introduced sandwiches to their menu, customers were more likely to assume that the same quality found in other Tim Hortons products would be found in the new item. Another restaurant without the same reputation for quality might not have success when introducing a new item.

The strong General Mills brand name makes the introduction of new products easier.

A strong brand allows a company to charge more for its goods and services. Most customers believe "you get what you pay for." Better quality is often associated with a higher price. This, in turn, can lead to greater markup margins and profits for the firm.

Further, firms with strong brands have more loyal customers. Customer loyalty results in patrons purchasing more products over time. Loyal customers also are less likely to make substitution purchases when other companies offer discounts, sales, and other enticements to switch brands.

Heightened levels of customer loyalty are often associated with positive word-of-mouth endorsements. Favourable comments help generate additional sales and attract new customers. Most consumers have more faith in personal references than in any form of advertising or promotion.

Positive consumer attitudes create corporate equity, which provides greater channel power. Retailers offer brands that are viewed positively by customers. Retailers buy the brands that pull customers into stores. As a result, a company that has a strong brand has more control and power in the channel and with retailers.

Another advantage of a strong brand is attracting quality employees. Just as consumers are drawn to strong firms, potential workers apply for jobs at companies with solid reputations. Consequently, recruiting and selection costs are reduced. All things being equal, there is less employee turnover at these companies.

A strong brand often results in a more favourable rating by Wall Street analysts and by other financial institutions. This is especially helpful when a company seeks to raise capital. Further, legislators and governmental agencies tend to act in a more supportive manner toward companies with strong and positive reputations. Lawmakers are less inclined to pursue actions that might hurt the business. Members of regulatory agencies are less likely to believe rumours of wrongdoing.

Customer Benefits	Company Benefits
◆ Assurance of product quality	◆ Brand extensions are easier
◆ Assurance when not familiar with product category	◆ Can charge a higher price
◆ Reduces search time	◆ Higher customer loyalty
◆ Psychological and social acceptance	◆ More frequent purchases
	◆ Positive word-of-mouth communications
	◆ Ability to attract quality employees
	◆ More favorable view by financial analysts

FIGURE 2.3
Customer and Company Benefits of a Strong Brand

The Road to Brand Value

Because a brand really only exists in the mind of the customer, the value generated from a strong brand relies on a number of attitudes and behaviours related to the mindset of the customer. Previous research has identified five key dimensions to mindset that essentially follow the customer, from introduction to the brand to post-purchase behaviours.[2] First is brand awareness, or the extent to which customers recognize the elements associated with the brand. Second are the associations that customers make with brands. These are thoughts customers have pertaining to one or more aspects of the brand. For example, BMW has built a brand based on driving performance. Customer brand associations for the BMW brand are such things as speed, handling, and precision. The third dimension involves attitudes that customers have on the ability of a brand to outperform competitors on a relevant association. Fourth is brand attachment, characterized by how loyal customers feel toward a brand. Some brands, such as BlackBerry, generate an almost cult-like devotion among customers. U.S. president Obama famously fought to keep his BlackBerry after he became president, even though secrecy concerns led to pressure for him to give it up. The last dimension is brand activity—how do customers use the brand, talk to others about it, and so on? Many brands do an excellent job of creating an environment that fosters brand activity, such as the Jeep Jamboree events that encourage Jeep owners to connect with one another and that offer driving tips for off-roading.

Approaches to Branding

Marketers take many different approaches when it comes to using their brands to generate revenue for the company. Figure 2.4 identifies several types of approaches.

Many brands produce family trees. A **family brand** is one in which a company offers a series or group of products under one brand name. For example, the Black & Decker brand is present on numerous power tools. The advantage of a family brand is that consumers usually transfer the image associated with the brand name to any new products added to current lines. When Black & Decker offers a new power tool, the new item automatically assumes the reputation associated with the Black & Decker name. These transfer associations occur as long as the new product is within the same product category. When additional products are not related to the brand's core merchandise, the transfer of loyalty might not occur as easily.

Leveraging an existing brand to enter a new market is known as **brand extension**. The extension may or may not be related to the core brand. For example, Nike has been successful in extending its brand name to a line of clothing to the point that Nike is now known as an apparel company as much as a shoe company. Black & Decker has been successful in extending its brand name to new types of power tools. It has not been as successful, however, in extending its line to small kitchen appliances. Other marketers use brand extension exclusively for products within the same category and use a multiple brand approach for products outside this category. For example, Coke uses the Coke brand on many soft drinks, including Coke, Diet Coke, and Coke Zero. But they use the Dasani brand for their bottled water and Minute Maid for orange juice products.

FIGURE 2.4
Types of Brands

- **Family brands.** A group of related products sold under one name.
- **Brand extension.** The use of an established brand name on products or services not related to the core brand.
- **Flanker brand.** The development of a new brand sold in the same category as another product.
- **Co-branding.** The offering of two or more brands in a single marketing offer.
- **Ingredient branding.** The placement of one brand within another brand.
- **Cooperative branding.** The joint venture of two or more brands into a new product or service.
- **Complementary branding.** The marketing of two brands together for co-consumption.
- **Private brands.** Proprietary brands marketed by an organization and sold within the organization's outlets.

ON THE JOB

Should you extend your brand?

- Brand extension is an attractive strategy for many marketers because it allows them to capitalize on the value of an existing brand. However, brand extensions are not always successful. Harley-Davidson enjoys strong brand equity in the motorcycle category and has been able to extend that brand into other areas, such as the co-branding effort with Ford trucks. However, when Harley-Davidson tried to extend its brand into perfume, consumers rejected it.

The main problem with brand extensions is that they can dilute the value of the original brand, or even kill the brand completely. In the case of Harley perfume, the **parent brand** did not suffer long-term harm, but some argue that brand extensions always harm at least some of the parent brand value.

In order to avoid product flops, or even worse, harming a valuable brand, there are a number of factors that managers should consider before extending their brands.

1. If the conviction for the parent brand is high, brand extensions are more likely to be successful.

2. When consumers have more experience with a brand, they are more likely to accept a brand extension.

3. If the reputation for quality in the parent brand is high, the extension is more likely to be successful.

4. If the brand has been extended successfully before, brand extensions are more likely to be successful in the future.

5. When a brand extension receives a high degree of marketing communications support, the extension is more likely to be more successful.

6. If retailers accept the brand extension, the extension is more likely to be successful. This is because retailer support can help "push" the product to customers.

7. If the degree of fit between the brand and the brand extension is high, the extension is likely to be successful. An example of a fit extension would be using the Coke brand on a new soft drink, while an example of a low fit extension is using the Coke brand on a new automobile.

8. When preference for the parent brand is driven more by physical attributes than by brand name, brand extensions are less likely to be successful.

9. If the perceived risk with a trial of the brand extension is low, the brand extension is more likely to be successful.

10. If target consumers are more innovative, they will be more likely to accept a brand extension.

The reader should note the important role that marketing communications plays in the majority of these success factors. Apart from the actual degree of marketing communications support for the brand extension itself (item 5), marketing communications can help develop longer-lasting and more meaningful relationships with customers (items 1 and 2), establish a reputation for quality (item 3), establish strong ties with retailers (item 6), and reduce the risk associated with trial (item 9).

Source: Adapted from: Franziska Volckner and Henrik Sattler (2006), "Drivers of Brand Extension Success," *Journal of Marketing, 70* (April), 18–34.

Brand extension is often used to take a brand into a completely new category. Gillette is a brand that was traditionally firmly entrenched with men. Then the company launched a massive campaign to position itself in the women's market. New products, including the Sensor Excel razor and Satin Care Shave Gel, were offered by mail to consumer homes, and free samples were placed in homeroom bags for 14- and 15-year-old girls at school. Gillette's advertisements encouraged women to view the products as a key part of being physically and psychologically ready for anything. The ad copy asked "Are you ready?" and answered "Yes, I am!" This positioning matches with the position of Gillette's products for men, which are marketed using the "Best a man can get" slogan.[3]

An alternative to a brand extension program is a flanker brand. A **flanker brand** is the development of a new brand by a company in a good or service category in which it currently has a brand offering. For example, Procter & Gamble's primary laundry detergents are Cheer and Tide. Over the years, P&G has introduced a number of additional brands, such as Ivory Snow. In total, P&G offers 11 different brands of detergents in North America; 16 in Latin America; 12 in Asia; and 17 in Europe, the Middle East, and

Africa. Figure 2.5 lists Procter & Gamble's various brands of laundry detergents, cosmetics, and hair-care products. The company's marketing team introduced these flanker brands to appeal to target markets in which the main brand was not reaching customers. Thus, using a set of flanker brands can help a company offer a more complete line of products. This creates barriers to entry for competing firms.

Sometimes a flanker brand is introduced when company leaders think that offering the product under the current brand name might adversely affect the overall marketing program. Hallmark created a flanker brand known as Shoebox Greetings. These cards sell in discount stores as well as Hallmark outlets; however, the Hallmark brand is only sold in retail stores carrying the Hallmark name. Shoebox Greeting cards are lower priced and allow Hallmark to attract a larger percentage of the market. Firms operating in high-end markets often use this strategy when they compete in low-end markets. It also is used in international expansion. For example, Procter & Gamble sells Ariel laundry detergent in Latin America, Asia, Europe, the Middle East, and Africa, but not in North America. Offering different brands for specific markets is a common flanker brand strategy that helps a firm to expand into international markets using more than its current brands.

Flanker brands are also used in business-to-business markets. Hotels, for example, rely heavily on business travellers for a consistent revenue stream. InterContinental Hotels Group, which owns, among other brands, InterContinental, Crowne Plaza, Holiday Inn,

FIGURE 2.5
Brands Sold by Procter & Gamble

Product Category	North America	Latin America	Asia	Europe, Middle East, and Africa
Laundry and cleaning brands	Bold	Ace	Ariel	Ace
	Bounce	Ariel	Bonus	Alo
	Cheer	Bold	Bounce	Ariel
	Downy	Downy	Cheer	Azurit
	Dreft	Duplex	Doll	Bold
	Dryel	InExtra	Ezee	Bonux
	Era	Limay	Gaofuli	Bounce
	Gain	Magia Blanca	Lanxiang	Dash
	Ivory Snow	ODD Fases	Panda	Daz
	Oxydol	Pop	Perla	Dreft
	Tide	Quanto	Tide	Fairy
		Rapido	Trilo	Lenor
		Ridex		Maintax
		Romtensid		Myth
		Supermo		Rei
		Tide		Tide
				Tix
Cosmetics	Cover Girl	Cover Girl	Cover Girl	Cover Girl
	Max Factor	Max Factor	Max Factor	Max Factor
	Oil of Olay			Ellen Betrix
Hair Care	Head & Shoulders	Drene	Head & Shoulders	Head & Shoulders
	Mediker	Head & Shoulders	Mediker	Mediker
	Pantene Pro-V	Pantene Pro-V	Pantene Pro-V	Pantene Pro-V
	Physique	Pert Plus	Rejoy–Rejoice	Rejoy–Rejoice
	Rejoy–Rejoice		Pert Plus	Pert Plus
	Pert Plus		Vidal Sassoon	Vidal Sassoon
	Vidal Sassoon			

and Holiday Inn Express, understands the needs of business travellers and offers unique services that add value to the businessperson's stay. High-speed Internet access is available at all of the properties, and at the Crowne Plaza, wireless connections are available at any location on the property. Understanding that time and convenience are important to business travellers, InterContinental Hotels offers an online wireless reservation system that allows business guests to review, cancel, or modify reservations. To ensure that business guests have a good night's sleep, Crowne Plaza offers a guaranteed wake-up call, quiet floors, sleep amenities, sleep CDs, and relaxation tips.[4] The Holiday Inn brand, especially Holiday Inn Express, emphasizes economy in its marketing communications. Speed is also an important positioning attribute for the brand, as can be seen in ads that include its breakfast-to-go offering.

In addition to flanker brands and brand extensions, marketers also use co-branding to reach new customers or generate new revenue. **Co-branding** takes three forms: ingredient branding, cooperative branding, and complementary branding. **Ingredient branding** is the placement of one brand within another brand, such as Intel microprocessors in HP computers. **Cooperative branding** is the joint venture of two or more brands into a new good or service. WestJet offers a MasterCard that allows users to collect points they can redeem on WestJet flights. This card takes advantage of the strength of both brands. Each company benefits from the relationship the other has with customers. **Complementary branding** is the marketing of two brands together to encourage co-consumption or co-purchases. One of the most common forms of complementary branding involves the co-location of two retail outlets within the same physical space. Subway sandwich shops can be found in many convenience stores, McDonald's are sometimes found in Walmart stores, Tim Hortons and Wendy's share many locations across Canada, and BMO branches can be found in Safeway supermarkets.

Co-branding succeeds when it builds the brand equity of both brands. For example, when Monsanto created NutraSweet, consumer trust was built by placing the NutraSweet logo on venerable brands consumers trusted, such as Diet Pepsi, Wrigley's Chewing Gum (Wrigley's Extra), and Crystal Light. The strategy worked so well that NutraSweet became the standard of quality in the sweetener industry.[5]

Conversely, co-branding is not without risk. If the relationship fails to do well in the marketplace, normally both brands suffer. To reduce the risk of failure, co-branding should be undertaken only with well-known brands. Co-branding of goods and services that are highly compatible generally will be less risky. Ingredient and cooperative branding tend to be less risky than complementary branding because both companies have more at stake and devote greater resources to ensure success.

Critical Thinking Exercise

Assume that MuchMusic is looking to expand its audience. The CEO recently came back from a seminar where she heard about co-branding, and she thinks this is a good idea to help increase the presence of the brand in the market. Identify three potential co-branding opportunities for the company. In each case, what will the company gain from the partnership? Why would the partners be interested in the partnership; what will they get out of it?

For small companies and brands that are not as well known, co-branding is an excellent strategy. The difficult part is finding a well-known brand that is willing to take on a lesser-known product as a co-brand. Yet, if such an alliance can be made, the co-brand relationship often builds brand equity for the lesser-known brand, as in the case of NutraSweet. Co-branding also provides access to distribution channels that may be difficult to obtain because of either lack of size or dominance by the major brands.

Private brands (also known as *private labels* and *store brands*) are proprietary brands marketed by an organization and normally distributed exclusively within the organization's outlets. Private brands have experienced a rollercoaster ride in terms of popularity and sales. To many individuals, private brands carry the connotation of a lower price and inferior quality. Historically, the primary audiences for private labels were price-sensitive individuals and low-income families. This is no longer true; retailers are investing marketing dollars to develop their private brands, which now account for approximately 15 percent of all retail sales and 19 percent of food items sold. According to ACNielsen, in the last 10 years store brand sales increased 64 percent, compared with 30 percent for major manufacturers' brands.[6]

Over the past few years, several changes have occurred in the private brand arena. Although private labels still tend to be priced between 15 and 30 percent lower than national brands, they also generate higher gross margins than national brands, because there is no channel intermediary. This higher margin enables retailers to earn higher profits on private brands, or, alternatively, to reduce the price of the private brands to make them more attractive to price-sensitive consumers. Retailers that maintain the higher markup on private labels have the opportunity to use some of the margin for advertising and promotions of the brands.

Another emerging trend in retailing is that loyalty toward retail stores has been gaining while loyalty toward individual brands has been declining. Rather than going to outlets that sell specific brands, many shoppers go to specific stores and are willing to buy from the brands offered by that store. This increase in loyalty to retailers has caused several department and specialty stores to expand the number of private-brand products that are offered. To do so, however, requires that the retailer develop a private brand that is congruent with a customer's image of the retailer.[7]

Savvy retailers recognize the value of private labels and how they can be used to differentiate the store from competing retailers and from national brands. These stores promote these labels as distinctive brands aimed toward specific market segments. Emphasis is on meeting the needs of consumers with a quality product. It is not based on price.

New trends in the use of private labels are emerging. Many retailers treat private brands more like national brands. Marketing dollars are spent on improving the actual label, on more noticeable in-store displays, and on packaging.[8] Retailers without large national ad budgets must rely more on displays and attractive packaging. A drab, cheap display does not convey the message that a private brand is as good as or better than a national brand. For many consumers, the two are indistinguishable. Unless they are familiar with the store's private brand labels, they may think they are purchasing a national brand.

Many Canadian grocery retailers have developed their own private label brands to compete with manufacturers' brands.

♦ Focus on core brands.	♦ Focus on in-store selling and packaging.
♦ Increase advertising.	♦ Use alternative methods of marketing.
♦ Introduce new products.	

FIGURE 2.6
Tactics Used by Manufacturers to Fight Gains Made by Private Labels

Source: Based on Vanessa L. Facenda, "A Swift Kick to the Privates," *Brandweek* 48, no. 31 (September 3, 2007), pp. 24–28.

How do manufacturers respond to the inroads made by private labels? Figure 2.6 lists some of the strategies.[9] Many manufacturers focus on a few core brands rather than split advertising dollars among a large number of brands. The core brands are advertised heavily. This helps the manufacturer maintain its brand name and reinforces the message that consumers are making the right decision when they purchase the manufacturer's national brand. The goal is to make an emotional connection with consumers both before and after the purchase.

Manufacturers may attempt to reduce the impact of private labels on sales by expanding product offerings. Private labels are normally copies of national brands. By aggressively introducing new products and new versions of current products, a manufacturer can maintain the loyalty of its current customers and be seen as an innovator. Hanesbrands Inc. owns a number of name brand apparel companies, such as Bali, Playtex, Champion, Ocean, and Hanes. The company expanded into the active wear market with the Hanes Sport casual collection. The surge in popularity of active lifestyle clothing created an increase in sales of other related products, such as the sports underwear featured in the Hanes ad in this section. Hanesbrands Inc. now manufactures products for women, men, and children.

Manufacturers must improve in-store displays and packaging to counter private labels. In displays and on packages, the manufacturer's brand must have a clear and compelling place. In some cases, it is the package that sells the product. Vendors of condiments, such as ketchup and mustard, know that the container has become extremely important to consumers.

In addition to using advertising, many manufacturers have turned to alternative product promotion methods. Gillette's marketing team realized that to encourage young males to use company products they needed to place samples in their hands. Consequently, the Fusion razor is mailed to men within one month of their 18th birthdays. Both Huggies and Pampers have developed websites that furnish usable information for young mothers. The sites also allow young mothers to communicate with each other.

Brand Names

A corporate name is the overall banner under which all other operations occur. According to David Placek, president and founder of Lexicon, Inc., "The corporate name is really the cornerstone of a company's relationship with its customers. It sets an attitude and tone and is the first step toward a personality."[10] Corporate names can be divided into the following four categories based on their actual, implied, or visionary meaning (see Figure 2.7).[11]

Overt names include Midwest Airlines and BMW Motorcycles USA. *Implied names* include FedEx and

Hanesbrands Inc. is one company that has introduced new products into the active lifestyle wear market.

©1999 Hanes Sport

Introducing Hanes Sport™ Underwear
THE CLOTHES YOU'D RATHER BE IN

HANES SPORT™
CASUAL COLLECTION
NEW

Hanes Sport Underwear for your active lifestyle
www.hanessport.com

FIGURE 2.7
Categories of Corporate Names

- ◆ **Overt names** reveal what a company does.
- ◆ **Implied names** contain recognizable words or word parts that convey what a company does.
- ◆ **Conceptual names** capture the essence of what a company offers.
- ◆ **Iconoclastic names** represent something unique, different, and memorable.

IBM (International Business Machines). *Conceptual names*, such as Google and Krispy Kreme, take a different approach. The name Google evokes a vision of a place where an endless number of items can be found, and Krispy Kreme suggests confectionaries filled with tasty cream. Monster.com and Fathead.com are examples of *iconoclastic names*.

Critical Thinking Exercise

It can be argued that the first two categories (overt and implied) are better for marketing communications purposes because they make it easier for consumers to recall the good or service, and they aid in the overall communications objective. However, the success (and associated value) of many brands calls this into question. For example, the Starbuck's name in itself didn't mean anything to most consumers until they associated it with a brand experience. Do you think examples like Starbuck's are the exception or the rule? Can the choice of a name create an advantage for marketing communications, or is it irrelevant?

To prevent cannibalism of its other teas, Celestial Seasonings positions each version for individual target markets.

POSITIONING

An important aspect in brand management is positioning. **Positioning** is the process of creating a perception in the consumer's mind regarding the nature of a company and its products relative to competitors. Positioning is created by such variables as the quality of products, prices charged, methods of distribution, packaging, image, and other factors. A product's position is based on two elements: (1) the product's standing relative to the competition and (2) how the product is perceived by consumers.

Consumers ultimately determine the position a product holds. Marketing programs are designed to position a product effectively. To do so, marketing communications must either reinforce what consumers already believe about a product and its brand name, or shift consumer views toward a more desirable position. The first strategy is certainly easier to accomplish. The goal of positioning is to find that niche in a consumer's mind that a product can occupy.

Positioning is vital for companies such as Celestial Seasonings® brands, because it helps prevent cannibalism among various brands within the product portfolio. Celestial produces teas that appeal to a wide variety of consumer segments. The one pictured in this section is being marketed to individuals who are concerned about their health and may not want to give up taste in their diet.

Effective positioning can be achieved in seven different ways (see Figure 2.8). Although companies might try two or three approaches, such efforts generally only confuse customers. The best method is to use one of these approaches consistently.

♦ Attributes   ♦ Product user
♦ Competitors   ♦ Product class
♦ Use or application   ♦ Cultural symbol
♦ Price–quality relationship

FIGURE 2.8
Positioning Strategies

An *attribute* is a product trait or characteristic that sets it apart from other products. The Sony ad in this section is aimed at business customers. The advertisement promotes the attribute of quality, because the projector provides stronger light. The ad attempt to convey the message that the attribute featured by the brand outperforms the competition.

Another common tactic is to use *competitors* to establish position. This is done by contrasting the company's product with others. For years, Avis ran advertisements comparing itself with Hertz. Avis admitted it was not number one, but turned that position into an advantage, because Avis was willing to "try harder" for business. Subway often takes aim at other quick-service restaurants in its marketing communications, comparing the nutritional content of its food directly with other options.

Use or *application* positioning involves creating a memorable set of uses for a product. Arm & Hammer has long utilized this approach in its attempt to convince consumers to use its baking soda as a deodorizer in the refrigerator. Arm & Hammer has also been featured as a co-brand in toothpaste, creating yet another use for the product.

Businesses on the extremes of the price range often use the *price–quality relationship*. At the top end, businesses emphasize high quality, whereas at the bottom end, they emphasize low prices. Hallmark cards cost more, but they are for those who "only want to send the very best." Other firms seek to be a "low-price leader," with no corresponding statement about quality. Walmart consistently strives for the low-cost position in the marketplace with its "rollback pricing" messaging strategy.

A *product user* positioning strategy distinguishes a brand or product by clearly specifying who might use it. Marketing communications for GMC trucks uses the idea that its customers have very difficult jobs that require tough, durable, and dependable trucks. Inherent in this message is that GMC trucks are for people who work with their trucks, as opposed to people who buy a truck to take their kids to soccer practice. The positioning based on the users (often defined as construction workers) gives the trucks their image of toughness and strength.

Sometimes firms seek to position themselves in a particular *product class*. Orange juice was long considered part of the breakfast drink product class. Years ago, those in the industry decided to create advertisements designed to move orange juice into a new product class, with slogans such as "it's not just for breakfast anymore." This repositioning has been fairly successful. Many consumers drink orange juice at other times during the day. This result was due, in part, to the perception that orange juice is a healthy drink. To be successful, this approach must position orange juice as an alternative to soft drinks such as Pepsi or Coke.

Identifying a product with a *cultural symbol* is difficult but, if done successfully, can become a strong competitive advantage for a firm. Playboy has evolved into an entertainment empire by becoming a cultural symbol, albeit a controversial one. In its advertisement shown in this section, Stetson cologne is tied to the American cowboy and the spirit of the West. The ad copy states that "the attraction is legendary." The purpose of placing this ad in *Glamour* magazine was to entice women to purchase the product for the men in their lives.

This business-to-business ad for a research firm positions the service based on the research sample attribute.

Toluna
In touch with people

Learning what's on their mind has never been in better hands.

Many brands, such as Stetson cologne, use the cultural symbolism of the cowboy as the positioning strategy.

An image-building ad for BMW Motorcycles.

Maintaining, Rejuvenating, and Repositioning a Brand

One of the most important aspects of any strong brand is its consistency. Strong brands are consistent in their positioning over time. They also deliver a consistent brand promise in every contact with the customer (more on this later in this chapter). In the BMW advertisement in this section, the goal is to reinforce the idea that BMW is a quality product and the top brand in the motorcycle industry. The message is that "BMW Motorcycles are the indisputable mark of a real ride," according to BMW brand manager Kerri Martin.[12] When an image is well established, other promotions can be built around the reputation. This fuels long-term customer loyalty and future sales.

Maintaining a strong brand over time is difficult; as a consequence, some brands can become stale. Rejuvenating a brand helps a firm build revenue and can attract new customers. At the same time, reinforcing previous aspects of a brand assists the company in retaining loyal patrons, who are comfortable with the firm's original image. The key to successful brand rejuvenation is to remain consistent with a previous image, while at the same time building to incorporate new elements to expand the firm's target audience.

Rejuvenating a firm's image can be difficult. It takes time and effort. McDonald's faced this problem when the company encountered negative publicity about health-related concerns over its menu. According to Wendy Cook, McDonald's Vice-president of Menu Innovations and Marketing, the key to rejuvenating the company's image was to send the message that it is possible to buy healthy food at McDonald's. The main product leading the effort was a series of salads. Before launching the new salad line, McDonald's marketing team talked to women, the target market. The team learned that women notice details, such as all-natural dressings with low-fat options and the 16 different kinds of lettuce. Using this information, new advertisements were developed using a "girl talk" approach, where women discovered a great salad with a variety of options. This integrated marketing approach helped modify McDonald's image for working women who might stop there for lunch.[13]

Holiday Inn faced a similar situation. Consumers viewed the hotel chain as consisting of outdated hotels with old decor. To regain its image as a mid-level hotel, over $1 billion was spent on interior and exterior renovations and updates; 150 properties that did not meet the new standards were sold, and the proceeds were invested in the remaining hotels. Helen Travers, a corporate travel planner, stated, "It's about time. My clients haven't stayed in Holiday Inns in years [because] the chain hasn't kept up." Holiday Inn's marketing team also created a new logo. The goal was to rejuvenate the brand and regain the business travellers it had lost.[14]

Sometimes a complete brand overhaul is necessary, and repositioning is the best approach. Changing a brand positioning becomes necessary when target markets have begun to shrink or disappear, or the firm's image no longer matches industry trends and consumer expectations. At that point, company leaders must carefully consider what they wish to change, why they wish to change it, and how they intend to accomplish the task. It is difficult to completely change the image people have of a brand.

Let's just say tailgaters aren't a problem.

BMW

Motorcycles

One brand that faced a situation of declining market share and changing customer tastes was Labatt Blue. For years, Blue was the leading beer in Canada. The brand enjoyed high levels of loyalty and strong market share. However, over time consumer tastes began to change and drinkers steered away from beer to other forms of alcohol. Making matters worse, the brand was being increasingly overtaken by brands that were positioning themselves for drinkers under 25 years of age, such as Canadian and Kokanee (which is a flanker brand to Labatt Blue). Despite having one of the most widely recognized brand names in the country, with almost iconic status, Labatt was seen by younger drinkers as being "old"—a beer perhaps their father would drink, but not something for them.

The result was that the market share began to decline and Canadian overtook Blue as the number-one selling beer in Canada. The brand managers were faced with a dilemma: how to sop up the decline in market share and entice more younger drinkers to the brand without alienating the older drinkers who were still loyal to the brand. Although older drinkers tend to drink less than younger drinkers, the volume sold to current customers was still considerable, and the managers could not afford to alienate older customers when attempting to connect with younger ones.

The brand was slowly repositioned toward a younger market. This was mainly accomplished through marketing communications that used the idea of spontaneity to position the brand as "fun and youthful." The television ads, in particular, were instrumental in balancing the attributes of youthful and fun for younger viewers, while reinforcing the beer's tradition and reputation for quality, which helped older drinkers to still feel connected to the brand.

Critical Thinking Exercise

In the NBC sitcom *The Office*, paper company Dunder Mifflin is under perpetual pressure from so-called big box retailers such as Staples and Office Depot. Because Dunder Mifflin is a small company, they likely cannot compete against these firms on price (as the doomed Michael Scott Paper Company demonstrated). Prepare a perceptual positioning map that places Dunder Mifflin against these competitors on two axes (other than price) that you think are salient to a target audience. Don't forget to define your target audience as part of this exercise.

THE COMPONENTS OF A BRAND

People encounter many things as they interact with a company or an organization. Each one of these encounters adds, over time, to a perception about the company and/or the brands it offers. Every brand consists of a unique set of components. The brand of an automobile such as Porsche, Mazda, Toyota, or Chevrolet may be based on evaluations of vehicles in test drives, whether the company is foreign or domestic, customer views of each brand's advertisements, and even other cars of the same brand that the consumer sees on the road. Further, the brand perception may include consumer assessments of company employees. In fact, the mechanic trying to repair a vehicle at a local dealer could become the dominant factor that shapes a customer's image of General Motors. Every time the customer comes into contact with the brand, it is an opportunity to reinforce the brand position. In some cases, these contacts occur on a daily basis. Although many customer **contact points** are beyond the control of marketers (e.g., an 18-year-old may see a senior citizen working on an Apple computer in a coffee shop and feel that Apple products are better suited to a younger, more technically savvy audience), many contact points are within marketers' control. It is critical that each of these contact points be managed to deliver a consistent brand experience in line with marketers' objectives.

Recently, Subaru and Mazda created programs that were designed to emphasize the importance of the dealership as an influence on consumer assessments of an automobile company's brand. Both firms launched aggressive remodelling plans for local dealerships, with the goal of providing a more pleasant shopping environment. These new-look dealerships helped boost the brands of both Subaru and Mazda, resulting in higher sales. Subaru dealerships that remodelled using the new retail format sold 54 percent more vehicles in the following year. Mazda dealerships that adopted the new retail design sold 30 percent more vehicles.[15] Toyota, recognizing that many women purchase automobiles, and that an even greater number have a significant influence on the purchase decision, launched a program aimed at women. The program's recommendations suggested that every Toyota dealer provide a children's play area in the showroom, a coffee bar in the service area, and nicely decorated restrooms.[16] The idea was to make the dealership experience more attractive to female customers to enhance the company's brand.

Pepperidge Farm has taken the idea of connecting with consumers even further. The company has a new campaign theme, "Connecting through cookies." The primary component of the campaign is a website, **www.artofthecookie.com**, where women can keep in contact with each other. One quote on the site is, "Our friendship with our girlfriends makes our lives much richer." In addition to allowing women to connect with each other, the site also displays video clips of Sally Horchow's cross-country trip from Las Vegas to Nantucket. During the trip, Ms. Horchow spoke to women about making and maintaining friendships. She serves as a co-host for the site and is the author of the book *The Art of Friendship: 70 Simple Rules for Making Meaningful Connections*.[17]

The website has been supported by print ads as well as a public relations initiative that involved a survey of American women on the topic of friendship. The ads ran in such magazines as *Country Living, Good Housekeeping*, and *Redbook*. The headline for each was "Friendship. Is yours an art form or a lost art?" The goal of the website and the print ads is to forge an emotional connection with customers that is difficult to achieve using broadcast advertising alone.

Pepperidge Farm is not alone in the move to social network marketing. A growing number of other companies, such as Circuit City, Coca-Cola, Sony, and Microsoft, now advertise on social networking websites such as Bebo, Buzznet, Facebook, and MySpace. According to eMarketer, a research firm, over $2 billion per year is spent on advertising on these types of websites.[18]

A brand also contains invisible and intangible elements. When consumers learn that a pharmaceutical or cosmetic company has a policy that prohibits product testing on animals, this information will be integrated into their attitudes toward the brands of that firm. Personnel policies and practices impact a brand. Strikes and labour disputes often have a negative impact on a brand. The beliefs and attitudes that consumers have about Japan might influence their views of brands such as Sony and Toyota.

MARKETING COMMUNICATIONS AND BRAND EQUITY

Strong brands are often achieved largely through marketing communications. But marketing communications also benefit from strong brands in a self-reinforcing cycle, because when consumers encounter marketing communications from a brand with high brand equity, the marketing communications are usually more effective. This is because consumers are generally more willing to attend to the marketing communications, spend time thinking about it, or recall it later on. Therefore, brand equity is central to marketing communications both as an end goal, and as a mediator to other end goals, such as awareness, recall, or revenue.[19]

Because brand equity exists only because of the perceptions, feelings, and attitudes that customers have toward the brand, marketing communications play a vital role in the development and maintenance of brand equity. Keller[20] portrays the development of brand equity in the form of a pyramid, as shown in Figure 2.9. The ultimate objective for a brand manager is to have **resonance** between a brand and a customer, which leads to a close relationship and loyalty.

At the most basic level, marketing communications helps establish brand awareness with customers. However, simple awareness is not enough to create the building blocks for a relationship with a brand. Marketing communications must strive to create

Stages of Development

4. Relationship =
What about you and me?

↑

3. Response =
What about you?

↑

2. Meaning =
What are you?

↑

1. Identity =
Who are you?

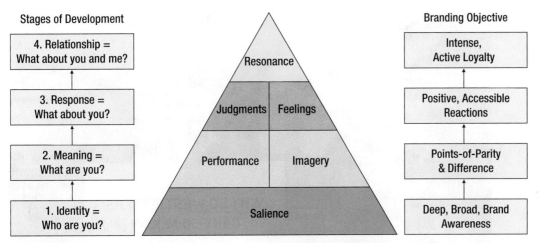

Resonance

Judgments | Feelings

Performance | Imagery

Salience

Branding Objective

Intense,
Active Loyalty

↑

Positive, Accessible
Reactions

↑

Points-of-Parity
& Difference

↑

Deep, Broad, Brand
Awareness

FIGURE 2.9
Brand Equity Model Pyramid

Source: Kevin Lane Keller (2007), "Advertising and Brand Equity," in *The Sage Handbook of Advertising*, Gerard J. Tellis and Tim Ambler (eds.), pp. 54-70. Sage: London, p. 57

brand salience for the customer. Customers must know how the brand can satisfy their needs. They must recall the brand not just in general, but at specific times and consumption experiences. Marketing communications plays a role in helping this happen. Point-of-purchase material in stores reminds people of the brand when they are shopping and considering a purchase. Advertising for a portable instant soup reminds people to have some on hand while at work so they don't hit the "3-o'clock wall." In addition to building brand awareness, these ads build brand salience because they help the consumer see how the brand can help them satisfy their particular needs.

Brand meaning is built upon brand salience. **Brand meaning** consists of both performance-related attributes related to functional needs and the abstract social or psychological needs of the customer. Marketing communications is critical in establishing both building blocks. With brand performance, it can clarify for customers how the ingredients, features, or attributes add value. It can also influence how people diagnose product performance. In a series of studies examining consumer preferences for orange juice, consumers who were shown ads for orange juice that described the high quality and taste of the brand ranked the brand higher on memory taste tests than did consumers who did not see ads that described taste and quality.[21] Brand meaning is also created when the brand creates intangible value for customers. Corona beer, for example, uses the idea of a laid-back beach holiday to create an image that consumers associate with consumption of the brand. Running Room creates marketing communications that are based on personal health and wellness, as opposed to other retailers that focus more on fashion.

Once brand meaning is established, the objective in building brand equity is generating **brand responses**, which are generated after customers examine the content of marketing communications designed to build identity and meaning. As is the case with brand meaning, responses are separated into two categories. The first deals with judgments customers make regarding product or service attributes. For example, after being exposed to marketing communications for the Petro-Canada brand, they may decide that the brand possesses a high degree of trustworthiness and quality, or see it as superior to other brands in the same category. They can also put the brand on their consideration list for purchase. The second category of responses concerns feelings toward the brand. These have to do with

Running Room focuses on personal health and fitness instead of fashion.

Source: Courtesy of WestJet

WHY DO WESTJETTERS CARE SO MUCH?

A Canadian brand that has developed a high degree of resonance with consumers is WestJet.

how the brand makes the customer feel when consuming, or contemplating consuming, the brand, and these feelings can be highlighted through marketing communications. For example, brands such as Coke generate feelings of excitement in their advertising, while the greeting card company Hallmark generates feelings of warmth. Alarm Force security seeks to generate feelings of security through their ads, while marketing communications for many fashion brands seek to generate feelings of social approval and inclusivity.

Once customers judge a brand favourably it can lead to **resonance**, or the psychological bond between the customer and the brand. This is where many of the benefits of strong brands come from. Resonance can lead to higher levels of loyalty or referring the brand to others. Consumers often talk of "loving" a brand, and they can promote it to others with almost evangelical zeal. Many users of Apple products, for example, are famous for their devotion to the brand. Marketing communications can play a strong role in developing both active and intense brand relationships. For example, social media allow current users of a brand to connect with other users and foster a sense of community, or promote the brand to non-users. Direct marketing can target customers with high-value relationships and ensure they get special perks not available to other customers.

THE IMC PLAN

Marketing communications planning is grounded in the overall marketing plan of the firm. The marketing plan outlines the four Ps: distribution planning, product enhancement, production plans, and pricing strategies. The marketing communications plan must work toward the same overall objectives as the other elements of the marketing plan. These overall marketing objectives are often based in metrics, such as market share or revenue gains over a period of time. For example, a marketing objective of a clothing manufacturer can set a marketing objective of increasing market share from 10 percent to 15 percent within the next year. Each element of the marketing plan must then work in concert to support this objective. This may include the addition of new lines, new distribution channels, new pricing strategies, and, most importantly for our consideration here, marketing communications.

The marketing plan typically involves background in the form of situation analysis, competitive intelligence, and some customer research. Based on this, along with the overall marketing objectives, the first step in the IMC plan is to define the objectives of the marketing communications. Objectives for IMC plans are discussed in Chapter 4, and often include such objectives as repositioning a brand, increasing awareness, or encouraging some form of customer behaviour, such as purchase or trial.

Closely tied to the marketing communications objectives is the definition of a target audience for the campaign. This may include multiple audiences if the brand wishes to penetrate multiple segments or communicate with different audiences involved in meeting the objective. For example, the Stetson cologne campaign mentioned earlier may involve two audiences. First, an audience of men can be targeted to ensure they see the brand as rugged and desirable. Next, women can be targeted as the gift-givers of the product. In order for the gift-giving strategy to work, the giver needs to know not only where she can buy it, but also that the recipient will value the gift. The definition of the audience is perhaps the most crucial part to any marketing communications plan because it will determine the appropriate communications tactics to use, along with the appropriate message strategy and timing. In other words, it is impossible to build an effective communications plan if you don't know with whom you are communicating.

Based on the objective and audience definition, the next step is to set a budget for the plan. This will be based on how aggressive the objective is relative to the current attitude or behaviour of the target audience. For example, if a modest 5 percent trial rate for a new brand extension is sought, and the target audience has high **brand resonance**, the budget should be fairly modest. However, if the objective is aggressive, such as increasing household penetration by 50 percent, or the target audience has a low degree of awareness or negative perceptions of the brands, the budget will have to be significantly larger.

The next step in the plan is to outline the specific communication vehicles to be used in the plan, their specific objectives (i.e., what role they play in achieving the overall objective), their specific tactics, the allocation of the budget, and the specific measures that will be used to determine success. The overall plan process and format can be found in Figure 2.10.

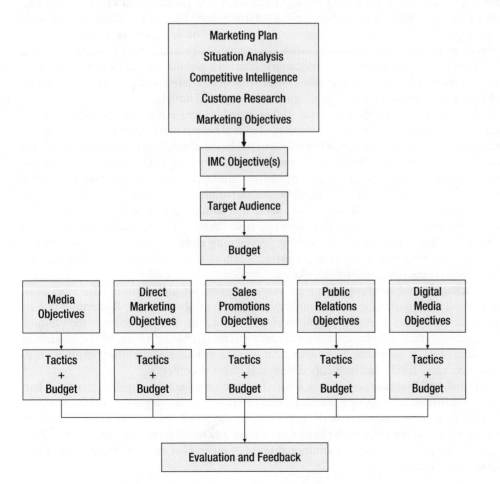

FIGURE 2.10
The IMC Plan Framework

The final step in the IMC plan, determining evaluation measures, should provide a link back to the objective so that the plan can be evaluated both within individual communication vehicles and overall. This is important because the manager must know now not only whether the overall objective was reached, but also how each element of the plan performed. For example, if television advertising is to be included in the plan with the intent of generating a high degree of awareness, this is a specific outcome related to this element of the IMC plan. If, however, the ultimate objective of product trial was not achieved, the manager could then diagnose why awareness through television advertising did not lead to trial. Perhaps other elements did not perform adequately, or perhaps other elements are needed to ensure the link between awareness and trial is made.

COMMUNICATING ACROSS CULTURES

In international markets, product development, branding, and maintaining an image are more complex. Firms can use either an *adaptation* strategy or a *standardization* strategy in promotional programs. These two approaches can be applied to the products themselves as well as to brand names. With standardization, the same brand name and product are sold in all countries. With adaptation, the brand and/or the actual product may be different in each country or region. This can mean that a product may be viewed as a local brand. Mr. Clean uses the adaptation brand approach for the same products. Mr. Proper and Maestro Limpio are just two of the brand names used by the company in other countries.

Using a standardized global brand reduces costs. Instead of advertising each local brand with a separate communication strategy, one standardized message can be sent. Standardized global brands also allow for the transference of best practices from one country to another. Further, purchasing a standardized global brand can be viewed by consumers as a better choice than buying a local brand. The global brand might have a higher perceived quality. The consumer's self-concept of being cosmopolitan, sophisticated, and modern can be enhanced when buying a global brand.[22] As the world continues to "shrink" through advances in telecommunications, consumers are becoming increasingly similar, displaying comparable consumer characteristics and purchase behaviours. This may lead to even greater use of standardized global brands.

Despite all of the advantages of global brands, some efforts to standardize brand names have met with resistance. A number of global brands that were introduced were not received with enthusiasm. Although consumer behaviour may have converged somewhat throughout the world, there are still many local idiosyncrasies. Global brands enjoy the most success in high-profile, high-involvement products. Local brands have performed the best in everyday, low-involvement products. Automobiles and computers have done well as global brands. Food, candy, and some soft drinks have done better using a local brand approach.[23] A common IMC strategy is to "think globally, but act locally." This approach can also be applied to branding. Developing global brands may be the ultimate goal; still the marketing team should consider each local market's unique features and be sensitive to supporting and developing local brands.

Packaging and labelling issues are more complex for global firms. The label must meet the legal requirements of the country where the product is sold. Remember that an attractive label is an attention-getting device that can draw the consumer to the product. For example, many purchases in Asia are, in part, driven by the appeal of the label.[24] At the same time, some culturally sensitive items, such as lingerie and other personal products, may carry labels that basically disguise or hide the contents.

Brand building and positioning issues become complicated in global markets. Part of the confusion may be that a particular country is held in low regard by other countries. Consequently, these negative feelings transfer to any products sold by companies from that country. Positioning may be harder to achieve due to differences in language, restrictions on advertising messages, additional taxes or tariffs that raise prices, and other less controllable factors.

The TELUS brand promise is "the future is friendly." "The brand promise drives everything we do across all products, in all the categories where we compete," says Kate Baillie, Director of Marketing for Broadband and Core Services for TELUS. Although the brand promise began initially, in part, due to a burgeoning technology development phase where new products may have been intimidating to customers, the brand promise is still relevant. "In fact, it's probably more relevant today than it ever was," explains Kate. "Many people are looking for someone to act as an editor to help them understand how all this new technology can help them improve their lives. What's available, what do I need, do I need all three of these features or can I get by with only one or two? These are questions we hear from customers who tell us they can sometimes be simply overwhelmed at the sheer number of products and options now available to them."

Lara Johnson agrees: "Our brand represents a promise that whatever technology comes along we will ensure it's integrated seamlessly and simply into our customers' lives. Take, for example, the TELUS Learning Centre that is available online and in our stores. Customers can visit the Learning Centre and learn how to make the most of their Smartphone features. Online tutorials provide simple to follow step-by-step visual instructions and tips to help you get the most out of your phone, but the in-store experience is interactive and customized to the customer's needs. We don't want to just sell a product and then make our customers figure it out on their own; we want to help them see how they can make the best use of what technology has to offer."

TELUS designs simplicity into all of its messages

Source: Courtesy of TELUS.

As part of the TELUS brand, the marketing team tries to ensure that the same qualities come through in every piece of marketing communications. "Across every single execution, we look for our brand attributes to be represented. Attributes like simplicity, intelligence, economy, and charm."

"It begins, first and foremost, with simplicity. When they hear from us, we want the audience to say 'I get it.' We want the language and message to be focused and easy to understand. This goes far beyond the use of white space or fonts, for example. It's at the very heart of the messages we design."

Second, Kate reconciles the attribute of simplicity with intelligence. "Intelligence is about not talking down to the audience. People are not dumb. So simplicity doesn't mean dumbing down a message to the point where someone may be insulted. We can create simple messages but still respect our audiences."

An important brand attribute in the category is economy. This isn't just a pricing issue. "We're not interested in competing just on price," says Kate. "Economy is in part the price, but as it relates to the brand it's about getting people the message quickly and efficiently. So our audience doesn't need to spend a lot of time thinking about what we're trying to say. We get to the point quickly and succinctly."

Finally, the brand attribute that many people recognize is charm. "When people take the time to engage with our message, we want to reward them for their time. So we try and entertain people at the same time as delivering a marketing message." This is accomplished by the now famous use of animals in the marketing communications. "In our television ads, for example, we try to create entertainment through the use of music and a relevant icon from nature." This has created many memorable campaigns, including the famous holiday 2005 campaign that began to the tune of "I Want a Hippopotamus for Christmas."

Working in such a competitive industry means that marketing communications plans for TELUS need to be nimble. As Lara Johnson explains, "from a financial standpoint we have a yearly plan accompanied by a locked down budget for the year. So we know what we will spend across the various marketing communications tools, agency fees, and things like that. But the industry moves so fast that we plan our marketing communications messaging more on a quarterly basis. So in October, for instance, we would be planning for January. That lets us stay flexible based on new products that are introduced, or activities by our competitors."

Source: Used with permission of Kate Baillie, TELUS Communications.

Source: Courtesy of TELUS.

The TELUS campaign has produced many memorable ads.

For help developing your IMC Plan, go to **www.pearsoncanada.ca/clow**.

SUMMARY

A strong brand is vital to the success of most companies. Brands that have a high degree of brand equity provide many benefits for both customers and the company behind the brand. For customers the benefits include, among other things, saving on search costs and being able to feel confident that they have made a good choice. For companies the benefits of brand equity include increased power over channel partners and the ability to charge premium prices. In many cases, this brand equity is the single most valuable asset of a firm.

Branding is used in many different ways by companies. Many companies create a family of brands that use the same brand name on many different products. Typically done through brand extension, this allows the brand equity established in one product to be transferred to other products. Other companies use a flanker approach and market several products within the same category under different brand names. In each case companies can use co-branding to extend the value of their brand, or capitalize on the value in other brands. Many retailers have

introduced their own brands, known as private label brands, to compete with national brands.

Brands do not exist in isolation. Rather, they are evaluated by audiences relative to other brands within the same category. Successful brands are able to position themselves in the market relative to competitors on one or more attributes that are salient for customers. Many different brand strategies are available to firms, but the most important thing is to reinforce a consistent positioning over time. When brands become stale or markets decline, it may be necessary to rejuvenate or even reposition a brand. Although this is difficult, it has been done successfully many times.

The positioning of a brand is impacted by the many contact points it has with customers. These contact points occur frequently, and they always represent an opportunity for the marketer to present a consistent brand experience to the customer. Many of the contact points, such as retail showrooms or employee interactions, are not typically associated with the marketing communications function. However, a consistent brand experience across these types of customer contact points can be crucial at reinforcing a brand positioning.

Success in marketing communications is easier when promoting a brand with a high degree of brand equity. However, marketing communications can also build brand equity. They do so across four stages. First, marketing communications can build brand identity and tell customers what the brand stands for and what it is. Second, marketing communications can develop brand meaning and reinforce either functional or image-related product attributes. Third, they can encourage brand responses in the form of judgments related to attributes or of feelings such as warmth or self-esteem. Finally, they can lead to resonance, which is the stage at which customers become loyal fans of a brand—or even its most effective salespeople.

The building of a brand and associated marketing objectives through marketing communications is achieved through the development of an integrated marketing communications plan. This plan is based on the overall marketing plan of the firm and should be developed in concert with product development, channel, and pricing plans. The plan begins with a statement of the objectives and target audience, followed by a budget. Then, each tactic in the marketing plan is outlined, along with reasons for its inclusion. Finally, a feedback and evaluation mechanism allows the manager to determine how each tactic in the plan helped meet overall objectives.

KEY TERMS

brands Names generally assigned to goods, or a service or group of complementary products.

brand extension The use of an established brand name on goods or services not related to the core brand.

brand equity The value that stakeholders assign to a brand over and above the value of an equal but unbranded product.

brand identity The adjectives or terms used to describe a brand.

brand meaning Functional and social or psychological aspects of a brand as they relate to a customer's needs.

brand metrics Measures of returns on brand investments.

brand resonance A psychological bond between a customer and a brand.

brand responses Judgments or feelings a customer makes concerning a brand based on what they know.

brand salience The degree to which customers feel a brand meets their needs.

co-branding Offering two or more brands in a single marketing effort.

complementary branding A form of co-branding in which the marketing of two brands together encourages co-consumption or co-purchases.

cooperative branding A form of co-branding in which two firms create a joint venture of two or more brands into a new good or service.

family brand When a company offers a series or group of products under one brand name.

flanker brand The development of a new brand by a company in a goods or service category in which it currently has a brand offering.

ingredient branding A form of co-branding in which the name of one brand is placed within another brand.

positioning The process of creating a perception in the consumer's mind about the nature of a company and its products relative to the competition. It is created by the quality of products, prices charged, methods of distribution, image, and other factors.

private brands (also known as *private labels*) Proprietary brands marketed by an organization and normally distributed exclusively within the organization's outlets.

REVIEW QUESTIONS

1. What is meant by the term *brand*? How is it different from *brand equity*?

2. How does a brand help customers? How does it help the company behind the brand?

3. Name five dimensions of brand value.

4. What are the four types of brand names?

5. What is the difference between brand equity and brand parity?

6. Why is brand equity important? How is it measured?

7. Describe the use of brand extension and flanker brand strategies.

8. How can one tell if a brand has potential for brand extension?

9. Identify and describe three types of co-brands.

10. How has private branding, or private labelling, changed in the past decade? How have competitors with private brands responded?

11. What is brand positioning? Give examples of various types of positioning strategies.

12. What are the principal components of an IMC plan?

13. What are four ways in which marketing communications can contribute to brand equity? How do the concepts of standardization and adaptation apply to products, brand names, and marketing strategies?

INTEGRATED LEARNING EXERCISES

1. Websites are an important vehicle by which brands communicate with audiences. Access the websites of the following companies to get a feel for the intended brand position each one tries to project. Is the image projected on the website consistent with the image portrayed in the company's advertisements? How would you improve the website to make it more consistent or effective?

   a. Bell Mobility

   b. Johnson and Johnson

   c. RBC Financial

   d. McDonald's

   e. Canadian Tire

2. Social media such as Facebook are an important tool for marketers who seek create resonance between customers and a brand. These media allow for regular communications between the brand and its customers and also allow customers to interact with each other. Find a Facebook fan page for a consumer brand and one for a business-to-business brand. Do you think the companies are effectively utilizing the media to create resonance with customers? What features or content would you add to help increase the potential for resonance?

3. Brand extension and flanker branding are common strategies for large corporations. Access the following websites. Identify the various brand extension strategies and flanker brands used by each company. Identify differences in the target audiences for each brand.

   a. Marriott Hotels (**www.marriott.ca**)

   b. Procter & Gamble (**www.pg.com**)

   c. General Motors (**www.gm.ca**)

   d. The Gap (**www.gapcanada.ca**)

4. Sporting goods marketer Fozani Group operated as a retailer under several brand names, including Sport Chek, Sport Mart, Atmosphere, and Athletes World, to name a few (a complete list can be found at **http://www.forzanigroup.com**). Do you agree with this approach? Perform an analysis of the Forzani brand strategy. As part of your analysis, discuss at least two benefits of this approach and two benefits that would be associated with reducing the number of brands, or even consolidating the outlets under one brand.

STUDENT PROJECT

Creative Corner

The brand name and positioning of a brand are two critical elements a marketing manager must consider when introducing a new product. Pick one of the products from the following list. Assume that you are the new product manager and that your company has introduced a new brand within the product category. Your first task is to decide how you will position your brand in the marketplace. Identify by name at least three competing brands. How are they positioned? How will your position be different? Part of this decision will be your target market.

Who will be your target audience? Which of the seven positioning strategies will you use? Once you have made the positioning decision based on your target market, create a brand name for your product. Discuss why you chose the name.

1. A new brand of ski boat used for recreational water-skiing

2. A new optical store that sells eyeglasses and contacts

3. A new brand of chocolate candy bar

4. A new brand of jeans

5. A new energy drink

→ ETHICS IN ACTION

A major objective for brand managers is to create loyalty. This is facilitated when there is resonance between a customer and a brand. Other behaviours that can result from resonance are referral behaviours and the willingness to pay a premium price for products with the brand name. But some critics argue that the development of brands, and the objective of brand resonance, promotes excessive materialism. They charge that when people begin to "fall in love" with brands, they lose sight of reality and can put their experiences with brands ahead of their experiences with other people in their lives.

One way that brand resonance can manifest itself is through something known as brand community. Brand communities are groups of users of a brand who share a similar sense of self, a sense of moral commitment to other users, and even some rituals.[25] Examples include the Harley-Davidson "posse rides," Jeep Jamboree weekend events, and any number of online Apple discussion forums. One of the hallmarks of these communities, is not only a shared sense of self among members, but a strong detachment from users of competing brands. On a fairly harmless level this can lead an Apple user to chide a PC user, or vice

versa. But it can also perpetuate stereotypes among rival brand communities and pleasure in the misfortune of others.[26] Taken to extremes, however, this can result in people neglecting their families due to perceived commitments to others in the brand community. The most extreme examples of this are people who spend up to a dozen hours a day playing in virtual worlds such as Second Life, or following what others are doing on Facebook. In an ironic twist, a number of websites have even sprung up to help people deal with addictions to Second Life.

1. Do you think a target of resonance or of fanatical devotion to a brand is an appropriate goal for marketers? What are three possible negative effects of consumers' extreme devotion to brands?

2. Find an example of an online brand community. Pose the question to members in the community to find out what value they receive from their membership in the community and why they belong. What are the top three reasons people offer for their membership? ●

CASE STUDY | Can Zellers Be Canada's Target?

Throughout its history, retailer Zellers has been somewhat of a fixture on the Canadian retail landscape. Beginning in 1931, the brand has always stood for value and low prices. With stores across the country, the brand is familiar to virtually every Canadian. But in the 1990s perhaps the greatest threat in the company's history came to Canada when Wal-Mart purchased the operations of Zellers' rival, Woolco. This move instantly gave Wal-Mart a presence in Canada, with over 100 Walmart stores.

The Wal-Mart Threat The Wal-mart model in Canada was largely the same as the American system, with which many Canadian shoppers were familiar from trips south of the border. Like Zellers, the Walmart brand was also built on low prices and value for consumers, but exceeded far beyond the success achieved by Zellers. Its inventory management expertise is legendary, and its power over manufacturers means Walmart gets deep concessions on pricing and other value-added benefits from retailers, which it uses to its advantage.

The Walmart brand uses marketing communications in a variety of ways. Most visible is its television advertising, which combines two key messages. First, it focuses on the low prices consumers can find at Walmart. The company positions itself using the "live better" tagline, which is meant to tell consumers they can do more because of the money they save by shopping at Walmart. The second message is about the support for local community events, and the Canadian economy in general. Many commercials

have featured Canadian suppliers to Walmart that enjoy their channel relationship and share in Walmart's success. These commercials appear to be an attempt to prevent Canadians from seeing the company's operation as a Canadian invasion by a U.S. retail giant.

HBC and Zellers Zellers is owned by HBC. It is the "mass merchandise retailer" of the company and a leading mass merchandise retailer in Canada, with 279 stores nationwide. The stores offer customers "clear value and price competitiveness on national and private label merchandise." [27] HBC also operates retailers under the following brands: The Bay, which is the company's flagship store name, with 92 stores across Canada; Home Outfitters, which specializes in kitchen, bath, and bedroom accessories and operates in 62 stores across Canada; and Field's, which is the extreme discount brand of the company. This brand began in western Canada but has since expanded into eastern Canada and now operates 196 stores across the country.

Zellers launched their own private label, Truly, in 1999. It includes products from a range of categories in the store, from food and beauty aids to pharmacy items and clothing. Most Zellers outlets across the country also feature restaurants within the stores, under the "Zellers Family Diner" name in English-speaking Canada and under "Restaurant familial Zellers" in Quebec. Some locations even feature hair salons. Zellers has also launched a smaller version of its stores—Zellers Select—to serve smaller markets.

Some argue that the Target branding model is a good template for Zellers.

Zellers also uses marketing communications to position itself. The most notable campaign, which ran for many years, was based on the tagline "the lowest price is the law." The campaign was featured on national television advertising, local print advertising, and flyers to promote items as part of a co-branding effort with manufacturers. The current emphasis for the brand is everyday low pricing, which deliberately targets mothers.[28]

The Zellers brand also participates in the HBC Rewards program, where shoppers can collect points with any purchase and redeem the points either at Zellers or at one of the other HBC retailers. The program includes a co-branding venture with MasterCard where shoppers can collect even more points when using their MasterCard to shop anywhere.

The Target Template Many companies who compete with Walmart look to the United States to understand how retailer Target competes effectively with Wal-Mart. The Target brand is Wal-Mart's largest U.S. competitor, and has positioned itself very effectively by differentiating itself from Wal-Mart's low-price message. The Target positioning is based on selection and an overall shopping experience based in "cheap chic."[29] This message is consistently reinforced in the marketing communications for the brand, which features popular recording artists and fresh, contemporary themes. Some shoppers even jokingly pronounce the store name as "tarjay" (pronounced like French, with a soft *g*) to connote the brand's high fashion at affordable prices.

Many see a move toward a Target-style positioning as the next logical move for the Zellers brand. They argue that the

"everyday low price" message is getting lost in the low-price positioning of Walmart. Others argue that the Zellers brand has been able to successfully fend off the Walmart threat for almost two decades and shows no sign of capitulation. Imagine you have been hired as a branding consultant to Zellers. Use your expertise to guide the brand into future success.

1. Do you think the Target approach to branding and competing with Wal-Mart has potential for Zellers in Canada? Write a memo to the VP of Marketing for Zellers outlining an argument for or against a move toward such an approach. In particular, outline whether you think this approach will harm any of the other brands within the HBC portfolio.

2. If Walmart "owns" the lowest price position in the category, where is the opportunity position Zellers? Develop a perceptual map that positions Zellers and Walmart on two axes that you think matter to the Canadian consumer.

3. Building on your map from question 2, develop a 30-second television commercial script to deliver this message.

4. Why do you think Zellers has been able to stay in business despite the presence of the Walmart brand in Canada? What aspects of the brand do you think have value for Canadian consumers? Prepare a 10-minute presentation with an analysis of which programs you think are most effective for Zellers, and which (if any) can be deleted from the company's strategy.

ENDNOTES

1. Don E. Schultz, "Mastering Brand Metrics," *Marketing Management* 11, no. 3 (May–June 2002), pp. 8–9; Daniel Baack and Mark N. Hatala, "Predictors of Brand Rating and Brand Recall: An Empirical Investigation," *Regional Business Review* 17 (1998), pp. 17–34.

2. Kevin Lane Keller and Donald R. Lehmann (2003), "How Do Brands Create Value?" *Marketing Management*, May–June, pp. 27–31.

3. Pat Sloan, "Gillette Bets $80 Mil on Women," *Advertising Age* (May 4, 1998), p. 63.

4. "Intercontinental Hotels Group," *Business Travel News* 21, no. 6 (April 19, 2004), p. 67.

5. Kusum L. Ailawaldi, Scott A. Neslin, and Donald R. Lehman, "Revenue Premium as an Outcome Measure of Brand Equity," *Journal of Marketing* 67, no. 4 (October 2003), pp. 1–18.

6. Sonia Reyes, "Saving Private Labels," *Brandweek* 47, no. 19 (May 8, 2006), pp. 30–34.

7. Dongdae Lee, "Image Congruence and Attitude Toward Private Brands," *Advances in Consumer Research* 31 (2004), pp. 435–41.

8. Thomas J. Ryan, "Private Labels: Strong, Strategic & Growing," *Apparel Magazine* 44, no. 10 (June 2003), pp. 32–39; Reyes, "Saving Private Labels."

9. Vanessa L. Facenda, "A Swift Kick to the Privates," *Brandweek* 48, No. 31 (September 3, 2007), pp. 24–28.

10. Paul McNamara, "The Name Game," *Network World* (April 20, 1998), pp. 77–78.

11. Max Du Bois, "Making Your Company One in a Million," *Brand Strategy,* no. 153 (November 2001), pp. 10–11.

12. Interview with Kerri L. Martin, brand manager for BMW Motorcycles USA (October 12, 2002).

13. Kate MacArthur, "Salad Days at McDonald's," *Advertising Age* 75, no. 50 (December 13, 2004), p. S-2.

14. David Kiley, "Holiday Inn's $1 Billion Revamp," *Businessweek Online* (October 39, 2007), p. 19.

15. Kari Greenberg, "Mazda, Subaru Racing to Upgrade Dealerships," *Brandweek* 45, no. 39 (November 1, 2004), p. 10.

16. Joan Voight, "The Lady Means Business," *Adweek* 47, no. 15 (April 10, 2006), pp. 32–36.

17. Stuart Elliott, "Making Social Connections and Selling Cookies" (**www.nytimes.com/2007/11/21/business/media/21adco.html**).

18. Ibid.

19. Kevin Lane Keller (2007), "Advertising and Brand Equity," in *The Sage Handbook of Advertising*, Gerard J. Tellis and Tim Ambler (eds.), p. 54–70. Sage: London.

20. Ibid.

21. Kathryn A. Braun (1999), "Postexperience Advertising Effects on Consumer Memory," *Journal of Consumer Research*, 25 (4), pp. 319–334.

22. Johnny K. Johansson and Ilkka A. Ronkainen, "Consider Implications of Local Brands in a Global Arena," *Marketing News* 38 (May 15, 2004), pp. 46–48.

23. Ibid.

24. Ibid.

25. Albert M. Muniz and Thomas C. O'Guinn (2001), "Brand Community," *Journal of Consumer Research* 27, no. 4, pp. 412–432.

26. Thomas Hickman and James Ward (2007), "The Dark Side of Brand Community: Inter-Group Stereotyping, Trash Talk, and Schadenfreude," *Advances in Consumer Research* 34, pp. 314–319.

27. HBC website: **http://www.hbc.com/hbc/about/default.asp,** accessed on April 23, 2010.

28. DSN Retailing (2002), "Zellers Reorganizes Stores, Adopts EDLP Strategy," February 25.

29. Patrick Barwise and Sean Meehan (2004), *Simply Better: Winning and Keeping Customers by Delivering What Matters Most*, Harvard University Press: Cambridge.

CHAPTER OBJECTIVES

After reading this chapter, you should be able to answer the following questions:

- **What** are the steps and issues associated with the consumer buying decision-making process?
- **How** does marketing communications play a role in developing each step of the process?
- **How** do attitudes and values influence buyer behaviours?
- **What** are the roles people other than the purchaser or consumer can play in the decision-making process?
- **How** do social influences impact the decision-making process?
- **How** do business and consumer buying decisions differ, and how are they the same?
- **How** can marketers communicate and sell to both consumer and business markets at the same time?
- **What** are the important emerging trends in buying behaviour?

INDUSTRY PROFILE

So You Want to Work in Marketing Communications?

Erin Leigh, Client Services Coordinator, Impact Communications, Halifax

Erin Leigh saw an opportunity and she took it. "While I was going to St. Mary's in their commerce program I was working at a pub called Your Father's Moustache. It's a well-known place here in Halifax. And Impact Communications was the agency that did, and still does, all of the brand development for the restaurant. Everything from the advertising right down to the menus. I was interested in working in the marketing field, so I decided I should get to know people from the agency. We're a small shop so it was easy to get to know everyone, and I would always try to be their server when they would come in."

"Eventually, as I got closer to graduation I asked our founder and CEO, Bruce Thompson, if he would give me a shot at the agency. At first I offered to do a volunteer or job shadow position to learn the business, but as luck would have it, the person who was in my job was just promoted so they needed a person to take over."

Although Erin still had to go through the formal interview process, her relationship with the agency certainly gave her a leg up. "They already knew my personality and had a chance to see the kind of colleague I would be."

The qualities that the agency saw in Erin have been essential to helping her succeed in her role as Client Services Coordinator. "Because we are a small agency, my role has a bit of everything. There are some administrative aspects to my position—things like taking care of the phones, printers, ordering supplies, and things like that. Then there's the work that I do as part of the team, working as a bridge between our clients and the rest of the resources in our agency."

Her role involves an almost unlimited number of different tasks, so Erin needs to be master of many skills. "One thing I do a lot of is contact reports, which are a tool that we use to make sure that our conversations with clients are accurately captured. After a meeting with a client, the reports allow everyone on the team to understand what decisions were made, and what their next steps are. But I'm also involved in leading a number of those steps. For instance, I'm responsible for getting quotes from some of our suppliers. I work with companies like printers,

Buyer Behaviours

promotions companies for things like coasters and other promotional items like that, video production companies, and radio stations to get estimates for projects and work to manage those companies when we work with them."

Another key aspect to Erin's work is to understand who the target audience is for a campaign, and to make sure others on the team—especially those people working in the creative department—share this understanding. "When I brief the creative team I need to understand who we are communicating with. That might include some demographic information, insight into their lifestyle, or anything that is relevant to help us do a better job of communicating. I also spend a lot of time analyzing what our clients' competitors are doing in the market so I can help our team create communications that are differentiated and take advantage of market opportunities."

Erin Leigh, Client Services Coordinator, Impact Communications

"Part of the value of truly understanding the audience and how our clients fit into the market is that we can take opportunities to make real connections with customers. In the case of Your Father's Moustache, which is now one of my clients, a big part of our communications is to take advantage of the fact that they are seen as somewhat of an institution in the city. So we place the guy with the big moustache in the logo in different scenes, like holding a lobster, for example. The communications are not only relevant to the business but also relevant to the city."

Perhaps the biggest demand on someone in a position like Erin's is the need to pay close attention to detail while working in an always busy, even chaotic environment. "In meetings, either internally or with a client, I need to be able to pinpoint the things that matter and capture those in a way that I can follow up with people to make sure things are getting done. Discussions happen quickly, and if I'm responsible for recording outcomes, decisions, or next steps, I need to be an active listener to what others on the team are saying."

"Of course, all of this takes place in an environment that is always changing. Every day I create a list of things to do that day. If I get done 5 out of the 20 things on that list, it's a good day. So many things come up during the day that require urgent attention, and I need to be able to switch gears in a moment's notice."

When asked for advice for aspiring marketers, she offers three pointers. "First—and I know this might sound obvious—be sure to actually pay attention in class. I know it may seem like some of the material is irrelevant to the real world, or overly theoretical, but it actually is quite relevant. A lot of the terminology, for example, from my classes and textbooks is actually used at our agency. So if I didn't have that exposure I would be at a big disadvantage in my job."

"Second, love what you do. Find a career where you have a passion and go for it. Especially in marketing communications, it can be a tough job sometimes. The learning curve is steep, and it is incredibly stressful. But if you love the work you do, it's easy to stick with it."

The third tip involves confidence. "It's important to be confident in what you do. Even sometimes if you aren't 100 percent confident, it's important to project confidence to others because people need to know that you are on top of your game. When I think back to how I got my start in this company, it was because I had the confidence to seek out the people I needed to know and ask them for a chance. If I didn't take that opportunity, who knows where I'd be now."

OVERVIEW

Developing effective methods to persuade audiences is necessary for success in an integrated marketing communications campaign. Although some campaigns seek to change attitudes, or target stakeholders other than customers (more on this will be discussed in Chapter 4), many IMC campaigns have sales as an ultimate objective. Therefore, in order to develop effective IMC plans, we need to understand how customers make purchase decisions. When the steps followed in making purchasing decisions are more fully understood, it becomes possible to develop stronger marketing communications programs.

This chapter outlines how marketing communications can influence customers' purchase behaviour through the five steps of the purchase decision process: *need recognition, information search, evaluation of alternatives, purchase*, and *post-purchase evaluation*. In each stage, this chapter will examine the process from both a consumer and business decision-making point of view. This is because the processes are very similar for both, given that decisions are made within companies by individuals who exhibit many of the same processes and tendencies that consumers do when purchasing for themselves.

The entire process begins when a customer decides the product or service of the marketer is needed. At this point, however, the customer has not yet decided which brand will be purchased. That decision begins with the information search, when the customer seeks to determine which brands meet their needs most effectively. Next, the customer evaluates the differences between the brands that could potentially fill the need. A decision is then made. But the process is not over, because customers regularly engage in evaluation after they have made the purchase to determine how well their decision meets their needs. As will be shown in this chapter, marketing communications plays a vital role in each of these five steps.

This chapter will also explore emerging trends in buying behaviour that impact how marketers plan and execute their campaigns. Buyer behaviour is constantly changing because it takes place in the context of our society. This means that some needs become more or less important over time. For example, teenagers as a group are much more powerful consumers today than they were only two generations ago. Teens now have their own disposable income, have access to technology their parents could only dream of, and wield much more power over family decision making than in the past. Marketers need to understand this new reality, whether they wish to communicate with teens directly, or market products or services to their households.

FIGURE 3.1
Purchase Decision-Making Process

```
┌──────────────┐
│   Problem    │
│ Recognition  │
└──────────────┘
        ↓
   ┌──────────────┐
   │ Information  │
   │   Search     │
   └──────────────┘
           ↓
      ┌──────────────┐
      │ Evaluation   │
      │     of       │
      │ Alternatives │
      └──────────────┘
              ↓
         ┌──────────────┐
         │  Purchase    │
         │  Decision    │
         └──────────────┘
                 ↓
            ┌──────────────┐
            │ Postpurchase │
            │  Evaluation  │
            └──────────────┘
```

THE PURCHASE DECISION-MAKING PROCESS

Finding ways to influence the purchasing process is a vital activity in marketing communications. Figure 3.1 models the purchase decision-making process. Each step of the decision-making process is important, and marketing communications plays a vital role in ensuring that each step is successfully achieved.

STEP 1: NEED RECOGNITION

The first step in the decision process for both businesses and consumers is the point at which someone decides a need exists. Needs can be highly complex, and simultaneous needs can exist within the same purchase process. For example, when considering the need for a car, a buyer might consider the functional need (e.g., a car provides transportation from point A to point B) as well as emotional or social needs (e.g., a car makes me feel independent and free and also makes me look more attractive to others).

Some need recognition occurs without any exposure by marketing communications. For example, when a buyer notices that a regularly used item (e.g., milk) is low in quantity, the need occurs without any marketing communications stimulation. In the same way, a mechanical breakdown in a vehicle can signal the need for repair services. Changes within the buyer or to his or her lifestyle can also stimulate need recognition. For example, when parents adopt a baby, they immediately have needs for a host of new items, such as diapers.

However, most need recognition occurs in ways where marketing communications can play an instrumental role in either creating and/or shaping the need. Consider the example mentioned above of the couple who just adopted a baby. While some items, such as diapers or baby clothes, are fairly standard needs for any parent, many of the items purchased by parents can be shaped by marketing communications. For example, Disney's Little Einstein products were promoted with a claim that they can aid in a child's development. (Note: This claim later turned out to be false.) In this case, the need for the product may not be apparent to the parents until they receive marketing communications and decide that their child should be exposed to these products.

Marketing communications for some children's toys produce need recognition for some parents.

Source: © Shutterstock.

In other cases, marketers can induce dissatisfaction with currently used products, and thus stimulate a need within a buyer. For example, many advertisements use comparative claims that position a product relative to that of a competitor. A parent may see an advertisement for Little Einstein products and decide that other learning aids she purchased are not adequate (perhaps because they lack the credibility of the Disney brand).

One more way in which marketing communications can induce a need is through the purchase of a complementary product. Consider the new parents who purchased a digital camera to record the growth of their baby. Another, complementary need may have been created at the point of the retail purchase, or even in promotions that ran through advertising, for a printer to go with the new camera. The purchase of a new product provides marketers with the opportunity to induce needs for complementary products.

Need Recognition in Business Decision-Making Processes

Just as consumers identify needs (hunger, protection, social interaction), businesses also make purchases because of needs, ranging from raw materials to professional services. The major difference, however, is the way many business needs are determined. Many business needs are created by derived demand. **Derived demand** is based on, linked to, or generated by the production and sale of some other good or service.[1] The demand for steel is largely based on the number of cars and trucks sold each year. When the demand for vehicles goes down because the economy experiences a recession or downturn, the demand for steel also declines. Steel manufacturers find it difficult to stimulate demand because of the nature of derived demand. Derived demand also exists for services. Most of the demand for mortgages depends on housing sales.

One of the principal benefits of inducing needs through marketing communications, apart from creating a market, is that it creates a situation where the buyer moves through the remaining stages of the purchase process quickly. For example, the couple who is purchasing the camera may be exposed to a retail promotion for a printer. This promotion can encourage them to move through the remaining steps to purchase the printer on the spot, without the benefit of an information search or formal evaluation of options. These steps are discussed next.

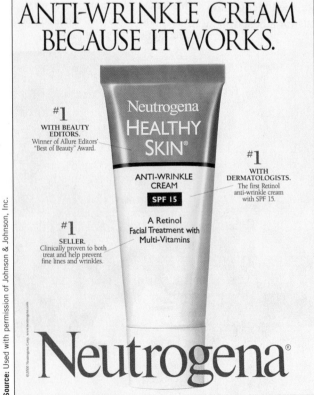

A Neutrogena ad designed to convince consumers that the product should be the first choice when selecting an antiwrinkle cream.

STEP 2: INFORMATION SEARCH

The second step of the purchase decision-making process occurs when the buyer, whether a business centre or individual consumer, conducts a search for information. Typically, a buyer begins with an internal search, mentally recalling products that might satisfy or meet the need. Often, the individual remembers how the need was met in the past. If a particular brand was chosen and the experience with that brand was positive, the buyer will likely make the same purchase decision. When this happens, the information search ends. If, however, the previous experience did not work out, the buyer conducts a more complete internal search. This includes memories of past experiences as well as the examination of other brands.

Internal Search

When conducting a more complete internal search, the buyer thinks about the brands he or she is willing to consider. This group does not normally contain every possible brand the buyer has experienced. The buyer removes brands that were tried but that did not result in a positive experience. The buyer also eliminates brands he or she knows little about. This means that during the information search process, the buyer quickly reduces the number of brands to a more manageable group.

Making sure a specific brand becomes part of the buyer's set of potential purchase alternatives is a key objective for marketing communications professionals. Achieving this goal greatly increases the chance that the brand will be purchased. A brand that has obtained a high level of brand equity is more likely to be included in the buyer's set of potential alternatives. The Neutrogena advertisement shown in this section uses "#1" four times to persuade consumers that Neutrogena is the number-one anti-wrinkle cream. The idea is to cause consumers who want an anti-wrinkle cream to think about Neutrogena, hopefully as the first and best choice.

External Search

Following an internal search, the buyer makes a mental decision regarding an *external search.* If the customer has sufficient internal information, he or she moves to the next step of the decision-making process: evaluating the alternatives. When the buyer remains uncertain about the right brand to purchase, an external search takes place.

External information may be gathered from a variety of sources, including friends, relatives, experts, books, magazines, newspapers, advertisements, public relations activities, in-store displays, salespeople, and the Internet. The amount of time a buyer spends on an external search depends on three factors: (1) ability, (2) motivation, and (3) costs versus benefits, (4) knowledge of the product (see Figure 3.2).[2]

The *ability to search* partially determines the extent of an information search. Ability consists of a person's education level combined with the specific knowledge he or she has about a product and the brands in that product's category. Educated individuals are more likely to spend time searching for information. They are also more inclined to visit stores prior to making decisions. Buyers possessing extensive knowledge about individual brands and product categories are better able to conduct a more involved external search. Thus, someone who knows a great deal about digital cameras has a more sophisticated ability to examine information than does someone who knows little about the technology. In addition, a person with more comprehensive knowledge of a product area often collects additional data, even when he or she is not in the market for the product.[3]

In terms of the amount of time an individual devotes to the external search process, a different phenomenon occurs. Although extensive product category knowledge provides individuals with a greater ability to search for external information, these buyers normally spend less time on the external search process. With knowledge already stored internally, there is no need to conduct an extensive external search for additional information. Buyers at the other end of the spectrum also spend less time in the external search process, but for the opposite reason. They do not have knowledge about the product category and do not know what type of information to ask for or even what type of information is needed, which means they lack the ability to search for information. Individuals in the middle, who have some knowledge of a product category but feel they need additional information to make intelligent decisions, typically spend the most time searching for external information.

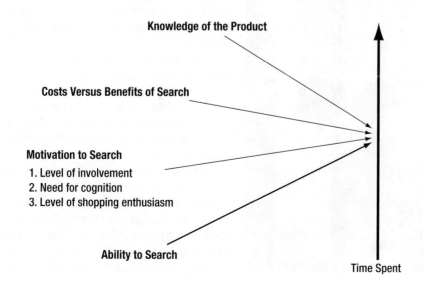

Knowledge of the Product

Costs Versus Benefits of Search

Motivation to Search
1. Level of involvement
2. Need for cognition
3. Level of shopping enthusiasm

Ability to Search

Time Spent

FIGURE 3.2
Factors Impacting the Amount of Time a Consumer Spends Conducting an External Search

The degree to which an external search takes place also depends on the buyer's *level of motivation.* The greater the motivation is, the greater the extent of an external search. Motivation is determined by the buyer's

- Level of involvement
- Need for cognition
- Level of shopping enthusiasm

Individuals are motivated to search for information when their involvement levels are high. **Involvement** means the extent to which a stimulus or task is relevant to a buyer's existing needs, wants, or values. When a buyer deems a product to be important, it becomes more likely he or she will engage in an external search. The amount of involvement is based on such factors as the *cost* of the product and its *importance.* The more a product costs, the more time an individual is willing to spend searching for information. Consider the amount of time a buyer spends when shopping for a new car versus the amount of time spent buying cough syrup. In the case of the car, the cost is significant and important because the purchase occurs only once every few years. In the case of cough syrup, the cost is relatively low and may occur several times throughout a cold.

Critical Thinking Exercise

Consider two recent purchases that cost more than $50. Think about one where you would characterize your process as containing a significant external search and one where the process contained no external search. Did your external search involve any form of marketing communications? Which ones were most instrumental to your decisions and why?

The same holds true for importance. Choosing clothes may not be an important decision to some young males, which suggests their clothing purchases typically have low involvement. Picking a tux for the high school prom, however, may spur greater involvement and a higher level of information search due to the social ramifications of dressing poorly at such an important event. The higher level of involvement emerges due to the addition of a new element—a major occasion in the person's life.

The **need for cognition** is a personality characteristic an individual displays when he or she engages in and enjoys mental activities. These mental exercises have a positive impact on the information search process. People with high needs for cognition gather more information and search more thoroughly than do individuals with a lower need for cognition.

The search also depends on a person's **enthusiasm for shopping**. Buyers who like to shop will undertake a more in-depth search for goods and services. Involvement, need for cognition, and enthusiasm for shopping combine to determine an individual's motivation to search for information.[4]

The third factor that influences an information search are the *perceived costs* versus the *perceived benefits* of the search. Higher perceived benefits increase the tendency to search. One benefit that a buyer often seeks while examining external information is the ability to reduce purchase risk. By obtaining additional

Enthusiasm for shopping has an impact on the amount of time spent on an external search.

information, the buyer lowers the chances of making a mistake in the purchase selection. The cost of the search consists of several items:

- The actual cost of the good or service
- The subjective costs associated with the search, including time spent and anxiety experienced while making a decision
- The opportunity cost of foregoing other activities to search for information (e.g., going shopping instead of playing golf or watching a movie)

The greater the perceived subjective cost of the external information search, the less likely the buyer will be to conduct a search.[5]

The fourth factor is *knowledge of the product category,* and the related amount of use or experience with the product category. For example, people who have educational backgrounds in technology may spend less time searching for information when purchasing a computer because they enter the process with a higher level of understanding than most. Similarly, if consumers have worked with computers daily as part of their job for years, they are less likely to require an extensive search because of their familiarity and experience with the product.

The four factors that make up an external search are normally considered simultaneously. From an integrated marketing communications perspective, the search process represents an important time to reach the buyer with information about a particular brand. The buyer's objective in making the effort to perform an external search is to acquire information leading to a better, more informed decision. The marketing team should try to provide information that leads buyers to view the company's products as ideal for meeting the specific needs recognized. Most critical is the development of favourable attitudes toward the product.

One difference in the information search process in a buying centre, compared with consumer decision making, is that the stage begins with the establishment of specifications. This is especially true in cases where the purchase is for a new good or service and not a reorder. Many times, various vendors are involved in helping the buyer develop clear specifications. In repeat purchase situations, specifications are examined to ensure that they are current and that they meet the company's needs.

Once specifications have been identified, potential vendors are identified and notified to find out if they are interested in submitting bids. In most business situations, written, formal bids are required. A vendor's ability to write a clear proposal often determines whether the company will present a successful bid. Effective proposals spell out prices, quality levels, payment terms, support services, and any other condition requested by the company looking to purchase goods or services.

Buyer Attitudes

Marketing communications has the ability to influence consumers' attitudes. An **attitude** is a mental position taken toward a topic, a person, or an event that influences the holder's feelings perceptions, learning processes, and subsequent behaviours. Whether we explicitly realize it or not, we have attitudes toward everything we know. Think about your attitude toward healthy eating or exercise. If your attitude is favourable, chances are you see it as an important part of your life and you do it regularly. If your attitude is negative, chances are you frequently make less healthy food

Consumers who are highly familiar with computers are more likely to purchase online through a vendor such as NCIX.com than to go to a more mainstream retailer such as Best Buy.

Canon injected humanity into a brand known for technological sophistication.

choices and avoid exercise. Marketing communications play a role in developing, maintaining, or changing attitudes toward brands or behaviours. In the case of a new brand launch, no attitude exists, and the task of marketing communications includes the development of positive attitudes. In the case of existing brands, such as Pepsi, most marketing communications are designed to maintain existing attitudes toward the brand (e.g., reinforcement of its youthful image). But for many well-known brands, marketing communications can set out to changes consumer attitudes from negative to positive, or change how consumers view the brand on one or more dimensions, such as quality or reliability.

Attitudes consist of three components: (1) cognitive, (2) affective, and (3) conative.[6] The cognitive component refers to a consumer's mental images, understanding, and interpretations of an ad or a brand. Essentially, it is how a person *thinks* about an ad or brand. The affective component consists of the emotions a consumer has about an ad or brand; how a person *feels* about it. The conative component includes a consumer's intentions and behaviours—things related to what a consumer *does* in response to marketing communications.

Consumers develop attitudes based on all three of these components, but the sequence of development is not the same for all products. This sequence is referred to as the *hierarchy of effects*, and it can take one of three sequences. Each of these is discussed in turn.

Cognitive—Affective—Conative

For many products, a consumer first develops an understanding of the product category or brand. This understanding can be developed through such aspects of marketing communications as advertising, brochures, websites, or even conversations with salespeople. This sequence is common for what are known as high involvement products—products where a consumer puts in effort to learn about the product category first, and comparison shopping is common. For example, when purchasing a new television, a consumer is likely to understand the features and benefits of different brands. This understanding will then result in the consumer feeling a certain way about a brand, which will then translate into purchase intentions.

Affective—Conative—Cognitive

Some product's categories are driven by emotions and feelings. Attitude formation for these products begins with the way a consumer feels about a product or in response to marketing communications. For example, ads for perfume or skin care products often associate the brand with emotional images of beauty or nature, with no product information at all. These ads develop a strong emotional response from consumers, who buy the product based on this emotion. Only after they have acted do they learn more about the product benefits and features, through such things as packaging and directions for use.

Conative—Cognitive—Affective

Still other purchases are associated with attitudes that begin with the behaviour, followed by thoughts and emotions. These products are usually low involvement goods where the consumer puts little effort into the decision-making process; often these are impulse purchases. Take, for example, a consumer who sees a deal on a new brand of cookies. Given that the product is new and the cost is relatively low (and it's on sale), she decides to try the cookies. She then learns about

Marketing communications for charities often rely on an emotional response.

the taste, texture, and other nutritional information, which then leads to the development of a feeling toward the product. This feeling, if positive, can then translate into future purchase intentions. But if the feeling is negative, the result can be avoidance or even explicitly negative behaviours, such as telling her friends not to buy the product.

It is important to note that the development of an attitude across all three components need not occur as the result of a single piece of marketing communications. Attitudes can take time to develop, with many different consumer touch points. For example, in the case of the television buyer in the first sequence, the cognitive stage might be impacted by a website search, a visit to a retail location, and a print ad. The affective stage could then be aided by television advertising, and the conative stage might be developed through discussions with friends and neighbours, or the launch of a limited-time promotion by the retailer.

Buyer Values

Implicit in our attitudes are our values. **Values** are strongly held beliefs about various topics or concepts. Values frame attitudes and lead to the judgments that guide behaviours. Values tend to be enduring. They normally form during childhood, although they can change as a person ages and experiences life.

Figure 3.3 lists some of the more common personal values. Individuals hold them to differing degrees. Factors that affect a person's values include the individual's personality, temperament, environment, and culture. By appealing to basic values, marketers hope to convince prospective customers to buy the company's products by acting on those values.

Critical Thinking Exercise

Study the list of personal values presented in Figure 3.3. Identify the five most important to you. Rank them from first to last. Beside each value, identify at least two products you have purchased to satisfy those values. Then, gather into small groups of three to five students. Using the information from your list of values, discuss differences among members of the group. Identify a way to send a marketing message that will appeal to the top value from each person's list.

◆ Comfortable life	◆ Pleasure
◆ Equality	◆ Salvation
◆ Excitement	◆ Security
◆ Freedom	◆ Self-fulfillment
◆ Fun, exciting life	◆ Self-respect
◆ Happiness	◆ Sense of belonging
◆ Inner peace	◆ Social acceptance
◆ Mature love	◆ Wisdom
◆ Personal accomplishment	

FIGURE 3.3
Personal Values

Marketing communications experts should consider both attitudes and values. If a good or service can be tied to a relatively universal *value*, such as patriotism, then the firm can take advantage of the linkage to present a positive image of the product. Following the Canadian men's and women's gold medal hockey wins at the Vancouver Olympics, many firms attempted to tie their brands to Canadian patriotism. Similarly, all forms of marketing communications represent an opportunity to shape attitudes. Most people consider being "put on hold" to be a nuisance. Marketers can tap into that insight and use it to present a good or service in a more favourable light. By making the time pass pleasantly while you are on hold, they turn a negative attitude into a more positive experience. Callers to the WestJet call centre are treated to a series of jokes while on hold.

FIGURE 3.4
Roles in the Decision-Making Process

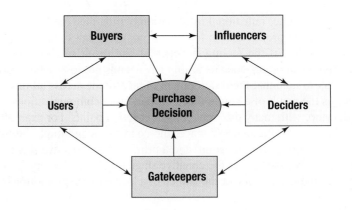

The Social Aspects of Buyer Behaviour

Purchase decision-making processes rarely involve only one person. In some cases, where there is no external search and the product is relatively low involvement, perhaps there is no impact of others around the buyer. For example, someone at the supermarket checkout may grab a package of gum without thinking much about what others will think of the decision, and certainly is unlikely to consult others for information to help him or her make a better decision. However, in many cases, the role of other people besides the buyer can be significant.

Roles within the Consumer Buying Process

For many purchases there are many more people involved in the purchase process than just the person who makes the purchase. There are five unique roles within the purchase process that people can take. These are listed in Figure 3.4.

- Users—The person or people who will actually use the product or service
- Buyer—The person who actually makes the purchase transaction
- Influencers—People who shape purchasing decisions by providing or influencing the criteria utilized in evaluating alternatives
- Deciders—People who decide whether or not something will be purchased and which product or service will be chosen
- Gatekeepers—People who control the flow of information to others in the purchase process

Of course, not every purchase will have someone occupying each of these fives roles. In other purchases, the same person might occupy multiple roles simultaneously. Consider some of the purchases made by a family of five people—two parents and three children, aged 14, 9, and 5, to see how various roles take shape.

Each member of the family can play a role in the decision-making process.

- Mother is in the grocery store examining the yogurt section. She has seen advertising for yogurts that contain probiotics that aid in digestion. She was also given a pamphlet about probiotics by her doctor the week before. She decides to purchase a container of Activa from Danone. In this situation, the mother is the buyer (she's the one in the store buying groceries), the decision maker, and probably the only user (although others in the house may also eat this yogurt). Her doctor may have played an influencer role, and also a gatekeeper role by deciding to provide information on the benefits of probiotics.

- Mother then goes down the cereal aisle. She chooses a box of Honey Nut Cheerios. She likes this for her nine- and five-year-olds because it's a little sweet but not too sugary. In this case she is the purchaser but not a user. Her children are users and definitely influencers. They may even be deciders, since some parents give their children a list of cereals they can choose from.

- The entire family is on holiday in Florida. Nice. As they drive their minivan along I-95, they decide to find a hotel for the night. At the next interchange, there are five hotels to choose from. One is a Super 8 budget motel, another is a high-end Marriott property. There is also a Residence Inn by Marriott, a Hampton Inn, and a Holiday Inn Express. They decide to stay at the Residence Inn because it has a pool with a water slide, offers a free hot breakfast, and has suites with two bedrooms. In this case, father may be the actual buyer (he checks in and uses his credit card to pay for the room). Mother and father are probably both deciders. All family members are users, since they all stay at the hotel. The children are influencers because they prefer the hotel with the water slide. Mother is also an influencer on the father's thinking because she wants the kids to have a good breakfast in the morning. She also prefers the two-bedroom suite so the kids can have their own room and beds (hey, it's been a long drive).

- After they return from vacation, the minivan breaks down and it's time for a new one. Father goes shopping on a Saturday afternoon and picks up some brochures. Although mother and father may be the deciders and purchasers, father, mother, and the 14-year-old are all users because the 14-year-old will be driving soon. The 14-year-old may be an influencer, at least on the options that are chosen for the vehicle, such as an MP3 player. The salesperson in the showroom can act as gatekeeper by discussing an upcoming promotion or sharing product information. Other influencers can be friends or family who also have minivans.

As these examples show, consumers regularly make purchases whereby they interact with others who occupy roles within the purchase process, or assume multiple roles themselves. In each case, marketers must understand when these roles exist so they can understand how purchase decisions are made. Those marketers that are able to identify and reach others in the process will be more successful because they are able to influence the entire purchase process, not just the buyer. For example, in the case of the yogurt, a marketing communications plan that also includes health professionals may aid in helping the purchase occur. Similarly, in the case of cereal, marketing that reaches the children is no doubt helpful in influencing the product selection.

Information Search in Business Decision-Making Processes

The buying decision-making process for businesses is often more complex due to the number of people involved. The **buying centre** is the group of individuals making a purchase decision on behalf of a business. The buying centre consists of same five different roles found in the process. As with consumer purchases, these five roles often overlap. A gatekeeper might also be the user. Oftentimes, the gatekeeper is the entire purchasing department, and this group might determine what information reaches members of the buying centre. The purchasing department usually controls the amount of access a salesperson has to members of the buying centre.

The behaviours of members in the buying centre are influenced by a series of organizational and individual factors.[7] These influences change the manner in which decisions are made and often affect the eventual outcome or alternative chosen.

Organizational Influences

Several organizational factors affect the ways in which individuals make purchasing decisions for a company. These organizational factors include the company's goals and its operating environment (recession, growth period, lawsuits pending, etc.). Decisions are further constrained by the organization's finances, capital assets, and market position; the quality of its human resources; and the country in which it operates.

FIGURE 3.5
Individual Factors Affecting the Behaviours
of Buying Centre Members

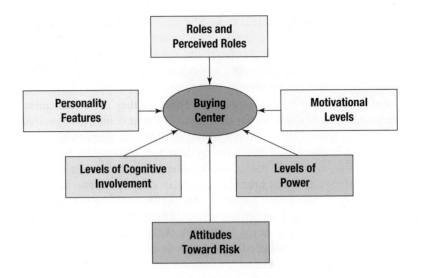

Studies of organizational decision making indicate that employees tend to adopt *heuristics*, which are decision rules designed to reduce the number of viable options to a smaller, manageable set. Company goals, rules, budgets, and other organizational factors create heuristics. One decision rule often employed is *satisficing*, which means that when an acceptable alternative has been identified, it is taken and the search is completed. Rather than spending a great deal of time looking for an optimal solution, decision makers tend to favour expedience.[8]

Individual Factors

At least six factors affect each member of the business buying centre: (1) personality features, (2) roles and perceived roles, (3) motivational levels, (4) levels of power, (5) attitudes toward risk, and (6) levels of cognitive involvement (see Figure 3.5).[9] Each impacts how the individual interacts with other members of the centre.

The first factor is *personality.* A decisive person makes purchase decisions in a manner different from someone who vacillates. Confidence, extroversion, shyness, and other personality traits affect both the person performing the decision-making role and others in the process. An aggressive "know-it-all" type affects the other members of a decision-making team, and such a personality feature does not always benefit the organization. An extrovert tends to become more involved in the buying process than a more introverted individual, but might spend too much time talking. The introvert might spend more time listening but might be too timid with salespeople, and consequently may not ask important questions.

The *roles* people play are influenced by an individual's age, heredity, ethnicity, gender, cultural memberships, and patterns of social interaction. Roles are socially constructed, which means people define how they intend to play roles as part of the negotiation process with others. A person's perception of how the role fits into the buying centre process and the overall organization affects how the individual is involved in the purchase. If a buying centre member perceives the role as merely giving approval to decisions made by the boss (the decider), then the individual will not actively participate. When members feel their inputs are important and are being solicited, they become more active.

Motivation depends on how well the individual's goals match the organization's goals. If a factory supervisor has a personal goal of becoming the vice president of operations, that supervisor is more likely to become involved in all purchasing decisions that affect his performance and that of his department. If a purchasing agent has been charged by the CEO to cut expenses, that person might take a more active role to ensure that cost-cutting selections are made.

A person's *level of power* in the buying process is derived from his or her formal position in the buying centre and in the organization, and the impact of the purchase decision on a specific job. When a particular purchase decision directly affects an employee, that person tries to gain more power in the buying process. For instance, a factory supervisor may have greater power within the buying centre in the purchase of raw materials, whereas the maintenance supervisor has more power in the purchase of maintenance supplies. In these situations, each strives to influence the decision that affects his or her area.

Risk also affects members of the buying centre. Many vendors are chosen because buyers believe the choice represents the lowest risk. Risk avoidance leads buyers to stay with current vendors rather than switching. In marketing to businesses, reducing risk is a major concern, especially when signing large contracts or when the purchase might affect company profits. People tend to think that taking risks (especially when a failure follows) can affect performance appraisals, promotions, and other aspects of an individual's job.

Levels of cognitive involvement impact the buying centre. Individuals with higher levels of cognitive capacity want more information prior to making decisions. They also ask more questions when interacting with a sales rep. These individuals spend more time deliberating prior to making decisions. Clearly stated message arguments are the important ingredients in persuading people with higher cognitive levels (as noted in the discussion of consumer buyer behaviours).

STEP 3: EVALUATION OF ALTERNATIVES

The third step in the consumer buying decision-making process is the evaluation of alternatives. As we saw previously, the purchase decisions process can contain many different roles, and these can influence the evaluation process. In the case of consumer decisions, the actual decision maker may not be the user, and may be heavily influenced by friends or family members. Similarly, in business decision-making processes, the buyer may be influenced by those who will actually use the product. The first step in evaluation is the development of the evoked set, which is followed by one of two evaluative processes—the multiattribute approach or affect referral.

The Evoked Set

A person's **evoked set** consists of the brands he or she considers in a purchasing situation. An evoked set might be reviewed during both the information search and evaluation stages of the buying decision-making process. Two additional brand sets become part of the evaluation of purchase alternatives: (1) the inept set and (2) the inert set. The **inept set** consists of the brands that are part of a person's memory that are *not considered* because they elicit negative feelings. These negative sentiments are normally caused by a bad experience with a vendor or particular brand. They can also originate from negative comments made by a friend or by seeing an advertisement that the potential customer did not like.

The **inert set** holds the brands that the consumer is aware of, but the individual has neither negative nor positive feelings about the products. A lack of knowledge about these brands usually eliminates them as alternatives. In other words, in most purchase situations the only brands considered are those that are present in the evoked set.

Critical Thinking Exercise

Without looking in your bathroom or going into a store, how many brands of toothpaste can you name? Now go into a supermarket and look at the toothpaste aisle. How many of the total number of brands on the shelf could you name? Why do you think you didn't recall the ones you did not, and why do you think you were able to recall the names of the ones you did? If a company were launching a new brand of toothpaste, how would you suggest they go about getting into your evoked set?

One of the primary goals of marketing communications is placing the brand name in the evoked sets of consumers. To do so normally requires promoting the brand name and the brand's primary benefit extensively and consistently. Extensively means using multiple marketing communications tactics. By tying the brand with its primary benefit, the intent is to embed the brand's name into the consumer's long-term memory. The message should be designed to establish or reinforce linkages between benefit and the brand name. When a consumer who is ready to evaluate alternatives uses his or her evoked set and the company's brand reaches the part of the set being considered, the marketing communications have been successful.

The Multiattribute Approach

Particularly for products with higher levels of involvement, consumers evaluate purchasing alternatives using the multiattribute approach. Consumers often examine sets of product attributes across an array of brands. The multiattribute model suggests that a consumer's ultimate attitude toward a brand is determined by:[10]

- The brand's performance on product or brand attributes
- The importance of each attribute to the consumer

This model includes the assumption that consumers rate choices by the degree to which they contain an attribute (e.g., low price, style, convenience) and the degree to which that attribute is important to them personally. When brands are rated highly on attributes with high personal importance, they are more likely to be purchased. Figure 3.6 notes products, along with some of the characteristics that affect their selection, each with potentially a lesser or greater value to individual consumers.

Marketing communications has the potential to greatly impact how this model formulates consumer attitudes. Marketing communications can certainly impact how a consumer views the *performance of a brand on a particular attribute*. Let's consider a food product, such as pre-packaged, frozen dinners. This category has become quite crowded over the years, with many brands, such as Stouffers' and Michelina's, now competing for revenue and shelf space in the frozen food section. Marketing communications for one brand can include messaging that is intended to lead consumers to rate it higher on the attribute of taste. This can be done through a number of ways, including communication of key ingredients; appetizing, full-colour photos; and endorsements by well-known chefs. The effect is that the consumer will rate this brand higher on taste and as a result, assuming that taste is an important attribute, be more likely to purchase this brand.

Another method by which marketing communications can generate more positive attitudes toward a brand using the multiattribute model is to analyze several different brands against each other on a variety of attributes. In addition to improving perceptions of performance on a brand, marketing communications can also impact how a consumer views *performance of a competing brand on a particular attribute*. In this case, the objective is to lead consumers to view the other brand as less desirable. In the case of taste,

FIGURE 3.6
The Mutliattribute Model

Product	Characteristics				
Computer	Price	Style	Service contract	Software	Memory storage
Telephone	Price	Style	Speed dial	Caller ID	Cordless feature
Car	Price	Style	Safety	Room	Other features
T-bone steak	Price	Age	Fat content	Degree cooked	Seasonings
Sunglasses	Price	Style	UV protection	Durability	Prescription lenses
Sofa	Price	Style	Foldout bed	Stain resistance	Color
Credit card	Interest rate	Fees	Billing cycle	Access to ATM	Credit limit

Consider each item. Which characteristic is most important to you personally? Least important?

marketing communications that include taste tests where a competing brand fails can be very effective.

A third way that marketing communications can alter attitudes formed through the multiattribute model is to *influence the importance of an attribute*. For example, many consumers may simply assume that frozen pre-packaged dinners are not very tasty. Therefore, they may rate the importance of the taste attribute as low in overall attitude formation. Marketing communications can play a role in helping consumers see taste as a more important aspect of their evaluation by taking it out of the freezer section and into the deli section, for example. This can not only enhance the performance of a given brand on the taste attribute, but also encourage consumers to think about taste as an important attribute when making a decision.

A fourth way that marketing communications can influence attitudes is through the *introduction of new attributes* that are not currently salient for consumers. Although this often requires some product modification as well as marketing communications, this is not always the case. For example, a brand of frozen dinners may introduce a cause-related marketing program that includes a donation of 25 cents to a charity with each purchase. This introduces a new brand attribute—altruism—that consumers can consider when deciding among brands.

Michelina's uses Facebook to connect with consumers.

Source: Courtesy of Bellisio Foods Canada.

How Does the Multiattribute Approach Work?

Let's assume a consumer is evaluating four high-definition television brands. She knows very little about HDTVs and has spent considerable time conducting external research. In making this purchase, she bases her evaluations on five criteria: (1) picture quality, (2) the speakers and quality of sound, (3) the styling and appearance of the HDTV, (4) the price, and (5) the type of screen. The importance ratings in Figure 3.7 indicate that the consumer is most interested in picture quality, because she gave it a rating of 5. Quality of sound with external speakers and style of the HDTV are next, with ratings of 4. The price and the type of screen are the least important.

The next column of numbers shows her evaluation of each attribute for each brand. In terms of picture quality, the Pioneer flat-panel plasma HDTV was the best, followed by Samsung and Westinghouse, and then Vizio. She can calculate evaluation scores in several ways. One method is to multiply each attribute's importance rating by the corresponding evaluation for each brand. Summing these results in the scores is shown in the

Attribute[a]	Importance[b]	Pioneer	Samsung	Vizio	Westinghouse
Picture quality	5	5	4	3	4
Speakers/sound quality	4	3	4	4	5
Styling of HDTV	4	4	5	2	3
Price	3	3	3	5	4
Screen type	3	4	2	5	4
Compensatory score[c]		74	71	69	76

FIGURE 3.7
Example of a Multiattribute Evaluation Approach for an HDTV

[a]Each attribute is ranked on a scale of 1 to 5, with 5 being high performance and 1 being low performance.

[b]Importance is ranked on a scale of 1 to 5, with 5 being very important and 1 being very unimportant.

[c]The compensatory score is the sum of the importance times the brand evaluation for each brand

Many consumers are loyal to MEC because of the fact that it is member-owned.

row labelled Compensatory Score. Using this method, she would choose the Westinghouse flat panel LCD HDTV, because of its overall score. This method of evaluating alternatives is called **compensatory heuristics**.

The compensatory heuristics method assumes that no one single brand scores high on every attribute and that individual attributes vary in importance. When considering several brands, consumers make tradeoffs. Although the Pioneer had the best picture quality, it was not the best brand for Kelli because of the poor ratings on other attributes.

A second computational form consumers can use to make evaluations is called **conjunctive heuristics**. In this method, she establishes a minimum, or threshold, rating. She considers only brands that meet this threshold, even when one product ranks high on individual criteria. Going back to Figure 3.7, assume that she has mentally established a minimum threshold of 4. She discards a brand if it scores 3 or lower on any criterion important to her. Using this method, she would eliminate all four brands because of low scores on individual attributes.

Consumers can also use an iterative approach. Picture quality is most important, so she starts there. She rated the Vizio a 3, and because this is below the minimum this brand is eliminated. Next, she goes to her next-most important criterion—quality of the sound and external speakers. She ranks both sound quality and styling of the HDTV with a 4 in terms of importance. Before she can eliminate any more brands, she has to decide which of those two criteria is more important. Assuming that sound quality is next, she would eliminate Pioneer due to its rating below the threshold. Now she has narrowed her choice to two models, Samsung and Westinghouse. The next attribute she considers is styling. Because the Westinghouse is below the threshold, she eliminates it. Thus, she chooses the Samsung brand because it is the only one left.

Another calculation can be made using a phased heuristic approach. This method is a combination of the others. Going back to Figure 3.7, assume that she eliminates any brand with a score lower than 3 on any criterion. This leaves Pioneer and Westinghouse. To make the decision between these two brands, she can use the compensatory heuristic approach. Consumers often use a phased approach similar to this when they have many brands to evaluate. This method easily reduces the evoked set to a smaller and more manageable subset.

Role of Social Influences in the Evaluation of Alternatives

An addition to the multiattribute model takes into account the role of social influences in alternative evaluation. In addition to the judgments made by the consumer about the performance of brands on several attributes and the importance of those attributes, an expanded model also adds the evaluations of others and the importance the consumer places on the judgments of those people. Here, again, marketing communications can play a critical role in shaping brand preference in the evaluation stage in two ways.

First, marketing communications can influence how the consumer sees the evaluations of others. A mother who buys food for her young children, for example, is likely to consider the evaluations of her children of the food she buys. If she believes that her children will not enjoy pre-packaged applesauce as a snack, she is unlikely to buy Dole brand applesauce, for example. Through marketing communications targeted toward mothers, the company can help change the perception mothers have of their children's evaluations of this product. Once mothers believe that their children will enjoy the snack, they are more likely to buy the product.

The second way that marketing communications can affect attitudes through social influences is to influence the importance of the opinions of others to the consumer. Consider the same example of the mother who is buying food for her children. Imagine that her children really don't like applesauce and she knows it. One way to encourage her to buy the

This ClikSTAR ad effectively uses others who share concerns about diabetes to create credibility for the product.

product anyway is to reduce the importance of the children's evaluations in favour of some other salient influencer. For example, a campaign can feature medical professionals talking about the importance of fruit in children's diets and how the brand is a perfect solution to introduce fruit. The mother is more likely to consider the taste evaluations of her children as less important in the face of more positive opinions of medical professionals.

Referent Groups

In addition to those in direct contact with the buyer in the decision-making process (like friends or family), two additional types of social influences are particularly important in evaluating alternatives using the multiattribute approach. These influences are known as referent groups. There are two types of referent groups—associative and dissociative. Associative referent groups are those to which the consumer wishes to belong. For example, a television ad for Callaway gold clubs portrays four golfing buddies on a golfing weekend in the Rockies. They are all good friends and take golf seriously. For men who are golf enthusiasts, the men in the ad may represent an associative referent group. They represent the kind of people many golf enthusiasts aspire to be.

For other marketers, the use of dissociative reference groups is an even more powerful mechanism. This is because the drive to be separate from some people is more powerful than the desire to be included with other people. We often define ourselves as much by who we not as by who we are.[11] Dissociative referent groups represent an opportunity for marketers to define the competition as undesirable, or even repulsive. For example, the famous ads for Apple that feature the Mac and PC played by two individuals use both associative and dissociative reference groups. But the dissociative reference group is arguably more powerful. The PC is portrayed by a bumbling, somewhat stocky man wearing an unattractive suit and tie. The consumers in the target audience for Apple want to be seen as the hip young man wearing the T-shirt as much as they want to avoid being seen as the bumbling man in the suit.

Critical Thinking Exercise

Find an advertisement that uses a dissociative reference group. Do you think the use of the group is effective? Why or why not?

Affect Referral

In addition to the multiattribute approach, a second model of how consumers evaluate purchase alternatives is called **affect referral**. It suggests that consumers choose brands they like the best or the ones with which they have developed emotional connections. This means the individual does not evaluate brands or think about product attributes. Instead, the consumer buys the brand he or she likes the best or the one that incites positive feelings. Toothpaste, ketchup, soft drinks, and milk are some of the products consumers normally select in this way. These purchases typically have low levels of involvement. They are also frequently purchased products.

The affect referral model also explains purchases of higher priced items as well as purchases of products that are "socially visible." It is the emotional bond that has been established between the consumer and the brand that leads to a purchase under those circumstances.

The affect referral model is a reasonable assumption for three reasons. First, using this approach to product evaluation saves mental energy. A quick choice seems easier than going through the process of evaluating every possible alternative. Some purchases basically don't deserve much effort. The affect referral model explains those situations.

Second, a multiattribute model type of approach might have been used previously when making a purchase. This means the person has already spent a great deal of time considering various product attributes, deciding which are most critical, and reaching a decision about the brand with the greatest number of advantages. Therefore, going through the process again would be "reinventing the wheel." For example, a teenager buying jeans may have already spent considerable time evaluating styles, prices, colours, durability levels, and "fit" of various brands. After making the purchase, this teenager continues to purchase the same brand as long as the experience remains positive. The affect referral model explains this buying behaviour—the repurchase is simple and convenient.

Third, consumers often develop emotional bonds with brands. In terms of the purchase decision, an emotional bond with a product can be the strongest and most salient factor in the decision.[12] It is more important than any attribute or benefit the product can offer. Successful brands establish emotional bonds with consumers. A bond generates brand loyalty, enhances brand equity, and reduces brand parity. This means consumers do not have to evaluate alternatives because of their bond with the brand. Harley-Davidson has developed such a bond with many of the company's customers. So has Nike. For these customers, these feelings toward Harley-Davidson and Nike are so strong that they do not even think about other alternatives.

Alternative Evaluation in Business Decision-Making Processes

While still influenced by the same factors as consumer decisions (e.g., referent groups, attitudes, etc.), the alternative evaluation stage is more formalized for businesses than it is for consumers. Evaluations of vendors in the business decision-making process normally occur at three levels. The first level is an *initial screening* of proposals. This process narrows the field of vendors down to three to five competitors. The second level of evaluation occurs as the firm undertakes a *vendor audit*. An audit is especially important when members of the company want to develop a long-term relationship with a supplier. Vendors that are the primary sources for critical components or raw materials recognize that long-term bonds benefit both the vendor and the purchasing firm. The third and final level of evaluation takes place as various members of the buying centre *share vendor audit information*. At that time, company leaders consider purchase procedures. A company might require the manufacturer to share its production schedule. Sharing information, such as the production schedules, with suppliers requires a degree of trust in the vendor.

STEP 4: PURCHASE DECISION

Although the purchase decision itself is not traditionally considered part of the marketing communications mix, savvy marketers know that this contact point with the customer can mean the difference between a one-off sale and the beginning of a long-term relationship. In fact, the purchase decision may not represent the actual purchase in some cases. Often, a decision is made to purchase something at a later time. Or, if a purchase decision is made while shopping online, the consumer may find out the item is out of stock and decide to go to a retail store near his or her home to buy the item. While the consumer is in the store, any number of things can happen to reverse the purchase decision.

It is important that the purchase experience be consistent with the overall brand experience that is promised throughout the previous steps in the purchase process. This includes the presentation of any warranties or service agreements, and the way the product is wrapped or delivered. This is especially important for certain product categories or groups of consumers. In Asian cultures, for example, the presentation of something can be equally important as the thing itself. Therefore, a store clerk who hastily shoves a product into a bag will deliver a poor brand experience for many customers, and those customers are less likely to return. This stage also represents an opportunity to introduce other products or services, as noted in the need recognition stage.

Purchase Decisions in Business Decision-Making Processes

In the decision process, members of the buying centre experience all of the individual and organizational pressures discussed earlier. The final decision is normally based on a comparison of per-dollar values offered by various vendors. When selection criteria are used, the most common include quality, delivery, performance history, warranties, facilities and capacity, geographic location, and technical capability.[13] It is not likely that any one vendor will be deemed superior on all selection criteria. Therefore, the marketing team for each seller will emphasize the company's specific strengths as part of the selling process. In reality, however, politics and other forces also have a significant impact. Successful marketing communications requires an understanding of these forces.

Critical Thinking Exercise

Think of a time when you had made a purchase and were disappointed with either the purchase experience itself or the post-purchase experience. What did the company do that created the disappointment? What about the experience was different than the "promise" made by the brand through marketing communications up to the actual purchase decision?

STEP 5: POST-PURCHASE EVALUATION

Again, savvy marketers know that the experience after the customer has received the product is critical to the development of a brand relationship and to repeat purchases in the future. Consumers seek to reduce **cognitive dissonance** after they have made

FIGURE 3.8
A Comparison of the Business-to-Business (B-to-B) Buying Process to the Consumer Buying Process

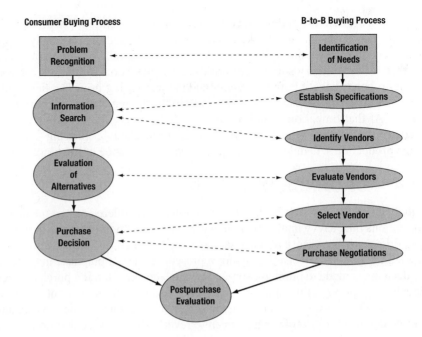

3M Post-it Sortable Cards are sold to both retail customers and in business-to-business markets.

purchases, and marketing communications can play an important role to assist them. Simply seeing advertising of brands they have chosen can make them feel good about their purchases. Tactics such as mail, email follow-up, or surveys are all good ways to ensure customers have positive experiences with the brand once they have purchased.

Post-Purchase Evaluation in Business Decision-Making Processes

When repurchasing, vendors that provide high-quality products, follow-up, and service often avoid most of the steps involved because they are the chosen vendor until something changes. Even for products that are purchased occasionally, the firm that gives attention to the post-purchase component of the selling process is likely to have an edge the next time a purchase is made. Figure 3.8 summarizes the purchase process found in businesses and compares that process to a typical consumer decision-making process.

DUAL CHANNEL MARKETING

Firms sell virtually the same goods or services to both consumers and businesses in a program known as **dual channel marketing**.[14] Perhaps the most common scenario occurs when a product sold in business markets is then adapted to consumer markets. For example, the BlackBerry was initially developed and sold as a productivity tool to businesses. Now, the consumer market for the entire smart phone category is an integral part to the future of the brand. New products often have high start-up costs, including R&D expenditures, market research, and so forth. Businesses tend to be less price sensitive than retail consumers. Thus, it is logical to sell to them first.

As sales grow, economies of scale emerge. Larger purchases of raw materials combined with more standardized methods of production make it possible to enter consumer markets. The benefits of economies of scale entice manufacturers to sell products previously supplied to the business sector in the retail markets. To make the move to the retail arena possible, prices must come down and products need to be user-friendly.

Approximately 30 percent of Holiday Inn's business customers also stay with the chain on private vacations.

Another type of dual channel marketing results from spin-off sales. Individuals who buy a particular product at work often have positive experiences and, as a result, purchase the product for personal use. This situation often occurs with computers and computer software. Favourable feelings about more expensive items can also result in spin-off sales. A salesperson who drives a company-owned car for work might like it so well that one is purchased for personal use. Holiday Inn's marketing team discovered that many of its private stays come from business-related spin-offs. Approximately 30 percent of Holiday Inn's business customers also stay with the chain on private vacations.[15]

In dual channel marketing, a primary decision that must be made is how to represent the product in each channel. The firm can either emphasize similarities between the two markets or focus on differences. Consumers and businesses looking for the same benefits and product features probably will see marketing messages that are quite similar in both channels. When consumers and business buyers value different product attributes or desire different benefits, the marketing strategy develops more customized messages for the separate markets.

When there are substantial differences between the two channels, the typical tactics are to

- Use different communication messages
- Create different brands
- Use multiple channels or different channels

In many instances the product attributes are the same, but the value or benefit of each attribute is different. Messages should focus on the benefits each segment can derive from the product. Cell phones marketed to businesses can stress the area coverage and service options. For consumers, cell phone marketing messages can centre on the fashionable design of the product, its ease of use, or a lower price.

To avoid confusing individuals who might see both messages from the same producer, companies often utilize dual branding. For instance, when Black & Decker decided to launch a professional line of power tools, the DeWalt brand name was chosen. This avoided confusion with the Black & Decker name and prevented any negative image transfer from home tools to professional tools.

In addition to creating economies of scale, integrating consumer markets has an additional advantage: the potential to create synergies. Synergies arise from increased brand identity and equity. An image developed in the consumer market can then be used to enter a business market, or vice versa. Using one brand makes it easier to develop brand awareness and brand loyalty. A business customer who uses a company-owned American Express card is likely to have a separate card from the same company for personal use.

Scanning both types of customers for new opportunities is an important part of dual channel marketing. For example, the firm Intuit, which sells Quicken software, discovered that individuals who use Quicken at home also are willing to use a similar version for their small businesses. Capitalizing on this need or demand, Quicken added features such as payroll and inventory control to a business software package. At the same time, Quicken maintained its easy-to-use format. By finding business needs for a consumer product, Quicken adapted a current product and captured 70 percent of the small-business accounting software market.[16]

Dual channel marketing can create a major competitive advantage as products are sold in both markets. A complete IMC planning process includes the evaluation of potential business market segments as well as consumer market segments. Firms that integrate messages across these markets take a major step toward reaching every potential user of the company's goods or services.

TRENDS IN THE CONSUMER BUYING ENVIRONMENT

Studying the steps consumers take while making purchasing decisions is essential when creating marketing communications. At the same time, the environment in which purchases are made is always changing and evolving. Several trends in the consumer buying environment affect purchasing patterns. Some of these are listed in Figure 3.9.[17]

Age Complexity

Information has changed the way children grow up. Children are bombarded with advertisements, video games, television shows, movies, and a myriad of other sensory perceptions from an early age. Most know a great deal about sex by the age of 12. Female teenagers, and even preteens, wear cropped tops, miniskirts, and low-rider jeans. The result is that many believe children are "growing up" at a much earlier age.

At the other end of the spectrum, many adults are refusing to "grow old." They still wear the fashions that resemble those worn by college students. Some still drive fast sports cars or convertibles. Many middle-aged adults apparently do not want to grow old, so they act like younger people and buy products normally purchased by them. This trend challenges marketers to create messages that reflect these behaviours but do not offend the traditional middle-aged component of society.

Gender Complexity

A second new trend in the consumer buying environment can be called gender complexity. The traditional roles, lifestyles, and interests of men and women are becoming blurred. Women increasingly enter male-dominated occupations. Men now work in occupations that were once considered only for women. Many women attend college, delay marriage, and wait to start families. Some do not marry or have children, choosing instead to focus on moving up the corporate ladder.

Men, meanwhile, are more likely to play an active role in parenting and help more with household chores. Today's men spend more on personal care products and plastic surgery. Traditionally, a company such as General Foods would advertise food and grocery shopping to women and an automaker such as General Motors would target car ads to men. That type of approach is no longer useful. Advertisements for food manufacturers may be targeted at the large percentage of men who do the grocery shopping. Ads for automobiles may be targeted at the large number of women who either purchase cars or have a major influence on vehicle purchases decisions.

Individualism

Individualism has become more pronounced, especially in the purchase of goods and services. Customers want companies to develop products just for them. To meet this trend,

Understanding the issues created by age and gender complexity, Guess created these two advertisements.

Nike now allows consumers to design their own shoes using the company's website. Levi Strauss allows for personalized jeans, made to fit the exact measurements given to them by the consumer, again over the Internet. Recognizing this trend, food manufacturers have increased the varieties, sizes, and flavours of foods. In the beverage industry, a total of 450 new products were introduced within a single year. Many of these new beverages were health-related items, touting that they were vitamin fortified, organic, all natural, or low calorie.[18]

Health Emphasis

The North American population continues to age. Two outcomes of this trend are a blossoming interest in health and maintaining one's youthful appearance. Many consumers are trying to develop a balanced lifestyle. This includes a regular emphasis on nutrition, exercise, and staying active without feeling too guilty about an occasional overindulgence.[19]

Developing better eating habits has had an impact on many families. Some companies were caught off guard by this change. Kraft, whose best-selling products included macaroni and cheese, Oscar Mayer hot dogs, Philadelphia cream cheese, and Kool-Aid, faced a new landscape. Rising concerns about obesity caused the company to shift its approach, and Kraft began to produce healthy, diet-oriented foods. In addition, Kraft reduced the fat content in over 200 products. The marketing message was changed to promote Kraft foods as part of a healthier diet.[20]

Although consumers want healthier foods, they also want convenience. Busy lifestyles mean consumers are less willing to cook from scratch. They want prepared foods that can be assembled easily and cooked quickly. Food products that combine health attributes with convenience are likely to sell well in the future.[21]

Active, Busy Lifestyles

Active lifestyles have had a dramatic impact on consumer behaviours. In one survey, 47 percent of respondents stated that they would prefer additional free time over more money. In another poll, 53 percent of respondents said they would be willing to give up one day's wages per week in exchange for a day off to spend with family and friends. Many consumers now focus less on material possessions and more on experiences, such as vacations, entertainment, and events with friends and family.[22]

Time pressures account for increases in sales of convenience items, such as microwave ovens, and in the use of drive-through dry-cleaning establishments and one-stop shopping outlets, most notably Walmart's Supercenters. People on the go use cell phones, BlackBerries, or answering machines to make sure they stay in touch with others and do not miss any important messages during busy days. The demand for convenience continues to increase.

Cocooning

One of the side effects of a busy and hectic lifestyle is cocooning. The stress of long hours at work with additional hours spent fighting commuter traffic has led many individuals to retreat and cocoon in their homes. A major part of cocooning is making the home environment as soothing as possible. Evidence of cocooning includes major expenditures on elaborate homes, expensive sound systems, satellite systems with big-screen televisions, swimming pools, saunas, hot tubs, and gourmet kitchens and large dining rooms.

Many advertisements emphasize cocooning aspects of shops and services. Recently, Internet ads focused on the utility of shopping from home during the Christmas season to offer the consumer a method to avoid the hustle and bustle of the holidays. In general, time spent online leads to cocooning because people simply don't need to leave the house as much as they used to.

Changes in Family Units

Divorce and remarriage have altered many family units. Remarried divorcees represent about 10 percent of the population. Divorcees tend to develop a new outlook on life. They often desire to cocoon, which changes their purchasing patterns. This group, called *second chancers,* is usually between the ages of 40 and 59 and has a higher household income. Second chancers are more content with life than are average adults. They tend to be happy with their new families but also have a different life focus. Second chancers spend less time trying to please others and more time seeking fuller, more enriching lives for themselves and their children or spouse. Although the home and cocooning is a major emphasis, entertainment and vacation services also appeal to this group.[23]

Pleasure Pursuits

Some people handle the stress caused by a hectic, busy lifestyle through occasional indulgences or pleasure binges, such as expensive dinners out and smaller luxury purchases. Pleasure pursuits also include "getaway" weekends in resorts and on short cruises. These self-rewarding activities make the consumer feel that all the work and effort is "worth it." The implications for marketing experts are to note the indulgence aspects of products.

◆ Monitor consumer environment for changes.

◆ Create goods and services that are compatible with the changes.

◆ Design marketing messages that reflect the changes.

FIGURE 3.9
How Marketers Should Respond to New
Trends in the Consumer Buying Environment

Many people respond to stress through exciting adventures. From theme parks to virtual reality playrooms, consumers enjoy the mental relaxation of experiencing things that seem almost unreal. Many gambling establishments cater to these more exotic types of vacations. IMAX theatres generate a much more exciting experience than do normal movie theatres. As the technology of fantasy continues to develop, more firms enter the marketplace to profit from consumer desires to "get away from it all."

The Environment

One of the most pervasive trends over the past decade has been an increased awareness of the importance of environmental considerations when making purchases. These so-called "green products" feature both supply chains that engender environmental protection (such as fair trade products or emissions reduction at the point of production) and products that offer environmental benefits that are created when the product is consumed (such as hybrid automobiles). Consumers regularly report that they prefer products that are associated with a degree of environmental protection. However, care must be taken when communicating these attributes to consumers. Too much emphasis on the environmental aspects may leave consumers assuming that the purchase requires a trade-off on other aspects of the brand related to performance. For example, in one study consumers reported that they expected fair trade coffee to taste worse than coffee sourced through more traditional channels.[24]

In sum, these new trends in the consumer buying environment create several challenges for marketing experts, as shown in Figure 3.9. The first is to monitor for changes so that the company is not surprised by them. The second is to create goods and services that are compatible with changing values. The third is to design marketing messages that reflect and build on the values of people in various target markets express. The idea is to incorporate new trends into the marketing program while at the same time being careful not to alienate current customers who might not like the trends.

COMMUNICATING ACROSS CULTURES

The messages included in marketing communications often vary widely across cultural divides. For example, the types of appeals found in North American advertising media tend to mirror individualistic values, such as independence and personal success. Many brands feature such cues to rugged individualism, such as the Marlboro man. Many Asian cultures, on the other hand, feature a more collectivistic set of values that prioritizes the success and needs of society over the needs of the individual. Studies find that in advertising in countries like South Korea and China, the collectivistic value is represented to a greater degree.[25] Interestingly, some differences in consumer values have appeared in China, which may signal a changing of the values caused by that country's adoption of some Western ideals.[26]

A number of other elements of marketing communications also differ widely across countries, reflecting marketers' integration of local values and norms. Humour, for example, is much more common in advertising in the United Kingdom than in North America.[27] Gender is also an important aspect of marketing communications that must be considered when crossing cultural boundaries. In Australia, for example, women are more likely to be portrayed as powerful executives in marketing communications than in North America.[28] Although Canadians tend to have typically "Canadian" values, such as support for universal health care, values do differ slightly between regions of the country. For example, the use of sex in ads is often more acceptable in Quebec, where the values related to marketing communications are more accepting of sexual appeals, than in the rest of Canada, which tends to mirror more broad North American values.

Communicating with audiences across cultures requires the marketing team to understand cultural differences related to products, messages, and selling techniques. Consumers and buyers within companies from other countries will also exhibit cultural differences as they consider purchasing alternatives. It is crucial to understand the nuances of the purchasing process in any transaction that takes place in a foreign country. For example, at Canadian trade shows it is unlikely that an actual purchase will be finalized. Instead, information is collected and transferred between the buyer and the seller. At international trade shows, however, sales are often completed. Higher ranking members of the purchasing company attend the shows and are more inclined to buy on the spot. Knowing these kinds of differences will help a company succeed in international trade.

IMC IN PRACTICE

Source: Courtesy of TELUS

"Of course, we have many different stakeholders that we communicate with, but on the buying side it really comes down to three: consumers, businesses, and wholesale clients that purchase our network capacity and resell TELUS solutions to their consumer and business clients under their own brand," says Kate. "Certainly our customers follow the same five-step buying process for our products and services that they do for other products and services, but this impacts our marketing communications planning more for our business customers than our consumer customers."

Because businesses typically have a more formal buying process, and tend to be more concerned with issues like technical specifications and lifetime cost of ownership, marketers at TELUS can be more deliberate about helping customers move through each step. "Businesses tend to have a much longer buying cycle," explains Kate. "Need recognition is probably the most important step here because many businesses don't spend a lot of time thinking about some of their telecommunications support functions. And new technology that becomes available needs to be presented to businesses in a way that helps them see the value it can bring to their bottom line.

"In the consumer wireless market, our potential market is virtually everyone who would purchase a cell phone, so we have a relatively large marketing budget and always have a campaign running. For that reason, the five-step buying process drives our campaigns less than it might other companies. However, because technology is always changing and there are always new features and functionality available, we do follow the AIDA model: awareness, interest, desire, and then action. One of the more critical steps is the point at which the purchase decision itself is made. As Jehan Lalkaka, Marketing Analyst at TELUS explains, it is often the point of contact with the consumer that can make or break the sale. "All of the marketing communications the consumer receives up to that point are an implicit promise about our brand. So when they come into a store, or phone our call centre, or go online, if they have a bad experience there is a disconnect and we risk losing the customer."

Part of Jehan's mandate at TELUS was to examine the consumer buying process from start to finish, and look for ways to improve the experience. "I looked for what I call 'pain points,'" says Jehan. "So my focus wasn't so much on the marketing communications we sent out to people, which people generally enjoy. My focus was on the experience they had when they responded to one of these communications and moved through their purchase process. In the information-gathering stage, for instance, our advertising might ask people to call a phone number for more information. I examined—by actually going through the purchase process to sign up for products—how consumers experience the brand once they respond to one of these initiatives." The importance of this customer understanding is especially true with a brand like TELUS. "When consumers buy our products and services, it's a logistic issue. We sell a complex product with a lot of moving parts, like installation, billing, engineering and service. All of these take coordination, and we need to make sure that we take care of the customer not only up to the purchase decision, but through that decision and beyond."

Source: Used with permission of Kate Baillie, TELUS Communications.

For help developing your IMC Plan, go to **www.pearsoncanada.ca/clow**.

SUMMARY

Buyer behaviours are part of the purchasing process in both consumer markets and business-to-business transactions. An effective IMC program accounts for the ways in which goods and services are purchased in both markets. The goal is to tailor marketing messages to target audiences that address the particular steps in the buying process.

The buying decision-making process consists of five steps: need recognition, information search, evaluation of alternatives, the purchase decision, and post-purchase evaluation. After a consumer recognizes a want or need, the individual searches for information both internally and externally. Marketing messages must be directed to placing the product or service in the consumer's evoked set of viable purchasing prospects. The more involved the customer is in the search, the more likely the product will have a longer-lasting impact once purchased. Those with greater needs for cognition are attracted to the process of thinking through a decision. Those with a greater degree of enthusiasm for shopping spend more time analyzing the available alternatives. Customers consider the benefits and costs of searches and make more or less rational decisions about how extensively they will seek out information.

Customers develop attitudes toward brands, which are shaped in part by marketing communications. Attitudes consist of cognitive, affective, and conative components. The development of attitudes, and the role of each of these elements, differs across product categories. It is important for marketers to match their messages with the primary attitudinal element in their product category.

In both consumer and business markets, people play a number of different roles within the overall purchase decision, including user, buyer, influencer, purchaser and gatekeeper. The same person can often play more than one role at the same time. The influence of others is also important in the development of attitudes because people are influenced by the opinions of others. Marketers can use this social influence to help position their brands by using either associative reference groups to attract people to the brand or dissociative reference groups to help consumers use the brand to define who they are not.

Because purchasing decisions in businesses are still made by people working at those businesses, the process is generally the same as the consumer decision-making process. However, the roles are usually more formally defined, through job descriptions, and the steps are often more formalized as well. The steps in business buying decisions are: need recognition, establishing specifications, identification, evaluation and selection of vendors, negotiating terms, and post-purchase evaluation.

Dual channel marketing means that the firm sells virtually the same goods or services to both consumers and businesses.

Dual channel marketing creates both economies of scale and synergies for the vendor company. It also enhances the chances that a product will be sold to every available customer. The challenge to the marketing team is to create strong and consistent marketing messages to every potential buyer, accounting for how buyer behaviours are present in purchasing processes.

Several emerging trends present a changing buying decision-making environment to marketers. New cultural values and attitudes, time pressures, and busy lifestyles influence what people buy, how they buy, and the manner in which they can be enticed to buy. Many families try to isolate themselves from everyday pressures by cocooning. They also try to escape through indulgences and pleasure binges, by finding excitement or fantasy, and by planning to meet social needs while having greater concern for the environment. Marketing communications can address these needs and lead customers to purchases based on them.

KEY TERMS

affect referral   A purchasing decision model in which the consumer chooses the brand for which he or she has the strongest liking or feelings.

attitude   A mental position taken toward a topic, person, or event that influences the holder's feelings, perceptions, learning processes, and subsequent behaviours.

buying centre   The group of individuals who make a purchase decision on behalf of a business.

cognitive dissonance   The feeling of doubt a customer often feels after making a purchase.

compensatory heuristics   A purchasing decision model that assumes that no one single brand will score high on every desirable attribute and that individual attributes vary in terms of their importance to the consumer.

conjunctive heuristics   A purchasing decision model that establishes a minimum or threshold rating that brands must meet in order to be considered.

derived demand   Demand based on, linked to, or generated by the production and sale of some other good or service.

dual channel marketing   Selling virtually the same goods or services to both consumers and businesses.

enthusiasm for shopping   Customers who like to shop will undertake a more in-depth search for details about goods and services.

evoked set   Consists of the set of brands a consumer considers during the information search and evaluation processes.

inept set   Part of a memory set that consists of the brands that are held in a person's memory but that are *not considered* because they elicit negative feelings.

inert set   Part of a memory set of brands that hold the brands that the consumer has awareness of but has neither negative nor positive feelings about.

involvement   The extent to which a stimulus or task is relevant to a consumer's existing needs, wants, or values.

need for cognition   A personality characteristic an individual displays when he or she engages in and enjoys mental activities.

values   Strongly held beliefs about various topics or concepts.

REVIEW QUESTIONS

1. What are the five steps of the consumer buying decision-making process?

2. How can marketing communications stimulate the need recognition phases of the decision-making process?

3. What is the difference between an internal search and an external search in a purchasing decision?

4. What three factors predict how extensive an external search will be?

5. Define attitude. What are the three main components of attitude, and how are they related to purchasing decisions?

6. How do values differ from attitudes? Name some personal values related to purchasing decisions.

7. How can consumers exhibit selectivity when it comes to marketing communications?

8. Name and describe the five roles played in the purchase process.

9. What are the six factors of individuals that determine their participation in the organizational buying centre?

10. What is an evoked set? Why are evoked sets, inept sets, and inert sets so important to the marketing department?

11. What are the key features of the multiattribute approach to evaluating purchasing alternatives?

12. What is meant by affect referral? When is a person likely to rely on such an approach to evaluating purchasing alternatives?

13. What new trends in the consumer buying environment affect consumer purchasing decisions?

14. Name the steps in the business-to-business buying process. How do they compare with the steps in the consumer process?

15. Describe dual channel marketing and explain why it is important to a company's well-being.

INTEGRATED LEARNING EXERCISES

1. Marketing communications for some products rely heavily on need recognition as part of their message. For example, advertisements for home security systems often try to get people to realize the need for security by showing what can happen if they do not have an alarm system. Similarly, insurance companies illustrate the need for their products by demonstrating the consequences of not carrying insurance. However, for many products the need recognition component of marketing communications can be more subtle.

   Find examples of marketing communications from each of the following product categories that include need recognition as part of the message and write a brief summary of how they have integrated this into their message:

   a. Soft drinks

   b. Automobiles

   c. Fast food

   d. Airlines

   e. Building supplies

2. Almost everyone has an opinion about tattoos. Some attitudes are positive, whereas others are negative. Few are neutral. Go to **www.tattoos.com** and examine the material that is on the website. Did this information modify your attitude toward tattoos? What factors on the website influenced your attitude? Find at least one additional website of a company that offers tattoos. Discuss the components of the website in terms of which components of attitude it is trying to influence (i.e., cognitive, affective, or conative).

3. United Raw Material Solutions, Inc., is a business-to-business marketplace that brings together buyers and seller of textiles, petrochemicals, plastics, and electronics. Access the website at **www.urms.com**. Which members of the buying centre would be most interested in this site? What services and benefits do you see for buyers? For suppliers?

4. Environmental messages are becoming more commonplace in mainstream marketing communications. For example, an ad campaign from the Canadian Association of Petroleum Producers showcases efforts to reduce the environmental impacts from the oil sands in Alberta. However, some companies have faced a backlash against these types of ads, with critics charging that they simply mask the fact that the company isn't doing enough to protect the environment. It's a catch-22 situation for many firms. If it doesn't promote environmental responsibility, critics may charge that the firm is not doing anything, but if the firm promotes environmental responsibility, critics may charge that it is only window dressing. How can companies avoid this problem? What techniques do you think companies should use when including environmental messages in their marketing communications?

STUDENT PROJECT

Creative Corner

A local travel agency has decided to advertise in the student newspaper on your campus to promote spring break packages. They have hired you to do the creative work. They are not sure which type of advertising approach to use. They know that attitude consists of three parts: cognitive, affective, and conative. They also know that an advertisement can appeal to any one of the attitude components. The agency's management team is not sure which component to use. Consequently, they have asked you to design three ads, with one ad designed to appeal to the cognitive component of attitude, the second ad to the affective component, and the third ad to the conative component. After you have finished designing the ads, discuss the pros and cons of each ad and make a recommendation to the travel agency on which one to use. The ads should be for a five-day spring break vacation on the beach in Fort Lauderdale, Florida.

→ ETHICS IN ACTION

Little of what we buy as consumers can truly be considered "needs." Although we may enjoy consuming products such as coffee, a Big Mac, or soft drinks, driving a sporty car, or wearing $150 jeans, the reality is that these things are better described as wants rather than needs. Considering Maslow's famous hierarchy of needs, the basic safety and physiological needs have long since been satisfied for most Canadians. Marketers know this, and now appeal to our higher level "needs," such as self-esteem or social needs. Some critics argue that a focus on these needs has created an overly materialistic society, where we spend money to achieve needs that require constant shopping in order to be fulfilled. This argument is grounded on one side of the age-old question: Does marketing communications lead buyer behaviours in our society, or does it merely mirror our society in an attempt to be relevant?

The difference between these two viewpoints has significant implications. For example, consider an advertisement that portrays someone with a new pair of pants as being more popular because the pants make him or her look more attractive. Proponents of the view that marketing mirrors society would argue that this is reflective of reality; people who are attractive are more popular. However, proponents of the argument that society is led by marketing communications argue that such an advertisement is not reflective of the societal norm, but rather that it is *responsible* for the societal norm.

1. Find an example of an advertisement that can be considered both leading to and reflecting the fact that, in our society, people who are attractive tend to be more popular. Which of these two processes do you think is taking place in the ad and why?

2. Some marketers use dissociative referent groups to position their brand against another brand using negative stereotypes. Find an example of marketing communications that uses a dissociative referent group to position itself. Propose a different form of the ad that takes a more positive view, one that does not use dissociative referent groups. ●

CASE STUDY | Recycling Works!

The blue box has become almost ubiquitous in Canadian towns and cities. Since its humble days in a 1981 pilot program in Kitchener, Ontario, to the one-millionth box in 1991, to the almost 1 million tonnes of material recycled in 2008, recycling has taken hold as a consumer behaviour.[29]

And yet, more can be done to encourage consumers to recycle. Our landfills are still crowded with

Source: Courtesy of Stewardship Ontario; Photo © Shanghoon

material that can easily be recycled. A number of challenges remain, and one initiative designed to overcome these challenges is the Stewardship Ontario "Recycling Works!" marketing communications campaign. Stewardship Ontario was established in 2002 under the Waste Diversion Act of 2002 to develop, implement, and operate a waste diversion program for paper materials and packaging wastes and, more recently, municipal hazardous and special wastes. They operate under the direction of the Minister of the Environment. Their goal is to promote the reduction, reuse, and recycling of recyclable materials.[30]

A cornerstone of the campaign is the website, **www.blueboxmore.ca.** On the site are also listed a number of other elements from the campaign, including television advertising and various versions of printed material. The idea is to show the things that can be made from recycled material so the consumer understands how recycling can save resources. For example, in the print ads shown here, the message is that recycled material is turned into things most consumers would not expect, such as wool or deck chairs.

The campaign also provides information to consumers about what things can and can't be recycled, and how material should be sorted, since the comingling of recycled material reduces the value of the material in after-markets.

The objective of the marketing communications initiative, along with other production improvements behind the scenes, is to achieve a 70 percent recycling rate of all recyclable material, up from the current 65.9 percent. This represents an increase of approximately 60,000 tonnes of material. The Recycling Works! marketing communications is intended to encourage natural growth among current recyclers and to encourage current non-recyclers to recycle.[31] Recyclable material includes glass, metal, paper, plastic, and textiles.

Although the campaign is meant to speak to virtually everyone in Ontario, the target audience was fairly well defined:[32]

- Women between the ages of 25 and 60 who work out of their homes

- Live-in single-unit family dwellings (i.e., houses) and multiple family dwellings (i.e., apartments, condos). However, recycling rates among single-family homes tends to be higher, and reaching those in multiple-family dwellings is more difficult due to mail and flyer restrictions.

A recent study suggests that there two primary barriers to recycling.[33]

Inconvenience. If people perceive it to be inconvenient, they will not recycle. Commonly cited reasons for not recycling are a lack of time, a lack of space for storage, pest concerns with retaining material near the home, general messiness, difficulty with moving material to the curb, or a lack of convenient facilities.

Lack of knowledge. A lack of knowledge of what is recyclable is related to a lower recycling participation rate. Quite simply, when consumers aren't sure what it is to go in the box, they are less likely to use it for anything.

Still, with the popularity of recycling programs, those people who don't recycle often experience a sense of guilt. When engaging in behaviour that contravenes overriding social norms, such as environmental stewardship, we feel guilty. In fact, at one environmental festival a Catholic priest was reportedly taking "green" confessions.[34] Yet this guilt hasn't led to marked shifts in the recycling behaviour for many people, and recycling rates have generally stalled. Therefore, the push for the 70 percent goal is significant, and will require a well-planned

Source: Courtesy of Stewardship Ontario

This message from Stewardship Ontario and the City of Brockville.

marketing communications campaign to encourage more recycling from those who do it sometimes, and to encourage those who do not currently recycle to adopt the behaviour.

1. Can marketing communications stimulate need recognition for one or both of these consumer audiences (those who recycle sometimes or not at all)? Do you feel the campaign as executed gets past the need recognition stage?

2. In recycling behaviour there isn't an information search stage per se because there is no alternative to recycling in your blue box (except of course for using the garbage). Is recycling a high involvement decision? How do people

develop attitudes? Write a two-page report outlining how a consumer in either of the two categories noted might move through each stage of the five-step decision making process.

3. If we know that people sometimes feel guilt about not recycling, do you think there is an opportunity to use social influences to help the campaign? Develop a 10-minute presentation that outlines your plan for either targeting multiple roles within the decision process (e.g., gatekeepers, influencers) or using social norms within the communications message itself to stimulate social norms.

ENDNOTES

1. Eugene F. Brigham and James L. Pappas, *Managerial Economics,* 2nd ed. (Hinsdale, IL: Dryden Press, 1976).

2. Jeffrey B. Schmidt and Richard A. Spreng, "A Proposed Model of External Consumer Information Search," *Journal of Academy of Marketing Science* 24, no. 3 (Summer 1996), pp. 246–56.

3. Merrie Brucks, "The Effect of Product Class Knowledge on Information Search Behavior," *Journal of Consumer Research* 12 (June 1985), pp. 1–15; Schmidt and Spreng, "A Proposed Model of External Consumer Information Search."

4. Laura M. Buchholz and Robert E. Smith, "The Role of Consumer Involvement in Determining Cognitive Responses to Broadcast Advertising," *Journal of Advertising* 20, no. 1 (1991), pp. 4–17; Schmidt and Spreng, "A Proposed Model of External Consumer Information Search"; Jeffrey J. Inman, Leigh McAllister, and Wayne D. Hoyer, "Promotion Signal: Proxy for a Price Cut," *Journal of Consumer Research* 17 (June 1990), pp. 74–81; Barry J. Babin, William R. Darden, and Mitch Griffin, "Work and/or Fun: Measuring Hedonic and Utilitarian Shopping Value," *Journal of Consumer Research* 20 (March 1994), pp. 644–56.

5. Jeffrey B. Schmidt and Richard A. Spreng, "A Proposed Model of External Consumer Information Search."

6. Richard P. Bagozzi, Alice M. Tybout, C. Samuel Craig, and Brian Sternathal, "The Construct Validity of the Tripartite Classification of Attitudes," *Journal of Marketing* 16, no. 1 (February 1979), pp. 88–95.

7. Patricia M. Doney and Gary M. Armstrong, "Effects of Accountability on Symbolic Information Search and Information Analysis by Organizational Buyers," *Journal of the Academy of Marketing Science* 24, no. 1 (Winter 1996), pp. 57–66.

8. Herbert Simon, *The New Science of Management Decisions,* rev. ed. (Upper Saddle River, NJ: Prentice Hall, 1977).

9. Doney and Armstrong, "Effects of Accountability on Symbolic Information Search and Information Analysis by Organizational Buyers"; James A. Eckert and Thomas J. Goldsby, "Using the Elaboration Likelihood Model to Guide Customer Service-Based Segmentation," *International Journal of Physical Distribution & Logistics Management* 27, no. 9–10 (1997), pp. 600–15.

10. Discussion of heuristics and multiattribute model based on William L. Wilkie and Edgar A. Pessemier, "Issues in Marketing's Use of Multiattribute Models," *Journal of Marketing Research* 10 (November 1983), pp. 428–41; Peter L. Wright, "Consumer Choice Strategies: Simplifying vs. Optimizing," *Journal of Marketing Research* 11 (February 1975), pp. 60–67; James B. Bettman, *An Information Processing Theory of Consumer Choice* (Reading, MA: Addison-Wesley, 1979).

11. Katherine White and Darren W. Dahl, "To Be or Not Be? The Influence of Dissociative Reference Groups of Consumer Preferences," *Journal of Consumer Psychology,* 16, no. 4) (2006), pp. 404–414.

12. Mark Sneider, "Create Emotional Ties with Brand for Sales," *Marketing News* 38 (May 15, 2004), pp. 44–45.

13. Charles A. Weber, John R. Current, and Desai Anand, "Vendor: A Structured Approach to Vendor Selection and Negotiation," *Journal of Business Logistics* 21, no. 1 (2000), pp. 134–69.

14. Discussion of dual channel marketing is based on Wim G. Biemans, "Marketing in the Twilight Zone," *Business Horizons* 41, no. 6 (November–December 1998), pp. 69–76.

15. Ibid.

16. Ibid.

17. This section is based on "Are Latest 'Megatrends' a Road Map for New Products?" *Candy Industry* 170, no. 1 (January 2005), pp. 14–15; "The Changing Face of 2005," *International Food Ingredients* (February–March 2005), p. 20; "Global Consumer Trends," *Datamonitor* (**www.market-research-report.com/datamonitor/DMCM0683.htm**, July 21, 2004).

18. Elizabeth Fuhrman, "Consumer Trends Driving New Products," *Beverage Industry* 98, no. 4 (April 2007), pp. 4–8.

19. "Boomers Bend the Trends," *Private Label Buyer* 21, no. 4 (April 2007), p. 14.

20. Dave Carpenter, "Diets Force Kraft to Change Marketing Approach," *Marketing News* 38 (September 15, 2004), p. 37.

21. Christine Blank, "Convenience, Health Top Consumer Trends," *Supermarket News* 55, no. 23 (June 4, 2007), p. 45.

22. Mark Dolliver, "Alas, Free Time Comes at a Price," *Adweek* 45, no. 34 (September 13, 2004), p. 42; Mark Dolliver, "More Money or More Time?" *Adweek* 42, no. 11 (March 12, 2001), p. 44.

23. Discussion of second-chancers based on Richard Halverson, "The Customer Connection: Second-Chancers," *Discount Store News* 37, no. 20 (October 26, 1998), pp. 91–95.

24. Carl Obermiller, Chauncey Burke, Erin Talbott and Gareth P. Green, "'Taste Great or More Fulfilling': The Effect of Brand Reputation on Consumer Social Responsibility Advertising for Fair Trade Coffee," *Corporate Reputation Review,* 12, no. 2 (2009), pp. 159–176.

25. S.P. Han and S. Shaviit, "Persuasion and Culture: Advertising Appeals in Individualistic and Collectivist Societies," *Journal of Experimental Social Psychology* 30 (1998), pp. 326–350.

26. Y. Zhang and J.P. Nellankavil, "The Influence of Culture on Advertising Effectiveness in China and the USA: A Cross-Cultural Study," *European Journal of Marketing* 31 (2, 1997), pp. 134–149.

27. M.G. Weinberger and H.E. Spotts, "A Situational View of Information Content in TV Advertising in the US and UK," *Journal of Marketing* 53, no. 1 (1989), pp. 89–94.

28. M.C. Gilly, "Sex Roles in Advertising: A Comparison of Television Advertisements in Australia, Mexico, and the United States," *Journal of Marketing* 52, no. 2 (1988), pp. 75–85.

29. **http://www.stewardshipontario.ca/bluebox/consultation/work_web.htm,** accessed on April 30, 2010.

30. **http://www.mass.gov/dep/recycle/reduce/crbdrop.pdf,** accessed on May 18, 2010.

31. Ibid.

32. **http://www.stewardshipontario.ca/bluebox/eefund/orw/orw_archive.htm,** accessed on April 30, 2010.

33. **http://www.stewardshipontario.ca/corporate/index.html,** accessed on May 18, 2010.

34. Janet Kornblum, The Guilty Green (Gasp!) Don't Always Recycle," *USA Today*, September 16, 2007. **http://www.usatoday.com/news/nation/environment/2007-09-16-green-guilt_N.htm**.

4

After reading this chapter, you should be able to answer the following questions:

- **What** activities are involved in completing a promotions opportunity analysis?
- **What** trends can represent opportunities for marketing communications campaigns?
- **What** are the characteristics of the major consumer market segments?
- **How** can a company identify and reach key business-to-business market segments?
- **What** characteristics define an attractive market segment?
- **How** should objectives for IMC plans be developed?
- **How** can firms determine budgets to support IMC programs?

INDUSTRY PROFILE

So You Want to Work in Marketing Communications?

**Marc Belcourt, Brand Communications Manager,
BMW Canada, Toronto**

Although Marc has the dream job of many young men, he didn't plan on making automotive marketing his career. "I wanted to be Jerry McGuire," jokes Marc. "I was a tennis professional and worked as an instructor, so my real aim was to get into athlete representation." Marc was able to land an unpaid internship at a U.S. agency that he hoped would give him an entree into that industry, but ended up taking him straight to BMW's door. "The internship was executing event marketing programs for BMW Canada. It was with an agency that managed all their event marketing for Canada, but the office was actually inside BMW's offices. So I got a chance to learn the business and the brand from the inside."

Because he was already working with the company through his internship, he was a logical choice when the company needed someone to work on their motorcycle business. Marc used the opportunity to demonstrate his abilities and quickly moved the annual sales of the brand in Canada from around 600 units to over 1,000. It got him noticed and he was tapped to take on the event marketing for the automotive side of the business.

"In each case, I worked by butt off to prove myself. Part of it was using what I was learning to develop smarter plans, but at its heart my initial success came from lots of hustle." At the event marketing post Marc oversaw all events, sponsorships, product launches, drive events, and driver training for the brand. "It was an incredible way to learn the business, but incredibly exhausting. For those four years at that position, our team would manage over 300 event days per year." After moving to the MINI brand for two years, Marc landed his current position with the company as the Brand Communications Manager for the BMW brand.

As Brand Communications Manager, Marc oversees a team of marketing professionals to develop and execute campaigns to both maintain and build the BMW brand over the long term and also to deliver short-term sales targets for the company. "It's a diverse set of projects, everything from BMW.ca to all of the media we buy, to all of the targeted direct marketing campaigns. My mandate is to

Promotions Opportunity Analysis

4

strengthen and increase the desirability of the brand and products, all while delivering the sales volume the company sets each year."

The role involves considerable use of analysis, internal coordination, and internal promotion. "My job is to keep the brand strong, and sometimes this can be a challenge. For example, if sales are not tracking as highly as we'd like, there can be increased pressure to deviate from the longer term objectives of the brand focus in exchange for driving sales today. I need to find a balance between the two and make sure that anything we achieve today also puts us in a position to succeed tomorrow."

"At the end of the day, our objectives are all about sales. But what is the process that we need to facilitate before a sale happens? We sell premium products, and the purchase often occurs over multiple years. So we need marketing communications that match that purchase process and to think about our efforts over a longer time period."

The analysis Marc uses is often based on how the BMW brand is perceived, along with what competitors are doing in the market. "With brand tracking research we can see how we are performing and adjust as needed. So, for example, if we see that one of our competitors comes out with a campaign that focuses on technological advancements, and we see that show up in our brand tracking, we would take steps to correct it and create messaging to re-establish our dominance on that particular brand dimension."

Another part of Marc's job is to spot opportunities to gain incremental sales for the brand using partnerships with other brands. "I see value in corporate partnerships where we can share our efforts

Marc Belcourt, Brand Communications Manager, BMW Canada.

and add value for each other's customers. Right now we are launching a direct marketing campaign with Fairmont Hotels where we are speaking to their high-end clients. We are given access to a very targeted customer base, and, in return, they get to offer additional value to their clients through the incentives we offer in the campaign." For Marc, one of the attractive qualities about this type of program is their measurability. "If we can show definitively that these programs deliver incremental sales for us—and we can do that—that's about as close to the holy grail in marketing communications as we can get."

Another opportunity involves a targeted campaign to connect with East Asian Canadians. "As a community, East Asians represent 5 percent of the population but 11 percent of our customers, so we clearly have an opportunity to connect with them. We are working with

Canada Post and their GeoPost service to target those people who are likely to be future buyers of our brand by linking their data with our own customer data. Here again we are seeing how efficient marketing communications can directly link to our sales."

Marc is always on the hunt to spot new opportunities. A recent campaign used bathroom mirrors at upscale bars and restaurants to engage potential customers through mobile marketing. The campaign involved teaser lines written on bathroom mirrors that would encourage the audience to go online to find out more. The writing was made to look like lipstick writing, and featured suggestive lines like "I'll make your heart pound" or "My body is absolutely stunning," which attracted the young male audience. "The media is an opportunity to connect with one of our audiences in a unique and unexpected way," says Marc. "Think of a typical Bay Street young professional. He has the money to buy our product, is very aspirational, eats at the right places, carries a smart phone. So this media is a great way to connect with them."

The campaign also allows Marc to gain learning for future campaigns. "We know that mobile marketing—using smart phones—is part of the future of marketing communications. But it's new, so we need to set benchmarks for our brand and our audience. What would our response rates be to this kind of media message? Being one of the first luxury brands to execute a smart phone campaign, we couldn't simply apply the established existing benchmarks. Well, we now know that we got about a 70 percent click through on this campaign. Compare that to about 0.5 percent on traditional online benchmarks, and I'd say this works pretty well for us."

Because the BMW brand is so prestigious, Marc has seen more than his share of young aspiring marketers in his office. "Anyone interested in working for this brand should keep in mind a number of things. First, work ethic and a passion for the work you are doing will take you further than you can imagine. Second, understand your strengths and look for opportunities to showcase those strengths. Mitigate your weaknesses and show that you are working on them. Third, practise winning over others. For example, when talking to the sales team, we need to understand what the sales team needs, and how they need to hear it. And, of course, stay current on the industry. BMW is a high-performance brand, and we demand a culture of high performance. These are some basic things that we look for to identify someone as a high performer."

OVERVIEW

People receive a myriad of marketing communications messages every day. From pens marked with logos to radio advertising to calendars containing both advertisements and tear-off discount coupons, consumers and businesses encounter marketing materials in an increasing variety of ways. These contacts do not occur by accident. At some point, a marketer decided to invest in these messages. Someone decided that there was an opportunity to make contact with someone in their target audience. In other words, skilled professionals decided to invest marketing resources into a communications message because it was felt that some response by the audience would provide a return back to the firm. Maybe this return comes in the form of a sale, or maybe it comes in the form of a changed attitude, or the recognition of a need to stimulate the purchase decision process. In each case, an analysis of the opportunity, including the objectives and costs of the marketing communications, precedes the message delivery.

This chapter describes the nature of a promotions opportunity analysis. The purpose is to identify customers and competitors in the marketplace and to discover opportunities to create and deliver successful marketing communications messages.

When these opportunities are found, the firm's overall IMC message can be adapted to various target markets. An effective promotional analysis specifies the audiences and markets the company intends to serve. Locating key market segments helps the company's leaders more accurately define whom they are trying to reach with an IMC program. Importantly, marketing communications are not only used to reach customer audiences. Marketers often include other stakeholders, such as employees, regulators, or non-profit organizations (NGOs), in their target audiences. In this chapter, target markets, campaign objectives, and budget allocation are described. Each of these activities is a key component in preparing an IMC program.

PROMOTIONS OPPORTUNITY ANALYSIS

Every effective marketing communications plan begins with a promotions opportunity analysis. A **promotions opportunity analysis** is the process marketers use to identify target audiences for an organization's message and the communications strategies needed to reach these audiences. A promotions opportunity analysis must accomplish two objectives: (1) determine which promotional opportunities exist for the company and (2) identify the characteristics of each target audience so that suitable advertising and marketing communications messages can reach them. The more a marketer knows about an audience, the greater the chance a message will be heard, be understood, and result in the desired outcome (i.e., a purchase, increased brand loyalty, increased employee satisfaction, etc.).

There are three steps in developing a promotions opportunity analysis, as shown in Figure 4.1. The upcoming sections describe each part of this planning process in greater detail.

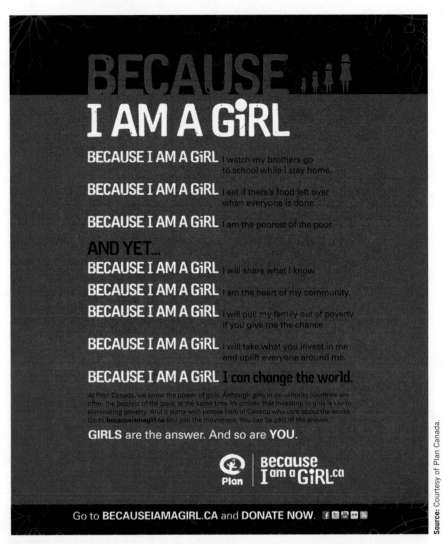

Marketers such as Plan Canada often have very limited budgets for their marketing communications and must set objectives accordingly.

Communication Market Analysis

The first step of a promotions opportunity analysis is a communication market analysis. A **communication market analysis** is the process of discovering the organization's strengths and weaknesses in the area of marketing communications and combining that information with an analysis of the opportunities and threats present in the firm's external

---

- ◆ Conduct a communication market analysis.
- ◆ Establish communications objectives.
- ◆ Create a communications budget.

FIGURE 4.1
Promotions Opportunity Analysis

environment. The analysis is from a communications perspective. A communication market analysis examines three areas:

- Competitors
- Opportunities
- Target markets

These three ingredients are studied together rather than sequentially. Each contributes key information about the marketplace.

Competitors

In examining competitors, the objective is to discover who they are and what they are doing in the areas of marketing communications. The marketing tactics competitors use are identified to understand how they are contacting the marketplace. Consumers integrate information from a variety of sources. It is helpful to know what potential customers see, hear, and read about the competition.

Every domestic and foreign competitor is identified. After listing the competing firms, a competitive analysis includes gathering *secondary data* about those companies. The first items to look at are statements that competitors make about themselves. These statements can be found in

- Advertisements
- Promotional materials
- Annual reports
- A prospectus for a publicly held corporation
- Websites

The next task is to study what *other people* say about the competition. Marketers often read trade journals. The library might yield additional news articles and press releases about competitor activities. The marketing team will try to discover how competing companies view them. This provides a sense of how any given company is viewed in comparison with its competition.

Another part of an analysis of the competition is *primary research*. In the retail business, it is helpful to visit competing stores to see how merchandise is displayed and to observe as the store's employees deal with customers. The marketing team should also talk to vendors and suppliers who have dealt with the competition, along with wholesalers, distributors, and agents. For businesses other than retail, marketers can contact salespeople in the field to obtain additional information about the competition.

The ultimate objective of the analysis of competitors is to determine where they are positioned relative to the brand in question and uncover gaps in the market—the next step in the communication market analysis.

Opportunities

The Canadian market for hardware and home building stores is fiercely competitive. Local player Home Hardware seeks to create a unique, local positioning to compete with global giants such as Home Depot.

Once the competitive landscape has been analyzed, marketers can conduct the search for opportunities. Some of the questions the marketing team asks are listed in Figure 4.2.

The purpose of these questions is to explore new communications opportunities. These opportunities are present when there is an unfilled market niche, when the competition is doing a poor job of meeting the needs of some customers, when the company offers a distinct competence, or when a market niche is not being targeted with effective marketing communications.

Critical Thinking Exercise

The single largest marketer in Canada, as measured by media spending, is the federal government. In this case, there are rarely any organizations that can be considered "competitors." However, competition can sometimes be viewed as an alternative to something the government wants you to do. For example, in 2009 the federal government undertook a massive campaign to promote immunization against the H1N1 flu. Competition, in this case, can be conceived to include things like natural or herbal remedies, or the decision to change one's behaviour to avoid coming into contact with the flu. What other examples of competition can you think of in this case? Can you think of other marketing communications from governments that may face these types of obstacles in achieving their objectives?

An opportunity can exist because demand of a growing segment of the market is not being met by competitors, or technology has enabled a new opportunity for companies to meet customer demand. For example, when Amazon launched in the 1990s, it was enabled by the adoption of the Web in both consumer and business markets. The company was among the first to recognize and perfect the online model of shopping, and this required a completely different marketing communications strategy from that used by their competition at the time.

Another source of opportunity can be trends within the target audience. In the case of marketing communications designed to attract potential employees, marketers can use the balance between work and personal life as a message to attract more qualified younger employees who value this balance. This balance was not prevalent in previous decades.

It is helpful to ascertain how customers perceive individual elements of marketing communications as well as what they think about the larger company. Service Metrics (see the advertisement in this section) examines a firm's website from the customer's perspective and, more importantly, compares the website to the competitions'. This type of analysis identifies all of a firm's communications avenues. It also tells the company how its website compares to the competition.

This ad for Molson Canadian, part of a larger campaign, takes advantage of a growing trend of Canadian pride among consumers.

TRUE CANADIAN TASTE

Source: Courtesy of Molson Coors Canada.

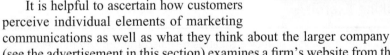

- ◆ Are there customers that the competition is ignoring or not serving?
- ◆ Which markets are heavily saturated and have intense competition?
- ◆ Are the benefits of our goods and services being clearly articulated to the various customer market segments?
- ◆ Are there opportunities to build relationships with customers using a slightly different marketing approach?
- ◆ Are there opportunities that are not being pursued, or is our brand positioned with a cluster of other companies in such a manner that it cannot stand out?

FIGURE 4.2
Questions for an Opportunity Analysis

Part of a customer analysis includes an examination of a firm's Web site from the customer's perspective

By identifying opportunities for marketing communications based on a firm's competitive position in the market, the marketer can clearly define the target audience for marketing communications, which is discussed next.

Target Markets

The third communication market analysis activity is examining various target markets. The questions asked during this part of the analysis are similar to those posed while looking for opportunities. The focus shifts to defining target markets more precisely. Beyond target market groups, marketers attempt to decipher the needs and wants of individual groups. The goal is to divide the overall market into smaller market segments. The company can then develop marketing programs and advertising campaigns for each of these smaller groups.

Market Segmentation

Marketers use market segmentation to distinguish between specific purchasing groups. **Market segmentation** is the process of identifying specific purchasing groups based on their needs, attitudes, and interests. A **market segment** is a set of businesses or group of individual consumers with distinct characteristics. Market segmentation efforts are of great value in completing a promotions opportunity analysis because they guide where a marketing communications campaign will focus, both in message and medium. The primary advantages are listed in Figure 4.3.

Critical Thinking Exercise

A promotions opportunity analysis of movie theatres revealed the primary moviegoer to be between 18 and 24 years of age. Twenty years ago, 44 percent of the individuals in this age bracket went to movies frequently. Today, less than 34 percent are frequent moviegoers.[1] Conduct a customer analysis by interviewing five individuals between the ages of 18 and 24. Based on their responses, what suggestions would you make to movie theatres to reverse this declining trend?

FIGURE 4.3
Advantages of Market Segmentation

◆ Identifying company strengths and weaknesses

◆ Locating market opportunities

◆ Matching the company's strengths with the most lucrative sets of customers

◆ Focusing budget expenditures on specific consumer or business segments

Market researchers spend considerable resources and amounts of time working to identify quality market segments. Market segments are grouped into two broad categories: (1) consumer markets and (2) business-to-business markets. The following section describes each of these segments in greater detail.

Market Segmentation by Consumer Groups

Effective IMC programs identify sets of consumers who are potential buyers and who have things in common, such as attitudes, interests, or needs. These consumer market segmentation approaches are listed in Figure 4.4.

Segments Based on Demographics

As shown in Figure 4.4, the first method of segmentation uses demographics. **Demographics** are population characteristics. Typical demographic segmentation variables include gender, age, education, income, and ethnicity. Companies create goods and services to meet the needs of individual demographic segments.

Gender

One key demographic is gender. Males and females purchase different products, buy similar products with different features (e.g., deodorants), buy the same products for dissimilar reasons (stereos, televisions), and buy the same products after being influenced by different kinds of appeals through different media.

Source: House of Bijan, Rodeo Drive, Beverly Hills.

An advertisement for Bijan targeted to females.

Women have become a major market for unique getaways, and travel agencies are now marketing specific travel opportunities for women. A survey found that 24 percent of women have gone on a getaway with one or more other women in the past three years and 39 percent plan on going on a girls-only getaway in the future.[2]

Marketing to women involves more than just creating and selling female-oriented products. A recent study revealed that women have an enormous impact on the spending habits of men. BMW Motorcycles recognized that women exert a considerable amount of influence on purchasing decisions for luxury touring motorcycles. A subject in one of the company's research programs explained, "If mama ain't happy, nobody's happy." Couples most often use luxury touring motorcycles for long-distance touring. This became an important factor in the development of a new motorcycle and in creating its market position. BMW's K 1200 LT has heated seats and backrests, with separate controls for both the passenger and the rider. A man tends to look at a motorcycle in terms of style, horsepower, torque, and handling. A woman has other concerns—most notably, comfort. In this case, BMW Motorcycles took what was learned from market research and made sure the motorcycle reached two target audiences: men as the primary purchasers and women as the decision-making influencers. Each was an important part of the promotional campaign.[3]

◆ Demographics	◆ Geodemographics
◆ Psychographics	◆ Benefits
◆ Generations	◆ Usage
◆ Geographic	

FIGURE 4.4
Methods of Segmenting Consumer Markets

Critical Thinking Exercise

Make a list of five consumer goods or services segmented on the basis of gender but sold to both genders. Are there any differences in the product or service attributes? Are there differences in how they are marketed? What are those differences? Do you think using a different marketing approach has worked?

Looks like two weeks vacation isn't going to cut it anymore.

Motorcycles

A BMW Motorcycle ad targeted toward men as the primary purchasers and women as the decision-making influencers.

Age

A second demographic characteristic is age. Marketing campaigns target children, young adults, middle-age adults, and senior citizens. Some campaigns combine age-related factors with other demographics, such as gender. Creating logical combinations with other segments is a common segmentation approach. For example, older women may be primary targets for specific types of vitamins and other age-related products. Young working women with children are more likely to notice ads for conveniences (ready-made foods and snacks, quick lube oil change facilities, etc.). Other groups might buy vitamins, snack foods, and change their car's oil, but individual segments can be targeted with messages that reach a particular set of needs.

Children have a major impact on the purchasing decisions of their parents. Appeals to children can tie several items together, including advertisements, merchandise based on the ads, and selections from other media. Children attracted to Harry Potter can buy toys, watch the movies, buy the books, and witness advertisements using the Harry Potter theme, such as when Burger King, KFC, and Taco Bell all combined to sponsor a campaign.

Besides children, another age-based demographic group that appeals to many firms is *seniors,* defined as individuals over age 55. In the past, all seniors were treated as one market and tended to be stereotyped in ads. They were portrayed as elderly grandparents; as feeble, avid gardeners; or as enjoying a blissful retirement demonstrated by walking down the beach together holding hands. Seniors are not a homogeneous group. They do not like to be told they are getting older. Companies that have been successful with this market segment understand seniors and know how to relate to them by understanding the value seniors place on friendships, their communities, and their involvement in life. Marketing professionals recognize that the segment called "seniors" is actually a compilation of smaller groups of individuals each with different lifestyle, interests, and opinions.[4]

Income

An important demographic segmentation variable for many goods and services is an individual's or a family's income. Spending is normally directed at three large categories of goods: (1) necessities, (2) sundries, and (3) luxuries. Lower levels of income mean consumers primarily purchase necessities, such as food, clothing, cleaning supplies, and so forth. As income increases, household members can buy more items categorized as sundries, which are things that are "nice to own," but not absolutely necessary. Sundries include televisions, computers, CD players, and other durable goods. Vacations are also sundry expenditures. Luxuries are things most people cannot afford or can afford only once in a lifetime, unless the family is a high-income household. Luxuries include yachts, expensive automobiles, extravagant resort vacations, and other high-cost goods and services. Marketers tailor messages to various income groups and to select media that match those groups.

Ethnic Groups

Although Canada is one of the most multicultural countries in the world, many marketing communications are still written from a white, Anglo-Saxon perspective. This represents both an opportunity and a threat: an opportunity for companies able to adapt their messages to other cultures and heritages, and a threat to those that do not.

Ethnic marketing includes more than spending money with ethnically owned radio stations or hiring ethnically owned advertising agencies and translating advertisements from English into Spanish. It is more than including African Canadians or Asian Canadians in advertisements. Successful ethnic marketing requires understanding various ethnic groups and writing marketing communications that speak to specific cultures and values.

Although different in many ways, several common threads exist among ethnic groups. They all tend to be more brand loyal than their white counterparts. They value quality and are willing to pay a higher price for quality and brand identity. They value relationships with companies and are loyal to those that make the effort to establish a connection with them.

To market effectively to ethnic groups, marketers look for creative approaches that respect Canada's ethnic differences while also highlighting similarities. Achieving this requires marketing agencies that understand the subtleties of multiculturalism. Becoming involved in sponsorships of minority and ethnic events helps establish ties with specific ethnic groups.

Ethnic marketing is similar in some ways to global marketing. It is important to present one overall message that is then tailored to fit the needs and values of various groups. Successfully achieving this integration of the overall message with characteristics of individual cultures should result in valuable gains in loyalty to a company and its brands and diversify the markets the company can effectively serve.

Psychographics

Demographics are relatively easy to identify. They do not, however, fully explain why people buy particular products or specific brands, or the type of appeal that can be used to reach them. To assist in the marketing effort while building on demographic information, psychographic profiles have been developed. **Psychographics** emerge from patterns of responses that reveal a person's activities, interests, and opinions (AIO). AIO measures can be combined with demographic information to provide marketers with a more complete understanding of the market to be targeted.[5]

SRI Consulting Business Intelligence provides a popular classification of lifestyles using psychographic segmentation. The VALS2 typology categorizes respondents into eight different

Source: Used with permission of Deutche Inc. on behalf of the Milk Processors Education Program.

An advertisement for milk based on nutritional benefits directed to men.

TELUS uses ethnic marketing to reach the multicultural Canadian market.

Source: Courtesy of TELUS.

groups based on resources and on the extent to which they are action-oriented.[6] The VALS2 typology includes the following segments:

- **Innovators** Successful, sophisticated, and receptive to new technologies. Their purchases reflect cultivated tastes for upscale products.
- **Thinkers** Educated, conservative, practical consumers who value knowledge and responsibility. They look for durability, functionality, and value.
- **Achievers** Goal-oriented, conservative consumers committed to career and family. They favour established prestige products that demonstrate success to peers.
- **Experiencers** Young, enthusiastic, and impulsive consumers who seek variety and excitement and spend substantially on fashion, entertainment, and socializing.
- **Believers** Conservative, conventional consumers who focus on tradition, family, religion, and community. They prefer established brands and favour North American–made products.
- **Strivers** Trendy, fun-loving consumers who are concerned about others' opinions and approval. They demonstrate to peers their ability to buy.
- **Makers** Self-sufficient consumers who have the skill and energy to carry out projects, respect authority, and are unimpressed by material possessions.
- **Survivors** Concerned with safety and security, they focus on meeting needs rather than fulfilling desires. They are brand loyal and purchase discounted products.

Because psychographics don't always align with easily identifiable characteristics of people, they are not always useful in placement of messages. For example, no media exists that only caters to achievers. However, psychographics can be immensely helpful in developing the messaging of marketing communications. When marketers can tap into the underlying value system of an audience they are much more likely to make a connection. For instance, if the target audience for a product is characterized as believers, marketing communications should focus more on tradition and North American values.

Segments Based on Generations

Many marketing efforts target generational cohorts. Although this approach does not require the use of psychographic information to enrich the demographics, it does possess some of the richness of the psychographics. The concept behind marketing to generational cohorts is that common experiences and events create bonds between people who are about the same age.

Segmentation based on generations notes that as people experience significant external events during their late adolescence or early adulthood, these events impact their social values, attitudes, and preferences. Based on similar experiences, these cohorts of individuals develop common preferences for music, foods, and other products. They also tend to respond to the same types of marketing appeals. Based on this idea, six cohorts or generations have been identified. Figure 4.5 identifies these cohorts along with some of their basic characteristics.

Segmentation by Geographic Area

Another form of segmentation is by geographic area or region. This method is especially useful for retailers seeking to limit marketing communications programs to specific areas. It also helps a company conduct a direct-mail campaign in a target area. The primary disadvantage of this approach is that everyone in a geographic area receives the marketing communication or is exposed to the advertisement, regardless of interest in the product or service. Geographic segmentation does not allow a firm to focus on a more specific target market containing only those most likely to make purchases.

Geodemographic Segmentation

A hybrid form of geographic segmentation allows companies to enrich geographic approaches to segmentation. This powerful new form of segmentation, called *geodemographics*, identifies potential customers from demographic information, geographic information, and psychographic information.

Geodemographic segmentation is especially beneficial for national firms conducting direct-mail campaigns or using sampling promotions. It is expensive and unwise to mail a sample to every household. Through geodemographics, samples are only sent to households

Name of Segment	Year of Birth	Characteristics
Generation Y	1978–2002	Spend money on clothes, automobiles, college, televisions, and stereos. Ninety percent live at home or in a dorm or rent an apartment.
Generation X	1965–1977	Focus on family and children. Spend on food, housing, transportation, and personal services.
Younger boomers	1954–1964	Focus on home and family. Spend on home mortgage, pets, toys, playground equipment, and large recreational items.
Older boomers	1952–1953	Spend on upgrading homes, ensuring education and independence of their children, and luxury items, such as boats.
Seniors	Up to 1951	Most have fixed incomes. Spend heavily on health care and related medical items.

Source: Based on Dana-Nicoleta Lascu and Kennth E. Clow, *Essentials of Marketing* (Cincinnati, OH: Atomic Dog Publishing, 2007).

FIGURE 4.5
Characterization of Generation Segment

that match the profile of a target market. For instance, colleges and universities use geodemographics to locate postal codes of communities that match student profiles.

Canada Post offers a service called GeoPost that helps companies pinpoint specific segments using geodemographics. The service locates regions of Canada where 65 unique segments of consumers can be found in high percentages. The concept is that people who tend to be similar tend to live close together, so certain neighbourhoods have concentrations of specific types of people. The segments are based on consumer clusters system known as PSYTE. Each of the clusters is unique in many respects from the others, and offers marketers a very specific profile of their target audience. For example, in the cluster labelled "Cruising Commuters" the service can help marketers identify consumers that commute from the suburbs to downtown, have children, and have an average household income of almost $100,000. Such a target audience would be very applicable for marketers looking to sell vehicle repairs, for example.

Geodemographic marketing has been expanded to the Internet. Adfinity is a program designed by Intelligent Interactions. It allows an advertiser to direct specific ads to Web users based on user-defined demographics. When users visit websites, they often provide their names and addresses along with other demographic information. While the user is surfing a site, Adfinity's software can access the user's file in order to place a targeted ad on the page. Based on the lifestyle and interests of that cluster, messages are sent that match the user.

Benefit Segmentation

Benefit segmentation focuses on the advantages consumers receive from a product rather than the characteristics of consumers themselves. Demographic and psychographic information can be combined with benefit information to identify segments. Then, the marketing team can seek to further understand each segment's consumers.

Benefit segmentation has been used in the fitness market. Regular exercisers belong in one of three benefit segments. The first group, "winners," do whatever it takes to stay physically fit. This segment tends to be younger, upwardly mobile, and career oriented. The second group, "dieters," exercise to maintain their weight and enhance their physical appearance. This group tends to be

Benefit segmentation is often used in the wine industry.

Source: © Dorling Kindersley.

females over the age of 35. They are primarily interested in reliable wellness programs offered by hospitals and weight-control nutritionists. The third group, "self-improvers," exercise to feel better and to control medical costs. The understanding that individuals exercise for different reasons provides excellent material for designing marketing programs and can help guide the messaging strategy in marketing communications. For example, if a fitness centre wants to attract self-improvers, they can focus their message on the cost-benefit analysis of the membership versus costs of medication and illness.

Usage Segmentation

The final type of consumer segmentation is based on customer usage or purchases. The goal of usage segmentation is to provide the highest level of service to a firm's best customers while promoting the company to casual or light users, or possibly attracting non-users.

Many company marketing teams identify heavy users by utilizing internal databases. With bar-code scanners, point-of-sale systems, and data from credit, debit, and transaction cards, in-house marketers can accumulate a wealth of information about customers. Many have learned that between 10 and 30 percent of a company's customers generate 70 to 90 percent of total sales. Firms develop customer clusters from these databases. Customers are placed in clusters based on common attitudes, lifestyles, and past purchase behaviours. This technique offers a business the following advantages:[7]

1. A meaningful classification scheme to cluster customers based on a firm's actual customers.
2. The ability to reduce large volumes of customer data down to a few concise, usable clusters.
3. The ability to assign a cluster code number to each customer in the database. Each number is based on the customer's actual purchases and other characteristics (e.g., address, amount spent, credit versus cash, etc.).
4. The capacity to measure the growth and migration of customers over time and from one cluster to another, which allows for the evaluation of marketing programs.
5. The capability of using a database to develop multiple clusters based on different benefits or usages.

In summary, consumer market segments can be identified in a number of ways. The best segmentation approaches are based on the company's circumstances. In choosing market segments to approach, a marketer looks for groups that best match the company's goods and services, as well as the overall marketing message. Then the message can be structured to meet the needs of the various market segments.

ON THE JOB

What Makes a Segment Attractive?

How does a marketer know when a segment represents an opportunity? There are five criteria that can be used to determine the viability of a segment as a target audience.

1. Is the segment *heterogenous* with the general population? This is the first and most obvious criterion for a market segment. If it doesn't differ from other parts of the population, then by definition it is not a segment. The more heterogeneity between the segment and the population, the more likely the marketing communications can deliver an impactful message. It is also may be more likely that the message can efficiently be placed in front of that audience. Take the example of two groups of students. One group is aged between

18 and 22, enrolled full time in a Canadian post-secondary school. The other is aged between 25 and 40 and enrolled part time. Both are post-secondary students, but the first group of students has significantly more heterogeneity from the general population than the second. To use their budget more effectively, marketers can use this to take advantage of certain media that only reach full-time students. They can also use certain pop culture references, language, or spokespeople more effectively if they are linked more closely with the target audience.

2. Is the segment *homogeneous* within itself? The next criterion for a good market segment is that the segment be relatively homogenous. This is because, in order for a segment to be efficient, each member

should be capable of being reached by the same approach to communication. This may vary by product category. For example, an age-based segment of seniors over 65 is likely not to be very homogenous when it comes to attitudes about vacations. Many seniors are not happy with sedate cruises that are stereotypical of previous generations of seniors, so a marketer selling vacations would need to be careful about using age as a segment criterion. But seniors over age 65 are likely very homogenous when it comes to their family situation. Almost all will now live in homes without children, most likely either alone or with their spouse or partner. So, for example, a marketer selling a home security system could use this information to make assumptions about the company's target audience by using age segmentation.

3. Is the segment *substantial*? For a segment to be attractive, it must represent a meaningful business opportunity with a high likelihood of delivering positive return on investment. So, for example, a marketer may define a segment as those people in the VALS2 innovator category living in Mississauga. This may represent only a few hundred people. Therefore, any marketing communications campaign specifically designed for them may be unlikely to deliver positive business returns because of the relatively high costs of reaching this small segment. Indeed, many marketers that sell online now benefit from being able to design very specific marketing messages for narrow

segments. Because their market is now the entire world, they are able to successfully use this targeted approach for specific segments.

4. Is the segment *able to respond*? Similar to point number 3, in order for a segment to represent a business opportunity, it must have the ability to respond to the marketing communications. For example, although a high-end car manufacturer like Ferrari might define strivers (from the VALS2 typology) as an attractive segment because of their need for social status, most of these people are unlikely to be able to buy a Ferrari. Therefore, any money invested in communicating with this group as a defined market segment will likely be wasted.

5. Is the segment *reachable*? The final criterion for a successful segment is that the marketer must be able to effectively reach the segment through one or more forms of marketing communications. The key word here is *effectively*, because if a marketer spends enough money, in theory everyone can receive the message. But the key is to focus the message on only those people in the segment. So, for example, if a marketer promoting hair colouring wishes to define red-haired people as a market segment, it is virtually impossible for them to deliver any communications that will not also be delivered to people without red hair. Such a campaign is likely to never become profitable.

Business-to-Business Segmentation

Some approaches that help identify consumer market segments can also be used to discover business-to-business market segments. Alternate methods also are available. Figure 4.6 lists the various types of business-to-business market segments. Keep in mind that, as with consumer markets, the primary goals of segmentation are to provide better customer service and to group homogeneous customers into clusters to enhance marketing efforts.

Segmentation by Industry

One method used to examine potential customers is by industry. Many marketers use the NAICS (North American Industry Classification System) coding system. NAICS allows the marketing team to examine specific industries, such as construction (23) or wholesale trade (42). They also can study segments within specific categories. For example, NAICS codes health care and social assistance services as 62. A company that

---

◆ Industry (NAICS/SIC codes) ◆ Product usage
◆ Size of business ◆ Customer value
◆ Geographic location

FIGURE 4.6
Methods of Segmenting Business-to-Business Markets

manufactures health-related products can divide the market into four segments based on the subsections. These four market segments are:

- 621   Ambulatory Health Care Services
- 622   Hospitals
- 623   Nursing and Residential Care Facilities
- 624   Social Assistance

If these segments are too broad, each can be broken down into smaller subcomponents. For example, Ambulatory Health Care Services includes physicians, dentists, chiropractors, and optometrists.

The NAICS divides the economy into 20 broad sectors using a 6-digit code rather than the SIC 4-digit code. The 6-digit code allows greater stratification of industries and provides greater flexibility in creating classifications. The federal government records corporate information and data using the NAICS, making it a logical system to choose for identifying market segments.

Segmentation by Size

Market segments can be identified based on company size. Large firms have needs that are different from smaller companies, and each should be contacted in a different manner. Typically, the marketing effort is often focused on the company's purchasing department when the firm is large. For smaller firms, the owner or general manager often makes the purchase decisions and is therefore the target of marketing messages. When developing marketing communications, campaigns directed at larger firms should take into account that the buying centre will likely contain a number of different people, and the process may be more formal.

Segmentation by Geographic Location

As with consumer segmentation, identifying market segments by geographic location can be a successful tactic. This approach benefits businesses with customers who are concentrated in geographic pockets, such as Canada's technology triangle centred around the Waterloo region. It works for other firms as well. When Applied Microbiology developed a new antimicrobial agent, the goal was to market the product to dairy farmers. The traditional agricultural marketing and distribution channel required to launch such a new product nationally was estimated at $3 million. Such a traditional marketing plan involved national advertising in agriculture magazines plus recruiting sales agents and brokers to introduce the product. Instead, Applied Microbiology used geodemographics, which combined geographic areas with demographic and psychographic data. Applied Microbiology used geodemographics to find areas with dairy herds consisting of 1,000 or more cows per farm. These farmers were contacted for two reasons. First, large dairy farmers who adopted the product would buy greater quantities of it. Second, the company's leaders believed that the larger farmers were opinion leaders who would influence smaller farmers, thereby causing them to adopt the product as well.

Several separate direct-response mailings offering discounts for and samples of Applied Microbiology's new product were sent to larger farms. After sales started rising, farmers were asked for testimonials. The testimonials were extremely powerful, and they were then incorporated into new direct-marketing pieces. One brochure contained three testimonials and validation of the product by Cornell University. After a dairy farmer adopted the product, direct-marketing pieces were sent to farmers in the surrounding area. Not only did this method bring excellent results, but the marketing costs were

Operators of nursing homes are a valuable audience for many business-to-business marketers, including those who sell catering, laundry, property maintenance, and employment services.

Source: LEMOINE/BSIP/MaXxImages.com

one-third of the traditional approach. Using geodemographics cost only $1 million rather than the proposed $3 million.[8]

Segmentation by Product Usage

Business markets can be segmented based on the manner in which the good or service is used. Many services (financial, transportation, shipping, etc.) have a variety of uses for distinct customers. For example, in the hotel industry a major source of revenue is booking business events and conferences. A hotel or resort can identify business market segments based on various types of events. Single-day seminars require only a meeting room and refreshments. A full conference may involve renting rooms for lodging, preparing banquets, furnishing meeting rooms, and planning sightseeing excursions. By segmenting the market based on the use of the hotel's facilities and staff, a manager can prepare marketing materials that address the needs of each specific type of conference. The advertisement for Edgewater Beach Resort, shown in this section, is an example of this type of approach.

An advertisement targeted to the large business conference segment.

Segmentation by Customer Value

The final method of business segmentation is based on customer value. This approach is much easier for business-to-business firms to utilize than it is for consumer businesses, due to the availability of in-depth data about each business customer. A more precise value can be assigned to each individual business through sales records and other sources of data and information.

ESTABLISHING MARKETING COMMUNICATIONS OBJECTIVES

An effective communications market analysis identifies a clear target audience for a marketing communications campaign. This lays the foundation for the development of communications objectives, the second step of a promotions opportunities analysis. Communications objectives guide the development and delivery of messages.

As stated in Chapter 2, the objectives for the marketing communications should be aligned to the overall marketing objectives of the organization. However, these broader objectives, such as increased market share, do not usually provide sufficient guidance for the development of an IMC plan. For example, these goals do not take into account any specific segments, or what the people in those segments may know (or do not know) about the organization. This guidance must come from the market analysis, performed through the promotions opportunity analysis.

It's also important that specific marketing communications objectives be defined since marketing communications must work in concert with the other elements of the marketing mix—product, price, and distribution. For example, if the objective of a campaign is merely to increase sales, these other elements play a major role in achieving this broad goal. Marketing communications cannot make up for a poor product, or account for poor logistics that result in out-of-stock items when customers wish to purchase. In order to be developed and judged effectively, objectives must be specific to the role marketing communications can play in the overall marketing plan.

There are four criteria that should be used when defining objectives for marketing communications:

1. *Specific Target Audience.* Building on the first step of the promotions opportunity analysis, the objective should include a specific target audience to whom the objective applies. For example, an objective of an IMC campaign can include the audience of non-users of a product, or users of a competitor's product. The selection of this is a target audience—and the associated objective—are very different than if the target audience is current users of a product.

2. *Specific Tasks.* The objective should relate to some defined behaviour or attitude on the part of the target audience. For example, with the target of non-users, one objective might be to change levels of non-users' awareness of a product. Another objective might be a trial of the product. Choosing one of these two objectives would lead to a very different message and delivery in the IMC plan since trial requires more effort than merely changing attitudes.

3. *Specific Changes.* Apart from specifying tasks, objectives should also state the precise nature of the changes in the task that the IMC plan is expected to bring about. For example, if the marketer knows that only 10 percent of non-users have ever tried the product, one of the tasks might be to develop a trial level of 50 percent among non-users. This includes the initial benchmark measure and the desired measure for the end of the campaign.

4. *Specific Time.* As suggested by the third criterion, a good objective is to set a specific time period during which the task should be completed. In this case, the objective might be expected to be complete after one year, which is a typical timeframe for marketing communications planning cycles.

Taken in sum, the objective from the example used in the above criteria might read something like this: *The objective of the marketing communications campaign is to increase the trial level among non-users from 10 percent to 50 percent over a period of one year.*

Objectives can be stated as overall objectives for the campaign, as above. However, each element of the entire IMC plan can play a specific role in delivering this overall objective. Thus, there may be objectives that fall under the overall plan objective. For example, if a marketer knows that his or her target audience is not yet aware of the brand (see the three-step process outlined in Chapter 3), the first objective should be awareness, since this precipitates need recognition. This is the necessary first step toward the overall objective of the trial. The campaign can also include elements designed to provide information, impact the attitudes of the target audience, or impact the evaluation criteria used to make the decision to purchase (in this case, trial of a product).

The five-step purchase process represents a useful framework for examining marketing communications objectives.

1. *Need Recognition.* As noted earlier, the objective in this step can be as simple as creating a level of awareness so the audience is aware of the product or service. Or the objective can go further to actually stimulate a sense of need within the audience. Often this can be done at times when the audience is facing a personal situation where a latent need can be activated. For example, across every campus one can find automotive manufacturers offering promotions to pending graduates to buy a car upon graduation.

2. *Information Search.* Here the relevant objective relates either to providing information that will help the audience make an informed decision, or to the attitude the audience has toward a particular brand. In the case of the automotive brand on campus, one objective might be to shift attitudes toward a particular brand as being more stylish or affordable. This can be accomplished through a number of outlets, including flyers, campus newspaper advertising, and websites. One specific objective might be to encourage website visits, or a visit to a showroom.

Porter Airlines has specific objectives for customer traffic among a business traveller audience.

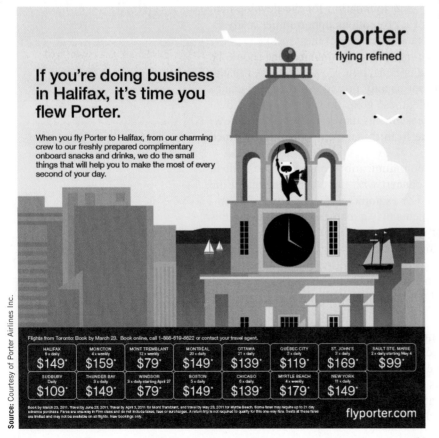

3. *Evaluation Criteria.* A relevant objective here might be to change the relevance of one product attribute, such as social status. An advertisement for the car could feature a message designed to suggest that the car sends a signal to others that one has "arrived." Or the car could lead the audience to think about how their future co-workers might look at their vehicle and suggest a particular brand is more suited to a professional career than others.

4. *Purchase Decision.* Obviously the automotive companies who promote the car to pending graduates would like everyone to move to this stage. Some of the tactics used to help encourage the objective of purchase are the promotions offered to graduates. Many companies offer pricing or financing specific to new graduates.

5. *Post-Purchase Evaluation.* At this stage, the objective of the marketer might be to increase or maintain customer satisfaction rates, or to encourage repeat purchase. Those who purchase a car can expect to receive one-to-one communications from the company designed to ensure the car meets their expectations and to encourage them to return for service visits.

The specific objectives for each marketer will vary widely, and many marketers combine multiple objectives into a single campaign. But in each case, the ultimate objective is to ensure that as many as possible within the target audience move through one or more of the five decision-making steps.

Critical Thinking Exercise

Go through your inbox or mailbox. Find a piece of communications you received from a marketer from whom you purchased something. Is the communication trying to influence your post-purchase evaluation? How is it doing that? Is it successful? Are there any other objectives you feel are built in to the communication?

ESTABLISHING A COMMUNICATIONS BUDGET

The third step of a promotions opportunity analysis is preparing a communications budget. Managers often make unrealistic assumptions about a communications budget. This occurs, for example, when a manager assumes there is a direct relationship between expenditures on marketing communications and subsequent sales revenues, which is highly unlikely. A more realistic relationship is shown in Figure 4.7. Several factors influence the relationship between expenditures on communications and sales, including

- The objective of the communication
- Threshold effects
- Carryover effects
- Wearout effects
- Decay effects
- Random events

The objective of the campaign is probably the single largest factor impacting communications budgets. For objectives that are relatively modest, it is possible that a relatively small budget will suffice. For example, if a target market is very concentrated, and the objective involves a small increase in awareness levels, much less budget will be required than if the audience contains millions of people, or the objective is a significant change in attitude from negative to positive.

Because the impact from marketing communications on sales can take time to occur, it is useful to examine the impact of **threshold effects**. As shown in Figure 4.7, the early effects of marketing communications are minimal. The same is true for most communications expenditures. At first, there may be little behavioural response, especially if

FIGURE 4.7
A Sales Response Function Curve Combined
with the Downward Response Curve and
Marginal Analysis

An unrealistic assumption about
the relationship between promotional
expenditures and sales

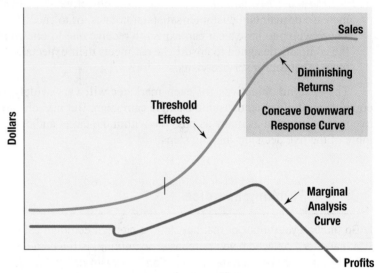

Marketing Communications Expenditures

only advertisements are used. Over time, a consumer who is exposed repeatedly to a company's marketing message recalls the company and eventually is willing to make a purchase.[9] Coupons, free samples, and other marketing tactics can help a good or service reach the threshold point sooner. Threshold effects are easy to reach in some circumstances, for instance, when the good or service is so innovative that consumers are quickly aware of its advantages and are willing to buy the item immediately. Also, when companies introduce new products under an established, strong brand name, reaching the threshold point normally occurs quicker. In others, capturing enough attention to spur sales is a lengthy process.

A point exists at which a promotional campaign has saturated the market. At that point, further expenditures have a minimal impact. The S-shaped curve displayed in Figure 4.7, which is known as the **sales-response function curve**, indicates when *diminishing returns* are present. Diminishing returns are part of the **concave downward function**. This means that incremental increases in expenditures in marketing communications result in smaller and smaller increases in sales. A **marginal analysis** shows that further communications expenditures might even adversely affect profits.

Another factor that influences the relationship between communications and sales is a **carryover effect**. Many products are only purchased when needed, such as washing machines and refrigerators. Promotions for these products must be designed to generate carryover effects. This occurs when the consumer has been exposed to the company's message for so long that, when the time comes to buy, the individual remembers the focal company. In other words, when a washing machine breaks down and requires a replacement, the goal of Maytag is for the consumer to remember the "lonely repairman" and his assistant. This means that Maytag's products will be considered and that the advertisements have carried over until the right time.

Wearout effects also complicate the marketing communications budgeting process. At a certain point, an advertisement or particular promotion simply becomes "old" or

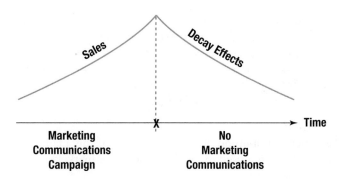

FIGURE 4.8
A Decay Effects Model

"boring." In such cases, consumers tend to ignore the advertisement or just tune it out.[10] It is even possible for consumers to develop negative attitudes toward the brand if they become annoyed at the marketing communication and believe it should be discontinued. The challenge for marketing communications is to keep an ad beyond the threshold effects and long enough to capture carryover effects, but not so long that wearout effects begin to take place.

Also, **decay effects** are present. When a company stops using marketing communications, consumers begin to forget the message. In some instances, the degree of decay is dramatic. In others, the carryover effects are strong enough that some time can lapse before the brand drops out of the consumer's consciousness. The promotional budget must be structured to avoid the problems of decay effects, which are illustrated in Figure 4.8.

Finally, random events affect promotions. A natural disaster or some other event can reduce the impact of any given campaign. Many retailers blame poor results on big shopping weekends on severe weather, which causes potential shoppers to stay home. Such events normally cannot be predicted.

Therefore, as the marketing team constructs the budget, the assumptions that drive the process should be considered. The newness of the product, the economy, and other complicating factors must be considered during the process of tying budgeting expenditures to marketing and communications objectives.

Critical Thinking Exercise

Think of an example of an advertisement you have seen at least 10 times. Are you sick and tired of the ad, or has the wearout effect not occurred? If you feel wearout has taken place, what could the company have done differently to help reduce wearout? If you don't feel wearout has taken place, why do you think this is the case?

Types of Budgets

A communications budget can be prepared in a number of different ways. Figure 4.9 provides a list of the various methods that are used.[11]

The Percentage of Sales Method

One common approach to setting the communications budget is the **percentage of sales method**. This budget is derived from either (1) sales from the previous year or (2) anticipated sales for the next year. A major reason for using this method is its simplicity. A percentage of sales budget is relatively easy to prepare.

The approach also has problems. First, it tends to change in the opposite direction of what is typically needed. That is, when sales go up, so does the communications budget.

◆ Percentage of sales	◆ Objective and task
◆ Meet the competition	◆ Payout planning
◆ "What we can afford"	◆ Quantitative models

FIGURE 4.9
Methods of Determining a Marketing Communications Budget

When sales decline, the communications budget also declines. In most cases, when sales are declining the communications budget should be increased to help reverse the trend. Further, during growth periods the communications budget may not need to be increased. The second major disadvantage of this method is that it does not allocate money for special needs or to combat competitive pressures. Therefore, many marketing experts believe the disadvantages of the percentage of sales method tend to outweigh its advantages.

The Meet-the-Competition Method

Some firms use the **meet-the-competition method**. The primary goal of this method is to prevent the loss of market share. It is often used in highly competitive markets where rivalries among competitors are intense.

The potential drawback to meet-the-competition budgeting is that marketing dollars might not be spent efficiently. Matching the competition's spending does not guarantee success. Market share can still be lost. It is important to remember that it is not *how much* is spent, but rather *how well* the money is allocated and how effectively the marketing campaign works at retaining customers and market share.

The "What We Can Afford" Method

A third strategy is the "**what we can afford**" method. This technique sets the marketing budget after all of the company's other budgets have been determined. Money is allocated based on what the company leaders feel they can afford. This method suggests that management may not fully recognize the benefits of marketing communications. Instead, company leaders may view marketing communications expenditures as non-revenue-generating activities. Newer and smaller companies with limited finances often use the "what we can afford" approach.

The Objective and Task Method

Another technique is the **objective and task method**. To prepare this type of communications budget, management lists all of the communications objectives to pursue during the year and then calculates the cost of accomplishing each objective. The communications budget is the cumulative sum of the estimated costs for all objectives.

Many marketing experts believe that the objective and task method is the best budgeting method because it relates dollar costs to achieving specific objectives. Unfortunately, it is difficult for a large company, such as Procter & Gamble, to use. With hundreds of products on the market, producing a budget based on objectives for each brand and product category is very time-consuming. Despite the challenge, some form of the objective and task method of setting marketing budgets is used by about 50 percent of firms.[12]

Payout Planning

Payout planning establishes a ratio of marketing communications to sales or market share. This method normally allocates greater amounts in early years to yield payouts in later years.[13] By allocating larger amounts at the beginning of a new product introduction, brand awareness and brand equity are built. Then, as the brand is accepted and sales build, a lower percentage of marketing communications dollars is needed to maintain a target growth. This budgeting approach is based on the threshold effects concept and the idea of diminishing returns. This is captured in Figure 4.10. A company that has reached the maximum threshold point should not continue pouring money into marketing communications that only results in diminishing returns. Instead, a company can maintain awareness and brand equity by more effective expenditures of marketing dollars. Future promotions will target specific market segments and consumer groups rather than simply increasing the volume of marketing dollars spent.

Quantitative Models

In some instances, computer simulations can be developed to model the relationship between advertising or promotional expenditures with sales and profits. These models are far from perfect. They do have the advantage of accounting for the type of industry and product as the model is created. In most cases, quantitative models are limited to larger organizations with strong computer and statistics departments.

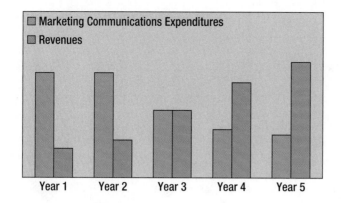

FIGURE 4.10
A Payout Planning Example

Budgeting Expenditures

A budget is finalized when the company has specified how funds will be spent on each of the major communications tools. Media advertising normally accounts for about 41 percent of a marketing budget. Trade promotions receive about 28 percent, and consumer promotions average about 28 percent (see Figure 4.11).[14] These percentages, however, vary considerably from industry to industry. Consumer product manufacturers spend more on trade promotions directed toward retailers. Service companies tend to spend more on media advertising. Budgets also vary by product types. For example, for dolls and stuffed toys the average expenditure on media advertising as a percentage of sales is 11.2 percent, whereas for men's clothing expenditures on media advertising represent only 3.3 percent of sales.[15]

The United States leads the world in annual advertising expenditures at $263.7 billion. This figure is approximately seven times more than the next closest nation.[16] See Figure 4.12 for a graph of the top 10 countries in terms of total advertising expenditures. Although Canada is in tenth place, the $6.4 billion spent on advertising is significant, and this figure, of course, doesn't include any other form of marketing communications.

When a promotions opportunity analysis is complete, marketers should have a firm understanding of where the most promising opportunities for marketing communications lie. This includes an analysis of both internal and competitive marketing communications and positioning, a specific target market, a specific objective related to that market, and a budget designed to deliver the objective.

The rest of this book is dedicated to executing the opportunity defined in the promotions opportunity analysis. We will next discuss the design of the messages that will be communicated to various target audiences (Chapters 5 and 6), the media and promotional vehicles available to deliver those messages (Chapters 7 through 11), ethical and regulatory considerations (Chapter 12), and the need for formal evaluation of IMC programs (Chapter 13).

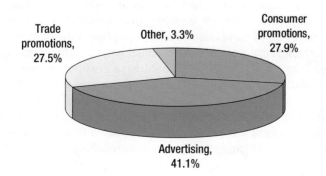

FIGURE 4.11
Breakdown of Marketing Communications Expenditures

FIGURE 4.12
Advertising Expenditures
of Top 10 Countries

Source: Based on "100 Leading National
Advertisers," *Adverising Age Datacenter 2007
Marketing Profiles Yearbook* (June 25, 2007), p.7

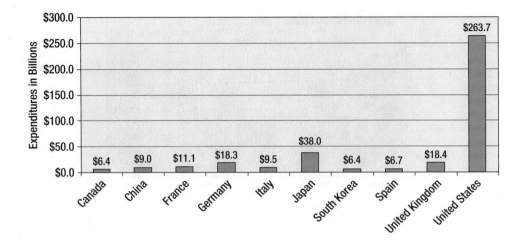

COMMUNICATING ACROSS CULTURES

As was first presented in Chapter 1, integrated marketing communications programs that take into account different cultures are vital for international firms. The world consists of many different languages and cultures. Brand names, marketing ideas, and marketing communications campaigns designed for one region of Canada do not always translate correctly to another. Nor do campaigns created for the Canadian market always translate when taken elsewhere, or vice versa. Consequently, understanding the local market is essential.

Recognizing the many cultural nuances throughout Canada and beyond is one key. This does not mean that different marketing campaigns must always be developed for each country and each cultural group within a country. Still, marketers must understand the region and its culture in order to tailor messages to individual audiences.

The first challenge in stretching across cultural boundaries is that there may be very different competitive positionings, or even different competitors across different cultures. For example, when Coke and Pepsi target the Muslim cola drinker, they do not compete only with each other. They also compete with the Qibla and Mecca brands. Both of these brands position themselves as "Muslim" colas, and they have a powerful connection with these consumers. When considering multiple cultures, segmentation is critical. The goal is to design a communications plan that effectively reaches every market segment.

One key to a successful cross-cultural campaign is developing local partnerships. Local partners can be marketing research firms or advertising firms that are familiar with the local language and culture. These partnerships sometimes are formed by hiring someone from a particular country with a full understanding of the market. Such a person is sometimes referred to as a **cultural assimilator**. It is vital that the chosen individual has a clear understanding of the language of the parent firm and the parent firm's business.

Next, objectives for IMC plans may vary from culture to culture, depending on at least two factors. First, one brand may have very low levels of awareness in one province, yet have high levels in another. Entering into markets with low brand awareness necessitates the inclusion of these intermediate steps prior to the objective of purchase or trial. In addition, brands can experience attitudinal barriers when entering new markets. For example, although most consumers would have positive attitudes toward seafood that comes from Malaysia, they may hold negative attitudes about cars manufactured in Malaysia.

Tied to the communications market analysis and objectives are the budgets required to achieve success across cultures. For cultures where there are negative attitudes toward the brand, or strong competitors entrenched, much larger budgets may be required.

Lara Johnson summarizes the overall marketing communications objective for TELUS: "TELUS' strategic intent is to unleash the Internet to deliver the best solutions to Canadians at home, in the workplace, and on the move. TELUS' marketing communication efforts are focused on communicating the information, entertainment, and communications solutions we provide our customers. We focus on driving new acquisitions and reducing the number of clients who deactivate their accounts."

"In our consumer markets, we have different segments for whom we develop relevant product and service variations," says Kate Baillie. Most of our communications are seen by everyone, and that's

Back to school is a peak season for TELUS.

a good thing for us because of the efficiencies in communicating with one voice. We use direct marketing to augment our mass campaigns with segment-specific messaging and offers." That one voice speaks to a large portion of the Canadian population, according to Lara Johnson. "Our look and feel is not intimidating; it's approachable. As a result, customers that may not be as comfortable with technology are more apt to come to us instead of a competitor."

Kate Baillie considers TELUS, in many ways, to be a retail business in the consumer market. "One of the big objectives for us in our marketing communications is to drive retail traffic. And our budgets are built around supporting periods when the industry as a whole tends to see increased retail traffic. The August–September "back to school" period has become one of our most important retail periods, rivalling Christmas. So when we set our budgets, we think about the year in a series of individual periods that are really about retail domination."

In consumer markets, Kate explains that the competition for market share is fierce, and most companies simply try to get as many customers as they can, but it's important to understand the needs of existing clients too. "We develop communication programs to certain existing customers that we think are likely to add television, high-speed Internet or mobility to their home phone service, for example. So much of our segmentation in consumer markets is aimed at upselling existing customers by using direct marketing and telemarketing."

The most prominent segmentation exercise for TELUS is between consumer and business markets. "Because we know businesses typically buy our products and services very differently from consumers, we have a different set of marketing communications programs for the business market, which is then segmented further into large enterprise businesses, small and medium businesses, and very small businesses. Business programs tend to include more online and email/direct marketing, sales tools, and personal selling, whereas in our consumer markets we do a lot more mass media advertising. Basically, we adapt the marketing communications to match what we know about how each segment buys."

Another important segment for TELUS includes investors. "We again have a unique set of marketing communications programs for the investor community, to make sure we reach our objectives for that audience," says Kate. But the great thing about the

TELUS creates unique marketing communications pieces for the investor audience.

TELUS brand is that the things that make us attractive to consumer and business audiences also help us in investor communications. Our annual report has won numerous awards for its clarity and transparency. So our brand attribute of simplicity carries over to our investor communications and helps us achieve our objectives across multiple segments."

Source: Used with permission of Kate Baillie, TELUS Communications.

For help developing your IMC Plan, go to **www.pearsoncanada.ca/clow**.

SUMMARY

A promotions opportunity analysis is the process by which marketers identify target audiences for the goods and services produced by the company. It consists of three steps: conduct a communications market analysis, establish communications objectives, and create a communications budget, prepare promotional strategies, and match tactics with strategies.

A thorough understanding of competitive strengths and weaknesses, specifically as they relate to marketing communications and their brand perception in the market is the first step. This analysis can lead to recognition of underserved audiences, or emerging audiences that represent valuable opportunities for marketing communications. Any number of trends can lead to new marketing opportunities, including technological, social, or even political trends. Based on this analysis, market segments should be identified with one or more representing a target audience for the marketing communications campaign.

Market segmentation is identifying sets of business or consumer groups with distinct characteristics. Segments must be heterogeneous to the general population, homogeneous within themselves, large enough to support a marketing campaign, responsive, and reachable through some type of communications vehicle. Consumer groups that can be segmented include those identified by demographics, including gender, age, income, and ethnic heritage. Markets can also be identified using psychographic, generational, and geographic delineations. Geodemographic segmentation combines demographic, psychographic, and geographic information together. Other ways to categorize consumers are by the benefits they receive from goods or services and by the ways they use products.

Business-to-business segmentation can be accomplished by targeting business customers by industry, business type, the size of the company, geographic location, usage, and customer value calculations. Marketing managers should carefully specify the company's consumer and business market segments. All other promotions opportunity analysis processes are tied to the identification of key customers.

After a target audience is defined, marketers must set specific objectives for the IMC plan. These include objectives related to a specific target audience, with a specific task measured against a benchmark over a specified period of time. Objectives of marketing communications can be considered in one of the five purchase decision-making steps: need recognition, information search, evaluation of alternatives, purchase decision, and post-purchase evaluation.

Based on the target audience and objective, a budget for the IMC plan must be set. Budgeting will depend first and foremost on the objective of the plan. More aggressive objectives will require more resources. A number of methods exist for setting budgets, including the percentage of sales, meet-the-competition, and "what we can afford" methods, objective and task, payout planning, and quantitative methods, which use computer modelling and simulation.

A promotions opportunity analysis program is the first step in developing a complete IMC plan, and is the foundation for the rest of the IMC program.

KEY TERMS

carryover effects   When products are only purchased when needed, promotions for those products must be designed to generate a situation in which the consumer has been exposed to the company's message for so long that when the time comes to buy, the consumer remembers the key company.

communication market analysis   The process of discovering the organization's strengths and weaknesses in the area of marketing communication.

concave downward function   A model of the diminishing returns of advertising expenditures on sales.

cultural assimilator A person who is familiar with the local language and culture of a given country who can help marketing efforts in that particular country.

decay effects Declines in advertising effectiveness that occur when advertising stops and consumers begin to forget about the company.

demographics The study of population characteristics.

marginal analysis A model that shows when additional expenditures on advertising and promotions have an adverse affect on profits.

market segment A set of businesses or group of individual consumers with distinct characteristics.

market segmentation The identification of specific purchasing groups based on their needs, attitudes, and interests.

meet-the-competition method A method of communications budgeting in which the primary rationale is to prevent the loss of market share, which occurs in highly competitive markets where rivalries between competitors are intense.

objective and task method A form of communications budgeting in which management first lists all of the objectives it wants to accomplish during the year and then budgets to meet those objectives.

payout planning A budgeting method that establishes a ratio of advertising to sales or market share.

percentage of sales method A form of communications budgeting in which budgeting is based on the sales from the previous year or anticipated sales for the coming year.

promotions opportunity analysis The process marketers use to identify target audiences for a company's goods and services and the communications strategies needed to reach these audiences.

psychographics The study of patterns of responses that reveal a person's activities, interests, and opinions (AIO).

sales-response function curve An S-shaped curve that indicates when threshold effects are present and when diminishing returns are present.

threshold effects For new products, initial advertisements yield little behavioral response; however, over time, a consumer who is exposed enough times to a company's marketing message will recall the company and eventually become willing to make a purchase.

wearout effects Declines in advertising effectiveness that occur when an ad or marketing communications becomes "old" or "boring."

"what we can afford" method A method of communications budgeting in which the marketing budget is set after all of the company's other budgets have been determined and communications monies are allocated based on what the firm feels it can afford to spend.

REVIEW QUESTIONS

1. What is a promotions opportunities analysis? What makes it a critical part of a company's marketing efforts?

2. What are the three parts of a promotions opportunities analysis planning process?

3. What are the characteristics of a good market segment?

4. Define demographics. How are they used to segment consumer markets?

5. How can firms take advantage of target markets by gender?

6. What generational cohorts have marketing experts identified?

7. What problems are associated with markets segmented according to geographic areas?

8. What are geodemographics? Why have they been so successful in defining marketing segments?

9. Describe usage segmentation and benefit segmentation.

10. What are the common business-to-business market segments?

11. Describe the NAICS approach to business market segmentation.

12. Describe a usage segmentation approach in a business-to-business setting.

13. Describe a segmentation approach based on company size.

14. What are the characteristics of a good marketing communications objective?

15. What are examples of marketing communications objectives for each step of the five-step decision-making process?

16. Name and describe the types of communications budget methods. Which is best? Why?

INTEGRATED LEARNING EXERCISES

1. Does the five-step process only apply to objectives for customer audiences? What about audiences such as employees or regulators? Companies regularly engage in marketing communications designed, at least in part, to communicate with non-customer audiences. In addition, other organizations such as non-profits or governments engage in marketing communications that can have objectives different from the objectives of companies. Find an

example of marketing communications from a company that you think includes at least one non-customer audience, and one example from a non-profit or government that you think has different objectives than those used by companies. Explain why you chose the communications you did.

2. *Marketing Magazine* provides useful insight on trends taking place within marketing communications. Go to the website at **www.marketingmag.com**. Scan through the news stories and identify two that highlight some trend that is impacting how organizations market to their audiences. Write a short summary report about the contents of each article.

3. For consumer markets, Canada Post offers GeoPost as a tool for marketers. Go to their website at **www.canadapost.ca** and explore the various methods of segmentation using PSYTE clusters. What information does Canada Post provide? Assume you have a small retail shop that sells flowers. How would you use this service as part of an integrated marketing communications plan? What advantages would it bring, and which clusters would interest you the most? What objective(s) would you set for your campaign using this cluster?

4. Values and lifestyles (VALS) psychographic segmentation can be a valuable tool for marketers as they prepare their marketing materials. Access VALS2 through Strategic Business Insights at **http://www .strategicbusinessinsights.com/vals/presurvey.shtml**. Once at the VALS site, examine the characteristics of each of the groups. Then take the test to determine which group you belong to. How can VALS2 help marketers develop marketing communications messages?

STUDENT PROJECT

Creative Corner

The VALS2 typology has been used by a number of companies and marketing communications agencies to create marketing materials. Your task is to design two print advertisements for your school. Pick one of the following pairs of VALS segments and design an advertisement promoting your school for each segment. When you are finished, write a paragraph explaining how you believe the ads you created will appeal to their respective VALS segment and how the two ads are different. Before you begin work on the ads, go to the Strategic Business Insights website at **http://www.strategicbusinessinsights.com/vals** to obtain more information about the two segments you will be targeting with your ads.

Pair 1: Innovators and survivors
Pair 2: Thinkers and makers
Pair 3: Believers and achievers
Pair 4: Strivers and experiencers

⮕ ETHICS IN ACTION

Unlike many companies that perform poorly in a recession, the rent-to-own industry does very well. These companies offer rental contracts to consumers who may not otherwise be able to afford to buy such things as appliances and furniture. So in a recession, many people lose some or all of their income and these rent-to-own contracts are a way to avoid sacrificing. The industry's ability to provide goods to people with low incomes makes lower income segments a very attractive market for them.[17] But critics charge that the customers don't really understand what they end up paying in the end because either the financing details are not properly disclosed, or the consumer is not financially literate enough to understand the implications of the rent-to-own model versus outright purchase. In the case of one retailer, they might rent a TV to a customer for $99 a month for 24 months, but the TV would only cost $800 to purchase.[18] Effectively, by targeting consumers who feel they have no other choice, the industry "can charge whatever they want."[19] Others charge that the industry promotes a lifestyle without sacrifice that truly can't be afforded by most of the people they target.

1. Find an ad for a rent-to-own retailer in your province. By targeting lower income consumers, do you feel the company is responsible for "gouging" consumers who might not be aware of the true price of financing? Do you feel they are promoting excessive consumption to a target audience that should learn to restrain wants due to a lack of income? Draft a letter to the retailer and either support or criticize their marketing communications on this issue. Be sure to outline your reasons for your position.

2. Some legislation has been passed to try and help potentially vulnerable consumers understand the true costs of rent-to-own contracts. Through your library database, review the legislation on this issue. Write a report outlining (a) what legislation currently is in place for consumer protection on this issue, (b) whether you think it is sufficient, and (c) what other elements you would add to the legislation to further protect consumers. ●

CASE STUDY | Promoting Cancer Prevention

Jill Vinall had landed her dream job as the marketing coordinator at the head office of the Canadian Cancer Society (CCS). Working for one of the most recognized and respected charities in the country gives Jill a great sense of pride. "I get to do a job where I not only get to work in marketing but I get to make a real difference in people's lives every day."

But part of the challenge in working with such a large organization is that the mandate is quite broad. This creates challenges for any one program because the focus of the marketing team can be easily distracted by programs in other areas. "There are so many needs, and so many great programs, and our budgets are fairly small, so a job in the charity sector is probably the biggest challenge a marketer can take on," says Jill.

As Jill heads to work on Monday morning, the challenge on her mind is the role of the CCS in promoting cancer prevention. A key part of the mandate of the CCS is to encourage Canadians to make better lifestyle choices to help reduce their risk of getting cancer. As you might imagine, this includes promotion and information on many different risk factors, including smoking, exercise, and diet. One program in particular—the component related to diet—can

be a challenge because it spans so many aspects of nutrition. The CCS website provides information on health issues related to fruits and vegetables, salt, and red meat, just to name a few.

Today Jill was re-examining the role of the CCS in the partnership known as Mix it Up! (**www.fruitsandveggies.ca**). She knew the site provided good information from a nutritional point of view but wondered how effective it was at getting this message out to Canadians.

"I know that most people don't really spend a lot time thinking about their diet," explains Jill. "And on top of that, the lifestyle for most people today makes it tough to eat a healthy diet with fresh fruits and vegetables." In addition, research shows that most people don't know how many servings of fruits and vegetables they should be eating, or what a serving looks like.[20] "And if that wasn't a big enough challenge, just getting people to think about cancer can be a challenge because it's a scary disease and a lot of people just shut down when a message about cancer is put in front of them."

The website is at the heart of the Mix It Up! program. It features recipes, information on preparing and storing fruits and vegetables, and tips on meal planning. But the campaign involves a number of other elements designed to raise awareness of the issue and, in many cases, encourages people to go to the website, where they can find more information. "A big challenge when promoting healthy eating is that it's not the kind of thing you can do in a 30-second television ad," says Jill. "It's a complex message that people are unlikely to adopt after just seeing one ad. We do what we can. We do have a TV spot, and we're on Facebook and Twitter, and whatever else we can do cost effectively." This challenge is exacerbated by the fact that the budget for the campaign is dwarfed by the budgets spent by marketers encouraging people to eat things other than fresh fruits and vegetables.

"Part of our challenge is that the industry selling foods that are not healthy has so much more money than we do," says Jill. Indeed, apart from selling products that more easily fit into today's busy lifestyles, the food industry has massive marketing communications budgets. Estimates for North America peg the overall budget at over $10 billion annually. This is particularly challenging because much of this money is spent marketing products to

Source: Courtesy of Canadian Produce Marketing Association.

The Mix it Up!™ Campaign includes many executions for both parents and kids.

Source: Digital Vision/Jupiter Images.

Today's lifestyles make it challenging to convince consumers to eat fresh fruits and vegetables.

children. An estimated $1.6 billion is spent on marketing communications by major firms only on the 12-to-17 age demographic.[21] Another study finds that children and adolescents see up to 6,100 televised food advertisements a year, with only 5 percent of them promoting healthy foods and beverages such as dairy products and fruit juice.[22]

"The partnership with the Heart and Stroke Foundation on Mix It Up! helps a little bit," says Jill. "But the reality is that we can never outspend the food companies that promote products other than fresh fruits and vegetables."

Part of Jill's mandate for the program's coming year is to revaluate the program entirely. "I need to look at the program from the ground up and try to establish some metrics around it. When it started it was based on the stated benefits of fresh fruits and vegetables in cancer prevention. But when our donors and other stakeholders ask how the program is working, we really can't tell them because the issue of nutrition is just so huge, with so many moving parts.

One of my main priorities is to set some specific objectives for the Mix It Up! campaign. I firmly believe in the program and "want to see it succeed, but if it's going to be sustainable over the long term we need to be more specific on how the program helps people." Part of the pressure facing Jill on this program is that other programs tend to have more specific objectives and success metrics. "We set objectives when we fund cancer research, for example, and we can see progress being made each year. Or in things like our anti-smoking campaigns, we watch smoking

rates or legislation that prevents dangers of second hand smoke and we can point to our work as part of what's behind that. But I wonder if I'll be able to do the same thing on this program."

As part of the coming year's planning cycle, Jill has been asked to perform a promotions opportunity analysis for the campaign. Assume that as part of your effort to gain some industry experience, you are a volunteer for the CCS in the marketing department. She has asked you to help her on this project.

1. Do a market communications analysis for the campaign. Who are the "competitors"? What are their strengths and weaknesses? Write up your results in a two-page memo to Jill.

2. Using whatever segmentation criteria you feel are appropriate, outline at least two market segments that can be considered as target audiences for this campaign. Do you think the five-step purchase process described in this text can be used to help guide the campaign?

3. Using your knowledge of objectives from this chapter, set some objectives for the campaign. Create a 10-minute presentation where you begin by listing as many options as you can think, and then narrow it down to only a few or even one. Justify why you chose the one(s) you did.

4. Based on what you know about the food industry and their budgets, can you determine an appropriate budget method for this campaign? What do you think an appropriate annual budget is for this campaign?

ENDNOTES

1. Shannon Shannon Dortch, "Going to the Movies," *American Demographics* 18, no. 12 (December 1996), pp. 4–8.

2. Kitty Bean Yancey, "More Women Head Out, Leave the Menfolk Behind," USA Today (**www.usatoday.com/travel/destinations/2007–10–25-gal-getaways_N.htm**, October 25, 2007).

3. Interview with Kerri Martin, brand manager of BMW Motorcycles, July 18, 2000.

4. Chris Cormack, "Why Vega Got It So Wrong," *B&T Weekly* 56, no. 2574 (July 28, 2006), p. 14.

5. Rebecca Piirto Heath, "Psychographics," *Marketing Tools* (November–December 1995), pp. 74–81.

6. SRI Consulting Business Intelligence (**www.sric-bi.com**, accessed January 3, 2008); Dana-Nicoleta Lascu and Kenneth E. Clow, *Essentials of Marketing* (Cincinnati, OH: Atomic Dog Publishing, 2007), p. 169.

7. Susan Pechman, "Custom Clusters: Finding Your True Customer Segments," *Bank Marketing* 26, no. 7 (July 1994), pp. 33–35.

8. Gene Koprowski, "Bovine Inspiration," *Marketing Tools* (October 1996), pp. 10–11.

9. Margaret Henderson Blair, "An Empirical Investigation of Advertising Wearin and Wearout," *Journal of Advertising Research* 40, no. 6 (November–December 2000), pp. 95–100.

10. Ibid.

11. Lionell A. Mitchell, "An Examination of Methods of Setting Advertising Budgets:

Practice and Literature," *European Journal of Marketing* 27, no. 5 (1993), pp. 5–22.

12. James E. Lynch and Graham J. Hooley, "Increased Sophistication in Advertising Budget Setting," Journal of Advertising Research 30, no. 1 (February–March 1990), pp. 67–76.

13. James O. Peckham, "Can We Relate Advertising Dollars to Market Share Objectives?" in M. A. McNiver (ed). How Much to Spend for Advertising, (New York: Association of National Advertisers, 1969), p. 30.

14. "Higher Gear," *Promo Industry Trends Report* (**www.promomagazine.com**, accessed January 2, 2008).

15. "2004 Advertising to Sales Ratios for 200 Largest Ad Spending Industries," *Adage* (**www.adage.com**, accessed February 26, 2005).

16. "Top Advertisers in Top 10 Countries, Excluding the U.S.," *2006 Fact Pack, Advertising Age* (February 27, 2006), p. 14.

17. Suzanne Kapner (2009), "Rent-to-Own Makes a Comeback," *Fortune International*, June 8, p. 15.

18. Ibid.

19. Ronald Paul Hill, David L. Ramp and Linda Silver (1998), "The Rent-to-Own Industry and Pricing Disclosure Tactics," *Journal of Public Policy & Marketing*, 17, no. 1, pp. 3–10.

20. Canadian Cancer Society (2003), "Research Shows Canadians Don't Have Time to

Eat Well and Don't Know the Benefits of Healthy Eating," (**http://cis.cancer.ca/Canada-wide/About us/Media centre/CW-Media releases/CW-200**, accessed May 17, 2010).

21. Federal Trade Commission (2008), "Marketing Food to Children and Adolescents: A Review of Industry Expenditures, Activities and Self-Regulation." A Report to Congress. (**www.ftc.gov/opa/2008/07/foodmkting.shtm**, accessed May 17, 2010).

22. Kaiser Family Foundation (2007), "Food for Thought: Television Food Advertising to Children in the United States." (**http://www.kff.org/entmedia/upload/7618ES.pdf**, accessed May 17, 2010).

PART

2

Message Design

After the analysis of the environment, identification of the intended audience(s), and development of the objectives, the next step in the marketing communications process is to develop the message intended for the audience.

In this second section of the book, we examine the strategies and tactics used to design marketing communications messages. The strategy, discussed in Chapter 5, broadly refers to the decisions made based on an understanding of how the target audience perceives the company, how the process of marketing communications works, and the efficacy of different appeal types. We then consider creative tactics, or how the strategy is used to develop specific messages—right down to the words and images—along with the production processes, in Chapter 6.

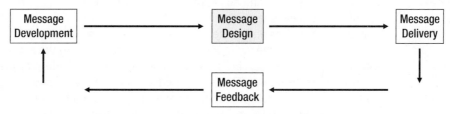

Step 2 in the Communications Process

CHAPTER 5   Creative Strategy   **CHAPTER 6**   Creative Tactics

CHAPTER OBJECTIVES

After reading this chapter, you should be able to answer the following questions:

- **What** are the components of a creative brief?

- **What** is the function of a creative brief in the overall marketing communications plan?

- **How** does marketing communications create impact with target audience?

- **What** roles do attitudes and values play in developing marketing communications messages?

- **What** appeals are used in the creative development process, and why are they successful?

- **Are** there differences in creating communications for consumer, for business-to-business, and across cultures?

INDUSTRY PROFILE

So You Want to Work in Marketing Communications?

Brent Mykyte, Creative Lead, City of Calgary, Calgary, Alberta

Brent Mykyte is one of those rare individuals who can speak from experience on both the strategy and the creative side of a communications project. He began his career with an undergraduate degree in communications with a focus on advertising, and worked in the marketing industry for seven years before returning to school to complete a design degree at the Alberta College of Art and Design (ACAD).

"To be truly effective in creative development, I believe there are two sets of necessary skills," says Brent. "First, you need the academic training side. In my case, my degree from ACAD gave me the ability to understand the visual side of communications. It allows me to translate the strategy of a campaign into the language of the campaign. Most people with business or commerce degrees find the creative of the business extremely difficult without those visual skills.

"The second skill is the ability to meet the people working on the strategy side halfway of what I call 'The Great Divide.' The people who work on the strategy side, or in account management, tend to be linear thinkers focused on the bigger picture aspects of a campaign—the objectives, the budget, and things like that. It's up to the people working on the creative side of that campaign—the translation of the objectives and strategy into a tangible piece of communications—to be able to also think in the same way. When we present ideas to the account team, for example, we need to be able to understand how they will interpret the ideas and where their priorities lie. That's why I encourage the creatives working for me to take some intro marketing courses, or seminars that help them understand where their counterparts on the account side are coming from."

But Brent cautions that the strategists also bear some of the responsibility in making the relationship work. He advises strategists to also become bilingual and be able to understand the language of creative development. "Learn how to use both the left and right sides of your brain," says Brent. "It will make you a much more effective colleague and at the end of the day make for much better campaigns if the strategists are able to appreciate the creative process and how it can add value.

Creative Strategy

"Here at the City of Calgary, we take a very pragmatic approach to creative development. This is in part because we are a public entity and our investments in marketing communications need to be justified to the public. We need to show that we are investing our budgets wisely and that our campaigns get results," explains Brent. "It's important that the creative side and the strategy side both work together. If someone gets a flyer in his mailbox that promotes a city recycling program, he needs to feel that it was worth the investment it took to produce that flyer.

"So we are not as focused on what I call 'haute couture' creative the same way a lot of agencies might be." Brent says his team doesn't value creative development for the sake of aesthetics but rather for how creative can help serve the needs of his clients. "Certainly the creative needs to be developed with what we know about visual design and communication, but all of that is lost if a campaign doesn't get the job done. So it's a balance between design and business."

But despite all that, Brent's campaigns aren't boring. One recent campaign won a coveted Gold Quill award from the International Association of Business Communicators. "The campaign objective was to promote Calgary parks. We have so many fantastic parks right here in the city, but many people don't know about them. Our task was to either remind or inform people about this wonderful resource right in their own backyard.

Brent Mykyte, Creative Lead, City of Calgary

We could've gone the traditional route and put up some billboards with a shot of the park and a line like 'Come Visit Fish Creek Park.' But we thought there was an opportunity to do something more special. So we dug further, went out and visited the parks, learned the history, learned why they were started, and read the plans for the future of Calgary parks. This background work gave us the insights for what became the award-winning Almost This Close campaign. In this campaign, the media was an important part of the creative as the actual message. "We wanted to put the message in highly urban, highly unexpected places to surprise people. We wanted an extra element of surprise when they learned that these wide open vistas were found within the city limits. So we bought media on the backs of elevators, escalator facing, bathroom stalls—anywhere that the audience would not expect to see a shot of an endless horizon from the top of Nose Hill, for example."

One of the things Brent enjoys most about his job is working with new graduates who bring an entirely new energy and perspective to the work. "Last year we had two students from ACAD join us and it was a great experience for me. Mentoring them was incredibly rewarding, and they brought so much passion to their work it was infectious. I especially liked the fact that they weren't afraid to speak up and challenge an idea if they felt they had something better to offer."

Brent has one more piece of advice for aspiring marketers who seek to enter the creative field, although the advice is sound for anyone seeking a career in marketing communications. "Get out there and experience life," urges Brent. "One of the most important things in this job is to understand that we create communications that speak to people within the context of their lives. But people are different, and contexts are different. With experience we learn to speak more languages, so to speak, and can understand how to communicate effectively with a wide variety of people in a wide variety of contexts. This makes you much more attractive to a potential employer simply because you can offer much more value."

OVERVIEW

This chapter represents an important and challenging part of the marketing communications development process. It is the first step in the coding process described in the model of communication presented in Chapter 1, and begins our examination of the message design component of the textbook.

This is a challenging step because it represents the interface between the "business" side of the marketing communications process, where most readers of this text are and will be based, and the "creative" side of the process. These two sides are often characterized by a clash of cultures. People working on the business side—sometimes referred to as "suits" within the industry—tend to be linear, left-brain thinkers. The people working on the creative side tend to be nonlinear, right-brain thinkers. Although each is necessary for development of a successful IMC plan, there is a need for a common language and understanding between the two sides.

This chapter represents this "hand-off" from the business side to the creative side. Up until this point, the content of this book has been on the work done by people working on the business side to understand the brand, analyze the customer, identify opportunities, and set objectives and budgets. People in the creative department are needed to turn these things into the tangible pieces of marketing communications that we experience every day. One challenge is that people who work on the business side have a different approach to business. They tend to be linear thinkers and grounded in quantitative analysis. Creative teams are typically non-linear thinkers and have often chosen their profession to specifically avoid quantitative analysis. As one marketing communications professional put it: "Advertising is a craft executed by people who aspire to be artists, but is assessed by people who aspire to be scientists. I cannot imagine any human relationship more perfectly designed to produce total mayhem."[1]

In considering creative development, this chapter takes the perspective that the reader is both an initiator and evaluator of the creative product, but not the actual producer. We will focus our examination, therefore, on aspects of the process likely to be faced by the reader in a future career. The focus on initiation will include the distillation of the strategic work done up until this point in the process into a focused creative strategy. This is delivered in the form of a creative brief. The focus on evaluation will include an examination of how different types of marketing communications work, and why they work. It is important for the person evaluating the creative from a business perspective to understand if and why the creative is likely to be effective.

This chapter focuses on the strategic aspects of creative development. This includes the development of the key message strategy and an understanding of why and how marketing communications works, and how different approaches to creating marketing communications can be effective. The next chapter in Part 2, Chapter 6, will focus on the tactical aspects of creative development. This will include how the messages and approaches are actually articulated through various media.

THE CREATIVE BRIEF

The document used to articulate this strategy to the creative department is known as the **creative brief**. This document includes a number of items that are essential for the creative team to understand in order to deliver a focused, effective message. Each marketer and agency uses his or her own slightly tailored version of this document. But, in general, there are a number of questions answered in the brief that are consistent to all versions, as listed in Figure 5.1

Who are we talking to? As discussed earlier, the entire IMC plan is based around a definition and understanding of a specific target audience. In the creative brief, a succinct summary of the key attributes of the target audience is necessary. This can include a number of segmentation criteria, as defined in Chapter 4. In can include attitudinal information, or information about their influencers, as described in Chapter 3. It should always include a discussion of how they perceive the brand or product category that is the subject of the briefing. For example, are they aware of our brand? Have they used our brand in the past? What do they think of our brand? What are their barriers to purchase, or other behaviours?

What is the objective? Building from the objective-setting exercise described in Chapter 4, the briefing should contain a specific objective for the communication. If it is purchase, it might describe any intermediary steps that are expected to be required prior to purchase, such as awareness or attitudinal shifts. But there should always be one focused overall objective for the brief so the people developing the communications know what they are expected to achieve.

What is the one thing we are trying to tell them? This question is sometimes worded differently on different versions of the brief, but it is always asked in a similar fashion. And it is perhaps the most important part of the brief because it gives a focus to the creative strategy. Indeed, it can be considered the actual creative strategy. This should be grounded in an insight into the target audience; give consideration to competitors' positions in the market; and, to be most effective, should be absolutely single-minded. Marketers should avoid adding multiple "one things" because it results in unfocused messages that do neither thing particularly well. Think of the memorable marketing communications from your own past. Most, if not all of them, can have their messages distilled into one simple phrase.

Why should they believe us? This represents the support for the "one thing" the creative is to convey to the audience. So, for example, if the "one thing" is about the quality of the customer service, the response to this question should include information relevant to supporting the customer service claim. This can include awards received for customer service, testimonials from previous customers, or rankings of independent organizations that verify service levels. Information that is not relevant to the creative strategy—the focused message in the communication—is superfluous and only complicates the creative development process.

Where and when are we telling them? This may appear to be a straightforward question, but it can be a very important element of the brief. For example, if the brief is for a Christmas campaign that will only run for a number of weeks before December, the development process should take this into account. Another problem with not being

---

◆ Who are we talking to?	◆ Why should they believe us?
◆ What is the objective?	◆ Where and when are we telling them?
◆ What is the one thing we're trying to tell them?	

FIGURE 5.1
Components of the Creative Brief

CAPP seeks to respond to accusations that the oil sands producers do not take their environmental impact into consideration

specific on the delivery mechanisms for the message is that, in the absence of specific direction, the creative team may develop ideas in media that are simply not options for the campaign. For example, television is the preferred medium for many creative teams, but it is expensive and not affordable by many marketers. Or the brief can specify that the campaign will be done through direct marketing because a targeted list is available. This question highlights the importance of understanding the various options available for message delivery and including experts working in each of those delivery media early in the creative process.

One final aspect of many creative briefs is what is known as *mandatories*. These include things that must be included in any message created, such as legal disclaimers (common, for example, in messages for automotive leases), the inclusion of phone numbers or websites, or certain logos.

Although some people believe that providing the creative team with more freedom is helpful, a relatively restrictive brief is generally considered a good thing by people in the creative department. By keeping a brief too loose, the creative team lacks focus and guidance, and is less likely to produce creative that will be effective. In fact, many agencies require their briefs to be kept to under one page. This process ensures that the account manager has thoroughly thought through only the most salient points to include, and narrowed down the message to only those necessary to dictate the strategy.

Critical Thinking Exercise

Find an advertisement that you have seen in the last 30 days that you think is impactful. Why was it impactful? Articulate the objective that you think the ad is trying to achieve. Compare this ad to other ads from the same product category. Why are the other ads not as impactful?

MARKETING COMMUNICATIONS THEORY— HOW AND WHY IT WORKS

If managers are to effectively initiate and, more importantly, evaluate the creative development process, they must understand how marketing communications effectively impacts audiences. Three useful theoretical frameworks are presented here. The first is the hierarchy of effects model. The second is a means–end chain. Both the hierarchy of effects model and a means–end chain can be used to develop leverage points. A leverage point moves the consumer from understanding a product's benefits to linking those benefits with personal values. The third model presented is the elaboration likelihood model (ELM). This list is not exhaustive, but it represents some of the primary theories used by marketers to understand how message design impacts the success of an IMC plan. Also, the models are not mutually exclusive. For example, the hierarchy of effects model is useful for understanding how certain types of creative strategies can be successful for different products, and this can be combined with the ELM to evaluate the likely success of a given piece of marketing communications.

Hierarchy of Effects

The **hierarchy of effects model** aids in clarifying the objectives of an IMC plan and the development of individual executions within the plan. The model parallels the buyer decision-making model first presented in Chapter 3, and suggests that there are six steps a consumer or a business buyer moves through when making a purchase. The steps in the hierarchy of effects model, and their relationship to the buyer decision-making model, are outlined in Figure 5.2.

These steps are sequential. A consumer will spend a period of time at each step before moving to the next. Thus, before a person can develop a liking for a product, he or she must first have sufficient knowledge of the product. Once the individual has the knowledge and develops a liking for the product, the advertiser can try to influence the consumer to favour a particular brand or company.

The hierarchy of effects approach can help a creative understand how a consumer reaches purchase decisions; however, some of the theory's assumptions have been questioned. For one, it is possible that these six steps are not always the route taken by consumers. For instance, a person makes a purchase (such as an impulse buy) and then later develops knowledge, liking, preference, and conviction. Also, shoppers may purchase products when little or no preference is involved, because coupons, discounts, or other purchase incentives cause them to choose one brand instead of another. At other times, someone may not even remember the name of the brand purchased. This is often the case with commodity products such as sugar and flour or even clothing purchases such as socks and shirts.

Still, the major benefit of the hierarchy of effects model is that it is one method used to identify the typical steps consumers and businesses take when making purchases. To encourage brand loyalty, all six steps must be included. A consumer or business is unlikely to be loyal to a particular brand without sufficient knowledge of the brand. Purchasers must like the brand and build a strong preference for it. Next, they must cultivate strong convictions that the particular brand is superior to the other brands on the market. None of this occurs without first becoming aware of the product. Thus, the components of the hierarchy of effects approach highlight the various responses that marketing communications must stimulate. This is true in both consumer and business-to-business markets.

The hierarchy of effects model has many similarities with theories about attitudes and attitudinal change, including the concepts of cognitive, affective, and conative elements first

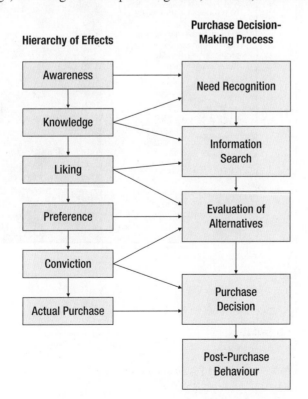

FIGURE 5.2
The Hierarchy of Effects and the Decision-Making Process

presented in Chapter 3. The *cognitive* component is the person's mental images, understanding, and interpretations of the person, object, or issue. The *affective* component contains the feelings or emotions a person has about the object, topic, or idea. The *conative* component is the individual's intentions, actions, or behaviour.

Any combination of these components is possible. This suggests that the structured six-step process of the hierarchy of effects model may be more rigid than is actually the case. Creative development can take into account these processes by developing communications that help the audience move through each of the three phases of attitude development. Let's assume that the process for soap is cognitive, affective, and conative. In this case, a marketing communications campaign can be launched with a television advertisement for Dove soap that takes a cognitive approach by examining how it works to fight bacteria or moisturize the skin. In the next part of the campaign, the brand can include elements designed to stimulate the affect component of attitude by sponsoring

Neutrogena understands that both conative and affective elements drive purchases.

Although it uses humour in the headline, this ad uses a largely rationale appeal to encourage farmers to build wind breaks on their farms.

FIGURE 5.3
The FCB Grid

	Rational	**Emotional**
High Involvement	<u>Process:</u> Cognitive → Affective → Conative <u>Product Example:</u> Appliances <u>Critical Campaign Elements:</u> Websites/Newspapers	<u>Process:</u> Affective → Cognitive → Conative <u>Product Example:</u> Clothing/fashion <u>Critical Campaign Elements:</u> Magazine/Out-of-Home
Low Involvement	<u>Process:</u> Conative → Cognitive → Affective <u>Product Example:</u> Frozen food <u>Critical Campaign Elements:</u> Coupons/Sampling	<u>Process:</u> Conative → Affective → Cognitive <u>Product Example:</u> Chewing gum <u>Critical Campaign Elements:</u> Point-of-Sale

an event to build self-esteem in young girls, for example. Finally, the campaign can then feature an element designed to stimulate the conative portion by using retail shelf space in sales promotions, or mailing a free sample to a targeted list of potential users. On the other hand, if the marketer believes that the necessary approach for Dove is to begin with conative, followed by affective, followed by cognitive, the approach could be reversed. In this case, the sales promotion or sampling program would precede the other elements of the marketing communications campaign.

When evaluating creative development, the manager can consider whether the elements of the campaign are sufficient to move the audience through the necessary steps in the purchase process. This includes both evaluation of the content of the individual components and consideration of how each component can work together toward an overall objective. One useful tool in the evaluation of the hierarchy of effects model for a given product is the FCB grid, shown in Figure 5.3. The distinction between products that are driven by rational thinking and those that are driven primarily by feelings and emotion determines which order the campaign should introduce each type of message. Similarly, the distinction between the high and low-involvement processing determines the specific types of marketing communications that should be included in a campaign.

Means–End Theory

A second theoretical approach to the effectiveness of marketing communications messages is a **means–end chain**. This approach suggests that marketing communications should contain a message, or *means,* that leads the consumer to a desired end state. These *end* states include the personal values that are listed in Figure 5.4. The purpose of

FIGURE 5.4
Personal Values

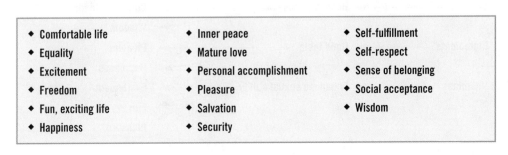

- ◆ Comfortable life
- ◆ Equality
- ◆ Excitement
- ◆ Freedom
- ◆ Fun, exciting life
- ◆ Happiness
- ◆ Inner peace
- ◆ Mature love
- ◆ Personal accomplishment
- ◆ Pleasure
- ◆ Salvation
- ◆ Security
- ◆ Self-fulfillment
- ◆ Self-respect
- ◆ Sense of belonging
- ◆ Social acceptance
- ◆ Wisdom

A Got Milk? advertisement illustrating the use of a means–end chain.

the means–end chain is to start a process in which the marketing communications leads the consumer to believe that using the product will help him or her reach one of these personal values.

Means–end theory is the basis of a model called the **Means–End Conceptualization of Components for Advertising Strategy** (MECCAS).[2] The MECCAS model suggests using five elements in creating ads:

- The product's attributes
- Consumer benefits
- Leverage points
- Personal values
- Message tactics

The MECCAS approach moves consumers through the five elements. The attributes of the product are linked to the specific benefits consumers can derive. These benefits, in turn, lead to the attainment of a personal value.

To illustrate the MECCAS method, consider Figure 5.5 and the milk advertisement shown. The product attribute calcium is linked to the benefits of being strong and healthy. The personal value the consumer obtains from healthy bones is feeling wise for using the product. The leverage point in the advertisement is the link between the benefit of health and the personal value of feeling wise. The tactics of the white moustache and the text in the advertisement are designed to help the viewer remember that drinking milk is healthy. In this case, the specific issue is preventing osteoporosis in women.

The MECCAS approach can also be applied to business-to-business messages. Members of the buying centre can be influenced by personal values, organizational values, and corporate goals. Consider the advertisement for Greenfield Online in this section and the means–end chain in Figure 5.6. Each attribute is presented in terms of the benefits business customers can obtain. Although not explicitly stated, the personal values of members of the buying centre choosing Greenfield Online might include job security for making good decisions, self-fulfillment, wisdom, and social acceptance by other members of the buying group.

FIGURE 5.5
Means-End Chain for Milk

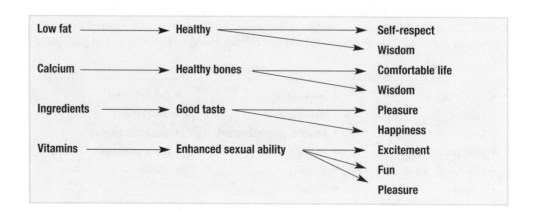

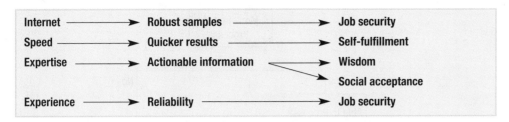

FIGURE 5.6
B-to-B Means-End Chain for Greenfield
Online

Leverage Points

Both the hierarchy of effects model and the means–end chain approach lead to leverage points. A leverage point is designed to move the consumer from understanding a product's benefits to linking those benefits with personal values. To construct a quality leverage point, the creative builds the pathway that connects a product benefit with the potential buyer's value system.

In the hierarchy of effects model, the initial level of awareness begins the process of exposing consumers to product benefits. As the viewer moves through the six stages, he or she eventually develops the conviction to buy the product. At that point, the benefit has indeed been linked with a personal value. In the milk advertisement used to illustrate the means–end chain, the leverage point is the phrase "There's one person I won't be," which is tied with the copy message "a woman with osteoporosis." The copy goes on to explain that because of calcium (a product attribute), women can have healthy bones (product benefit). Making a conscious decision to use milk to prevent osteoporosis demonstrates the personal values of wisdom and seeking a healthy lifestyle.

In the Greenfield Online business-to-business advertisement, the leverage point is the picture of an old-fashioned woman using an old telephone sandwiched between the headline "Are you still buying marketing research done the old-fashioned way?" and the first sentence of the copy explaining that companies can "Do it better on the Internet." The picture creates an excellent mental image of marketing research done the old-fashioned way and the opportunities Greenfield Online can provide.

The means–end chain and MECCAS approaches are based on the product's attributes and its benefits to the consumer. The leverage point is the message that links these attributes and benefits with consumer values. In the execution itself, the message tactics are the plot or scenario used to convey the message designed to complete the linkage. Chapter 6 discusses creative tactics in detail, in which dramatizations and other methods of telling the ad story help build successful leverage points.

An effective leverage point can also be associated with an attitudinal change, especially when the sequence is cognitive ▶ affective ▶ conative. As the attitude is formed, the individual first understands, then is moved emotionally, and then takes action. A leverage point can help the viewer of an ad move through these three stages, thereby tying cognitive knowledge of the product to more emotional and personal values.

A Greenfield Online business advertisement illustrating the use of a means–end chain in a business ad.

Elaboration Likelihood Model (ELM)

A third theoretical approach to understanding how marketing communications works is the **elaboration likelihood model**, or ELM, which is depicted in Figure 5.7. Put simply, this

FIGURE 5.7
The Elaboration Likelihood Model (ELM)

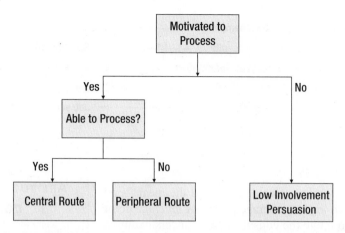

Source: Gerard J. Tellis (2004), *Effective Advertising: Understanding When, How and Why Advertising Works.* Thousand Oaks, Sage pg.113. Adapted from Cacioppo, John T., and Richard E Petty (1985), "Central and Peripheral Routes to Persuasion: The Role of Message Repetition," in Linda F. Alwitt and Andrew A. Mitchell (eds.), *Psychological Processes and Advertising Effects: Theory, Research and Applications,* Hillsdale, NJ: Lawrence Erlbaum, 90-111. pg. 92. Copyright 1985 Reproduced with permission of TAYLOR & FRANCIS GROUP LLC - BOOKS in the format other book via Copyright Clearance Center.

model examines how likely a person is to spend time thinking deeply (i.e., elaborating) about any specific piece of marketing communications. The underlying premise of the model is that marketing communications influences audiences based on how much the audience thinks about the message. The different ways in which audiences think about and process messages are known as the routes to persuasion. When an audience is able to think about a message, and has motivation to do so, their elaboration will be high. For example, someone relaxing and reading a magazine who suffers from migraines will likely spend a relatively large amount of time reading and thinking about an ad for migraine mediation placed in that magazine. In this case, the use of arguments and specific product information is appropriate because it is what the audience is looking for. This route of elaboration is known as the **central route of persuasion** under the ELM.

However, if the audience has the motivation but not the ability to spend time thinking about a message, they will respond more to cues in the message that are not related to arguments or product detail. In this case, cues such as the use of a celebrity endorser or images will be used to evaluate the marketing communication. For example, if an ad for running shoes is placed on the side of a bus, one cue that might be effective is the use of a high-profile athlete endorser. This route of persuasion is known as the **peripheral route** of persuasion.

Still, in other cases, the audience is neither able nor motivated to process the message in marketing communications. This is known as **low-involvement persuasion** because the audience is not interested in spending time thinking about marketing communications. An example of a product that usually faces low-involvement processing by consumer audiences is cola. This is why most marketing communications for brands like Pepsi and Coke usually feature the use of humour as opposed to arguments.

Critical Thinking Exercise

Although cola is best described as a product category where consumers are not motivated to elaborate on marketing communications, one message approach used in the past for both Pepsi and Coke is the idea of a "taste test." In this approach, the main argument is that people prefer the taste of one brand over another. This approach often does not use humour or any other cue that would normally be associated with either peripheral or low-involvement processing. Do you think this approach can be effective for either of these brands? Why or why not? Do you think the approach of the taste test argument would be applicable to a new brand entrant to the cola category?

The three routes to persuasion do not have equal effects. For example, processing under the central route of persuasion is typically more permanent than persuasion using other routes. This is because the audience has engaged in careful and detailed analysis and theoretically worked out some conclusions based on the message and their existing beliefs. The effects of the peripheral route, on the other hand, tend to be relatively fleeting. However, the use of the peripheral route of persuasion does allow the marketer to use repetition, which can help in aiding the permanence of persuasion under peripheral persuasion. Repetition is not generally found in marketing communications messages that seek the central route of persuasion, since repeated arguments tend to lead to boredom or annoyance.

Low-involvement persuasion—considered by some to be ineffective—can indeed be effective, but not in the same way as the other routes. Since the audience is not involved, and only passively consumes the message, they may be more likely to believe any trivial statements included in the message. This is because people tend to evaluate the truth of statements based on their reasoning, but if they are not involved, then evaluation is based on repetition. Simply, when an audience is less involved in a message, they are more likely to believe it to be true.[3] For example, marketing communications for milk are typically low-involvement messages. Over time, these are likely to be believed by the audience due to their low involvement.

In summary, all of the theoretical models presented in this section provide useful ideas for the message design component of the IMC plan. Each one suggests that some kind of sequence must be followed as the message is prepared and delivered. In the next section, we examine the different types of appeals that are available to marketers when crafting their messages.

Milk ads are created understanding the low-involvement process of consumers.

Source: Used with permission of Philip Rostron, photographer. Dairy Farmers of Canada.

TYPES OF MARKETING COMMUNICATIONS APPEALS

Throughout the years, advertisers have employed a wide variety of appeals in marketing communications. Appeals are the approach used to achieve the objectives for the message. For example, one approach to deliver a message is to use a rational appeal, where the arguments for a product or service are clearly laid out. In this case, the effectiveness of the appeal relies on largely cognitive processing by the audience, because the appeal is designed to appeal to rational thought. On the other hand, creative development can use an emotional appeal. In this case, the appeal is made more to the heart than the head. In this case, the effectiveness relies on the audience to feel a certain way, or to use a certain emotion to achieve objectives.

Within any one piece of marketing communications, both appeals can be present. For example, marketing communications for automobiles often use both, since both play important roles in the decision-making process for cars. Also, across an entire campaign and multiple types of marketing communications, creative development often includes both types of appeals to make sure the audience moves through each step of the purchase process. For example, the evaluation of alternatives step might be influenced by emotions and therefore benefit from a more emotional appeal, but the actual decision process can be swayed by a more rational appeal, such as the use of price comparisons.

FIGURE 5.8
Examples of Creative Appeals

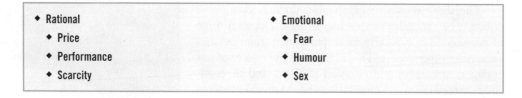

- ◆ Rational
  - ◆ Price
  - ◆ Performance
  - ◆ Scarcity
- ◆ Emotional
  - ◆ Fear
  - ◆ Humour
  - ◆ Sex

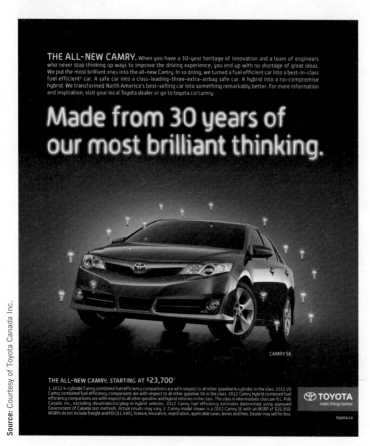

Source: Courtesy of Toyota Canada Inc.

The decision-making process for cars involves both emotional and rational elements.

The decision about which type of appeal to use should be based on a review of the creative brief, the objective of the marketing communications, and the means–end chain to be conveyed. The final choice depends on a number of factors, including the product being sold, the personal preferences of the creative and account teams, as well as the wishes of the client. Each of these two types of appeals, and some of the various forms they take, are listed in Figure 5.8 and explained in detail below.

Rational Appeals

A rational appeal can be useful at any stage of the hierarchy of effects: awareness, knowledge, liking, preference, conviction, and purchase. Communications oriented to the knowledge stage will transmit basic product information. In the preference stage, the objective shifts to presenting logical reasons why one particular brand is superior, such as the superior gas mileage of an automobile or a better safety record. A rational message leads to a stronger conviction about a product's benefits, so that the purchase is eventually made.

Rational appeals rely on consumers actively processing the information presented in the marketing communications. The audience must pay attention to the communication, comprehend the message, and compare the message to existing knowledge. Messages consistent with the current knowledge strengthen it. New messages help the person form cognitive beliefs about the brand and establish new knowledge. A business customer who sees a Kinko's advertisement about videoconferencing services already may have the company in his cognitive structure. The customer may have used Kinko's in the past but was not aware that the company offers videoconferencing.

Content-rich media such as newspaper, magazine, direct mail, or websites offer the best outlets for rational appeals. They allow the audience greater opportunities to process copy information. They can pause and take time to read the verbal content. Television and radio commercials, for example, are so short that it is difficult for viewers to process message arguments.

Business-to-business advertisers use printed matter extensively. These marketers take advantage of print's ability to feature rational appeals. Many marketing communications professionals believe trade publications are the best way to reach members of the buying centre. Those in the industry read trade publications carefully. Placing an ad in a trade publication, or targeting that publication in a PR campaign, means the firm has an excellent chance of hitting its primary target market. Further, trade publications allow marketers the opportunity to convey more details to potential buyers.

Buying centre members who scan trade journals while in the information search stage of the buying process are quite likely to notice the message, read it, and process the information. Buying centre members who are not looking for information about the particular product probably will ignore the same message. Magazines do not have intrusion value and readers can easily skip or ignore messages. A rational appeal usually focuses on a primary appeal, and no strong peripheral cues grab the reader's attention.

Conventional wisdom states that rational appeals are well suited for high-involvement and complex products. High-involvement decisions require considerable cognitive activity, and consumers spend more time evaluating the attributes of the individual brands. Thus, a rational appeal is the best approach to reach them. For some consumers, however, emotions and feelings even influence high-involvement decisions. For instance, life insurance involves both rational and emotional elements. Various insurance companies can use both in seeking to influence consumers.

In general, rational appeals are effective when consumers have high levels of involvement and are willing to pay attention to the message. Message arguments and product information can be placed in the copy. Consumers can then more fully absorb information.

A rational appeal is superior to other appeals in developing or changing attitudes and establishing brand beliefs. This is mainly true when the audience has a particular interest in the product or brand behind the message. Otherwise, the consumer will often ignore an ad using a rational appeal.

Rational appeals can take many forms. Some of the more common ones are listed below.

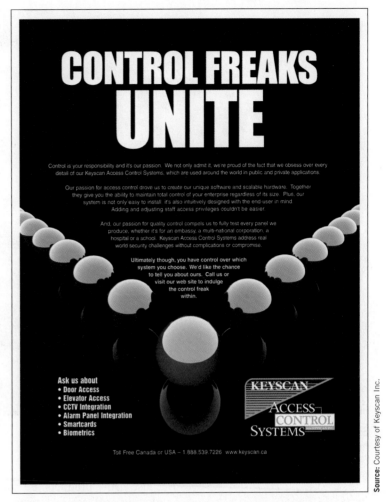

B-to-B ads often contain more copy than do ads for consumers.

Source: Courtesy of Keyscan Inc.

Critical Thinking Exercise

What is an example of marketing communications you've come across in the past week that uses a rational appeal? Do you think it was an effective use of the appeal? Which of the hierarchy of effects processes do you think is applicable to the product that was being marketed, and which objective do you think is behind the message?

Price Appeals

Price is a commonly used base for messages using a rational appeal. In this form, the price and associated value (often relative to competitors' prices) are the focus. Price appeals are common at later stages of the purchase decision process, where it can be used to provide a rational reason to choose one product over another, similar product. Therefore, this appeal is typical in sales promotions and is indeed the basis for virtually all coupons.

Performance Appeals

Performance appeals are similar to price appeals because they inherently involve some aspect of the overall **value equation** for the audience. Many products base their appeals simply on the premise of outperforming competitors' products, suggesting that their product is a better value or will perform in situations where competitors' products will not. For example, in the ad shown here, the appeal to the business buyer is on the performance of the server system compared to that of competitors.

Shaw uses its fibre optic network to compete with other telecommunications firms for business customers.

Scarcity Appeals

Scarcity appeals urge consumers to buy a particular product because of a limitation. It can be that a limited number of the products is available or, more often, that the product is available for only a limited time. When there is a limited supply of a product, the value of that product increases. At the turn of the millennium, General Mills introduced a Cheerios line called Millenios as a limited-time product. Tiny 2s were added to the familiar O-shaped Cheerios.[4] McDonald's, Wendy's, and Burger King offer sandwiches (McRib, Hot N' Spicy Chicken, Dollar Whoppers) for limitedtime periods throughout the year. The scarcity concept is also used for musical compilations, encouraging consumers to buy the product because of its limited availability. By making sure it is not available in retail stores, marketers increase its scarcity value.

Like other forms of rational appeals, a scarcity appeal is often tied to multiple promotional tools. For example, a manufacturer may advertise a limited price discount offer to retailers who stock up early for Christmas or some other holiday season. Contests and sweepstakes also run for limited times. The primary benefit of scarcity appeals is that they encourage consumers to take action.

Emotional Appeals

Because many products are sold into markets with high degrees of brand parity, most marketing professionals view emotional advertising as the key to brand loyalty. They want customers to feel a bond with the brand. So it's not surprising that most marketing communications contain, at least in part, some form of emotional appeal. The forms of emotional appeal are literally limited only to the number of emotions experienced by humans. Figure 5.9 displays some of the more common emotions presented in marketing communications. Fear, humour, and sex appeals are among the more popular appeals that are generally considered to be emotional in nature. Each is discussed next.

Fear Appeals

Marketers use fear to sell numerous products. Life insurance companies focus on the consequences of not having life insurance when a person dies. Shampoo and mouthwash ads invoke fears of dandruff and bad breath. These problems can make a person a social outcast. Fear is used more often than most casual observers realize.

FIGURE 5.9
Emotions Used in Marketing
Communications

◆ Trust	◆ Protecting loved ones
◆ Reliability	◆ Romance
◆ Friendship	◆ Passion
◆ Happiness	◆ Family bonds
◆ Security	◆ with parents
◆ Glamour–luxury	◆ with siblings
◆ Serenity	◆ with children
◆ Anger	◆ with extended family members

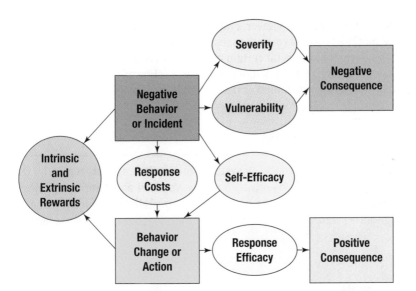

FIGURE 5.10
Behavioural Response Model

Simply stated, marketers use fear appeals because they can be highly effective. Fear increases both the viewer's interest in a message and the persuasiveness of the message. Many individuals remember advertisements with fear appeals better than they do warm, upbeat messages.[5] Consumers who pay more attention to a message are more likely to process the information it presents. This information processing makes it possible to accomplish objectives of marketing communications.

A theoretical explanation regarding the way fear works is the *behavioural response model* (see Figure 5.10).[6] As shown, various incidents can lead to negative or positive consequences, which then affect future behaviours.

In developing messages using fear appeals, the idea is to include as many aspects of the behavioural response model as possible. A business-to-business advertiser offering Internet services tries to focus on the severity of downtime if a company's Internet server goes down. Another ad describes the firm's vulnerability by showing the high probability that a company's server is going to crash. The Service Metrics advertisement in this section features a picture of a blindfolded man ready to step into a manhole to illustrate the danger of e-business pitfalls. The goal of the advertisement is to make business leaders realize their companies are more vulnerable than they think. Service Metrics can help them identify these potential problems before they turn into disasters.

When using fear, one issue is the strength of the appeal. Research suggests that a moderate level of fear is the most effective.[7] A low level of fear may not be noticed, and the fear level may not be convincing in terms of severity or vulnerability. Further, a message with too high of a fear level can backfire, because the message is so strong that it causes feelings of anxiety. This leads the audience to avoid watching the message.[8] Therefore, the goal for a fear appeal should be to make it

A business-to-business advertisement using a fear appeal.

powerful enough to capture a viewer's attention and to influence his or her thinking, but not so scary that the person avoids the message entirely.

Fear appeals match well with certain types of goods and services, especially products that eliminate problems or threats to a consumer's sense of personal security. Marketers must decide if fear is a good choice or if some other type of appeal offers greater promise.

Critical Thinking Exercise

Marketers promoting home security systems employ fear appeals regularly. Do you think these are effective? Why or why not? Can you find an example of a message for a home security system that does not use a fear appeal? Is it effective? See if you can design an ad for a home security system that does not use a fear appeal.

Humour Appeals

Clutter presents a significant challenge for marketing communications. Capturing the attention of an audience is difficult. Even after a marketer has garnered the audience's attention, keeping that attention is even more challenging. Humour has proven to be one of the best techniques for cutting through clutter. Humour can be effective at both getting attention and keeping it. Audiences, as a whole, enjoy messages that make them laugh. Something that is funny has intrusive value and grabs attention.[9]

Humour is used in about 24 percent of prime time television advertisements and 35 percent of radio ads. Humorous ads often win awards and tend to be favourites among judges at the International Advertising Film Festival at Cannes as well as for other types of marketing communications awards. At a recent Clio Awards ceremony for radio ads, 62 percent of the winners used some type of humour.[10] In *USA Today*'s consumer survey of the most likeable advertising campaigns for the year, simplicity and humour were the key ingredients.[11]

The success of humour as an advertising appeal is based on three things. Humour causes the audience to: (1) watch, (2) laugh, and, most importantly, (3) remember. In recall tests, consumers most often remember humorous messages. To be successful, the humour should be connected directly to the product's benefits. It should tie together the product features, the advantage to customers, and the personal values of the means–end chain.

Humorous messages pique viewer interest. This makes it is easier to gain more careful consumer consideration of the message. A funny message captures the viewer's attention, which leads to improved comprehension and recall of the advertising message and tagline. Advertising research indicates that humour elevates people's moods and that happy consumers associate a good mood with the advertiser's products. Humour helps fix the company in the consumer's cognitive structure with links to positive feelings.

Although humour captures the viewer's attention, cuts through ad clutter, and enhances recall, unfortunately, humorous messages can also go wrong. Marketers must be careful to avoid letting the humour overpower the message. When humour fails, it is usually because the joke in the message is remembered but the product or brand is not. In other words, the message is so funny that the audience forgets or does not catch the sponsor's name. Although humorous messages often win awards, they can fail in terms of accomplishing the objectives of the marketing communications plan. To avoid this problem, the humour used in the ad should focus on a component of the means–end chain. The humour should relate to either a product's attributes, a customer benefit, or the personal value obtained from the product. The most effective ads are those in which the humour incorporates all three elements.

One example where humour was not effective was the Snickers ad during the 2007 Super Bowl. The ad featured two mechanics eating from opposite ends of the same candy bar until they accidentally ended up kissing. The two men responded in disgust by

- ◆ Captures attention.
- ◆ Holds attention.
- ◆ Often wins creative awards.
- ◆ High recall scores.
- ◆ Consumers enjoy ads that make them laugh.
- ◆ Evaluated by consumers as likeable ads.

FIGURE 5.11
Reasons for Using Humour in Marketing Communications

ripping out their own chest hair. The outcry against the ad was so loud and strong that it was immediately pulled from television.[12]

Some evidence suggests that humour is universal; however, there are particular executions of humour that may not be. Humour is often culturally based. It may be difficult to transfer wit from one culture to another. Not all audiences will see a humorous ad in the same way. It is important for advertisers to pretest a message before it is launched in another country to ensure it will be liked and, more important, that it will be considered funny and not offensive.

Humour is being used more frequently in various countries. A humorous ad developed for McDonald's in Singapore had the highest recall rate (90 percent) of all ads shown in the month it was released. In Germany, Ford deviated from traditional ads that concentrated on promoting product quality and value to a humorous ad approach. The humorous ad shows a pigeon sitting on tree branch with a Ford Ka parked nearby. The bird swoops down to bomb the car, but at the last minute the car hood springs up and knocks the bird out. The advertisement was first shown on Ford's U.K. website. Word about the ad quickly spread until more than 1 million people had visited the website to see the ad. German dealers requested the ad so they could show it on television. The feedback and popularity of the ad in the United Kingdom caused Ford's marketing bosses to agree to run the ad in Germany. The ad resonated with young, affluent buyers, which Ford had been trying to reach. The new ad was seen as witty, gutsy, and edgy, which worked well with Ford's theme of projecting the Ka as a stylish car.[13]

Figure 5.11 summarizes the major reasons for using humour.

Sex Appeals

Like humour appeals, sexual appeals are often used to break through clutter. Marketing communications in North America and other parts of the world contain more visual sexual themes than they have in the past. Nudity and other sexual approaches are common. Sexual themes in ads, however, no longer sell the way they used to. Sex no longer has shock value. People today have grown up in societies immersed in sex. Seeing another sexually oriented ad gets very little attention. Currently, many advertisers are shifting to

---

ON THE JOB

Getting Emotional at Work

Marketers with business audiences are now beginning to use emotional appeals. In the past, only 5 to 10 percent of all business-to-business communications messages had emotional appeals. Today, the figure is around 25 percent. A magazine advertisement for a product to treat racehorses switched from a rational appeal to an emotional appeal. The target market for the ad was veterinarians. In the past, the ad would have opened with a very rational appeal, featuring such ad copy as "For swelling in joints use . . ." The emotional ad has the horse thinking, "I will prove them wrong. I will run again. I will mend my spirits."[14]

The underlying principle for changing to more emotional business-to-business marketing communications is that emotions can be part of every type of purchase decision. Members of the buying centre consider product information in making decisions, but, at the same time, they are likely to be affected by emotions. Although a member of the buying centre may try to minimize the emotional side of a purchase, the person is still likely to be affected. The affective component of attitudes is just as important as the cognitive component.

FIGURE 5.12
Sexual Approaches Used in Marketing
Communications

- ◆ Subliminal techniques
- ◆ Sensuality
- ◆ Sexual suggestiveness
- ◆ Nudity or partial nudity
- ◆ Overt sexuality

Source: John Davis © Dorling Kindersley.

more subtle sexual cues, suggestions, and innuendos.[15] Sexuality has been employed in marketing communications in the five ways listed in Figure 5.12.

Subliminal approaches place sexual cues or icons in messages in the attempt to affect a viewer's subconscious mind. In an odd paradox, truly subliminal cues are not noticed, nor do they create any effects. Consumers pay little attention to messages already. A subliminal message that registers only in the subconscious mind is not going to be effective. If it did, there would not be the need for stronger sexual content in messages.

Sexual appeals can also be based on *sensuality.* Many women respond more favourably to a sensual suggestion than to an overtly sexual approach. An alluring glance across a crowded room can be sensual and draw attention to a product. Many view sensuality as a more sophisticated approach, because it relies on the imagination. Images of romance and love can be more enticing than raw sexuality.

Many ads feature a *sexually suggestive* approach. The Bijan ad shown on the next page features Bo Derek. The ad states, "Bo Derek is wearing Bijan Eau de Parfum and nothing else," which is a sexually suggestive message. In a similar manner, the Clairol Herbal Essence Shampoo ads borrowed the "yes, Yes, YES!" scene from the movie *When Harry Met Sally* to make the product seem more sensuous by suggesting sexual activity.

A recent trend in sexual suggestiveness is to use gay and lesbian themes. Swedish retailer IKEA was among the first in North America to use a gay theme. A television commercial showing two gay men shopping for a dining room table together first appeared in 1994.[16]

Nudity or *partial nudity* is still used to sell products that have sexual connotations, such as clothing, perfume, and cologne. Some messages are designed to solicit a sexual response. Others are not. For example, starting in 1987, underwear companies could use live models in television ads. The first commercials were modest and informational, emphasizing the design or materials used in the undergarment. The first Playtex bra commercials using live models drew strong criticism from organizations such as the

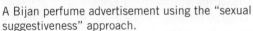

A Bijan perfume advertisement using the "sexual suggestiveness" approach.

An advertisement by Benetton using partial nudity.

American Family Association. Now, advertisements for undergarments go much further and involve superstars, such as actress Jennifer Love Hewitt, who appeared in television and print ads for Hanes for their All-Over Comfort bra and their Perfect Panty. The campaign even included an online element with footage from the photo shoots, a "bad bra toss" game, and a blog about bad bra moments.[17]

A common sexual approach in marketing communications is to use decorative models. Decorative models are individuals placed in a message whose primary purpose is to adorn the product as a sexual or attractive stimulus. The model serves no functional purpose in the message except to attract attention. In the past, commercials for automobiles, tools, and beer often used female models dressed in bikinis to stand by their products. A number of studies have been conducted to determine how effective decorative models are. The basic conclusions are listed in Figure 5.13.[18]

- *The presence of female (or male) decorative models improves ad recognition, but not brand recognition.*
- *The presence of a decorative model influences emotional and objective evaluations of the product among both male and female audiences.*
- *Attractive models produce a higher level of attention to ads than do less attractive models.*
- *The presence of an attractive model produces higher purchase intentions when the product is sexually relevant than if it is not sexually relevant.*

FIGURE 5.13
Factors to Consider Before Using Decorative Models

Using *overt sexuality* in messages for products that are sexually oriented is normally accepted, but it often becomes controversial when used for other types of products. When Procter & Gamble launched a television advertising campaign for Dentyne, eyebrows were raised. The ad shows two teens in a living room. The girl pops a piece of Dentyne Fire bubble gum into her mouth and then rips off her blouse and jumps on her boyfriend. At first the parents stare in shock. Then, the mom tries a piece of Dentyne Fire and promptly jumps on the dad. The controversy centred on whether the ad promoted teenage sexuality by suggesting that parents should openly display sexual feelings and desires.[19]

Critical Thinking Exercise

Collect 5 to 10 examples of marketing communications that use sex appeals. How many of these sex appeals are germane to the product or service being promoted? Do you feel those that include appeals only when they have a logical link to the brand are more effective than those that do not?

A Guess advertisement featuring both a male and a female model using a sexual appeal.

Are Sex Appeals Effective?

In addition to research on the use of decorative models, there are numerous studies that have examined the effectiveness of sexual appeals and nudity in marketing communications. Almost all of them have concluded that sex and nudity do increase attention, regardless of the gender of the individual in the message or the gender of the audience. Normally, the attention is greater for opposite-sex situations than same-sex situations. That is, a male viewing a female in a sexually provocative message pays more attention than a male viewing another male in a sexually provocative message. The same is true for females. To encourage both males and females to pay attention to its ads, Guess often uses both a male and a female in a sexually provocative manner in a single message.

Although sexually oriented messages attract attention, brand recall for messages using a sex appeal is lower than messages using some other type of appeal. Thus, it appears that although people pay attention to the message, the sexual theme distracts them from paying attention to the brand name.[20]

Sexually oriented messages are often rated as being more interesting. Those messages deemed to be highly controversial in terms of their sexual content were rated as more interesting by both males and females. The paradox, however, is that although the controversial ads are more interesting, they fail to increase the transmission of information. Respondents are less likely to remember any more about the message.[21]

Messages using overt sexual stimuli or containing nudity produce higher levels of physiological arousal responses. These arousal responses have been linked to the formation of both affective and cognitive responses. If the viewer is male and the sexual stimulus is female, such as a naked female in an ad for cologne, then the viewer tends to develop a strong feeling toward the ad based on the arousal response his body experiences. Female viewers of male nudity in an ad often experience the same type of response, although the arousal response tends not to be as strong.

The cognitive impression made on viewers of a sexually oriented message depends on whether the viewer feels the message is pleasant or offensive. If a viewer likes the message, then a positive impression of the brand will result. If, however, the viewer thinks the message is in poor taste, then negative feelings and beliefs about the brand may result. When sex works, the message increases sales. When it does not, the message may create strong negative feelings toward the company.[22]

In determining the level of sex appeal to use in creative development, it is important to consider society's view and level of acceptance.[23] Just as economies go through cycles, attitudes toward sex in marketing communications experience acceptance swings. The use and acceptance of sexual themes in advertising had swung to a high level of tolerance in the early part of the 2000s, until the Super Bowl of 2004. The public reaction to Janet Jackson's breast-baring halftime show sent ripples throughout the industry. Shortly afterward, Victoria's Secret dropped its TV lingerie fashion show. Abercrombie & Fitch killed the company's quarterly catalogue, which had been strongly criticized for featuring models in sexually suggestive poses. Anheuser-Busch dropped some of its risqué ads.[24] The pendulum was still swinging in the opposite direction a year later when ads for Super Bowl 2005 were unveiled. Fewer ads used sexual appeals. Those that featured sex were much tamer. The only controversial ad was by GoDaddy.com. Only one of the two ads for GoDaddy.com was shown; the other was rejected by the network because of its highly sexual content. The network feared upsetting the Super Bowl audience.

Many researchers, both in academia and in industry, believe society is becoming more conservative and that youth are returning to more traditional values. Recent research suggests that many teens are offended by the widespread use of sexually provocative marketing messages and are often embarrassed by sexual innuendos. As one study concluded, "Sexually explicit advertising has lost its potency. Young people of today are more interested in traditional family values and wholesome ad messages than the flash of a breast to sell shampoo or the promise of limitless sex if your engine is big enough."[25]

In contrast, a study of clothing ads geared to teens revealed that teens had a stronger, more favourable opinion of brands featuring sexually oriented messages. A 17-year-old male, upon seeing a non–sexually oriented clothing ad, complained that the ad was "too boring. If I saw it somewhere, it wouldn't stick in my mind. A good ad is either funny, sexy, or provocative. This is neither. The models aren't even sexy—what is this, a Wal-Mart ad?"[26]

It is clear that the use of sex in marketing communications will continue. Marketers must carefully determine the level and the type of sexuality to use and the target audience. What will work at one particular point in time may not work at another.

The use of sexual imagery has become popular with both genders.

Critical Thinking Exercise

This section presents two contrasting views on how teenagers view the use of sex appeals in marketing communications. On the one hand, research suggests that teens are more interested in family values, and may even be embarrassed by sex appeals. Other research suggests that sex appeals are necessary to win over a teen audience. What can account for these opposing views?

Disadvantages of Sex Appeals

One major criticism of sexually based marketing communications is that it perpetuates dissatisfaction with one's body. Females in print advertisements and models in television advertising are often thin. The key to success seems to be the thinner the better. As models have gotten thinner, body dissatisfaction and eating disorders among women have risen. Research indicates that women feel unhappy about their own bodies and believe they are too fat after viewing advertisements showing thin models. What is interesting is that these same ads have an impact on men, but the reverse. Men feel they are not muscular enough and are too thin or too fat. It does not make any difference whether the male is viewing a male model or a female model in advertisements.[27]

An effective example of a sexual appeal to promote milk.

I'm here in the middle of Times Square to show off my best feature. My bones. What's my secret? Milk. It helps give bones the calcium they need to stay strong. And since they grow until about age 35, I'd say that's news worth putting on display.

got milk?

REBECCA ROMIJN-STAMOS ©1998 NATIONAL FLUID MILK PROCESSOR PROMOTION BOARD

In response, some firms have begun using "regular person" models in their creative. Wal-Mart has employees pose in clothing to be sold, and with other products. This approach has met with many positive results, which means other companies may need to rethink their positions on body image advertising. The Dove brand has been a pioneer in this field, with its Campaign for Real Beauty.

The problem with the stereotyping of females in creative takes a different twist in other countries. For example, in Saudi Arabia and Malaysia women must be shown in family settings. They cannot be depicted as being carefree or desirable to the opposite sex. In Canada, as well as in countries such as France and Sweden, sexism should be avoided in any communication directed toward children. Marketers refrain from associating toys with a particular gender, such as dolls for girls or soldier figures for boys.[28]

In general, the use of sex to make products more appealing is a legitimate tactic for many companies, products, and marketing communications agencies. The goal should be to use sex in a manner that is interesting, germane to the product, and within the ethical standards of the region. From there, taste and other more personalized standards serve as guides. The milk industry advertisement shown in this section has been very effective. Although the model is dressed in a swimsuit, it is germane to the product. It is a very effective way to persuade women that milk not only is good for healthy bones, but also enhances one's appearance. By telling women that bones continue to develop until the age of 35, the ad reinforces one of the reasons to consume milk.

ON THE JOB

In a recent awards ceremony for the Effie Awards in New York, 21 of the 34 Effie Gold Awards presented used emotional appeals. The most common approach winners used was to combine humour with emotions. The second most common approach among the emotional appeal ads was a focus on the consumer's life and feelings.[29] The MasterCard "Priceless" campaign uses this approach.

The basic tagline is "There are some things money can't buy. For everything else, there's MasterCard." One of the most popular ads featured a father and son at a baseball game. The ad successfully created warm feelings in viewers. It also increased both awareness and use of the MasterCard. Mothers responded as favourably as fathers to the spot. The same theme is used in international markets. Commercials are adjusted to local customs. In Australia, instead of a baseball game, the father and son attend a cricket match.[30]

Emotional appeals tend to be more effective than rational appeals. This is due to a number of reasons:

1. Emotional appeals are more likely to gain the attention of the audience, breaking through the clutter in the market. Of course, this theory may only hold as long as there are at least some rational appeals found in any given market.

2. The audience requires less concentration to process an emotional appeal than a rational appeal. The message in emotional appeals tends to be simpler, and allow the message to get through without taxing cognitive resources.

3. When an audience is presented with a rational appeal, they are likely to engage in counterarguments. This is part of the natural defence system that we all have and is activated when we are faced with marketing communications. We assume the message is trying to persuade us and naturally seek to "find holes" in the arguments presented. Emotional appeals, because they make arguments in a less direct fashion, tend to trigger this defence less often.

4. Emotional appeals tend to be more memorable for audiences. The message is more likely to be stored in memory and activated at a later time when the audience accesses relevant information about a given product category.

5. Emotional appeals are more likely to lead to action than rational appeals. They are closer to the action in the purchase decision process for most products and most consumers.

The reader should note that the reasons for the success of emotional appeals cover every aspect of the purchase decision-making process, up to the purchase decision itself. They begin with helping ensure awareness and ensure information is presented, comprehended, retained, and ultimately accessed to make a purchase decision.

Source: Adapted from Gerard J. Tellis (2004), *Effective Advertising: Understanding When, How and Why Advertising Works.* Thousand Oaks: Sage.

OVERCOMING AUDIENCE SELECTIVITY

Unfortunately most consumers don't spend as much time thinking about marketing communications as readers of this text do, and they certainly spend less time thinking about the professionals working in the industry. This has ramifications for the creation and delivery of marketing communications messages in the field. This is because senders must be aware of the obstacles to reaching and communicating effectively with an audience that cares much less about your message than you do. Target audiences can exhibit several forms of selectivity, which can make effective communication difficult.

One way an audience can exhibit selectivity is through **selective exposure**. This occurs when an audience chooses not even to be exposed to the message in the first place. This is a fairly common occurrence. For example, many people get up and leave the room or change the channel while watching television. Many people sort their email with a junk folder that automatically collects all emails flagged as spam. In order for marketing communications to avoid this problem, marketers have become creative about where they place their messages. Product placement is one practice that is changing rapidly, where marketers place their messages directly in entertainment content such as television, movies, music, or video games rather than relying on standalone commercials. Marketers also place messages where an audience simply can't avoid them, such as in move trailers and the back of bathroom stall doors.

Even if an audience is exposed to marketing communications, it doesn't mean they will pay attention. Many consumers exhibit **selective attention** by not actively perceiving the messages. For example, during a commercial break during a hockey telecast, many people engage in conversation and don't pay attention to the advertising on television. Many people sort their mail over the blue box recycling bin and simply don't pay attention to flyers or other mail that looks like marketing. In order to secure attention, marketers need to create compelling or eye-catching visuals, use attention-getting sounds, or even use shock tactics to get attention. The use of humour can also be a way to ensure people pay attention to communications.

Even if people are exposed to a message and give it their attention, they still may exhibit **selective comprehension**. This occurs when an audience interprets the message according to their own biases or beliefs. In short, even though the message gets through, it might not be understood. This can occur for simple reasons, such as the use of overly technical language, or because of deeply held prejudices, such as gender bias, on the part of audience members. For example, a woman portraying a doctor may simply lack credibility for some male audience members who still see the profession as the domain of men. A deep understanding of the audience and their decoding processes is necessary to avoid this problem.

Finally, even if the audience is exposed to the message, gives attention, and correctly interprets the message, they still may exhibit **selective retention**. This occurs when a consumer lacks the ability to activate the message at a later date when it can impact the purchase process. As we saw earlier in this chapter, the use of humour in marketing communications can lead people to not remember the brand name that appears in a message. Marketers can help avoid this problem by creating easy to recall mnemonics and simple, focused messages that are consistent across all communications. Brand recognition builds over time—just think of the cute bunny that now has a firm association with the Energizer brand.

COMMUNICATING ACROSS CULTURES

Many of the international implications of both marketing communications theory and the various types of appeals have already been described. In summary, leverage points lead to customer values. These values may be influenced by the culture or country in which the consumer lives. Therefore, advertisements must be constructed in ways that will express those values appropriate for the market.

When crossing cultural boundaries, one of the most controversial and delicate forms of appeals is the sex appeal. This is because sex tends to be an explosive issue for some cultures and perfectly acceptable in everyday life for others. What is deemed appropriate in terms of sexual appeal varies across countries. Something that is acceptable in one country may not be in another. In Chile, a campaign featuring nude celebrities touting the benefits of drinking milk was recently launched. The ads' producers stated, "Chile is a country of stuffed shirts, so this campaign is going to shake them up, and at a relatively low cost, thanks to nudity." The Chilean dairy federation believed the idea of rebellion rather than nudity is an easy sell to Chilean youth. As more Chilean kids travel and see a world filled with teens with green and blue hair and body piercings, public nudity will become associated with freedom. Despite opposition by conservatives, the new "naked" milk campaign aroused the attention of Chilean young people, and milk sales grew.[31]

Other parts of the world, such as Europe, also tolerate sex in marketing communications that would never be acceptable in North America.[32] Even within Canada, the values in Quebec tend to be more aligned with Europe, and therefore sex appeals are more common in the province of Quebec. Other provinces, such as Alberta, are more conservative in nature, and sex appeals may be less likely to be effective there than in other provinces.

In many Middle Eastern countries, sex and gender issues are taboo subjects. Sexual appeals are not used in creative, and even sexually related products are difficult to promote. In Egypt, Procter & Gamble hosted a call-in TV show directed toward young girls. The show's panel contained health experts, and topics ranged from marriage to menopause. The call-in show was followed up with a TV talk show (called *Frankly Speaking*) about feminine hygiene. The goal of the show was to tackle some of the more sensitive issues facing young Egyptian girls. Although the show discussed what happens during puberty, it was P&G's policy not to discuss sexuality. P&G sponsored the show, and the primary product advertised was P&G's feminine sanitary pads, Always.[33]

IMC IN PRACTICE

"When we brief our agencies for a campaign, they have a clear and concise understanding of what our brand is and what it stands for. The brand has been consistent since the late 90s, and it helps that we always have a clear starting point," explains Kate.

The "big idea" in TELUS marketing communications isn't about any one campaign. The brand pillars discussed in Chapter 2—simplicity, economy, intelligence, and charm—are the foundation for the big idea that positions the brand consistently as the helpful, approachable brand for telecommunications. "And a visual articulation of the brand that includes nature makes sense because it fits each of these attributes so beautifully."

Kate feels the communications for the brand blend the necessary components of rational and emotional thought in purchasing. "Each of our brand attributes resonates with consumers on both an emotional and a rational level. We need to appeal to both the hearts and the heads of our audience because of the categories in which we compete.

Enlightening digital TV. Down-to-earth price.

With all digital TELUS TV® you will:
- Enjoy superb picture and sound quality
- Start with 70 channels, including 45 commercial-free music channels
- Get access to HD Video On Demand

Plus, sign up now and receive a FREE HD PVR rental*

Add TELUS TV to a home bundle for $20/mo.*

TELUS
the future is friendly®

Source: Courtesy of TELUS.

TELUS focuses on simplicity as one of its key brand pillars.

"A TELUS purchase involves the emotional components of 'I want to feel good about the company I'm with,' and for many people buying these services is an exciting experience. Who doesn't love a new gadget or service that is going to make their lives easier and entertain them at the same time? Or, they may be moving their services, which we all know can be stressful."

But the rational side of the appeal can be just as important for customers. "People make decisions based on the perceived value. The value proposition to the customer—what they get for what they pay—is still the core of our marketing communications. So, while our marketing communications always include some elements that are designed to help people feel a certain way about the TELUS brand, they are almost always accompanied by a message that helps people decide very rationally that TELUS is good value for their money."

For Lara Johnson, Director, Marketing Communications at TELUS, her background in sociology makes her keenly aware of the drivers behind customer behaviour and how strong creative development is based on key consumer insights. "If you are going to impact the way someone behaves you have to understand what leads them to that action. Then you have a head start for determining the one compelling piece of information that will change what they believe so their behaviour is altered. And, of course, the way people behave is heavily influenced by factors like their upbringing, their demographics, attitudes, and things often associated with the field of sociology."

Source: Used with permission of Kate Baillie, TELUS Communications.

The most smartphones on Canada's largest High Speed network.

MOTO Q 9c	Next Generation BlackBerry® Pearl™	BlackBerry® Curve™ 8330	HTC S720	HTC S640
$149.99*	$99.99*	$249.99*	$0*	$49.99*
(3 year term)	(3 year term)	(3 year term)	(3 year term)	(3 year term)

ADD UNLIMITED personal email and instant messaging for only $15/month.*

TELUS

Source: Courtesy of TELUS.

Some marketing communications from TELUS feature rational appeals.

SUMMARY

In the model of communications presented in Chapter 1, the work in message development includes the background, competitive research, positioning, and development of objectives for marketing communications. This chapter introduced the second stage in the model, the coding process. The first step in the coding process is the development of a creative strategy that will guide the development of the message itself. This strategy is articulated through the development of a creative brief and represents the point at which the account team actively works with the creative team to develop the messages that they will presented to target audiences.

The creative brief contains a number of specific pieces of information that are critical to the development of effective creative. The first is a concise summary of the target audience. Only information salient to the product or service being promoted should be included. This target audience definition should be accompanied by a specific objective that the message is expected to achieve. Next, the "one thing" that will motivate the audience to act in way that will satisfy the objective is stated, along with any necessary support statements. Finally, details on any timing or geographic constraints or opportunities are presented.

The effectiveness of messages created and presented to a target audience can be explained through a number of theories. The hierarchy of effects model suggests consumers move through a series of stages as they are persuaded to make a purchase. The steps are: (1) awareness, (2) knowledge, (3) liking, (4) preference, (5) conviction, and (6) the actual purchase. Although the process probably is not a lock-step model that every buyer follows, the hierarchy of effects approach does provide important information about which mental issues to account for in various advertising campaigns. The hierarchy of effects model can be combined with the three main elements present in attitudes: (1) cognitive, (2) affective, and (3) conative components. Ads are designed to influence affective feelings, cognitive knowledge, or conative intentions to act or behave based on an attitude. A means–end chain displays the linkages between a means to achieve a desired state and the end or personal value at issue. Advertisers can select personal values that mesh with the key characteristics of the target market and then construct ads designed to provide them the means to achieve these ends by purchasing the good or service. These ideas help the creative develop a leverage point to move the buyer from understanding the product's benefits to incorporating those benefits with his or her personal values.

The elaboration likelihood model (ELM) accounts for the effects of the audiences' ability to process information presented in a marketing communications message. Audiences with higher involvement or in product categories characterized by high-involvement decision making will process messages based on the central route, which focuses on arguments and details presented in the message. Consumers who lack the ability or motivation to process such detail take the peripheral route, and in this case other cues such as spokespeople or images lead to attitude or behaviour change. Finally, in low-involvement processing, even when the audience is not actively processing information, messages can change attitudes and behaviours due to repetition.

Regardless of the relevant process an audience uses when coming into contact with marketing communications, one of the most critical decisions in the creative strategy is the type of appeal that will be used. The two main categories are rational and emotional appeals. Rational appeals focus on factual information presented to convince the audience to act based on such elements as price, product performance, or scarcity. Emotional appeals focus less on cognition and more on affect. Although virtually any emotion can be used in an appeal, some of the most common emotional appeals are based on fear, humour, and sex. Emotional appeals tend to work better than rational appeals for many products. However, with a given campaign or even within a given piece of marketing communications, both types of appeals can be combined effectively to move the audience through one or more of the steps in the purchase decision process.

Messages with business audiences often contain rational appeals because the purchase decision variables are more complex. At the same time, many marketers have recently discovered that emotional appeals can be effective, which expands business-to-business marketing communications beyond traditional venues, such as print, and into other venues, such as television, radio, the Internet, and social networking.

The process of designing ads for international markets is quite similar to that for domestic ads. The major difference is careful consideration of local attitudes and customers, with due care given to the language, slang, and symbols of the area. For example, Sega recently discovered that its product's name is slang for "masturbation" in Italian, after a major advertising campaign had started. Obviously, these types of mistakes should be carefully avoided.

KEY TERMS

central route of persuasion Audience processing of a message that uses arguments or information presented in the message.

creative brief The document used to articulate the creative strategy, containing five key questions: Who are we talking to? What is the objective? What is the one thing we're trying to tell them? Why should they believe us? When and where are we telling them?

elaboration likelihood model A model for interpreting how an audience processes marketing communications messages.

hierarchy of effects model A marketing approach suggesting that a consumer moves through a series of six steps when becoming convinced to make a purchase: (1) awareness, (2) knowledge, (3) liking, (4) preference, (5) conviction, and (6) the actual purchase.

low-involvement persuasion Audience persuasion that occurs even when an audience is not actively processing a marketing communications message.

means–end chain An advertisement approach in which the message contains a means (a reasoning or mental process)

to lead the consumer to a desired end state, such as a key personal value.

Means–End Conceptualization of Components for Advertising Strategy (MECCAS) An advertising approach that suggests using five elements in creating ads: (1) the product's attributes, (2) consumer benefits, (3) leverage points, (4) personal values, and (5) the executional framework.

peripheral route of persuasion Audience processing of a message that focuses on cues, such as spokespeople, images, or colours.

selective attention When an audience is exposed to a message but chooses not to pay attention.

selective comprehension When an audience fails to properly comprehend the message in marketing communications.

selective exposure When an audience avoids a marketing communications message.

selective retention When an audience fails to retain information presented in a marketing communications message.

REVIEW QUESTIONS

1. What are the five main elements of a creative brief? How do they affect the choice of message appeals?

2. What are the six stages of the hierarchy of effects model? Do they always occur in that order? Why or why not?

3. How are the three components of attitudes related to the hierarchy of effects model?

4. In a means–end chain, what are the means? The ends? How do they affect advertising design?

5. What is a leverage point? How are leverage points related to the hierarchy of effects model, attitudinal changes, and means–end chains?

6. What are the routes to persuasion according to the elaboration likelihood model? How do they differ?

7. What are three examples of rational appeals used in marketing communications messages?

8. What are three examples of emotional appeals used in marketing communications messages?

9. When do humour appeals work in marketing communications? What pitfalls should companies avoid in using humorous appeals?

10. What types of sexual appeals can messages contain?

11. When are sexual appeals most likely to succeed? To fail?

12. What are five reasons that emotional appeals tend to be more effective than rational appeals?

13. Why are emotional appeals being used more often in business-to-business marketing communications?

14. What factors should marketers using sex appeals across cultural boundaries take into consideration?

INTEGRATED LEARNING EXERCISES

1. Ipsos is one of the leading online research firms. Access the website at **www.ipsos.ca**. What types of products and services does the company offer? How would this information help a creative in developing marketing communications creative? How would this information assist a marketing communications agency in understanding the target audience for a campaign?

2. Develop a means–end chain similar to the one in Figure 5.6 for each of the following branded products:
   - Clorox bleach
   - Zippo lighters
   - Kool-Aid
   - Apple iPods

Share your results with the class. How were your means–end chains similar or dissimilar to others in class?

3. Find at least two elements from the same marketing communications campaign. For example, find an example of a television ad and communications using social media. Do you think they are intended to work at different points along the hierarchy of effects? How do the two pieces work together to deliver different stages of the overall process?

4. Access an online database search engine through your library. Pick one of the appeals listed in the chapter. Find at least three different articles that discuss the appeal. Write a report of your findings.

STUDENT PROJECT

Creative Corner

You have been hired to help solve a market positioning problem with the school in which you are enrolled. Specifically, your challenge is to help promote your specific faculty to future students. Your boss, the Dean, tells you that she thinks the school lacks differentiation among students and feels that marketing communications can help. You were hired because of your keen understanding of the target audience and competitors within this market. Your first job is to brief the creative team that will work with you to develop the campaign. Using the creative brief template provided in this chapter, write a creative brief.

Be sure to be clear about what objective(s) you feel the marketing communications can and should achieve. Remember, you will be judged on the ability of the marketing communications to meet this objective. Also, although it is not called for in the brief, offer any suggestions you have on the specific types of appeals that you think would work best for this brand, and why.

➜ ETHICS IN ACTION

A U.S. fast food chain recently airedaired a television commercial featuring a schoolteacher dancing on top of her desk while a room full of guys performed a rap song entitled "I Like Flat Buns." The song seemed appropriate since the ad was for a new sandwich on a flat bun. Instead, the ad received considerable flack because the sexy blonde school teacher was wearing a short, tight skirt. Teachers associations complained that it was inappropriate because it was a "sexually exploitive assault" on teachers, students, and schools.

1. Do you think this type of ad is appropriate or not? What are three arguments in favour of allowing this type of ad to run? What are three possible negative societal outcomes that can result from the airing of such commercials?

2. Do you think this type of sex appeal is germane to the product or not? Develop an idea for a message that uses a humour appeal and present it to the class. Have a vote to see if they like your idea better than the sex appeal version of the ad. ●

CASE STUDY | The Greening of Benoit Motors

Roger Benoit has pretty much "seen it all" over several decades of selling used cars. His business, Benoit Motors, had experienced a series of high and low points related to buyer whims and the nature of the industry. As a small fish in an industry that sold over 1.5 million cars each year, Roger was quite pleased to earn a living selling a few hundred cars a year.[34] But he is quick to point out that his strongest ally has always been a marketing communications agency in Montreal that has helped him negotiate the troubled waters.

From the beginning, Roger has seen opportunities rise up and drift away. When he opened his modest lot in 1973, the first gas crisis was just emerging. People were dumping gas hog cars and diligently looking for high-mileage cars and those fuelled by diesel. In fact, Roger distinctly remembers offering a practically brand new Ford LTD II, one of the most popular models of the time, at $3,000 below its "blue book" value and not being able to find a buyer for weeks due to consumer fears about oil shortages and rising gas prices.

At that time, Roger's new agency account executive, Sheila Unrau, pointed out an old technique that had worked wonders for years. It comes from the Sun Tzu book known as *The Art of War*. In it, the Chinese military general tells those who have a weakness in war to find a way to exploit that weakness so it becomes a strength. In the car business, there was a relevant example in one of the most celebrated print ad campaigns of all time. That's where Sheila got the idea. The original Volkswagen "bug" was promoted as being ugly, but economical. Many restaurants during that era bought ads pointing out that the reason they were so "slow" was due to their higher-quality food, making it "worth the wait."

Consequently, Benoit Motors placed ads in newspapers and on the radio focusing on the "value" an individual could obtain by trading down or across. Sales reps were instructed to convey to individual buyers that a person would have to buy an awfully large amount of gas at 55 cents per gallon before a large car would actually be costly, especially when mpg

(miles per gallon) differences between midsize and smaller cars were so small. Benoit managed to buy cars that other companies did not want to carry, at drastically reduced prices, and sell them to the customers they could educate concerning the shift from disadvantage to advantage. Within a few years, those high-priced (and hard to maintain) diesel cars disappeared, and people once again fell in love with larger gas hogs. By then Roger's company was well established in the marketplace.

The next challenge was in the 1980s, when Roger weathered the invasion of foreign cars into North America by once again seeing an advantage in the disadvantage. Using patriotic themes, his company subtly pointed out that people buying foreign-made cars hurt the local economy, especially because Quebec was home to a major GM production facility. Sales presentations always included the question "Are you in a union?" Those who responded "yes" were easy targets for the company's "Buy Domestic" theme during the early 1980s.

From there, Roger spent a great deal of energy making sure he understood the needs of his aging client base. Those who started families in the 1980s needed minivans in the 1990s. Those who were older and facing retirement often wanted low-maintenance cars. By carefully constructing his original message, that a person would gain an advantage by shopping at his lot, the business continued to succeed.

The next major challenge for Benoit Motors is what Roger sees as the "greening" of the world's auto fleet. At first, Roger wasn't sure if this shift was for real. He saw consumers steering away from larger cars and moving heavily into smaller, more fuel-efficient vehicles. He wondered if this was just like the 1970s all over again. For a while he thought he would simply replay his strategy from the 1970s, and buy up lots of the cheap SUVs that were flooding the market or sitting unsold on other dealers' lots. But after thinking carefully about what he was seeing in the market, Roger realized that the shift wasn't just about money this time.

Sure, the price of gas has risen dramatically, almost as much on a percentage basis as it did in the 1970s. And customers were again today steering away from larger vehicles on a cost basis. Lower operating costs for cars meant that companies such as Toyota were announcing 50 percent year-over-year production increases for cars like their Prius hybrid.[35] But this time Roger couldn't use the same technique of selling people on larger cars on a simple, low upfront price because of the other driver of this trend.

The second driver of the green trend was that consumers were becoming more aware of their impacts on the environment. It was also a social issue. People who were seen in their neighbourhood driving a gas guzzler were seen somewhat as social outcasts. No one wanted to be seen driving a car that they thought people would label as bad for the environment. Even the large North American car companies, that for years built larger and larger SUVs for the local market, began to shift their lines to smaller, more efficient vehicles.[36] So even if a larger car didn't end up costing any more than a small one, the pollutants created by larger cars—especially the older, used ones on his lot—meant that Roger needed to find a new approach. Once again he would need to reinvent his business to keep pace.

Roger decided that for Benoit Motors to stay alive he would need to adapt his business to this new green environment. He would need to radically shift the product sitting on his lot. He made plans to sell off his larger cars in the wholesale market, and replenish his inventory with smaller cars. He even considered changing the name of his dealership from Benoit Motors to Green Motors to help align his company with what he felt was going to be a paradigm shift in the automotive market. If he moved quickly, he could have an advantage over other dealers that still sold a wide variety of cars. By focusing only on smaller, more efficient, and environmentally friendly cars, Roger wanted Benoit Motors to be the place to shop for a car for buyers who were concerned about saving money for themselves and saving the planet in the process. Roger knew that a marketing communications campaign to "relaunch" his brand in the Montreal market was an important element of his new marketing plan. He picked up the phone to call his old friend Sheila at the agency to set up a meeting.

1. Assume you are Roger. Write a creative brief for your agency.

2. Do you think a rational or creative appeal is the best approach to take for this campaign? What specific type of appeal would you suggest the agency use and why? Develop a five-minute presentation that you will deliver in the meeting with the agency to try and convince them to use your appeal in the creative development.

3. In explaining to the creative team why you think you should invest in marketing communications to take advantage of this green opportunity, outline how you think the marketing communications will be effective using either the hierarchy of effects or the means–end chain.

4. Assume you have decided one night after a few drinks that maybe you don't need the creative team after all, and decide to take a shot at developing the creative yourself. Your first task is to do the next print ad that will appear in *The Gazette*. Each week for the past 20 years you have run a half-page ad in the paper. The ad usually features a series of pictures of cars for sale, and you want to keep this in. But you reserve half of the ad for your new green message. Take a shot at designing the ad yourself.

ENDNOTES

1. John Ward (1994), "Four Facets of Advertising Performance Measurement," in Chris Baker, ed., *The Longer and Broader Effects of Advertising.* London: Institute of Practitioners in Advertising, p. 44.

2. Jerry Olson and Thomas J. Reynolds, "Understanding Consumers' Cognitive Structures: Implications for Advertising Strategy," *Advertising Consumer Psychology,* L. Percy and A. Woodside, eds. (Lexington, MA: Lexington Books, 1983), pp. 77–90; Thomas J. Reynolds and Alyce Craddock, "The Application of the MECCAS Model to Development and Assessment of Advertising Strategy," *Journal of Advertising Research* 28, no. 2 (1988), pp. 43–54.

3. Scott A. Hawkins and Steve J. Hoch (1992), "Low-Involvement Learning: Memory Without Evaluation," *Journal of Consumer Research,* 19 (September), 212–225.

4. Stephanie Thompson, "Big Deal," *Mediaweek* 7, no. 44 (November 24, 1997), p. 36; Judann Pollack, "Big G Has Special Cheerios for Big '00,'" *Advertising Age* (June 14, 1999).

5. Olson and Reynolds, "Understanding Consumers' Cognitive Structures"; Reynolds and Craddock, "The Application of the MECCAS Model to Development and Assessment of Advertising Strategy."

6. Based on Rosemary M. Murtaugh, "Designing Effective Health Promotion Messages Using Components of Protection Motivation Theory," *Proceedings of the Atlantic Marketing Association* (1999), pp. 553–57; R. W. Rogers and S. Prentice-Dunn, "Protection Motivation Theory," *Handbook of Health Behavior Research I: Personal and Social Determinants,* D. Gochman, ed. (New York: Plenum Press, 1997), pp. 130–32.

7. Robin Coulter and Mary Beth Pinto (1995), "Guilt Appeals in Advertising: What Are Their Effects?" Journal of Applied Psychology, 80 (6), 697–705.

8. Michael S. Latour and Robin L. Snipes, "Don't Be Afraid to Use Fear Appeals: An Experimental Study," *Journal of Advertising Research* 36, no. 2 (March–April 1996), pp. 59–68.

9. Martin Eisend, "A Meta-Analysis of Humor Effects in Advertising," *Advances in Consumer Research–North American Conference Proceedings* 34 (2007), pp. 320–23.

10. Karen Flaherty, Marc G. Weinberger, and Charles S. Gulas, "The Impact of Perceived Humor, Product Type, and Humor Style in Radio Advertising," *Journal of Current Issues and Research in Advertising* 26, no. 1 (Spring 2004), pp. 25–37.

11. Theresa Howard, "Windex Birds Make Clean Sweep as Most-Liked Ads," *USA Today* (December 18, 2006), p. 7B (Money).

12. Matthew Creamer, "Marketing's Era of Outrage," *Advertising Age* 78, no. 7 (February 12, 2007), pp. 1, 26.

13. Jimmy Yap, "McDonald's Finds Humor a Hit with Singapore Viewers," *Media Asia* (February 7, 2004), p. 22; Bill Britt, "Ford Tries Witty, Edgy Advertising to Promote the Kia," *Automotive News Europe* 9, no. 2 (January 26, 2004), p. 4.

14. Joanne Lynch and Leslie de Chernatony, "The Power of Emotion: Brand Communication in Business-to-Business Markets," *Journal of Brand Management* 11, no. 5 (May 2004), pp. 403–420; Karalynn Ott, "B-to-B Marketers Display Their Creative Side," *Advertising Age's Business Marketing* 84, no. 1 (January 1999), pp. 3–4.

15. "Sex Doesn't Sell," *The Economist* 373, no. 8399 (October 30, 2004), pp. 62–63.

16. Laurel Wentz, "Global Village," *Advertising Age* 68, no. 10 (March 10, 1997), p. 3; Michael Wilke, "A Kiss Before Buying," *Advocate* (April 27, 1999), pp. 34–35.

17. Sandra O'Loughlin, "Hanes Shows Some 'Love' in Battle for Intimates," *Brandweek* 48, no. 9 (February 26, 2007), p. 11. pp. 1–2. Gregg Cebrzynski, "Teachers Hot about Hot Teacher Dancing in 'Sexually Exploitive' Hardee's TV Spot," *Nation's Restaurant News* 41, no. 37 (September 17, 2007), p. 12.

18. Tom Reichart, "Sex in Advertising Research: A Review of Content, Effects, and Functions of Sexual Information in Consumer Advertising," *Annual Review of Sex Research* 13 (2002), pp. 242–74; D. C. Bello, R. E. Pitts, and M. J. Etzel, "The Communication Effects of Controversial Sexual Content in Television Programs and Commercials," *Journal of Advertising* 3, no. 12 (1983), pp. 32–42.

19. Bob Garfield, "Dentyne Spot Makes It Seem That Naysayers Have a Point," *Advertising Age* 76, no. 5 (January 31, 2005), p. 41.

20. Jessica Severn, George E. Belch, and Michael A. Belch, "The Effects of Sexual and Non-Sexual Advertising Appeals and Information Level on Cognitive Processing and Communication Effectiveness," *Journal of Advertising* 19, no. 1 (1990), pp. 14–22.

21. Ibid.

22. Reichart 2002.

23. "Note to Chrysler: Gutter Humor Has No Place in Ads," *Automotive News* 78, no. 6064 (October 27, 2003), p. 12.

24. Bruce Horovitz, "Risqué May Be Too Risky for Ads," *USA Today* (April 16, 2004), p. 1B.

25. Ibid.

26. Claire Beale, "What Now for Ad Industry As Sex No Longer Sells?" *Campaign (UK),* no. 36 (September 3, 2004), p. 23.

27. Gerard Stamp and Mark Stockdale, "Sex in Advertising," *Advertising Age's Creativity* 7, no. 6 (July–August 1999), pp. 35–36; Bob Garfield, "Pushing the Envelope: The Performing Penis," *Advertising Age International,* (July 12, 1999), p. 4. Jean J. Boddewyn, "Sex and Decency Issues in Advertising: General and International Dimensions," *Business Horizons* 34, no. 5 (September–October 1991), pp. 13–20.

28. Elizabeth Bryant, "P&G Pushes the Envelope in Egypt with TV Show on Feminine Hygiene," *Advertising Age International* (December 14, 1998), p. 2.

29. Scott Rockwood, "For Better Ad Success, Try Getting Emotional," *Marketing News* 30, no. 22 (October 21, 1996), p. 4.

30. Mae Anderson, "A Priceless Promotion," *Adweek* 45, no. 44 (November 22, 2004), pp. 24–25.

31. Daniel A. Joelson, "Rebel Sell," *Latin Trade* 12, no. 8 (August 2004), p. 16.

32. Gerard Stamp and Mark Stockdale, "Sex in Advertising," *Advertising Age's Creativity* 7, no. 6 (July–August 1999), pp. 35–36; Bob Garfield, "Pushing the Envelope: The Performing Penis," *Advertising Age International*, (July 12, 1999), p. 4. Jean J. Boddewyn, "Sex and Decency Issues in Advertising: General and International Dimensions," *Business Horizons* 34, no. 5 (September–October 1991), pp. 13–20.

33. Bryant 1998.

34. Grace Macaluso (2010), "Canadian Car Dealers Expect Sales Jump to Level Off," *Windsor Star*, May 7, p. B1.

35. Michael Hastings, Keith Naughton, and Masato Kawaguchi (2004), "The Gas Miser," *Newsweek*, September 20, p. 4.

36. David Kiley (2006), "Suddenly Revved About Small Cars," *Businessweek*, January 10, p. 6.

6

After reading this chapter, you should be able to answer the following questions:

- **How** do cognitive, affective, and conative message strategies differ?
- **How** do message tactics affect the development of leverage points and executional frameworks?
- **What** is an executional framework?
- **How** do executional frameworks fit with message appeals?
- **Which** characteristics are most important when selecting a source or spokesperson?
- **How** does consistency help ensure the effectiveness of marketing communications?
- **What** are the steps involved in creating print and broadcast marketing communications?

INDUSTRY PROFILE
So You Want to Work in Marketing Communications?

Lisagh King, Director of Creative Services, McKim Cringan George, Winnipeg

If people who meet Lisagh aren't exactly sure what she does in her job, they have good reason. She is probably the only person in the country who does—or is able to do—exactly what she does at McKim Cringan George. Not that other agencies wouldn't love to have someone in her role, but her unique blend of skills and background make her perfectly and uniquely suited to act as an interface between the account and creative functions of a marketing communications agency.

Explaining how her role came about, Lisagh says, "It was done to facilitate what we needed at our agency—someone who understands the creative process but was pragmatic and understood the business side as well." As the lynchpin between creative and accounts, there isn't too much that goes on in the agency that Lisagh doesn't see. "My job involves working with production and account services to assist in creating estimates and timelines for projects, and to help them make sure things like work orders and change orders for projects are thorough and well thought out. I also work with the creative teams to figure out what they need, who has time to work on which projects, who is best suited to projects and to help them figure out ways to get things finished if we are in a time crunch. And all of this spans virtually any kind of marketing communications you can imagine, from magazine ads to TV and radio spots, to huge branding projects or annual report."

Lisagh is well suited to this role because she has a clear understanding of each part of the process. "I'm formally an art director. I have a Fine Arts degree, but over time I lost interest in the graphic design and art direction side of the business. I'm probably the only art director out there who can't really draw. In fact, when I used to work with my writing partner on creative projects, I used to do some of the writing and she would do some of the design. So as much as I understand the creative side of this business, as time went on I started to feel more comfortable on what eventually became the role I have now."

A big part of her perspective about the business is no doubt due to her personality. "The pragmatic side of me goes back as long as I can remember. A few years

Creative Tactics

ago I took the Myers-Briggs test, and I came out something like 90 to 1 on the thinking versus feeling side. I guess I'm just not a right-brained person at heart. But this, along with the personal knowledge I have for the creative process, makes me a great fit to play this role."

The role provides value to clients of the agency because it helps the process run more smoothly and productively. "The people on the account side get help in preparing jobs or any direction on work that requires creative input, so that even before the work starts it is succinct, focused and thorough. This then adds value to the people on the creative side because they are getting better, more focused direction and can spend less time deciphering feedback or tracking down details and more time adding value." In this way, the role of gatekeeper between the two departments ensures that things happen the way they should, and nobody tries to take any shortcuts. "I'm kind of the like the agency cop," jokes Lisagh.

Being the one who is always demanding that process be followed may not always make Lisagh the most popular person in the agency, but her demand for consistency has paid off more than once. "One time we had a student intern working with us in our design department. She was using a version of software that was different than the one we used in our studio. She had worked on a project that went back and forth with the client many times, and had changed significantly from the original ver-

Lisagh King, Director of Creative Services, McKim Cringan George

sion. So when she left we couldn't open the files. We had to go back to the original version and re-do all of the changes that had been made over several rounds of feedback." This situation is not uncommon to anyone who has been working on a file and had their computer crash. It is sometimes impossible to recreate the work that had been done prior to the last saved version of the file. But at McKim Cringan George the team had every change documented so it was easy to go back and re-trace all of the changes. "I always demand that any work coming into the creative department or studio be documented in full, precisely for occasions like this. It doesn't happen very often, but when problems like this come up it can be devastating. It happens when people are rushed and do something in a voicemail, or a casual email, or a conversation in the hallway. If there is no record, there is no control, and if there is no control, there is the potential for chaos."

Luckily situations where Lisagh is needed to avert crises are rare, and she can generally enjoy her work at the agency. "I love it here first for the people. We've got a great team. But we also have great clients and that allows us to work on some really interesting projects. The Blue Bombers are one of my favourites. We've had a long relationship with them so there is a level of trust, and we have a bit more leeway and creative freedom which is nice." But Lisagh also enjoys the mix of projects at the agency. "We have a wide range of clients: Governments, public utilities, retailers. The list goes on. Some are local, some are national. Some need mainly advertising, and others need more branding work, or web design, or event management. So every day brings a new challenge."

When asked for her advice to aspiring young account people, she lists two things. "First—and I can't take credit for coming up with this, but nothing is more true—people need to learn that three aspects define any project. It can be good, it can be fast, and it can be cheap. But generally, we can only deliver two out of these three at one time. Part of my job is to help account managers, who expect projects to be high quality and on budget, understand why it's a challenge to deliver projects for the next day. Luckily, the team here is good at miracles, but an understanding of the realities of the production process would be a huge asset for someone new to the business."

The second suggestion is avoid what Lisagh calls *get-it-off-my-desk-itis*. "This is when an account person simply takes feedback or direction they get from a client and passes it on to me. It's using cut and paste, but no value has been added. It's important that people in the account role add value to the process by distilling feedback into a succinct, focused brief and provide the necessary background to do work, or whatever the project requires. When an account manager comes to me with a specific request and I ask them to tell me 'why' before I pass it on to the team, if their answer is 'I don't know,' we've got a breakdown in the creative process."

"I give them a hard time sometimes, but I really have empathy for people that work on the account side. It's tough. I couldn't do it. I'm between the account and creative side, but they are between the client and the entire agency, so it's a big job. But the ones that come in and take the time to learn how to develop their skills, and enjoy the work, are the ones that will thrive."

OVERVIEW

The previous chapter examined the creative strategy in marketing communications, examining the questions of why marketing communications can be effective, and why certain appeals are useful at reaching objectives. This chapter examines the tactics involved in turning these broad appeals into tangible elements of a marketing communications plan.

For example, a rational appeal can be executed in a number of different ways. The message can be formatted to provide detail directly by comparing one product with a competitor's, on a range of performance metrics or prices. Or the message can be formatted to demonstrate someone using the product and enjoying the benefits. In each case, the overall appeal can be quite rational, but how the appeal is executed is quite different.

Once again, we will review this stage of message development from the position of the initiator and evaluator of the creative development as opposed to the actual development itself. However, it must be noted that the creative development process consistently defies the use of rules or specific guidelines to suggest that one tactic is always appropriate. The specifics of a given market, target audience, and objectives must always be taken into account when evaluating creative tactics.

For example, one of the most common "rules" associated with marketing communications messages in print media is the use of a product logo or tagline in the bottom right corner of the page. However, one of the most memorable campaigns in print media did not use the product logo or even mention the name of the product. The campaign was a series of print ads for a brand of scotch whisky called Chivas, and was developed by one of the most lauded creative directors of the 20th century, Neil French. The campaign featured headlines and visual cues of the product that only current users of the brand would recognize. For example, using only the shape of the bottle, the headline read: "If You Don't Recognize It, You're Probably Not Ready for It." In one headline, this ad instantly told people who currently use the brand that they were special, and somehow elite, creating significant brand appeal. In addition, non-users of the brand were motivated to seek out the brand by the shape of the bottle because they wanted to be included in this elite club of scotch drinkers.

This chapter will examine three types of message tactics that marketing communications can include. These are cognitive, affective, and conative message tactics that match with the stages of attitudinal development. Next, we will examine the various executional frameworks that can be used to structure both rational and emotional appeals in marketing communications messages. Then, we will examine how spokespersons can be used effectively, followed by an examination of the production process for a number of different marketing communications tactics.

MESSAGE TACTICS

Under the broad strategy of either rational or emotional appeals, marketing communications messages can use a number of message tactics. These are essentially how the appeal is manifested in a piece of marketing communications. For example, a rational appeal can be presented using a number of different message tactics, including the use of exaggerations or direct head-to-head comparisons with competitors. Overall, these tactics are based on knowledge of the stages of attitudinal development—cognitive, affective, and conative—described earlier in this textbook.[1]

Cognitive Tactics

A **cognitive message tactic** is the presentation of rational arguments or pieces of information to consumers designed to stimulate cognitive processing. When a cognitive message tactic is used, the key feature of the message is about the product's attributes or benefits. Customers can obtain these benefits by using the product.[2]

The point of the cognitive message tactic is to impact on a person's beliefs and/or knowledge structure. This can be accomplished by suggesting any one of a wide variety of potential product benefits. Foods may be described as healthful, pleasant tasting, or low calorie. A tool can be shown as durable, convenient, or handy to use. A drill press machine used in a manufacturing operation may be portrayed as being more reliable or faster than comparable machines on the market. Cognitive message strategies make these benefits clear to potential customers. The five major forms of cognitive strategies are:

1. Generic messages
2. Preemptive messages
3. Unique selling proposition
4. Hyperbole
5. Comparative messages

Generic messages are direct presentations of product attributes or benefits without any claim of superiority. This type of tactic works best for a firm that is clearly the brand leader and is the dominant company in the industry. The goal of the generic message is to make the brand synonymous with the product category. Thus, Campbell's Soups can declare "Soup is good food" without making any claim to superiority. This is because the company so strongly dominates the industry. When most consumers think of soup, they think of Campbell's. Of the hundreds of millions of bowls of soup consumed each year, 69 percent are a variety of Campbell's.[3]

Generic message tactics are seldom found in business-to-business messages, because few firms dominate an industry to the extent of Campbell's. One major exception is Intel, which currently controls 80.2 percent of the microchip market.[4] The generic message "Intel inside" has been used for years to convey to both businesses and end users that the processor inside is made by Intel.

Generic message tactics can also be used to create brand awareness. The goal of the marketer may be to develop a cognitive linkage between a specific brand name and a product category, such as Sketchers and sporty footwear. The ad may contain very little information about the product's attributes. The intent of the ad is simply to put the brand name in a person's cognitive memory.

Preemptive messages claim superiority based on a product's specific attribute or benefit. The idea is to prevent the competition from making the same or a similar statement. For example, Crest toothpaste is well known as "the cavity fighter." The brand preempts other companies from making similar-sounding claims, even though all toothpastes fight cavities. The key to effectively using a preemptive message is to be the first company to state the advantage. This keeps competitors from saying the same thing. Those that do are viewed as "me-too" brands or copycats.

Critical Thinking Exercise

Find an example of a preemptive message tactic in any category. In other words, find one message that "owns" a claim in that product category, such as the Crest example given above. Then find an example of another message from a different marketer in the same category. If the brand using the preemptive message "owns" that message, what does the other brand use instead? Can you think of a message that would be more effective to compete with the one "owned" by the preemptive brand?

An advertisement for Kal Tire featuring a unique selling proposition.

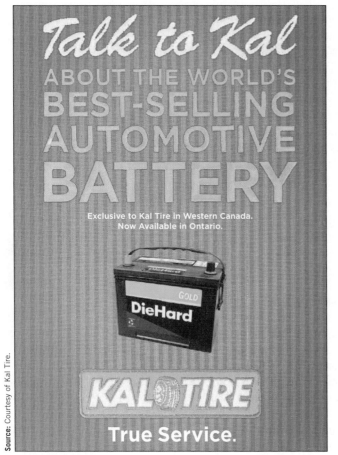

Source: Courtesy of Kal Tire.

A **unique selling proposition (USP)** is an explicit, testable claim of uniqueness or superiority that can be supported or substantiated in some manner. In the Kal Tire advertisement shown on the this page, the company proposes a unique selling proposition aimed at car owners. The message that the DieHard battery is the "the world's best-selling automotive battery" highlights the popularity of the product.

The **hyperbole** approach makes an untestable claim based upon some attribute or benefit. When CBC states that its programming contains the nation's favourite comedies, the claim is a hyperbole. These claims do not have to be substantiated, which makes this cognitive tactic quite popular.

The final cognitive message tactic includes **comparative messages**. When a marketer directly or indirectly compares a good or service to the competition, they are using the comparative method. The advertisement may or may not mention the competitor by name. Sometimes, a marketer simply presents a "make-believe" competitor, giving it a name like brand X. This approach, however, is not as effective as comparative advertising that states the actual competitor's name. To provide protection from lawsuits, company leaders must be sure any claim concerning the competition can be clearly substantiated.

Bell, Rogers, and TELUS compare network capabilities and rates. VISA notes that many merchants will not accept American Express. Burger King explains the advantages of flame broiling as opposed to frying, which McDonald's and Wendy's use. In the business-to-business sector, shipping companies compare delivery times and accuracy rates.

The major advantage of comparative messages is that they often capture the audience's attention. When comparisons are made, both brand awareness and message awareness increase. Consumers tend to remember more of what the message says about a brand than when the same information is presented in a noncomparative format.

The negative side of using comparative messages is in the areas of believability and consumer attitudes. Many consumers think comparative messages are less believable. They view the information about the sponsor brand as exaggerated and conclude that the information about the comparison brand probably is misstated to make the sponsor brand appear superior.

Another danger of comparative messages is the negative attitudes consumers may develop toward the message itself. If the audience acquires negative attitudes toward the message, these negative attitudes can transfer to the sponsor's product. This is especially true when the sponsor runs a *negative comparative message*. This form of message portrays the competition's product in a negative light. Research has shown that negative comparative messages typically result in lower believability of the claims and create less favourable attitudes toward the brand.[5]

In psychology, the concept of *spontaneous trait transference* suggests that when someone calls another person dishonest, other people tend to remember the speaker as also being less than honest. When a comparative message criticizes the competition's brand based on some particular attribute, the audience may attribute that deficiency to the sponsor brand as well. This is most likely to occur when the consumer uses the comparative brand, not the sponsored brand.[6] Company leaders must be careful in choosing an appropriate comparison firm and must be even more careful about using a negative comparative message format.

The comparative message tactic can be beneficial if used with caution. The comparison brand must be picked carefully to ensure consumers see it as a viable competing brand. Actual product attributes and customer benefits must be used, without stretching the information or providing misleading information. If there are actual differences to compare, then comparative messages work well. If the comparisons are all hype and opinion, with no substantial differences, comparative messages do not work as well.

In general, comparing a low-market share brand to the market leader works well, because viewers concentrate more carefully on the content and message of the ad. On the other hand, comparing a high-market share brand with another high-market share brand is often not effective. In these cases, a better strategy may be to simply make the comparison without naming the competitor.

Car rental company Avis is one classic case study in comparative messages. When Avis was 10th in market share in the rental car industry, a series of ads was developed for Avis, comparing its service to the market leader, Hertz, mentioning the Hertz name specifically. Consumers began to believe that Avis provided the same level of quality as Hertz. After gaining market share and becoming one of the top three brands, Avis changed its approach and now usually does not mention Hertz in marketing communications. Still, when comparisons are made, consumers still know which competitor is involved.[7] More recently, the car company Hyundai used this approach to compare its fleet of cars to other more prestigious brands such as BMW. The message compared tangible claims such as the number of awards for product quality or warranties in order to improve the perception of quality of Hyundai cars.

All five of these **cognitive message tactics** are based on some type of rational logic. The message is designed to make sure consumers pay attention to the ad and take the time to cognitively process the information. In terms of attitudes, the sequence of *cognitive → affective → conative* is the plan of attack when developing a rational approach. The intention of a cognitive message tactic is first to present consumers with rational information about a good, service, or company,

The AVIS "We Try Harder" campaign was an effective comparative advertising approach.

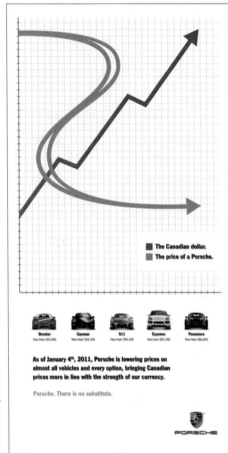

Porsche combines informational and emotional appeals in its communications.

Wiser's and their agency, John St., used an affective appeal to help attract a younger demographic to the brand.

and then to help them develop positive feelings about the same product or company.

Affective Tactics

Affective message tactics invoke feelings or emotions and match those feelings with the good, service, or company. Such messages are prepared in order to enhance the likeability of the product, recall of the appeal, or comprehension of the message. Affective strategies elicit emotions that, in turn, lead the consumer to act, preferably to buy the product, and subsequently affect the consumer's reasoning process.

An emotion such as love can be featured in order to convince consumers that a product such as Cheerios is a superior breakfast cereal for loved ones. The consumer group is then led to believe Cheerios is a rational choice because the company's messages mention the cereal's positive effects on cholesterol levels. This approach is demonstrated by the advertisement for Cheerios in this section. The ad features a photo of three generations of a family combined with the words "Your heart has better things to do than deal with heart disease." Family memories and emotions combine with the product feature of being a heart-smart cereal.

Just as with emotional appeals, which can be based on any number of possible human emotions. Many emotions can be connected to products, including trust, reliability, friendship, happiness, security, glamour, luxury, serenity, pleasure, romance, and passion.

Affective tactics are a common approach to developing a strong brand name. For example, when an advertisement gets you to like a brand and have positive feelings for a brand, then the hope is that you will also purchase that brand. Cognitive beliefs about the brand then follow. This approach relies on the attitude development sequence of *affective → conative → cognitive.* For some products, affective messages are an effective approach because they can create a meaningful point of difference between brands, like this ad for Tetley.

Conative Tactics

Conative message tactics are designed to lead more directly to some type of consumer response. They can be used in the development of sales promotions, such as coupon redemption programs, Internet "hits" and orders, and in-store offers such as buy-one-get-one-free. The goal of a conative tactic is to elicit behaviour. For example, a conative tactic is present in any television advertisement for music CDs that seeks to persuade viewers to call a toll-free number to purchase the music. These ads typically encourage quick action by stating that the CD cannot be purchased in stores and is available for only a limited time. And, yes, some old people still buy music on CDs.

Action-inducing conative messages create situations in which cognitive knowledge of the product or affective liking of the product may come later (after the actual purchase) or during product usage. For instance, a point-of-purchase display is designed (sometimes through advertising tie-ins) to cause people to make *impulse buys.* The goal is to make the sale, with cognitive knowledge and affective feelings forming as the product is used. In terms of an attitude sequence, conative message tactics typically utilize the *conative → cognitive → affective* approach.

Cognitive, affective, and conative tactics can be matched with the hierarchy of effects approach described in the previous chapter. The hierarchy of effects model suggests that consumers pass through a series of stages, from awareness to knowledge, liking, preference, conviction,

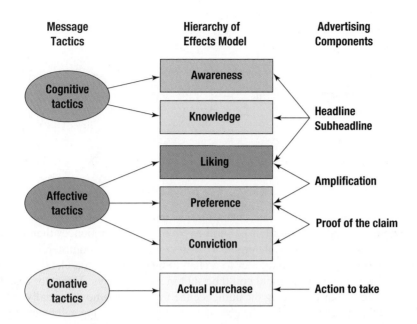

FIGURE 6.1
The Hierarchy of Effects Model, Message Tactics, and Marketing Communications Components

and, finally, to the purchase. As shown in Figure 6.1, each message strategy can highlight a different stage of the hierarchy of effects model.

Choosing the right message tactic is a key ingredient in creating a successful marketing communications program. To be effective, the message tactic must be carefully matched with the leverage point and executional framework that have been selected. In the following section, the next element, the executional framework, is described.

EXECUTIONAL FRAMEWORKS

After the appeal type has been selected, and the appeal tactics have been determined, the executional framework is selected. The **executional framework** is the manner in which an appeal tactic is presented. Figure 6.2 displays the various frameworks that are described in this section.

Slice-of-Life

In slice-of-life executional frameworks, marketers attempt to provide solutions to the everyday problems consumers or businesses face. This format was made famous by Procter & Gamble during the early days of television advertising in the 1950s. The messages normally show the common experiences, and especially the problems, people encounter. Then, the good or service is made available to solve the problem. The most common slice-of-life format has the four components identified in Figure 6.3. In some of the messages, the actors portray the dilemma or problem and solve the problems themselves. In others, a voiceover or accompanying copy explains the benefits or solution to the problem that the good, service, or company provides.

A typical slice-of-life message could start with a child playing soccer and her parents cheering (the encounter). Her dirty uniform is then shown with comments by the child

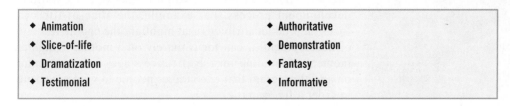

* Animation
* Slice-of-life
* Dramatization
* Testimonial
* Authoritative
* Demonstration
* Fantasy
* Informative

FIGURE 6.2
Executional Frameworks

FIGURE 6.3
Components of a Slice-of-Life Message

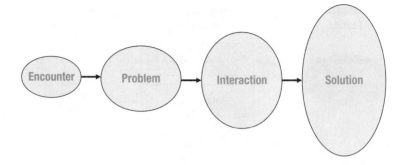

Encounter → Problem → Interaction → Solution

that it will never come clean for the championship game, or a voiceover can be used to state the same message (the problem). Another parent or the announcer then introduces the benefits of the new laundry detergent (the interaction). The commercial ends with the proud parents taking their daughter to a championship game in a clean uniform (the solution). Note that this commercial could be shot in various ways. The actors can talk to each other in the scenario, making the audience the third party who essentially is "eavesdropping" on the conversation. Or, the commercial can be shot using a voiceover to highlight the problem and solution portions of the commercial, with the announcer speaking directly to the audience.

In print messages, slice-of-life frameworks are difficult, but not impossible, to prepare. In the business-to-business advertisement for Messagemedia shown in this section, the encounter is the potential female customer. The problem is that the "average single female breaks up with 4.3 men, avoids 237 phone calls, and ignores approximately 79 red lights per year." The interaction occurs through the copy "What are the chances she'll read your e-mail message?" The solution to this problem is Messagemedia's "E-messaging campaign."

A business-to-business advertisement for Messagemedia.com containing a slice-of-life execution.

Business-to-business messages also heavily use the slice-of-life method. The execution is popular because it allows the marketer to highlight the ways a product can meet business needs. For example, a typical business-to-business message begins with a routine business experience, such as a sales manager making a presentation to the board of directors. Then, the projector being used by the salesperson does not have a clear picture. The ad offers the solution: a projector from Sony. The presentation is made with great clarity, and the board of directors accepts the customer's bid for the account. As with many slice-of-life messages, a disaster is avoided. By using the brand behind the message, a happy ending is the result.

The slice-of-life executional framework is an excellent example of how one framework can be used to manifest either a rational or an emotional appeal. For example, in the laundry detergent example used above, the slice-of-life story can be told in a very factual manner, highlighting some of the product characteristics that allow the detergent to work as well as it did, or it can be told with humour, for example. Also, the framework can be matched with a cognitive, affective, or conative message tactic, depending on where the marketer thinks it will be effective in the attitude development process. For example, the slice-of-life can focus on product attributes that highlight the cognitive stage of development, it can focus merely on a mother–daughter moment of bonding for the affective stage, or it can centre on a trial program that encourages people to visit a website to order a free sample.

Animation

Animation is a popular type of executional framework. In recent years, the use of animation in marketing communications has increased dramatically. This is due, in part, to the growing sophistication of computer graphics programs. The animation technology available to creative teams are far superior to the cartoon-type technology that was previously used.

One new animation technique is *rotoscoping*. Rotoscoping is the process of digitally painting or sketching figures into live sequences.[8] This makes it possible to present both live actors and animated characters in the same frame. The creative can also merge or modify various live scenes within the same frame. Another animation method, *clay animation*, was made popular by commercials featuring the Pillsbury Doughboy.

Animation characters can be human, animal, or product personifications. Animation was originally a last-resort technique for advertisers who did not have money to prepare a live commercial. Most agencies did not hold it in high regard. Animation has become one of the most popular advertising techniques. Successful films such as *The Incredibles* and *Bee Movie* continue to create a great deal of interest in animation in marketing communications.

Animation is used mostly in television spots. It is also used in movie trailers and Internet ads. Single shots of animated characters, such as Tony the Tiger, are also placed into print ads, packaging, websites, and coupons. For years, animation was rarely used in business-to-business advertising. Many agencies had negative views of it. Agency leaders tended to believe animation appealed to children but not to businesspeople. These views have changed. Business ads shown on television can now take advantage of high-quality graphics technologies to illustrate a product's uses with animated figures and graphics.

A recent example of animation in business-to-business advertising comes from United Airlines. A commercial shows a father gently adjusting the blankets where his son is sleeping, just as he is getting ready to leave on a business trip. The son is dreaming that the father is flying away on the wings of a swan. The point is to make an emotional connection with the viewer through animation.[9]

A Green Giant advertisement using animation.

Critical Thinking Exercise

Find an example of a message that uses an animation executional framework. Does it use a rational or an emotional appeal? Do you think it is an example of a cognitive, affective, or conative tactic? Based on the application of the slice-of-life executional framework to both rational/emotional appeals, and the cognitive/affective/conative tactics, write a summary of how the animation executional framework can be used for both types of appeals, and matched with all three message tactics.

Dramatization

A dramatization is similar to the slice-of-life executional framework. It uses the same format, in which a problem is first presented and then a solution is offered. The difference lies in the intensity and story format. Dramatization uses a higher level of excitement and suspense to tell the story. A dramatization story normally builds to a crisis point leading to a suspenseful climax.

An effective and dramatic message is difficult to create, because the drama must be completed in either 30 or 60 seconds. Building a story to a climatic moment is challenging, given such a short time period. The early "What's in Your Wallet" advertisements for Capital One credit cards did manage to create the level of excitement needed. They were, however, later replaced with humorous executions. Not all dramatic execution styles can accomplish the high level of suspense required to make them successful. It is often easier to simply produce the message using the slice-of-life framework.

Demonstration

A demonstration execution shows how a product works. A demonstration is an effective way to communicate the attributes of a product to the audience. For example, advertising for the Swiffer brand of cleaning tools regularly shows the product in action to demonstrate the benefits. The demonstration highlighted the product's multiple uses by cleaning a television screen, a wooden floor, a saxophone, and light fixtures on the ceiling. Thus, consumers were being shown how to use the product while at the same time hearing about its advantages.

Business-to-business messages often present demonstrations. They allow a business to illustrate how a product can meet the specific needs of another business. For example, GoldTouch, Inc. can demonstrate the InstaGold Flash System, which deposits a bright and uniform gold surface finish on products, such as jewellery, through a nonelectrical current process of immersion plating. Such demonstrations can be offered via Flash media ads on the Internet.

Demonstration messages are especially well suited to television and Internet media. To a limited extent, the print media can feature demonstrations, especially when a series of photos outlines the sequence of product usage.

Fantasy

Some products lend themselves to a fantasy-type executional framework. Fantasy executions are designed to lift the audience beyond the real world to a make-believe experience. Some fantasies are meant to be realistic. Others are completely irrational. Often, the more irrational and illogical messages are, the more clearly consumers recall them. Fantasies can deal with anything from a dream vacation spot or cruise ships to a juicy hamburger or an enticing DiGiorno pizza. This approach is commonly used for goods and services targeted at homemakers, and encourages them to picture a fantasy world where they can relax in a bath without screaming kids, a dirty house, or clutter. The scene that is depicted is a quiet, dark room with scented candles and soothing music. Sometimes there is a handsome bath attendant thrown in for good measure.

The most common fantasy themes, however, still involve sex, love, and romance. According to some marketing experts, raw sex and nudity in marketing communications are losing their impact. Instead, marketers can feature a softer, more subtle presentation of sex. Fantasy fits nicely with target audiences that have a preference for a tamer presentation of sexuality. Instead of raw sex and nudity, which may be offensive, fantasy takes them into a world of romantic make-believe.

One product category that frequently uses fantasy executions is the perfume and cologne industry. In the past, the most common theme was that splashing on a certain cologne causes women to flock to a man. For women, the reverse was suggested. Although used extensively, these messages were not particularly effective because people didn't believe them. Currently, perfume advertisers tend to portray the product as enhancing the love life of a couple or even making a man or woman feel more sensuous, rather than turning a man into a "babe magnet" or a woman into a "diva." One exception is, of course, the line of Axe products, which regularly use a sex-based fantasy for young men: young women who can't help themselves when they see a man using Axe products.

Critical Thinking Exercise

Similar to the discussion in Chapter 5 examining sex appeals in general, the sex fantasy executional framework can be confusing because the effects are not consistent across all segments of the population. Although many consumers do not believe the overt sex fantasies in many ads, the success of the Axe brand suggests that their customers do find the ads effective. Why do you think this is the case? Who is the target audience for Axe products? Why would they be more likely to respond positively to the Axe commercials than, say, a 45-year-old man or a 32-year-old woman?

The business-to-business advertising field has not used fantasy a great deal, primarily because of fear that members of a buying centre will not take it seriously. At the same time, marketers are sometimes able to feature a fantasy in a business-to-business ad by showing a product helping the buyer achieve some type of unrealistic result or outcome. For example, being promoted from sanitation engineer to president because of the correct choice of a cleaning product would be a fantasy aimed at people using or purchasing janitorial supplies.

Informative

One common executional framework uses informative messages, which present information to the audience in a straightforward manner. Agencies prepare informative messages extensively for radio advertisements, where only verbal communication is possible. Informative messages are less common in television and print, because consumers tend to ignore them. Other marketing communications tools, such as sales promotions, often rely heavily on informative executions because they simply present a deal, discount, or other premium.

Customers who are highly involved in a particular product category, or actively in the market for a product, pay more attention to an informational message. For example, if a business is not in the market for a particular product, buying centre members do not pay much attention to informative messages. However, many marketers believe that business buyers need detailed information to make intelligent buying decisions and value informative executions. As a result, the informative framework continues to be a popular approach for business-to-business advertisers.

One of the keys to informative executions is the placement of the message. An informative message from a restaurant placed on a radio station just before noon is listened to more carefully than one that runs at 3:00 p.m. An informative ad about a diet product in an issue of *Glamour* that has a special article on weight control or exercising will be noticed more than if it is placed in the fashion section of the magazine. An informative business ad featuring a new piece of industrial equipment works well next to an article about the capital costs of equipment. An informative direct mail package for cruises will be more effective if it is targeted to people who are more likely to go on cruises, and coupons that merely inform consumers can be highly effective if placed on the shelf in the retail store. Consequently, informative messages have limited uses but can be effective when placed properly.

Testimonials

The testimonial type of executional framework has been successful for many years, especially in the business-to-business and service sectors. When a customer is presented in a message telling about a positive experience with a product, it is a testimonial. In the business-to-business sector, testimonials from current customers add credibility to the claims being made. In many business buying situations, prospective vendors are asked for references. Testimonials provide references in advance. Further, most buyers believe what others say about a company more than they believe what a company says about itself. Thus, testimonials by someone else offer greater credibility than self-proclamations.

Now Open...
The Original Taste of South India!

"One step into HSB and you're greeted with the aroma of South India. It is a real treat for vegetarians especially Dosa lovers. But hey, wait a minute; it is not about Dosa alone. HSB offers many other excellent lunch and diner items. The Saravanaa meal is a feast and a treat. For people with a sweet tooth, there is a whole variety to choose from. Dining at HSB is not just eating – it is an experience..."
Toronto Vegetarian Association.

Experience the Spice Trail...

A Sumptuous Feast of Vegetarian Cuisine...

Dine In • Take Out • Weekday Buffet

Weekend Buffet • Tandoori Delights • Catering

SARAVANAA BHAVAN

955 West Broadway (At Oak Street) • Vancouver • V5Z 1K3

Timings: 11:30 AM to 3 PM & 5 PM to 10 PM Everyday of the week.

Finest Spices • Authentic Recipes • Menu of Choices

WWW.SARAVANAABHAVAN.CA   TEL: 604.732.7700

Because restaurants rely so heavily on referrals, many use testimonials in their communications

Testimonials also are an effective method for promoting services. Services are intangible; they cannot be seen or touched. Consumers cannot examine services before making decisions. A testimony from a current customer is an effective method of describing the benefits or attributes of the service. This matches the method most consumers use in selecting a service. When choosing a dentist, an attorney, or an automobile repair shop, consumers often ask friends, relatives, or co-workers. A testimonial for a service simulates this type of word-of-mouth recommendation.

One major reason companies choose testimonials is that they enhance company credibility. Endorsers and famous individuals do not always have high levels of credibility, because consumers know they are being paid for their endorsements. In testimonials, everyday people, often actual customers, are the main characters. At other times, they are paid actors who look like everyday consumers.

Authoritative

When using the authoritative executional framework, the marketer is seeking to convince the audience that a given product is superior to other brands. One form is expert authority These ads employ a physician, dentist, engineer, or chemist to state the particular brand's advantages compared to other brands. Firms also can feature less recognized experts, such as automobile mechanics, professional house painters, nurses, and aerobics instructors. The message presents each of these as an expert or authority in a particular field. These experts normally talk about the brand attributes that make the product superior.

Many authoritative messages include some type of scientific or survey evidence. Independent organizations such as the Canadian Medical Association undertake a variety of product studies. Quoting the results gives a message greater credibility. Survey results are less credible. Stating that four out of five dentists recommend a particular toothbrush or toothpaste is less effective, because consumers do not have details about how the survey was conducted or even how many dentists were surveyed (5 or 50). In contrast, when the Canadian Medical Association states that an aspirin a day reduces the risk of a second heart attack, it is highly credible. A company such as Bayer can take advantage of the finding by including the information in the company's marketing communications. The same is true when a magazine such as *Consumer Reports* ranks a particular brand as the best.

Any scientific, independent, unpaid source makes a claim more powerful. For example, the Canadian Heart and Stroke Foundation has developed a relationship with the margarine brand Becel to promote the benefits of the product to heart health. The authoritative voice of he Heart and Stroke Foundation is featured in marketing communications and on the packaging itself, making any health claims more believable to consumers.

Authoritative messages have been widely incorporated into business-to-business sector marketing communications, especially when scientific findings are available to support a company's product claims. Independent test results are likely to have a more profound influence on members of the buying centre, especially if they are actively looking for rational information to help them make decisions.

The authoritative executional framework assumes consumers and business decision makers rely on cognitive processes when making purchase decisions. This means that they will pay attention to a message and carefully think about the information conveyed. The authoritative framework works well in printed media, because the buyers are willing to take the time to read the claim or findings provided in the message.

Authoritative executional frameworks perform especially well in specialty magazines and on specific websites. For example, in a hunting magazine, having an expert hunter discuss the superiority of a particular gun is effective, because readers have an interest in hunting. Brides observe the endorsements of wedding experts in special bridal magazines and bridal websites. Readers notice these specialized messages, and the claims made have greater credibility. The same is true in business-to-business magazines. Trade journals in the business world are similar to specialty magazines in the consumer world.

One of the most critical aspects of using either authoritative or testimonial appeals is the decision to use a specific spokesperson. Although a specific person is not always chosen, as in the Becel example, usually these executional frameworks feature a specific person. In addition, the other executional frameworks discussed here regularly use people as part of the message delivery. The choice of the individual to deliver the message has significant impact on how the audience will decode the message, and must be done carefully. The next section examines issues related to the selection of spokespersons.

SOURCES AND SPOKESPERSONS

Figure 6.4 identifies four types of sources available to marketers. Of the four types listed, *celebrity spokespersons* are perhaps the most noticeable, but their appearance in messages has been declining. According to the research firm Millward Brown, 17 percent of all television ads in 2001 used some type of celebrity endorser. Today, that proportion is around 6 percent.[10]

Companies still use celebrity endorsers because his or her stamp of approval can enhance the product's brand equity. Celebrities also help create emotional bonds with the products. The idea is to transfer the bond that exists between the celebrity and the audience to the product being endorsed. This bond transfer often is more profound for younger consumers. Older consumers are not as likely to be influenced by celebrity endorsements. Still, many advertisers believe they are effective. Figure 6.5 lists the top eight Hollywood celebrities and their recent endorsements.

Agencies also use celebrities to help establish a "personality" for a brand. The trick is to tie the brand's characteristics to those of the spokesperson, such as the late Elizabeth Taylor's love of the finer things in life being attached to her line of scents and perfumes, as well as other products. In developing a brand personality, the brand must already be established. The celebrity merely helps to define the brand more clearly. Using celebrities for new products does not always work as well as for already established brands.

Apart from the traditional paid celebrity endorsement, there are three additional variations of celebrity endorsements: (1) unpaid spokespersons, (2) celebrity voiceovers, and (3) what may be called *dead-person endorsements*.

FIGURE 6.4
Types of Sources and Spokespersons

- Catherine Zeta-Jones, T-Mobile, $20 million
- Angelina Jolie, St. John clothing, $12 million
- Nicole Kidman, Chanel 5 perfume, $12 million
- Jessica Simpson, Guthy-Renker direct response TV, cosmetics, $7.5 million
- Gwyneth Paltrow, Estée Lauder fragrances, $6 million
- Charlize Theron, Dior fragrance, $6 million
- Julia Roberts, Gianfranco Ferré fashion, $5 million
- Brad Pitt, Heineken beer, $4 million

FIGURE 6.5
Top Hollywood Celebrity Endorsers

Source: Based on Gail Schiller, "Top 10 Ad Deals," *Adweek* 47, no. 17 (April 24, 2006), pp. 20–22.

FIGURE 6.6
Top-Earning Dead Celebrities

◆ Kurt Cobain	$50 million	◆ Andy Warhol	$19 million
◆ Elvis Presley	$42 million	◆ Theodor Geisel (Dr. Seuss)	$10 million
◆ Charles M. Schultz	$35 million	◆ Ray Charles	$10 million
◆ John Lennon	$24 million	◆ Marilyn Monroe	$ 8 million
◆ Albert Einstein	$20 million	◆ Johnny Cash	$ 8 million

Source: Based on "Top Earning Dead Celebrities" (October 20, 2006) (**www.forbes.com/2006/10/20/tech-media_06deadcelebs_cx_pf_top-earning-dead-celebrities.htm**).

Unpaid spokespersons are those celebrities who support a charity or cause by appearing in an ad. These types of endorsements are highly credible and can entice significant contributions to a cause. Sarah McLachlan's appearance in ads for the SPCA is a recent example of this type.

Many celebrities also provide voiceovers for television and radio ads without being shown or identified. Listeners often respond to the ads and try to figure out who is reading the copy. This adds interest to the ad but may also serve as a distraction when the individual does not hear the message while trying to identify the speaker. Sometimes celebrities are chosen for voiceovers simply because they have an appropriate voice for the task. Morgan Freeman does voiceovers for VISA, and Donald Sutherland is the voice used in ads for RBC.

A dead-person endorsement occurs when a sponsor uses an image or past video or film featuring an actor or personality who has died. Dead-person endorsements are somewhat controversial but are becoming more common. Bob Marley, Marilyn Monroe, John Wayne, John Lennon, Elvis Presley, and many others have appeared in ads and have even become spokespersons for products after death. Colonel Sanders has become a spokesperson in animation for KFC. Figure 6.6 identifies the top-earning dead celebrities and the amount each of their estates earned in just one year.

Celebrity spokespersons work because of **meaning transfer theory.** This theory suggests that meaning transfer between celebrities and brands occurs in three stages.[11] First, the celebrity is imbued with meaning through his or her role in popular culture. In this stage, the meaning is encoded in the persona of the celebrity. Celebrities are known for many things, ranging from being kind or charitable to fashion-forward to typifying beauty. In the second stage, the celebrity becomes associated with the brand through endorsement in marketing communications. In the third stage, the consumer buys and consumes the product in an effort to capture some of the meaning associated with the celebrity. This theory assumes that purchases are not always made for functional value exclusively. They are also made for cultural or symbolic/social value embedded in the product through celebrity endorsement.

The use of the CEO as the spokesperson or source is another popular tactic. Dave Thomas of Wendy's was possibly the most famous CEO in commercials in the 1990s. Michael Dell has appeared as the spokesperson for Dell. The CEO of General Motors appeared in marketing communications in an effort to bring credibility and personality to the brand as it emerged from bankruptcy in 2009. A highly visible and personable CEO can become a major asset for the firm and its products. Many local companies succeed, in part, because their owners are out front in small-market television commercials. They then begin to take on the status of local celebrities.

Expert sources include physicians, lawyers, accountants, and financial planners. These experts tend not to be famous celebrities or CEOs. Experts provide backing for testimonials, serve as authoritative figures, demonstrate products, and enhance the credibility of informative advertisements. These spokespersons are used in authoritative executional frameworks.

The final category of spokesperson is *typical-person sources*, which are the people who typically deliver messages in the testimonial executional framework. Typical persons are one of two types. The first category consists of paid actors or models who portray or resemble everyday people. The second is actual, typical, everyday people used in communications. Wal-Mart, as already mentioned, features its own store employees in freestanding insert advertisements. Home Hardware also features local store owners in all of its ads. Agencies also create "man-on-the-street" types of messages. For example, PERT shampoo recently prepared ads showing an individual asking people if they would like to have their hair washed. Dr. Scholl's interviews people about foot problems that might be resolved with cushioned shoe inserts.

Real-people sources are becoming more common. One reason for this is the overuse of celebrities. Many experts believe that consumers have become saturated with celebrity endorsers and that the positive impact today is not as strong as it was in the past. One study conducted in Great Britain indicated that 55 percent of the consumers surveyed reported that a famous face was not enough to hold their attention. Celebrities held a greater appeal for the 15- to 24-year-old age bracket. Sixty-two percent of that group stated that a famous person in an ad would get their attention.[12]

Source Characteristics

In evaluating their choices for people to serve as sources for marketing communications messages, marketers consider several characteristics. The effectiveness of a message that utilizes a spokesperson depends on the degree to which the person has one or more of the characteristics. As illustrated in Figure 6.7, the source-selection characteristic of a spokesperson's *credibility* is derived from the composite of attractiveness, similarity, likability, trustworthiness, and expertise.[13] Credibility affects a receiver's acceptance of the spokesperson and message. A credible source is believable. Most sources do not score highly on all four attributes, yet they need to score highly on multiple characteristics to be viewed as credible. One reason for using celebrities is that they are more likely to possess at least an element of all characteristics. A CEO, expert, or typical person probably lacks one or more of them.

Attractiveness has two forms: (1) physical characteristics and (2) personality characteristics. Physical attractiveness is usually an important asset for an endorser. Bijan used Michael Jordan's and Bo Derek's physical attractiveness to promote its line of menswear, perfume, and jewellery. Messages with physically attractive spokespersons fare better than those with

Nigel Mohammed
Manager
Community Services

Good *things* happen *here.*

"At the heart of it all, it's really a question of how we can impact the community.

We listen and we look beyond just profit to see potential other financial institutions wouldn't see. That puts us in a better position to provide our members with the support they need to meet their goals. That means businesses thrive, organizations are sustainable and our members have options. In return, our entire community benefits. Good things really do happen here."

(1-877) 958-8588 or www.assiniboine.mb.ca

Assiniboine
CREDIT UNION

Decision-making for financial services tends to be more rational and highly involved.

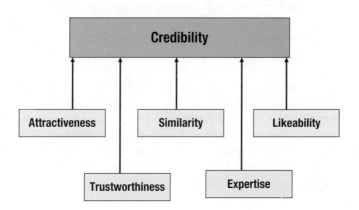

FIGURE 6.7
Characteristics of Effective Spokespersons

Attractiveness is often used as a source characteristic.

less attractive people. This is true for both male and female audiences. At the same time, the attractiveness of the spokesperson's personality is also important to many consumers. This personality component helps viewers form an emotional bond with the spokesperson. If the spokesperson is seen as having a sour personality, even if physically beautiful, consumers are less likely to develop an emotional bond with the individual and the product.

Closely related to attractiveness is the concept of **similarity.** Consumers are more inclined to be influenced by a message delivered by a person who is somehow similar. For example, a "stay at home" mom is more likely to be influenced by an advertisement that starts out with a woman saying, "Since I made the decision to stop working and care for my family full-time…" Similarity allows the viewer to *identify* with the spokesperson in some manner. At times this may involve the fantasy of identifying with a rich person buying a BMW. At other times, **identification** is based on believing the source has similar beliefs, attitudes, preferences, or behaviours or is in the same or a similar situation as the customer.

Closely related to the personality components of attractiveness and similarity is *likeability.* Consumers respond more positively to spokespersons they like. This liking arises from various sources, including situations in which viewers like either the actor or the character played by the actor in a movie. An athlete gains likeability if he or she plays on the consumer's favourite team. Other individuals are likeable because they support the favourite charities of consumers. If consumers do not like a particular spokesperson, they are likely to transfer that dislike to the product the celebrity endorses. This is not an automatic transfer, because consumers recognize that endorsers are paid spokespersons. Still, there is almost always a negative impact on attitudes toward the brand.

A celebrity may be likable or attractive, but he or she may not be viewed as *trustworthy.* Trustworthiness is the degree of confidence or the level of acceptance consumers place in the spokesperson's message. A trustworthy spokesperson helps consumers believe the message. One highly trusted celebrity is Oprah Winfrey. Likeability and trustworthiness are highly related. People who are liked tend to be trusted and people who are disliked tend not to be trusted.

The final characteristic advertisers look for when examining sources is *expertise.* Spokespersons with higher levels of expertise are more believable than sources with low expertise. Richard Petty and Jeff Gordon are seen as experts when automobile products and lubricants are advertised. Often when expertise is desired in an ad, the ad agency opts for the CEO or a trained or educated expert in the field. American Express features Maria Barraza, a small-business owner and designer, to promote its Small Business Services.

In choosing spokespersons, marketers typically must make tradeoffs between these five characteristics. For example, a CEO may have a high degree of expertise on a particular subject. This is valuable because expertise can be persuasive in messages designed to change opinions or attitudes. Spokespersons with high levels of expertise are more capable of persuading an audience than someone with zero or low expertise.[14] However, that same individual may lack some of the other key characteristics (attractiveness, likeability, or trustworthiness). These tradeoffs are discussed in the next section.

Matching Source Types and Characteristics

Celebrities tend to score well in terms of trustworthiness, believability, persuasiveness, and likeability. These virtues increase if the match between the product and celebrity is a logical and proper fit. For example, Phil Mickelson endorsing golf merchandise is a good fit. An athlete endorsing any type of athletic product fits well. Companies can be creative but also use common sense in making quality matches. For instance, the match of boxer George Foreman to his Lean Mean Grilling Machine is a great success.[15]

Several dangers exist in using celebrities. The first is negative publicity about the celebrity caused by inappropriate conduct. For example, Michael Vick's arrest and conviction for dog fighting created considerable negative press. Britney Spears' battles with depression and the courts have created a superstar that brands do not want to touch. Then there was Lindsay Lohan's drunk driving arrests and subsequent jail stint. Still, in other cases, like the highly lucrative endorsement of Tiger Woods for Nike, the effects of indiscretions in the personal lives of celebrities don't always lead to trouble. Although marketers like celebrity endorsers because of the potential they have for developing an attraction to their brands, they have to weigh the positive benefits against the potential risks.[16]

The potential for negative publicity has led some marketers to use deceased celebrities. Companies have concluded that there is no need to risk bringing embarrassment or injury to themselves or the brand. It is also a reason that more ads use cartoon characters. Practically everyone likes cartoons, and they don't get caught with drugs.

The second danger of using celebrities is that their endorsement of too many products can tarnish their credibility. Consumers know celebrities are paid, which detracts from their believability. If the celebrity endorses a number of products, consumer evaluations of that person's credibility decline further. Some advertising research indicates that when a celebrity endorses multiple products, it tends to reduce his or her credibility and likeability as well as consumers' attitudes toward the ad.[17]

As a result, careful consideration must be given to the choice of a celebrity. The individual cannot simply be famous. The person should possess as many of the characteristics as possible, match the good or service being advertised, not be "spread too thin" or overexposed, and promote a positive image that can be transferred to the good, service, or company.

A *CEO* or other prominent corporate official may or may not possess the characteristics of attractiveness and likeability. CEOs should, however, appear to be trustworthy, have expertise, and maintain a degree of credibility. A CEO is not a professional actor or model. It might be difficult for the CEO to come across well in marketing communications. Many companies train their top executives in media tactics so they can be more polished when engaged in media interviews or other PR efforts on behalf of the firm.

Companies must be aware of the trustworthiness issue. For example, many times the owner of a local auto dealership represents it as the spokesperson. The primary problem is that many consumers view used-car salespeople as untrustworthy. Other local business owners may be highly trustworthy, such as restaurant owners, physicians, eye care professionals, and so forth.

Source: House of Bijan, Rodeo Drive, Beverly Hills.

Michael Jordan is a rare celebrity who can endorse multiple products and maintain a high level of credibility.

Marketers should be careful about asking a CEO or business owner to serve as a source. They first must be convinced that the individual has enough key characteristics to promote the product and gain the consumer's interest and trust.

Experts, first and foremost, of course, should embody a high degree of expertise. The marketer should also seek out an expert who is attractive, likable, and trustworthy. Experts are helpful in promoting health-care products and other high-involvement types of products. Recent research has indicated that experts are more believable than celebrities when it comes to high-technology products, and, as a result, the use of an expert will reduce consumers' level of perceived risk in purchasing the product.[18] These types of endorsers can be effective when consumers or businesses perceive there are higher levels of risk involved in making purchases. Therefore, when selecting an expert spokesperson, agencies should be certain that the person has valid credentials and will be able to clearly explain a product's benefits. Doing so will reduce the level of perceived risk.

Critical Thinking Exercise

Find a magazine that is aimed at a business audience, such as a trade journal, and one magazine with a consumer audience. Do you see a difference in the use of spokespersons in the ads? Is there a difference in the type of executional frameworks used? What do you think accounts for either the differences or lack of differences?

Many ads use models that are actually paid actors designed to look like "ordinary" people.

Source: © Digital Vision/Thinkstock.

Typical-person messages are sometimes difficult to prepare, especially when they use real persons and not paid actors. First, typical-person sources do not have the name recognition of celebrities. Consequently, marketers often use multiple sources within one message to build credibility. Increasing the number of sources in the message makes it more effective. Hearing three people talk about a good dentist is more believable than hearing only one person. By using multiple sources, viewers are motivated to pay attention to the message and to process its arguments.[19]

Real-person messages are a double-edged sword. On the one hand, trustworthiness, similarity, and credibility rise when the source is bald, overweight, or has some other characteristic that would lead them to be judged as less physically attractive by many people. This can be especially valuable when the bald person promotes a hair replacement program or the overweight source talks about a diet program. On the other hand, attractiveness and likeability may be lower.

Using customers in media such as television can be difficult, because they will flub lines and look less natural on the screen. These difficulties with actual customers and employees lead many agencies to turn to professional models and actors to portray ordinary people. Professional actors make filming and photographing much easier. Also, the agency is in the position to choose a likable, but plain, person. The desired effects (trustworthiness, similarity, and credibility) are often easier to create using professional actors and models.

In general, the agency should seek to be certain that the source or spokesperson has the major characteristics

		Ability to Process Information	
		High	Low
Motivation to Process Information	High	Expert/Typical Person	Expert
	Low	Typical Person	Celebrity

Source: Adapted from Gerard J. Tellis (2004), *Effective Advertising: Understanding When, How and Why Advertising Works*, Sage. Thousand Oaks.

FIGURE 6.8
A Model to Determine Effective Spokespersons

the message needs. When the appeal is humour, likeability is very important. In a rational or informational message, expertise and credibility are crucial, especially in business-to-business contexts. In each case, the goal is to try to include as many of the characteristics as possible when retaining a spokesperson.

One approach to choosing spokespersons is to return to the elaboration likelihood model for an understanding of how an audience will perceive marketing communications. Using the axes of motivation and ability to process, Figure 6.8 highlights the opportunities for different types of spokespersons.

Along the top row of Figure 6.8, where products are characterized as higher involvement (due to the higher motivation to process information), let's assume that Lenovo is looking to create marketing communications for its computers and is unsure whether or not spokespersons are appropriate, and, if so, which type they should use. In the top left quadrant, the audience may be highly familiar with computers and have a high ability and motivation to process the message. In this case, the use of celebrity endorsements is probably inappropriate, since the audience will not be swayed by the paid opinion of an endorser. The use of spokespersons in this case would be limited, at best, to the use of experts or typical-person endorsers who would deliver product information and specifications. In the case of the upper right quadrant, the use of an expert endorser would make sense. In this case, the customer may be new to computers and anxious to make a good decision. The recommendation of an expert, such as a computer science professor, would be very influential.

Along the bottom row of Figure 6.8, let's assume the product is a household floor cleaning product where the motivation to process information may be low. If the ability to process information is high, say, for a homemaker who has considerable experience with the product category, typical-person endorsers may be appropriate, perhaps in a demonstration or slice-of-life execution. In the bottom left quadrant, where the audience has low motivation and ability, celebrity endorsers are worth consideration due to the peripheral processing of the information.

CONSISTENCY

One of the most important elements of effective marketing communications is consistency. Consistency in marketing communications can be considered in three ways. First, communications should be repeated over time, they should also contain consistent appeals and frameworks, and they should be used in multiple marketing communications vehicles across that time.

The first element—consistency over time—takes into account the fact that audiences often do not pay attention to marketing communications. This makes the length or duration of a campaign important. Using

MasterCard has used the same core idea behind its marketing communications for years.

darkness: priceless

For blinds, ibuprofen and everything you need New Year's Day, there's MasterCard® Accepted coast to coast. *MasterCard*

mastercard.ca

the same message over time helps embed the message in the consumer's long-term memory. The ad should be changed before it becomes stale and viewers become bored with it; however, changing ads too frequently impedes retention. Repeating a message can increase brand and message recall. Repetition is especially effective in increasing recall if no competitor ads are present. When competitor messages are present, repetition does not help the competitive ad interference problem and does not stimulate greater recall.

An example of a highly successful campaign is the MasterCard campaign noted previously. It has used the same general appeal and tactics for over a decade: "There are some things money can't buy. For everything else, there's MasterCard."

However, mere repetition of a message does not always work. The next element of consistency concerns the consistent use of appeals over a period of time. Visual consistency is especially important because consumers, whether individual consumers or members of a business buying centre, spend very little time viewing or listening to marketing communications. In most cases, it is just a casual glance at a print advertisement or a cursory glimpse at a television ad. Visual consistency causes the audience to move the message from short-term to long-term memory. Consistently used logos and other long-standing images help fix the brand or company in the consumer's mind. For example, people remember Frosted Flakes because of the visually consistent use of Tony the Tiger. They know Green Giant products by the cartoon spokesperson. Logos such as the Nike swoosh and the Prudential Rock emblem are well established in the minds of many consumers.

Another common element used in marketing communications is taglines. Visual consistency combined with consistent taglines can be a powerful approach. The message may change, but either the visual imagery or the tagline remains the same. For example, ING Direct has included the "Save Your Money" line in its marketing communications for over 15 years. Taglines help consumers tie the message into current knowledge structure nodes that already exist in their minds. Figure 6.9 contains some of the more common taglines. See how many you can identify.

The MasterCard campaign has used a number of visual and verbal cues consistently across the life of the campaign. The tagline is the most obviously recognized aspect of the campaign, but the voice used in the television ads has also been consistent. So has the use of a small number of related items that cost money. There is never a laundry list, always just three or four. The result is that the audience becomes comfortable and familiar with the message more easily over time.

The third way marketers use consistency uses the principles present in **variability theory**.[20] The theory suggests that variable encoding occurs when a consumer sees the same message in different environments over time. These varied environments increase recall and effectiveness by encoding the message into the brain through various methods.

The MasterCard message can be found across a number of advertising media as well as direct mail, the company website, and various co-branding efforts for its cards. A message placed in more than one medium also reduces competing ad interference. Consumers seeing a message in multiple media are more likely to recall the ad than if it is always seen in only one medium. Varying the context of the message increases recall and is an effective method for overcoming competitive interference.[21]

FIGURE 6.9
Which Taglines Can You Identify?

1. A diamond is forever.	6. Always fresh.
2. Don't leave home without it.	7. The ultimate driving machine.
3. Banking can be this comfortable.	8. What can Brown do for you?
4. Just do it.	9. You deserve a break today.
5. Look, mom, no cavities.	10. For days like today.

Answers: DeBeers, Amex, TD Canada Trust, Nike, Crest, Tim Hortons, BMW, UPS, McDonald's, Canadian Tire.

ON THE JOB

The Structure of a Print Advertisement

Most people have heard the old line that print ads should move the eye from the top right of the page to the bottom left of the page. Maybe so. But high-profile examples such as the Chivas campaign cited earlier in this chapter suggest that the deployment of such typical rules stifles some of the best ideas from creative teams. Still, there are some things that are fairly consistent in print advertising and important to know. The majority of ads prepared for publication or broadcast tend to contain five elements. They are:

- The promise of a benefit (the headline)
- The spelling out of the promise (a subheadline)
- Amplification
- Proof of the claim
- Action to take

In print advertising, the *headline* is crucial. A typical reader is going to look at the artwork, figure, or illustration first. Next, the reader scans the headline. To keep the potential customer interested means finding some method (rational, emotional, humour, etc.) that moves the reader to the rest of the copy. Typical features of a headline are that the words are short, simple, and limited (less than 12); are inviting or interest-provoking; are action-oriented; and supply enough information to let the buyer know about the product while appealing most directly to the target audience.

A headline should not be mistaken for a tagline. The tagline is a key phrase that is usually placed near the end of an advertisement's copy. The *subheadline*, or

spelling out of the promise, accompanies the headline. In some instances, the headline is powerful enough by itself, so this step is skipped. A subheadline is similar to a second headline in a newspaper story. It delivers additional information and leads the reader to the copy.

The *amplification* is the text or body copy of the advertisement. The wording should be concise. The *unique selling proposition* or the *major selling idea* is portrayed in the copy. The company can be factual, imaginative, or emotional in its approach. Factual copy often is part of comparison advertising, where one product or company is directly contrasted with another. Amplification copy is especially important in business-to-business advertisements, in which more complex features of a product must be explained or summarized.

Proof of the claim can be generated from many sources. These include seals of approval (e.g., Good Housekeeping), guarantees (money back if not fully satisfied), trial offers and samples, warranties, demonstrations, and testimonials. A company with strong brand equity is in a better position to make a claim because of the brand's power.

Finally, the consumer must be made aware of the *action to take.* "Buy now," "stop by for a free sample," and "tell your friends" are statements declaring the action the consumer should take. Less direct actions might be to "give us a try" or "stop by for a test drive." The action should mirror the stage in the hierarchy of effects model: awareness, knowledge, liking, preference, conviction, or purchase.

CREATING MARKETING COMMUNICATIONS

For both the account and creative teams, the delivery of the creative brief is just the tip of the iceberg when it comes to the production of marketing communications. The brief kicks off the process that will examine the different appeals that can be used, and the creative team will weigh their options with various tactics and executional frameworks. The first step, once the creative team has developed the idea for the marketing communications campaign, is an internal meeting at the marketing communications agency between the creative and account teams. (In the case of a company with an internal marketing agency function, this meeting would be between the people developing the campaign creative and the brand manager.)

At this first meeting, which can take place anywhere from a couple of days to several weeks after the creative briefing, the account team will usually provide feedback on the campaign. This feedback can include evaluations of the creative concerning the appropriateness of a certain appeal, executional framework, or other element of the creative. This feedback is important because the account team is the voice of the client within the agency. If the account team knows the client will not respond positively to an aspect of the creative, it is important to make this change internally before moving forward. This may result in several meetings and internal creative presentations within the agency.

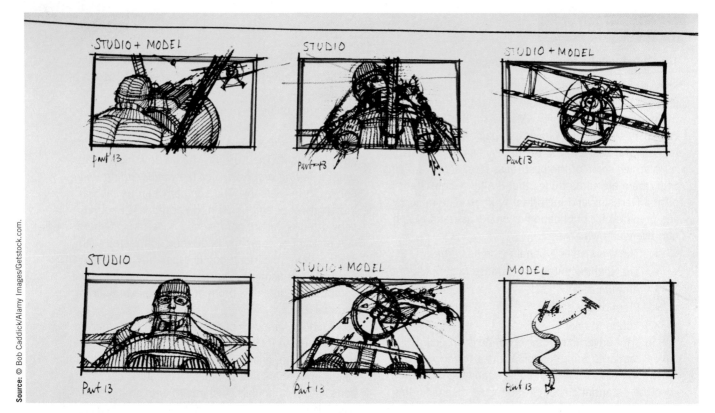

Storyboards are used to illustrate the idea for marketing communications before they are actually created.

An important aspect to this internal process is that both the creative and account team assume "ownership" of the creative. When moving forward to present the work to clients, account people need to be comfortable with the creative so they can properly support the creative team.

The next step is a meeting between the agency and client. Usually this meeting includes both the account and creative teams, as well as several people from the client organization. The meeting involves the presentation of the work itself, along with a discussion of the rationale for the work. For example, if a spokesperson is to be used, details of that person are discussed along with an explanation as to why the person will help the message succeed. At this stage, the creative may only be crude mock-ups or storyboards to give an impression of what the final communications will look like. So, for example, although the campaign may require original photography, the creative team will use stock photos in place of the actual photography to create an impression.

Quite often, the client will request that research be undertaken to test the creative with various audiences. Most often, if research is to be done at this stage, it is done through a focus group. Creative teams are notorious for being suspicious of focus groups evaluating marketing communications, and for good reason. The creative process involves an understanding of the audience and the context in which marketing communications occurs, and a certain degree of intuition. A poorly executed focus group can result in suggestions for the communications that are offered by consumers who are not reacting as they would when they see the message in the course of their daily lives, but as people who are expected to be experts in marketing communications. Consumers often don't consciously know how marketing communications affects them, so when they are given a chance to design a message, their ideas must be tempered with a degree of skepticism. However, focus groups can be an effective way to ensure that the message doesn't anger or otherwise give people the wrong impression.

The process of presentation and feedback between agency and client, even without research, can take up to several weeks. Assuming the approval is given to create the campaign, the next step depends to some extent on which elements of the marketing communications mix will be included in the campaign. For example, if the campaign is

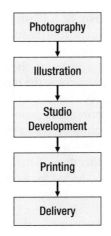

FIGURE 6.10
The Print-Based Production Process

to include television advertising, there will be activity specific to that media. Next we outline two main categories of marketing communications—print-based and broadcast-based—and illustrate the production process for each.

Print-Based Marketing Communications Production

Print-based communications include the majority of elements in a marketing communications campaign. For example, they include traditional print advertising for newspapers and magazines, but also the many other elements of a campaign, such as direct mail; many sales promotion elements, such as flyers and coupons; out-of-home advertising, such as billboards and bus shelters; and even the majority of marketing communications done online, since the two-dimensional presentation on screen most closely resembles the print format.

First, the copy and layout specifics are finalized. These may be already finalized in the client presentation, but usually—especially for elements that are copy-intensive, such as direct mail—the writing is only done once the overall campaign is approved. This finalization process can take only a few days for simple executions, or many days or weeks for complex campaigns. Based on this copy and layout, a number of subsequent activities occur, as depicted in Figure 6.10.

Photography. This includes the selection of any necessary models, props, locations, and, of course, the hiring of a specific professional photographer. In some cases, photo shoots for a single ad can last all day and easily cost in the thousands of dollars. The preparation for the shoot, including photographer selection, can take up to three or four weeks. This is especially true where photography requires significant preparation, as is the case with photos of food. In rare occasions, or when budgets are limited, stock photos are sometimes used to replace original photography. Although offering far less flexibility, stock photos can be mush less costly, costing as little as a few hundred dollars for a national print campaign.

Illustrations. Communications can also include illustrations, either as a main feature of a message or as one small element of a message. The process for illustration mirrors that of photography. Once the specifics of the illustration are defined by the art director, an illustrator is chosen (usually on the basis of his or her particular style, selected to match the intended style and tone of the overall message). Simple illustrations can be done in a matter of one or two days, but more complex illustrations can take weeks.

Studio Development. Once the copy is written and any photos or illustrations are chosen, the work then proceeds to the studio within the agency. The studio process is where the actual electronic files for the messages are created. This process can easily take days for complex projects such as direct mail packages. The studio chooses among a myriad of typefaces for fonts, and arranges spacing and a host of other technical details behind the scenes. An important aspect of the studio work is sizing and file creation dictated by the message delivery media. So, for example, if a message will run in newspapers, the ad may need to be created in multiple sizes since each newspaper has its own unique dimensions (i.e., a full page in the *Toronto Star* is not the same size as a full page in the *Saskatoon Star Phoenix*). In the case of online material, the coding

Organizations with small budgets often find creative ideas and layouts to save on production and studio costs.

may be a Flash animation, or another specific platform that requires coding of elements into one electronic format.

Printing. If the final product is to be printed in hard copy, the next stage is the actual printing itself. For media such as newspaper and magazines, this printing is done by the publisher. But in the case of campaigns like direct mail or coupons, the agency hires a printer. Printing timelines depend on the specifics of the job, but at least a week should be budgeted for a relatively small print job (in terms of either complexity or the number of copies).

Delivery. Once the materials are printed, the final step in the process is delivery to the intended audience. Once again, the details and timelines for this process vary, depending on the type of job. In the case of direct mail packages, the printed material goes to a letter shop. There, the various elements are arranged and inserted into the final package you receive in the mail. In the case of coupons, delivery could be to various retailers or other outlets. In the case of brochures they might be delivered to salespeople in offices across the country, who will then use them as part of their sales presentations. A typical timeframe for material delivery is anywhere between one to two weeks.

Throughout each of the steps involved, the account team is responsible to ensure those involved in the process have the resources they need, understand the timelines, and stay within the prescribed budget for the campaign. In some cases, such as photography, the account team plays a secondary role to the creative team. In others, the account teams works directly with someone who manages the studio or outside vendors, such as printers. In still other cases, such as delivery, the account team may have direct responsibility for this final step.

As can been seen from the above, the process of the creative brief is only the beginning. The entire process, from development of the creative brief to the final delivery of printed material for use in a marketing communications campaign, can take anywhere from around one month to over five months. The broadcast-based production process, described next, can take even longer.

Critical Thinking Exercise

The ad for the marathon presented in this section provides a number of benefits to the marketer. It saves on costs since only photography is necessary, and it saves on studio time since the layout is simple. It also adds flexibility, since the company can create new messages for the campaign very quickly. So what are the downsides to using this approach to creative execution? Does the marketer give anything up when it gains these advantages?

Broadcast-Based Marketing Communications Production

Broadcast-based elements of a campaign include television, radio, video, or audio to be used in online media, or other elements, such as DVDs or video to be sent to customers or developed as a means of sales support. Again, the finalization of the elements, such as the script, is done first, which can take several weeks from the point of client approval of the campaign. There are three main stages in the production process as outlined below and depicted in Figure 6.11.

```
┌─────────────────┐
│  Pre-production │
└─────────────────┘
         │
         ▼
┌─────────────────┐
│   Production    │
└─────────────────┘
         │
         ▼
┌─────────────────┐
│ Post-Production │
└─────────────────┘
```

FIGURE 6.11
The Broadcast-Based Production Process

Pre-Production. This phase includes a number of activities similar to the photography stage for print-based marketing communication. But instead of issues related to photography, the necessary decisions need to be made for either audio or video production. For audio production, which can include radio advertisements, voiceovers for videos, or any message delivered orally, such as the on-hold message people hear when they call a phone line, the decisions are simpler. The main decision concerns the selection of the talent—the person whose voice will be used. A recording studio is also arranged. This process can be done quickly, often in a matter of a few days. The creative often has a specific person in mind when they create the copy for the audio script. For many audio messages, music is an integral component. In the case of existing music, rights can be purchased to use the music in the desired medium. Or, if original music is needed, a composer is hired to record the music for the production. Samples are given to determine the right "feel" for the music.

For video production, one of the first tasks is to hire a director. Directors play the same role as they do in the movie business; they help translate the idea from the script and the creative team into reality, and are involved in every aspect of production, including the planning. Other steps include the casting, development of any props, and location scouting. For some video production, the planning can be significant. Imagine the planning involved for television advertising for a car commercial where in addition to the normal planning issues at stake, there are also stunt drivers and perhaps weeks of practice. Overall, even without special considerations like stunts, the preparation for video production can take anywhere from a few weeks to several months.

Production. This stage is the actual recording of the script. For audio that includes voice, the event usually lasts a matter of hours in a recording studio. The talent will say the lines, usually several dozen times, until everyone agrees that the right tone and quality has been reached. This can include everything from small voice inflections to timing the recording so it fits a time constraint, such as a 30-second radio ad. It also includes any necessary sound effects. For music production, the recording typically happens with the composer over a period of days or weeks, and the creative and account teams hear the music once it is completed.

For video production, the process is very much like a Hollywood production. The recording takes place on either a studio set or a location, and usually takes one or two days. This length of time is needed to create a simple 30-second advertisement because there are always multiple takes, and takes from different camera angles. Sometimes things don't go as planned, especially when working with animals or small children, or in outdoor shoots, where issues like the weather can postpone production. Even things like an airplane passing overhead can stop a shoot, and force a new take. Because of the high cost of arranging elements necessary for the shoot—including the director, lighting and electrical technicians, talent, props, and the like—it is important that everyone involved be on the set to approve the takes as they happen. This means many account teams and clients sit idle for hours as the teams prepare each scene and take in the production.

Many car commercials take months to prepare.

Source: © iStockphoto/Thinkstock.

Post-Production. During this process, all of the elements come together to form the final product. In the case of audio production, this may be as simple as creating a final sound mix and recording in a format that can be played back. For example, in the case of a radio ad, a digital file is created. In the case of phone on-hold messages, a physical tape may be created. The recordings are then shipped to wherever they will be used to ultimately deliver the message to an audience. In the case of radio advertising, this could mean sending files to any number of radio stations across the country. If the audio production is to be used as part of a video production (such as a voiceover), the digital file is sent to an editing studio where it is combined with the other video elements.

For video post-production, the process is more time consuming and costly. The first significant function in post-production is the edit. This is the process whereby all the video that was shot during the production is cut down to form a video of whatever length is needed. In the case of television advertising, the usual formats are either 30 or 60 seconds. In the case of other formats, such as online video, time may not be a restriction, but an editor is still required to take footage from several different scenes, takes, and angles, and create one cohesive story. From here, the sound is mixed to ensure that any voices are at the right levels with any other sound effects or music. Again, like in audio production, the material is then shipped to where it will be required to deliver the message to the ultimate audience, such as television broadcasters, website managers, or a sales force that will use the video as part of their sales presentations. The entire post-production process usually takes at least two weeks to complete, but it can take much longer.

As with print-based production, the broadcast production process is complicated and lengthy. For many video productions, it is also quite costly. Imagine the costs for a location shoot in Mexico, including hiring and transporting talent, directors, crew, an agency staff; hiring equipment for the shoot; followed by editing, original music, and voiceovers. It is not uncommon for a 30-second television ad to cost six figures to produce.

COMMUNICATING ACROSS CULTURES

Many common themes and messages translate well across cultures. The major challenge is to make sure that the message strategy and form of executional framework match the tendencies and preferences in a region. For example, some cultures tend to be more rational in decision-making processes, whereas others favour more emotional approaches. This may, in turn, affect the selection of a message tactic in a given nation.

Comparison ads are less common in other countries. This is due to both social and cultural differences as well as legal restrictions. It is critical to be aware of these issues. For example, in many European countries comparative advertising is illegal. In Japan, it is not illegal, but it runs against the society's cultural preferences. In Brazil, the advertising industry is so powerful that any attempt to create a comparative advertisement has been challenged and stopped. Often, international consumers not only dislike the advertisements, but often transfer that dislike to the company sponsoring the ad.[22]

Choices of message strategies will affect selections of executional frameworks. Once again, someone familiar with the tendencies of a given country should be consulted before the creative begins work. A cultural assimilator who is familiar with advertising practices becomes invaluable.

The slice-of-life executional framework has become popular in Japan in recent years. The slice-of-life style is suited to Japan's soft-sell approach to marketing. A more hard-sell attitude is often found in the United States and, to a lesser extent, here in Canada. Japanese marketing communications tend to be more indirect, and the slice-of-life approach allows advertisers to present a product in a typical everyday situation. Benefits can be presented in a positive light without making brazen or harsh claims and without directly disparaging the competition.[23]

Other patterns and changes in preferred forms of executions can be discovered by watching local media and reading about trends in magazines and trade journals in the country involved. While maintaining an overall message and idea, the advertiser must adjust to social customs present in a region.

IMC IN PRACTICE

"Apart from helping us deliver our brand message strategically, the use of nature in our marketing communications is a wonderfully efficient tactic." Whereas some Hollywood actors talk of the horrors of working with animals on set, for TELUS the use of animals as the centrepiece of any piece of marketing communications carries many benefits. "For one thing, we don't have the usual talent costs that are associated with the use of human actors in marketing communications. Apart from the studio costs there are additional repeated fees that have to be paid if we want to use those human actors in the future."

Using animals saves on talent costs for TELUS.

Lara Johnson explains how testing helps ensure a link between the "critter" and the message being delivered. "When we launched the new Optik™ TV and High Speed powered by the TELUS Fibre Optic Network, we used a lion cub. That's in part because in testing, when we asked for words people associated with various animals, the lion cub came out as a great fit with the services. Strong, powerful, leader, revolutionary. These are things that relate to how we wanted to position the new service to the market."

Another benefit is that, over time, the communications remain contemporary. "Our imagery can be used for a number of years because there is effectively no expiry date on it. We don't have issues with fashion trends or anything like that because the animals stay the same year after year. And, of course, the universe has literally thousands of species that have yet to star in our marketing communications, so in theory we have content to extend the campaign well into the next centuries." Very few brands can say anything close to this about their marketing communications.

"One other thing that a lot of people don't realize is that our television advertising does not generally have voiceovers. The music always helps to deliver "the message." But it does so in a subtle way. So instead of saying 'here's a great gift for Christmas' our advertising might use the "I want a Hippopotamus for Christmas" song and people get the same message. But the message is delivered in a way that entertains the audience, and one that creates a more emotional connection than a simple retail ad telling people to give TELUS products as gifts."

For Lara, the beauty of the TELUS campaigns is the simplicity that comes through the use of metaphors. "The cover of one memorable direct mail piece had a monkey sitting in a pile of bananas with a couple of bananas flying through the air heading his way. The monkey was clearly overwhelmed by the experience. The campaign was for Home Phone calling features that helped customers manage their in-coming calls, services such as Call Display and Voice Mail. It was a brilliant metaphor for how people sometimes feel when keeping track of so many things in their lives. The metaphors used in our messages transcend almost everything—gender, age, race, education level, you name it. Metaphor is perhaps the most basic way to communicate a message."

Web hosting that grows with you

⌁TELUS·
the future is friendly·

Clean design and the use of animals means the ads stay contemporary over years and even decades.

Source: Used with permission of Kate Baillie, TELUS Communications.

For help developing your IMC Plan, go to **www.pearsoncanada.ca/clow**.

SUMMARY

Three types of message tactics are present in marketing communications. Cognitive tactics emphasize rational and logical arguments to compel consumers to make purchases. Affective tactics are oriented toward buyer emotions and feelings. Conative tactics are linked to more direct responses, behaviours, and actions. These tactics should be integrated with various types of appeals through the marketing communications campaign elements.

Executional frameworks tell the story in the message. Animation has become more sophisticated and provides many new creative approaches in the design of messages. The slice-of-life approach and dramatizations are problem-solving types of frameworks, leading the consumer to something better by using the product. Testimonials are rendered by individuals who have realized the benefits of a product. An authoritative expert can build consumer confidence in a product or company. Demonstrations show how products can be used. A fantasy takes people away from the real world to a make-believe place. This makes the product more exotic and desirable. Informative messages render basic information about the product. Each execution can be used effectively to persuade consumers and business-to-business buyers to consider a company's offerings.

Celebrities, CEOs, experts, and typical persons can be chosen to be "out front" in the message. Each has advantages and disadvantages. The marketing team selects sources or spokespersons based on the individual's attractiveness, similarity, likeability, trustworthiness, expertise, or credibility. The more of these characteristics that are present, the stronger the spokesperson. Most spokespersons have at least one weak category of the five and should be chosen based on a combination of factors related to both the product and the audience.

Consistency in marketing communications helps ensure success. Consistency is achieved through three means. The first is simply sticking with a message over a period of time. Many effects of marketing communications occur through simple repetition. But consistency is enhanced by ensuring that over time the message is presented with as many consistent elements as possible, including taglines, colours, or executional frameworks. The third aspect of consistency refers to consistency of the message through various marketing communications elements, including such things as advertising in different media, sales promotions, and direct marketing.

The production of both print- and broadcast-based messages is complex and requires a considerable amount of time and management. The print-based production process can include photography, illustration, studio development, printing, and delivery. The broadcast-based production process includes three stages: pre-production, production, and post-production. In either case, the production process can mean that several months pass between the creative brief and the presentation of a message to a target audience.

KEY TERMS

affective message tactics   Messages designed to evoke feelings and emotions and match them with the good, service, or company.

cognitive message tactics   The presentation of rational arguments or pieces of information to consumers.

comparative messages   The direct or indirect comparison of a good or service to the competition.

conative message tactics   Messages designed to stimulate actual purchase or that arise during usage of the product.

executional framework   The manner in which an ad appeal is presented.

generic messages   Direct promotions of product attributes or benefits without any claim of superiority.

hyperbole   Making an untestable claim based upon some attribute or benefit.

identification   Occurs when the receiver is able, in some manner, to identify with the source, either through a fantasy; or by similar beliefs, attitudes, preferences, behaviours; or by being in the same or a similar situation.

meaning transfer theory   The process of transferring a persona of a celebrity in pop culture to the brand that is endorsed by that celebrity.

preemptive messages   Claims of superiority based on a specific attribute or benefit of a product that preempt the competition from making the same claim.

similarity   Consumers are more inclined to be influenced by a message delivered by a person who is somehow similar.

unique selling proposition (USP)   An explicit, testable claim of uniqueness or superiority that can be supported or substantiated in some manner.

REVIEW QUESTIONS

1. Name the three types of message tactics that are used to generate marketing communications.

2. What types of products or services best match cognitive message tactics? List the five types of cognitive tactics.

3. When will an affective message tactic be most effective? Give an example of one.

4. What is the primary goal of a conative message tactic?

5. How is an executional framework different from a message appeal? How are they related?

6. How are slice-of-life and dramatization executional frameworks similar? How are they different?

7. How are authoritative and informational executional frameworks similar? How are they different?

8. What types of testimonials can advertisers use? Give an example of each.

9. What kinds of products or services are best suited to fantasy-based executional frameworks? What products or services are poor candidates for fantasies?

10. Identify the four main types of sources or spokespersons. What are the advantages and disadvantages of each?

11. List the five key criteria used when selecting a spokesperson.

12. What are the three aspects of consistency in marketing communications?

13. What are the five steps in the print-based production process?

14. What are the three steps in the broadcast-based production process?

INTEGRATED LEARNING EXERCISES

1. If you were the VP of Marketing at the following organizations, would you use a celebrity spokesperson? What value would the celebrity spokesperson bring to the brand? In each case, develop a short list of three celebrities (living or dead) whom you would approach to be your spokesperson. Why did you choose the ones you did?

   - Tim Hortons
   - Canadian Tire
   - Scotiabank
   - Rona
   - Roots
   - Canadian Cancer Society

2. Studies involving comparative advertisements and non-comparative ads produced the following findings. Discuss why you think each statement is true. Try to think of comparative ads you have seen that substantiate these claims.

   a. Message awareness was higher for comparative ads than for noncomparative ads if the brands were already established brands.

   b. Brand recall was higher for comparative ads than for noncomparative ads.

   c. Comparative ads were viewed as less believable than noncomparative ads.

   d. Attitudes toward comparative ads were more negative than those toward noncomparative ads.

3. In Canada, many of the iconic ads that run every year during the Super Bowl are blocked by Canadian broadcasters who show Canadian ads instead. But there is good news! Current as well as past Super Bowl ads are available at **www.superbowl-ads.com**. Access the site and compare Super Bowl ads for the past several years. What types of executional frameworks are most popular? Who and what types of endorsers were used? Compare and contrast these three elements of ads.

4. Most marketing communications agencies provide examples of their work on company websites. The goal is to display the agency's creative abilities to potential clients. Using a search engine, locate three different Canadian agencies. Locate samples of their work. Compare the work produced by these three agencies in terms of message appeals, executions, and spokespersons. What similarities do you see? What differences do you see? Which agency, in your opinion, is the most creative? Why?

5. A surfing school in Tofino, British Columbia, wants to develop a print ad highlighting surfing lessons as an activity over the school breaks in the winter. The ad will be placed in campus newspaper across the country. The target market will be postsecondary students. Discuss the merits of each of the following approaches. In your opinion, which one would be the best? Why? Develop a print ad for the one you think is best suited to the situation.

   a. Hyperbole cognitive message tactic, humour appeal, and demonstration execution

   b. Affective message tactic, emotional appeal, and slice-of-life execution

   c. Conative message tactic, scarcity appeal, and informative execution

   d. Affective message tactic, sex appeal, and fantasy execution

   e. Comparative message tactic, fear appeal, and a testimonial execution

STUDENT PROJECT

Creative Corner

It is time to try your creativity with a television advertisement. Using your cell phone or a borrowed camcorder, develop a 30-second television spot for one of the following brands, using the suggested appeal. Be sure to develop a means–end chain prior to creating the advertisement.

a. Wilson tennis racket, humour appeal
b. Chapman's ice cream, emotional appeal
c. Jamieson vitamins, fear appeal
d. Callaway golf clubs, rational appeal
e. This textbook, emotional or rational appeal

→ ETHICS IN ACTION

Children, especially those under the age of eight, are highly susceptible to marketing communications because they lack the ability to distinguish a message designed to persuade them from a message designed to inform them. Although Canada has a number of laws to protect children from advertisers who seek to promote products through media such as television and out-of-home, the Internet is largely an unregulated free-for-all. Using animation as the primary executional framework, many companies offer websites with games and other activities for children. For example, Pop Tarts offers a number of games and activities for children who sign up through their website (**www.poptarts.com**), listed under the "for kids" section. The products are included in every game, sometimes overtly. On top of this, links to product promotion are easily accessible from the games.

1. Take the position that this practice is unethical. Write a two-page memo outlining three arguments against the practice, *and* three points to counter your arguments that you would expect from those who would argue the practice is not unethical.

2. If you were a regulator concerned that this practice circumvents Canadian laws protecting children from marketing communications, how would you stop the practice? If you couldn't stop it, what steps would you take to ensure that the potential for harmful effects is minimized. Write a one-page memo to your MP outlining your ideas. ●

CASE STUDY | Can You Get Emotional about Plumbing?

The story of Delta Faucets is a classic story of opportunity. In the 1920s, an immigrant named Alex Manoogian founded Masco Company, which provided auto parts. Twenty-five years later, Manoogian was contacted by an inventor who had created the first washerless faucet. Although it was not related to his current business, Manoogian saw the potential and refined the item, which was first sold out of the trunks of salesmen's cars, as the first Delta Faucet. The name was chosen because a key part of the product resembled the shape of the Greek letter delta.

The Delta Faucet Company became a separate part of the original Masco Company and relocated. Over the next two decades, it expanded quickly to an entire line of products. Currently, Delta Faucet Company is a multinational firm with locations in Canada, the United States, and China. It sells over 1 million faucets per month. The overall Masco Company now sells door hardware and locks, cabinets, and glass products in addition to faucets.

The faucet line of Masco has expanded to include a number of brands. Delta is the "flagship" brand and is positioned as the faucet for everyday water needs for the majority of consumers and homes. The Brizo brand is positioned as the high-end faucet and competes not only on functionality and performance, but also on fashion. Consumers who buy this brand are as interested in making a fashion statement as they are a new faucet. Finally, the Peerless brand of faucets is positioned as the faucet for the do-it-yourselfer (DIY). It is less expensive than the other brands, and the customer who buys this brand is usually interested in a low-cost, functional faucet.[24]

The primary marketing challenges for the company appear to exist in four main areas. First, company leaders must make sure that one brand does not cannibalize the others. The brands must remain as distinct products offered to separate sets of consumers. This is done in part through marketing communications, but also in part by where the faucets are sold. Peerless is almost exclusively in stores like Home

Depot and Rona, which cater to the DIY audience, and Brizo is usually found in higher-end showrooms that offer complete renovations for consumers. Second, the brands must be viewed as the primary choices and must be remembered by consumers when the time comes to buy a plumbing fixture. Third, there cannot be brand confusion. Builders and plumbers must believe that the fixtures are distinct along several lines, including quality and durability, ease of installation, and strong warranties, but they must also perceived them as being fashionable. Fourth, innovation has become a new part of the plumbing fixture industry. A wide variety of options exist. Delta's products must compete with all the new faucet variations and the company must retain its position as the one of the premier manufacturers.

Consumers and plumbers are two audiences that the firm considers when developing marketing communications. Many plumbers and builders are simply looking for a low-cost option, especially when lower-end rental properties and similar units are being developed. Plumbers may be willing to install a wide variety of products, but usually have their favourites that they prefer to install. These brands will be the ones that have worked for them in the past and provided few problems of breakdowns requiring follow-up service calls. They will consider the costs of a product but also want something that will be easy to install and durable.

Consumers, on the other hand, can be interested in other product qualities, such as novel features and the look of the product. But the fact is that most consumers don't really give their faucets a second thought unless one of two things takes place. First, if a plumbing product is being purchased for the first time, such as when a home is being built or an area is being refurbished, consumers will take considerable time in selecting the product. The second is when an item is defective and must be replaced. The first occasion is usually characterized by purchases of other, related products in addition the faucets, and the purchase decision may take place over several days or weeks. The second occasion usually requires immediate attention and the purchase decision may be made within a matter of hours or even minutes.

While plumbers tend to be homogenous, consumers fall into segments that roughly match the three product lines of Masco. Consumers who bought the Peerless line were very price sensitive. They wanted something that provided a good mix of reliability, ease of installation, and, most important, low price. These faucets often went into rented apartments or basement bathrooms. The consumers who bought Brizo, on the other hand, wanted something stylish and considered the faucet as a showpiece for their home. Price was not an obstacle, and these buyers tended to hire professional designers to remodel. Often the designer would show the consumers samples from the showroom, which is where many consumers first learned of the Brizo brand.

In some ways these two segments were very distinct from the consumer segment that bought the Delta line of faucets. But in some ways they were not. For example, although the

MAGNETIC NORTH HAS GUIDED TRAVELERS FOR CENTURIES.

OUR MAGNETIC DOCKING FAUCET, HOWEVER, IS HAPPY TO STAY WHERE IT BELONGS.

Goes far when you need it, stays put when you don't. It's the Delta® faucet with MagnaTite™ docking and it's a new solution to an age-old problem. With a powerful magnet built into its pull-down spray head, there's no need to worry about it staying docked when it's not in use. It's one of the many ideas that make Delta® more than just a faucet

△DELTA
see what Delta can do™

deltafaucet.com/magnatite

ALLORA™

Delta is just one of the brands offered in the portfolio, each targeted at different consumer segments.

Brizo buyers wanted style for their kitchen, they were happy with a functional product in the basement. The person who was happy with a Peerless faucet in the basement apartment, wanted something a little more stylish in his or her own bathroom or kitchen. This created a challenge for the marketers of the Delta brand, which was really only able to be met through marketing communications.

Using marketing communications, managers can effectively move a target audience through the purchase process by creating differentiation between the Delta, Peerless, and Brizo brands. But this requires detailed insight into how the consumer moves through the stages of the purchase process.

It also means the marketing team needs to understand the various roles involved in the marketing communications process. The person who actually makes the purchase is not always the person who decides, or even the person who uses the faucet. For example, about half of the consumers who buy the Delta brand do so through a plumber. In some cases, if the plumber was loyal to a different brand, the consumer could be talked out of the Delta line and into something else.

Source: © iStockphoto.

Plumbers can be highly influential in the purchase decisions of consumers.

Imagine you have been hired by Masco to work on the Delta line of faucets. You report directly to the VP of Marketing who oversees all three brands of faucets. He has told you that he would like to see an emotional appeal used in the marketing communications for the brand to help differentiate it from the Peerless brand, and to help build a bond between the consumer and the brand to insulate the consumer from the influence of plumbers who might try to push other, competing brands.

As your first order of business, you set up a meeting with your marketing communications agency. You tell them about the idea for a new direction, and they are excited to exercise some creative muscle for the Delta brand. They ask you to prepare answers to a few questions in advance of the meeting:

1. Which of the three attitudinal development paths do you think is dominant in this product category? Justify your answer.

2. If you had to pick one of the executional frameworks presented in this chapter, which one would you favour for the creative development? Develop an example of a print ad to be placed in a home decorating magazine that you think would be effective for Delta Faucets. Be sure to consider how the ad might impact consumer perceptions of the other brands.

3. Do you think the same message should be communicated to both consumers and plumbers? Can the same appeal and executional framework work for both? What are the respective purchase processes for each audience? Which audience do you think is a priority? Write a two-page memo to the VP of Marketing explaining why you think (or don't think) the same creative should be used for both audiences, and justify your response by using information about each audience's purchase process. If you think a new creative approach is needed for the plumber audience, sketch out a print ad to go with the one you developed from question #2.

4. Do you feel a spokesperson will be effective for the campaign? What type of spokesperson do you have in mind? Would it matter if it is for the consumer or plumber audience? In a five-minute presentation, describe the perfect spokesperson for this campaign.

ENDNOTES

1. Henry A. Laskey, Ellen Day, and Melvin R. Crask, "Typology of Main Message Strategies for Television Commercials," *Journal of Advertising* 18, no. 1 (1989), pp. 36–41.

2. David Aaker and Donald Norris, "Characteristics of TV Commercials Perceived As Informative," *Journal of Advertising Research* 22, no. 2 (1982), pp. 61–70.

3. **www.campbellsoupcompany.com/atw_usa.asp**, accessed January 12, 2008.

4. Tony Smith, "Intel Extends Market Share Gains," *Register Hardware* (**www.reghardware.co.uk/2007/04/20/intel_vs_amd_q1_07/print.html**, April 20, 2007).

5. Shailendra Pratap Jain and Steven S. Posavac, "Valenced Comparisons," *Journal of Marketing Research* 41, no. 1 (February 2004), pp. 46–56.

6. Dhruv Grewal and Sukumar Kavanoor, "Comparative Versus Noncomparative Advertising: A Meta-Analysis," *Journal of Marketing* 61, no. 4 (October 1997),

pp. 1–15; Jain and Posavac, "Valenced Comparisons."

7. Joseph R. Priester, John Godek, D. J. Nayakankuppum, and Kiwan Park, "Brand Congruity and Comparative Advertising: When and Why Comparative Advertisements Lead to Greater Elaboration," *Journal of Consumer Psychology* 14, no. 1/2 (2004), pp. 115–24; Grewal and Kavanoor, "Comparative Versus Noncomparative Advertising: A Meta-Analysis."

8. Jim Hanas, "Rotscope Redux," *Creativity* 10, no. 1 (February 2002), pp. 40–41.

9. "Drawing Attention to Animation," *BtoB* 91, no. 7 (June 12, 2006), p. 46.

10. Matthew Warren, "Do Celebrity Endorsements Still Work?" *Campaign (UK)* 44 (November 2, 2007) p. 13.

11. Grant McCracken, "Who Is the Celebrity Endorser? Cultural Foundations of the Endorsement Process," *Journal of Consumer Research* 16 (December 1989), pp. 310–321.

12. Claire Murphy, "Stars Brought Down to Earth in TV Ads Research," *Marketing* (January 22, 1998), p. 1.

13. Kamile Junokaite, Sonata Alijosiene, and Rasa Gudonaviciene, "The Solutions of Celebrity Endorsers Selection for Advertising Products," *Economics & Management* 12, no. 3 (2007), pp. 384–90.

14. Roobina Ohanian, "Construction and Validation of a Scale to Measure Celebrity Endorsers' Perceived Expertise," *Journal of Advertising* 19, no. 3 (1990), pp. 39–52.

15. Cathy Yingling, "Beware the Lure of Celebrity Endorsers," *Advertising Age* (**www.adage.com/print?article_ide=120560,** September 24, 2007).

16. Carolyn Tripp, Thomas D. Jensen, and Les Carlson, "The Effects of Multiple Product Endorsements by Celebrities on Consumers' Attitudes and Intentions," *Journal of Consumer Research* 20 (March 1994), pp. 535–47.

17. Dipayan Biswas, Abhijit Biswas, and Neel Das, "The Differential Effects of Celebrity and Expert Endorsements on Consumer Risk Perceptions," *Journal of Advertising* 35, no. 2 (Summer 2006), pp. 17–31.

18. Ibid.

19. Raymond R. Burke and Thomas K. Srull, "Competitive Interference and Consumer Memory for Advertising," *Journal of Consumer Research* 15 (June 1988), pp. 55–68.

20. A. W. Melton, "The Situation with Respect to the Spacing of Repetitions and Memory," *Journal of Verbal Learning and Verbal Behavior* 9 (1970), pp. 596–606.

21. H. Rao Unnava and Deepak Sirdeshmukh, "Reducing Competitive Ad Interference," *Journal of Marketing Research* 31, no. 3 (August 1994), pp. 403–411.

22. Naveen Donthu, "A Cross-Country Investigation of Recall of and Attitudes Toward Comparative Advertising," *Journal of Advertising* 27, no. 2 (Summer 1998), pp. 111–21.

23. Michael L. Maynard, "Slice-of-Life: A Persuasive Mini Drama in Japanese Television Advertising," *Journal of Popular Culture* 31, no. 2 (Fall 1997), pp. 131–42.

24. **http://www.masco.com/our_companies/delta_faucet.html,** accessed May 18, 2010.

PART

3

Message Delivery

Once the marketer has identified the target audience and crafted the specific message to be delivered to that audience, the next step is the actual delivery.

In this third section of the book, we examine the different means by which marketers can place messages in front of target audiences. Broadly known as the marketing communications mix, all or any combination of these different delivery options can lead to effective delivery of the message. We examine advertising media such as television and magazines, direct marketing through methods like mail and email, sales promotion including contests and other incentives, public relations including sponsorships and corporate social responsibility, and digital marketing including participation in networks such as Facebook.

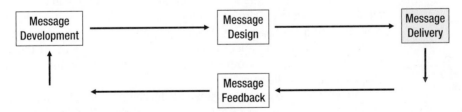

Step 3 in the Communications Process

CHAPTER OBJECTIVES

After reading this chapter, you should be able to answer the following questions:

- **What** activities are involved in creating a media plan?

- **How** do the roles played by media planners and media buyers differ from others in the delivery of marketing communications?

- **What** are reach, frequency, continuity, impressions, and CPM?

- **What** are the advantages and disadvantages of the various forms of traditional media used in advertising?

- **Why** is the mix of media a key part of an advertising campaign?

INDUSTRY PROFILE
So You Want to Work in Marketing Communications?

Carmen Hunt, Media Director, TBWA, Vancouver, British Columbia

Like many students, when Carmen had completed her undergraduate degree she saw herself working in the marketing communications industry. As a communications major with an arts background, she was interested in an Art Director position. But she was always fascinated with the impact of media and how the medium in which a message is conveyed could change the message itself. "The medium really is the message, and I thought this especially true in the case of marketing communications," says Carmen. "I would look at print ads for products that were all about image and building certain attributes about the product like quality or prestige. But then I'd hear a radio ad for that same product and the message would be all about urgency. Buy now. And I realized that the nature of the media itself—print being a long-life media and radio being fleeting, here one minute and gone the next—influenced how marketers could use each media differently."

Just like many students who envision themselves working in the marketing communications industry, Carmen's entry into the profession did not go according to plan. Instead of finding an Art Director job, a friend who knew she wanted to work in the industry told her about a media job he'd heard about. "I thought it would be a great way to break into the industry and further my interest in how media can shape consumer behaviour."

Carmen's first job was with a small media company in Edmonton. "It was great," recalls Carmen, "there were only four of us working there so I was able to learn from very close relationships with people with much more experience than I had. We would help clients decide which media they should use, and how much they should buy. And then we'd buy it for them. Because we were a small company, I was able to see every aspect of the media buy from start to finish."

But the first couple of years were not particularly glamorous. "I started off like pretty much everyone in media starts off," says Carmen. "I maintained media contracts, which involves literally checking thousands of facts in media contracts. When we bought some media, a contract was prepared and it was my job to make sure the details in the contract—which media we bought, how much of it, when

Advertising

and where—were all correct. Then after the media buy was finished and the ads ran, it was my job to make sure we got what we paid for."

This early career experience required tremendous attention to detail and organizational skills. Also, because it was mainly working with numbers, being comfortable with spreadsheets really helped.

Building on this solid base, Carmen began to take on more responsibility in subsequent jobs. "After a while I started getting more involved in the actual negotiations of the media purchase—working out deals with sales reps from media companies to buy air time, newspaper ads, and things like that. But the thing that really excited me was the opportunity to work with media plans that integrated multiple aspects of a campaign," says Carmen.

"Probably the most exciting project I've ever worked on was for Vancity, and it was their BikeShare program. Even though the project had no traditional mass media, it serves as a great example of how a campaign should fire on all cylinders." Vancity (**www.vancity.com**), which positions itself on a platform of social responsibility, gave away 45 bikes to consumers. The bikes were meant to be shared among people who could use them instead of cars. Initially, the bikes were given to people who, for three weeks, would blog about the experience. After three weeks, they would give the bikes to someone else, who would in turn blog about their experience, and so on. The whole campaign was launched with a pancake breakfast, where the bikes were on display in a main intersection in downtown Vancouver.

Carmen Hunt, Media Director, TBWA Vancouver.

Apart from the uniqueness of the project, Carmen recalls the campaign because of the results it generated. "This campaign—which cost something like $20,000—generated at least $300,000 in unpaid media coverage. And it wasn't just the space we could have bought. We received coverage on the front page of the local newspapers, which we could not have bought at any price. One radio station even discussed the program for a total of 23 minutes straight on air."

Carmen's advice for people interested in coming into the media field? "There are two things that people need to balance—essentially, a left brain and right brain balance. On the left-brain side, there is a lot of detail that people need to learn how to master. The first couple years can be tedious. Everyone has to go through it. But for those who can also engage their more creative side—the right brain—they can be inspired by the potential of where media is going in the future."

Technology, in particular, will change the media landscape in the coming years. "Obviously social media like Facebook are becoming a major part of many media plans now. And looking out a few years, we can see things like mobile marketing coming to North America in a big way. In Japan, for example, consumers take a photo of an outdoor billboard, send it to the company, and receive a coupon in exchange. So there's a campaign that marries traditional media (the billboard) with a mobile platform (the smart phone) with a direct marketing application (the customers identify themselves) and a promotional element (the coupon). The potential for media to become even more tightly integrated with the overall campaign is only going to grow. And technology means that our only limit is our imagination."

OVERVIEW

Advertising media is one element of the **marketing communications mix**, or the tools that marketers have at their disposal to deliver their messages to audiences. This section of the textbook covers a number of these tools in addition to advertising media: direct and database marketing, sales promotions, public relations, and digital marketing. But it is advertising media that are often the most noticed and memorable of all the tools in the communications mix. Think of some of the more noteworthy marketing communications you've seen over the past year. Chances are they are television ads. In fact, the yearly ads on the Super Bowl are among the most highly anticipated and impressive ads produced each year.

Media such as television, radio, billboards, magazines, and newspapers all tend to be very good at reaching large numbers of people, and often deliver some of the most memorable marketing messages. However, their ability to place messages in front of large numbers of people makes advertising media often a very blunt tool, with a limited ability to target specific, narrow audiences. Each of the media outlined in this chapter possess specific benefits and drawbacks that make them more or less useful as part of a marketing communications mix. Of note, although some forms of media on the Internet share similarities with more traditional media, our examination of digital marketing (including Internet media) is reserved for Chapter 11.

This chapter will examine the objectives that are reached through the use of advertising media, the processes by which media are selected and bought, and the specific forms of media that are available to marketers, along with summaries of each of their strengths and weaknesses.

ADVERTISING MEDIA OBJECTIVES

Marketers can include advertising media as part of their overall effort to achieve the objectives set out in the marketing communications plan. You'll recall that in Chapter 4 we examined the objective setting process, and identified opportunities to set marketing communications objectives that move audiences through the purchase process: need recognition, information search, evaluation criteria, purchase decision, and post-purchase evaluation. Advertising media can play a useful role in achieving any or all of these steps in customer decision making. For example, radio advertising can play a useful role in stimulating the need for a quick and easy meal. Many ads played on the radio during the evening commuting period are specifically designed to encourage drivers to consider a restaurant as an option for an easy meal at the end of a long work day. On the other hand, newspaper advertising for automobiles often features a large amount of product and pricing information, which can help customers through the information search stage.

The usefulness of media as part of the IMC plans for many products is evidenced by the investment many marketers make in media. As Figure 7.1 illustrates, the automotive sector, for example, invests almost $20 billion a year in media.

Category	Total	Magazines	Newspapers	Outdoor	Television	Radio	Internet
Automotive	$19.799	11.0%	25.4%	1.7%	50.4%	7.8%	3.7%
Retail	$19.114	11.0%	35.4%	2.0%	33.8%	11.2%	6.6%
Telecommunications	$10.950	8.2%	19.8%	2.5%	48.7%	7.1%	13.6%
Financial services	$ 8.689	13.7%	21.8%	2.8%	36.3%	8.3%	17.0%
Food, beverages, candy	$ 7.225	27.6%	0.7%	1.1%	64.2%	4.5%	1.8%
Restaurants	$ 5.291	2.5%	3.5%	4.5%	78.4%	10.1%	0.9%
Apparel	$ 2.911	75.1%	2.0%	1.0%	19.8%	0.7%	1.3%

Source: Based on "100 Leading National Advertisers," *Advertising Age* (June 25, 2007), p. 9. Reprinted with permission, Advertising Age (2007) Copyright Crain Communications Inc.

FIGURE 7.1
Advertising Media Expenditures for Select Categories

Critical Thinking Exercise

What specific objectives, or stages in the purchase process, can media advertising deliver for each of the sectors listed in Figure 7.1? Why do some sectors, such as automotive, invest heavily in television, while others, such as apparel, invest heavily in magazines? What does each medium, as well as media overall, deliver to marketers in these sectors?

If a marketer has determined that advertising media can play a role in achieving the overall objectives of the IMC plan, the next step is to outline the specific objectives for the media component. The technical terms used to describe outcomes are listed in Figure 7.2.

Reach is the number of people, households, or businesses in a target audience exposed to a media vehicle or message schedule at least once during a given time period. A time period is normally four weeks. In other words, how many targeted buyers did the ad reach at least once during a four-week period?

Frequency is the average number of times an individual, household, or business within a particular target market is exposed to a particular advertisement within a specified time period, again, usually four weeks. Or, how many times did the person see the ad during the campaign? A regular viewer sees the same ad shown each day on *Wheel of Fortune* more frequently than an ad shown once on *Grey's Anatomy*, even though the latter program has a far greater reach. In media planning, instead of frequency, **opportunities to see (OTS)** is commonly used. Opportunities to see refers to the cumulative exposures achieved in a given time period. For example, if a company places two ads on a television show that is televised weekly, then during a four-week period there are eight OTS (four shows × two ads per show).

One continuing issue facing marketers is deciding how many times a person must be exposed to a message before it has an impact. Most agree that a single exposure is not enough. Discovering the actual number has inspired a great deal of debate. Some argue it takes three exposures. Others say as many as 10. The basic rule, developed by Herbert Krugman,

- ◆ Reach
- ◆ Frequency
- ◆ Opportunities to see (OTS)
- ◆ Gross rating points (GRP)
- ◆ Cost per thousand (CPM)
- ◆ Cost per rating point (CPRP)
- ◆ Ratings
- ◆ Continuity
- ◆ Gross impressions

FIGURE 7.2
Advertising Objective Terminology

Pepsi uses high frequency in its marketing communications.

states that it takes a minimum of three exposures for an advertisement to be effective. This is the *three-exposure hypothesis.* Most media professionals have assumed it for many years.[1]

However, many advertisers think three exposures are not enough to create an impression in the consumer's mind, primarily because of the amount of clutter that exists. Clutter also affects the types of objectives firms try to accomplish. For instance, increasing brand awareness is usually easier than building brand image. Attention-getting is easier than holding someone's interest long enough to make a point about the firm's image. Also, a well-known brand that is the first choice of the majority of consumers can accomplish its objective with fewer ad exposures than a less well-known brand.

Seeking to discover the minimum number of exposures needed to be effective is based on two concepts: effective frequency and effective reach. **Effective reach** is the *percentage of an audience* that must be exposed to a particular message to achieve a specific objective. **Effective frequency** refers to the *number of times* a target audience must be exposed to a message to achieve a particular objective. The concept of effective frequency implies that some minimum number of exposures exists.

Effective frequency and effective reach are crucial. Too few exposures means the advertiser will fail to attain its intended objectives. On the other hand, too many exposures waste resources. The goal is to discover the optimal reach and frequency mix to accomplish the intended objectives without experiencing diminishing returns from extra ads. Remember that the optimal mix for an objective dealing with brand recognition is different than for an objective involved brand recall.

When the objective is to increase brand awareness, the emphasis will be on the visual presentation of the product and/or logo. The goal is to create or strengthen a linkage in the person's knowledge structure between the brand and other nodes of knowledge that already exist. Rather than have the individual recall the brand name from memory, the advertiser wants the person to recognize the brand name and logo at the retail store or in an advertisement. In this situation, advertisers want to increase reach, exposing a maximum percentage of the target audience to the brand's name, logo, and selling point.

When the objective is to increase brand recall, frequency is more important than reach. Repetition is required to embed a brand in the consumer's cognitive memory. Repetition increases the odds that a particular brand will come to mind.

Other elements can also enhance effective frequency and effective reach. They include the size, placement, and the length of an ad. A small magazine advertisement does not create the same impact as a larger ad. In television advertising, a spot in the middle of an ad sequence usually has less of an impact than the ads shown at the beginning and end of the series. If a firm uses 15-second television ads, effective frequency may require six exposures. In comparison, a longer 45-second spot may require only four exposures to be remembered.

Another important factor that affects these objectives is the number of different media used in an advertising campaign. In general, a campaign featuring ads in two types of media, such as television and magazines, has greater effective reach than a campaign in only one medium, such as magazines only.

In recent years, numerous media companies have designed computer models to optimize reach and frequency, including *Nielsen SAVE*, which examines cable TV alternatives and calculates the value of each using criteria such as Nielsen TV audience data (ratings), product purchasing information, customer preference cluster data, and specific systems data. Another version, *ADPlus* software, combines reach and frequency information with media mix information, budgeting data, and customized information for the individual advertiser. *Adware* provides Arbitron and Nielsen rating information, calculates media costs, and is designed to project GRP.

The programs that evaluate effective reach and frequency are based on probability theory and are designed to help the marketing team effectively allocate advertising dollars. An interaction of an attention-getting television ad with a magazine ad with copy explaining a product's features may have a synergistic effect in which the combined ads are more potent than the impact of either ad alone.

As an alternative, because of traditional concerns about reach and frequency, a new theory challenges the traditional three-exposure hypothesis. It is called **recency theory**. The theory suggests that a consumer's attention is selective and focused on his or her individual needs and wants. It is also based on the idea that because of clutter, advertising has only a short-term effect and responses to advertising dissipate rapidly, with few carryover effects.[2]

The traditional three-exposure hypothesis is based on the intrusion value of advertisements and the idea that advertisements can make an impact on an audience regardless of individual needs or wants. **Intrusion value** is the ability of media or an advertisement to intrude upon a viewer without his or her voluntary attention.

Recency theory's premise is that consumers have selective attention processes as they consider advertisements. They give the most attention to messages that might meet their needs or wants. The closer or more recent an ad is to a purchase, the more powerful the ad will be. Also, when a consumer contemplates a future purchase of the product being advertised, it becomes more likely that the consumer will pay attention to and react favourably toward an ad. This means that a member of a buying centre from a business in the market for a new copier will more readily notice copier advertisements. An individual who is not in the market for a copier ignores the same ad. The same is true in consumer markets: An individual needing a new pair of jeans notices clothing ads, especially ones that feature jeans.

Recency theory also suggests that the impact of advertising dissipates over time, even if the ad is noticed by individuals. The clutter and information overload that consumers experience means that the carryover effects of advertising tend to be low. Therefore, companies must advertise on an almost continuous basis to ensure an advertisement is in front of the buyer when he or she is thinking of making a purchase.

One primary difference in recency theory is the idea that one ad exposure is enough to affect an audience when that person or business needs the product being promoted. Additional exposures actually may not be necessary. The advertising strategy that matches recency theory spreads the message around using a variety of media, each one providing limited exposure per week or time period. In the case of selling supplemental health insurance to the elderly, magazines such as *Senior Living*, television's spots on local news and weather programs, and newspaper ads can quickly reach the target audience in a cost-effective manner. Such an approach, which maximizes reach, accomplishes more than increasing frequency.

Based on recency theory, a female looking for ski boots is likely to notice this ad.

Critical Thinking Exercise

Which of these ideas do you find more compelling: optimal reach, frequency, or recency? Do you think there are some products for which recency theory is a better approach, and others for which repetition is necessary? What is it about some products that makes one targeted exposure enough to stimulate a response while other products might require several exposures?

Gross rating points (GRP) are a measure of the impact or intensity of a media plan. Gross rating points are calculated by multiplying a vehicle's rating by the OTS, or number of insertions of an advertisement. GRP gives the advertiser an idea about the odds of the target audience actually viewing the ad. By increasing the frequency, or OTS, of an advertisement, the chances of a magazine reader seeing the advertisement increase. An advertisement featured in each issue of *Time* during a four-week period is more likely to be seen than one that appears only once in a monthly periodical.

Cost is a measure of overall expenditures associated with an advertising program or campaign. But, to be able to compare how cost-effective one medium or ad placement is compared with another, a measure called **cost per thousand (CPM)** is calculated. CPM is the dollar cost of reaching 1,000 members of the media vehicle's audience. CPM is calculated by using the following formula:

$$CPM = (Cost\ of\ media\ buy\ /\ Total\ audience) \times 1{,}000$$

Figure 7.3 shows some basic cost and readership information. The first three columns of the table provide the name of the magazine; the cost of a four-colour, full-page advertisement; and the magazine's total readership. The fourth column contains a measure of the CPM of each magazine. Notice that the CPM for *National Geographic* is $16.44. This means that it takes $16.44 to reach 1,000 *National Geographic* readers. Notice that the CPM for *Sports Illustrated* is $71.11 and for *Travel & Leisure*, $83.09. The readership of *Travel & Leisure* is the lowest, and yet its CPM is the highest of all eight magazines.

One critical concern is the cost of reaching a firm's target audience. Therefore, a measure called the **cost per rating point (CPRP)** was developed. The cost per rating point is a relative measure of the efficiency of a media vehicle relative to a firm's target market. **Ratings** measure the percentage of a firm's target market that is exposed to a show on television or an article in a print medium. The following formula is used to calculate the cost per rating point:

$$CPRP = Cost\ of\ media\ buy\ /\ Vehicle's\ rating$$

Magazine	Cost for 4-Color Full-Page Ad	Total Readership (000s)	CPM Total	Target Market (20M)	
				Rating (Reach)	Cost per Rating Point (CPRP)
National Geographic	$ 346,080	21,051	$16.44	16.1	$21,496
Newsweek	780,180	15,594	50.03	12.2	63,949
People	605,880	21,824	27.76	9.4	64,455
Sports Illustrated	965,940	13,583	71.11	10.5	91,994
Time	1,324,282	21,468	61.69	15.9	83,288
Travel & Leisure	183,216	2,205	83.09	2.3	79,659

FIGURE 7.3
Hypothetical Media Plan Information for Select Magazines

The ratings in Figure 7.3 were generated for potential buyers of a 35 mm digital camera. The table shows that the rating for *National Geographic* is 16.1, which means that 16.1 percent of the defined target market for 35 mm digital cameras read *National Geographic*. The CPRP for *National Geographic* is $21,496. This is the average cost for each rating point, or of each 1 percent of the firm's target audience (35 mm digital camera buyers). Not all readers of a magazine are part of the firm's target market. The CPRP more accurately measures an advertising campaign's efficiency than does CPM. Notice that the CPRP is the lowest for *National Geographic*.

CPRP provides a relative measure of reach exposure in terms of cost. For example, it costs $21,496 to reach 1 percent of the people in this firm's target market using *National Geographic*. It costs $91,994 to reach 1 percent using *Sports Illustrated*. Because some magazines are cheaper than others, why wouldn't a marketer just do all of the advertising in those magazines? The answer lies in both the size and targetability of the audience for any given magazine. Some magazines have a relatively small readership and therefore miss larger portions of the total target audience. Further, some magazines offer a more targeted readership. Consider the readership of *National Geographic* versus that of *Sports Illustrated*. If you were a marketing manager working for Under Armour, which magazine would provide an audience more likely to be interested in your product? Very likely a higher percentage of *Sports Illustrated* readers will be interested in athletic gear, and therefore the higher cost may be justified.

To further analyze whether an ad has reached the target market effectively, a **weighted (or demographic) CPM** value can be calculated, as follows:

$$\text{Weighted CPM} = \frac{\text{Advertisement cost} \times 1,000}{\text{Actual audience reached}}$$

For example, if the cost of an advertisement in *Sports Illustrated* is $115,000 and the magazine reaches 4,200,000 readers, the standard CPM would be $27.38. If the ad targets parents of Little League baseball players and research indicates that 600,000 of *Sports Illustrated*'s readers are Little League parents, the result would be:

$$\text{Weighted CPM} = \frac{\$115,000 \times 1,000}{600,000} = \$191.66$$

This figure could be compared to figures for *Sporting News, ESPN Magazine,* and other sports magazines.

The final objective advertisers consider is the concept of *impressions*. The number of **gross impressions** is the total exposures of the audience to an advertisement. It does not take into consideration what percentage of the total audience will see the advertisement. Figure 7.3 indicates that the total readership of *National Geographic* is 21,051,000. If six insertions were placed in *National Geographic*, multiplying the insertions by the readership would yield a total of 126 million impressions.

BUILDING THE MEDIA PLAN

The media plan refers to the specific media elements to be included in the marketing communications mix. It is often represented in a blocking chart that allows all of the various media (e.g., television, radio, newspaper, etc.) to be plotted over the year. The selection and timing of each medium is optimized to achieve the overall IMC objectives and work in concert with other marketing communications tools, such as direct and digital marketing or sales promotions.

The media plan begins with a careful analysis of the target market. It involves understanding the process consumers and businesses use in making a purchase and what influences the final decision. One method of addressing media planning is to study the media choices that members of a specific, defined target market might make

FIGURE 7.4
Examples of Times Workers Are Exposed to Media

◆ A favourite wake-up radio station or one listened to during the commute to work	◆ Favourite magazines read during the evening hours
◆ A favourite morning news show or newspaper	◆ Favourite television shows watched during the evening hours
◆ Trade or business journals examined while at work	◆ Internet sites accessed during leisure time
◆ A radio station played during office hours at work	◆ Shopping, dining, and entertainment venues frequented
◆ Favourite computer sites accessed during work	

at different times during the course of a day. Some of the more common choices are listed in Figure 7.4.

Specific details of this type are extremely valuable when developing a media strategy. Simply knowing demographic information such as age, sex, income, and education is not enough to determine the media habits of a person in a target market. Information about the listening and viewing patterns of customers helps the marketing team design messages that appeal to the right people. The message can also be made available at the best times and in the best places.

No two media plans are alike. Each plan should integrate the overall IMC strategy with specific marketing tactics. The typical components of a media plan include the following elements, which are also identified in Figure 7.5.

A *marketing analysis* is a comprehensive review of the fundamental marketing environment. It includes a statement of current sales, current market share, and prime prospects to be solicited (by demographics, lifestyle, geographic location, or product usage). These elements should reflect a compatible pricing strategy based on the product, its benefits and distinguishing characteristics, and an analysis of the competitive environment.

An *advertising analysis* states the fundamental advertising objectives and budget to be used in meeting those objectives. The *media strategy* spells out the media to be used and the creative considerations. The *media schedule* notes when ads will appear in individual media. The *justification and summary* states the measures of goal achievement and the rationale for each media choice.

The plan is usually developed and executed by a team consisting of a media planner and a media buyer.

Media Planning

The **media planner** formulates a media program stating where and when to place advertisements. Media planners work closely with other members of the marketing communications team, particularly people working to develop the creative strategies. This is to ensure that the development of the message is done in concert with the selection of the media used to deliver the message. Obviously, television ads are constructed in a different way than radio or newspaper ads.

Marketing experts at companies such as Procter & Gamble and Unilever consider media planning to be the heart of a communications strategy. At P&G, the first step is to set brand priorities and objectives. Next, a media channel communications plan is agreed upon before the actual communications plan and creative brief are prepared. The challenge for media buyers in this environment, according to Carl Fremont of the worldwide media services company Digitas, is "to integrate marketing messages across a range of media, and sometimes this involves working with several agencies to accomplish the client's goals."[3]

FIGURE 7.5
Components of a Media Plan

◆ Marketing analysis	◆ Media schedule
◆ Advertising analysis	◆ Justification and summary
◆ Media strategy	

Critical Thinking Exercise

Why might marketers for companies like P&G and Unilever consider media planning to be the heart of their communications strategy? These types of companies use media more than other elements of the marketing mix, such as public relations or digital marketing. Why do you think that is? What is it about their products, their target customers, or both that makes media such an important element of their success?

In most instances, the media planner conducts research to help match the product with the market and media. If a product's target market is 18- to 25-year-old males with college degrees who love the outdoors, then the media should match those characteristics. The media planner then identifies the most ideal locations for the advertisements. The New Balance running shoe ad in this section was placed in *Runner's World* near an article about running. The media plan should be designed to find the best ways to reach the client's customers.

Part of the media planner's research is gathering information about various media. This includes newspaper and magazine circulation rates and the characteristics of those who use the medium. The audience for a television show may be quite different from that of a radio station or a magazine. Careful research improves the chances of selecting appropriate media.[4]

Almost everyone has heard of S.O.S. soap pads. A few years ago, however, S.O.S. sales began to decline. The product was no longer the top-of-mind brand. The task of rebuilding awareness for the S.O.S. soap pads in Canada was assigned to the Palmer Jarvis DDB agency. The agency's media planners began by examining the media habits of the primary target market for S.O.S. soap pads. The group consisted of women, ages 35 to 54, who work; have kids; and are in a busy, active household. Women in this target group are heavy magazine readers. They have interest in home decor, entertaining, gardening, and cooking. As a result, media buys were made in *Canadian Living, Cooking at Home, Canadian House & Home*, and *Homemaker's*. These magazines were the best match of product, market, and media habits of the main consumer group.[5]

Media Buying

After the media are chosen, someone must buy the space and negotiate rates, times, and schedules for the ads. This is the work of the **media buyer**. Media buyers stay in constant contact with media sales representatives. They have a great deal of knowledge about rates and schedules. Media buyers also watch for special deals and tie-ins between different media outlets (e.g., radio with television, magazines with the same owner, etc.).

The media planner works with the media buyer in the design of an advertising campaign. Each plays a critical role in the development of an integrated marketing communications program. The challenge of coordinating the efforts of these individuals intensifies when they are from different companies, which is typically the

An advertisement featuring New Balance shoes that was placed in *Runner's World* magazine.

When does a jogger become a runner?

On a day like this.

achieve new balance

case for large clients and national brands. For example, because of the benefits of buying a large amount of media, many firms now outsource their media buying to centralized buying companies that purchase media for many clients. Although this may allow for lower media costs, the costs of coordination increase.

The size of the marketing communications agency or media buying firm alone does not ensure effective media purchases. Research indicates that there is little connection between the size of a firm and the prices it can negotiate. One study indicated that differences in media costs are based on the time of the actual purchase (closer to the day the ad is to run) rather than the size of the agency.[6] Other major factors in cost differences are knowledge of the marketplace and the ability to negotiate package deals. Spot television media plans vary by as much as 45 percent in the price of the spot. A **spot ad** is a one-time placement of an ad on a local television station. Rates are negotiated individually by the number of times ads appear with individual stations. For example, a media plan costing one firm $1 million can cost another firm $1.5 million. Radio time slots vary by as much as 42 percent and national print ads by as much as 24 percent.[7] More importantly, differences in effectiveness of advertising are often related to:

- The quality of media choices (the right ones) made by each agency
- Creativity
- Financial stewardship ("bang" for your advertising buck)
- Agency culture and track record
- Computer systems to analyze data
- Relationships between the agency and the medium's sales representative

The negotiated price is only one element in the success of an advertising program. Effectiveness in advertising is also determined by quality of the selections made by the marketing team and the content of the ad itself. Media should be selected and purchased with specific advertising objectives in mind.

One of the most significant issues that media planners and buyers must address is continuity of the media schedule. **Continuity** is the exposure pattern or schedule used in the media campaign. Media planners and buyers can choose among three types of patterns: continuous, pulsating, and discontinuous. A continuous schedule uses media time in a steady stream. Typically, this is done through the placement of media continually for a 12-month period, since most media plans are based on a one-year timeframe. By using different ads and rotating them, readers will not get bored, because they will see more than one ad for the same product or brand. This type of schedule is used for many consumer goods companies, such as Kraft or Coca-Cola.

A retailer such as The Bay might use a pulsating schedule by placing ads in various media throughout the entire year, but then increasing the number of advertisements in small, short bursts around holidays, including Christmas, Hanukkah, Thanksgiving, Victoria Day, Labour Day, Mother's Day, Father's Day, and Easter. The goal of pulsating advertising is to reach consumers when they are most likely to make purchases or buy special merchandise, such as during the holiday shopping season. Thus, a Canadian Tire advertisement just prior to Christmas can encourage consumers to purchase gift cards.

Companies can also select what is called a flighting schedule, whereby ads are presented only during peak times, and not at all during off seasons. A flighting (or discontinuous) campaign schedule might be used by Whistler-Blackcomb in B.C. or Blue Mountain Ski Resort in Ontario to promote activities during the fall and winter seasons, but none during the spring and summer. This type of schedule can also be used by marketers in other product categories in an attempt to stretch media dollars further. Recall the presence of the carryover effect in advertising. For many products, residual effects from advertising might eliminate the need to purchase media every month, allowing, for example, media every other month.

Critical Thinking Exercise

Continuous media schedules are very expensive because they require media to be purchased throughout the year. This can be especially costly when very expensive media, such as television, are included in the mix. Why do you think some marketers opt for continuous scheduling? What is it about their customer or their product that requires such frequent message placement? Do you think these companies are wasting their money and should opt for a flighting approach to take advantage of the carryover effect? What factors would you consider that would help determine the appropriate interval between flights?

MEDIA SELECTION

A variety of advertising media are available. Effectively mixing these media is an important part of designing quality advertising. To do so, the advantages and disadvantages of each individual medium must be understood.

Television

For many years, television had the reputation of being the most glamorous advertising medium. A company featuring a television advertising campaign enjoyed more prestige. To some, television advertising is still the best option, although its dominance of the media landscape has dwindled.

Figure 7.6 lists the advantages and disadvantages of television advertising. As shown, television offers advertisers the most extensive coverage and highest reach of any of the media. A single ad can reach millions of viewers simultaneously. Even though the total cost of running the ad is high, the cost per contact is relatively low. This *low cost per contact* justifies, for example, spending $3 million for a 30-second spot during the Super Bowl.

Further, television has the advantage of *intrusion value*, which is the ability of a medium or advertisement to intrude upon a viewer without his or her voluntary attention. Television ads with a catchy musical tune, sexy content, or humour can quickly grab a viewer's attention. Television provides many opportunities for creativity in advertising design. Images and sounds can be incorporated to capture the viewer's attention and present persuasive messages. Products and services can be demonstrated on television in a manner not possible in print or using radio advertisements.

Clutter is the primary problem with television advertising. Five years ago, prime-time averaged 16 minutes and 26 ads per hour of programming. That has slowly crept upward to about 19 minutes and 31 ads per hour. One particular television show had a total of 24 ads within the 30-minute show, which meant 11 minutes out of the 30 was devoted to advertising. Four- and five-minute commercial breaks are no longer unusual.[8] As a result, many viewers switch channels during commercial breaks. Thus, messages at the beginning or near the end of the break have the best recall. Those in the middle often have virtually no impact. Therefore, clutter makes it difficult for a single message to have much influence.

Advantages	Disadvantages
1. High reach	1. Greater clutter
2. High frequency potential	2. Low recall due to clutter
3. Low cost per contact	3. Channel surfing during commercials
4. High intrusion value (motion, sound)	4. Short amount of copy
5. Quality creative opportunities	5. High cost per ad
6. Segmentation possibilities through cable outlets	

FIGURE 7.6
Television Advertising

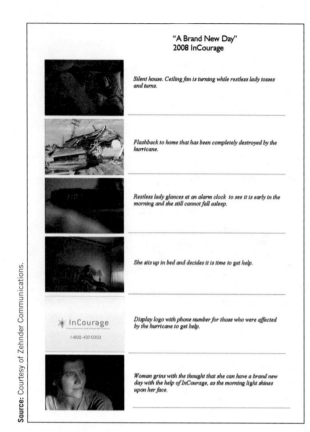

"A Brand New Day"
2008 InCourage

Silent house. Ceiling fan is turning while restless lady tosses and turns.

Flashback to home that has been completely destroyed by the hurricane.

Restless lady glances at an alarm clock to see it is early in the morning and she still cannot fall asleep.

She sits up in bed and decides it is time to get help.

InCourage
1-800-437-0303

Display logo with phone number for those who were affected by the hurricane to get help.

Woman grins with the thought that she can have a brand new day with the help of InCourage, as the morning light shines upon her face.

A storyboard produced by Zehnder Communications for a television commercial.

Another method some viewers use to cope with clutter is a DVR, recording favourite programs and watching them later. Currently, 20 percent of television viewers use a DVR. The fear advertisers have is that consumers will skip over the commercials. Some research indicates, however, that fewer than half fast-forward through commercials. Also, the majority watches the television show the same day it is recorded, and 75 percent have watched it by the end of the next day. This means that time-sensitive ads are being seen close to when they first were shown.[9]

Television commercials have *short life spans.* Sixty-nine percent of the national ads produced during the past year were 30-second ads. Occasionally an advertiser purchases a 15-, 45-, or 60-second ad, but those are rare. Another disadvantage of television is the high cost per ad, not only for the media time, but also in terms of production costs. Outstanding commercials often are expensive to produce. The average cost to produce a 30-second national ad is $358,000. Production fees account for the largest portion of the cost, an average of $236,000. Other costs include director fees ($23,000), editing and finishing the ad ($45,000), and creative/labour fees and music ($34,000). Of course, many television ads are produced for far less, with some costing as little as a few thousand dollars.[10]

When television advertising spots are shown too frequently they quickly lose the ability to attract the viewer's interest. Companies are forced to replace the ads with something new before consumers get tired of them and tune them out, even though the marketing team wants to run an ad long enough to recover production costs.

Choosing the best television advertising outlets for an ad is challenging. The goal is to match a firm's target audience with specific shows. Many cable television programs provide well-defined audiences. For example, Home and Garden Television (HGTV) delivers an audience that skews older with a lifestyle interest in gardening, renovation, and so forth, while MuchMusic delivers a young demographic with an interest in music.

To gain a sense of how well an advertisement fared in terms of reaching an audience, a given program's *rating* can be calculated. The typical ratings formula is:

$$\text{Rating} = \frac{\text{Number of households turned to a program}}{\text{Total number of households in a market}}$$

In Canada, approximately 30 million households have television sets. To calculate the rating of an episode of *The Bachelor,* if the number of households tuned to the season finale was 3.85 million, the rating would be:

$$\text{Rating} = 3{,}850{,}000 / 30{,}000{,}000 = 12.8$$

Next, if the advertiser were interested in the percentage of households that actually were watching television at that hour, the program's share could be calculated. If 18 million of the 30 million households had a television turned on during the hour in which *The Bachelor* aired, the share would be:

$$\text{Share} = 3{,}850{,}000 / 18{,}000{,}000 = 21.3$$

A 12.8 rating would mean that 12.8 percent of all televisions in the country were tuned to *The Bachelor.* A 21.3 share means 21.3 percent of the households with a television actually turned on were watching the program.

However, there is no guarantee that the viewers saw the commercial. Viewers might have ignored the commercial, or left the room during the commercial break. Ratings and shares are only indicators of how well the program fared relative to other programming. Ratings are used to establish rates for advertisements. The higher a show's rating over time, the more that is charged.

ON THE JOB

What does it cost to run an ad? Many people outside the advertising industry are surprised at how expensive it is to advertise through media. Further complicating matters is the ability to purchase media at either a local level or a national level. Below are some examples of costs for various media, in both local regions/cities and nationally.

Carmen Hunt, of TBWA in Vancouver, states that posted costs for media can almost always be negotiated lower by media buyers, but offers the following as a starting point for various media in her local market of Vancouver:

Television:

30-second spot on local 6 p.m. *Global News* broadcast	$2,725
30-second spot on local broadcast of the drama series *House*	$9,402
30-second spot on local broadcast of *Survivor*	$8,441
30-second spot on game #1 of *Hockey Night in Canada* (national)	$43,088

Radio:

30-second spot on QM-FM	$140
30-second spot on The Beat	$140

Newspapers:

Full-page, full-colour ad in *Vancouver Sun* Saturday edition	$50,095.87
Full-page, full-colour ad in *Vancouver Province* Sunday edition	$25,999.15
Full-page, full-colour ad in *The Globe & Mail* Saturday edition (national)	$89,805.60

Magazines:

Full-page, full-colour ad in *Maclean's*	$31,815

Out-of-Home:

1 billboard in Lower Mainland for 4 weeks	$2,250
1 transit shelter in downtown Vancouver for 4 weeks	$2,625

ACNielsen is the primary organization that calculates and reports ratings and shares. The company also provides local channel information regarding shares of stations in local markets, known as *designated marketing areas* (DMAs). Data gathering techniques used by ACNielsen include diaries written by viewers who report what they watched, audience meters that record what is being watched automatically, and people meters that allow the viewing habits of individual members of families to be tracked.

These numbers can be further refined to help media buyers and planners understand whether an advertisement reached a target market. Within rating and share categories, viewers can be subdivided by certain demographics, such as:

- Age
- Income
- Gender
- Educational level
- Race or ethnic heritage

Organizations that prepare this kind of information include Nielsen Media Research; Starch INRA; Hooper, Inc.; Mediamark Research, Inc.; Burke Marketing Research; and Simmons Market Research Bureau. An advertising team may find it extremely helpful to know that viewers of *CSI: Miami* tend to be college educated, older than the age of 40, and have annual incomes of more than $50,000. If psychographic information can be added in (such as that the show is mostly watched by people who voted Liberal in the previous election), then the marketer has a good sense of whether this is the best audience for the media element of the campaign.

For local and regional advertisers, spot TV is the best option for television advertising. In many cases, national brands supplement national commercials with spot TV purchases in select markets. Media planners do this primarily because of the high cost of national ad time and because 75 to 80 percent of prime-time slots are sold out during the spring, shortly after they go on the market. By selecting local early news, late news,

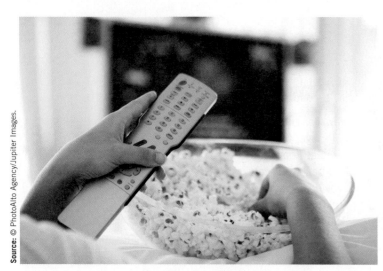

Snack foods are often advertised on television.

and prime access, a media planner can generate higher GRP at a lower cost than if only national ad time is purchased.

Two measures, the brand and category development indices, can be used to help pick spot TV times (or indeed any form of local media). The *brand development index* (BDI) is the market's percentage of sales of a particular brand divided by the percent that local market represents of total Canadian households. The *category development index* (CDI) is the particular market's percentage of a category's sales divided by the percent of the market's share of the Canadian households.[11] To illustrate, the province of Saskatchewan has a population of just over 1 million, or 3 percent of the total Canadian population. To calculate the BDI and CDI for a product such as Ivory bar soap, several figures are needed. First, 4.6 percent of Ivory's total Canadian sales occur in Saskatchewan. This yields a BDI of 153 (4.6 / 3). The category sales of bar soap in Saskatchewan are 3.3 percent of total Canadian sales of bar soap. This makes the CDI 110 (3.3 / 3). The BDI and CDI indices indicate that Ivory has a higher percentage of the total bar soap sales in the Saskatchewan market than it does in other Canadian markets, and that Saskatchewan residents buy approximately 10 percent more soap than the average Canadian. This information can then be compared to sales figures in other markets in order to gain a sense of where Ivory is doing well and where sales are less strong. Subsequently, the media planner can make decisions about where media spending can be increased or decreased.

Another factor that may be considered before making a decision to purchase spot TV time in Saskatchewan is *trend information.* If the BDI has been declining during the last few months or years, additional spot TV time may be purchased to reverse the declining trend. On the other hand, if the trend analysis shows a steady market share or increasing market share, Ivory's marketing team may reduce spot TV time in the province and shift those advertising dollars to other local markets where sales are less robust.

In general, television still has a wide audience that appeals to companies selling goods and services with general target markets. These markets include most durable goods (washers, dryers, cars, etc.), staple items (detergent, soap, deodorant), general appeal products (snack foods, beers, soft drinks, and Internet sites), and various luxuries marketed to larger groups (cruise ships, theme parks, and credit cards).

Although less frequent, business-to-business products are also found on television for several reasons. First, members of the business buying centre watch television. Second, increasing ad clutter in trade journals and traditional business outlets makes television spots more desirable. Third, business advertisements now use more emotional appeals, and television portrays emotions effectively. Fourth, a strong brand identity is a growing factor in the business-to-business sector, and television ads can increase it. Finally, television reaches members of the buying centre when they are not preoccupied with other business concerns. Consequently, they may be more open to advertising messages.

Radio

Although perhaps not as glamorous as television, a well-placed, clever radio ad is a one-on-one message that can have significant impact. Many smaller local companies rely heavily on radio advertising. Most radio ads are produced locally and with small budgets. Figure 7.7 summarizes the advantages and disadvantages of radio advertising.

Radio offers several advantages. Skilful radio advertisers help the listener remember the message by creating a powerful image to visualize or by using repetition. It is important to help the consumer move the ad from short-term to long-term memory. Various sound effects and lively tunes assist in this process. Through repetition a person hears an advertisement often enough to assist in recall—just like repeating a phone number or email address helps you remember numbers or letters.

FIGURE 7.7
Radio Advertising

Advantages	Disadvantages
1. Recall promoted	1. Short exposure time
2. Narrower target markets	2. Low attention
3. Ad music can match station's programming	3. Few chances to reach national audience
4. High segmentation potential	4. Target duplication when several stations use the same format
5. Flexibility in making new ads	5. Information overload
6. Able to modify ads to fit local conditions	
7. Intimacy (with DJs and radio personalities)	
8. Mobile—people carry radios everywhere	
9. Creative opportunities with music and other sounds	

A radio station has definable target markets based on its format. Certain formats (talk radio, "lite" mix, oldies, etc.) attract similar audiences. This means a firm can advertise on a specific type of station across the country. Campbell's found that radio spots were an effective way to promote its Chunky Soup using a tie-in with the National Football League. The company advertised on sports stations with primarily male audiences and featured professional football players praising Chunky Soup.[12]

Radio stations offer considerable *flexibility* and a short lead time. Commercials can be recorded and placed on the air within a few days, and sometimes within hours. Ads can be changed quickly. This is especially helpful in volatile markets or in the retail sector for companies that want to change the items featured on sale. A national company can modify advertisements to fit local conditions. A manufacturer can develop one national advertisement and change it for each dealer or retailer that carries the manufacturer's merchandise. General Motors offered its hundreds of dealers across the country nationally produced radio spots to advertise the GM certified brand of used vehicles. The national ad was higher quality than can usually be produced locally and provided consistency across Canada for GM. Local dealers can customize the spots with local information, such as the dealer's address, phone number, or Website.[13]

Another major advantage of radio is *intimacy*. Listeners often feel personally close to some DJs and radio personalities. This closeness grows over time. Listening to the same individual becomes more personal and intimate, especially if the listener has a conversation with the DJ during a contest or when requesting a song. The bond or intimacy level gives the radio personality a higher level of credibility and gives an edge to goods and services the radio celebrity endorses. No other medium offers this advantage.

Elizabeth Arden used radio to launch the Skinsimple line of skin-care products. Sales increased by an average of 18 percent in the three weeks following the run of advertisements in 30 markets. According to Greg Griffin, vice president of marketing for Elizabeth Arden, "The radio listener is more open to your message . . . especially when the DJs are given leeway to have fun with the promotions and chat about the brand, consumers don't feel like it's an ad."[14]

Radio is also *mobile*. People carry radios to the beach, the ballpark, work, and picnics. They listen at home, at work, and on the road in between. Few other advertising media stay with the audience quite like radio.

Radio also has disadvantages. One is the *short exposure time* of an ad. Like television, most radio advertisements last only 15 or 30 seconds. Listeners involved in other activities, such as driving or working on a computer, may not pay attention to the radio. Further, people often use radio as a background to drown out other distractions, especially at work.

Radio also suffers from advertising *clutter*. One study indicated that after six ads in a block only 20 percent of the listening audience is still there. Yet, radio advertisers continue to build larger and larger blocks of ads. In Australia, ad blocks have reached a high

Radio enjoys the advantage of intimacy.

of 13 straight ads. With the advance of MP3 players and digital technology, ad clutter in radio is going to become an even more serious problem, because listeners now have new alternatives for listening to music.[15]

For national advertisers, covering a large area with radio advertisements is challenging. To place a national advertisement requires contacting a large number of companies. Few large radio conglomerates means contacts must be made with multiple stations. Negotiating rates with individual stations based on volume is difficult. Local businesses can often negotiate better rates than national advertisers because of the local company's relationships with the radio stations.

In large metropolitan areas, another problem is target duplication. Several radio stations may try to reach the same target market. For instance, Toronto has several rock stations. Advertising on every station is not financially feasible, yet reaching everyone in that target market is not possible unless all rock stations are used. The rock music audience is divided among those stations, with each having its own subset of loyal listeners.

Another new challenge to traditional radio is satellite radio. These stations charge a fee for listening, but then do not run advertisements. The growth in satellite radio may hurt both national and local radio stations and networks.

Finally, many locally produced commercials often have too much information crammed into the spot. It overloads the consumer, and very little is retained.

Radio advertising is a low-cost option for a local firm. Ads can be placed at ideal times and adapted to local conditions. The key to radio is careful selection of stations and times, and quality construction of the ad. Tests can be created to see if ads effectively reach customers. Immediate response techniques, contest entries, and other devices provide evidence about whether customers heard and responded to ads. Radio *remotes* occur when the station broadcasts from a business location. Remotes are a popular method of attracting attention to a new business (restaurants, taverns, small retail shops, etc.) or to a company trying to make a major push for immediate customers. Effective radio promotions can be combined with other media (local television, newspapers, etc.) to send out a more integrated message.

Toronto's Yonge Street is state-of-the-art when it comes to out-of-home media.

For business-to-business advertisers, radio provides the opportunity to reach businesses during working hours, because many employees listen to the radio during office hours. More important, radio can reach businesspeople while they are in transit to or from work. Both radio and television usage has increased for business-to-business marketing.

Out-of-Home Advertising

Billboards along major roads are the most common form of out-of-home (OOH) advertising, and have been in use in North America since the late 1800s. Billboards, however, are only one form of OOH advertising. In a search to reach an ever-increasing number of consumers more and more often, media companies can now place advertising messages virtually

Advantages	Disadvantages
1. Able to select key geographic areas	1. Short exposure time
2. Accessible for local ads	2. Brief messages
3. Low cost per impression	3. Little segmentation possible
4. Broad reach	4. Cluttered travel routes
5. High frequency on major commuter routes	
6. Large, spectacular ads possible	

FIGURE 7.8
Out-of-Home Advertising

anywhere in a public setting: signs on cabs, buses, public transit stops, park benches, sports arenas, escalators, and elevators. One of the most noticeable forms of OOH advertising is found in restrooms, where advertisers can deliver a message while the audience is truly captive. On virtually all campuses across Canada, ads can be seen in areas that historically have been off-limits to for-profit advertisers.

OOH advertising has changed dramatically with advances in technology. Annual expenditures on outdoor advertisements now total in the hundreds of millions of dollars in Canada. Global positioning systems, wireless communications, and digital display technology have transformed outdoor advertising. The most popular outdoor technology, LED, is used by companies such as Procter & Gamble and McDonald's. LED technology is used to create video screens for animated videos high traffic locations such as Toronto's Yonge Street. It can create both static messages and visuals that change electronically.[16]

The cosmetics industry spends heavily on OOH advertising. On average, 6.7 percent of a cosmetics company's budget is reserved for OOH, compared to an industry average of 2.6 percent. In the past few years, billboards have been used to feature Dove and Neutrogena. Taxi-top ads helped launch the Visibly Even line of products for Neutrogena.[17] Other fast-growing outdoor ad programs are found in the fashion industry. The Gap, Calvin Klein, Ralph Lauren, and DKNY regularly buy outdoor space. Because OOH media is so varied, there are differences in the relative strength and weakness of OOH as a general media category. However, many are common, and the most prominent are listed in Figure 7.8.

One primary advantage of OOH advertising is *long life*. For local companies, OOH is an excellent media option because the message is seen primarily by local audiences. Services such as restaurants, hotels, resorts, service stations, and amusement parks are heavy users of OOH. It also provides an effective way to communicate a firm's location to travellers. For example, individuals who want to eat at a particular restaurant (Wendy's, Burger King) while on the road can normally spot a billboard for that restaurant.

OOH advertising is a low-cost media option when measured by cost per impression. OOH advertising also offers a broad reach and a high level of frequency if multiple locations or formats are purchased. Every person who travels past a billboard or sees an advertisement on a taxi has the potential for being exposed to the message. Many OOH media companies provide rotation packages, in which an ad moves to different locations throughout an area during the course of the year, thereby increasing the ad's reach.

Some OOH media can be *large* and *spectacular*, making them major attention-getting devices. For example, a billboard's large size creates the impression that the product and message are important. Movement and lighting through LED

HSBC uses a domination approach at many airports to reinforce its message of being "the world's local bank."

Source: John Peloza. Used with permission of HSBC Bank Canada.

A billboard for Wendy's breakfast meal.

technology add to the attention-capturing qualities of billboards. At the other extreme, OOH advertising can be small, yet stir attention. Another way that marketers use OOH advertising to create impact is through domination strategies, where an entire bus or subway platform is "owned" by one brand.

A major drawback of OOH media is the *short exposure time.* Audiences must pay attention to their surroundings as well as the ad. When the ad is on a vehicle, pedestrians often get only a quick look. Most either ignore outdoor ads or give them just a casual glance. Ironically, in large cities along major arteries the cost of some OOH media is increasing. The reason: traffic jams. People stuck in slow-moving traffic spend more time looking at ads when they are strategically placed.

To counter the short exposure time and take advantage of traffic jams, another outdoor technique that is now being used is a mobile billboard, which is a truck covered with a two-sided billboard. For $500 to $800 a day, customers can tailor a mobile billboard to exact routes they want driven or to specific postal codes, or they can even have it parked outside a specific event. Although some cities ban mobile billboards and some citizens are raising concerns about added pollution and drivers being distracted by reading billboards on moving vehicles, the popularity of mobile billboards is rising. Mobile billboards provide the opportunity to beat ad clutter and the short exposure times of static billboards. They reach consumers where they are—stuck in traffic.[18]

A short exposure time means the message must be extremely brief. People usually ignore a complicated or detailed message. Further, OOH media typically offer limited segmentation opportunities. A wide variety of people may view the message. To help overcome this problem, some companies use geodemographic software technologies to identify the profile of individuals who will pass by a particular outdoor location. Such an approach works well on local streets of cities and towns but is not very effective along major highways, because of long-distance traffic.

Today, OOH advertising is seen as a critical component of the media plans for many local and national marketers and, in some cases, the primary medium. When promoting the movie *Avatar*, the media planning company IMA Outdoor created a dominant presence in Toronto's Union Station including wall murals, column wraps, decals on doors and floors, and a series of backlit posters.[19] Movies often heavily use OOH as part of their IMC plans. Figure 7.9 highlights other major industries and how much each spent on OOH advertising during one quarter. As the chart indicates, local services and amusements spend considerably more than any other industry.

Magazines

Research indicates that in many cases magazines are an excellent media option. One study concluded that every dollar a company spends on magazine advertising yields an average of $8.23 in sales. The average return on investment for all other media is $3.52 per dollar spent on advertising. The reason given for this difference is magazine advertising's ability to target consumers more efficiently by demographics and lifestyles.[20]

A billboard advertisement for Sunkist.

Naturally, the validity of these results has been staunchly debated by executives from other media. Figure 7.10 displays the pros and cons of magazine advertising.

As mentioned previously, one major advantage of magazines is the high level of *market segmentation.* Magazines are highly segmented by topic area. Specialized magazines

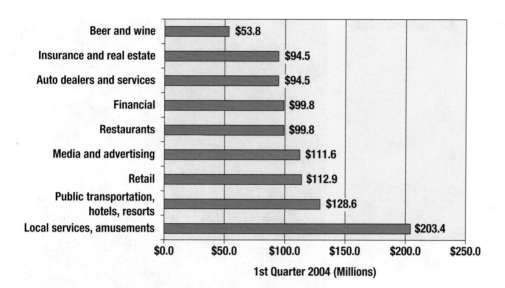

FIGURE 7.9
Expenditures on Out-of-Home Advertising in a Typical Three-Month Period

are much more common than general magazines with broad readerships. Even within certain market segments, such as automobiles, a number of magazines exist. High audience interest becomes another advantage. An individual who subscribes to the bridal magazine *Wedding Bells* has an attraction to weddings. People reading magazines also tend to view and pay attention to advertisements related to their needs and wants. Often, readers linger over an ad for a longer period of time because they read magazines in waiting situations (e.g., doctor's office) or during leisure time. This high level of interest, segmentation, and differentiation is ideal for products with precisely defined target markets.

Trade and business journals are a major medium for business-to-business marketing. Businesses can target advertisements to buying centre members. The ad copy can then provide a greater level of detail about products. Readers, if interested, take time to read the information in the ad. Ads can provide toll-free telephone numbers and Web addresses so that interested parties can obtain further information.

Magazines offer *high-quality colour* and more sophisticated production processes, providing the opportunity to produce intriguing and enticing advertisements. Colour and unusual images can be used to attract attention. Magazines such as *Glamour*, *Chatelaine*, and *Cosmopolitan* may include scratch-and-sniff ads to entice women to notice the fragrance of a perfume or cologne. Even car manufacturers have ventured into this type of advertising by reproducing the smell of leather in ads.

Magazines have a *long life* that reaches beyond the immediate issue. Subscribers read and reread them. It is not unusual for an avid magazine reader to examine a particular issue several times and spend a considerable amount of time with each issue. This appeal is attractive because advertisers know the reader will be exposed to the ad

Advantages	Disadvantages
1. High market segmentation	1. Declining readership (some magazines)
2. Targeted audience interest by magazine	2. High level of clutter
3. Direct-response techniques (e.g., coupons, Web addresses, toll-free numbers)	3. Long lead time
	4. Little flexibility
4. High color quality	5. High cost
5. Availability of special features (e.g., scratch and sniff)	
6. Long life	
7. Read during leisure time (longer attention to ad)	

FIGURE 7.10
Magazine Advertising

Source: Reprinted with permission from *Marketing News*, published by the American Marketing Association, Deborah L. Vence, "Outdoor Ads Leverage New Technology," vol. 38, no. 15 (September 15, 2004), pp.11–13

What is your China strategy?

King & Wood advises on and implements intellectual property protection and IP litigation strategies for multinational and high-tech companies. We have gathered a highly recognized team of intellectual property practitioners who have successfully advised clients on matters in China, including: patent, trademark, IP litigation and other legal affairs relating to intellectual property.

If you seek a depth of Chinese experience combined with an international perspective, then look to King & Wood.

Patent | Trademark | Copyright | Unfair Competition | IP Litigation

金杜律师事务所
KING & WOOD
PRC LAWYERS

Beijing | Shanghai | Shenzhen | Chengdu | Guangzhou | Xi'an | Chongqing | Hangzhou | Tianjin | Suzhou | Qingdao | Hong Kong | Tokyo | Silicon Valley | New York

China Depth. International Expertise.   ip@kingandwood.com

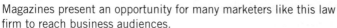

Magazines present an opportunity for many marketers like this law firm to reach business audiences.

Magazines allow marketers like the Upper Canada College to target specific audiences.

more than once and is more likely to pay attention. Other individuals may also look at the magazine, since people often pass along magazines to friends when they are finished reading them. In the business-to-business sector, trade journals are often passed around to several individuals or members of the buying centre. As long as the magazine lasts, the advertisement is still there to be viewed.

One major disadvantage facing magazine advertisers is a *decline in younger readers.* The Leo Burnett Company's *Starcom Report* stated that magazines lost 61 million readers from the 18- to 49-year-old age bracket in just a year.[21] However, overall magazine readership for the top 300 magazines is down only 0.5 percent from 1997.[22]

Although circulation has remained relatively stable, the number of ad pages has declined in recent years. Ad pages for the top 300 magazines are down 21 percent from 1997 and 26 percent from 2000. Despite the decline in ad pages, total ad revenue has not declined nearly as much, due to the increased cost of magazine ads. A magazine such as *Maclean's*, therefore, charges over $31,000 for a full-page colour ad.[23]

Clutter is another big problem for magazine advertisers. A recent 318-page issue of *Glamour* contained 195 pages of advertising and only 123 pages of content. Ads can be easily lost in those situations. To be noticed, the advertisement must be unique or stand out in some way.

Long lead times are a major disadvantage of magazines, because advertisements must be submitted as much as six months in advance of the issue. Consequently, making changes in ads after submission is very difficult. Also, because of the long life of magazines, images or messages created through magazine advertising have long lives. This is good for stable goods or services, but not for volatile markets or highly competitive markets wherein the appeal, price, or some other aspect of the marketing mix changes more frequently.

Magazines continue to proliferate even with the problems of *declining readership.* The wide variety of special interests makes it possible to develop and sell them. Many advertisers still can target audiences and take advantage of various magazine features, such as direct-response Internet addresses and coupon offers. This is especially true in the business market. Although business-to-business marketers increasingly use other media, trade journals and business magazines remain an effective method of reaching their target markets. As a result, the nature of advertising in magazines may change, but individual companies still will find effective uses for the outlets.

Newspapers

For many smaller local firms, newspaper ads, along with OOH media and radio, are the most viable advertising options, especially if television ads are cost-prohibitive. Newspapers can be distributed daily, weekly, or in partial form as the advertising supplements found in the front sections of many grocery stores and retail outlets. Figure 7.11 displays the basic advantages and disadvantages of newspaper advertising.

Many retailers rely heavily on newspaper ads because they offer *geographic selectivity* (local market access). Promoting sales, retail hours, and store locations is easy to accomplish in a newspaper ad. Short lead time allows retailers to change ads and promotions quickly. This *flexibility* is a major advantage. It allows advertisers the ability to keep ads current. Ads can be modified to meet competitive offers or to focus on recent events.

Newspapers have *high levels of credibility.* Readers rely on newspapers for factual information in stories. Newspaper readers hold high interest levels in the articles they read. They tend to pay more attention to advertisements as well as to news stories. This increased audience interest allows advertisers to provide more copy detail in their ads. Newspaper readers take more time to read copy, unless simply too much information is jammed into a small space.

ATMOSPHERE
The Great Outdoors Starts HERE

Columbia MERRELL ARC'TERYX OSPREY M'KINLEY. DAKINE THE NORTH FACE MOUNTAIN HARD WEAR Marmot KEEN

BRITISH COLUMBIA ALBERTA ONTARIO NOVA SCOTIA NEWFOUNDLAND QUEBEC
atmosphere.ca

Source: Courtesy of The Forzani Group.

This Atmosphere ad appeared in a special section of Maclean's magazine dedicated to the outdoor lifestyle, called the "Great Canadian Getaway."

FIGURE 7.11
Newspaper Advertising

Advantages	Disadvantages
1. Geographic selectivity	1. Poor buying procedures
2. High flexibility	2. Short life span
3. High credibility	3. Major clutter (especially holidays)
4. Strong audience interest	4. Poor quality reproduction (especially color)
5. Longer copy	5. Internet competition with classified ads
6. Cumulative volume discounts	
7. Coupons and special-response features	

Source: Courtesy of Toyota Canada Inc.

Newspapers are a staple media for many national advertisers such as Toyota.

Recognizing the good match between newspaper readers and its customer base, Starbucks launched a unique newspaper campaign designed by the agency Wieden + Kennedy of Portland, Oregon. Starbucks invited coffee drinkers to stop at their local Starbucks for a free cup of coffee on March 15. Four-page full-colour ads were placed in daily newspapers of 11 major markets, including New York, Los Angeles, Chicago, Boston, and Dallas. The ads were placed in the newspapers one week before the giveaway and again the day before. Then, on the day of the giveaway, Starbucks hired street vendors to pass out free copies of the newspapers that contained the Starbucks ad. The newspapers were banded with the distinctive Starbuck's coffee cup sleeve. The campaign resulted in half a million customers going into a Starbucks store. In some locations lines wrapped around the block. Starbucks estimated that the newspaper campaign resulted in 12 million impressions.[24]

Newspaper advertisers receive volume discounts for buying larger *column inches* of advertising space. Many newspapers grant these volume discounts, called *cumulative discounts*, for one-month, three-month, or even yearlong time periods. This potentially makes the cost per exposure even lower, because larger and repeated ads are more likely to garner the reader's attention.

There are limitations and disadvantages to newspaper advertising. First, newspapers cannot be targeted as easily to specific market segments (although sports pages carry sports ads, entertainment pages contain movie and restaurant ads, and so forth). Newspapers also have a *short life*. Once read, a newspaper normally is cast to the side, recycled, or destroyed. If a reader does not see an advertisement during the first pass through a newspaper, it probably will go unnoticed. Readers rarely pick up papers a second time. When they do, it is to continue reading, not to re-read or re-scan a section that has already been viewed.

Newspaper ads often suffer from *lower production quality*. Many companies do not buy colour ads because they are much more expensive. Photos and copy tend to be harder to read and see clearly compared with other print media, especially magazines.

Apart from either *The Globe and Mail* or *National Post*, newspapers suffer *poor national buying procedures*. For a national advertiser, this means contacting numerous companies and using rate cards that vary by market. Also, newspapers tend to favour local companies instead of national firms. Local businesses generally receive better advertising rates than do national advertisers, because local companies advertise on a more regular basis and receive volume discounts. Also, newspapers want to have a strong local appeal. By favouring local companies in ad rates, they can meet this goal and seem more desirable to local patrons.

MEDIA MIX

Just as media, in general, can prove useful in achieving overall IMC objectives—such as trial of new products or brand positioning—each specific media possesses unique strengths that make it applicable to specific objectives. Selecting the proper blend of media for advertisements is crucial. Media planners and media buyers are both excellent sources of information about the most effective type of mix for a particular media plan. It is a challenge to the creative team to design ads for each medium that speak to the audience and that also tie in with the overall theme of the IMC program.

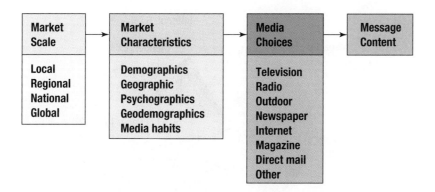

FIGURE 7.12
Developing Logical Combinations of Media

Figure 7.12 shows the process for choosing the best media for a particular advertising message. Consider the many possible options and combinations. Media experts work continually to decide which go together for individual target markets, goods and services, and advertising messages.

As we saw earlier, there are considerable differences in media mixes used by various industries. Recent studies by Millward Brown and ACNielsen highlight the benefits of combining different media.[25] In a telephone survey, Millward Brown reported that ad awareness was strongest when consumers were exposed to an advertisement on television and in a magazine. Ad awareness was much lower for those who only read the magazine ad and even less for those who only saw the television ad. The increased impact of using two or more media is called a **media multiplier effect**, which means that the combined impact of using two or more media is stronger than using either medium alone. The media multiplier effect is equally important in business-to-business advertising. In one survey, 89 percent of the business respondents indicated that an integrated marketing approach raised their awareness of a company or brand. Seeing advertisements in more than one medium caused the company or brand name to become top-of-mind. It also resulted in more individuals making purchases.[26]

The ways in which advertising media dollars are allocated among the various media are shown in Figure 7.13. Spot TV are ads purchased from a local television station for that station only. Cable and network advertising are national ads and are broadcast on all systems that carry those channels. The fastest growing media outlet is the Internet.[27]

As mentioned earlier, more and more business-to-business marketers are using media outside the traditional workplace to reach audiences. Taking lessons from brand giants such as Nike, Campbell's Soups, Wal-Mart, and Procter & Gamble, business marketers see the value of strong brands, because the name helps a company gain the attention of members of the buying centre. Office Depot recently launched an advertising campaign directed toward the business buyers that make up approximately 80 percent of the company's customer base. The campaign, titled "Takin' Care of Business,"

Media advertising hasn't traditionally been a big part of how Canadian universities attract students, donors, or potential employers. But as this magazine ad shows, many universities are now more aggressively promoting their programs and their students.

For both sides of the brain.

Tabasum Akseer
MEd candidate, Education.
Passions: flute, viola, painting, photography, humanitarianism.
Goals: Educate children. Enlighten society.

Welcome to Brock, a university designed to develop well-rounded human beings. It's a place that not only recognizes but nurtures both sides of the brain – where diverse passions are not only welcomed but celebrated, and students become better versions of themselves. And what could be more important than that?

Just ask Tabasum Akseer, a voice for cultural and racial diversity and how they're reflected in the classroom. She's taken her academic interests out of the classroom and into Afghanistan where she's helped to build two all-girl schools. Growing knowledge in Niagara and half-way 'round the world.

For your own Brock experience, visit brocku.ca or tour our campus in St. Catharines, Niagara, Ontario.

Brock
Both Sides of the Brain

FIGURE 7.13
Advertising Expenditures by Media

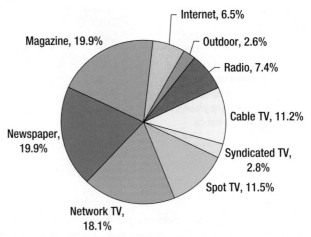

Source: Based on "100 Leading National Advertisers," *Advertising Age Datacenter 2007 Marketing Profiles Yearbook* (June 25, 2007), p. 7. Reprinted with permission, Advertising Age (2007) Copyright Crain Communications Inc.

FIGURE 7.14
Business-to-Business Advertising
Expenditures

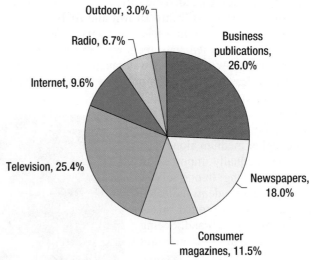

Source: Based on Kate Maddox. "Top 100 B-to-B Advertisers Increased Spending 3% in '06," *B to B* 92, no. 11 (September 10, 2007), pp. 25–30. Reprinted with permission, Advertising Age (2007) Copyright Crain Communications Inc.

highlighted the company's commitment to business customers. The campaign included TV spots, along with radio, print, online, and search marketing ads. Office Depot also signed a sponsorship deal to be the official office products partner of NASCAR.[28] Figure 7.14 shows the media allocation among business-to-business marketers.

Critical Thinking Exercise

The biggest difference between Figure 7.13 (Advertising Expenditures by Media) and Figure 7.14 (Business-to-Business Advertising Expenditures) is that consumer marketers use more television media (43.6 percent overall compared with 25.4 percent for business-to-business) and business-to-business marketers use magazines more often (37.5 percent overall compared with 19.9 percent for consumer). Why do you think this difference exists? Why do you think business-to-business marketers use the Internet as a media vehicle almost 50 percent more than consumer marketers?

COMMUNICATING ACROSS CULTURES

Understanding media consumption habits in both international and regional markets is important for successful media planning. In Japan, television is a major advertising media tool; in other countries, it is not as prevalent. In Europe, the best way to reach consumers is through print media; magazines and newspapers account for 51.5 percent of total ad spending compared with less than 40 percent in North America. Outdoor is used relatively little in North America and Europe (3.1 percent and 6.1 percent, respectively) but consists of 11.6 percent of the total media spending in Japan.[29]

Although there are a large number of media buying agencies throughout the world, nearly three-quarters of all media buying is conducted by only six large global agencies or their holding agencies. The largest global media company is the WPP Group, which holds 22 percent of the market share.[30] To combat these large media networks, a global media consortium has been formed. The consortium is made up of a number of smaller independent agencies and offers services in Europe, North America, the Russian Federation, and Asia. Central offices are located in New York and London to serve business clients and to pitch for regional and national accounts.[31] The large global media agencies have faced some criticism in recent years from marketing managers. They complain about the inability to provide effective media buys throughout all the countries where the clients operate. Although a few agencies do cover the world, it is difficult to be strong in every country where an agency may have a presence. The global agency just cannot be the best option in every country. For this reason, local media agencies and the consortium of independent agencies believe they have a chance to increase their market share.

China offers an excellent example of the difficulties the global media agencies face. A recent study revealed that the average multinational agency has a relationship with Chinese clients for 2.4 to 2.8 years, which is two to three times shorter than the typical agency–client relationship in the United States and Europe. The challenge the multinational agencies face is to provide a seamless delivery to far-flung cities and provinces throughout China and to provide it cheaper, faster, and better than the local Chinese agencies. It is a monumental task. For instance, one client required media buys in 120 Chinese cities. With 55,000 local Chinese agencies vying for business in China, the global companies face a stiff challenge.[32]

In general, the tactics used to develop advertising campaigns and choose appropriate media in North America apply to other countries throughout the world. What differs is the nature of the target markets, consumer media preferences, the processes used to buy media, and even availability of certain media. Also, company representatives must carefully attend to cultural mores to make sure the buying process does not offend the cultural and religious attitudes prevalent in any given region. It is important to fully understand the target market as a company purchases media as part of its overall IMC campaigns.

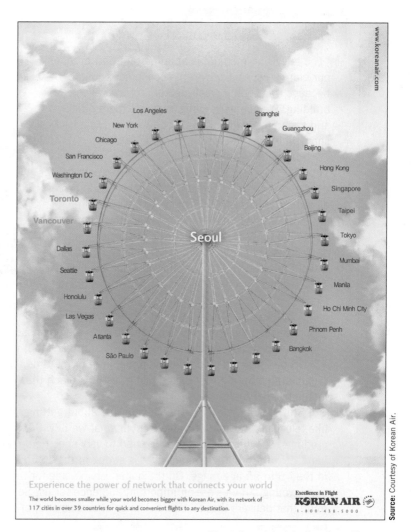

Magazines local to the Canadian market provide global brands like Korean Air an excellent opportunity to target Canadian travellers heading to Asia.

IMC IN PRACTICE

"The television medium is an important part of all of our plans—especially with the consumer audience—because it is such a great medium for awareness building. We can get our message out there quickly and generate very high levels of awareness in a very short time using television."

But the medium also delivers other benefits for TELUS. "The medium also lets us appeal to both the head and heart of the audience. It enables us to express all attributes of the TELUS brand at the same time."

For consumer marketers, Kate sees television as integral to success. "We see it as a cornerstone of our campaigns," she says. "We've run consumer campaigns without television before, but they just don't deliver the same results. First the levels of awareness and brand likability are never as high without television in a campaign, but we also see a difference on the revenue side. Television helps build that initial awareness that leads people through the entire process right down to the purchase decision."

TELUS uses advertising extensively because it has such a broad target audience.

As a major advertiser in Canada, and a company that wants almost every Canadian to hear its message, TELUS purchases a lot of television media in prime time, between the hours of 8 p.m. and 11 p.m. "The programming during prime time just gives us a reach that we can't match with any other time, or any other media for that matter."

Still, buying television media isn't just about getting a high number. "Even with a broad reach media like television, we try to be smart about what we buy. So, for example, in the advertising for TELUS Mobility products, specific handsets can be tied to very specific demographics. So we match the messages for one handset with the programming that is strong in the 18 to 24 segment, and others that deliver more viewers in the 45 to 55 age range. On the home service side for things like home phone, long distance, and broadband, young families are an important audience for us. So you'll see our ads skewed more toward programming that delivers these viewers. Things like news and, of course, hockey."

Source: Used with permission of Kate Baillie, TELUS Communications.

For help developing your IMC Plan, go to **www.pearsoncanada.ca/clow**.

SUMMARY

Traditionally, advertising media was seen as the dominant force behind marketing communications success. This has lessened significantly as other marketing communications tools, such as digital marketing and sales promotion, prove their value. However, the importance of media to overall IMC objectives, and the value of media planning and buying, continues to gain clout in the marketing community. Speaking about the advertising media component of IMC, Bob Brennan, Chief Operating Officer of Chicago-based Leo Burnett Starcom USA, says that in the past, "Ninety-five percent of your success was great creative and 5 percent was great media. Now it's much closer to 50–50."[33]

We started this chapter with an examination of why and when advertising media should be considered for inclusion in an IMC plan. The ability for media to deliver on objectives such

as need recognition or brand positioning makes it an excellent choice for many marketers. Next, we examined the objectives specific to the media portion of the IMC plan: reach, frequency, opportunity to see, gross rating points, effective rating points, cost, continuity, and gross impressions drive the media selection process. Reach is the number of people, households, or businesses in a target audience exposed to a media vehicle or message schedule at least once during a given time period. Frequency is the average number of times an individual, household, or business within a particular target market is exposed to a particular advertisement within a specified time period. Gross rating points (GRP) measure the impact or intensity of a media plan. Cost per thousand (CPM) is one method of finding the cost of the campaign by assessing the dollar cost of reaching 1,000 members of the media vehicle's audience. Cost per rating point

(CPRP) is a second cost measure, which assesses the efficiency of a media vehicle relative to a firm's target market. Ratings measure the percentage of a firm's target market that is exposed to a show on television or an article in a print medium. Continuity is the schedule or pattern of advertisement placements within an advertising campaign period. Gross impressions is the number of total exposures of the audience to an advertisement.

In addition to these basic concepts, advertising experts often utilize the concepts of effective frequency and effective reach. Effective frequency is the number of times a target audience must be exposed to a message to achieve a particular objective. Effective reach is the percentage of an audience that must be exposed to a particular message to achieve a specific objective.

We explored how the media planner and media buyer develop the media plan. This plan includes the marketing and advertising analyses, media strategy, schedule, and justification. The plan consists of a consideration of a range of potential media options, each of which possesses unique strengths and weaknesses. Thus, television, radio, out-of-home, magazines, and newspapers should all be considered as potential ingredients in a campaign. Logical combinations of media must be chosen to make sure the intended audience is exposed to the message. The three-exposure hypothesis suggests that a consumer must be exposed to an ad at least three times before it has the desired impact; other experts believe even more exposures are necessary. In contrast, recency theory suggests that ads truly reach only those wanting or needing a product and that the carryover effect of advertising diminishes rapidly. The selection of media continuity, then, depends on determining how many times and how often the audience needs to be exposed to the message. Media planners and buyers choose between continuous, pulsating, and flighting schedules.

Finally, we examined how the media multiplier effect works and the advantages of using more than one media in conjunction with one another (in addition to the other tools in the marketing communications mix) to create synergies. This effect is present in both consumer and business-to-business markets.

Advertising across cultures dictates that a media plan be developed within each local jurisdiction because media buying processes differ, as do media preferences of locals in various countries. At its most basic, however, the process of media selection is quite similar: Marketing experts choose media they believe will reach the target audience in an effective manner.

KEY TERMS

continuity   The schedule or pattern of advertisement placements within an advertising campaign period.

cost per rating point (CPRP)   A measure of the efficiency of a media vehicle relative to a firm's target market.

cost per thousand (CPM)   The dollar cost of reaching 1,000 members of the media vehicle's audience.

effective frequency   The number of times a target audience must be exposed to a message to achieve a particular objective.

effective reach   The percentage of an audience that must be exposed to a particular message to achieve a specific objective.

frequency   The average number of times an individual, household, or business within a particular target market is exposed to a particular advertisement within a specified time period.

gross impressions   The total number of exposures of the audience to an advertisement.

gross rating points (GRP)   A measure of the impact or intensity of a media plan.

intrusion value   The ability of media or an advertisement to intrude upon a viewer without his or her voluntary attention.

marketing communications mix   The combination of tools used to promote a product or service, including advertising media, direct marketing, sales promotion, public relations, and digital marketing.

media buyer   The person who buys the space and negotiates rates, times, and schedules for the ads.

media multiplier effect   The combined impact of using two or more media is stronger than using either medium alone.

media planner   The individual who formulates the program stating where and when to place advertisements.

opportunities to see (OTS)   The cumulative exposures to an advertisement that are achieved in a given time period.

reach   The number of people, households, or businesses in a target audience exposed to a media vehicle or message schedule at least once during a given time period.

spot ad   A one-time ad placed on a local television station.

ratings   A measure of the percentage of a firm's target market that is exposed to a show on television or an article in a print medium.

recency theory   A theory that suggests that a consumer's attention is selective and focused on his or her individual needs and wants, and that therefore advertising has little to no carryover effect.

weighted (or demographic) CPM   A measure used to calculate whether an advertisement reached the target market effectively.

REVIEW QUESTIONS

1. What is a media plan? How does it relate to the creative brief and the overall IMC plan?

2. What does a media planner do?

3. Describe the role of media buyer in an advertising program.

4. What is reach? Give examples of reach in various advertising media.

5. What is frequency? How can an advertiser increase frequency in a campaign?

6. What are gross rating points? What do they measure?

7. What is the difference between CPM and CPRP? What costs do they measure?

8. What is continuity?

9. Describe the three-exposure hypothesis.

10. How does recency theory differ from the three-exposure hypothesis?

11. What is effective frequency? Effective reach?

12. What are the major advantages and disadvantages of television advertising?

13. What are the major advantages and disadvantages of radio advertising?

14. What are the major advantages and disadvantages of out-of-home advertising?

15. What are the major advantages and disadvantages of magazine advertising?

16. What are the major advantages and disadvantages of newspaper advertising?

17. Is the strong intrusion value of television an advantage? Why or why not?

INTEGRATED LEARNING EXERCISES

1. Assume that HP wants to sell a new line of colour printers to businesses. Market research determined that the most promising segments are governments, universities, and colleges because of their relative immunity to economic cycles and a relatively steady investment in updating technology over time. A $2.5 million marketing communications budget has been allocated for the Canadian market. Should advertising media be considered for the marketing communications plan? Why or why not? Which specific media do you recommend and why? Come up with four specific media outlets that you recommend to reach the target audience at these institutions—two while they are at work, and two while they are not at work.

2. A significant source of media planning information in Canada is BBM (Bureau of Broadcast Measurement).

Access their website at **www.bbm.ca.** What type of information is available on the site? How can it be used to develop a media plan for Canada?

3. Although executing a media campaign across two or more media provides benefits for marketers, it provides creative challenges. It can be difficult for a creative idea to work in more than one medium, especially when one is a broadcast medium such as television, and another is a print medium such as newspaper or outdoor. Find an example of a campaign currently running in your market that you think does a good job of executing a campaign idea across two or more different advertising media, or one that you think does a poor job of executing across two or more media. What is it about the specific ads and the underlying idea that leads you to your conclusions?

STUDENT PROJECT

Creative Corner

Advertising and marketing of colleges and universities is a recent phenomenon. Promoting a college of business or a marketing department within a university is even more rare. One of your recent marketing alumni made a large donation for media buys to advertise the marketing program. She is especially interested in the nontraditional student who is married, has a family,

and is working full time. What message would you want to convey about the marketing program to this specific target market? Choose one medium that you think will be particularly critical to your media plan and justify your recommendation. Then design the ad you plan to use (e.g., if it's a billboard, magazine, or newspaper ad, do the layout and copy; if it's a radio ad, provide the script; if it's a television ad, develop a storyboard).

→ ETHICS IN ACTION

It's Spring break and you are in Mexico. Nice. Imagine you are lying on a beach on a beautiful sunny day, staring out at the ocean. Then along comes a floating billboard with loud music announcing the opening of a bar near the beach. At first you think maybe you'll try it out that night, but then you notice that a plane is also approaching, carrying a large banner announcing the same opening. This gets you wondering; was it right that the bar used the public space to promote itself? The intrusion into a public space of an advertising message is something that beach goers simply cannot avoid, and this creates an ethical dilemma. Are there some spaces—public spaces—that should be protected against commercial messages? Where is the line between the sanctity of shared public

space and the availability of that space for a member of the public to use as their free medium?

1. Think of an example of an advertising message that you saw recently that was placed obtrusively, and for free, by the advertiser in a public space. Did it annoy you? Did you have the opportunity to avoid the message?

2. What are the factors that might predict when a member of the public will be upset over the intrusion of private advertising messages into public spaces, and when they will accept it or even see it as valuable? Is there a specific type or amount of advertising or a specific public space in which you feel that advertising should never be permitted? ●

CASE STUDY | Diversity in the New Haven Fire Department

Ask most people to describe a typical firefighter and you will hear about a man, physically strong, aged somewhere between 25 and 40. And for the most part, that description is fairly accurate. But fire departments today, and the role of firefighters, largely don't reflect the profession. Decades ago, physical strength was required as firefighters hauled ladders and other heavy equipment in their firefighting duties. Today, although firefighters are still required to carry some equipment and possess reasonable physical fitness, there is no reason why the profession should be limited to young, strong men.

Last year in the city of New Haven only 4 percent of the incidents to which the fire department responded were fires. Over 60 percent of incidents were medical incidents from 911 calls, and a further 22 percent of incidents were motor vehicle accidents. Firefighters attend medical incidents as "first responders," and New Haven is served by their fire department from 11 fire halls throughout the city.

Additionally, firefighting equipment has changed significantly over the years. Heavy ladders that were once raised manually are now electronically operated. Self-contained breathing apparatus—a heavy steel air tank strapped onto the back of firefighters—have been upgraded to smaller lightweight versions. Advanced techniques have been introduced to make the job less reliant on brute strength.

A total of 219 career firefighters combined with approximately 75 paid, on-call volunteers make up New Haven's fire department. When one looks closely at the workforce profile of the department, it is almost exclusively Caucasian and male. Only 5 percent of all firefighters belong to one of the four recognized employment equity groups—four females and seven visible minorities. The first two female firefighters was hired approximately 15 years ago. There are currently no Aboriginal firefighters or firefighters with disabilities.

This stands in sharp contrast to the composition of New Haven. Statistics indicate that the population of the city grew from 276,345 to 321,871 in the past five years. Approximately one-half of the city's population is female. The city has a fairly large visible minority population, accounting for approximately 76,005, or 23.6 percent, of its total population. The South Asian population, which consists of various ethnic groups including East Indian, Pakistani, and Sri Lankan, accounts for approximately 27.5 percent of the total city population and 51 percent of visible minorities. Additionally, while the Aboriginal population is comparatively small, it is the most youthful and fastest growing population in Canada and will be entering the labour force at an exponential rate over the next 20 years.

The vast majority of the city's population speaks English or French; however, statistics reveal that approximately 5.5 percent of the city's population does not speak either official language. Given Canada's ongoing efforts to encourage immigration to help address its skilled labour shortages, it is expected that the percentage of individuals speaking languages other than English and French will continue to rise.

Vacancies for firefighter positions are typically associated with population growth or retirements. Few vacancies become available due to firefighters who leave the profession. This is largely due to the fact that firefighting provides full-time and year-round work, offers higher pay than many professions with similar educational requirements, and provides good opportunities for promotion and comprehensive insurance plans. Additionally, good working conditions, prestige, camaraderie, and dedication to the service contribute to a low attrition rate.

One study developed a benchmark for the expected female representation among firefighters by computing the proportion of women in the nation-wide labour force of typical firefighter age (20–49) and educational background (high-school graduate but no college degree), employed at least 35 hours per week in one of 184 occupations resembling firefighting in requiring strength, stamina, and dexterity, and/or involving outdoor, dirty, or dangerous work. These comparable occupations included: bus mechanics, drywall installers, enlisted military personnel, highway maintenance workers, loggers, professional athletes, refuse collectors, and roofers, among others. The proportion of women among these persons in the labour force nationwide is 17.0 percent. The benchmark for visible minorities is even higher, suggesting that the New Haven Fire Service is lagging well behind other professions and simply does not reflect the city that it serves.

Additionally, careers in the fire department were often seen as a family tradition. Over the years, firefighters were looked up to as trusted, almost heroic community figures, which in turn helped fuel a degree of elitism from within the department. Over many years, the department developed to the point where it consisted of a majority of Caucasian males, helping to feed the perception that women were perhaps incapable of carrying out the duties of a firefighter and that visible minorities, women, and Aboriginal peoples were not wanted or would not be accepted.

This is a problem for a number of reasons. First, as a public service, the department should reflect the diversity of the city. Second, when citizens feel identification with the fire department, they are more likely to call upon them in times of need. New Haven is ranked one of the most diverse communities in Canada and strongly believes that building a diverse workforce is necessary to better serve the community and build trust among its citizens.

Source: © Stockbroker/MaxxImages.com.

Firefighters who are not white males are uncommon.

Recognizing the benefits of a diverse workforce, and the fact that new applications still largely reflect the white male stereotypes of the fire department, Chief Bill Bailey decided to appoint a committee to oversee a communications campaign to encourage applications across the community. The goal is to, over time, evolve the workforce of the New Haven Fire Department so that it's representative of the demographic composition of the city of New Haven.

The committee has organized appearances at various community fairs, including several multicultural events, in an effort to drive recruitment. But feedback from those staffing the booths is that the stereotypes are very strong, and that most people simply ignored the firefighter booth. A decision was made to undertake a media campaign in an effort to change the perception of the fire department to support these local events. As one of the first orders of business, the committee has reached out to your school to ask for input on how it should approach the recruitment process. Media often donate time to public service causes such as the fire department, but the committee wonders where to start. With so many media options, and such a bias to overcome, what would be the best approach?

1. If you were advising the committee, what objectives would you set for the media portion of the campaign? Using the approach to objectives discussed in Chapter 4, write a specific recommendation for the committee.

2. Although the city of New Haven has options in television, radio, newspapers, local magazines, and plenty of out-of-home media, the committee has asked for a priority list. Develop a two-page report to the committee where you outline two media you recommend they use as a focus. In the report, analyze each of the five media options, and discuss how each of their respective strengths and weaknesses are applicable to the challenge of the New Haven Fire Department.

3. The committee has asked you to also provide input on the message strategy that will accompany your media recommendation. Since changing stereotypes is a long-term proposal, one of the key challenges will be to match the media strengths with the message. Prepare a 15-minute presentation in which you outline your ideas (e.g., print layout, radio script, storyboard, etc.) for your two proposed media.

ENDNOTES

1. Herbert E. Krugman, "Why Three Exposures May Be Enough," *Journal of Advertising Research* 12, no. 6 (1972), pp. 11–14.

2. Erwin Ephron and Colin McDonald, "Media Scheduling and Carry-over Effects: Is Adstock a Useful Planning Tool," *Journal of Advertising Research* 42, no. 4 (July–August 2002), pp. 66–70; Laurie Freeman, "Added Theories Drive Need for Client Solutions," *Advertising Age* 68, no. 31, p. 18.

3. Kate Maddox, "Media Planners in High Demand," *B to B* 89, no. 13 (November 8, 2004), p. 24.

4. Jack Neff, "Media Buying & Planning," *Advertising Age* 70, no. 32 (August 2, 1999), pp. 1–2.

5. Melanie Johnston, "That Little Blue Pad," *Marketing Magazine* 107, no. 4 (April 8, 2002), p. 10.

6. Arthur A. Andersen, "Clout Only a Part of Media Buyer's Value," *Advertising Age* 70, no. 15 (April 5, 1999), p. 26.

7. Ibid.

8. Diane Holloway, "What's On? Ads, Ads, and Maybe a TV Show," *Austin American Statesman* (**www.austin360.com/tv/content/movies/television/2005/10/11tvcolumn.html**, accessed January 17, 2008).

9. Gregory Solman, "Forward Thought: Ads A-Ok on DVRs," *Hollywood Reporter* (**http://hollywoodreporter.com**), December 27, 2007.

10. "AAAA Survey Finds Eight Percent Hike in Cost to Produce 30-Second TV Commercials," *Film & Video Production & Postproduction Magazine (ICOM)* (**www.icommag.com/november-2002/november-page-1b.html**, accessed January 14, 2005).

11. Roger Baron, "Spot TV Strategy No Simple Matter," *Television Week* 23, no. 39 (September 27, 2004), p. 57.

12. Stephanie Thompson, "Food Marketers Stir Up the Media," *Advertising Age* 70, no. 42 (September 11, 1999), p. 18.

13. Arlena Sawyers, "GM Certified Offers Dealer Ads," *Automotive News* 79, no. 6138 (March 14, 2005), p. 58.

14. Stephanie Thompson, "Arden Scores with Radio Promotions," *Advertising Age* 75, no. 47 (November 22, 2004), p. 8.

15. Camille Alarcon, "War of Words over Radio Ads," *B&T Weekly* 54, no. 2508 (February 25, 2005), p. 9.

16. Deborah L. Vence, "Outdoor Ads Leverage New Technology," *Marketing News* 38, no. 5 (September 15, 2004), pp. 11–13.

17. Dana Wood, "The Great Outdoors," *WWD: Women's Wear Daily* 188, no. 121 (December 10, 2004), p. 6.

18. "Mobile Billboards Get Exposed in Traffic," *Marketing News* 38, no. 14 (September 1, 2004), p. 12.

19. IMA Outdoor. Accessed on June 4, 2011 from: **http://www.imaoutdoor.com/content/view/19/35/**

20. Jamie LaReau, "Magazines Are Pricey—But a Bargain, Publishers Say," *Automotive News* 79, no. 6139 (March 21, 2005), p. 46.

21. Ann Marie Kerwin, "Magazines Blast Study Showing Reader Falloff," *Advertising Age* 70, no. 10 (March 8, 1999), pp. 3–4.

22. "Reports of Mag-Industry Demise Greatly Exaggerated," *Advertising Age* 78, no. 14 (April 2, 2007), p. 14.

23. Lisa Granatstein, "Ups and Downs," *Brandweek* 45, no. 34 (September 27, 2004), p. SR11; Jamie LaReau, "Magazines Are Pricey—But a Bargain, Publishers Say," *Automotive News* 79, no. 6139 (March 21, 2005), p. 46.

24. Bill Gloede, "Best Use of Newspapers," *Adweek* 48, no. 25 (June 18, 2007), pp. SR22–23.

25. Lindsay Morris, "Studies Give 'Thumbs Up' to Mags for Ad Awareness," *Advertising Age* 70, no. 32 (August 2, 1999), pp. 16–17; Rachel X. Weissman, "Broadcasters Mine the Gold," *American Demographics* 21, no. 6 (June 1999), pp. 35–37.

26. "ABM Releases Harris Study Data: B2B Advertising Highly Effective," *Min's B2B* 9, no. 26 (June 26, 2006), p. 8.

27. Larry Percy, John R. Rossiter, and Richard Elliott, "Media Strategy," *Strategic Advertising Management* (2001), pp. 151–63.

28. Carol Krol, "Office Depot Puts Focus on 'Business' in New Year," *BtoB* 90, no. 1 (January 17, 2005), p. 3.

29. Colin MacLeod, "Global Adspend Trends," *International Journal of Advertising,* 24 (2, 2005), 261–262.

30. Joe Mandese, "Power Shift," *Broadcasting & Cable* 135, no. 53 (December 12, 2005), p. 12.

31. Martin Croft, "Media Indies Take on Networks with Consortium," *Marketing Week* 29, no. 28 (July 13, 2006), p. 13.

32. Greg Paull, "Act Local, Think Local as China Gets Even Tougher," *Media: Asia's Media & Marketing Newspaper* (April 21, 2006), p. 19.

33. Jack Neff, "Media Buying & Planning," *Advertising Age* 70, no. 32 (August 2, 1999), pp. 1–2.

CHAPTER OBJECTIVES

After reading this chapter, you should be able to answer the following questions:

- **What** objectives can direct marketing fulfill in an overall IMC plan?
- **How** do marketers compile a data warehouse?
- **What** are the means by which marketers can code and analyze data to build marketing programs and direct marketing communications?
- **What** formats are included in direct marketing?
- **What** are the strengths and weaknesses of direct marketing?

INDUSTRY PROFILE
So You Want to Work in Marketing Communications?

Brigitte St-Germain, Director of Corporate Relations, Canadian Red Cross, Quebec Division Montreal, Quebec

Brigitte St-Germain sleeps well at night. After 20 years as a criminal defence attorney, she finally has a career where she feels fulfilled and rewarded in ways that money never could provide. "When I was a lawyer, there were a few times when I was actually sad that I won a case!" says Brigitte. "As a criminal lawyer I didn't always get the greatest sense of satisfaction from my work. But now, when I see the immediate results of the work of the Red Cross, or see the gratitude from those that we help . . . it just feels great to help people."

Her move into the Red Cross was somewhat of an accident. "I knew I wanted a change, and my sister-in-law worked at the Red Cross. I asked if there were any openings at the organization. It didn't matter to me if it was in finance, fundraising, or whatever. As luck would have it, they needed someone to work in the fundraising department, so that's where I got my start."

"Fundraising for the Red Cross was an interesting challenge," says Brigitte. "Although the brand is recognized by virtually everyone and enjoys a level of trust that most brands can only dream about, most people don't actually understand what we do on a day-to-day basis." The problem, says Brigitte, is that the organization is so well known for its international disaster relief that raising money for ongoing needs doesn't fit most donors' perceptions of the brand. "When the Haiti earthquake happened, for example, across Canada we raised $140 million virtually overnight. Canadians are so generous when they see these events happen around the world, and we are the first and sometimes only brand that comes to mind as a way for them to help."

Even when raising money for domestic efforts, the success comes easily for high-profile events. "When the big ice storm hit Quebec in the 90s, or during the Déluge du Saguenay, people opened their hearts and wallets and wanted to help," says Brigitte. But the problem is that every day, smaller events affect people and these don't make the news. "We helped over 6,000 people in the

Direct Marketing

province of Quebec last year, responding to over 1,200 disasters. These are things like house fires where the family is left with nothing. The Red Cross comes in to help. Most people don't know about this work, so the only time they donate is when they hear of a high-profile, major disaster."

Like most nonprofit organizations, the Red Cross relies heavily on direct mail for its ongoing fundraising efforts. "We do two types of mailings," says Brigitte. "The first, and most important, is our own list of people who have donated to us before. This is an important list because these people know who we are and what we do in addition to the high-profile international disasters. We are fortunate to have very loyal donors, and because our brand is so trusted, they know when they donate to us the money will be used for the purpose they intended."

"The second type of mailing at the Red Cross is donor acquisition mailings. These are done through rented lists where we can choose people based on their age, where they live, or other factors that we think will make them likely donors to the Red Cross." The targeted mailings are a way to focus the specific message of the Red Cross, and the education of the domestic efforts on people who may not yet know what the Red Cross does with Quebec, but are likely to want to help.

Brigitte St-Germain, Director of Corporate Relations, Canadian Red Cross.

"An important audience for us in acquisition programs are younger donors. Brigitte explains: "Donors to most charities tend to be older than the average Canadian. So it's important that we continually attract new, younger donors. The ideal is that someone begins a relationship with us in their 20s and becomes a lifelong donor."

But Brigitte knows that direct mailings, like many traditional communication vehicles, may not be the best way to attract younger donors. "Of course, we are rounding out our direct mailing program with activities in places like Facebook. If we want to communicate with an audience, we have to go where they are and do it on their terms."

The Red Cross also communicates with corporate donors. "One of our biggest events is our annual charity ball. A lot of companies get involved, and each year a CEO from one of the high-profile Quebec-based companies gets involved as co-chair of the event." The relationships built over time with corporate donors are an important link between fundraising in the traditional sense and newer forms of corporate support for the Red Cross. "When I moved from fundraising to the my new role as Director of Corporate Relations, I saw the power of existing relationships and the benefit of having people know who we are and what we do."

The latest innovation, based on a successful campaign in the United States, is to partner with companies to allow employees to volunteer in disaster relief for two full days, with full pay. "For this new campaign, it's important that the project receive endorsement from the top levels of the company. One of the first companies to sign on was Bombardier. They were a natural company for us to approach because the CEO Pierre Beaudoin had been involved with our charity ball for the previous six years. So we had a relationship, and he knew that our organization was a worthwhile partner in this program."

For this new corporate program, targeting is also important. "We need to be specific in who we approach, and not just ask anyone who knows us. Part of the reason for this is that we need to be sure the company is large enough to justify the efforts of the program. For example, we know that a relatively small percentage of employees sign up. Maybe 3 or 4 percent. So if there are only five people volunteering from a company, it's inefficient to manage. It's also nice if the employees of the company have some experience that might be relevant in a disaster. So, for instance, companies like Hydro Quebec and Bell are is a great fit for this program."

Because nonprofits tend to have fewer resources for formal training, Brigitte tells young people considering the field to be sure to bring their initiative. "We need people who aren't afraid to grab the bull by the horns and take on a project, or to speak up when they see something that can be done better. But we need people to stand on their own two feet relatively quickly once they join."

The good news is that there is no shortage of young people with initiative who want to work in the nonprofit field. "We have a lot more interest from younger people these days who say they are looking for a career where they can get more than just money. They are looking for a sense of satisfaction from their work. It's why I joined the Red Cross, but it took me 20 years to figure it out. Younger people today seem to have figured this out already. The pay is usually lower, and the hours can sometimes be longer, but I wouldn't trade it for the world."

OVERVIEW

The second tool in the marketing communications toolbox is, much like advertising media, actually a collection of tactics that share a number of things in common. Grouped under the heading of direct marketing, all of these tactics rely on a conversation that takes places between the marketers and an individual, one audience member at a time. Examples include letters that come addressed to the recipient personally or emails that contain information specific to the person receiving it.

The defining characteristic of direct marketing is that it does not assume that all members of an audience are equal. The ability to target messages specifically to individual members of an audience group means the marketers can tailor their message based on what they know about that individual. For example, if an individual has recently purchased a car from a dealer, the dealer can follow up with offers for service and maintenance that are specific to vehicle that was purchased. This can be much more effective than advertising dealer service through more mass media such as newspapers or out-of-home media, since every member of the target audience is already pre-screened as a customer who purchased a car from that specific dealer. Further, after a number of years, the dealer can send a direct response message to the same customer with the objective of having them buy a replacement vehicle. This can again be highly effective since the dealer knows, with a reasonable degree of certainty, the age of the customers' car, and the likelihood that they will be in the market for a new vehicle. Because of the highly targeted nature of direct marketing, it can be particularly effective at the purchase and post-purchase stages of the customer decision-making process.

At the heart of direct marketing is data. Data can be used to either target specific messages to specific individuals, as in the case of the car dealer above. This data can, in turn, be used to produce higher levels of retention, loyalty, and ultimately profitability.

The first part of this chapter examines issues related to data and database management, as well as various sources of data available to marketers. We then examine how this data can be organized and analyzed to provide the marketer with useful insights. Finally, we examine how these insights can be used to craft marketing programs and guide the development of specific direct marketing tactics that add value to the IMC plan.

DATA AND DATABASE MANAGEMENT

Database marketing involves collecting and utilizing customer data for the purposes of enhancing interactions with a target audience. Although most databases house a collection of information on customers, communications with any stakeholder of an organization can be through direct marketing. For example, a firm that wishes to manage relationships with members of parliament can compile a database containing information on each MP and use that data to craft specific messages to each individual MP. Apart from allowing riding-specific messages to each individual, such a program may be one of only a few options to reach some audiences.

Successful database marketing emphasizes two things: identifying customers and building relationships with them. This includes understanding the lifetime values of various customers and the development of customer retention efforts, especially for the firm's best customers. Harry Rosen is a high-end men's clothing store. When shoppers visit the store, the sales staff has access to data regarding their preferences, sizes, previous purchases, and other information. Purchases are followed up with thank-you notes. Customers receive notices when new shipments of clothes arrive, and they are given invitations to special events. Loyalty to the store remains high. One vital ingredient in this success story stands out: Data is used to make customers feel special and to develop relationships them. While selling may occur, it does not drive the database program.

Building a Database

Successful database marketing requires a quality data warehouse. The **data warehouse** holds all of the customer data. In building one, the IT department and marketing team first distinguish between an operational database and the marketing database. The operational database contains the transactions individuals have with the firm and follows accounting principles. The marketing department manages the marketing database, which contains information about current customers, former customers, and prospects. Examples of data and analyses found in a standard marketing data warehouse include:

- Customer names and addresses
- E-mail addresses and the cookies that record Web visits to the company's website
- History of every purchase transaction
- History of customer interactions, such as inquiries, complaints, and returns
- Results of any customer surveys
- Preferences and profiles supplied by the customer
- Marketing promotions and response history from marketing campaigns
- Appended demographic and psychographic data from sources such as Knowledge Base Marketing or Claritas
- Database coding through customer analyses, such as lifetime value, customer segment cluster, and RFM (recency, frequency, monetary) analysis

Collecting customer names and addresses is the easiest part of developing the database. The challenge is collecting all of the other information that turns the data warehouse into a powerful marketing and communication tool.

Source: © iStockphoto.

Keeping an up-to-date data warehouse requires constant management.

The marketing team typically has a system for updating addresses, because approximately 20 percent of Canadians move each year. When individuals fill out a change of address form with Canada Post, the information is sent to all of the service bureaus authorized to sell the information to businesses. A company that sends database names to one of these service bureaus receives address updates for only a few cents per hit, or per individual that moves. Updating mailing addresses should occur at least once each year, depending on how the database is used and the frequencies of contacts.

Data for the data warehouse comes from either the company's internal operations or external sources where companies can purchase information about individuals. Each of these is discussed below.

Internal Data Sources

Ongoing interactions between a company and individuals create many opportunities to collect data that can then become an integral part of a data warehouse.

Email Addresses and Other Personal Identification Data

Email addresses are essential elements of a most databases because they provide excellent, cost-effective channels of communication which can be used in building relationships with customers. Many customers provide email addresses when signing up for newsletters, inquiring about products or services, or simply accessing a customer service function. Other address information is routinely gathered as part of a company's operations when a customer purchases products. For example, when a customer purchases a new washer and dryer from The Brick, the delivery requires the collection of address information.

Purchase and Communication Histories

Effective database programs maintain detailed purchase histories of customers. The database records every interaction the company has with a customer. This can include not only sales but other interactions such as customer service or tech support inquiries. Purchases and interaction histories determine future communications with customers and assist the marketing department in evaluating each customer's lifetime value, as well as other customer value metrics.

Critical Thinking Exercise

What are the factors that should determine how a marketer deals with customers who show a high usage of tech support, or make an unusually high number of calls to a customer service department? Do these customer represent an opportunity to invest marketing communications dollars in order to help the relationship with the company, or should this information be used to eliminate them from future communications since they are likely to cost the company more than they are worth in revenue?

ON THE JOB

Many companies gather data on customers by using advertising media to encourage customers to contact them directly, or even buy from them directly. The use of media to generate a dialogue between the company and the customer provides two advantages, depending on the objective of the media placement.

For ads that promote direct selling, the benefit is obvious—revenue without the expense of a distribution channel. The company invests heavily in television advertising focused on specific direct-response offers. Dell's marketing team recently discovered that the company's television spots generated the largest number of responses, as measured by inbound calls and hits on the company's website. Dell also places ads in free-standing inserts (FSIs) in newspapers and on the radio. Both have also proven to be more successful than anticipated in driving traffic to Dell's website and driving sales.[1]

For some advertisements, the objective is to offer additional information on a product or service. For example, the Canadian Home Income Plan encourages seniors to call and order a brochure on reverse mortgages. In this case, the benefit is the identification of a qualified prospect, and the delivery of materials than can result in an eventual sale. The purchase process for a reverse mortgage is characterized by high involvement. For instance, by getting a brochure into the hands of a qualified prospect, the company moves one step closer to a sale.

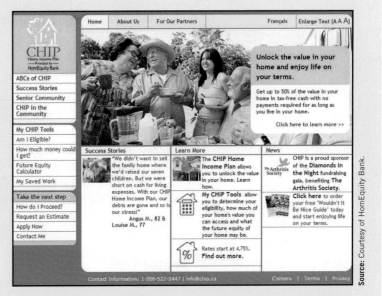

Source: Courtesy of HomEquity Bank.

The Canadian Home Income Plan asks consumers to request a brochure or visit a website for more information.

Therefore, it is important that direct marketing—like all elements of the marketing communications mix—be integrated tightly into the overall plan. In the past, media has dominated the mix, with elements like direct marketing added as an afterthought. These examples show how the lines between direct response and advertising media are blurred and necessitate a truly integrated approach to marketing communications.

Personal Preference Profiles

Purchase and visit histories are not sufficient. Quality data warehouses include customer profiles with specific information regarding each customer's personal preferences. The manner in which these profiles and personal preference files are constructed varies from company to company. Some may be obtained from customer surveys. Others gather information on the website or in retail stores.

External Data Sources

Geocoding

One way to append demographic information is **geocoding**, which is the process of adding geographic codes to each customer record so that customer addresses can be plotted on a map. Geocoding helps decision makers finalize placements of retail outlets and can be used to direct marketing materials to specific geographic areas. Geocoding allows for combining demographic information with lifestyle data.

As mentioned in Chapter 4, Canada Post offers a service called GeoPost that helps companies pinpoint specific segments using geodemographics. The service identifies 65 unique segments of consumers and geographic areas (defined by postal codes) where they can be found in high percentages. The segments are based on consumer clusters system known as PSYTE. Each of the clusters is unique in many respects from the others, and offers marketers a very specific profile of their target audience. Marketers can use this service to append information to their internal data and supplement sales data with other types of data related to lifestyle or demographics.

Critical Thinking Exercise

Go to the Canada Post website and learn more about the GeoPost service. How might some of the attributes available through GeoPost be useful to marketers in tailoring more effective direct marketing messages? If a company has address and sales history data, what value can knowing other lifestyle information such as whether or not the person has children and their ages, or their approximate income, add to the direct marketing development process?

Rented Lists

Companies that wish to go further than appending external data to their internal lists can rent information about individuals. These rented lists are typically standalone data warehouses that allow a marketer to target and execute direct marketing programs without building their own data warehouses. They are also useful for new customer acquisition programs because most internal data warehouses consist of existing or previous customers of a firm, and relying only on this source data doesn't allow for growth of the customer base. Further, external lists are valuable for companies that do not have transactional data. Consider the example of Kraft. When a person buys a Kraft product at a grocery store, the company has no way of tracking that customer in the same manner as other firms such as Bell or Rogers can track their customers. Through rented lists the company can target specific individuals who they know have an interest in cooking and tailor specific, targeted messages to them.

Typically the rental of lists is for a one-time use, although some lists can be rented for multiple uses. After using the data for the number of times agreed upon, marketers are supposed to destroy any data from the list. However, any responses from the effort (where a customer responds directly to the firm) are available for inclusion in the company's internal data warehouse.

There are three types of list available for rent.

1. **Response Lists.** Some organizations rent the information on customers who have previously made specific purchases, or responded previously to some other direct marketing campaign. The most interesting example of rented responses lists is the rental of charity donor lists. When a charity receives a donation, it often records information on the donor such as the name and address, size of the donation, and perhaps some other basic demographic information such as age or gender. Many charities rent this information to other charities who then use it to build their own direct marketing campaigns. Why would a charity rent information on its donor to other charities? Because research shows that when people donate to one charity, they typically also donate to several others. When a charity rents the names of its current donors, the most likely outcome is that the donor will continue to make donations and possibly add donations to any new charities that approach them. The charity renting the names first gains revenue through the initial donation and then again on subsequent list rentals. Because these lists are highly targeted and based on previous behaviours, they tend to be expensive.

2. **Compiled Lists.** Organizations collect data on individuals' purchases and other behaviour and make this data available to marketers. In Canada, one prominent organization goes by the name of Shopper's Voice. They regularly mail out

surveys to Canadians in which they collect data on usage of various products, both generic categories and specific brands. Many marketers pay to be included in this survey and therefore "own" the data once it is collected, but the company also rents data, which can be very valuable to marketers. For example, one recent survey contained questions about yogurt consumption. Consumers responded with the amount of yogurt they consume and which brands they consume (e.g., Activia, Source, etc.). Assume the survey identifies 10,000 people across the country who consume Activia yogurt four or more times per week. This information would be valuable to both the marketers of Activia (who may have no other way of knowing who their high volume customers are directly) and certainly this information would be valuable to the marketers of competing brands of yogurt. Although the data is self-reported by consumers (i.e., not based on actual observed purchases or use), the data can still be expensive because of its high degree of targetability.

3. **Subscription Lists.** These are lists that contain information on individuals who subscribe to things like magazines or blogs. They are valuable sources of data for many companies because they often contain groups of people with similar lifestyles or interests. For example, if Jeep wants to target individuals who have a love of the outdoors when promoting its new sports vehicle, the subscribers to Field and Stream represent a very targeted list of people who are likely to be avid outdoors people. It can further narrow down the selection to individuals who live in certain provinces or fit other criteria that the magazine might also have, such as income or age. Because the list is targeted only in terms of general interests or lifestyles, these lists can be the least expensive options for many direct marketing campaigns. An example of a rented list spec sheet, along with rental costs, is provided in Figure 8.1.

FIGHTING FOR A NEW SCHOOL IN ATTAWAPISKAT

CANADIAN Geographic

DECEMBER 2010 $7.95
www.canadiangeographic.ca

HEART-STOPPING WILDLIFE
ACTION SHOTS

WILDLIFE PHOTO CONTEST WINNERS

Life on the **International Space Station**
The **species-at-risk** list is getting longer
A new **world-population** map

Source: Canadian Geographic, December 2010.

Magazines such as Canadian Geographic provide lists that allow marketers to target highly qualified audiences with relevant messages.

Critical Thinking Exercise

Assume you are a manager working at Canadian Tire and your responsibility is to promote the camping equipment sold both through the physical stores and online. Purchases in the physical stores often don't come with any transactional data since customers don't provide even their names and addresses. For online purchases, only names and addresses are collected. How would you use these two sets of data and augment them with external data sources to build a direct marketing campaign? Which type of external list would you prefer and why? What advantages would your preferred list source provide over the others?

FIGURE 8.1
A Sample List Rental Selection Sheet

ORDER # :	S-DE110504-1-TECHWEB-1
Contact Name:	Mike Podmore
Company:	Tech Web Direct
Billing Address:	14133 Burrows Road
City/Prov/Pcode	Richmond, BC V6V 3B4
Phone:	
Fax:	
Email:	

Qty	Description	Code	Rate	Total
6000	**Consumers Census List** - Contact and full postal address		$0.140	$840.00
	Geo = FSA'S Victoria-Vancouver Island			
	V8K,V8L,V8M,V8N,V8P,V8R,V8S,V8T,V8V,V8W,V8X,			
	V8Y,V8Z,V9A,V9B,,V9C,V9E,V9G,V9H,V9J,V9L,V9M,			
	V9N,V9P,V9R,V9S,V9T,V9V,V9W,V9X,,V9Y,V9Z, V0R,V0S			
	Age = 35 – 80			
	Gender = Females			
	HHI = $50K+			
5000	**Readers Digest** - Contact and full postal		$0.195	$975.00
5000	Geo = FSA'S Victoria-Vancouver Island			
	V8K,V8L,V8M,V8N,V8P,V8R,V8S,V8T,V8V,V8W,V8X,			
	V8Y,V8Z,V9A,V9B,,V9C,V9E,V9G,V9H,V9J,V9L,V9M,			
	V9N,V9P,V9R,V9S,V9T,V9V,V9W,V9X,,V9Y,V9Z, V0R,V0S			
5000	**Canadian Multi-Donors** - Contact and full postal		$0.195	$975.00
5000	Geo = FSA'S Victoria-Vancouver Island			
	V8K,V8L,V8M,V8N,V8P,V8R,V8S,V8T,V8V,V8W,V8X,			
	V8Y,V8Z,V9A,V9B,,V9C,V9E,V9G,V9H,V9J,V9L,V9M,			
	V9N,V9P,V9R,V9S,V9T,V9V,V9W,V9X,,V9Y,V9Z, V0R,V0S			

Comments:		Total Data		$2,790.00
		Delivery		$210.00
		Subtotal		**$3,000.00**
		HST	12.0%	$360.00
		Due	**CDN**	**$3,360.00**

By my signature below, I agree to the above statements and provisions.

Please sign here and see following Page for Terms & Conditions and Payment Options.

_____   _____

Signature   Date

Source: Used with permission of Tech Web Direct.

DATABASE CODING AND ANALYSIS

Once the data warehouse is created, the next component in building a database is database coding and analysis. This process essentially helps the marketer "make sense" of the data and provides the foundation upon which subsequent communications can be built. For example, which criteria should be given highest priority when planning communications to customers—the amount of times they purchased in the last year, the total amount they spent in the last year, or some other criteria such as age or income? Three common practices of database coding and analysis are lifetime value analysis, RFM analysis, and data mining/modelling.

Lifetime Value Analysis

The first procedure that may be used is the calculation of the lifetime value of a customer or market segment. **Lifetime value** is a figure that represents the profit revenue of a customer throughout the lifetime of a relationship. Some companies calculate the value for individual customers. Others calculate it for customer segments. Many marketing experts believe the latter value is more accurate, because it includes costs across a market segment. Individual lifetime value calculations normally only contain costs for single customers.

The key figures in calculating the lifetime value of a consumer or set of consumers are revenues, costs, retention rates, and visits or purchases per time period, normally one year. Revenue and costs are normally easy to obtain, because many companies record these numbers for accounting purposes. Retention rate and purchases per year require an accurate marketing database system.

The cost of acquiring a new customer is important. It is calculated by dividing the total marketing and advertising expenditures in dollars by the number of new customers obtained. As an example, if $1,000 dollars are spent and the company acquires 10 new customers as a result, then the acquisition cost is $100 per customer.

Another key figure is the cost of maintaining a database. This figure represents the number of dollars spent to keep records and enter new information. Typically, its does not include any costs associated with customer retention or dollars spent on marketing efforts targeted at customers in the database.

One method for calculating lifetime value is shown in Figure 8.2. The table presents a lifetime value calculation for the database customers of Lilly Fashions. This small retailer has 3,200 customers in its database. Approximately 50 percent of the customers who provide information and join Lilly's database through a membership card stay with the club during the first year. In the second year following the sign up, 60 percent continue with the club. By the third year, approximately 70 percent stay with the club. As indicated by the data from Lilly's Fashions, loyal customers make more purchases and also increase the amounts they spend on each visit. Retaining customers is clearly more efficient and effective than constantly seeking to acquire new customers.

Lilly Fashions chose to calculate a customer's lifetime value for three years. There is nothing magic about that figure. A firm can use any number of years, but the longer the period, the more difficult it is to estimate

Encouraging repeat purchases and maximizing lifetime value is important for automotive brands such as Mercedes.

A wolf in wolf's clothing.

It's the first fully fledged coupe to bare the C-Class name. Its road owning direct-injection performance engines get you there, but it's the aggressive AMG styling and panoramic sunroof that get you looks along the way. Visit your Mercedes-Benz dealer or mercedes-benz.ca to schedule a test drive.

The all-new 2012 C-Class Coupe.

Like Mercedes-Benz
facebook.com/MercedesBenzCanada

125! years of innovation

Mercedes-Benz
The best or nothing.

© 2011 Mercedes-Benz Canada Inc.

FIGURE 8.2
Lifetime Value for Lilly Fashions

	Year 1	Year 2	Year 3
Customers	3,200	1,600	960
Retention rate	50%	60%	70%
Visits per year	4	5	6
Sales per visit	$78.00	$94.00	$110.00
Total revenue	$998,400	$752,000	$633,600
Variable costs %	60%	60%	60%
Variable costs	$ $599,040	$451,200	$380,160
Acquisition costs ($72)	$230,400		
Database costs	($3) $9,600	$4,800	$2,880
Total costs	$839,040	$456,000	$383,040
Gross profit	$159,360	$296,000	$250,560
Cumulative gross profit	$159,360	$455,360	$705,920
Lifetime value per customer	**$49.80**	**$142.30**	**$220.60**

future behaviour. The calculations for Year 2 and Year 3 are for the Year 1 cohort only. Each year Lilly Fashions adds new members. The lifetime value for each year is kept separately.

Notice that the lifetime value of this set of customers over a three-year period is $220.60. This is the average amount of profit each of the loyal customers generates for Lilly Fashions. It gives Lilly Fashions an idea of what it can spend on maintaining the loyalty of these customers.

Critical Thinking Exercise

Review the data in Figure 8.2. The manager of Lilly Fashions knows that each customer in the database generates an average of $220.60 in profit over 3 years. In order to encourage loyalty, retention, and increased spending, the manager has decided to devote $30 per year per customer to this effort. Based on material presented in this chapter, what types of marketing and retention efforts would you encourage for Lilly Fashions? Justify your recommendations.

RFM Analysis

A second common approach used in database marketing is **RFM analysis**. RFM refers to the use of the terms *recency*, *frequency*, and *monetary*, which are used to predict customer behaviours. *Recency* notes the date of the last purchase. *Frequency* is the number of purchases within a specific time period, normally one year. *Monetary* refers to the monetary expenditures with a firm and is usually expressed as expenditures per year, or other suitable time period.

To code the database in terms of recency, the database will be sorted from the most recent purchase date to the most historic date. The data are then typically split into five equal groups, with each group being assigned a value of 5, 4, 3, 2, or 1. A code of "5" is given for the most recent purchasers, "4" for the second most recent group, and so forth, with the group making the *least* frequent purchases coded "1." The same procedure is used for the frequency, where "5" is assigned to the most frequent purchasers and "1" is assigned to the least frequent purchasers. Finally, the data are coded based on the total amount of money spent using the same procedure.

The end result of the RFM analysis is that each customer is assigned a three-digit code corresponding to recency, frequency, and monetary. Codes for an individual person would range from 555 to 111. A person with a score of 235, for instance, has not recently made a purchase, makes an average number of purchases in terms of frequency, but has spent a large amount of money in total.

The codes provide excellent information as a whole and for each separate number. Clearly a customer with a value of 555 holds the highest value to the company. Further, marketers know that recency has the most significant impact on future purchases. Individuals who have purchased recently (those with a score of "5" as the first number in the code) are more inclined to purchase again. The longer the time since the last purchase, the less likely they will make a purchase or respond to a marketing initiative. The same is true for frequency, although frequency is not as precise in predicting future behaviour as is recency. The more frequently an individual makes a purchase (with a score of "5" as the second number in the code), the more likely the person is to make another purchase.

The least predictive figure in the RFM analysis is monetary, the third number in the code. Past purchase size does not necessarily predict that the person will make a future purchase. Consequently, it gives a less clear indication of how valuable that customer may be.

Data Mining/Modelling

Similar to lifetime value and RFM analysis, data modelling is often used to understand which customers are likely to represent profitable future customers by using past behaviour as a benchmark. Data mining and modelling are done in two steps: (1) building profiles of customer segments, and/or (2) preparing models that predict future purchase behaviours based on past purchases. **Data mining** is the program used to develop a profile of the company's best customers. The profile, in turn, helps identify prospective new customers. The profile can be used to examine "good" customers to see if they are candidates for sales calls that would move them from "good" to a higher value. Companies offering different types of goods and services will develop multiple profiles. These profiles are used to target sales calls and to look for situations in which cross-selling is possible.

Retailer American Eagle used data mining to study how consumers responded to price markdowns. The information helped the marketing team determine when to cut prices and by how much in order to optimize sales. Markdown programs were geared to individual stores, because consumers responded differently in each outlet.

The second aspect involves developing models that predict future sales based on past purchasing activities. Staples, Inc., used a modelling program to examine the buying habits of the company's catalogue customers. The program identified the names of frequent buyers. Customized mailings were sent to those customers.

The method used to mine the data is determined by specific informational needs. Once the data have been mined for information, individual marketing programs can be designed. Profiles and models assist in designing the database best suited for each purpose or program. For example, an email campaign to current customers is different from one designed to attract new customers. The data provide clues about the best approach for each customer segment.

Source: Courtesy of BASF Canada Inc.

Companies such as BASF can use RFM analysis to help direct marketing tactics to farmers.

Data mining can also impact other elements of the communications mix, such as this print ad for Toyota that speaks to a female audience with a safety message.

Source: Courtesy of Toyota.

Data coding and analysis serve two purposes. First, they can be used to develop marketing programs designed to take advantage of the insights gained through the data. Second, they can be useful at helping marketers choose and design specific direct marketing communications. These are discussed next.

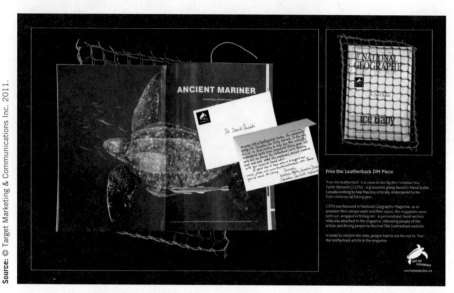

Halifax-based Canadian Sea Turtle Network (CSTN) used a targeted mailing to reach key influencers in the environmental media with its message. The campaign capitalized on an article featuring the CSTN in *National Geographic Magazine*, enclosing the issue in a fishing net to highlight the CSTN's expertise in disentangling endangered leatherback sea turtles from fishing gear.

DIRECT MARKETING PROGRAMS

Database-driven marketing programs take many forms. They may be used in conjunction with other marketing activities. Two of the more common programs—permission marketing and loyalty programs—are described here.

Permission Marketing

There has been a strong backlash by consumers regarding spam and junk mail. Consequently, many marketing departments have turned to **permission marketing**, a program in which promotional information is only sent to consumers who give the company permission to do so. Simply put, permission marketing is asking the customer permission to contact them using direct marketing media such as mail, telephone or email. Response rates are often higher in permissions programs, because consumers are receiving only the marketing materials they have asked for. Results are further enhanced if permission marketing programs utilize database technology and segment customers. Not everyone who signs up for a permission marketing program is a good customer.

Figure 8.3 lists the steps of a permission marketing program. Permission is normally obtained by providing an incentive for volunteering. Information, entertainment, a gift, cash, or entries in a sweepstakes are common incentives. The information provided is primarily educational and is focused on the company's product or service features. Reinforcing the incentive involves an additional new incentive beyond the original gift. Permission levels are increased by obtaining more in-depth information about a consumer, such as hobbies, interests, attitudes, and opinions. This information can be used to entice additional purchases by offering the individual participant a special deal, which creates a win–win situation for both parties.

Keys to Success in Permission Marketing

For a permission marketing program to succeed, the marketing team must make sure that the recipients have agreed to participate. Unfortunately, some consumers have been tricked into joining permission marketing programs. A common tactic is used when a customer completes an online survey or when the person makes an online purchase. To opt out of the permission marketing part of the program, the person must uncheck a box on the site. Although this increases the number of individuals enrolled in the program, the technique often creates negative feelings.

FIGURE 8.3
Steps in Building a Permissions Marketing Program

1. Obtain permission from the customer.
2. Offer the consumer an ongoing curriculum that is meaningful.
3. Reinforce the incentive to continue the relationship.
4. Increase the level of permission.
5. Leverage the permission to benefit both parties.

An email marketing piece must be relevant to the consumer receiving it in order for the program to work. Far too many people have joined a permission marketing program that turns into a situation where the consumer has no input and is bombarded with extraneous marketing messages. This does not create loyalty and runs counter to the purpose of a permission program.

One recent survey revealed that 80 percent of consumers stopped reading permission emails from companies because they were shoddy or irrelevant. Another 68 percent said the emails came too frequently, and 51 percent said they lost interest in the goods, services, or topics of the emails. On the whole, consumers delete an average of 43 percent of permission emails without ever reading them.[2]

To overcome these challenges, the marketing team should monitor responses and customize the permission program to meet the needs of individual customers. Database technology allows for such customization by tracking responses. For example, if a customer regularly accesses a website through a link in an email sent by the company to read the latest fashion news, then this behaviour can trigger email offers and incentives on fashions related to the news stories. An individual who does not access the website and does not appear to be interested in fashion news receives a different type of email offer. By capitalizing on the power of database technology, a company can enhance the permissions marketing program and make it beneficial to the company and the customer.

Permission Marketing Enticements

Krishnamurthy suggests that a number of factors will determine a consumer's level of interest in participating in permission marketing campaigns.[3] Ultimately, it is a matter of perceived costs and benefits that will drive consumers to participate, and this perception is created by message relevance and monetary benefit, as outlined in Figure 8.4 First, consumers will be more likely to participate in a permission marketing campaign if they perceive that the messages will be relevant. For example, an avid skier will participate in a program by a ski manufacturer because she will expect the messages to be relevant to a particular interest of hers. Consumers will also be more likely to participate if they perceive a monetary benefit, as in the case of programs that offer points in exchange for receiving messages, or in campaigns that are driven by coupons or other forms of monetary incentive.

These benefits are counterbalanced against perceived costs of participation. First, although most permission marketing campaigns have no out of pocket costs, there is a cost join in the form of providing detailed personal information. When consumers are forced to provide higher levels of detailed information it places transaction costs on the consumer and she is less likely to continue. Marketers can encourage participation by making the sign up process shorter and less involved. Another related cost is related to privacy. If consumers are asked to give more than basic information such as an email address, they may be concerned about the security of their data and thus abandon the sign up. Many marketers use third party endorsements such as eTrust to help consumers overcome such concerns. Finally, another cost comes in the form of information processing. If consumers perceive the messages to be complex or sequenced illogically, they are more likely to discard the message and subsequently abandon the program. Recognizing the context in which consumers receive messages and tailoring the content accordingly (e.g., short, simple messages) can help sustain consumer participation.

◆ Higher Perceived Relevance of Information	◆ Lower Perceived Privacy Costs
◆ Higher Perceived Monetary Benefit	◆ Lower Perceived Processing Costs
◆ Lower Perceived Entry Costs	

FIGURE 8.4
Factors Affecting Consumer Participation in Permission Marketing Campaigns

Source: Sandeep Krishnamurthy, "A Comprehensive Analysis of Permission Marketing," *Journal of Computer-Mediated Communication* 6 (2) January 2001. http://jcmc.indiana.edu/vol6/issue2/krishnamurthy.html#c4

Permission marketing programs have the potential to build strong, ongoing relationships with customers when the program offers something of value to the customer. To optimize permission marketing, firms must feature empowerment and reciprocity.[4] **Empowerment** means consumers believe they have power throughout the relationship and not just at the beginning when they agreed to join the program. They can make decisions and have choices about what is received.

To maintain positive attitudes, consumers should be given instant rewards along the way, not just at the beginning. This creates feelings of **reciprocity**, which is a sense of obligation toward the company. One mistake that is often made is rewarding consumers only for joining a permission marketing program. Empowerment and reciprocity lead the customer to believe the company values the relationship. This enhances the quality of the program and increases the chances that the consumer will remain an active participant in the program.

Loyalty Programs

When a company offers rewards for a series of purchases, the technique is known as a **frequency program** or **loyalty program**. These efforts encourage customers to make repeat purchases. Frequent flyer programs in the airline industry offer free flights after a certain number of miles have been accumulated by a traveler. Many photo development shops give consumers punch cards that track the number of times the individual brings in film or electronic versions of pictures. Following a certain number (usually 10), the next set will be developed for free.

Airlines use frequent flyer programs due to the presence of brand parity, or the perception that the service is basically the same regardless of which company is being given patronage. Figure 8.5 lists various reasons for developing loyalty programs. Loyalty programs were first developed to differentiate one brand from its competition; however, now they tend to be common across all competitors in an industry (credit cards, airlines, hotels, etc.).

Loyalty Program Goals

Loyalty programs target three goals. The first is, of course, developing customer loyalty. Matching or preempting the competition is a second objective. Third, higher income individuals tend to join loyalty programs more than lower income households, which make them an inviting market segment to reach. As evidence, marketers point out that 92 percent of households with incomes of $125,000 or higher are actively enrolled in a frequent flyer program compared to only 51 percent for households with incomes below $125,000. Further, participating in a loyalty program influences future purchase decisions. About 90 percent of the high-income households said a membership in a loyalty program had a moderate to strong impact on purchase decisions.[5] Keeping customers creates repeat purchases. It also makes it possible to cross-sell other goods and services.

A similar concept is known as **customer relationship management (CRM)**, where companies use databases to build bonds with customers. A major objective of CRM programs is **share of customer**, which refers to the percentage of expenditures a customer makes with one particular firm compared to total expenditures in

FIGURE 8.5
Loyalty Program Objectives

◆ Maintain sales, margins, or profits.	◆ Induce cross-selling to existing customers.
◆ Increase loyalty of existing customers.	◆ Differentiate a parity brand.
◆ Preempt or match a competitor's frequency program.	◆ Preempt the entry of a new brand.

Source: Grahame R. Dowling and Mark Uncles, "Do Customer Loyalty Programs Really Work?" *Sloan Management Review* 38, no. 4 (Summer 1997), pp. 71–82.

that product's category. Share of customer is a measure of a customer's potential value, with more loyal customers giving a firm a higher percentage of their total category purchases. The question becomes, "If more is invested by the company in developing a relationship, what will the yield be over time?" When a customer makes only one-fourth of his or her purchases of a particular product with a specific vendor, increasing the share of the customer would mean increasing that percentage from 25 percent to a higher level, thus generating additional sales revenues. The ultimate goal would be leading the customer to make 100 percent of his or her purchases with one vendor.[6]

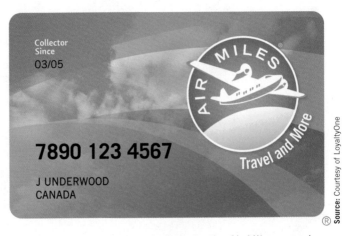

Loyalty Program Principles

Three principles guide the development of a loyalty program. The first principle, *design the program to enhance the value of the product*, means the program should add value to what the product offers or provide a unique new feature. The more effort a customer expends to participate in a loyalty program, the greater the value of the reward should be. Many consumers are willing to put forth greater effort to obtain luxury rewards as opposed to necessity rewards. Shoppers at a grocery store are more likely to be willing to give a higher level of effort in order to receive a free overnight stay at a nearby local resort or a free meal at a nice restaurant than they would for a $50 gift certificate for food.[7]

The second principle in building a loyalty program is to *calculate the full cost of the program*. This means the marketing team considers record-keeping as part of the cost. Many times the cost of maintaining a frequency account is greater than any additional profits.

The third principle is to *design a program that maximizes the customer's motivation to make the next purchase*. Moderate users of a product are most likely to be enticed by a loyalty program. The added incentive encourages loyalty to a particular company or brand.

Harrah's Entertainment, one of the world's largest casino operators, generates $4 billion annually through 45,000 slot machines in 28 casinos. Seventy-five percent of Harrah's 250,000 daily customers are members of the company's rewards program and use the company's "loyalty card." With every push of a button and every swipe of the loyalty card, data are sent to Harrah's computing centre. Over 100 million pieces of data are collected daily. The card can be used to track the machines or games a customer plays, how much that customer spends, how long the person stays at a particular machine, and how often the customer goes to a Harrah's casino. The marketing team tracks the gambling behaviour of 30 million people. By combining the information with slot records, the marketing team determines the games that are the most popular with various groups, such as men, women, tourists, and locals. The Harrah's staff also knows which slot machines are hot and which are not. The information is used to place slot machines in the best locations at each casino. Other data helps the managers decide which types of machines should be purchased and which ones should be phased out. Finally, the information suggests which customers should receive frequency rewards, such as room upgrades, show tickets, or free-dinner vouchers.[8]

The marketing team should monitor members within a loyalty program. RFM analysis is a useful tool. For example, a locally owned restaurant did a recency analysis of its Frequent Diner Club and located 4,000 club members who had not earned any points during the previous 3 months. The restaurant sent a letter to each of the 4,000 offering a

In Canada, the Air Miles name is ubiquitous, and retailers across dozens of categories use the AIR MILES Reward Program as the basis for their loyalty program.

Brands like Safeway tap into the equity of the AIR MILES Reward Program for their loyalty programs.

$5 discount on dinner. The offer was good for 35 days and the mailing cost $1,800. The results were as follows:

- The average number of member visits per day increased from 25 to 42 during the promotion and to 29 per day after the promotion ended.
- Average visits by individual members holding cards increased both during and after the promotion.
- Incremental sales increased by $17,100 during the promotion and by $4,700 after the 35-day promotion.

By spending $1,800, this promotion led to reactivations by 599 people who had not dined at the restaurant in 3 months. Of the 599 who came back during the promotion, 147 dined at the restaurant after the promotion was over.[9]

Critical Thinking Exercise

Although loyalty programs have been used with success around the world, some critics argue that they are merely a form of "bribery" and, ironically, can make customers less loyal in the true meaning of the term. What does it mean to be "loyal" to a company or brand? Are you enrolled in a loyalty program that you think has meaningfully enhanced your loyalty to the company behind it? If so, what aspect of the program has enhanced your loyalty? If your loyalty hasn't been enhanced, what else can the company add to the program to achieve this objective?

In general, direct-marketing-driven programs should be designed to enhance customer loyalty. When a hotel's check-in person knows in advance that a business traveler prefers a nonsmoking room, a king-size bed, and reads the *National Post*, these items could be made available as the guest arrives. Training hotel clerks and other employees to use the database helps them to provide better service, thereby building loyalty from regular customers. Any organization's marketing department can adapt these techniques to fit the needs of its customers and clients.

DIRECT MARKETING COMMUNICATIONS

When communicating with customers on a one-to-one basis in order to execute direct marketing programs, marketers have a number of options.

Direct Mail

While it may seem unfashionable or even wasteful to the environmentally conscious, paper-based direct mail, still represents the lion's share of direct marketing investment by companies. Over three-quarters of companies use direct mail to communicate with their customers, and almost the same amount use direct mail to communicate with prospects.[10] Direct mail allows consumers the chance to sit down with a piece of paper and digest the message in their own time.

Direct mail, unlike media which tends to be fixed in a particular format (e.g., a 30-second radio ad), can literally take any form that the marketer desires. Formats range from a standard envelope and letter delivered through third class mail, to complex packages with many pieces that are delivered by courier. The specifics of the mailing depend on a range of factors. These include the objective of the mailing (e.g., purchase versus providing information), the target audience (e.g., a high versus low degree of product knowledge), and even the properties of the product itself (e.g., a high-end sports car versus an entry level sedan). In many cases, receiving a catalogue is the first step in the buying cycle. Although some mailings may seem expensive, when these factors are taken into account the return on investment of mail campaigns can be very high.

Email Marketing

Email messages have also become a very popular form of direct marketing, with 55 percent of companies using email to communicate with current customers and almost 50 percent using it to communicate with prospects.[11]

Many of the same issues with paper-based direct mail are found in email campaigns. The largest issue is targeting a message to the right audience, and including a message that is relevant and compelling. This is especially true for email marketing, where backlash against "spam" tends to be greater than with physical "junk mail." Formats, like physical direct mail, can vary although the variation is usually found within the presentation of the email itself. Many marketers prefer the basic text-based email format to avoid problems with download speeds and display on email programs. Others opt for the formatted HTML format that can include graphics and photos, and a range of fonts.

Brands such as Porsche use direct mail formats that reinforce the high-end positioning of the brand.

Source: Photo: Dick Hemingway. Courtesy of Porsche Cars Canada, Ltd.

Apart from lower costs of production, one of the biggest benefits of email marketing when compared to physical direct mail is that the audience is already engaging in the medium that can be used to access further information, or even make a purchase. With a single click a prospect can enter the purchase process, or link to additional information on a website. A major drawback is that the filters on many email programs are designed to divert messages into a junk folder, so the audience is never even exposed to the message.

Telemarketing

A third means of direct marketing is telemarketing. Despite being traditionally derided for being ineffective and creating a high degree of annoyance among consumers, almost one quarter of all firms still use the telephone to deliver messages to a target audience.[12]

Telemarketing is most successful when it is tied into a database and either customers or prospects are being contacted. For example, a telemarketing program that contacts customers who have not purchased in a year can be successful at bringing those customers back and learning why they have not purchased recently. Or it can be used to obtain subsequent sales. For example, a company that purchases a copy machine can be called to see if they are interested in a contract that would supply it with paper and toner.

One of the largest benefits of telemarketing is that it provides the opportunity for the marketer to actively overcome objections. The message can be tailored specifically based on responses given by the audience to create a very compelling proposition. Responses are in real time. However, as mentioned, many marketers are reluctant to use telemarketing except for ongoing service calls or relationship management with current customers because so many people find them obtrusive. Further, it has become more difficult to effectively use telemarketing as the population moves away from published telephone numbers for landlines to unlisted cell phones, and adopts call-screening technologies.

Critical Thinking Exercise

Think of a time recently when you responded to a direct marketing communications message. Which format was it in? How did the format shape your decision to respond? If the format had been in a different format, would you have still responded? Why or why not?

STRENGTHS AND WEAKNESSES OF DIRECT MARKETING

As with advertising media (discussed in Chapter 7) and the tactics mentioned above, each form of direct marketing has specific advantages and disadvantages. However, there are a number of strengths and weaknesses that all forms of direct marketing have in common.

Strengths of Direct Marketing

Targetability. A significant benefit of direct marketing, when compared to other elements of the marketing communications mix, is the high degree of targetability. A well-targeted direct marketing campaign based on a well-maintained database can provide virtually zero wasted coverage. In theory, every person who receives the communication will be a highly qualified customer who is receptive to the message. This means every dollar invested in a direct marketing campaign is highly effective.

Customizability. Using data to guide the message, direct marketing provides the opportunity to create unique messages down to the individual customer level, in theory. Each message can be tailored to meet the specific needs of each individual member of the audience.

Measurable. Because many direct marketing programs have sales-oriented objectives, such programs are often more easily measured than other elements of the marketing communications mix. In the Dell example mentioned earlier, for instance, the company can understand exactly which direct marketing campaigns generated which results. This also makes testing within direct marketing communications relatively easy, and marketers can determine the optimal elements of the overall message. However, the desire to attribute all marketing outcomes to direct marketing when it is one element of an overall IMC plan must be tempered. The role of other elements such as media or digital marketing in supporting the direct marketing communications component of the integrated marketing plan must be recognized and accounted for.

Timely. For all forms of direct marketing, even paper-based direct mail, communications can be developed and delivered literally within the hour. This is useful for responding to competitive activity in the marketplace, or to communicate with stakeholders during a crisis such as a product recall.

Weaknesses of Direct Marketing

Image Limitations. Direct marketing can at best provide limited opportunities to develop brand image, and at worst can negatively impact the image of some brands. Many image-building messages simply aren't suited to direct marketing formats. For example, when Pepsi wants to position itself as the choice of a younger generation, they certainly can't email or call consumers with that message. It lends itself more to other elements of the marketing communications mix. Second, consumers may associate direct marketing with lower quality products, or become annoyed if they feel that they are being harassed.

Clutter. Most consumers receive numerous direct marketing offers on a daily basis. Direct marketing formats don't offer the same opportunity to create attention and take advantage of the consumers' environment like other elements of the marketing communications mix. Paper-based mail comes in a stack each day (often sorted over the recycling bin), emails can pile up in an inbox, and telemarketing can compete with any number of other distractions the consumer faces, such as a crying baby. Many consumers sign up for do-not-call and do-not-mail lists, which means marketers are unable to even put the message in their mail/inbox in the first place.

Selective Exposure. Similar to clutter, direct marketing communications are subject to significant selective exposure by consumers. Many consumers automatically drop any piece of mail that remotely resembles a marketing message into the recycling bin, and typically don't even see emails if their spam filters are set. Screening telephone calls is easy. Further, many consumers subscribe to do not mail/call lists (more on this in Chapter 12).

Cost Per Contact. Relative to other forms of marketing communications, direct marketing can be very expensive on a cost-per-contact basis—especially paper-based direct mail and telemarketing. This means their effectiveness for some IMC objectives is limited. However, the cost-per-contact may be justified if the value of a highly targeted audience is high enough. For example, many pharmaceutical companies spend hundreds of dollars a year mailing information to physicians. While expensive on a per-physician basis, the return on marketing investment can still be quite high if the list of physicians is targeted and their response (e.g., writing prescriptions for one drug over another) generates sufficient revenues. Although some critics argue that some tactics, such as free trips, cross an ethical boundary between these companies and physicians, the potential value of doctors as customers means companies continually push this boundary.

Source: © Photodisc/Thinkstock.

With so many marketers using direct mail to reach targeted customers, clutter at the mailbox creates a challenge for getting consumers' attention.

COMMUNICATING ACROSS CULTURES

Direct marketing faces the same challenges as other aspects of an IMC program when the program crosses cultural or national boundaries. These include differences in technology, which make data collection and analysis more difficult due to issues such as language and Internet availability. Further, local laws may limit the methods by which information can be collected as well as the types of information a company seeks and/or shares with other companies.

In many parts of the world, customers may only live a few miles apart yet at the same time are in a different country. For example, the European Union consists of many nations in close proximity. Therefore, decisions must be made as to whether data will be country specific.

Programs such as permission marketing, frequency, and CRM are subject to legal restrictions as well as cultural differences. In some instances, they may be highly accepted. This is the case for permission marketing in Japan. In many Asian cultures, the giving of gifts takes on added meaning. This may include stronger bonds between customers and companies.

Direct marketing tactics must also be adapted to local conditions. Mail delivery systems may be easier to access and more reliable in some countries than others. The same is true for telephone systems, Internet access, and other technologies. A company's marketing team should consider all local legal, social, cultural, technological, and competitive conditions while developing the direct marketing element of the IMC plan.

IMC IN PRACTICE

"At TELUS we define direct marketing quite narrowly because it helps us understand how it fits our plan," says Kate. "Although media are becoming much more interconnected, and targetability is becoming more sophisticated across almost all advertising media, we consider 'direct marketing' to include direct mail, email, SMS, and telemarketing."

TELUS uses targeted direct marketing to target offers to specific audiences.

TELUS uses all of these direct marketing tools to both communicate with current customers, and to try and acquire new customers. "For us and our competitors, getting customers to bundle our products is a big objective right now. So we always try to mine our customer data to see if a customer represents an opportunity to add a new product or service to what they currently use."

As the telecommunications space sees new entrants, the competition is fierce and is often waged using direct marketing. "We directly compete for customers. We try to encourage our competitor's customers to buy television services from us, and they try to encourage our customers to buy phone services from them. The place where this battle is truly being waged is in direct mail because it lets us speak directly to customers who are most likely to switch. It certainly lets us target the message only to those customers who we know have one service or another, so we aren't asking customers who already buy television services from us to do so again."

The direct mail communications channel is another place where the TELUS brand helps the company. "We find that particularly in the direct mail vehicles, our brand allows us more interactivity with our customers. It's a tactile communications message. We try to be somewhat playful and entertaining in our direct mail, so we use things like die cuts or unique folds to encourage people to interact with the direct mail package. It's part of the charm, and we do see higher than industry average response rates as a result."

"Our brand gives us licence to have a little bit more fun with this medium than other companies can. For example, we have done a scratch and sniff direct mail campaign. I don't think the brands of our competitors would allow them to do that."

Source: Used with permission of Kate Baillie, TELUS Communications.

For help developing your IMC Plan, go to **www.pearsoncanada.ca/clow**.

SUMMARY

Direct marketing has become a vital element of creating a complete IMC program. The two key activities involved at the most general level, identifying customers and building relationships with them, have an impact on numerous other IMC tasks. It is clearly more cost-effective to retain customers than to continually seek out new ones. Further, the actual message will change when communicating with long-time, loyal customers.

Building a data warehouse begins with collecting data to be used by the marketing department. Beyond basic information, such as a customer's name, address, and email address, other key data include the customer's purchase history and preferences. External data sources can be used to augment internal data sources. Geocoding is the process of adding geographic codes to customer records, which assists in selecting media and creating messages targeted to specific groups. List rentals are also available. Response, compiled, and subscription lists all provide a number of benefits to marketers looking to access data to drive their direct marketing programs.

Database coding and analysis leads to either a lifetime value analysis of customers and customer groups, or RFM analysis of customer spending patterns, or both. Data mining and modelling programs involve building profiles of customer segments and/or preparing models that predict future purchase behaviours based on past purchases. The information gathered from data coding and data mining leads to the development of direct marketing programs and communications.

Direct marketing programs include permission marketing and loyalty programs. Permission marketing is a selling approach in which the customer agrees to receive promotional materials in exchange for various incentives. Loyalty programs are incentives customers receive for repeat business. Both are designed to create customer loyalty over time.

Direct marketing communications are executed through either direct mail, email or telemarketing, or some combination of them. Although each provides unique advantages and disadvantages, in general, direct marketing strengths include targetability, customizability, measurability, and timeliness. Weaknesses include image limitations, clutter, selective exposure, and a high cost per contact.

In the new age of marketing communications, a case can be made that individual consumers desire greater intimacy with the companies that serve them. They are drawn to firms that take the time to build relationships through quality, customized communications and marketing programs. It seems likely that this trend will continue and that successful marketing teams must continue to emphasize methods for identifying customers and personalizing relationships with them.

KEY TERMS

compiled list   A list consisting of information about consumers who meet a specific demographic profile or behavioural profile.

customer relationship management (CRM)   Programs designed to build long-term loyalty and bonds with customers through the use of a personal touch facilitated by technology.

data mining   The process of searching a database to develop a profile of the company's best customers.

data warehouse   The place where customer data are held.

empowerment   When consumers believe they have power throughout the seller–consumer relationship, not just at the beginning when they agreed to join a frequency program.

geocoding   Adding geographic codes to customer records to make it possible to plot customer addresses on a map.

lifetime value   Sales revenues generated by a customer throughout the lifetime of his or her relationship with a company.

loyalty (or frequency) program   A marketing program designed to promote loyalty or frequent purchases of the same brand (or company).

permission marketing   A form of database marketing in which the company sends promotional materials to customers who give the company permission to do so.

reciprocity   A sense of obligation toward a company that results from receiving special deals or incentives such as gifts.

response list   A list of customers who have made transactions or who have responded to direct marketing offers in the past.

RFM analysis   The use of recency, frequency, and monetary figures to predict consumer behaviours.

share of customer   The percentage of expenditures a customer makes with one particular firm compared to total expenditures in that product's category.

subscription list   A list of individuals who subscribe to a source of information such as a magazine or a blog.

REVIEW QUESTIONS

1. What type of objectives within the overall IMC plan can be achieved through direct marketing?

2. What is a data warehouse?

3. What are the two sources of data for a data warehouse?

4. What are the three sources of external data in the form of lists?

5. What is geocoding?

6. Define "lifetime value." How is it determined?

7. What does RFM stand for? Explain what an RFM code describes.

8. Describe a permission marketing program. What are the key benefits of this approach?

9. What are the keys to an effective permission marketing program?

10. Describe a loyalty program. Which type of user pays off the best in a loyalty program—light, medium, or heavy users?

11. What is customer relationship management?

12. What is meant by the term "share of customer"?

13. What are the three main categories of media that can be used to execute a direct marketing campaign?

14. What are the strengths and weaknesses of direct marketing?

INTEGRATED LEARNING EXERCISES

1. Your first job in marketing communications after graduating is with the graduate school of one of the most well-known business schools in the country. What role can direct marketing play in your IMC planning? How would it play a role in the overall plan and complement the advertising that you are running in media such as magazine and newspaper? Why would you consider using direct marketing, and where would you start in building your data warehouse?

2. Demonstrating how mainstream direct marketing has become, and the importance of data-driven marketing communications across all elements of the marketing communications mix, the organization formerly known as the Canadian Direct Marketing Association changed its name to the Canadian Marketing Association (CMA). Visit their website at **www.the-cma.org.** What services does the CMA provide its members? What services does the CMA provide the Canadian public? If you find a job

in the marketing communications industry, how might you use the services of the CMA to help you perform in your career?

3. Visit the website of the list broker Prospects Influential (**www.prospectsinfluential.com**). The system lets you search for lists that are available. One of the options is a "new mover" list that contains information on households that have moved within the past six months. What marketers would be interested in using the new mover list? Run some searches based on cities to see how many people have moved within the past six months.

4. Almost all hotels have some type of frequency or loyalty program. Examine the loyalty programs of the following hotels. Critique each one. Which ones are best? Why?

 a. Best Western (**www.bestwestern.com**)

 b. Days Inn (**www.daysinn.com**)

 c. Doubletree Inn (**doubletree.hilton.com**)

 d. Marriott (**www.marriott.com**)

 e. Radisson (**www.radisson.com**)

 f. Wyndham Hotels & Resorts (**www.wyndham.com**)

STUDENT PROJECT

Creative Corner

Lilly's Fashions sells fashionable clothes in the mid-to-upper price range to females ages 15 to 30. Lilly's wants to capitalize on the direct marketing opportunity. The company has been collecting email addresses for years and sending out coupons and information on special sales to its customers. The company now wants to build a loyalty program and start to manage its customer relationships more closely.

a. What information do you suggest the company acquire in order to drive its loyalty program?

b. Design an email that will be sent to the current list to encourage them to sign up for the loyalty program. What incentives will you offer, and why do you think they will be successful?

c. Assume after one year there is a segment of customers that has not purchased anything from the store for over six months. Design a campaign to try and lure these customers back into the store. Which format(s) will you use? What offer will you make to entice them back? They have already received the email announcing the loyalty program and did not respond. What will your new offer be?

→ ETHICS IN ACTION

Loyalty programs are common. Most are fairly uncontroversial, found in categories such as gasoline (e.g., Petro Points) and grocery stores (e.g., Air Miles). The goal of these programs is, of course, to encourage customers to return to the same business for all of their purchases. Petro Points encourages customers to avoid Shell and Esso stations in favour of Petro Canada stations. But the program doesn't necessarily encourage people to buy more gasoline. However, critics charge that loyalty programs developed by provincial lottery corporations not only encourage people to gamble in only one way, but are effectively encouraging people to gamble more often.

One such program is in place at Casino Windsor. The program, Total Rewards from Harrah's Entertainment, provides consumers with a number of benefits. Essentially the program rewards users with points when they gamble, and they can redeem those points for a range of goods and services including food, hotel stays, and other forms of entertainment.

1. Is a loyalty program offered by a casino ethical? Do you feel it encourages gambling at only one location, or increased gambling overall?

2. Would your opinion of the loyalty program be any different if the gambling industry in Canada wasn't a government monopoly? Would your point of view change if it were private companies competing with one another, using loyalty programs as a point of difference?

3. What other goods or services do you feel overstep an ethical boundary with the use of a loyalty program? Propose a set of criteria that a manager can follow to determine if a loyalty program should be pursued or not. ●

CASE STUDY | Dorval Medical Supply

Natalie Ouellet has just taken on a unique dual role in her job at Dorval Medical Supply. She was to be in charge of the marketing database for the company and also would serve as liaison with the marketing communications team. Natalie was told her input would be heavily counted on to help with key decisions to build the size and scope of the company in the next several years.

Dorval Medical Supply was located in Dorval, Quebec. The company served business-to-business markets by selling and servicing various types of medical equipment, from items as basic as ankle braces to some as sophisticated as foetal monitors. The company was a distributor that resold various devices to other businesses who then either used them in their operations, or sold them to end-users. The company had achieved a great

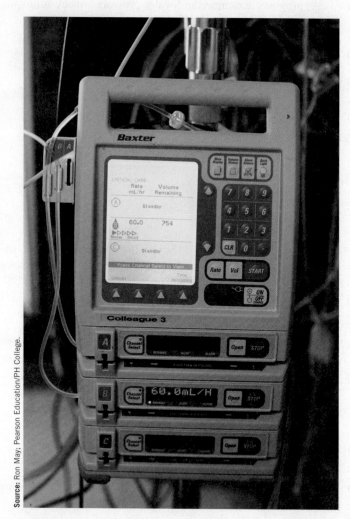

Source: Ron May; Pearson Education/PH College.

Dorval markets expensive medical equipment to doctors and hospitals.

deal of success simply through the sheer demand for various products, but the management team was concerned that no coherent marketing plan had ever been developed.

Natalie was told that the company had three basic customer groups:

- Retailers
- Physicians' offices
- Hospitals

Retail customers purchase the lower-cost, less intricate items, such as braces, bandages, and cold packs. The market is highly fragmented with many local, independent stores operating in cities across Canada. Although the company does sell some equipment to retailers like Shoppers Drug Mart, the majority of their items are found in more specialized medical supply stores. Physicians buy more elaborate equipment and also provide referrals for patients. Obviously, the physician market is extremely fragmented, with local doctor's offices covering the entire country. Hospitals order the big-ticket items, and represent a fragmented market with virtually all

hospitals purchasing their own equipment independently from one another. Each customer type generates a solid source of revenue for the organization, with about one-third coming from each.

Natalie's first challenge was to develop a database for each type of customer. Her potential sources for retail customers were insurance forms (many filed for insurance to pay for the items involved) and sales ticket information requested from each person. But she only had basic data on the retailers that purchased from Dorval. She didn't have detailed records of their purchases (although these were available through company records) or the retailers that have never purchased from Dorval. Doctors' offices could be sources of a great deal of information, but the company often had to "push" the staff to provide statistics on numbers of patients, types of expenditures, and other key facts. Hospitals could be assessed through internal company reports and by accessing data from external sources. Doctors' offices and hospitals presented the same problem—Natalie did not know how many of them weren't buying from Dorval, or whether or not they were different from Dorval's current customers.

Clearly the needs of each group were different, and therefore it seemed plausible that the marketing tactics used for each customer type would also vary. At the same time, Natalie wanted a consistent message sent—that Dorval Medical Supply stood for consistent, high-quality, and excellent service advantages. She knew the name "Dorval" didn't help, because so many companies in the city also used the name (e.g., Dorval Electric Supply, Dorval Party Favours) and outside the city the lack of an association between the name and medical supplies meant the name carried little equity.

Natalie held a meeting with the marketing team. The group told her the primary goal was to build greater brand equity in the name. Next, the company's leaders wanted to expand revenues from all three customer segments. They wanted to understand how they were viewed within their market segments and what opportunities were available to expand within them. With all of these challenges in mind, Natalie took a deep breath and started working.

1. What internal and external sources of data are available to Natalie? Write a brief, one-page compilation of potential external data sources for the firm and suggest options for internal data.

2. Which data sources do you recommend she focus on? Write a two-page report outlining recommendations on what her next steps should be to acquire the data. Be sure to outline how the data will help her achieve her objective of expanding the market for Dorval Medical Supply within each of the three segments.

3. How do you think Dorval might use direct marketing tactics to communicate with buyers? Which method(s) are most appropriate—direct mail, email, or telemarketing? Prepare a five-minute briefing to the senior management team in which you outline your approach to direct marketing communications, and help them understand how your proposed tactic(s) will help the firm meet its objectives.

ENDNOTES

1. Carol Krol, "Dell Sees Continued Success with DM," *BtoB* 89, no. 12 (October 25, 2004), p. 8.

2. Joseph Gatti, "Poor E-Mail Practices Provoking Considerable Customer Defection," *Direct Marketing* (December 2003), pp. 1–2.

3. http://jcmc.indiana.edu/vol6/issue2/krishnamurthy.html

4. J. Walker Smith, "Permission Is Not Enough," *Marketing Management* 13, no. 3 (May–June 2004), p. 52.

5. Arthur M. Hughes, *Strategic Database Marketing* (New York: McGraw Hill, 2006).

6. "CRM Metrics," *Harvard Management Update* 5, no. 3 (March 2000), pp. 3–4.

7. Ran Kivetz and Itamar Simonson, "Earning the Right to Indulge: Effort As a Determinant of Customer Preferences Toward Frequency Program Rewards," *Journal of Marketing Research* 39, no. 2 (May 2002), pp. 155–70.

8. Daniel Lyons, "Too Much Information," *Forbes* 174, no. 12 (December 13, 2004), pp. 110–14.

9. Arthur M. Hughes, "The Importance of Customer Communications," *Database Marketing Institute* (**www.dbmarketing.com/articles/ART233.htm**, August 23, 2007).

10. Richard H. Levey, "Prospects Looking Good," *Direct* 16 (December 1, 2004), p. 1–5.

11. Ibid.

12. Ibid.

CHAPTER OBJECTIVES

After reading this chapter, you should be able to answer the following questions:

- **What** are the two main categories of sales promotions and how do they differ?
- **What** are the major categories of trade promotions and how are they used?
- **How** can sales promotions stimulate behaviour in customers?
- **What** are the strengths and weaknesses of sales promotions?
- **How** can a marketing team tie consumer promotions to trade promotions and other elements of the marketing communications mix?
- **What** are the potential limitations when sales promotions programs are being developed for international customers?

INDUSTRY PROFILE

So You Want to Work in Marketing Communications?

Roman Hatashita, Founder and President, Hatashita International, Waterloo, Ontario

Given Roman Hatashita's background, it is no surprise that he is now a successful marketer of martial arts gear and apparel. He grew up in an entrepreneurial family. "My dad owned lots of small businesses. A jewellery store, a wallpaper store, gift stores. So I learned the retail business and how to spot and take advantage of opportunities at a very early age." In fact, Roman started his first business in grade 8 when he would buy fireworks during family trips to the Southern United States and sell them to his friends at school.

The focus on martial arts is also obvious given Roman's accomplishments in his teens and twenties. He was a member of Canada's judo team, and even competed at the 1992 Olympics in Barcelona. "After the Olympics I was looking for my next business venture. I had a successful business selling watches in kiosks at the mall, but when the malls realized they could charge way more rent, the profit was gone, so I closed the business." Although previous careers were profitable for Roman, he never felt the same passion for the work that he did for his judo career. "So I decided to bring my entrepreneurial background and my sports background together and start this business."

Hatashita has grown over the years from a small retailer of marital arts gear to a firm that sells a broad range of martial arts–related products, and even designs and produces its own brands of gear and apparel. "Where we are today is really serving retailers and martial arts clubs as a producer and wholesaler of gear and martial arts products," says Roman. "A key pillar of our revenue comes from working with martial arts clubs across the country. Instead of carrying their own inventory, martial arts clubs sell Roman's products to their members. And promotions are a big part of how Roman generates that revenue.

"We need to make it as easy as possible for these clubs to sell our products because most of them are very small operations run by people who have a passion for the sport but relatively little business savvy. They don't have the time or

Sales Promotions

expertise to do anything more than train, so when their members are looking for gear, it needs to be simple."

The system Roman designed is based on affiliate marketing programs found online. When clubs refer their members to the site (**www.hatashita.com**), they log in with a special club code and receive a 10 percent discount on all purchases. "So there is an incentive for the club member to buy through the club because of the discount. But the real beauty of the program is that we also let the club keep the full retail margin from the sale. We take the normal wholesale spread, but the retail margin helps ensure that clubs have an incentive to send their members our way."

Roman also implements programs around the wholesale website interface. "In order to help make it as easy as possible for clubs to promote our site, we provide each club with a few dozen business cards that outline the details of the discount for club members, and provide directions on how to order through the club's special code. That way we give an incentive to the club, to the member, and provide an easy—almost foolproof— program to make that happen."

The program allows Hatashita to attract dozens or even hundreds of individual customers at a time, and it's far more effective than traditional brand-building approaches through such vehicles as media advertising. "One of the realities of small business is that there just isn't the same level of resources that

Roman Hatashita, Founder and President, Hatashita International.

you find in large businesses. So I need to be smart and very efficient about how I promote my business. Promotions like this deliver far more return than I could ever get through traditional advertising, and for a small fraction of the cost," says Roman.

When talking to people who have a dream of starting their own businesses, Roman has some very specific advice. First, he says, be sure to understand your product and your market very well. "Start off small to make sure you build the business the right way. If you are into shoes, for example, don't run off and get funding for a complete line of shoes and have them stocked in every store in the country. It's better to have some unmet demand for a product after you have worked out the kinks than it is to have 20,000 pairs of shoes sitting in a warehouse."

Having said that, Roman's second piece of advice is to make sure you have adequate funding to run the business properly. Funding that is secured without the help of venture capitalists. "When VCs get involved, the business is ruled by them. And they might not have the same objectives as the original owner. But on the flip side, I talk to people who want to start marital arts clubs and many of them simply don't give themselves a chance because of underfunding. So they'll start a club without complete gear, or open without matting. It's a bad way to introduce yourself to customers, and you only get one chance to make that first impression."

The third piece of advice concerns the balance between growth and focus. "I learned a lot from my dad, and he had many successful businesses. But the one thing I learned to avoid was a lack of focus. When my dad bought a sailboat, instead of buying equipment from someone else, he opened up a sailing shop. In my business, I always need to balance the growth opportunities with the need to stay focused on not only my core business, but also my passion for the sport. So we started with judo suits. Then went on to karate suits. Then to producing our own karate suits. Now to our own Reevo brand of gear, and we're even into UFC-style cages and rings now. We keep expanding and it hasn't taken me down yet, so I must be finding the right balance."

OVERVIEW

Although the 4P framework of marketing tactics (price, place, product, and promotion) labels the entire marketing communications mix as promotion, the proper use of the term *promotion* refers to a subset of activities within the marketing communications mix. These activities, collectively known as **sales promotion**, are used extensively by marketers in virtually all product categories. Activities range from coupons and price-off discount tactics to the use of sampling and contests to generate a customer response. Although varied, these activities all tend to focus on behavioural objectives for customers. They are all designed to stimulate some form of specific action on the part of the customer. Although these behaviours are most related to the purchase decision stage in the customer decision-making process, sales promotions can be part of any stage in the process and can contribute to a broad range of marketing communications objectives.

Sales promotions take two forms: **consumer promotions** and **trade promotions**. Consumer promotions are the incentives that are directly offered to a firm's customers or potential customers. Consumer promotions are aimed at those who actually use the product, those who make the final purchase decision, or those who are the actual buyers.

Trade promotions are used only in the distribution channel. Trade promotions consist of the expenditures or incentives used by manufacturers and other members of the marketing channel to purchase goods for eventual resale. Trade promotions provided to other firms help push products through to retailers. In this sense the "customers" of the firm using sales promotions are the firms that buy the products and resell them to the ultimate end-users.

In the past, some marketing experts believed that any type of sales promotion, whether consumer or trade, eroded brand equity. They suggested that the incentives simply encouraged customers, businesses, and the distribution channel to focus on price. Recently, however, that view has changed. Many company leaders recognize that promotions can differentiate a brand from the competition. This increased differentiation builds brand awareness and improves a brand's image.[1]

This chapter examines consumer promotions first, followed by trade promotions. Although the presentations are separate, keep in mind that the marketing team designs both at the same time. After examining different types of sales promotion activities, we will examine how and why they can be effective at generating customer response, and consider their strengths and weaknesses as part of the overall IMC plan.

EARLY BIRD CLIP & SAVE OFFER

PJ'S PETS PETS UNLIMITED VALID THROUGH DEC. 18, 2011

TAKE **$10 OFF** ANY PURCHASE OF $50 OR MORE (before taxes)

Coupon is not redeemable for cash. Coupon has no cash value and must be presented at time of purchase. One coupon per transaction. Not available in-store. Coupon cannot be used towards the purchase of gift cards. Coupon cannot be combined with any other offer. Coupon is redeemable for purchases at any PJ's Pets location. Valid for one time use only until December 18, 2011.

Coupons and price discounts are forms of promotion found in almost every product category.

CONSUMER PROMOTIONS

Enticing a consumer to take the final step and make the purchase is one of the primary goals of a consumer promotions program. In addition to leading to the final decision to buy an item, consumer promotions programs can be highly effective in generating traffic to a store and enhancing brand loyalty.

In 2007, Taco Bell created a unique promotion program. The restaurant chain offered a free taco if one of the players in the World Series stole a base during the game. In the fourth inning of the second game, Boston Red Sox rookie Jacoby Ellsbury stole second base. The free tacos were given out between 2:00 to 6:00 p.m. the next day. The estimated cost of the giveaway was $1 million; however, when customers purchased a drink or other food with the free taco, the actual cost to the company was lower.[2] Marketing professionals estimated the value of the buzz and publicity to be $5.6 million. The figure was based on the idea that the giveaway created news that was featured on ESPN and other sports channels. It also resulted in chatter on blogs and social networks. The ensuing publicity was far better than any advertising the company could have purchased.

As the Taco Bell example suggests, consumer promotions can be highly effective. The two most general categories of consumer promotions are franchise-building promotions and sales-building promotions. *Franchise-building promotions* are designed to increase awareness of and loyalty to a brand. Building a favourable image by pointing out unique features and selling points is the goal. This also reduces reliance on discounts to increase sales. An example is when WestJet offers a free trip in a contest; the incentive is directly tied to the service provided by the company, and the contest allows the company to develop its positioning within the market. From the list of consumer promotions in Figure 9.1, we see that franchise-building promotions often consist of premiums, contests, sweepstakes, sampling, and bonus packs.

Sales-building promotions focus on immediate sales, rather than brand equity or loyalty, through discounts or other enticements. An example is the e-coupon, created by Pearl Fever, designed to stimulate immediate sales by offering a limited-time financial incentive. Sales-building promotions shown in Figure 9.1 include coupons, refunds, rebates, and price-offs. Each of these forms of promotions is described next.

FIGURE 9.1
Types of Consumer Promotions

- ◆ Coupons
- ◆ Premiums
- ◆ Contests and sweepstakes
- ◆ Refunds and rebates
- ◆ Sampling
- ◆ Bonus packs
- ◆ Price-offs

Critical Thinking Exercise

How can each type of promotion—franchise-building and sales-building—be used within the same IMC plan to deliver different objectives? Think of an example of a product or service you bought recently that included some type of promotion. What type of promotion was it? Did the promotion influence your decision to buy? Would another type of promotion have been more effective in your opinion? Why?

Coupons

A coupon is a price reduction offer to a consumer. It may be a percentage off the retail price, such as 25 or 40 percent, or an absolute amount, such as 50 cents or $1. In Canada, 2.6 billion coupons were distributed and over 100 million were redeemed within just a year. The 0.33 percent redemption rate represents approximately $105 million in savings for consumers, or about $1.05 per coupon. Approximately 78 percent of all households use coupons, and 64 percent are willing to switch brands with coupons.[3] Figure 9.2 provides a more detailed breakdown of coupon usage.

Coupon Distribution

Approximately 80 percent of all coupons are issued by manufacturers. Figure 9.3 lists the various forms of coupon distribution. Nearly 90 percent of all coupons are sent out through print media. Approximately 88 percent are distributed through **freestanding inserts (FSIs)**. FSIs are sheets of coupons distributed in newspapers, primarily on Sunday. The average person receives 850 freestanding inserts per year. Other methods of distribution include in-store, on-shelf, and electronically dispensed coupons, along with coupons attached to free samples of a product. The remaining coupons are distributed in or on product packages, online, by direct mail, and in magazines and newspapers.[4] One

FIGURE 9.2
Percentage of Consumer Coupon Usage

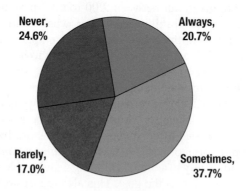

Never, 24.6%
Always, 20.7%
Rarely, 17.0%
Sometimes, 37.7%

FIGURE 9.3
Methods of Coupon Distribution

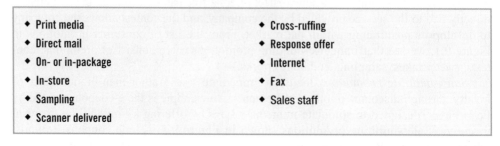

- ◆ Print media
- ◆ Direct mail
- ◆ On- or in-package
- ◆ In-store
- ◆ Sampling
- ◆ Scanner delivered
- ◆ Cross-ruffing
- ◆ Response offer
- ◆ Internet
- ◆ Fax
- ◆ Sales staff

outlet for coupons that has become wildly popular is Groupon (**www.groupon.com**). The site lets users access local coupons to products and services within their city, often with very large and time-sensitive discounts, and share those coupons with friends online.

FSIs and print media are used to distribute coupons for several reasons. First, a consumer must make a conscious effort to clip or save the coupon. Second, coupons create brand awareness. The consumer sees the brand name on the coupon even when the coupon is not redeemed. Third, FSIs encourage consumers to purchase brands on their next trip to the store. Consumers are more likely to purchase a couponed brand and remember the brand name when they redeem a coupon, which helps move the brand to a consumer's long-term memory. The consumer is more likely to recall the brand and buy it the next time the need arises, even without a coupon.

Types of Coupons

Coupons are often distributed in retail stores and placed on or near packages. The consumer can immediately redeem the coupon while making the purchase. This type of coupon is called an *instant redemption coupon*. These coupons often lead to trial purchases and purchases of additional packages of a product. Many grocery stores allow a company to cook a new food product and offer free samples along with coupon giveaways. Coupons are also placed in dispensers near various products, which provide convenient access for customers. All of these are forms of instant redemption coupons, because customers can use them immediately.

A cross-ruffing coupon for Tyson and Betty Crocker.

Coupons can also be placed inside packages so that customers cannot redeem them quite as quickly. This approach encourages repeat purchases. These coupons are called *bounce-back coupons.*

Some companies issue coupons at the cash register. These are called *scanner-delivered coupons*, because they are triggered by an item being scanned. The coupon that is delivered is often for a competitor's product. This approach is designed to encourage brand switching the next time a consumer makes a purchase.

Cross-ruffing is the placement of two promotional materials together. A cross-ruff coupon is placed on one product for another product. A coupon for a French onion dip placed on a package of potato chips is a cross-ruff coupon. Cross-ruff coupons should be on products that fit together logically and that are often purchased and consumed simultaneously. Occasionally, a manufacturer uses cross-ruffing to encourage consumers to purchase another one of its products. For example, Kellogg may place a coupon on a Rice Krispies box for another cereal, such as Frosted Flakes or an oatmeal product. This type of couponing tactic encourages consumers to purchase within the same brand or family of products.

Response offer coupons are issued following requests by consumers. Coupons are then mailed, faxed, or sent via the Internet to the consumer. Office supply companies and other vendors use them to entice business customers to make purchases or place orders. Some firms distribute coupons through sales representatives. This creates instant redemptions, because the salesperson also takes the order.

Critical Thinking Exercise

The few months after Christmas are traditionally very slow for most retailers. In an effort to stimulate sales in the January-to-March period, Lululemon, the popular yoga clothing store, is considering using coupons. Do you think this is a good idea? Discuss the pros and cons of each method of distributing coupons for Lululemon listed in Figure 9.3. Are some methods better choices than others? Why?

Problems with Coupons

The use of coupons as a promotional tactic does have some drawbacks, including:

- Reduced revenues
- Mass-cutting
- Counterfeiting
- Misredemptions

Customers who already have a preference for a brand redeem approximately 80 percent of all coupons.[5] Some argue that offering a price discount to customers who are willing to pay full price does not make sense. Manufacturers, however, point out that these consumers may be willing to stock up on the item, which means they won't use the competition's coupons or products. Consequently, manufacturers recognize that these brand-preference customer redemptions are a "necessary evil" if mass distribution is used. Some firms use direct mail to distribute the coupon primarily to customers who are not brand loyal. The goal is to target nonusers and the competitor's customers. The primary disadvantage of this method is the high cost of direct mail, especially in light of the low response rate associated with direct-mail coupons.

A common form of coupon fraud is *mass-cutting*. Coupons are "redeemed" through a fraudulent, nonexistent retail outlet, which is a mailbox set up by an illegal coupon-redemption ring. At \$.50 to \$3 per coupon, mass-cutting of coupons can be lucrative. Many times these rings take advantage of charitable organizations and religious groups that think they are helping a worthy cause by sending in coupons to the mailbox to receive a percentage of the proceeds. Instead, they actually are aiding an illegal activity.

Counterfeiting occurs when coupons are copied and then sent back to the manufacturer for reimbursement. The manufacturer pays for phony coupons. Newspaper-generated black-and-white coupons are the easiest to counterfeit. Colour copiers, however, have made other forms of counterfeiting easier. The major source of counterfeiting is the Internet. High-quality printer technology makes it possible for people to create bogus coupons and then sell or distribute them via the Internet. In most cases, the counterfeit coupons are sold in bulk and often are for inflated discounts or even free merchandise.

Retailers usually are not involved in mass-cutting or counterfeiting of coupons. They can, however, engage in the *misredemption* of coupons. For instance, a coupon for soup often states the size of can for which the discount applies. If the discount is used for another size, such as a 12-ounce can instead of the 24-ounce can, then a misredemption occurs. This may be due to an error on the part of the clerk who did not check the coupon carefully. Or, the clerk might have known it was the wrong-size can but did not want to bother finding the correct size or risk making the customer mad by denying the coupon. Other times, clerks honour coupons for merchandise that was not purchased when they take the coupon and subtract it from the customer's total without matching it to any actual product.

Brands like Budweiser often feature premiums found in packages of beer.

Premiums

A second form of consumer promotion is the offer of a premium. Premiums are prizes, gifts, or other special offers consumers receive when purchasing products. When a company presents a premium, the consumer pays full price for the good or service, in contrast to coupons, which grant price reductions.

Some marketing experts believe overusing coupons damages a brand's image. Conversely, premiums can actually enhance an image. The key is to pick the right type of premium.

ON THE JOB

The High Cost of Coupon Redemption

Many marketers mistakenly believe that coupons provide an effective way to encourage purchase while still making a profit on a sale. They argue that because the discount amount of the coupon is less than the margin on the product, the coupon is merely a way of "splitting" some portion of the margin with the customer. However, this is not always the case when the true cost of the coupon program is taken into account. Consider the following example:

A product sells at retail for $5.00, with a margin of $1.25. If a coupon for $.75 is issued, in theory the program can still be profitable because the marketer is still earning a $.50 margin on every sale. But this is not the case.

Let's assume that the coupon is distributed through printed form, which is still the most common format for coupons. That printing, although relatively inexpensive in quantity, still costs money. Let's assume that the printing costs for 5 million coupons are $15/thousand, or $75,000.

If we achieve a 2 percent redemption rate, the 100,000 redeemed coupons cost a total of $75,000 in margin.

Finally, the handling of the coupon through a clearinghouse is an additional expense, since many manufacturer coupons are processed by an intermediary between the manufacturer and retailer. Let's assume a cost of $.10 per coupon.

The total cost of the coupon program is $160,000 ($75,000 for printing, $75,000 in margin, and $10,000 for handling). But the total margin as a result of the coupon was only $125,000 ($1.25 per product × 100,000 units sold). Therefore, the coupon program actually lost money. This may be acceptable if the objective of the marketer was to introduce the product to new customers, for example. But the full cost of any discount program should be fully accounted for so that marketers can make the most appropriate decision based on facts.

Premiums can be used in the attempt to boost sales; however, they usually are not as successful as coupon sales. Nevertheless, premiums remain a valuable consumer promotional tool.

The four major types of premiums are shown in Figure 9.4. *Free-in-the-mail premiums* are gifts individuals receive for purchasing products. To receive the gift, the customer mails in a proof of purchase to the manufacturer, who then mails the gift to the customer. Sometimes more than one purchase is required to receive the gift. Credit card companies use premiums to entice individuals to sign up for credit cards. Instead of providing a proof of purchase, the consumer need only activate the card to receive the incentives, which can range from cash back on purchases to merchandise and frequent-flier miles.

In- or *on-package premiums* are usually small gifts, such as toys in cereal boxes. The gift may be disguised or packaged so the consumer must buy the product to find out which premium it contains. The most famous of these may be Cracker Jack's prizes. At other times the gift is attached to the package, such as a package of blades with the purchase of a razor.

Store or manufacturer premiums are gifts given by either the retail store or the manufacturer when the customer purchases a product. Fast-food restaurants offer children a toy with the purchase of a child's meal. To entice individuals to purchase high-end homes and real estate in Prime Nature Villa in Thailand, the contractors offered a number of unique premiums. One premium was a 525i BMW automobile that was given to individuals who purchased land plots larger than 1,600 square metres in the company's luxury-home project area. Individuals who purchased smaller plots of between 800 and 1,600 square metres received gift certificates for diamond jewellery.[6]

◆ Free-in-the-mail	◆ Store or manufacturer
◆ In- or on-package	◆ Self-liquidating

FIGURE 9.4
Types of Premiums

Premiums in cereal boxes aren't always toys meant for children. Products with adult target audiences also use in-box premiums to drive sales.

The fourth major type is called a *self-liquidating premium.* These require the consumer to pay an amount of money for a gift or item. For example, the premium may be offered for only $4.99 plus shipping and handling and two proofs of purchase from boxes of Cheerios. The premium is called self-liquidating because the $4.99 covers the cost of the premium. The manufacturer also receives money for shipping and handling. This means that consumers pay most or all of the actual cost of the item.

Keys to Successful Premium Programs

Successful premium programs have several common elements, as shown in Figure 9.5. First, the premium should match the target market. A target market such as older, high-income individuals can be reached with a premium such as china or fine crystal. If the market is children, a cartoon figure or a character from Disney or Sesame Street is more attractive.

The best premiums reinforce the firm's image. They should not be low-cost trinkets if the brand is positioned as higher quality. Offering cheap merchandise insults customers and can damage the firm's image. Premium programs succeed when they tie in with the firm's products in order to enhance the image of the product and the firm.[7]

Premiums should be integrated with the other components of the IMC program. Premiums provide an excellent means of adding value to a product instead of slashing prices or using coupons. Premiums can serve as a "thank you" to current customers or to attract new customers. *Sports Illustrated* has a rich history of premium programs, from DVDs to watches to phones, which are presented for either renewing a subscription to the magazine or ordering one for the first time.

Although premiums are an excellent method of adding value or enhancing a brand, they are not as effective at increasing profits. Therefore, a clear relationship between the premium's intention and IMC goals should be established. Logically, the goal is more about image than profit.

Critical Thinking Exercise

Beer companies are famous for using premiums in their packaging. Assume you are the brand manager for Molson Canadian. What role would premiums play in your sales promotion? What would your premium(s) be, and in what type of packaging would you insert them? What would you hope to achieve with this element of your sales promotion plan, and how could it complement other elements of the IMC plan?

Contests

Contests are popular consumer sales promotions. Approximately $1.8 billion is spent on various games and contests each year, which appear in consumer markets as well as business markets.[8] The prize list is the primary factor that determines the success or failure of these appeals. Members of the target market for the contest or sweepstakes must find the prizes desirable in order to entice them to participate.

FIGURE 9.5
Keys to Successful Premiums

- ◆ Match the premium to the target market
- ◆ Carefully select the premiums (avoid fads, try for exclusivity)
- ◆ Pick a premium that reinforces the firm's product and image
- ◆ Integrate the premium with other IMC tools (especially advertising and POP displays)
- ◆ Don't expect premiums to increase short-term profits

Source: Based on Don Jagoda, "The Seven Habits of Highly Successful Premiums," *Incentive* 173, no.8 (August 1999), pg. 104–105

In Canada, it is illegal to force a consumer to make a purchase to enter a contest. It is also illegal for a company to offer what is otherwise considered a lottery. Therefore, all contests in Canada feature a no-purchase option of entry, and require participants to answer at least some sort of skill testing question or show some other form of accomplishment prior to winning.

People enter contests that they perceive as being worth their time and attention. Consumers do not enter every contest they encounter. Instead, they selectively choose. The decision is often based on the perceived value of the contest prize combined with the odds of winning. The greater the perceived odds of winning, the more likely a person will participate in the contest.

Heinz encourages dialogue with consumers through the use of contests.

There are two primary categories of contests. The first is where consumers enter by simply identifying themselves as a contestant. Often this is done through ballots in the retail store, online, or through a mail-in. Consumers identify themselves using their name, address, and other personal information.

The second form is where consumers perform some act as part of their entry into a contest. An example is the Heinz Comfort Food Creations Recipe Contest. Consumers entered recipes online in which comfort food recipes were described in detail (of course, all using Heinz products). Winners received a range of cookware and Heinz products.

The second form of contest combines both extrinsic value and intrinsic value in the prizing. The *extrinsic value* is the actual attractiveness of the item (a car versus a free sandwich). The greater the perceived value, the more likely the person will participate. *Intrinsic values* are those associated with participating. A contest requiring the use of a skill, such as the one with recipes or an essay contest, entices entry by individuals who enjoy demonstrating a skill. In that case, extrinsic rewards become secondary. Instead, participants enjoy competing and demonstrating their abilities, which in part explains the popularity of fantasy football and baseball leagues and "pick the winner" sports contests.

Car makers such as Mazda often target sales promotions at new graduates.

The Internet can provide opportunities for individuals to participate for a prize's intrinsic value. It also can be used to create interactive games that can challenge a contestant's ability. The Internet provides promoters with data-capturing capabilities.

A mobile phone promotion developed by Hip Cricket, a mobile marketing and event company, provided instant notification of winning via text messaging. Hip Cricket developed a sweepstakes for Miller Brewing Company. The sweepstakes was the first to be conducted live, during a rock concert. Music fans 21 years old or older could enter the sweepstakes by text messaging the words "Pick Me" during the concert. At 10:00 p.m., one concertgoer, Melissa Hasty, received word via text message that she had won the grand prize, a five-day, four-night Caribbean cruise on the "Rock Boat." Other concert fans won secondary prizes throughout the night, again receiving notification via their cell phone's instant messaging system. For Melissa and others at the concert, winning instantly was even more exciting.[9]

To encourage consumers to continue participating in a contest, the extrinsic values of prizes can be increased by allowing small, incremental rewards. A consumer who wins a soft drink or a sandwich in a sweepstakes at Subway is more likely to continue participating. Scratch-and-win cards tend to be effective because the reward is instant.

Refunds and Rebates

Refunds and rebates are cash returns offered to consumers or businesses following the purchase of a product. Consumers pay full price for the product but can mail in some type of proof of purchase. The manufacturer then refunds a portion of the purchase price. A *refund* is a cash return on what are called "soft goods," such as food or clothing. *Rebates* are cash returns on "hard goods," which are major-ticket items such as automobiles and appliances. Normally, refunds are smaller and rebates are larger. For example, the typical refund offered on a food item may be $1; the typical rebate on a car may be $500, $1,000, or more, depending on the price and size of the car.

Only about 30 percent of all rebates are ever claimed. For rebates valued at $50 or more, however, the percentage of claims rises to about 65 percent. The major reason for the low response rate is the inconvenience associated with getting the rebate. Too many steps or long waiting times because of "snail mail" are common complaints about rebates. It is not unusual for consumers to wait up to 6 months to receive a rebate cheque.[10]

Many rebate programs suffer from diminished effectiveness, because consumers have come to expect them. For example, car dealers often find that customers won't buy until rebates are offered. As a result, there is no new purchase activity associated with the rebate, but rather a delay in the purchase process as consumers "wait out" auto manufacturers. According to J.D. Power and Associates, slightly more than 60 percent of all vehicle purchases involve some type of cash rebate.[11] Further, increasing the amount of a rebate no longer seems to spur additional sales activity, yet discontinuing or reducing rebate levels tends to have an immediate negative impact on sales.

Refunds and rebates achieve the greatest successes when they are perceived as being new or original. When they become an entrenched part of doing business, they are expected discounts. Rebates and refunds must have the impact of changing the buyer's behaviour, either by leading to more immediate purchases or by causing the customer to change brands.

Sampling

A popular method for enticing consumers to try new products is sampling. Sampling is the actual delivery of a product to consumers for their use or consumption. Most samples are provided free of charge. A coupon or price-off incentive is often given with the sample to persuade the consumer to purchase a larger version of the product, such as a full-size package.

In business-to-business markets, samples of products may be provided to potential clients. Sampling also can be featured in the service sector. For example, a tanning salon may offer an initial visit free to encourage new customers to try its facilities. Dentists and lawyers use sampling when they offer an initial consultation free of charge.

Figure 9.6 lists various ways samples are distributed. The most common consumer method is *in-store distribution,* such as when food product companies have personnel cooking the food and passing it out to individuals in the store. *Direct sampling* is a program in which samples are mailed or delivered door to door to consumers.

Various demographic target markets can be identified for free samples. In the business-to-business sector, salespeople often deliver direct samples. *Response samples* are made available to individuals or businesses responding to a media offer on television, on the Internet, from a magazine, or by some other source. *Cross-ruff* sampling plans provide samples of one product on another. A laundry detergent with a free dryer sheet attached to the package is a cross-ruff sample. *Media sampling* means the sample is included in the media outlet. For example, a small sample of perfume can be included in

FIGURE 9.6
Types of Sampling

◆ In-store distribution	◆ Media sampling
◆ Direct sampling	◆ Professional sampling
◆ Response sampling	◆ Selective sampling
◆ Cross-ruff sampling	

a magazine advertisement or with a newspaper. *Professional samples* are delivered to professionals, such as doctors, who may then provide patients with the free drug samples. *Selective samples* are distributed at a site, such as a parade, hospital, restaurant, or sporting event. For instance, many times Power Bars are given to people attending football or basketball games. There is a tie-in between the product (nutrition) and the event (athletics).

In recent years, marketers have increased usage of FSIs for the distribution of samples. A variety of products have been distributed in newspapers, such as breakfast bars, coffee, shampoo, snacks, tea, and automotive cleansers. Companies using newspapers utilize the FSI insert method because it breaks through the clutter and gets the attention of consumers. The newspaper is an "invited medium." Therefore, consumers are more receptive when samples are distributed with the paper.[12]

Benefits of Sampling

Product sampling is an effective way to introduce a new product, generate interest in that product, and collect information about consumers. Internet-based response sampling programs have also become popular with both consumers and manufacturers. Bristol-Myers/Squibb was one of the first companies to utilize the Internet for product sampling. The company offered a free sample of Excedrin to individuals who requested the sample and were willing to provide their name, address, and email information. In addition to the 12-pack sample of Excedrin, consumers received coupons for additional Excedrin purchases, along with the quarterly *Excedrin Headache Relief Update Newsletter*. The advantage of this form of response sampling is that only consumers who requested the product received it. Also, companies normally can gather additional information to be added to a database. Seventy percent of consumers who requested a sample online were willing to complete a survey to receive the sample.[13]

Problems with Sampling

The primary disadvantage of sampling is cost. Often, a special sample-size package must be developed. The package must be very similar to the regular-size pack, so consumers will be able to identify the product after using the sample. Many times samples are mailed, adding to the expense of the program. A sample given out in a store requires an individual to distribute it and some kind of permission from the store.

Successful Sampling Programs

The primary purpose of sampling is to encourage a trial use by a consumer or a business. Sampling is most effective when it introduces a new product or a new version of a product to a market. Samples also help promote a current product to a new target market or to new prospects.

Successful sampling means targeting the right audience. Mass sampling is not nearly as cost-effective as targeted sampling. Recently, Green & Black's launched a sampling campaign for organic chocolates at 21 outdoor concerts in England. Each audience member was given a bar of Green & Black's organic chocolate at the entrance. More than 80 percent of the audience, a total of 105,000 people, received sample bars. A tasting marquee was also set up in the concert area so that concert attendees could try other flavours. The goal was to build a brand experience between concert attendees and the Green & Black's brand name and to boost sales, which it did. Sales of the organic chocolate bar increased 79 percent in the months immediately following the concerts.[14]

Bonus Packs

When an additional or extra number of items are placed in a special product package, it is called a bonus pack. When a consumer buys four bars of soap for the price of three, it is a bonus pack promotion.

Bell used the Toronto International Film Festival to "sample" its new IPTV service, Fibe.

This B-to-B Polycom ad offers a free 30-day, risk-free trial.

A bonus pack offer for two packages of Lean Slices by Carl Buddig.

Recently, Energizer offered three free AA batteries in a bonus pack containing nine batteries. Typical bonuses range from 20 percent to 100 percent of the normal number of units in a package. A 30 percent bonus is the most common.

Types of Bonus Packs

Figure 9.7 identifies the major objectives of bonus packs. Increasing the size or quantity of the package can lead to greater product use. For example, if a cereal box is increased in size by 25 percent, the consumer is likely to eat more cereal, because it is readily available. This is not true for products that have a constant rate of consumption. For instance, if Colgate increases the size of a toothpaste container by 25 percent, consumers will not use more toothpaste. In effect, this delays the customer's next purchase. Still, manufacturers offer these types of bonus packs because they may preempt the competition. A consumer with a large quantity of the merchandise on hand is less likely to switch to another brand, even when offered some type of deal.

Benefits of Bonus Packs

A firm's current customers often take advantage of a bonus pack offer. When customers stockpile a quantity of a particular brand, they are less likely to purchase from a competitor. Bonus packs reward customer loyalty by offering, in effect, free merchandise.

Bonus packs can lead to brand switching if the consumer has used the brand previously. Facing purchase decisions, consumers may opt for brands that offer a bonus pack at the regular price. These products have an advantage that competitive brands are not offering.

Bonus packs tend to be popular with manufacturers, retailers, and customers. A retailer can build a good relationship with a manufacturer that uses a bonus pack to increase brand switching and stockpiling. Retailers gain an advantage because the bonus pack is a "bargain" or "value" offered through the retail outlet. Customers like bonus packs because they get additional product at the same price. For ongoing products with high competition, the bonus pack approach is one way to maintain brand loyalty and reduce brand switching at a minimal cost.

Problems with Bonus Packs

Bonus packs rarely attract new customers because the consumer is less likely to have previously purchased the brand. Obtaining an extra quantity does not reduce the purchase risk. In fact, it adds to the risk, especially when the customer does not like to waste a product by throwing it away if he or she is dissatisfied with the product.

Some marketing research indicates that consumers are sceptical of bonus pack offers. When the bonus is small (20 to 40 percent), consumers often believe the price has not

FIGURE 9.7
Reasons for Using Bonus Packs

◆ Increase usage of the product	◆ Develop customer loyalty
◆ Match or preempt competitive actions	◆ Attract new users
◆ Stockpile the product	◆ Encourage brand switching

truly changed. Unfortunately, when the bonus is large, such as a two-for-the-price-of-one sale, consumers tend to believe that the price was first increased to compensate for the additional quantity. Even though increasing the size of a bonus catches the consumer's attention, it may not convey the desired message.[15]

Price-Offs

A price-off is a temporary reduction in the price of a product to the consumer. A price-off can be physically marked on the product, such as when a bottle of aspirin shows the regular retail price marked out and replaced by a special retail price (e.g., $4.99 marked out and replaced by $3.99). Producing a label with the price reduction premarked forces the retailer to sell the item at the reduced price. This ensures the price-off incentive will be passed on to the consumer. At other times, the price-off is not on the actual item, but on a retail display, sign, or shelf.

Benefits of Price-Offs

Price-offs are excellent at stimulating sales of an existing product. They can entice customers to try new products because the lower price reduces the financial risk of making the purchase. They can encourage customers to switch brands in brand parity situations or when no strong brand loyalty exists. In cases where consumers do have a brand preference, a price-off on a favourite brand encourages stockpiling of the product and possibly

Many companies offer students special pricing.

increased consumption of the item.[16] A consumer who purchases additional breakfast bars because of a price-off tends to consume more breakfast bars. Again, this will not be true for products such as deodorant or toothpaste. Stockpiling for those types of products just delays the next purchase. It does not increase consumption. Similar effects are seen in the business-to-business arena when price-offs are used.

Price-offs have proven to be successful consumer promotions for two reasons. First, the price-off has the appeal of a monetary savings to consumers. Second, the reward is immediate. Unlike with rebates, refunds, contests, sweepstakes, and other promotional incentives, consumers do not have to wait for the reward.

Problems with Price-Offs

While price-offs are easy to implement and can have a sudden impact on sales, they can also cause problems. Although sales may increase, price-offs can have a negative impact on a company's profit margin. It normally takes at least a 20 percent increase in sales to offset each 5 percent price reduction.

Another danger of price-off programs is that they encourage consumers to become more price-sensitive. In the same way that customers respond to rebates, they can either wait for a price-off promotion or choose another brand that happens to be on sale. In addition, when used too often, price-offs can have a negative impact on a brand's image. As always, price-off programs should be incorporated into the firm's overall IMC program.

$29⁹⁵

$tudent pricing

For just $29.95, walk in with your taxes, walk out with your refund. Instantly. You'll also get a free SPC Card to save big at your favourite retailers.*

maximum
refund™
free SPC Card

we make taxes easy

  H&R BLOCK®

Follow us on Twitter and Facebook   **hrblock.ca**

© 2011 H&R Block Canada, Inc. *$29.95 valid for regular student tax preparation only. Cash Back service included. To qualify for student pricing, student must present either (i) a T2202a documenting 4 or more months of full-time attendance at a college or university during 2010 or (ii) a valid high school identification card. Expires December 31, 2011. Valid only at participating H&R Block locations in Canada. SPC Card offers valid from 08/01/10 to 07/31/11 at participating locations in Canada only. For Cardholder only. Offers may vary, restrictions may apply. Usage may be restricted when used in conjunction with any other offer or retailer loyalty card discounts. Cannot be used towards the purchase of gift cards or certificates. **If H&R Block makes any error in the preparation of your tax return that costs you any interest or penalties on additional taxes due, although we do not assume the liability for the additional taxes, we will reimburse you for the interest and penalties.

Companies like Procter & Gamble use tie-ins between brands to cross-promote to consumers. A box of detergent, for example, might make an excellent vehicle to offer samples of a fabric softener.

Overlays and Tie-Ins

At times companies combine two or more consumer promotions activities into a single campaign, called an *overlay*. To attract Chinese consumers in Canada, Tropicana combined sampling with coupons. Free samples (50,000 cups of orange juice) were given out along with 30,000 coupons at a Chinese New Year's celebration in Vancouver. Asians who live in the North America are not typically large users of coupons; however, Tropicana Canada's research showed that the Chinese consider oranges to be harbingers of good luck. A few weeks after the promotion, 40 percent of the coupons were redeemed, and sales of Tropicana orange juice among the Chinese community in Canada increased considerably.[17]

Another common strategy is to develop a consumer promotion with another product or company. This is called a *tie-in*. *Intracompany tie-ins* are the promotion of two different products within one company using one consumer promotion. An alternative method is partnering with another company, which is an *intercompany tie-in*. Fast-food restaurants often use tie-ins with movies and toys to creative attractive children's promotions.

Critical Thinking Exercise

According to the sales promotion manager at one leading national chain of drug stores, "The teen and preteen segments are important because they are developing buying habits and loyalties during these ages and are our future loyal consumers." In addition to established brands such as Cover Girl and Maybelline, the store also stocks brands that are specifically positioned toward younger audiences. Which consumer promotions would be the best to attract teens and preteens to the cosmetics department of the store? What tie-ins or overlays would you recommend?

Point-of-Purchase

Although not always associated with sales promotions, a common platform for execution of promotions at retailers is point-of-purchase (POP) displays. POP is any form of special display that promotes merchandise. POP displays are often located near cash registers in retail stores, at the end of an aisle, in a store's entryway, or any other place where they will be noticed. POP includes displays, signs, structures, and devices used to identify, advertise, or merchandise an outlet, service, or product. POP displays serve as an important aid to retail selling.

POP displays remain highly effective tools for increasing sales. About 70 percent of all purchasing decisions are made in the retail store. Nearly 50 percent of the money spent at mass-merchandisers and supermarkets is unplanned. These purchases are called *impulse buys.* When consumers make purchases, they often do not decide on the particular brand until the last minute. For food purchases, 88 percent of the decisions about brands are made in the store at the time of the purchase. In many instances, point-of-purchase materials and other in-store advertising materials influence the decision.[18]

Coca-Cola reports that only 50 percent of soft drink sales are made from the regular store shelf. The other 50 percent results from product displays in other parts of the store. American Express discovered that 30 percent of purchases charged on the American Express card came from impulse decisions by customers seeing the "American Express Cards Welcome" sign. Other research indicates that an average increase in sales of around 9 percent occurs when one POP display is used. Only about half of POP displays create an impact on sales. For the half that does make an impact, however, the average increase in purchases is about 20 percent. Consequently, POP advertising is quite attractive to manufacturers.[19]

Currently, manufacturers spend billions each year on point-of-purchase advertising materials. The largest users of POP advertising are restaurants, food services, apparel stores, and footwear retailers. The fastest-growing categories are fresh, frozen, or refrigerated foods, and professional services.[20]

Manufacturers view POP displays as an attractive method of getting a brand more prominently displayed before customers. Many retailers have a different perspective. Retailers believe POP materials should either boost sales for the store or draw customers in to the store. Retailers are not interested in the sales of one particular brand, but instead want to improve overall sales and store profits. Retailers prefer displays that educate consumers and provide information. As a result, retailers are more inclined to set up POP displays that match the retailer's marketing objectives.

POP displays are very helpful when selling products such as cosmetics, perfume, or cologne.

Source: House of Bijan, Rodeo Drive, Beverly Hills.

Designing Effective POP

To be effective, POP displays must clearly communicate the product's attributes. Pricing and other promotional information is also helpful. The display should encourage the customer to stop and look, pick up the product, and examine it. A customer who stops to examine a product on display is more likely to buy that product.

The POP display should make a clear, succinct offer that customers immediately understand. Many times the POP display only has three-tenths of a second to capture the customer's attention. If it fails, the customer simply moves on to other merchandise. Colours, designs, merchandise arrangements, and tie-ins with other marketing messages are critical elements of effective POP displays.

The best POP displays are those integrated with other marketing communications messages. Message themes used in other IMC components should appear on the POP. Customers more quickly recognize tie-ins with current advertising and promotional themes as they view displays. Figure 9.8 lists some additional pointers for point-of-purchase advertising.

Remember that the size of a display is important to retailers. Store space is limited. Customers do not respond well when freestanding displays at the ends of aisles block traffic through the store. Consequently, individual retailers normally will use only POP displays that fit the allocated space. Retailers prefer easy-to-assemble, easy-to-stock, and adaptable displays. A manufacturer's marketing team should remember that if a retailer does not like a display, it won't be used, no matter how great it looks.

The most common reason why retailers do not use displays furnished by manufacturers is that they are inappropriate for the channel. In other words, a display that works well in a discount store may not be appropriate for a supermarket or a specialty store. Various retailers and channel members have different needs in terms of what they want in a POP display design. Manufacturers should consult with each type of channel member to ensure the display meets their needs.

FIGURE 9.8
Effective POP Displays

- Integrate the brand's image into the display.
- Integrate the display with current advertising and promotions.
- Make the display dramatic to get attention.
- Keep the color of the display down so the product and signage stand out.
- Make the display versatile so it can be easily adapted by retailers.
- Make the display reusable and easy to assemble.
- Make the display easy to stock.
- Customize the display to fit the retailer's store.

Critical Thinking Exercise

Many manufacturers believe the best method for differentiating company brands from competitors is advertising. However, others believe that well-chosen promotional tactics can support brand differentiation. What forms of consumer promotions do you think are promising for building brands, and which ones do you think are limited in their brand-building ability?

TRADE PROMOTIONS

Trade promotions are incentives that members of the trade channel use to entice another member to *purchase goods for eventual resale.* Trade promotions are aimed at retailers, distributors, wholesalers, brokers, or agents. A manufacturer can offer trade promotions to convince another member of the trade channel to carry its goods. Wholesalers, distributors, brokers, and agents use trade promotions to entice retailers to purchase products for eventual resale.

Trade promotions account for a significant percentage of a supplier's or retailer's gross revenues. Twenty years ago they accounted for about 25 percent of a manufacturer's marketing communications budget; today it is nearly 70 percent of the budget. Trade promotions are often the second-largest expense for a manufacturer after the cost-of-goods-sold. Trade promotions account for 17.4 percent of gross sales of manufacturers.[21]

Retailers such as Metro are a very important audience for brands that want to get their products placed in front of shoppers.

Source: Courtesy of Metro Ontario, Inc.

Trade promotions are an integral part of an IMC program. Unfortunately, in many companies, the individual handling trade promotions is not involved in the IMC planning process. Leaders in these firms often view trade promotions as being merely a means for getting products onto retail shelves or satisfying some channel member's request. As a result, little consideration may be given to matching the IMC program when trade promotions programs are developed.

A variety of trade promotions tools exist. Individual companies select trade promotions techniques based on several factors. These factors include the nature of the business (manufacturer versus distributor), the type of customer to be influenced (e.g., selling to a retailer versus selling to a wholesaler), company preferences, and the objectives of the IMC plan. The primary types of trade promotions are listed in Figure 9.9.

FIGURE 9.9
Types of Trade Promotions

◆ Off-invoice allowance: A per-case rebate paid to retailers for an order.

◆ Slotting fees: Money paid to retailers to stock a new product.

◆ Exit fees: Money paid to retailers to remove an item from their SKU inventory.

FIGURE 9.10
Types of Trade Allowances

Trade Allowances

The first major type of trade promotion manufacturers and others use in the channel is a **trade allowance**. Trade allowances provide financial incentives to other channel members to motivate them to make purchases. Trade allowances can be packaged into a variety of forms, including the ones described in Figure 9.10. Each makes it possible for the channel member to offer discounts or other deals to customers.

Off-Invoice Allowances and Slotting Fees

Off-invoice allowances are financial discounts given for each item, case, or pallet ordered. They encourage channel members to place orders. Approximately 35 percent of all trade dollars are spent on off-invoice allowances, making them the largest expenditure among trade promotions tools.[22] Companies often feature off-invoice allowances during holiday seasons. This encourages retailers to purchase larger quantities. Orders must be placed by a specific date to receive a holiday off-invoice allowance. Manufacturers also can place a minimum order size as a further condition.

The most controversial form of trade allowance is a slotting fee. **Slotting fees** are funds charged by retailers to stock new products. Most retailers charge slotting fees and justify them in several ways.[23] First, retailers spend money to add new products to inventories and to stock merchandise. A product that is not successful means the retailer's investment in inventory represents a loss, especially when the retailer has stocked the product in a large number of stores.

Second, adding a new product in the retail store means giving it shelf space. Most shelves are already filled with products. Adding a new product means either deleting brands or products or reducing the amount of shelf space allocated to them. In both cases, the retailer spends both time and money on creating space for a new product.

Third, slotting fees make it easier for retailers to finalize decisions about new products. A typical supermarket carries 35,000 SKUs (stock-keeping units). The supermarket's managers must evaluate at least 10,000 to 15,000 new products per year. Most will fail. Consequently, retailers believe charging slotting fees forces manufacturers to weed out poor product introductions. The average total cost in slotting fees for a nation-

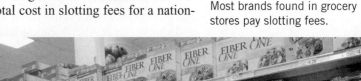

Most brands found in grocery stores pay slotting fees.

ally introduced product ranges from $1.5 million to $2 million.[24] Consequently, retailers contend that slotting fees force manufacturers to conduct careful test marketing on products before introducing them. Such testing reduces the number of new products offered each year. This, in turn, drastically reduces the number of new product failures.

Fourth, and finally, slotting fees add to the bottom line. Many products have low margins or markups. Slotting fees provide additional monies to support retail operations. It has been estimated that between 14 and 27 percent of trade promotion monies given to retailers go directly to the retailer's bottom line.[25]

The other side of the argument comes from manufacturers, who claim slotting fees are practically a form of extortion.

Many manufacturers believe slotting fees are too costly and are unfair in the first place. These fees compel manufacturers to pay millions of dollars to retailers that could be used for advertising, sales promotions, or other marketing efforts.

Slotting fees can prevent small manufacturers from getting products into stores simply because they cannot afford them. Some large retail operations have small-vendor policies; however, placing merchandise remains extremely challenging.

In addition to keeping small manufacturers out of the market, slotting fees favour incumbent suppliers. New entrants into the market face tremendous investment of up-front money already, and then must add on slotting fees. Unless company leaders are absolutely certain the new brand can compete, the firm may not enter a market simply because of slotting fees.

Instead of paying a slotting allowance, some retailers ask for **exit fees**, which are monies paid to remove an item from a retailer's inventory. This approach is often used when a manufacturer introduces a new size of a product or a new version, such as a three-litre bottle of Pepsi. PepsiCo already has products on the retailer's shelves. Adding a new-sized container or new variety of the product involves lower risk and is not the same as adding a new product. Rather than charging an up-front fee such as a slotting allowance, retailers request exit fees if the new version of the product fails or if one of the current versions must be removed from the inventory. Only 4 percent of retailers use exit fees, compared to the 82 percent that use slotting fees.[26]

Trade Allowance Complications

In offering trade allowances to retailers, manufacturers assume that a portion of the price reduction will be passed on to consumers. This occurs only about half of the time. When a portion of the price allowance is passed on to consumers, retailers often schedule competing brands, so they can have at least one special offer going at all times. It is not an accident that one week Pepsi offers a reduced price and the next Coke offers a discount. The two products are rarely promoted *on-deal* (passing along trade allowance discounts) at the same time. By offering only one on-deal at a time, the retailer always has a reduced-price competitor for the price-sensitive consumer. The retailer also can charge the brand-loyal consumer full price 50 percent of the time. While accomplishing these goals, the retailer receives special trade allowances from both Pepsi and Coke.

In an effort to increase their profit margins, retailers often engage in two activities: forward buying and diversion. *Forward buying* occurs when a retailer purchases extra amounts of a product while it is on-deal. The retailer then sells the on-deal merchandise after the deal period ends, saving the cost of purchasing the product at the manufacturer's full price. *Diversion* occurs when a retailer purchases a product on-deal in one location and ships it to another location where it is off-deal. For example, a manufacturer may offer an off-invoice allowance of $5 per case for the product in the Greater Toronto Area. Diversion tactics mean the retailer purchases an excess quantity in the GTA and has it shipped to stores in other areas. To do so, retailers first examine the potential profits to be earned, less the cost of shipping the product to other locations. Shipping costs tend to be relatively high compared to trade allowances offered. Consequently, retailers do not use diversion nearly as much as forward buying.

Trade Contests

To achieve sales targets and other objectives, manufacturers sometimes use trade contests. Rewards are given as contest prizes to brokers, retail salespeople, retail stores, wholesalers, or agents. These funds are also known as **spiff money**. The prizes offered in a trade contest can be items such as luggage, a stereo, or a television, or a trip to an exotic place such as Hawaii.

A contest can be held at various levels within the channel. It can be between brokers or agents who handle the manufacturer's goods. It can be for wholesalers, or it can be a sales volume contest among individual retail stores. Although contests can be designed between retail organizations (e.g., Canadian Tire versus Wal-Mart), they are seldom used because of conflict-of-interest policies in many large organizations. Buyers in large organizations are often prohibited from participating in vendor contests because they create conflicts of interest and unfairly influence their buying decisions. Although this is exactly what a contest is designed to accomplish, many large retail organizations do not want buyers participating, because these buyers make purchase decisions for as many as 500 to 2,500 stores. This places undue pressure on the buyer.

Demand for cruise ship vacations has steadily increased in the past few years. There is intense competition among the cruise lines. Cruise ship companies use a combination of advertising, consumer promotions, and trade promotions to attract patrons. For example, Royal Caribbean International offered travel agents cooperative advertising programs featuring TV commercials, newspaper ads, as well as an email template to contact potential travellers. Norwegian Cruise Lines enrolled 5,500 agents in a "Sale of All Sails" promotional contest. Prizes were based on bookings. Each agent who set up a Holland America cruise was enrolled in the trade contest. The prizes offered included a free cruise with five veranda staterooms.

The Princess Cruise line offered booking agents the chance to win a West Coast sailing cruise with a mini suite. One cruise was awarded each day during a 90-day period. This combination of advertising, consumer promotions, and trade promotions led to a year in which advanced bookings for summer cruises reached an all-time high. It is not surprising that offering travel agents the chance to win prizes and cruises for themselves causes them to be highly motivated to book cruises for the lines holding the contests.[27]

Most channel members agree that contests conducted at the individual store level work best when restricted to a specific region. Many times, they are also limited to exclusive dealerships, such as auto, truck, or boat dealers that sell a particular brand. For example B.F. Goodrich, a manufacturer of automobile tires, may run a contest among its retail operations within a specific region for highest sales within a given time period.

Norwegian Cruise Lines used trade contests to increase their bookings.

Trade Incentives

Trade incentives are similar to trade allowances. The difference is that trade incentives involve the retailer performing a function in order to receive the funds. The purpose, however, is the same as it was for trade allowances: either to encourage retailers to push the manufacturer's brand or to increase retailer purchases of that brand. The three major types of trade incentives are identified in Figure 9.11.

Cooperative Merchandising Agreements

The most comprehensive trade incentive is a *cooperative merchandising agreement (CMA),* which is a formal agreement between the retailer and manufacturer to undertake

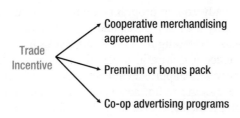

FIGURE 9.11
Types of Trade Incentives

a two-way marketing effort. The CMA can be for a wide variety of marketing tasks. For instance, a CMA can feature the manufacturer's brand as a price leader in an advertisement. A cooperative agreement can be made to emphasize the manufacturer's brand as part of an in-house offer made by the retail store or a by using a special shelf display featuring a price incentive. The advantage of creating a CMA agreement that features a price break is that the manufacturer is assured that the retailer will pass along the price allowance to the customer.

CMAs are popular with manufacturers because the retailer performs a function in order to receive the allowance or incentive. The manufacturer retains control of the functions performed. Also, if price allowances are made as part of the CMA, the manufacturer knows that the retailer passes a certain percentage of the price discount on to the consumer. CMAs allow manufacturers to create annual contracts with retailers. These longer-term commitments reduce the need for last-minute trade incentives or trade allowances.

CMAs also benefit retailers. The primary benefit of a CMA from the retailer's perspective is that it allows them to develop calendar promotions. *Calendar promotions* are promotional campaigns the retailer plans for customers through manufacturer trade incentives. By signing a CMA, a retailer can schedule the weeks a particular brand will be on sale and offset the other weeks with other brands. By using calendar promotions, the retailer will always have one brand on sale while the others are off-deal. Calendar promotions allow the retailer to rotate the brands on sale. This arrangement is attractive for price-sensitive customers, because one brand is always on sale. For the brand-loyal consumer, the retailer carries the preferred brand at the regular price some times and on sale at others. By arranging sales through trade incentives, the margins for the retailer are approximately the same for all brands, both on-deal and off-deal, because they rotate. Retailers can effectively move price reductions given to the customer to the manufacturer rather than absorbing them themselves. A store may feature Budweiser on-deal one week and Heineken the next. Loyal beer drinkers stay with their preferred brand, while price-sensitive consumers can choose the on-deal brand, and the store retains a reasonable markup on all beers sold.

Premiums and Bonus Packs

The second major type of trade incentive is a *premium* or *bonus pack*. Instead of offering the retailer a discount on the price, the manufacturer offers free merchandise. For example, a manufacturer can offer a bonus pack of one carton for each 20 purchased within the next 60 days. The bonus packs are free to the retailer and are awarded either for placing the order by a certain date or for agreeing to a minimum-size order. Often, to receive the free merchandise the retailer must meet both conditions: a specified date and a minimum order size.

Cooperative Advertising

The final trade incentive is co-op advertising. In a *cooperative advertising program,* the manufacturer agrees to reimburse the retailer a certain percentage of the advertising costs associated with advertising the manufacturer's products in the retailer's ad. To receive the reimbursement, the retailer follows specific guidelines concerning the placement of the ad and its content. In almost all cases, no competing products can be advertised. Normally, the manufacturer's product must be displayed prominently. There may be other restrictions on how the product is advertised as well as specific photos or copy that must be used.

In most cooperative advertising programs, retailers accrue co-op monies based on purchases. This is normally a certain percentage of sales. For example, B.F. Goodrich offers a 4.5 percent co-op advertising fund on all purchases by retailers such as Canadian Tire. This money can be accrued for a year, and then it starts over again. B.F. Goodrich pays 70 percent of the cost of an approved advertisement. Any of the media can be used for the advertisement, including radio, newspaper, magazines, television, and outdoor advertising. This unlimited media choice does not hold true for all manufacturers. For example, Dayton, another tire manufacturer, does not allow co-op dollars to be used for magazine advertising. B.F. Goodrich allows group ads for co-op monies; Dayton does not. Further, Dayton requires preapproval for some of the media buys and advertisements; B.F. Goodrich does not require any preapprovals. Thus, each manufacturer has a unique set of restrictions that must be followed by retailers seeking to qualify for co-op monies.[28]

Co-op advertising programs allow retailers to use the manufacturer's dollars to expand advertising programs. In a co-op ad, the retailer gains additional advertising coverage at minimal cost. Retailers also benefit from the image of a national brand, which can attract new or additional customers to the store. From the retailer's perspective, there is little to lose in co-op programs. The only negative side is that the retailer is reimbursed following the placement of the ad, which could lead to a cash flow problem for a smaller company.

Manufacturers also benefit from co-op ads. By sharing advertising costs with retailers, the manufacturer gains additional exposure at a reduced cost. More important, almost all co-op advertising programs are tied to sales. The retailer accrues co-op advertising dollars based on a certain percentage of sales. Thus, to get the co-op money, the retailer must not only promote the brand prominently, but must also purchase the product for resale. As a result, it is not surprising to see the wide variety of cooperative advertisements appearing regularly in every medium, for both consumer and business-to-business products.

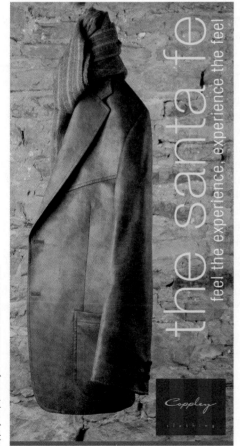

Many retailers defray the costs of marketing communications with co-op dollars.

Over $12 billion is spent on trade shows each year.

Trade Shows

Trade shows are used extensively in business-to-business marketing programs. They benefit both manufacturers and retailers. From a manufacturer's standpoint, a trade show offers the opportunity to discover potential customers and sell new products. Also, relationships with current customers can be strengthened at a show. A trade show often provides the chance to find out what the competition is doing. Many times, trade shows present a situation in which the manufacturer's sales team can meet directly with decision makers and buyers from business-to-business clients. A trade show can be used to strengthen the brand name of a product as well as the company's image.

From the retailer's perspective, a trade show allows buyers to compare merchandise and to make contacts with several prospective vendors in a short period of time. In some cases, the retailer can negotiate special deals. Trade shows represent an ideal place for buyers and sellers to meet in an informal, low-pressure setting to discuss how to work together effectively.

Some national and international trade shows are attended by thousands of buyers. To be sure the trade show will be successful, manufacturers seek out key buyers and try to avoid spending too much time with nonbuyers. Narrowing down the large number of contacts to those most promising is called *prospecting*. Figure 9.12 identifies five categories of buyers who attend trade shows. Many marketers try to weed out the education seekers, who are not interested in buying. Manufacturer's agents concentrate efforts on three groups:

FIGURE 9.12
Five Categories of Buyers Attending Trade Shows

- ◆ Education seekers: Buyers who want to browse, look, and learn but are not in the buying mode

- ◆ Reinforcement seekers: Buyers who want reassurance they made the right decision in past purchases

- ◆ Solution seekers: Buyers seeking solutions to specific problems and are in the buying mode

- ◆ Buying teams: A team of buyers seeking vendors for their business; usually are in the buying mode

- ◆ Power buyers: Members of upper management or key purchasing agents with the authority to buy

solution seekers, buying teams, and power buyers. Asking the right questions identifies solution seekers and buying teams. The power buyers are more difficult to find because they do not want to be identified. They often do not wear badges at trade shows, which means vendors are never sure who they are.

Buyers and sellers meet, discuss, and maybe even negotiate, but buys are seldom completed. Instead, manufacturers collect leads to be followed up later. This procedure varies for international customers. International attendees tend to be senior executives with the authority to make purchases. They fit into the power buyer category listed in Figure 9.12. North American manufacturers know that the international attendee often wishes to conduct business during the trade show, not afterward. The international attendees also spend more time at each manufacturer's booth. They stay longer in order to gather and study information in greater detail. The international guest, who pays more for travel expenses, wants more in-depth information than a North American counterpart usually needs.

The number of international trade show visitors has increased as competition continues to expand globally. The increase in international participants has caused trade show centres to set up more meeting spaces, conference centres, and even places to eat where buyers and sellers can meet and transact business.

HOW CAN SALES PROMOTIONS BE EFFECTIVE?

Researchers have identified three routes by which sales promotions can be effective in stimulating customer behaviour: economic, informational, and affective.[29]

Economic Effects

The most commonly discussed means by which promotions can stimulate behaviour is by enhancing the monetary value in the transaction for the customer. For example, by providing a rebate, a consumer now pays less for a product. Trade promotions are heavily influenced by economic factors because the majority of tactics explicitly provide reduced monetary costs to customers, whereas many consumer promotions offer other forms of value, such as contests. Economic benefits from promotions also come in indirect forms. They can provide heuristics that allow customers to spend less time in the decision-making process (e.g., "this one is on sale so it's the best option").

It should be noted that not all promotions result in enhanced economic value for the customer. Hidden costs can more than offset reduced costs and appear in the form of stockpiling costs, for example, when multiple purchases are required to receive economic benefit. They can also lead to foregone consumption or purchases as customers wait for better deals to emerge.

Informational Effects

The presence of sales promotions provides customers with significant informational cues. Certainly a promotion can help create brand awareness. It is also a way for some consumers to signal to others that they are savvy shoppers and able to get deals.

One major drawback is that discounts or other promotions can lead to perceptions of lower product quality for some customers. They can also lower price expectations, or lead to perceptions of higher prices when an item isn't offered through a promotion.

Affective Effects

Sales promotions offer customers an opportunity to feel both good and bad. On the positive side, some customers simply enjoy getting a deal. They may also feel like smarter shoppers for buying through the promotion, or fortunate because they were buying at the

Critical Thinking Exercise

The above effects of promotion suggest that promotions can be a way for a shopper to signal to others that he or she is a savvy shopper—and is good at getting deals. This is a positive effect of promotions. But the negative effect of appearing cheap to others is also given as a potential affective drawback to promotions. Can you reconcile these two effects? When will customers be likely to feel good about others seeing them affected by a promotion, and when might they avoid letting others know about the deal for fear of looking cheap? Are there characteristics of the products or the purchase situations, or other factors that you think can help explain this paradox?

time a promotion was offered. Promotions also provide the opportunity for consumers to feel the thrill of trying new products.

However, not all promotions produce positive emotions for customers. Many promotions can cause annoyance at having to deal with coupons or restrictions on promotions such as deadlines of purchase quantities. Promotions can also cause some consumers to worry that they will appear cheap to others.

STRENGTHS AND WEAKNESSES OF SALES PROMOTIONS

As with other IMC tools, each specific form of promotion has specific strengths and weaknesses. However, as an overall category, sales promotions have a number of things in common.

Strengths of Sales Promotion

Provides Extra Incentive to Act. Particularly through economic effects, many forms of sales promotion provide additional utility that can stimulate a purchase decision. Perhaps a consumer was considering buying a product, but was unsure for any number of reasons. The addition of a rebate or contest can add the extra value that leads to a decision to buy.

Creates Sense of Immediacy. Along with the above point, most sales promotions include a time-sensitivity component. Coupons expire, contests close, on-pack premiums sell out, and so on. By creating a sense of urgency, the consumer is often motivated not only to act, but to act immediately.

Stimulates Trial. One of the particular strengths of sales promotion—sampling in particular—is its ability to acquire new customers. The additional benefit offered by sales promotions can be the reduction in costs in cases where the price previously held some consumers back from trying the product. Perhaps it is a rebate that lowers the cost of trying a new product, or a sample that allows them to experience the benefits.

Increases Purchase or Usage Frequency. Promotions can stimulate purchase and/or usage frequency by consumers. The recipe contest mentioned earlier, for example, is a way for Heinz to encourage customers to experiment with their products, and therefore generate a need to replenish their stock more frequently.

Builds Databases. Similar to the point above, many sales promotions require customers to provide identifying information about themselves. Rebates, for example, are a means by which many manufacturers learn who has purchased their products when other options are not available. For example, if a customer buys a Sony television through Best Buy, they don't have information such as name and address of the customer who bought. Having customers identify themselves is one way that manufacturers can create future dialogue with customers.

Weaknesses of Sales Promotion

Adds clutter. The immediate nature of sales promotions can lead to a sense of clutter, overwhelming some consumers. If a retail environment, for example, becomes overloaded with POP displays, sampling booths, or other promotional tactics, each one can lose effectiveness because of the sheer weight of all promotions combined. Consumers simply become immune by tuning out promotions to some extent.

Sets False Retail Prices. Most consumers are fairly savvy; they know that if items are regularly promoted with either discounts, premiums, or some other form of incremental value, they can wait and purchase only when this value is offered. In doing so, the expected retail price is effectively reduced because the consumer is accustomed to greater value. Although the retail price itself might not be lowered, the value expected by the consumer in return is heightened.

Promotes Forward Buying. Similar to the above point, many consumers will simply forward purchase, or engage in **pantry loading** as a result of limited-time sales promotions. This can be true for virtually any product that is consumed on a regular basis. Many consumers will purchase canned soup while on sale, for example, and simply store it at home for use over time. As a result, the marketer may simply trade future sales at full margin for sales today at a discount. Potentially, no new customers are gained and the result is simply less profitable margins over time.

COMMUNICATING ACROSS CULTURES

Sales promotions should be adapted to any country in which they are offered. There are two complications: legal and cultural. Any coupon, premium, contest, or price change must fit with local legal regulations. The marketing team should investigate any potential legal problems before launching an international consumer promotions program. Legal considerations for contests and other forms of promotion are discussed in Chapter 12.

Culturally, citizens in some countries may take a dim view of some promotions, most notably coupons. Those who redeem them may be viewed as being of lower socio-economic status, which may dissuade others from using them. Participation in contests may violate religious norms in some nations. When considering a sales promotion, a cultural assimilator should be consulted to make sure the promotion is both legally and culturally viable.

Finally, the emphasis placed on sales promotions will be different, depending on the company involved and the country in which that company operates. Both small companies seeking to do business in foreign countries and large international conglomerates will need to adjust to local conditions when employing these marketing tactics. At the same time, the goal remains to be certain that the efforts match the company's image and overall approach to marketing communications.

IMC IN PRACTICE

"In our consumer markets, we are essentially a retail business, so we include a lot of sales promotion in our marketing communications plan," say Kate. "Back-to-school has become one of our biggest customer acquisition periods, so we always feature sales promotions as a big part of our campaign at that time. The sales promotions give us that extra bit to help customers make the decision to buy, and, of course, to buy from us instead of the competition."

TELUS does not position itself as a low-cost provider in the industry, so the sales promotions tend not to be overly focused on price. "We try to make whatever incremental value we offer to the customer relevant to the product. So, for example, on the broadband marketing communications we have included a promotion that offers a free computer with sign-up. It makes more sense to do that than to offer a trip or something unrelated. This is becoming more and more a part of our approach to sales promotion as we add to our product offering and look to sign customers up to bundles of services."

One play where price is an issue is in the joint promotions that are developed with retailers. "We are in most

Digital TV from TELUS has arrived.

Open your eyes to a new era in television. With no start-up costs and packages starting from $22 per month, see for yourself how far TV has come.

Win a mesmerizing prize.
Enter now for a chance to win*:

- LG® 52" LCD TV and 5-disc DVD home theatre system
- Logitech Harmony™ remote
- One year of FREE TELUS TV®, High Speed Enhanced Internet and home phone service

Visit **telus.com/tvcontest** for a chance to win and find out when you can see TELUS TV live.

*NO PURCHASE NECESSARY. Contest runs from May 13, 2008 to June 9, 2008. For complete contest rules visit telus.com/tvcontest. TELUS, TELUSTV, the TELUS logo and the future is friendly are trademarks of the TELUS Corporation, used under licence. LG is a registered trademark of LG Electronics. Logitech and Harmony are trademarks of Logitech and are registered in the U.S. and other countries. 03073 © 2008 TELUS. 04/08

Source: Courtesy of TELUS.

TELUS contests often feature products or services as an integral component to the promotion.

major electronics retailers. These retailers use flyers and sales as a cornerstone of their promotional activities. So consumers see flyers from retailers like Best Buy and Future Shop almost every week. What they don't see is the discussion that takes place behind the scenes where we negotiate with those retailers for inclusion in their sales promotions.

"The retailers know all of the competitors want to be featured in the flyers. We all compete for space, particularly the best spaces, like the front cover. The space and positioning is determined primarily by two things: our willingness to pay for the advertising opportunity and the richness of the offer that we're prepared to provide retail customers. We know these flyers, and the discounts that are offered, are often the final piece of the puzzle for consumers. If someone has seen our television advertising or received a direct mail package, and is thinking of buying, the promotion offered to close the deal at retail is a make-or-break time for us."

Source: Used with permission of Kate Baillie, TELUS Communications.

For help developing your IMC Plan, go to **www.pearsoncanada.ca/clow**.

SUMMARY

This chapter reviewed the techniques available to attract customers by using consumer promotions. These tactics include coupons, premiums, contests, refunds, rebates, samples, bonus packs, and price-off deals. These items should be combined with specific promotional goals to have the right impact on customers.

Consumer promotions are often used to boost sales. They can be an excellent short-term method to increase sales or a firm's market share. They can also be an excellent means of introducing new products. Often, a consumer promotion prompts consumers to at least try the product where selling it at the regular price will not. Coupons and contests have been successful tactics for attracting new customers. Consumer promotions can boost sales of a particular brand, and evidence suggests that they increase sales of the overall product category rather than just take sales away from competitors.

Trade promotions complement consumer promotions. The use of trade allowances, trade contests, trade incentives, and participation in trade shows helps the manufacturer or member of the marketing channel maintain positive contact with other organizations and moves products toward the retailer. Trade promotions work best when they are integrated into other IMC efforts rather than being viewed as a necessary evil or simply as a short-term tool to increase sales.

Sales promotions are effective because of three potential effects they create. Economic effects are present when the customer views the promotion as a means of changing the economic value that is perceived in the transaction. Informational effects occur when the presence of a sales promotion sends information to the customer about the brand attributes, the quality of the product, or the price. Affect effects take place when customers experience feelings or emotions tied to sales promotions. Emotions can be either positive (i.e., the thrill of getting a deal) or negative (e.g., annoyance with promotion restrictions).

Sales promotions are found in IMC plans of many firms. Their ability to provide extra incentives to consumers to act immediately, to stimulate trial and consumption of a product, and to build databases make them a popular choice. However, the resulting clutter from sales promotions, their tendency to falsify retail prices, and the potential for stimulating forward buying means that sales promotions should be carefully and strategically considered as part of an overall IMC plan. One further concern when planning across national or cultural boundaries is the difference between attitudes, laws, regulations, and cultural nuances in each market.

KEY TERMS

consumer promotions Incentives directly offered to a firm's customers or potential customers.

cross-ruffing The placement of two promotional materials together.

exit fees Monies paid to remove an item from a retailer's inventory.

freestanding inserts (FSIs) Sheets of coupons distributed in newspapers, primarily on Sunday.

pantry loading Purchasing multiple units of the same item and holding the inventory at home.

sales promotions All of the incentives offered to customers and channel members to encourage product purchases.

slotting fees A form of trade allowance in which funds are charged by retailers to stock new products.

spiff money Rewards given as contest prizes to brokers, retail salespeople, stores, wholesalers, and agents.

trade allowances Financial incentives to other channel members to motivate them to make purchases.

trade promotions Expenditures or incentives used by manufacturers and other members of the marketing channel to purchase goods for eventual sale.

trade incentives Funds given that require the retailer to perform a function in order to receive the dollars.

REVIEW QUESTIONS

1. Define sales promotion. What are the two main categories of sales promotions?

2. Name and describe five types of coupons. Which is the most popular with manufacturers? Which has the highest redemption rate?

3. What problems are associated with coupon programs?

4. What is a premium? What four types of premium programs can companies use?

5. What are the keys to successful premium programs?

6. What are the two main components of prizes rendered in contests?

7. What tactics can be used to improve the success rates of contests? What role might the Internet play in this process?

8. How is a refund different from a rebate?

9. What are the primary types of samples?

10. What benefits and problems are associated with sampling?

11. What are the benefits of offering bonus packs?

12. What benefits and problems are associated with price-off tactics?

13. What is an overlay?

14. What are the major types of trade allowances?

15. What is a slotting fee? An exit fee?

16. What is meant by the term on-deal?

17. What complications are associated with trade allowances?

18. How does the term spiff money relate to trade contests?

19. What are the main types of trade incentives?

20. Describe a cooperative merchandising agreement.

21. How are premiums or bonus packs used as trade incentives?

22. How can a cooperative advertising program benefit both a manufacturer and a retailer?

23. What are the three ways that sales promotions can lead to customer behaviour?

24. What are the strengths and weaknesses of sales promotion as part of the IMC plan?

25. What problems must be overcome when developing international sales promotions programs?

INTEGRATED LEARNING EXERCISES

1. Groupon has become a very successful company by promoting coupons that are regionally specific and offer significant discounts. The service lets users share coupons among friends, and even suggest businesses that the firm could add to their coupon inventory. One of the benefits of the service is that it lets small businesses have access a very large number of potential customers, and many businesses use it to acquire new customers and trial. Pick a small business in your city. Do you think participating in Groupon is a good idea for the company? Why or why not? If yes, design a coupon offer and justify it. If not, justify your decision by suggesting an alternative marketing tactic that they can use to acquire new customers or generate trial.

2. Electronic Arts is a leading manufacturer of video games. In addition to many popular sports games (e.g., NHL, FIFA) the companies makes a range of games across a range of genres. Assume you are the marketing manager in charge of the NHL franchise. One of the things the brand has tried in the past is "sampling" video games through a road show where people could come to a location and try the game. Building on the success of this, you decide that sampling should play a larger role in your IMC plan going forward. Develop your sampling plan. What are your objectives? Who are your target audience, and how will you distribute the game so they can experience it?

3. Many companies offer special consumer promotions on their websites. Examine the following company websites. What types of promotions are available? What are the objectives of the various consumer promotions? Do the promotions on the websites mesh with the company's advertising and consumer promotions at retail outlets?

   a. Taco Bell (**www.tacobell.ca**)

   b. Bell (**www. bell.ca**)

   c. Tim Hortons (**www.timhortons.com**)

   d. Kia Motors (**www.kia.ca**)

4. One widely read journal featuring promotional marketing is called *PROMO*. Go to the website at **www.promomagazine .com**. Examine the website headings and access the various areas. After exploring the site, write a short report on what is available at the website and how it can be used to assist companies wanting to develop various promotions.

STUDENT PROJECT

Creative Corner

Choose a hockey franchise that is local in your city. It can be either professional (e.g., Montreal Canadiens) or semi-professional (e.g., Vancouver Giants). Assume the marketing manager at that club has hired you to develop a sales promotion campaign for the team. She has specifically asked for three things related to two promotional events:

1. A special game at the arena where all fans who attend get a free toque. Design a flyer for the special day and the toque giveaway.

2. A tie-in with a local grocery store, where anyone who purchases over $150 in groceries is given a pass for four people to attend a special afternoon practice of the team. Design a webpage the team can put on its website to promote this tie-in.

Use whatever design skills and software you have (MS Word is fine) to do some preliminary layouts for each of the above items. Be prepared to present them in class.

ETHICS IN ACTION

Have you ever been given a free sample of a drug by your doctor? Chances are you have, since more than 90 percent of doctors receive free samples, and more than half of patients—most of them older—report getting at least one in a given year. One U.S. study put the annual value of samples from drugmakers to doctors at almost $16 billion, equal to more than a quarter of their marketing communications budgets in a typical year.[30]

At first glance this practice might look like a win–win–win situation for manufacturers, doctors, and patients. But sampling can have hidden costs. Doctors might pick a sub-optimal drug simply because they have a sample. Plus, only makers of expensive brand-name drugs are giving out samples; generic drug makers usually don't provide samples. Leaving pharmacists out of the equation only increases the risk of errors.

"Doctors think they're saving their patients money and helping them by giving out free medication," says David Miller, a general internist at the Wake Forest University School of Medicine in Winston-Salem, N.C. Paradoxically, Miller says, "they are likely costing those patients more money down the road." As evidence of the influence drug samples have on doctors' prescriptions, one study found that when samples were eliminated, doctors were three times more likely to prescribe less expensive generic drugs.[31]

1. Have you ever been given a free sample of a drug by a doctor? Did you take the medication? Did you buy more of the same brand of medication? Why or why not?

2. Do you agree with those who argue that drug samples to doctors should be banned? Draft a one-page letter to the Director of Health Canada either asking for a ban or lobbying to keep the practice legal.

3. Do you think samples mentioned in the example above encouraged people to try one brand over another, or to try a new drug where they wouldn't have otherwise bought any drugs? Are there other products where you feel that rather than encouraging brand switching, sampling can encourage new users to try the product category? For example, if someone tries a cracker sample and decides to start eating crackers, little harm is likely to occur. But if someone discovers drugs or alcohol through a sample, and begins to use those products, the potential for harm exists. Make a list of products for which you think offering free samples is ethically questionable. ●

CASE STUDY | Hot Rod Marketing

Terry Walsh knew the time was right to move from being a small, "garage-based" company to a much larger enterprise. After spending years as a research chemist, Terry had launched out on his own. His goal was to develop a top-of-the-line fuel injector cleaner for both domestic and foreign automobiles. For two years, he worked with various formulas until the right one emerged. The product was named Hot Fire Fuel Injector Cleaner, and the company's name was Hot Fire. Terry was positive Hot Fire would perform well against any competitive product.

The market for fuel-injector cleaners is diverse. Numerous backyard mechanics sell limited amounts of their concoctions to local merchants and over the Internet. Several formulas are even available on eBay. There is no guarantee of quality for these products, some of which may actually harm engine performance. At the other extreme, major companies such as STP, Gumout, and Dupont offer various grades of cleaners, from low-end products selling for around $3 per unit up to high-end versions priced as high as $30. The primary price determinant is the degree to which the product reduces congestion in a fuel injector. The higher-priced entries are more powerful and remove more "gunk."

Terry's Hot Fire Fuel Injector Cleaner was at the high end. The price would be $17 wholesale, per can. He hoped that dealers would charge no more than $25 as a retail price. Hot Fire sold in single containers as well as in multipacks of 6 and 12 cans. Each can held two treatments or applications.

Several potential markets are available for fuel-injector cleaners. The first is auto repair shops, including simple "lube and oil" change stores and more traditional repair shops. Many times, the proprietors of these stores welcome the idea of a small display of an auto repair or maintenance product, as long as the owner believes the product actually works.

The second type of outlet consists of all of the retailers that sell replacement parts and auto supplies, such as Canadian Tire and Napa Auto Parts. Most of these retailers only sell nationally

Hot Fire targets repair shops, specialty stores, and convenience stores.

based products from major manufacturers. Getting them to stock Hot Fire would be a major victory.

A third potential customer base is convenience stores. Again, the primary challenge would be convincing a chain such as 7-Eleven or Couche Tard to carry Hot Fire along with other, cheaper products such as STP's and Gumout's low-end products.

Terry knew that buyers in all of these outlets are extremely price sensitive. At the same time, the buyers want to be sure the product works and will not harm other engine parts. Once these objectives have been reached, the goal is to convince them to order larger quantities and continually stock the product. To encourage sales, seasonal discounts, such as for the summer driving season, may move more product to the shelves.

Hot Fire currently employs 20 workers in the production department and has a sales force of 5 people to cover the entire country. The company's website is designed to attract people who are willing to buy auto products online and to provide information to business customers.

Terry had a large enough budget to do some advertising. He mostly bought ads in magazines that featured high-performance cars and trade journals for auto body shop managers. One major advantage that had emerged was that Hot Fire sold well locally and was emerging as a product known by local and regional race car drivers. Hot Fire decals were placed on cars at races across the region.

Terry decided to take the company to the next level and take on a partner. The equity was used to improve and expand production, but a large portion was earmarked for marketing communications. Specifically, Terry felt that promotions were the key to supplement the media advertising he had been doing thus far. Expanding retailer coverage was critical, and he knew that promotions could help him achieve success, both in getting stocked on retail shelves and in selling to ultimate end-users from those retail shelves.

1. What should be the main trade promotions objectives for Hot Fire Fuel Injector Cleaner? What challenges or obstacles might keep the company from reaching those objectives? Write a two-page report that outlines your trade promotions objectives and details of how it will work. Will you use discounts, contests, or some other element in order to encourage retailers to carry the product? Will your program be consistent across all three types of retailers?

2. Once the product is on the retail shelf, promotions can also encourage consumers to purchase the product. Write a two-page report to go along with your trade promotion report from question #1 above. Outline your objective(s) for the consumer promotion and what elements your plan will include.

3. In an effort to tie the promotions into existing marketing communications, you will need to incorporate your promotion plan into the rest of the campaign. Develop a print ad for both trade journals and a consumer magazine that incorporates the promotion into the overall message.

ENDNOTES

1. Mariola Palazon-Vidal and Elena Delgado-Ballester, "Sales Promotions Effect on Consumer-Based Brand Equity," *International Journal of Market Research* 47, no. 2 (2005), pp. 179–205.

2. Emily Bryson York, "Why Taco Bell's World Series Play Was a Steal," *Advertising Age* (**http://adage.com/article_id=121563**, October 29, 2007).

3. "Do Coupons Make Sense," *Incentive* 177, no. 5 (May 2003), p. 19.

4. Noreen O'Leary, "Dealing with Coupons," *Adweek* 46, no. 8 (February 21, 2005), p. 29.

5. Elizabeth Gardener and Minakshi Trivedi, "A Communication Framework to Evaluate Sales Promotion Strategies," *Journal of Advertising Research* 38, no. 3 (May–June 1998), pp. 67–71.

6. Srimalee Somluck, "Prime Nature Villa: Cars, Jewelry on Offer," *The Nation (Thailand)* (**www.nationmultimedia.com**, accessed September 29, 2004).

7. Don Jagoda, "The Seven Habits of Highly Successful Promotions," *Incentive* 173, no. 8 (August 1999), pp. 104–105.

8. "Industry Trends Report 2007," *Promo* (**www.promomagazine.com/september2007**), pp. AR1–27.

9. Kathleen Joyce, "Not Just a Novelty," *PROMO* 17, no. 12 (November 2004), pp. 52–56.

10. Sandra Block, "Rattled About Rebate Hassles? Regulators Starting to Step In," *USA Today* (March 22, 2005), p. 3b.

11. Lindsay Chappell, "Rebates Eventually Become Ho-Hum, Researcher Says," *Automotive News* 79, no. 6133 (February 7, 2005), p. 36.

12. Pete Wetmore, "Inserts Branch Out Beyond Print Fliers," *Advertising Age* 75, no. 16 (April 19, 2004), p. N-6.

13. Betsy Spethman, "Introductory Offer," *PROMO* 16 (2004), p. 27; Jennifer Kulpa, "Bristol-Myers Squibb Breaks Ground with Direct Response Product Sampling Website," *Drug Store News* 19, no. 7 (April 7, 1997), p. 19.

14. Jennifer Hiscock, "The Two Faces of Sampling," *Event* (April 2004), pp. 25–26.

15. Beng Soo Ong and Foo Nin Ho, "Consumer Perceptions of Bonus Packs: An Exploratory Analysis," *Journal of Consumer Marketing* 14, no. 2–3 (1997), pp. 102–12.

16. David R. Bell, Ganesh Iyer, and V. Padmanaghan, "Price Competition Under Stockpiling and Flexible Consumption," *Journal of Marketing Research* 39, no. 3 (August 2002), pp. 292–304.

17. Showwei Chu, "Welcome to Canada, Please Buy Something," *Canadian Business* 71, no. 9 (May 29, 1998), pp. 72–73.

18. Michael Bellas, "Shopper Marketing's Instant Impact," *Beverage World* 126, no. 11 (November 15, 2007), p. 18.

19. "POP Sharpness in Focus," *Brandweek* 44, no. 24 (June 6, 2003), pp. 31–36; David Tossman, "The Final Push-POP Bloom," *New Zealand Marketing Magazine* 18, no. 8 (September 1999), pp. 45–51.

20. Betsy Spethmann, "Retail Details," *Promo SourceBook* 2005 17 (2005), pp. 27–28.

21. Miguel Gomez, Vithala Rao, and Edward McLaughlin, "Empirical Analysis of Budget and Allocation of Trade Promotions in the U.S. Supermarket Industry," *Journal of Marketing Research* 44, no. 3 (August 2007), pp. 410–24.

22. Ibid.

23. K. Sudhir and Vithala Rao, "Do Slotting Allowances Enhance Efficiency or Hinder Competition?" *Journal of Marketing Research* 43, no. 2 (May 2006), pp. 137–55.

24. Paula Bone, Karen France, and Richard Riley, "A Multifirm Analysis of Slotting Fees," *Journal of Public Policy & Marketing* 25, no. 2 (Fall 2006), pp. 224–37.

25. "Study: Trade Dollars Up," *Frozen Food Age* 50, no. 2 (September 2001), p. 14.

26. Walter Heller, "Promotion Pullback," *Progressive Grocer* 81, no. 4 (March 1, 2002), p. 19.

27. "Cruise Selling Season Kicks Off with Agent Promotions and Optimism," *Travel Agent* 319 (January 3, 2005), p. 9.

28. Roger A. Slavens, "Getting a Grip on Co-Op," *Modern Tire Dealer* 75, no. 3 (March 1994), pp. 34–37.

29. Priya Raghubir, J. Jefrey Inman, and Hans Grande, "The Three Faces of Consumer Promotions," *California Management Review,* 46 (4, 2004), p. 23–42.

30. Rita Rubin, "Doctors Ditch Drug Samples to Avoid Influencing Treatment," *USA Today*, December 1, 2008. Accessed on February 10, 2011, from: **http://www.usatoday.com/news/health/2008-11-30-drug-samples_N.htm**

31. Ibid.

10

After reading this chapter, you should be able to answer the following questions:

- **What** types of relationships are possible between a public relations team and a marketing communications team?

- **Who** are the stakeholders of a firm relevant to public relations?

- **When** should a marketing team consider cause-related marketing and green marketing programs?

- **How** can a sponsorship program hurt or enhance a firm's image?

- **What** role can product placement, branded entertainment, and buzz marketing play in a firm's IMC plan?

- **When** are event marketing programs most and least likely to succeed?

- **What** are the ways that public relations professionals can practice damage control?

INDUSTRY PROFILE
So You Want to Work in Marketing Communications?

Paul Joliat, Vice President, Lang Marketing Network, Toronto, Ontario

From his days of leading canoe trips at camp during his university summers, Paul Joliat always knew he wanted a career in sports. "I was always into sports. I played on the university soccer team in my undergrad, and my psychology thesis examined the effects of momentum in hockey. But I wasn't sure how this was going to translate into a career."

Seeking advice, Paul went back to his high school guidance counsellor to find some ideas. "I went to an all-boys school in Toronto that has a very strong alumni network. So I asked him if he could put me in touch with any alumni who are working in the sports field who would be willing to meet with me to talk about possible career paths. I met with sports lawyers, sports agents, and a number of agencies, all with the hope of finding where I might fit into the business and keep my personal passion part of my professional life."

When meeting with what was then known as Lang and Associates, Paul was told that if any jobs came up he would get a call. "I didn't think too much of it, but literally the next day I got a call. The work wasn't glamorous by any means—my very first task was stuffing envelopes for some sponsorship work connected with the Bell Canadian Open. From there I did some storage locker cleanout from some old Coke sponsorships. But slowly I started take on more meaty roles around event management, like working on a five-month road show for a camping promotion with Canadian Tire."

The small jobs eventually turned into a full-time position for Paul, and he began to work on the planning and strategy behind events and sponsorships in addition to the execution of the plans. "But I realized that with my degree in psychology and a minor in music, I really didn't have any 'business' background. So I thought about doing an MBA, and I eventually enrolled in a program at the University of Alberta that specialized in sports management. When I finished, despite some offers from traditional consulting companies like KPMG and Ernst & Young, I was lured back to Lang, which had become a much smaller and focused company by that time, focusing largely on helping organizations find corporate sponsors. Being able to see

Public Relations

the other side of the sponsorship deal, and work with organizations like Skate Canada and the Canadian Olympic Committee were a big draw for me."

Because of his ability to see both sides of sponsorship, Paul became active in bringing companies and sports organizations together to develop relationships. "I know what properties are looking for sponsorships, and what they can offer. I also know what companies are looking for out of sponsorships, and how the property can help their brand. With those two sides I'm able to put together deals that make sense for both sides."

One example of just such a pairing was Paul's work with HSBC, as they expanded their presence from the Lower Mainland in British Columbia to the rest of Canada. "When they came to Toronto, for example, we put together a deal with the Blue Jays that helped the HSBC brand to become instantly

Paul Joliat, Vice President, Lang Marketing Network.

associated with some iconic Toronto institutions. We did the same thing for them in Calgary, with a sponsorship with the Flames, and again with French-language sports broadcaster RDS when they entered the Quebec market."

Paul has expanded his role from sport sponsorships to include working as an advisor and broker for all sorts of organizations that seek sponsorships. "This job has opened my eyes to the whole other world of sponsorships out there beyond sports. Sports will always be a big part of many sponsorship deals, but we work with charities and non-profit groups, which is very rewarding."

In addition to planning sponsorships, Paul has taken on the challenge of evaluating and measuring their impacts. "One of the big criticisms of sponsorship has always been a lack of measurability. So, together with Angus Reid, I helped put together the CRSI (Corporate Reputation & Sponsorship Index). It's an ongoing survey that we use to track consumers' awareness of sponsorships in the market. Then we match that with other key outcomes such as perceptions of brand citizenship or industry leadership, so we are better able to see exactly how sponsorships can lead to key brand performance metrics over time."

Working on so many different initiatives, with so many different clients and organizations, means Paul's multitasking skills are pushed to the limit. "I've usually got at least 30 things on the go, so staying organized is key in this business. But so is staying flexible. Things don't always go the way I plan, and curveballs are regularly thrown at me, so being able to adapt quickly is another essential skill. Of course, the ability to relate to others and build relationships is a must because they can make negotiations go a lot smoother. For me these relationships are critical since negotiation is such a big part of my job."

Throughout all of this, however, Paul still says his most useful skill is finding a work–life balance. "I value the time I spend with my family, so it's important for me to find a way to do both. In this business I can't always dictate my hours, so it's tough. But instead of staying at work until 7, I'll leave at 5 and then work for a couple hours later, after the kids have gone to bed."

When asked for advice for young people looking to get into the field, Paul is clear. "If you know that you want to be in the marketing field, go get some experience. This usually means volunteering, but that's OK. That experience means that you have something on your résumé that you can talk about, and that we as a potential employer can use to see that you are serious about your career in marketing. It's something we look for in every intern we hire."

But experience is just the starting point. "You need to be persistent. The job you want may not be available right now, but you still need to stay in contact so that when it does come up, you'll be first in line." This means not just staying connected, but finding connections in the first place. "Technology today, with things like LinkedIn, makes it very easy to start building your network even while you are in school. So start building it. You'll be glad you did."

OVERVIEW

Public relations efforts, broadly speaking, are part of the overall IMC approach. The same unified message appears in every marketing endeavour, from the appearance of the company's letterhead and stationery to advertisements, promotional items, information in press releases, and in any sponsorship program. The goal of an IMC plan is to make sure that each component of a firm's communications plan speaks with one voice. Extending this goal to public relations and sponsorships is an important task for the marketing team.

The marketing communications activities under the heading public relations are perhaps the most diverse of all the tactics discussed thus far in this book (advertising media, direct marketing, and sales promotion). The term public relations traditionally refers to programs designed to encourage positive media coverage of a company or event, but it has come to include a much broader range of activities. These activities can enhance the reputation of the company overall, as well as play a specific tactical role in an IMC program designed to position and sell specific products.

Although not the only part of an IMC plan to target non-customers, public relations activities are usually more inclusive of non-customer target audiences, such as shareholders, governments, special interest groups, media, or employees. Public relations can therefore play a role in a wide variety of IMC objectives, from enhancing the reputation of a firm to create trust with a consumer audience (which can, in turn, support the effectiveness of other IMC components like direct marketing and sales promotion), to helping create an employee culture of customer service that can help with post-purchase evaluation by customers, to helping establish credibility of the firm with governments or corporate watchdogs.

This chapter begins with an evaluation of the responsibility for the public relations function, followed by an examination of various stakeholders of the company (potential audiences for public relations). From there, we examine a number of different public relations activities, followed by an assessment of the strengths and weaknesses of public relations as part of the overall IMC plan.

THE PUBLIC RELATIONS FUNCTION

In Hollywood, one well-worn phrase is "There's no such thing as bad publicity." This may be true for a bad-boy actor trying to get his name out to the public; however, in the world of marketing and communications bad publicity is *worse* than no publicity. Many business organizations spend countless hours fending off negative news while trying to develop positive and noticeable messages and themes.

The **public relations (PR) team** is a unit in the firm that manages publicity and other communications with every group that is in contact with the company. Some of the functions performed by the public relations department are similar to those provided by the marketing communications team. Others are quite different. Often, the public relations department is separate from the marketing communications team. The two may cooperate with and consult each other, yet each has a separate role to perform.

Some marketing experts argue that public relations should be part of the marketing communications team, just as advertising media, direct marketing, and sales promotions are under the jurisdiction of the marketing communications manager. Others suggest that public relations activities are different and cannot operate effectively within a marketing communications team. Instead, a member of the public relations department should serve as a consultant to the marketing communications team. Still others contend that a new division, called the department of communications, should be created to oversee both marketing and public relations activities. Regardless of where the public relations expertise lies within the organization, or whether it is handled internally or through an external agency, it is clear—just as with trade promotions—that it should be integrated with the overall IMC plan to make sure objectives are aligned and individual elements of the IMC plan support each other.

This ad for Cenovus likely is not meant for consumers, since they can't purchase directly from the company. What might the objectives and related target audience be for this ad?

IDENTIFYING STAKEHOLDERS

All the recipients of company communications are important. Any constituent who makes contact with a company should receive a clear, unified message. In this section, the stakeholders who are targets of public relations efforts are described. A **stakeholder** is a person or group who has a vested interest in the organization's activities. A vested interest can be a variety of things, including:

- Profits paid as common stock dividends
- Loan repayments that a lending institution seeks to receive
- Sales to the company or purchases made from the company
- Wages paid to employees
- Community well-being
- A special-interest topic

In essence, a wide variety of items can cause people or other companies to believe they hold a stake in the firm's activities.

To understand the nature of public relations programs, it is helpful to begin by identifying the publics that make contact with various companies. Figure 10.1 identifies the primary internal and external stakeholders that the public relations department should monitor.

Communications to each of these stakeholder groups are crucial. To ensure consistency, the company should develop a clear communications strategy

Welcome to a different kind of oil sands.

While some of the oil from Canada's oil sands sits near the surface, the majority is found deep underground. And even though you can't see it, innovative technology, pioneered here in Canada, allows us to reach that oil by drilling for it, so we disturb very little land. In fact, over 80% of the oil sands is only accessible using this type of recovery. Cenovus is a Canadian company committed to safely and responsibly unlocking this abundant natural resource for today and tomorrow. Discover more at adifferentoilsands.com.

cenovus ENERGY

New ideas. New approaches.

Source: Courtesy of Cenovus Energy.

FIGURE 10.1
Stakeholders

◆ Employees	◆ Media
◆ Unions	◆ Local community
◆ Shareholders	◆ Financial community
◆ Channel members	◆ Government
◆ Customers	◆ Special-interest groups

that fits well with the firm's IMC plan and corporate image that is to be conveyed. The overall message to each stakeholder should be the same. Then, each message will be tailored to meet the different expectations of the various audiences. By customizing the content, style, and channel of communication, each stakeholder group receives a message that best resonates with them, yet is consistent with other messages.

In addition to sending communications to each of the stakeholders, the public relations team closely monitors the actions and opinions of each group. When changes in attitudes, new views, or serious concerns develop, the public relations team should be ready to address the problem. Most importantly, it is the responsibility of the public relations team to be certain that all forms of communications to each of these publics remain consistent with the firm's message and image.

Internal Stakeholders

Company leaders should not underestimate the value of quality internal communications. Employees provide a powerful channel of communication to people outside of the organization. They can either enhance the firm's reputation or damage it. What employees say to those around them has a much higher level of credibility than what a company says about itself. Word-of-mouth communications, even informal statements by employees, impact decisions about purchasing and investing.[1]

Employees should receive a constant stream of information from the company. The same is true for other internal stakeholders, such as corporate shareholders and labour unions. Many of these individuals are quite distant from the marketing and public relations teams. They should be made aware of what the company is trying to achieve with its IMC program, even if this means only basic knowledge. Those closest to the marketing communications function, such as employees serving customers, are going to be more acutely aware of the nature of the IMC plan, including how the company's message theme is being sent to all other constituents.

To work effectively in communicating with employees, the public relations team must work closely with the human resources (HR) department. Publications and communications aimed at employees must be consistent with the image and message that the firm is espousing to customers and other groups. For example, any firm that uses advertising media to suggest that employees are always ready to assist customers should make sure those employees are aware of the message. Employee behaviours should then be consistent with the message theme that is being conveyed to customers. The HR department should hire the kind of employee who is attracted to such an approach and structure performance appraisals and rewards to favour those who "buy in to" the company's overall IMC approach. The emphasis on providing information about company activities must logically extend to every public relations event and sponsorship program.

Critical Thinking Exercise

Think about a job you've held in the past. What communications, if any, did the company deliver to you as an employee? If you didn't work in the marketing communications department, were you made aware of the IMC objectives of the organization? How might knowing this information have helped you perform your job?

Shareholders are another important internal audience, for two reasons. First, as the owners of the company, shareholders should be made aware of the marketing communications objectives of the firm and how it plans to compete in the market. Second, as shareholders, investors are also a form of "customer" for the company. If shareholders perceive the company as a better investment, share prices will rise. Since share prices are often tied to management compensation, the marketing communications team often has a vested interest in making sure the shareholder community understands the strategy and performance of the firm.

External Stakeholders

Overseeing external communications is a daunting task, because the company has little or no influence on how these external publics perceive organizational activities. External stakeholders include such groups as the media, the local community, the financial community, government, and special-interest groups. The company usually has little power over what these groups say or how they interpret information about the company. It is important, therefore, for the company to disseminate positive information and quickly react to any negative publicity or views that are expressed.

In general, a totally integrated communications program accounts for all types of messages that an organization delivers to both internal and external stakeholders. Every contact point provides the opportunity for a message to be sent. The marketing communications team tends to create contact points with customers and potential customers. To complement this effort, the public relations team deals with the myriad of contact points that are not created or planned, yet are just as critical as those that are planned. An unplanned contact point, such as a news story or an individual talking to an employee of the firm at a social gathering, allows the firm to build a positive image or reduce any negative messages that are being passed along. Naturally, it is more difficult to deal with unplanned contact points, because they cannot always be anticipated. The key is to monitor constantly what is going on around the firm in order to keep constituents as happy and satisfied as possible.

I'M GLAD MY PROSTITUTE MADE ME FINISH SCHOOL.

SEX WORKERS ARE MOTHERS TOO.
steppingstonens.ca
stepping stone

This is intended to influence a wide variety of attitudes including governments and other social institutions.

PUBLIC RELATIONS ACTIVITIES

The remainder of the chapter examines various forms that public relations activities can take.

Media Relations

The activities most associated with public relations are actually a number of activities targeted at one specific stakeholder—the media. The objective is to gain positive coverage through journalists who carry stories about a company or brand as part of their media content. For example, when the CTV morning news runs a segment on Wal-Mart's decision to open an additional 40 Super Centres across Canada, the company benefits from the exposure. But stories by journalists rarely happen by accident. They are usually part of a coordinated plan on the part of the public relations team to embed stories in the media. Working with journalists, they help create a compelling story that will interest the public and then provide access to data, interviews, or other materials that the journalist can use to create the story.

Press releases are a common tool used in media relations. These are developed and sent to journalists in an attempt to develop interest in a significant corporate news story. Often they contain enough information to be self-contained news items on their own, and journalists often cut and paste elements from press releases into news stories. Often, releases will direct journalists to an area on the company's website where more information, such as background, or images are available.

Critical Thinking Exercise

Imagine you are the editor of your school newspaper. You have just received a press release from Lululemon announcing the company is making a $50,000 donation to the school for the installation of a small space that students can use for meditation and yoga. Would you be inclined to give coverage to the story in the pages of your paper? Why or why not? What could the company include in its press release that might make it more compelling for you to include the story, or to help you write the story itself?

Press conferences are another tactic used in media relations to help generate a buzz among journalists and create hype around announcements. For example, when the junior hockey team the Halifax Lions changed their name to the Marauders and moved to a new arena, they held a press conference to announce the event, which dozens of journalists attended. Such an event is an opportunity to create greater excitement than a press release, allows for journalists to ask questions about a story, and offers a chance to develop personal relationships between marketers and journalists, which are helpful in future media relations activities.

Corporate Social Responsibility

Corporate social responsibility (CSR) is the obligation an organization has to be ethical, accountable, and reactive to the needs of society. Figure 10.2 outlines some of the general areas in which firms can either enhance or harm their reputation by impacting society's needs.

Some people criticize CSR activities for being more about public relations posturing than substantive investments in communities or societal welfare. However, business experts agree that genuinely socially responsible firms are more likely to thrive and survive in the long term. Companies engaged in positive activities generate quality publicity and customer loyalty that result in a positive image of the firm. Firms that work strongly toward reductions in unfair practices, pollution, harassment, and other negative activities are more likely to suffer fewer negative word-of-mouth comments by unhappy employees or consumers. By managing these activities properly, a firm can reduce damage to its public image and increase positive public perceptions of the organization.

A corporate social responsibility audit is usually undertaken by the organization's management team in conjunction with department managers. Often, external agencies provide guidelines. The purpose of a social responsibility audit is to make sure the organization has clear-cut ethical guidelines for employees to follow and that the

Press conferences are often used to make large announcements, such as when the city of Winnipeg was awarded an NHL franchise in 2011.

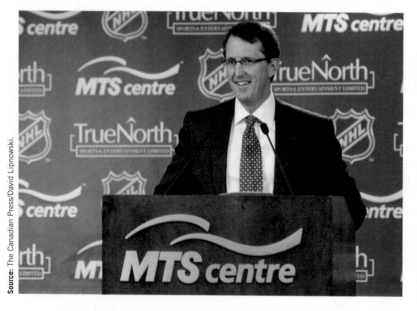

ON THE JOB

Although we have all been exposed to the outcomes of press releases (i.e., news stories that are placed in media such as television, the Internet, or newspapers), few people have actually seen a press release, let alone created one. Amnesty International Canada—an organization that relies heavily on media relations to implement its mission—provides a useful guideline for those seeking to impact coverage of a story through media.[2]

1. Start with a bang! Give all the most important information in the first paragraph. Get everyone interested enough in your event to read the rest of the news release.

2. Be simple and concise. Don't use fancy wording or long sentences. Get your point across quickly and clearly. Don't use exclamation points and try to write in the third person.

3. Be picky. Type your press release and double space it. Check carefully for accuracy—double-check names, dates, times, addresses, and telephone numbers.

4. Give opinions a voice. Use quotes instead of just making statements. For example, instead of saying,

"This event is a lot of fun," say "Jane Smith, who has attended for the last four years says, 'This event is so much fun! My kids just love it!'." (Naturally, make sure the quote is real.)

Before you send out the press release, be sure to check that all the information is there.

WHO . . . Tell which organizations are involved. When quoting people, give their full name and position.

WHAT . . . Be sure to say exactly what's going on— what exact activities are taking place?

WHEN . . . Give the full date and time, and don't forget to specify if it's a.m. or p.m.

WHERE . . . Give the exact location of your event. You may also wish to include directions or information such as where to park.

WHY . . . Why is this worth reading about? Why is the event happening? Why is the event so special that people will want to attend?

WHO CARES . . . Explain what impact this event has on your community.

CONTACT . . . Include a contact name and telephone number—and double-check to make sure it's right.

Image-Destroying Activities	Image-Building Activities
◆ Discrimination	◆ Empowerment of employees
◆ Harassment	◆ Charitable contributions
◆ Pollution	◆ Sponsoring local events
◆ Misleading communications	◆ Selling environmentally safe products
◆ Deceptive communications	◆ Outplacement programs
◆ Offensive communications	◆ Supporting community events

FIGURE 10.2
Examples of Activities that Affect a Company's Image

company acts to serve the interests of all publics. Guidelines include use of a corporate or professional code of ethics, specifying activities that would be construed as being unethical, and statements about the positive activities a company will pursue. Many firms also have access to "ethics hotlines," where employees can call or email to discuss specific ethical dilemmas.

If a firm is found to be deficient during a social responsibility audit, clear steps should be outlined to show how the issues will be resolved. Firms without codes of ethics should start by setting up committees or groups to develop them. Companies without other ethical guidelines should move quickly to establish them.

It is the task of the public relations team to make sure internal publics are aware of a corporation's social responsibility activities. The team can then inform the general public about these activities to help enhance the firm's image. CSR activities can take any number of forms, from donations to charities to workplace policies. Two of the activities particularly relevant to marketing communications are cause-related marketing and green marketing, which are discussed below.

Cause-Related Marketing

Cause-related marketing (CSR) is a program whereby a firm ties a customer exchange to a charity in order to generate goodwill. Most programs feature a specific donation (either a percentage or an absolute dollar amount) that is made every time a customer makes a purchase. This type of partnership agreement between a charity and a for-profit business is based on the idea that consumers are more likely to purchase from companies that are willing to help a good cause.

As noted previously, brand parity is the norm for many goods and services. Customers perceive that there are few notable differences between products and the companies that sell them. Many marketers use cause-related marketing to help develop stronger brand ties and to move consumers, as well as businesses, toward brand loyalty. A survey by Cone Communications and Roper Starch Worldwide revealed the following:[3]

- 78% of consumers are more likely to purchase a brand associated with a cause they care about.

- 54% would be willing to pay more for a brand that is associated with a cause they care about.

- 66% would switch brands to support a particular cause.

- 84% indicated that cause-related marketing creates a more positive image of a company.

One difficulty businesses can encounter is that what is a "good" cause to one customer may be disliked by another. One company found a large number of picketers outside company stores objecting to contributions the company made to Planned Parenthood, even as others praised the company's involvement.[4]

In the past, a number of companies donated to causes with little thought to the impact or benefit of such gifts. These philanthropic efforts were expected of big business. Today, most companies want to know what the benefit will be. Even if company leaders believe a charity is worthwhile, supporting that charity must, in some way,

Many products allow customers to contribute to a social good through their purchases.

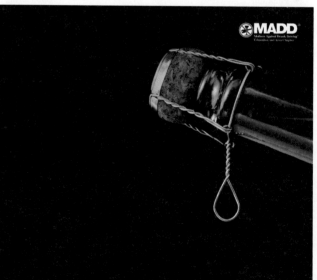

Organizations such as MADD Canada (Mothers Against Impaired Driving) are supported by a number of corporate donors.

FIGURE 10.3
Causes Customers Prefer

◆ Improve public schools	52%
◆ Dropout prevention	34%
◆ Scholarships	28%
◆ Cleanup of environment	27%
◆ Community health education	25%

Source: Bevolyn Williams-Harold and Eric L. Smith. "Spending with Heart," *Black Enterprise* 28, no. 12, (July 1998), p. 26.

result in a tangible benefit. Otherwise the company should not give support. Possible benefits include:

- Additional customers
- Increased profits
- Consumer goodwill for the future
- Better relations with governmental agencies
- Reduced negative public opinion

These benefits lead companies to get involved. Relationships that do not yield positive benefits to the business sponsor do not last long. Figure 10.3 highlights the top five areas consumers want businesses to consider as they seek causes to support.

In choosing a cause, the marketing team focuses on issues that relate to the company's business. Supporting these efforts makes the activity more credible to consumers. When the company supports an unrelated cause, consumers may feel that the business simply is trying to benefit from the charity's reputation. This may lead some consumers to stop buying the company's products or to believe the company is trying to cover up unethical behaviour. Consumers are becoming sceptical about the motives behind the increased emphasis given to various charities. Even though most people understand that a business must benefit from the relationship, they still tend to develop negative views when they believe that the business is exploiting a relationship with a charity.

When a good fit exists, positive reactions emerge. For example, a cosmetic dentist established partnerships with a homeless shelter for battered women and a residential education centre for former substance abusers and ex-convicts. The dentist offered free services to these centres. Several television and newspaper reporters showed up to observe him treating patients. Individuals who had been in pain for months were interviewed. When they stated that cosmetic dental work gave them relief, positive feelings in the community were the result. The publicity was extremely valuable. The dental services were something neither the centres nor individuals who were living in the centres could afford.[5]

Critical Thinking Exercise

Two problems exist for marketers seeking to promote cause-related marketing campaigns. First, many people don't know about them. Awareness levels tend to be very low. Second, if a person perceives the motive for the campaign to be self-serving, he or she will have more negative attitudes toward the company than positive outcomes from the campaign. Think back to an example of a cause-related marketing campaign. How did you become aware of it and what did you think of it? If you felt the campaign was self-serving, what could the company have done to change that perception? If you felt the campaign did not make the company look self-serving, what about it made you feel that way?

Hier,
planten uw
handdoeken bomen

Here,
YOUR towels
plant trees

Although many Canadian consumers integrate environmental thinking into their consumption, European consumers are generally more environmentally conscious.

Cause-related marketing is also an important source of donations for charities. Competition has increased in both the business world and the nonprofit world. An increasing number of charities are competing for contributions and gifts. Strategic relationships with businesses can boost contributions for a charity considerably. For instance, the CIBC Run for the Cure annual event has raised millions of dollars for the Susan G. Komen Breast Cancer Foundation. Using the slogan "Save Lids to Save Lives," Yoplait also makes donations to the charity when customers return lids from containers.[6] These relationships with businesses result not only in direct increases in revenues, but also in greater publicity for the charity.

The public relations aspect of cause-related marketing is complicated. To benefit from cause-related marketing, company leaders want publicity about what is being done. Yet, if the company publicizes too much, people will think the cause is simply being used for commercial gain. In a survey of British consumers, the vast majority said a company should spend funds on communications about their cause-related efforts. The same survey indicated that two-thirds also said the amount that should be spent should not be significant. At the same time, the majority of those surveyed said their purchase decisions are influenced by the causes a company supports. This makes informing people about what a company is doing important; however, doing so involves walking a thin line between publicizing and what might be perceived as corporate self-aggrandizement.[7]

Green Marketing

Green marketing is the development and promotion of products that are environmentally safe. When asked, most consumers strongly favour the concept of green marketing. One recent survey indicated that 58 percent of consumers try to save electricity, 46 percent recycle newspapers, 45 percent return bottles or cans, and 23 percent buy products made from or packaged in recycled materials.[8]

Although consumers favour green marketing and environmentally safe products, actual purchases of such products only occur when all things are considered equal. Most consumers are not willing to sacrifice price, quality, convenience, availability, or performance for the sake of the environment. In fact, according to a recent study, about 40 percent of consumers say they do not purchase green products because they believe the products are inferior to regular goods.[9]

To benefit from green marketing, the company should identify market segments that are most attracted to environmentally friendly products. Figure 10.4 divides consumers into five segments based on their propensity to use green products and their attitudes

Critical Thinking Exercise

Recent research suggests that the inclusion of a green message in marketing communications can lead consumers to change their perceptions of product quality. For example, if consumers learn that coffee is fair trade, they expect that it will not taste as good as conventional coffee (even though in actual taste tests there is no difference in consumers' perceptions).[10] This might not be what proponents of sustainability want to hear, but it is indeed the case. What products have you encountered where you felt the inclusion of a green message meant a trade-off on product performance? How can marketing communications overcome this potential downside to the promotion of green products?

FIGURE 10.4
Consumers Segmented on Their Attitudes
Toward and Support of Green Marketing

- ◆ **True Blue Green (9%)**—Have strong environmental values and are politically active in environmental issues; heavy users of green products

- ◆ **Greenback Greens (6%)**—Have strong environmental values, but are not politically active; heavy users of green products

- ◆ **Sprouts (31%)**—Believe in green products in theory, but not in practice; will buy green products, but only if equal to or superior to nongreen products

- ◆ **Grousers (19%)**—Are uneducated about environmental issues and cynical about their ability to affect change; believe green products are too expensive and inferior

- ◆ **Basic Browns (33%)**—Do not care about environmental issues or social issues

Source: Jill Meredith Ginsberg and Paul N. Bloom, "Choosing the Right Green Marketing Strategy," *MIT Sloan Management Review* 46, no.1 (Fall 2004), pp. 79–84.

about environmental issues. Notice that only 9 percent of consumers are classified as "True Blue Greens," and another 6 percent are classified as "Greenback Greens." The True Blue Greens are active environmentalists who support environmentally safe products and shop for brands that utilize green marketing. The Greenback Greens purchase environmentally safe products, but are not politically active.

Company leaders must carefully choose a green marketing strategy that matches the target audience. In making the decision on how much emphasis to put on green marketing, managers should ask three questions. First, what percentage of the company's customer base fits into the green marketing segments? Second, can the brand or company be differentiated from the competition along green lines in such a way that it can become a competitive advantage? Third, will the company's current target audience be alienated by adopting a green marketing approach?

Almost all firms say they are pro-environment and provide information on company websites about their environmental activities. The amount of effort given to publicize these activities varies widely.[11] For example, Coca-Cola tries to protect the environment, but most people are unaware of the company's efforts. Coca-Cola has invested heavily in various recycling programs and recyclable package designs. The activities are not publicized, because there is some fear that it would reduce the product's appeal to some of the company's audience. Overemphasizing the green aspects of Coca-Cola's operation may actually hurt sales through criticisms of **greenwashing**.

An alternative approach to being pro-environment is to promote the direct, tangible benefits of a product first, with the environmental benefits presented as a secondary factor. The Toyota Prius was launched with an emphasis on fuel efficiency. Consumers were told they would spend less on gas. The fact that the Prius was an environmentally advanced, fuel-efficient hybrid vehicle was mentioned, but not stressed. The idea was that strong environmentalists would believe a hybrid car is important. For those who were not strong environmentalists, it did not matter, because the car delivered fuel efficiency. Starbucks is another example. Renewable energy now accounts for about 20 percent of the power used in its company-owned stores.[12]

For a few companies, environmental activities are fully integrated into the business design and marketing approach because the primary customer base is True Blue Greens and the Greenback Greens. Examples of these types of companies include The Body Shop, Patagonia, and Nike. In 2008, Nike released its Trash Talk brand of basketball shoe.

Nissan is using the message of innovation to support environmental claims about its vehicles.

Many companies sponsor local events to embed themselves in the community.

The product is made from manufacturing waste. NBA player Steve Nash wore the shoes in the 2008 All Star Game. Nash has a longstanding interest in environmental causes. The free publicity was an excellent tie-in for the Trash Talk launch.

Most business leaders believe their companies should be involved in protecting the environment and creating green products; however, the marketing emphasis each one gives varies. If it thinks new customers will be gained or product sales will rise, the company will be more likely to aggressively promote its environmental stance. Other companies, such as Coca-Cola, may be less willing to make such bold statements. Each company's marketing team will decide whether green marketing should be a central part of the IMC message and how to position itself in terms of the environment.

Sponsorships

To build brand loyalty and other positive feelings toward a company, many marketing leaders utilize sponsorships and event marketing. These programs make it possible to meet with prospects, customers, vendors, and others in unique situations. People who attend sponsored activities or special events already have favourable feelings about the activity taking place. These positive attitudes are easily transferred to a company that has provided funding. In this section, sponsorship programs and event marketing are described in greater detail.

Sponsorship marketing means that the company pays money to sponsor someone, some group, or something that is part of an activity. A firm can sponsor a practically unending list of groups, individuals, activities, and events. For years, firms sponsored everything from local soccer teams to national musical tours to NASCAR drivers, and placed corporate names on sports stadiums.

Forms of Sponsorships

In North America, approximately $14.4 billion a year is spent on sponsorships and events.[13] Figure 10.5 provides a breakdown of how the money is spent. Sports represent

FIGURE 10.5
Marketing Expenditures on Sponsorships and Events

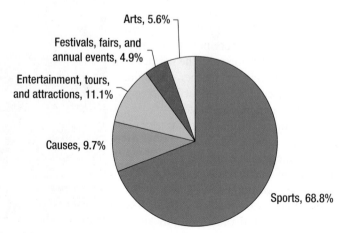

nearly 70 percent of all sponsorships. Sporting events are highly popular and often attract large crowds. In addition to the audience attending the game or competition, many more watch on television. Popular athletes can be effective spokespersons for various products. If possible, the firm should be the exclusive sponsor of the person or team. It is much easier to be remembered if the firm is the only sponsor rather than one of multiple sponsors.

Gillette's sponsorships are a major component of the company's marketing program. Gillette spends millions of dollars each year on various sponsorships, many of which are sports related. The company has an employee whose job description is to manage sponsorship activities. The Gillette Fusion razor was featured as part of a sponsorship for the television show *The Apprentice*. Gillette consistently sponsors the FIFA World Cup, including a $50 million global promotion featuring soccer star David Beckham. An integrated marketing campaign featured a $20 million Gillette Young Guns Campaign musical concert tour tied with six NASCAR drivers and a sampling and couponing program at the concerts.[14]

FedEx uses sponsorships to build customer loyalty. The company sponsors many sporting events and makes sure key customers not only get to attend them, but also are allowed to go into places they could not get into on their own. This includes access to NFL locker rooms; trackside passes at the Daytona 500; and access to famous golf courses such as Pebble Beach. These unique experiences create strong bonds with FedEx.[15] In addition, the marketing department tracks revenues from these customers before and after each event. Company figures indicate these activities generate positive revenues along with customer loyalty.

FedEx has relationships with the NFL, NBA, NASCAR, the PGA Tour, horse racing, and the NCAA. These programs create a great deal of company exposure. The NASCAR sponsorship, for example, costs $16 million but generates nearly $50 million in TV exposure. More recently, FedEx became the transportation carrier for many of the company's sponsored events. FedEx ships equipment for the halftime shows for the Super Bowl and Pro Bowl. The company also ships game films to every professional football team on a weekly basis.

Some organizations have moved away from sports sponsorships toward more cultural events, such as classical music groups and jazz bands, visual art exhibits by noted painters, dance troupes, and actors for various theatre performances. Cultural sponsorships are not the best match for every firm. They are most effective for products sold to affluent members of society. Consequently, financial institutions are the primary sponsors of these types of performers and performances. In the past, many institutions provided funds without receiving much recognition. Now these philanthropic efforts are being leveraged by having the name of the company strongly associated with the cultural activity. This includes printing the name of the firm on programs and regularly mentioning the brand or corporate name as being responsible for arranging for the artist to be present at the cultural event. Also, sponsors usually receive choice seats at performances that can be given to key clients.

Choosing Sponsorships

In choosing a sponsorship, it is important to match the audience profile with the company's target market. Sponsoring a participant at an event attended mainly by females works best when the company's primary customers are female. Marketing executives also consider the image of the individual participant or group and how it relates to the firm's image. For sponsors like Bell and Videotron, sponsorship of the annual Jazz Festival in Montreal is an obvious choice. The festival provides access to a wide range of consumers (both companies target a wide section of Canadians) and is a somewhat iconic local event in the Quebec market, where both companies are headquartered.

To maximize the benefits of a sponsorship effort, it is important to define the primary goals of the program. As with the other marketing tools, the goals of the sponsorships should be integrated with the firm's overall IMC theme. The public should easily recognize the link between the person or group being sponsored, the activity, and the company involved. To achieve the maximum impact for the sponsorship, the message should be combined with other advertising and promotional efforts, such as a sampling program or a giveaway (T-shirts, caps, etc.). Sampling is an effective method for encouraging people to try a product. Unless a sponsorship is surrounded by supporting marketing efforts, the money invested may not accomplish its objectives.

Product Placements and Branded Entertainment

Many marketers take their sponsorship one step further and actually embed their products within entertainment such as television shows and movies. **Product placement** is defined as the planned insertion of a brand or product into a movie, television show, and some other media program with the purpose of influencing viewers. **Branded entertainment** is the integration of entertainment and advertising by embedding brands into the storyline of a movie, television show, or other entertainment medium.[16]

Product Placements

Product placements have been a part of motion pictures since the beginning in the 1890s. Lever Brothers placed the company's soap brand in some of the early films. In the 1930s, Buick had 10-picture deal with Warner Brothers for placements. Several tobacco companies paid actors to endorse and use the brands. Early television programs were sponsored by brands, such as the *Colgate Comedy Hour*. The biggest surge in product placement may have occurred in 1982, when Reese's Pieces were used to lure E.T. out of hiding as part of the plot of the movie *E.T.* The placement of the Reese's Pieces spurred a 65 percent rise in sales following the movie's release.[17]

More recently, Coca-Cola and Ford chose to sponsor the popular television show *American Idol*. Each company paid for the right to be part of the show, to post online content, and to run off-air co-branded marketing programs. Ford featured its vehicles in music videos sung by the final 12 contestants. Coca-Cola made sure its branded cups were front and centre on the judges' tables and that Coke graphics were visible behind the contestants when they were being interviewed.[18]

Marketers believe that product placements lead to increased awareness and more positive attitudes toward the brand. In a few isolated cases, sales of a brand have increased. In most instances, however, there is not an immediate impact on sales. Research by Nielsen reveals the following about product placements:[19]

- Brands placed within "emotionally engaging" television programs were recognized by 43 percent more viewers.
- Brand recognition increased 29 percent for brands place in highly enjoyed programs compared to 21 percent for commercial spots.
- Positive brand feelings increased by 85 percent for brands placed in programs compared to 75 percent for commercial spots.

One key advantage of brand placement is the low cost-per-viewer. This is especially true for movies. After a movie has finished at the cinema, it is usually converted to a DVD for movie rental. From there, it is not unusual for the movie to be converted to television for viewing on syndication outlets or one of the premium movie channels. It may also be available on TV through video-on-demand. The end result is that the movie expands beyond the cinema screen to various venues and may be seen multiple times by individuals.

Branded Entertainment

In branded entertainment, the brand is woven into the storyline of the movie or television show. For instance, in an episode of the CTC drama *The Eleventh Hour*, Nicorette was integrated into a story about a character trying to quit smoking. By integrating the brand into the story, it is much more noticeable to the viewing audience. The use of branded entertainment increased sharply with the rise of reality television shows where there is a lack of scripts and the focus is on creating "real-world" situations. The success of branded entertainment in reality shows has led to its use in scripted television shows. Branded entertainment is now also found in novels, plays, songs, and movies.

Critical Thinking Exercise

A key difference between product placement and branded entertainment is the degree to which the brand is integrated into the entertainment. In branded entertainment, the product almost becomes the "star" of the production. Some critics argue that this goes too far, and creates a consumer backlash. They argue that consumers will revolt when they perceive the inclusion of brands in entertainment as too heavy-handed. Do you agree? Think of an example of a product or brand that you saw as part of a production that you feel was well done and one that was not. Why did you perceive a difference?

Achieving Success with Individual Consumers

Figure 10.6 identifies the major factors that influence the success of brand placements and branded entertainment. Notice that the media used has an impact on their effectiveness. Some television programs are losing clout because of placement clutter. For instance, in one recent season there were 4,349 product placements during Fox's *American Idol* shows.[20] Unless a brand was prominent, like the red plastic cups of Coca-Cola in front of the judges, most were lost in the clutter of other brands appearing on the show. The CTV production of *Canadian Idol* similarly featured products prominently placed within the broadcast, such as Oreo cookies.

High profile events give marketers an opportunity to tie sponsorships to their overall IMC objectives

Product placements and branded entertainment work because there is no call to action. The primary goal is to increase brand awareness and liking. When a consumer's favourite actor uses a particular brand or his or her favourite show contains a particular brand, it becomes more likely that the individual will transfer those positive feelings to the brand.

Some consumers are more receptive to brand placements than others. People between the ages of 15 and 34 are more likely to notice brands placed in a movie or show. Also, individuals in North America and the Asia-Pacific area are more receptive than people in Europe.

When a consumer sees a brand placement of a product that he or she has purchased, it may reinforce that idea that a wise decision was made, which further validates the original purchase decision.[21]

- ◆ Media
- ◆ Supporting promotional activities
- ◆ Consumer attitudes toward placements

- ◆ Placement characteristics
- ◆ Regulations

FIGURE 10.6
Key Factors Influencing Effectiveness of Product Placement and Branded Entertainment

Source: Based on Simon Hudson and David Hudson, "Branded Entertainment: A New Advertising Technique or Product Placement inDisguise?" *Journal of Marketing Management* 22, no. 5/6 (July 2006), pp. 489–504.

Company Tactics

The actual manner in which a brand is placed into a movie or show is important. Brand insertions work best when they seem logical. In other words, the most effective placements are those woven into the program in such a way that they appear to be a natural part of the story. Brands shown in the background that seem to be artificially inserted are not nearly as effective.

It is also important to examine the scene where the brand placement will occur. Will the viewer see the brand in a positive setting, or will it be seen in a negative situation? For instance, in the movie *The Hoax*, starring Richard Gere, McGraw-Hill is not seen in a positive light, because the star in the show deceived the publisher by proposing a fake biography of Howard Hughes.[22]

Many companies buy advertising spots on television programs that feature product placements of the brand. Additional promotional incentives may also be offered. The goal is to move beyond recognition and liking to the actual purchase.

Budgets for product placements and branded entertainment have been increasing for several reasons. First, a brand's appeal is stronger when it is shown in a context that doesn't appear as paid media. Second, the perception of what others think of a brand is important to consumers. For many it is more important than how the consumer views the brand. Seeing the brand being used in a television show, a movie, or a book makes the brand look acceptable and even desirable. Third, seeing the brand used by others provides post-purchase reassurance for individuals who have already purchased the item. Fourth, for individuals who place little value on brand names and branded products, having a brand placed in a program can provide evidence of the brand's advantages, and this evidence may be strong enough for them to consider purchasing the brand. In these cases, the brand does not have to persuade the consumer of its merits directly. It does so through the acceptance and use of the brand by the actor or program.

The Producer's Perspective

For moviemakers and television producers, the primary motivation behind product placements and branded entertainment is money. In the past, brand mentions were incidental or used by movie producers to create realism in a film. They now generate additional income. Martha Stewart charges $10,000 for a 30-second placement on her show. For a one-time mention in the show with a product close-up, the price goes up to $100,000. For a two-minute branded entertainment segment with two or three talking points, the price is $250,000+.[23]

Many producers and directors are critical of product placement and what they see as an infringement upon creative freedom. They argue that once entertainment becomes nothing more than vehicle to position products or create corporate image it ceases to have any real entertainment value. However, with more pressure on production companies to make profits in a media landscape filled with piracy and unlimited entertainment options for free online, product placement and branded entertainment shows no signs of slowing any time soon.

Buzz Marketing

Take product placement one step further, into real life, and you have buzz marketing. Buzz marketing is one of the fastest growing areas in alternative media marketing. Estimated expenditures for buzz marketing are now at $1 billion annually. **Buzz marketing**, which is also known as word-of-mouth marketing, emphasizes consumers passing along information about a product. A recommendation by another person carries higher levels of credibility than does an advertisement. It is also more powerful than the words of a paid spokesperson or endorser. Buzz, or word-of-mouth, can be generated in one of the following ways:

- Consumers who truly like a brand and tell others
- Consumers who like a brand and are sponsored by a company to tell others
- Company or agency employees posing as customers of the company, telling others about the brand

Consumers Who Like a Brand

The ideal situation occurs when a consumer truly likes a particular brand and tells others. This can take place in person or it can occur via the Internet in chat rooms, on blogs, or by email. Many musical groups have gained fame and fortune through the word-of-mouth support of those who have seen the bands in bars or as part of a small concert or tour. Companies can attempt to facilitate this word-of-mouth by using a presence on Facebook and other venues where consumers can share consumption experiences with each other. But this doesn't provide the company control over the form or frequency of the message, so some marketers are turning to more proactive approaches by either paying sponsoring customers or paying people to pose as customers.

Critical Thinking Exercise

Everyone has told someone else about a product or company. We all engage in word-of-mouth virtually every day. When was the last time you felt compelled to tell someone else about an experience with a product or company? Was it a positive or negative experience? What factors do you think lead you to tell someone about one experience but not many others? What can explain why someone will feel compelled to share an experience in only selected cases? Are there things that define consumers who are likely to spread word-of-mouth, define consumption experiences that are likely to be talked about, or define consumers who are likely to be told something through word-of-mouth?

Sponsored Consumers

Many companies sponsor individuals as agents or advocates to introduce new products. When Procter & Gamble launched a new cleaning product called Dawn Direct Foam, a set of consumers who were called "connectors" was identified. The group, which was named "Vocalpoint," consisted of 450,000 mothers who were assigned the task of starting discussions about P&G products. When Dawn Direct Foam launched, the pitch to these moms was that it would make dishwashing fun for children. Members of Vocalpoint received coupons and "fun for children" talking points. The moms quickly spread the word, increasing the sales of the new detergent by 50 percent.[24]

Sony used buzz marketing and brand advocates to launch its GPS camera. The product featured an emerging technology, and Sony's marketing department believed it was important to get people to physically try the product. The company selected 25 "ambassadors" from a pool of 2,000 applicants. The individuals chosen displayed high levels of interest in cameras and in taking pictures, and had plans either to travel or to participate in sporting events. Each ambassador was given a free camera and lessons on how to use it. The Sony ambassadors were encouraged to hand out discount coupons, show the cameras to anyone who asked, and blog weekly about their adventures on the Sony microsite. One of the ambassadors, Cheryl Gillet, described and photographed her trip to Australia, adding a map of her journey. Juxtaposed with destinations on the map were photos of beach scenes and her tanned friends in swimsuits. Even those applicants who were not selected were pleased because each was sent a 20-percent discount coupon for the GPS camera.[25]

Brand ambassadors or customer evangelists are typically individuals who already like the product that they are asked to sponsor. The company offers them incentives and rewards in exchange for advocacy. Companies select these ambassadors based on devotion to the brand and the size of their social circle. Once recruited, they are expected to deliver messages to their social circle, families, friends, reference groups, and work associates. Some

Dawn Direct Foam launched a buzz marketing campaign involving "fun for children" talking points for mom ambassadors.

Source: © Dorling Kindersley.

are expected to develop grassroots, no- or low-cost marketing events and to promote the brand on the Internet through blogs or social networks such as MySpace. Brand advocates are asked to be upfront and honest about their connections with the brand.

When the marketing team at Lee jeans decided to find ways to strengthen the brand's connection with younger, contemporary consumers, the company identified 1,000 brand ambassadors. Each received a free pair of One True Fit jeans, a promotional kit, a suggested list of people to contact, and a DVD. Six months later, 88 percent of the agents still wore the jeans and 50 percent bought at least one more pair.[26]

Company Employees

The final group of advocates, employees posing as customers, has been used by some companies. Doing so is risky. According to the Word of Mouth Marketing Association (WOMMA), the practice is dishonest and unethical, unless the person is upfront and clearly identifies him- or herself as being with the company. In the past, Wal-Mart used the tactic on a blog about two ordinary people, Laura and Jim, trekking across the United States in an RV staying in Wal-Mart parking lots. The blog received considerable attention, especially after *BusinessWeek* exposed Jim as a professional photojournalist employed by Edelman, Wal-Mart's public relations firm. Both Wal-Mart and Edelman received considerable criticism regarding the program.[27]

Hallmarks of this type of campaign include a fairly low-key approach to presenting the product to other consumers. To be overly aggressive would likely signal to consumers that the person they are dealing with has a vested interest in selling the product. A low-key approach was taken by Vespa scooters when they entered the Canadian market. Focusing on major cities, the company had very little marketing communications budget but still wanted to make an impression on a highly targeted group of young people likely to buy its scooters. So it staged a play in the streets of Toronto's entertainment district. Only the "audience" were patrons at local patios and they didn't realize they were seeing a play. The play involved one paid actor who parked his Vespa in a conspicuous place and then left. Minutes later a young woman came by and admired the scooter, asking patrons if it belonged to them. Then, on cue, the first actor returned. The two struck up a conversation, and then rode off on the scooter together. In one performance, hundreds of potential customers witnessed the potential for Vespa scooters to make them "cool." And it was all an act.[28]

WOMMA provides guidelines for companies that want to generate word-of-mouth communications through its employees, agency employees, or even sponsors or agents. It encourages

- Honesty of relationship—be honest about the relationship between consumers, advocates, and marketers.
- Honesty of opinion—be honest in presenting opinions about the brand, both good and bad.
- Honesty of identity—identify honestly who you are.[29]

Vespa used a street performance in downtown Toronto to help promote its scooters.

Event Marketing

Event marketing is similar to sponsorship marketing. The major difference is that sponsorship marketing involves a person, group, or team. **Event marketing** occurs when the company supports or hosts a specific event. Event marketing is closely related to lifestyle marketing. Both often include setting up a booth or display and having some type of physical presence at an event.

As is the case with sponsorships, many event marketing programs feature sports. Other events are more related to lifestyle, and can therefore be targeted to very specific target audiences. A Hispanic food festival funded by a food company, for example, is event marketing and a great to promote products to specific audiences.

A critical decision in event marketing requires a match between the event, the target audience, and specific objectives of the event. When the objective is to reward customers, it is crucial to find an event that major customers would be interested in attending. Objectives that are more internally oriented, especially those designed to get employees involved and boost morale, should be met by finding events internal members will enjoy. Many times, the goals of sponsoring an event are to help the firm maintain its market share, to build a stronger brand presence in the marketplace, to enhance the product's or firm's image, or to increase sales.

Some events turn out better than others for the sponsor. To help determine which events are most effective, employees can monitor how many pieces of literature were given to attendees, the number of samples distributed, and the number of visitors to the sponsor's display booth. When Victoria's

The marketing team at Victoria's Secret tracked the results of the "Pink" event marketing program.

Secret launched its new brand "Pink," it was coupled with a unique event marketing promotion during spring break. The goal was to reach 18- to 24-year-old females. The event began when a three-storey pink box was set up on a Miami beach. Advertisements, postings, street teams of employees giving out fliers, aerial signs, signs in nearby hotels, and public relations press releases built excitement during the five-day countdown. When 5,000 spring breakers showed up to the event, they were treated to a fashion show and a live concert. After the concert, Victoria's Secret Pink gift cards were passed out and the company hosted nightclub parties. The unique marketing event spurred sales of both the new Pink brand and other Victoria's Secret brands. The Victoria's Secret marketing team completed the evaluation stage and discovered that the Pink brand sales increase in the Miami area was huge and that the other Victoria's Secret brand sales also rose dramatically.[30]

A study by the Advertising Research Foundation (ARF) found that purchase intentions in buying a particular branded product increased from 11 to 52 percent among consumers who attended a brand-sponsored event, such as a sporting event, walkathon, or themed event. Further research found that purchase intentions translated into sales about half the time. The ARF study involved events sponsored by companies such as Frito-Lay, State Farm, and Coca-Cola. As with sponsorships, sports-related events tended to have the best results.[31]

Damage Control

A corporation's reputation is fragile. It also is valuable. Well-received corporate and brand names can enhance businesses during the good times and protect them when a crisis or problem occurs. Consumer preferences about which brands to purchase are influenced by a company's reputation. People make decisions about where to invest based on corporate reputations.

Different from the previous public relations activities, which proactively pursue opportunities to promote the company or brand in a positive light, damage control is designed to be in response to a negative event. **Damage control** is reacting to negative events caused by a company error, consumer grievances, or unjustified or exaggerated negative press. Corporate and brand images are quickly damaged by negative publicity and events. A strong company image that took years to build may be destroyed in just a few weeks or months. Toyota took a significant reputational hit when it announced a series of product recalls after consumer complaints about gas pedals sticking to the floor. Maple Leaf Foods faced a significant problem when listeriosis was found in its products and consumers avoided anything with the Maple Leaf brand. Both companies received criticism from experts on the way they handled the crisis. Toyota, for example, was criticized for not getting all the bad news out at once and letting a large number of small problems and recall notices come out over a period of weeks. "The result was a slow drip of bad news, which is one of the key things you always talk about avoiding in crisis management," says Gene Grabowski of Levick

FIGURE 10.7
Damage Control Strategies

> ◆ **Proactive Strategies**
>   Entitlings
>   Enhancements
> ◆ **Reactive Strategies**
>   Internet interventions
>   Crisis management programs
>   Apology strategy
>   Impression management techniques

Strategic Communications. "You want to rip off that Band-Aid all at once, so you don't have this slow torture that creates this heightening effect."[32]

Not all negative publicity is generated by the media. Sometimes negative publicity comes from word-of-mouth communication from customers, employees, or other individuals connected with the company. With the Internet, bad experiences and negative talk can be posted and spread to thousands, even millions, within a very short time.

Although damage control is by definition in response to negative events, it consists of proactive prevention as well as reactive strategies (see Figure 10.7).

Proactive Prevention Strategies

Proactive prevention means that rather than waiting for harmful publicity to appear and then reacting, firms engage in practices that can help serve as a buffer to negative press. These approaches may prevent negative publicity from starting in the first place. Two proactive prevention techniques are entitlings and enhancements.[33] **Entitlings** are attempts to claim responsibility for positive outcomes of events. **Enhancements** are attempts to increase the desirable outcome of an event in the eyes of the public.

Local retailers took advantage of the Maple Leaf Foods crisis to build their businesses.

Dear Customers

All recalled Maple Leaf products have been removed from our Deli Counter.

For inquiries please call :
CFIA- 1-800-442-2342
Maple Leaf Consumer Foods- 1-800-568-5801

Entitling occurs when a firm associates its name with a positive event. For example, being the official sponsor of the Canadian Olympic team that wins a gold medal attaches the company's name to the athletic achievements of people who don't work for the firm, yet the firm can claim responsibility for some aspect of their success.

Enhancements occur when a bigger deal is made out of something that is relatively small. For instance, many products now claim to be *fat free,* which makes it sound like they are diet foods. In fact, many fat-free products have just as many calories as do those that contain fat. At the same time, the fat-free label helps convince customers that the company is trying to help them to eat healthy food and watch their weight at the same time. Marketers mush take care when using enhancements, since consumers will punish firms (through negative word-of-mouth, boycotts, etc.) they perceive as deliberately trying to deceive.

Reactive Damage-Control Strategies

Company leaders often must react to unforeseen events, because they cannot anticipate every possible contingency. In these instances, managers must work diligently to blunt the effects of unwanted bad publicity by every means possible. Crisis management and other techniques should be designed to help the firm cope with circumstances that threaten its image. Reactive damage-control strategies include

- Internet interventions
- Crisis management programs
- Apology strategy
- Impression management techniques

Internet interventions are designed to combat negative word-of-mouth that is placed somewhere online. Many forums for sharing negative word-of-mouth and spreading bad experiences exist, including Twitter, chat rooms, rogue websites, and Internet blogs. All provide an environment in which consumers from every part of the world can share horror stories. Individuals can put any information they desire on the Internet, even when it unfairly portrays certain industries, companies, or brands. Although passivity can sometimes be the best approach, some companies fail to monitor these communications, and therefore are completely unaware of their existence.

Vigilant public relations officers realize the power of the Internet and what it can do to an organization's reputation. These leaders make sure someone monitors what is being said. When they see messages criticizing a company unjustly or proclaiming untruths, company representatives take action. Some log into a chat room and immediately identify themselves as company representatives. They then attempt to explain the company's point of view and try to correct misconceptions. In other situations, the company's public relations department prepares public statements and press releases. Not every activity warrants a formal reaction. Still, monitoring the Internet keeps the company's leadership informed about what people are saying and what they are thinking.

Crisis management involves either accepting the blame for an event and offering an apology or refuting those making the charges in a forceful manner. A crisis may be viewed as either a problem or an opportunity. Many times a crisis contains the potential to improve the firm's position and image. For example, when PepsiCo encountered claims that hypodermic needles were being found in its products, the management team quickly responded with photographs and video demonstrating that such an occurrence was impossible, because the bottles and cans are turned upside down before being filled with any soft drink. This fast and powerful answer eliminated the negative publicity, and Pepsi was able, at the same time, to make a strong statement about the safety of its products. Pepsi's reaction was quite effective in dealing with this particular crisis.

Unfortunately, some company leaders manage only to make matters worse, as was the case with the reaction of Ford and Bridgestone to the faulty tires on the new Ford Explorers. Instead of immediately seeking to correct the problem, both denied a problem existed and tried to put the blame on others. Ford CEO Jacques Nasser blamed Bridgestone/Firestone Inc. for the tire separation problems. Bridgestone blamed consumers, saying they did not inflate the tires to the correct pressure. This

When reports surfaced of hypodermic needles in Pepsi products, Pepsi quickly reacted by showing the public how cans and bottles were filled.

FIGURE 10.8
Elements of an Apology Strategy

1. An expression of guilt, embarrassment, or regret
2. A statement recognizing the inappropriate behavior and acceptance of sanctions for wrong behavior
3. A rejection of the inappropriate behavior
4. Approval of the appropriate behavior and a promise not to engage in inappropriate behavior
5. An offer of compensation or penance to correct the wrong

finger-pointing ended Ford's 100-year relationship with Firestone. Bitter words were exchanged and the public did not buy either excuse. The outcry was so strong that both companies lost sales and suffered image damage, and eventually Nasser lost his job at Ford.[34]

An **apology strategy** is another reactive form of crisis management and damage control. If the end result of the investigation is the revelation that the firm is at fault, an apology should be offered quickly. A full apology contains five elements, as shown in Figure 10.8.[35]

Apologies are most often used either in situations in which the violation is minor or in ones in which the firm or person cannot escape being found guilty. It is also a good strategy for creating a strong emotional bond with the public. It is more difficult to be angry with a company that admits a mistake was made. If people feel the apology is sincere and heartfelt, they not only will forgive the company, but they may also feel more positive about the company afterward.

The tendency to protect one's self-image is called **impression management**, or "the conscious or unconscious attempt to control images that are projected in real or imagined social interactions."[36] In order to maintain or enhance self-image, individuals and corporations attempt to influence the identities they display to others. The goal is to project themselves in such a manner as to maximize access to and the visibility of positive characteristics while minimizing any negative elements.

Any event that threatens a person's self-image or desired identity is viewed as a predicament. When faced with such predicaments, individuals make concerted efforts to reduce or minimize the negative consequences. If the predicament cannot be avoided or concealed, then an individual engages in any type of remedial activity that reduces the potentially harmful consequences. Remedial tactics include:[37]

- Expressions of innocence
- Excuses
- Justifications
- Other explanations

An *expression of innocence* approach means company leaders provide information designed to convince others (clients, the media, and the government) that they were not associated with the event that caused the predicament. In other words, they say, "We did not cause this to happen. Someone (or something) else did."

Excuses are explanations designed to convince the public that the firm and its leaders are not responsible for the predicament or that it could not have been foreseen. Thus, they should not be held accountable for the event that created the predicament. For example, they might say, "It was an act of God. It was totally unavoidable."

Justifications involve using logic designed to reduce the degree of negativity associated with the predicament. Making the event seem minor or trivial is one method. Making the argument that the firm had to proceed in the way it did (e.g., "We pollute because if we don't we'll be out of business, and our employees will lose their jobs") is another form of justification.

Other explanations may be created to persuade individuals that the cause of the predicament is not a fair representation of what the firm or individual is really like. In other words, the case was the exception rather than the rule, and customers should not judge the firm too harshly as a result. You will hear comments such as "This was a singular incident, and not indicative of the way we do business."

STRENGTHS AND WEAKNESSES OF PUBLIC RELATIONS

Because of the wide variety of activities that are included under the public relations umbrella, many strengths and weaknesses are specific to only certain elements. However, some generalizations can be made.

Strengths of Public Relations

Reaching Elusive Audiences. Public relations activities generally have the ability to reach audiences that are otherwise difficult to reach. For example, many consumers who avoid advertising media or sales promotions may still read the newspaper or attend sporting events. Further, tactics such as buzz marketing can be very effective at targeting highly specific target audiences.

Image and Reputation Management. Because of their ability to convey messages about the company behind the brands, tactics such as cause-related marketing can be very effective at enhancing the reputation of firms. The ability for tactics such as product placement to build associations with popular cultural figures creates further positive reputation effects.

Credibility. Although not all public relations tactics are delivered through third parties, many of them rely on the support of media to bring the message to consumers and other audiences. Media relations are often built into many other public relations tactics, such as event marketing or cause-related marketing, in an effort to help build their reach. In the case of damage control, the popular press is a central source of information for many consumers. When a message is delivered through a third party, the audience is more likely to believe it when compared with a message delivered directly from the firm. The media portrayal of a corporate response to a negative event, for example, can greatly sway the public's reaction.

Relatively Low Cost. All of the public relations tactics described here can have relatively low costs on a per-audience-member basis. Sponsorships, for example, can reach millions of people at a time if they are paired with popular sporting events. Product placement in popular TV shows can achieve even greater reach than advertising media on those same shows because viewers generally don't skip over product placements like they do with advertisements.

Weaknesses of Public Relations

Relative Loss of Control. For many public relations tactics, the marketer gives up a certain degree of control. Certainly in any media relations activity, the marketer does not control the message or slant taken by journalists. Product placements can sometimes place products in a negative light, events are subject to negative events given their public nature, and sponsorships can turn negative very quickly, as was the case when Tiger Woods's personal problems came to light.

Measurement Difficulties. Because many public relations activities carry very high-level objectives related to corporate reputation, they can be more difficult to measure when compared with other tactics. For example, event marketing measures, such as the number of people attending, provide very limited opportunities to understand the long-term impact that events can have on measures like sales or customer preferences. Further, because some of the audiences for public relations are explicitly non-customers, their behaviours can be difficult to link back to specific activities. For example, if Imperial Oil (the company behind Esso gas stations) receives a drilling permit in Northern Canada, it's difficult to determine what role, if any, cause-related marketing played in shaping the image of the company with regulators.

COMMUNICATING ACROSS CULTURES

One of the largest areas of concern for public relations professionals has become corporate social responsibility. This is because of two developments. First, companies have expanded internationally and greatly increased their footprint in emerging economies, whether through their supply chain or by selling products to end-users. This means that companies are operating across a greater range of cultures and social norms than ever before. Further, because some emerging economies do not have the same regulatory standards as some developed nations, there is a temptation to reduce the ethical responsibility of the company in areas where the minimum criteria are much lower.

The second development is the advent of telecommunications that allow for news—good, but especially bad—to travel instantly around the world. This means that any decision made by a company in a developing nation is made public in all of the markets in which it operates. In a 24/7 news environment, a crisis could unfold in Toronto at 3 a.m. because the evening newscast in Seoul just broke a news story about sweatshop labour in one of the firm's suppliers in Southeast Asia. By the morning news in Toronto, the crisis can be in full swing.

Simply obeying the law or other local minimum standards in developing country operations is not usually considered sufficient for firms headquartered in North America and Europe. Their constituents in their home markets, including consumers and politicians, will criticize a company if they feel it is engaged in moral relativism and taking advantage of people elsewhere in the world while preaching high standards at home. Many successful boycotts have resulted from companies taking these different positions across markets. Many firms now engage in corporate social responsibility activities that are consistent across all markets in order to avoid such problems.

IMC IN PRACTICE

"Our approach to sponsorship has changed over time," says Kate. "We are lucky in that we don't need to rely on sponsorships for logo recognition because we have such high levels of awareness among customers. So the majority of our programs in this area are now dispersed across the country and take the form of community-based events."

This is especially true in the area of corporate philanthropy for TELUS. "Our mantra is that 'we give where we live.' We have employees all over Canada (as well as in the Philippines and Central America), and we look at this as a way to build connections not just with our customers but with our employees too."

"Employees are often an overlooked audience for the brand and public profile of a company. But our employees are essential, not just because of the obvious benefits associated with having an engaged team, but because they are often on the front line communicating with customers." The program involves letting employees on a local level decide how the company should support their community. It also involves significant support for the charitable work by employees themselves. "TELUS matches employee donations on a dollar-for-dollar basis and will make a lump-sum donation if TELUS employees or retirees volunteer a certain amount of time. Also, we have a TELUS Day of Giving, where employees get out into their local communities for one day a year, doing whatever their chosen community partner needs; from walking dogs for the SPCA, to cleaning up parks, or building playgrounds. It's a great program that benefits everyone."

Donations are focused at the local level to ensure employee involvement.

But public relations isn't always about being proactive in trying to build the brand. Sometimes it is about responding to crises, and trying to protect the brand. As a telecommunications provider with a vast network of underground and overhead cables, we are often at the mercy of the weather, construction, and sometimes even thieves. Of course, these events can create massive inconvenience for our clients and they look to us to fix it, but often it's not that easy.

Several years ago, construction on a major roadway severed a main cable leading to downtown Vancouver. Our PR team invited the media to see the conditions under which our technicians were working (two technicians crammed into a tiny hole deep underground that kept filling with water) so that the community could at least understand that we were doing our absolute best to fix the problem. Once folks realize that the organization has team members that are passionate about fixing things when they go wrong, the response can be amazing. It can actually contribute to the strength of the brand."

Source: Used with permission of Kate Baillie, TELUS Communications.

For help developing your IMC Plan, go to **www.pearsoncanada.ca/clow**.

SUMMARY

The public relations team plays a major role in an integrated marketing communications program, regardless of where the responsibility for the public relations function lies. Public relations efforts are primarily oriented to making sure that every possible contact point delivers a positive and unified message on behalf of the company. This includes assessing a corporation's reputation and involvement in socially responsible activities.

There are many stakeholders inside and surrounding a company. Any person or group with a vested interest in the organization's activities is a stakeholder. Internal stakeholders include employees, unions, and stockholders. External publics include members of the marketing channel, customers, the media, the local community, financial institutions, the government, and special-interest groups.

To reach all intended audiences, the public relations team has a series of tools available. These include media relations, corporate social responsibility, green marketing, sponsorships, product placement and branded entertainment, buzz marketing, and event marketing. Media relations is often featured as a component of other public relations tools because it allows for external coverage and promotion of other activities by the firm, such as CSR or sponsorships.

Due care must be given to making certain that CSR and green marketing communications are not perceived with cynicism and skepticism. This means being certain that any good deed matches with company products and other marketing

efforts. A natural fit between an altruistic event and the company's brand is more readily accepted by various members of the public.

Sponsorship programs enhance and build the company's image and brand loyalty. A sponsorship of an individual or group involved in some kind of activity—whether a sporting event, a contest, or a performance by an artistic group—can be used to link the company's name with the popularity of the player involved. Sponsorships should match with the firm's products and brands. Some marketers have extended sponsorship to include their brands within entertainment content itself, or sponsored consumers to act on behalf of the company.

Event marketing occurs when a firm sponsors an event. A strong physical presence at the event is one of the keys to successfully linking an organization's name with a program. To do so, the firm must determine the major objective of the event sponsorship, match it with company customers and publics, and make sure the firm's name is prominently displayed on the literature accompanying the event.

In addition to proactive public relations like those described above, the public relations team is also responsible for damage control when negative publicity arises. Both proactive and reactive tactics are available to maintain a positive image for the company. Damage control tactics include Internet interventions, crisis management programs, and impression management techniques.

KEY TERMS

apology strategy   Presenting a full apology when the firm has made an error.

branded entertainment   The integration of entertainment and advertising by embedding brands into the storyline of a movie, television show, or other entertainment medium.

buzz marketing   Emphasizes consumers passing along information about a product to others, and is closely related to word-of-mouth marketing.

cause-related marketing (CSR)   Matching marketing efforts with some type of charity work or program.

corporate social responsibility An organization's obligation to be ethical, accountable, and reactive to the needs of society.

crisis management Either accepting the blame for an event and offering an apology or refuting those making the charges in a forceful manner.

damage control Reacting to negative events caused by a company error, consumer grievances, or unjustified or exaggerated negative press.

enhancements Attempts to increase the desirable outcome of an event in the eyes of the public.

entitlings Attempts to claim responsibility for positive outcomes of events.

event marketing When a company pays money to sponsor an event or program.

green marketing The development and promotion of products that are environmentally safe.

greenwashing Deceptive use of environmental messaging to create the perception that a company's policies or products are environmentally sustainable.

impression management The conscious or unconscious attempt to control images that are projected in real or imagined social situations.

Internet interventions Confronting negative publicity on the Internet, either in website news releases or by entering chat rooms, blogs, or social networks.

press releases Written or recorded information sent by companies to media outlets with the intent of having the media deliver the information as news.

product placement The planned insertion of a brand or product into a movie, television show, or other media program.

public relations (PR) team A unit in the firm that manages items such as publicity and other communications with all of the groups that make contact with the company.

sponsorship marketing When the company pays money to sponsor someone or some group that is participating in an activity.

stakeholder A person or group with a vested interest in a firm's activities and well-being.

REVIEW QUESTIONS

1. Describe the role of the public relations team. How is it related to the marketing communications department? Should both departments be called the department of communications? Why or why not?

2. What is a stakeholder?

3. Name the major internal stakeholders in organizations. Describe their interests in the company.

4. Name the major external stakeholders in organizations. Describe the major interest in the company of each one.

5. What are two tools used in media relations?

6. What is social responsibility? How is it related to public relations activities?

7. What is cause-related marketing? How can company leaders create effective cause-related marketing programs?

8. What is green marketing? How do different companies promote environmentally friendly activities?

9. What is sponsorship marketing? Name a pro athlete, a musician or musical group, or a performer of some other type who has been featured in a sponsorship program. Was the program effective or ineffective? Why?

10. What are product placement and branded entertainment? What do they have in common and how do they differ?

11. What is buzz marketing?

12. What three types of consumers pass along buzz marketing messages?

13. Describe an event marketing program.

14. Name and briefly describe two proactive prevention strategies companies can use to create a positive image.

15. What reactive damage-control techniques are available to the public relations team?

16. What four forms of impression management are used to combat negative events?

INTEGRATED LEARNING EXERCISES

1. In Canada, the primary trade association for public relations is the Canadian Public Relations Society. Access the website of this organization at **www.cprs.ca** or Public Relations Society at **www.prsa.org**. What type of information is available? What types of services are offered? How would these organizations be beneficial to various companies?

2. Many high-profile companies now feature special sections on their websites devoted specifically to members of the media. Find three examples of websites of companies that

contain "media" sections. What information do you see available? How can this be helpful to the public relations objectives of these firms? Is there something missing from the sites that you think should be included? What are the differences between media sections that you think are good and those you think are inadequate?

3. Corporate sponsorships are very important to charities. Without their financial assistance, many causes would not exist. Look up two organizations from the following list.

Who are their corporate sponsors? What benefits do the profit-seeking companies receive from these sponsorships?

a. Canadian Cancer Society (**www.cancer.ca**)

b. Ducks Unlimited (**www.ducks.ca**)

c. Habitat for Humanity (**www.habitat.ca**)

d. World Wildlife Fund (**www.wwf.ca**)

e. Sick Kids Foundation (**www.sickkidsfoundation.com**)

f. Second Harvest (**www.secondharvest.ca**)

4. Although the Internet has created a number of opportunities for marketing communications, it has created new challenges. One of those challenges is the rise of so-called anti-brand websites. These are sites set up by individuals who seek to attack well-known brands. Some are set up by disgruntled former employees, others by customers who feel they have been mistreated, and still others by activist organizations with a social or political agenda. In one high-profile case, Wal-Mart bought the domain to the site **www.walmartsucks.com** in an effort to stop it from being used against the firm. Visit the following websites (please note that the URLs are not misspelled). In each case, describe your recommended approach to the public relations manager for the target firm. Would you recommend a direct response? No response? A response through other forms of marketing communications or other marketing functions of the firm?

a. Best Buy (**www.bestbuy-s.com**)

b. Starbucks (**www.starbucked.com**)

c. United (**www.untied.com**)

d. Ticketmaster (**www.fantasyland.com/ticketbastard**)

STUDENT PROJECT

Creative Corner

Circle K Ranch has been selling, training, and boarding horses for almost 20 years. With the recent downturn in the economy, however, Circle K has experienced a decline in all facets of its business. In talking with some marketing students at the local university, the owner of Circle K Ranch, Kathy Kroncke, wondered about using cause-related marketing, sponsorships, and even event marketing to boost the awareness and image of her business. She recently added horseback riding to her list of services and developed a 10-mile ride that goes through a local national park. So far, business has not been what she expected, despite research that indicated a high level of interest in riding, especially by 15- to 40-year-old females. Design Kathy a cause-related marketing program, a sponsorship program, and an event marketing program. After you have designed each of the programs, choose the one you think would be the best for Circle K Ranch. Design a newspaper ad featuring the program. What other methods would you use to publicize the program you chose?

ETHICS IN ACTION

Product placement and other forms of marketing communications designed to be "under the radar" for consumers are generally considered effective. Maybe too effective. Especially when the audience has an already limited ability to discern the difference between entertainment and commercial messages, as is the case with young children. And yet, entertainment programming for children is filled with product placement. Critics of product placement in children's entertainment point out that marketers are taking advantage of children's inability to understand that brands often pay to be included in programming. But those who defend the practice suggest that shielding children from practices such as this only makes them more susceptible later in life to the influence of marketing communications. Besides, parents should be responsible for ensuring that children understand the difference between entertainment and commercials. By simply spending time with children while they watch entertainment (or switching the television off), parents can help their children understand how product placement works and consequently help their children to become more aware and not be so influenced by it.

1. What is your point of view on the subject of product placement? Do you think it is ethical to include it in children's programming? Do you have a different point of view for product placement in entertainment targeted at adults?

2. What are some of the potentially harmful outcomes that might result from product placement in children's entertainment?

3. What do you feel is the appropriate balance of responsibility between parents and marketers when it comes to protecting children? Should marketers bear any of the responsibility for potential harmful outcomes, or are these potential outcomes the fault of bad parenting?

4. Find out what Advertising Standards Canada (**www.adstandards .com**) is doing to protect children from persuasive advertising messages. Do you think they are doing enough to manage product placement? Write your recommended approach to regulating product placement targeted at children in a one-page memo. ●

CASE STUDY | Health Scare at the Barnacle

James Madison, manager of the Barnacle Restaurant in Moncton, couldn't believe it. But there it was in black and white in the press release from the South-East Regional Health Authority entitled "Hepatitis A Alert—Moncton Barnacle Restaurant." The restaurant had only been open for less than a year, and this type of thing can put even the most successful and established restaurant into a tailspin. The release was dated December 23, and was an early Christmas present James wished he could send back.

The report read: "South-East Health has identified a case of Hepatitis A in a food handler employed at the Barnacle Restaurant. This infection was acquired outside of the country, and the infected individual ceased employment with the restaurant on December 10. To date, there are no reported cases from customers of the restaurant. The restaurant is cooperating fully and assisting South-East Health in identifying patrons and staff who need to be contacted. The South-East Health Officer is encouraging the following individuals to get a Hepatitis A vaccination as soon as possible: People who ate salads or desserts at the restaurant before 8:00 p.m. on December 5, December 9, or December 10. It is possible for the Hepatitis A virus to be passed on to others through food. A safe and effective Hepatitis A vaccine is available which reduces the risk of illness, provided vaccination is received within 14 days of coming into contact with the virus. Anyone who ate at the restaurant on the dates noted above will be eligible for the vaccine as they may be at some risk for contracting Hepatitis A."

Hepatitis A is a viral illness that affects the liver. Symptoms may develop 15 to 50 days after exposure and include nausea, abdominal cramps, fever, dark urine, pale feces, and yellowing of the skin and eyes. Illness can last for several weeks and people generally recover completely. However, it may be more severe in the elderly or those with chronic liver disease.

If there is any one industry in which word-of-mouth can do great damage in a hurry, that industry would be food service—especially restaurants. A single problem can drive away customers for months. Any tale of contamination or unsanitary conditions that circulates in a local community creates a major crisis for a restaurant owner.

The Barnacle, which opened in 1974, specializes in seafood. Over the years the company expanded to nine locations throughout the Maritimes. Locations are always waterfront to complement the seafood focus. As such, the company positions itself as a somewhat upscale dining option.

The company also engages in a number of community events and sponsorships. One of its most prominent social responsibility initiatives is their participation in the Atlantic Fishery Foundation. Through a partnership, the Foundation and the company help conserve and restore various species of fish along the Eastern coast. The partnership started with the Barnacle's 2009 "Best of the East Coast Festival." While celebrating their 35th anniversary that year, the restaurant donated $1 from the sale of select wines, a donation of $3,500.

However, James knew that any of the efforts of the company relating to social responsibility weren't going to help his restaurant in this crisis. The news story was picked up by local and even national media, including the CBC. The issue even appeared on a local online restaurant review website. Making matters worse, the crisis came right in the heart of the holiday season, when the restaurant was at its busiest time all year.

James knew the company didn't have the money to launch a full-scale marketing communications campaign to attempt damage control. He felt the company overall had a good reputation, and was confident that the crisis would pass with time. But at the same time, he knew that he had to do something, if for no other reason than to try to salvage the Christmas season. Sales had already been less than half what they would normally be in the two days since the crisis broke, and he didn't want to wait for the situation to correct itself. As he finished wrapping his son's Christmas presents, he sat down at the kitchen table wondering what his first move should be when he went into the work the next day, Christmas Eve.

1. What public relations tactics should James consider for his restaurant and for himself as manager? Write an email to James outlining the choices he should consider and what he should hope to achieve with them. If business is down by 50 percent, how long would you advise James it will take to return to 100 percent?

2. It is important that James tell his side of the story and try to encourage at least some positive messages to counter the negative publicity. Write a one-page press release that James can send to local media.

3. Part of the problem in this situation is the timing. If James attempts to work too quickly, his message will get lost in the holiday noise. But if he waits, he runs the risk of letting the story get out of hand, and the possibility that rumours will swirl making damage control after the holidays even harder, if not impossible. Prepare two PowerPoint slides in which you outline the advantages and disadvantages of taking action before the holiday, followed by your recommendation on timing.

Health scares can decimate a restaurant's business.

Source: © Photos.com/Jupiter Images.

Note: This case study is fictional and any resemblance to real businesses is coincidental. The events of the case study are real; many businesses have gone through similar circumstances.

ENDNOTES

1. Jenny Dawkins, "Corporate Responsibility: The Communication Challenge," *Journal of Communication Management* 9, no. 2 (November 2004), pp. 106–17.

2. Amnesty International, "How to Write a Press Release," accessed on June 4, 2011, from: **http://www.amnesty.ca/youth/ youth_action_toolkit/how_to_write_ press_release.php**.

3. Larry Chiagouris and Ipshita Ray, "Saving the World with Cause-Related Marketing," *Marketing Management* 16, no. 4 (July–August 2007), pp. 48–51.

4. Brad Edmondson, "New Keys to Customer Loyalty," *American Demographics* 16, no. 1 (January 1994), p. 2.

5. Steven Van Yoder, "Make It Mean Something," *Successful Meeting* 53, No. 2 (February 2004), pp. 27–29.

6. Nan Xiaoli and Heo Kwangiun, "Consumer Responses to Corporate Social Responsibility (CSR) Initiatives," *Journal of Advertising* 36, no. 2 (Summer 2007), pp. 63–74.

7. Dawkins, "Corporate Responsibility: The Communication Challenge."

8. Jill Meredith Ginsberg and Paul N. Bloom, "Choosing the Right Green Marketing Strategy," *MIT Sloan Management Review* 46, no. 1 (Fall 2004), pp. 79–84.

9. Ibid.

10. Carl Obermiller, Chauncey Burke, Erin Talbott, and Gareth P. Green, "Taste great or more fulfilling: The effect of brand reputation on consumer social responsibility advertising for fair trade coffee," *Corporate Reputation Review* 12, no. 2 (2009), pp. 159–176.

11. Examples based on Ginsberg and Bloom, "Choosing the Right Green Marketing Strategy."

12. Valerie Seckler, "Causes and Effect," *Women's Wear Daily* 194, no. 93 (October 31, 2007), p. 9.

13. "Events & Sponsorships," *2007 Marketing Fact Book, Marketing News* 41, no. 12 (July 15, 2007), p. 31.

14. Jack Neff, "Gillette Amps Up Sponsorships," *Advertising Age* 75, no. 36 (September 6, 2004), pp. 4–5.

15. Tom Weir, "When You Absolutely, Positively Need $$$$$," *USA Today* (December 29, 2004), p. 3C.

16. Simon Hudson and David Hudson, "Branded Entertainment: A New Advertising Technique or Product Placement in Disguise?" *Journal of Marketing Management* 22, no. 5/6 (July 2006), pp. 489–504.

17. Ibid.

18. Gail Schiller, "Idol Sponsors Coke, Ford, AT&T Paying More," *Brandweek.com* (**http://brandweek.com**, January 15, 2008).

19. Linda Moss, "Nielsen: Product Placements Succeed in 'Emotionally Engaging' Shows," *Multichannel News*, December 10, 2007.

20. Cecily Hall, "Subliminal Messages," *Women's Wear Daily* 195, no. 2 (January 3, 2008), p. 12.

21. Jean-Marie Lehu, "Seamless Brand Integration," *Brand Strategy*, no. 211 (April 2007), pp. 34–35.

22. Hudson and Hudson, "Branded Entertainment."

23. Burt Helm, "Marketing: Queen of the Product Pitch," *BusinessWeek* (April 30, 2007), pp. 40–41.

24. Sinclair Stewart, "More Marketers Using Word of Mouth to Whip up Sales," *The Seattle PostIntelligencer*, December 23, 2007.

25. John Voight, "The New Brand Ambassadors," *Adweek.com*, December 31, 2007.

26. Stewart, "More Marketers Using Word of Mouth."

27. Angelo Fernando, "Transparency Under Attack," *Communications World* 24, no. 2 (March–April 2007), pp. 9–11.

28. Hollie Shaw, "Taking It to the Street," *National Post*, June 17, 2006, p. FP3.

29. Fernando, "Transparency Under Attack."

30. Betsy Spethmann, "A Winning Season," *PROMO* 18, no. 1 (December 2004), pp. 32–41.

31. Kenneth Hein, "Study: Purchase Intent Grows with Each Event," *Brandweek* 49, no. 4 (January 28, 2008), p. 4.

32. "Toyota's Digital Disaster," *Newsweek*, accessed on June 4, 2011, from: **http:/ /www.newsweek.com/2010/02/03/ toyota-s-digital-disaster.html**.

33. Marvin E. Shaw and Philip R. Costanzo, *Theories of Social Psychology,* 2nd ed. (New York: McGraw-Hill, 1982), p. 334.

34. "Jac Nasser Out as Ford's CEO," *Tire Business* 19, no. 16 (November 15, 2001), p. 1.

35. Shaw and Costanzo, *Theories of Social Psychology,* 2nd ed., p. 334.

36. Ibid, p. 329.

37. Ibid, p. 333.

CHAPTER OBJECTIVES

After reading this chapter, you should be able to answer the following questions:

- **What** is digital marketing and how does it differ from other forms of marketing communications?

- **What** forms can digital marketing take?

- **How** can different methods of pricing for digital media impact marketers' success?

- **How** do social networks democratize marketing communications to allow even small-budget marketers to find success?

- **How** can digital content create a dialogue with stakeholders that meaningfully changes how marketing communications creates relationships?

INDUSTRY PROFILE

So You Want to Work in Marketing Communications?

Nicole Armstrong, Associate Planner, Critical Mass, Calgary, Alberta

Critical Mass is a Canadian digital marketing agency with a world-class reputation and some of the world's most recognized brands as clients: Nissan, Infiniti, Budweiser, AT&T, and even NASA. And chances are you've never heard of them. That's because they focus on digital brand engagement, and are behind the scenes in some of the most compelling and cutting-edge online brand experiences in the business today.

"We focus on creating extraordinary experiences for our clients, bringing their brands to life online through immersive interactions and engagement," says Associate Planner Nicole Armstrong. The role comes easily for Nicole who presents almost evangelical vision of what great brands can do to engage and enrich customers' lives.

Branding has always been a passion for Nicole. "While I was going to school in my undergraduate program, I worked in several part-time jobs for marketing agencies. They were in more traditional agencies, but it was a great way to see how the business worked. I knew I wanted to work in this business, so I made an effort to meet people in the business to learn about the industry and learn about possible job opportunities. At first it was volunteering, but after I demonstrated the value I could add, I was able to convince them to keep my role on as a part-time paid position." Adding on to a good thing, the opportunity to work in the industry only strengthened Nicole's confidence and passion for branding because it helped her apply the marketing concepts she was learning in her degree program.

When she graduated, Nicole again used that same confidence and focus to seek out an employer that could provide the best challenge. "I had already made the decision to focus my career on branding, so then it was just a matter of choosing the best options. I wanted to work with a company that had a high calibre of brands because of the sophistication of the work and the scope of the challenge of managing some of the world's leading brands."

Critical Mass fit the bill perfectly. "The online environment is the perfect opportunity to enable a brand to come to life," says Nicole. "When a customer is

Digital Marketing

engaged through an online medium, we can actually deliver on the brand promise in a meaningful way. For example, I recently worked on a project for a customer support interface with Panasonic North America. We were able to design a brand experience for customers that produced an almost immediate lift in customer satisfaction. I look for what we in marketing call 'reasons to believe'—the things that prove to a customer that the brand promise has substance. And the digital environment is simply the best platform on which to build meaningful brand engagement."

In her position in the planning department, Nicole is focused on bringing the voice of the customer into the strategy process. "I use what I know about the customer to help establish the strategic direction to solve our clients' challenges. That means writing points-of-view documents and insight briefs that are based on sound strategy, good customer research, focused competitive intelligence, and a keen understanding of the trends that are shaping the marketplace."

"I use a lot of both primary and secondary research in my job. Primary research can be anything from site usability tests, where we hire a company to test the consumer experience in one of our projects, to any type of performance metric. Secondary research can be even more varied because you never know what new trend or technology is going to take hold."

Nicole Armstrong, Associate Planner, Critical Mass.

Nicole has learned to become extremely resourceful in her quest to acquire the customer and brand insights that can help her shape better strategy. "There is so much out there; the problem isn't so much finding something but it's finding something that is relevant and credible. I use **emarketer.com** a lot to see what's happening out there. **PSFK.com** is another cool site. **Trendwatching.com** is another one. And I also use the more widely read sources like *Brand Week* or *Ad Age*." Working for an agency gives Nicole the benefit of accessing Forrester Research reports as well. "The point is to take the best ideas that are out there and apply them to my client's challenge, their brand, and the brand experience that we want to create."

In the fast-paced environment, one challenge for Nicole is to keep learning and to make sure learning is shared among others in the agency. "Being able to work in a team is a big requirement of this job, or any job in this business. It moves so quickly, and we need to make sure that everyone on the team is up to speed." Presentation skills are another key to Nicole's success. "My presentations can't be just about content," says Nicole. "You can have great ideas, but if they don't inspire others on my team, my work will be overlooked. You can't be shy in this business. If you have a good idea you sometimes have to work to make sure it sees the light of day."

One of the ways Nicole tests herself, and ensures that she is current and relevant, is through her blog (**http://morethanalogo.blogspot.com**). "My blog has been a great avenue for me to force myself to stay on top of new topics and a chance for me to showcase my thinking. Going through the process of writing about something forces me to really think it through, to make sure my ideas are sound. It's especially useful for people who are more junior in an organization to help others know what they are capable of."

Nicole recommends a blog for anyone in the job market as a way to showcase their ideas and promote themselves to potential employers. "It's a digital portfolio that you can use to inform potential employers what skills you can bring to the organization. It's not specific to any one job, just an overall opportunity to show that you are passionate for the business and have useful insights." But she cautions not to rush to post too quickly. "The worst thing you can do is put up some half-baked ideas that haven't been properly thought through, because once they are out there, you can't take them back. I hovered over the post button for about five minutes in my first entry because I wanted to make absolutely sure I was ready to share my ideas with the world."

The only way to have confidence in your ideas, says Nicole, is to do the work to properly develop them. "People should pick an area where they have a passion because it takes work to be on top of your game. Get to know the business intimately. Read constantly. If you love the work you do, it honestly doesn't even feel like work."

OVERVIEW

The final tool in the marketing toolbox is, like previous tools such as public relations and sales promotions, a broad range of tools that fall under one common theme. They all employ a digital delivery system. Hence, the term digital marketing is used to describe them. Examples include banner advertising on webpages, websites used by companies themselves, and actual "content" on sites like Facebook with the use of brand pages.

Digital marketing has blurred the lines between traditional marketing functions in two respects. First, because consumers in an online environment can be only a click away from a purchase, the line between marketing communications and distribution has blurred. E-commerce is more tightly linked to specific marketing communications in an online environment than, for example, a billboard advertisement and a subsequent visit to a physical retail store.

The second way that digital marketing has blurred traditional lines within the marketing function is within marketing communications specifically. Examples of digital marketing—from the official Tim Hortons Facebook page to the Credit Unions of BC channel on YouTube to the selection of online banner ads on any given media website, such as the **theglobeandmail.com**—integrate features and benefits of virtually all other tools of the marketing communications mix. Media are represented with the traditional banner ads. But these ads can be highly targeted and customized based on user profiles, which makes them more like a direct marketing tactic than a traditional advertising media tactic. Many online campaigns integrate sales promotions, and some, such as the Heinz Comfort Creations contest, are exclusively managed online. Other elements, such as brand participation in online chat forums, can be compared to some of the public relations efforts by firms to engage different stakeholders. Still, because of their unique properties and growing importance in the marketing communications landscape, this chapter is exclusively focused on the collection of tactics known as digital marketing.

Arguably, other forms of marketing communications—particularly elements such as television, radio, and print—may be subsumed within a digital world. Much of the content in these media is delivered simultaneously through both traditional and digital formats (e.g., newspapers that offer content in both printed and online formats). More importantly, technologies in different delivery systems are converging to a digital platform. Eventually, all devices, such as televisions, radios, computers, and cell phones, will be nothing more than devices with a specific IP (**Internet protocol**) address. Content will be seamlessly portable between all of them. For example, today a consumer can plug in a laptop to a television screen and watch a sitcom at home, or stream the same sitcom to his or her phone while riding the bus. The specific device becomes less relevant to the delivery as all content converges to a digital platform. Evidence of this convergence can be found in the sheer number of IP addresses in existence. In 2011, the world technically "ran out" of IP addresses because the original designers of the Internet never envisioned so many connections. They "only" allocated 4 billion addresses.[1] In theory, any appliance can have an IP address. Imagine a refrigerator with a screen that can stream content and marketing communications from marketers of foods and beverages.

For this reason, digital marketing is the least stable of all the marketing communications tools. This chapter highlights the world of contemporary digital marketing tactics and examines some of the specific forms of digital marketing that are prevalent in marketing communications plans today. Because of the wide variety of tactics, and the ability for each one to provide strengths of various other marketing communications tools, we will examine the digital marketing world in its two main forms. The first is digital marketing that largely resembles marketing communications in other forms, including display or space media, search engines, and other means of placing messages in front of people in a digital environment. The second form includes the development of Web-based content that provides value to stakeholders while delivering marketing communications effects. These include company websites, participation in social networks, and virtual worlds.

DISPLAY/SPACE MEDIA

Display, or space, advertising is the most similar to traditional advertising media. Most commonly found in the form of banner ads, this media places ad messages in front of users. But included in this section is search engine optimization because of the similar manner in which marketing communications professionals can place messages in front of users. The difference is that banner ads are directed based on the content that appears on screen (e.g., someone browsing an automotive website is likely to be exposed to banner ads for cars or car accessories) while search engine optimization places messages in front of an audience based on their search (e.g., if I search for automotive websites, marketers can "buy" placements in the search results that are produced). Each of these types of digital marketing is discussed next, and highlighted in Figure 11.1.

Banner Advertising

Banner ads can be presented each time a webpage is viewed, also known as **impressions**. The market has virtually exploded in recent years, with the total number of impressions totalling well into the hundreds of billions worldwide for individual websites. Yahoo and Facebook, for example, each offer advertisers hundreds of billions of page impressions each year.[2]

In the early days of banner advertising, messages were fairly straightforward and resembled static digital billboards. Over the years, the term "banner advertising" has been used to encompass an ever-growing field of digital media that now includes full-motion video and sound, special effects when a mouse is dragged over an ad, or ads in forms that pop up when users click on a website. Online advertising is used by marketers in a wide range of industries, as shown in Figure 11.2.

◆ Banner advertising	◆ Mobile media
◆ Search engine optimization	◆ Video game advertising

FIGURE 11.1
Display/Space Advertising Forms

FIGURE 11.2
Online Advertising Spending by Industry Sector

◆ Automotive: 12%	◆ Entertainment: 5%
◆ Packaged Goods: 10%	◆ Leisure (travel, hotel, etc.): 5%
◆ Financial: 10%	◆ Media: 4%
◆ Technology: 9%	◆ Pharma/Health: 2%
◆ Retail: 7%	◆ Other: 31%
◆ Telecommunications: 5%	

Source: IAB Canada, *2010 Actual + 2011 Estimated Canadian Online Advertising Revenue Survey Detailed Report*, www.iabcanada.com, used with permission.

Banner ads like this for Grub Canada still create awareness and residual value even if consumers don't click through.

In addition to the tactics used to place messages in front of web browsers, the objectives of such ads have changed. Initially, success was largely determined by whether or not a browser clicked on an ad. By clicking on an ad, users are taken to a website where they can find out more information or even purchase the item. The model was very much based on direct marketing, where response rates dictate success or failure. Traditionally, response rates for banner advertising have been very low. Reach Students created a series of Internet ads to promote an offer from one of the major parcel delivery services. The ads ran in May and June, just as students were deciding what to do with their personal items over the summer. Should they keep them or ship them home? The timing seemed perfect for such a campaign. Unfortunately, only 0.04 percent—only 4 out of every 10,000—students who saw the web ad responded. Luke Mitchell, who ran the campaign, had anticipated at least a 1 percent response rate.[3]

As the field of banner advertising matured, the potential effects of banner advertising were widened to include more traditional objectives, such as awareness and brand-building commonly associated with such media as out-of-home billboards. As more dollars are shifted to banner advertising, there is concern about the impact of those ads. Web users, just like television viewers, are becoming immune to advertisements. The percentage of people who respond to banner ads is steadily shrinking. The click-through rate on major web destinations such as Microsoft, AOL, and Yahoo! has declined to less than 1 percent. A recent measurement showed a response rate of 0.27 percent.[4]

Despite their challenges, banner ads are increasingly popular. YouTube, for example, now generates billions of dollars annually in ad revenues for its parent company, Google. But the place where they are increasingly found is on social network sites such as Facebook. One recent study showed that social networking sites accounted for more than 20 percent of all display ads viewed online, with MySpace and Facebook combining to deliver more than 80 percent of ads among sites in the social networking category.[5] "Over the past few years, social networking has become one of the most popular online activities, accounting for a significant portion of the time Internet users spend online and the pages they consume," said Jeff Hackett, Senior Vice President of ComScore, a company that tracks online advertising trends. "Because the top social media sites can deliver high reach and frequency against target segments at a low cost, it appears that some advertisers are eager to use social networking sites as a new advertising delivery vehicle."[6]

In perhaps the ultimate intermingling of old and new media, some traditional media outlets are using their Facebook pages to create additional advertising revenue. For example, *US Weekly* sold sponsorship of its new Facebook profile to State Farm in what appears to be a first for a media company on the social networking website, as well as a first for a company's fan page. If the approach takes hold, imagine what sponsorships could mean for Facebook pages belonging to *The New York Times*, with 447,749 fans so far; *National Geographic*, with 453,013 fans; or even ABC's *Lost*, with 785,093 fans. "We do anticipate that this becomes another tool in our tool chest [of] meaningful ways to let brands reach our audience in a very credible, differentiated environment," said Steven Schwartz, chief digital officer at *US Weekly's* parent, Wenner Media.[7]

Canada's largest social networking site that focuses specifically on youth is Nexopia (**www.nexopia.com**). The site caters to a younger audience, primarily teens.

The selective audience for sites like this compared to Facebook means they offer more attractive, targeted media for advertising. For example, Alberta Employment ran a Nexopia campaign targeting the 15- to19-year-old demographic. Since workers who are under 25 are 33 percent more likely to be injured on the job than any other age group, the site offered a chance to get the message of workplace safety to those who need it most.[8]

In another effort to use online advertising to connect with difficult to reach younger demographics, Wal-Mart Canada launched a campaign to promote its environmental initiatives. The campaign included banner ads on such sites as theglobeandmail.com and Yahoo.ca.[9]

Search Engine Optimization

One way that marketers use to ensure higher click-throughs and other effects from online advertising dollars is to focus their budgets on users who are more predisposed to notice their messages. By far the most popular means of doing this is through the use of search engines, where messages are placed in front of users only when they identify their interests.

In fact, nearly 80 percent of all Web traffic begins at a search engine.[10] Therefore, one key marketing goal is to make sure that a company's name or brand is one of the first ones listed when a person performs a search. **SEO**, or **search engine optimization**, is the process of increasing the probability of a particular company's website emerging from a search.

SEO can be reached in one of three ways. The first is through a paid search insertion that comes up when certain products or information are sought. Companies can speed this process by registering with various search engines in order to have the site indexed. Even paying for insertions takes time. It can take months for a site to be listed prominently.

The Alberta government used social networks to communicate the importance of workplace safety to teens.

The second approach is to increase identification through the natural, or organic, emergence of the site. The idea is to develop efficient and effective organic results that will arise from the natural search process. Each search engine uses a slightly different set of algorithms to generate results. At the same time, these programs identify key phrases that match what the person types into the search box. To be listed first in an organic search requires time and effort. When a website is first built, it is unlikely that the site will emerge at the top of the search results. It takes time for the search engines to locate the site.

Some studies suggest that the impact of organic listings can be impressive. For sites that come up on the first page of a search or within the top 10, Web traffic increases nine-fold. For second- and third-page listings, Web traffic increases six-fold. In terms of sales, being a top 10 listing has resulted in a 42 percent increase in sales the first month and a 100 percent increase the second month.[11]

The third approach is to use paid search ads. Paid search advertising can be small text boxes that pop up when a particular word is typed in or it can take the form of paid link boxes at the top or side of a search result. Search advertising now accounts for 40 percent of online advertising dollars. More money has been shifted to search advertising, because it is more effective than regular online advertising. The typical click-through rate for online advertising is around 0.2 percent; for search advertising it is around 5 percent.[12]

Critical Thinking Exercise

It can be argued that search engine optimization is preferred to banner advertising since search engines place messages in front of an audience that has self-identified themselves as interested in a specific topic. But is this always the case? Clearly banner ads must serve a purpose, since they are used so often by advertisers. Can you think of examples where banner advertising might serve a purpose that makes it more attractive than search engine optimization?

Pay-Per-Impression or Pay Per Click?

As mentioned earlier, online media were originally focused on click-throughs. The assumption was that targeted media could deliver browsers to a company website, and the pricing model was based on paying for only those people who clicked on an ad. However, those with an appreciation for the more latent effects of advertising online advocated a pricing model based on the number of impressions, similar to the other forms of media discussed in Chapter 7.

Google AdWords is a good example of showing how **pay-per-click** (PPC) advertising works. Launched in February 2002, Google AdWords is a self-service advertising program that provides a way to advertise and pay only when the advertising "works" in the form of stimulating a browser to click it. Since advertisers are only charged by Google when search users click on ads, it is especially beneficial to small companies and entrepreneurs because they only pay when they have guaranteed visitors on their websites. The concept of AdWords is choosing keywords (search terms or search segments) that relate directly to an advertiser's business and create an ad for users to see. When a user searches on a keyword that an advertiser chose, he or she will see the ad in the "Sponsored Links" section of the search results. If the user is interested in what the ad says, he or she will click on it and visit the company's website. Because of this keyword-driven feature, it is suggested that advertisers pick relevant and high-quality keywords that fit their ads and make it easy to reach potential customers and be more profitable.[13]

Pay-per-impression (PPM) is an alternative pricing model that assumes some residual value is created even when a browser does not click on an ad. Many media that attract more specialized audiences opt for this form of pricing over pay-per-click, because of the benefits associated with such effects as awareness and brand recognition.

Critical Thinking Exercise

Which is a better pricing model—pay-per-click or pay-per-impression? What types of businesses might prefer to pay on a per-click basis and which ones might prefer to pay for impressions? What are the differences between the marketing communications objectives for these businesses?

Rogers could pay for this banner using either impressions or a pay-per-click model.

Mobile Media

Mobile advertising has raised considerable interest as mobile technology has advanced and companies world-wide are starting to use not only text messages, but also multimedia messages in their mobile commercial communication. Although a few years younger than its online counterpart, mobile advertising is growing rapidly.As more phones become Web-enabled, the mobile phone will likely become the primary means of communication for many people. As such, many of the tactics discussed already in this chapter are just as applicable to mobile phones as they are to any computer device. However, because the penetration of Web-enabled phones remains fairly low and marketers can create unique opportunities based on their portable nature, we examine mobile media in this separate section.

Apple formally got into digital advertising with the launch of iAds in 2010. In fact, many brands are already looking at Apple's iPad—as well as other devices with larger display areas—to see what they can do with the increased space.[14]

The two main types of mobile ads today are advertiser-to-user messages and content-embedded ads. Other mobile marketing options include smart phone apps that let advertisers carve out real estate on the mobile device and build ongoing dialogue with the consumer. Message ads are predominantly Short Message Service (SMS), EMS (Enhanced Messaging Service), and MMS (Multimedia Message Service). Each is a form of telemarketing that is more intrusive than embedded ads because messages cannot be ignored—phones flag their arrival with an icon or pop-up, and users must dismiss the notification to return to the phone's prior state.[15]

Content-embedded ads are typically injections, prep-ended clips, or Web-embedded ads. Injections occur when a message passes through an intercepting server that inserts an ad and forwards it to the recipient. Prep-ended clips are short audio-video segments played before a normal clip. Web-embedded ads are online ads viewed on the mobile browser.

The Mobile Marketing Association (MMA) estimated that advertisers spent about $2.16 billion on US mobile marketing in 2010. "Mobile is the most effective direct marketing channel," says Michael Becker, managing director for MMA's North America branch. "There's an immediacy to the message that you get on your mobile device. If a brand is not engaged with mobile consumers today, it's missing key parts of the market."[16] Although the Canadian market is much smaller, penetration of smart phones and similar consumer patterns suggest similar growth in mobile marketing will continue in the Canadian market.

P&G recently ran a campaign for its Herbal Essences hair care products in which consumers could click on a styling preview at home or on their way to a salon. In another example of how digital media are converging and allowing integration, the airline KLM recently ran a campaign known as "KLM Surprise." Passengers who checked in via Foursquare—a mobile application that uses global positioning to pinpoint the exact location of a phone—before their journey, or who tweeted about waiting to board a KLM flight, were randomly surprised with personalized gifts at the airport by an airline representative. The campaign garnered more than one million impressions via social media channels, while creating a deeper level of engagement on the part of its customers.

For marketers, mobile media offer a unique ability to reach out and touch a consumer at almost any location in real time—for example the use of search, display, text messages,, or mobile coupons to drive purchase behaviour at the point of sale. Mobile's ability to capture consumer behaviours also provides a host of rich analytic data to help marketers design effective campaigns. "Mobile allows businesses to interact with individual consumers in real time, and we are just scratching the surface of the possibilities," says Chris Rothey, VP of market development and advertising at NAVTEQ. "Mobile is the holy grail of retail marketing," Rothey says. "In fact, we think that hyperlocal advertising aimed at individual consumers will

BMW used mobile communications to connect with customers and encourage test drives.

actually grow the advertising pie, rather than compete with other channels. That's because consumers view these ad messages as a service, not as an interruption."[17]

Video Game Advertising

The computer and video games industry has become one of the dominant forms of mass-market entertainment, capturing the attention of people of all ages. The latest research by the Entertainment Software Association (ESA) in the US found the average age of gamers to be 30 years old—the largest demographic being those aged between 18 and 49, a group that represents 44 percent of the market. Game consoles like Wii have expanded the market to the point that those aged 50 years and over now make up a surprising 25 percent of the gamer market. According to eMarketer.com, it projects that US in-game advertising spending will surpass $650 million in 2012.[18]

The concept of **in-game advertising** (IGA) is to use computer and video games as a medium in which to deliver advertising. For example, a company's product might be an integral part of the game's virtual environment, such as a logo on the side of a racetrack, a beverage used by the protagonist for energy replenishment, an actual race vehicle, famous sporting personalities, film characters, popular music, or sports commentary. Companies such as IGA Worldwide and Massive Incorporated have recently been established specifically for the purpose of promoting and strengthening the links between advertisers and games developers. More significant, perhaps, is that companies are now employing simple interactive games, particularly those accessible via websites, as a direct source of advertising for their products, essentially making the advertising a game.

Collectively, the types of in-game content described above are commonly referred to by those in the games industry as "licensing," where games developers acquire the rights from famous entities to portray their product or image within the game. Clear examples of where licensing has been used extensively include Sony's Gran Turismo, Sega's Shenmue series, EA's Tiger Woods PGA Tour series, and Activision's Spider-Man. However, despite the obvious presence of advertising and/or product placement within these titles, it is often difficult to distinguish precisely the type and extent of advertising used, especially since the type of advertising is usually dependent on the type of game—for example, sports games usually feature sporting-related logos and banners, while racing games typically contain car-related imagery, such as company logos, tire manufacturers, and race sponsors.

These forms of advertising, in whatever form they may appear, are playing an increasingly important role in the development of interactive games. While some research has shown that passive advertising involving low levels of interaction can be ineffective, other reports suggest the potency of in-game advertising. One study suggests that 30 percent of in-game advertising can be recalled by gamers in the short term, compared with only 20 percent for TV advertising.[19]

Critical Thinking Exercise

Do certain goods or services lend themselves to video game advertising more than others? Because the age range of gamers has widened to include virtually all demographics of society, old stereotypes of gamers have changed. Therefore, products that target younger males might no longer be the only options for this media. What other goods or services would be good candidates? What ads have you noticed in video games and why do you think they have/have not been effective?

- ◆ Company websites
- ◆ Online social networks
- ◆ Blogs
- ◆ Viral marketing
- ◆ Virtual worlds

FIGURE 11.3
Digital Content Forms

DIGITAL CONTENT

Taking digital marketing one step further, many marketers have moved beyond merely advertising to the creation of digital content as a key pillar of their online presence. Essentially, digital content refers to the creation of material that in itself provides value for the target audience. The most obvious of these are the websites of companies themselves. But delivery of content has expanded into many other areas, including participation in social network sites, in addition to advertising on those sites, blogs, and discussion forums, and participation in online virtual worlds such as Second Life. Each of these is discussed next, and outlined in Figure 11.3.

Company Websites

Almost all businesses and organizations of any kind have websites as a key part of their communications with all types of stakeholders. Successful marketers have figured out ways to make their websites destinations that consumers actively want to explore and return to again and again. This means moving beyond a website that is merely an online catalogue or repository of information to one that actively engages stakeholders and provides value in exchange for screen time.

An excellent example of a website strategy that is integrated with other elements of the marketing communications mix—including social networks such as those described later in this chapter—comes from Starbucks. The brand launched **MyStarbucksIdea .com** as a forum for customers to make suggestions, ask questions, and even vent their frustrations. With hundred of thousands of registered users, the brand has received tens of thousands of suggestions, many of which have actually be implemented in stores.[20]

Understanding how customers and other stakeholders use the information available on websites is critical to help create more effective communications. In general, this analysis is referred to as **web analytics**, which is the process of analyzing where someone went to on a brand's website, what they did within the website, and what other sites they visited. If an individual spent 10 minutes examining merchandise within a particular section of the website, then that person is an excellent target for an email about the products he or she examined. If an individual visited several websites to look at similar merchandise, then that person is likely in the latter stages of the purchase process and is close to making the purchase decision or actual purchase.

Software such as the Relationship Optimizer and Prime Response by NCR uses powerful data analysis techniques to personalize marketing messages. The NCR software analyzes customer interactions such as click-stream data traffic—any type of customer interaction with the firm—and combines it with demographic information from external or internal databases. As the data are being processed, the software can launch complex interactive and personalized marketing materials.

Recent research indicates that about 40 percent of online shoppers abandon the shopping cart just prior to the checkout. Only about 30 percent of these shoppers ever return to complete the transaction. The IT department can identify those individuals who have abandoned a shopping basket. An email

Although not a business, the federal government has good reason to encourage Canadians to return to its website, and regularly updates content to encourage repeat visits.

Source: *Government of Canada Web site Banner*, [http://www.canada.gc.ca/home.html], Human Resources and Skills Development Canada, Service Canada Initiative, 2011. Reproduced with the permission of the Minister of Public Works and Government Services Canada, 2012.

sent to these individuals offering free shipping or a discount if they complete the order, or with a simple reminder that they have items in their shopping basket can lead to greater sales. Converting these individuals to customers is much easier and more lucrative than sending mass emails or other forms of advertising.[21]

Website Design Issues

The primary website design issues are to make sure that the site functions properly and that it can serve as a springboard for interactive marketing programs. E-commerce companies spend an average of $100 to acquire each new customer, and some companies spend up to $500.[22] It may appear that developing an effective website is cheap; however, it is not. Figure 11.4 offers some tips on how to create winning websites.

The high usage of search engines to locate products, brands, and companies has led to changes in the ways websites are designed. A search engine often will direct an individual straight to the page with the product on it. The front page will be skipped entirely. Therefore, it is important to design each page of the website as if it were the front page and the consumer is coming through on that page. Menus should be available to allow the site visitor to easily access other parts of the site. Brand awareness and marketing messages must be reinforced at every level.

Levi Strauss employs Blue Martini E-Merchandising software to customize both the **Levis.com** and the **Dockers.com** websites. The Home Shopping Network uses Edify's Smart Options software to track user preferences and suggest products based on the customer's past activities and current purchases. These technologies blur the line between selling and marketing, because the messages and products a customer sees are based on past purchasing and browsing activities. These programs are designed to increase the odds that the customer will discover something he or she wants rather than being forced to wade through scores of products he or she has no interest in purchasing at a more standardized website.[23]

Critical Thinking Exercise

Go to the websites of five different Canadian marketing communications agencies. You can find a listing at the Institute of Communications Agencies (www.icacanada.ca). How well do their websites follow the principles listed in Figure 11.4? What key stakeholders do you think the websites are trying to serve? Which ones do you think are most effective and why?

FIGURE 11.4
Tips for Creating Effective Websites

- The Web site should follow a strategic purpose such as to acquire new customers, serve existing customers, or to cross-sell goods and services.
- Make the Web site easy to access and quick to load.
- Written content should be precise with short words, short sentences, and short paragraphs.
- Remember that content is the key to success, not fancy graphics and design.
- Be certain graphics support content, and do not detract from it.
- Make some type of marketing offer to encourage a response.
- Ask for site evaluation.
- Provide easy-to-use navigation links on every page.
- Use gimmicks such as moving icons or flashing banners to gain attention at the beginning but do not use them deeper in the Web site.
- Change the Web site on a regular basis to keep individuals coming back.
- Measure results continually, especially designs and offers.

Source: Based on Ray Jutkins, "13 Ideas That Could Lead to Successful Web Marketing," *Advertising Age's Business Marketing* 84, no. 6 (June 1999), p. 27.

Consumer-Generated Reviews

One feature of many websites is the inclusion of consumer-generated reviews of the company's products. **Amazon.ca** is at the forefront of consumer-generated reviews. Each book offered online holds a space where individual customers can write reviews, both with words and with a one- to five-star rating. The site informs the shopper of the number of reviews and the average star rating, and notes if the reviews are written by anonymous critics or those who provide their real names. A person wishing to place his or her name on a review must authenticate it by presenting Amazon with a credit card number. The benefit to customers is that they can read the reviews before making purchases. Obviously the system is not perfect, because an author may use a pseudonym to write a highly favourable review and encourage friends and family members to do the same. At the same time, the author cannot control any outside review that is posted.

Electronics retailers like Best Buy are also incorporating consumer feedback into online retailing. They offer a blog section for consumers to read about and discuss various topics. For each product category, such as cameras, they provide a discussion forum on a variety of topics that relate to that product. In the digital camera discussion forum, consumers can post photos they have taken with various cameras. Customer reviews of each product are provided. Some are positive, some are negative. These reviews have considerable influence on which brands consumers consider and eventually purchase. By providing blogs, discussion forums, and consumer reviews, the marketer's goal is to offer consumers a variety of ways to search for and evaluate products and to make final purchase decisions without ever leaving the company's website.[24]

Online reviews let people research products, even if they eventually buy in a retail store.

Consumer-generated reviews and discussions can be important vehicles for reaching early adopters of products. They provide a forum that allows for the dissemination of information among consumers.[25]

There are several key implications of customer-generated reviews. First, too many negative reviews and low star ratings will be harmful to the company. The marketing team should carefully monitor them to see what is being said about the company. Second, reviews stress the importance of consistent, high-quality customer products and services. Third, reviews provide important information on how a company's product is being evaluated by customers and how the brand compares with competing brands. This information is critical in developing marketing plans, product modifications, and service strategies.

Clearly, the use of consumer-generated reviews is on the rise. The challenge for marketing departments is to manage this aspect of consumer word-of-mouth endorsement in a way that will enhance brand equity and increase sales.

Consumer-Generated Products

Taking consumer involvement one step further, many brands have engaged consumers to help them craft actual products. The basis for these efforts is often a dedicated **microsite**, a site that is attached to the main website of the brand but dedicated to a specific activity or promotion. One example of this type of effort is Doritos' invitation to allow consumers to name new flavours of its products. Although this type of activity is similar to some of the contests mentioned in Chapter 9, it is typically much more engaging for the consumer and of course allows consumers to feel much more "ownership" over the brand than does any other form of promotion.

One brand has taken customer involvement and "ownership" to a whole new level is Mountain Dew. Initially launched as the "Dewmocracy" campaign, the company shifted virtually all of its marketing communications dollars to digital marketing. A cornerstone of the campaign was involving customers in the selection of three new flavours of the brand, but in an effort to push the boundary of online engagement, the brand even allowed customers to select its marketing communications agency. Director of Marketing Brett O'Brien explained, "It became clear that the consumer had built these products and had a clear idea of the products. The consumers challenged us to say who is going to do our advertising, and how do we get some new thinking?"[26]

Online Social Networks

Although websites are typically a key pillar of any brand's online presence, they require that a person know about them. One way of promoting a site is through banner ads and search engines, as mentioned earlier. But many marketers now take content—such as videos—that would traditionally have been housed on a website and "push" it out to consumers. Online social networks have become extremely popular with people and with companies seeking to communicate with consumers by reaching out to them. The most well-known social networking sites are Facebook and MySpace. But there is a social network for just about every possible theme that can be imagined. **Yub.com** is for shopaholics; **Fuzzstar** is for pet lovers; **YogaMates** is for people who like yoga; **ONLoq.com** is for hip-hop fans; and **PassportStamp.com** is for avid travellers. Membership can vary widely, from a few hundred to millions.[26] These smaller sites provide companies the opportunity to zero in on an audience that provides an optimal match with what is being offered.

In social networks, marketers have two ways to attract an audience: joining groups that consist of like-minded audiences in Facebook and other such networking sites, and/or creating their own groups and community and sending invitations to potential members. Once a connection is made, the next stage is to establish expertise and relationship with audiences. The difference between communications in social media and advertising is that the content is usually not effective if it is overtly sales-oriented. Participation in online groups assumes a more subdued approach, where the company acts as an equal member of a community engaged in dialogue, versus a community leader engaged in a one-way monologue.

The term *social network* has come to encompass virtually any online forum where people can share ideas and communicate with each other. The challenge is that this defines a broad range of sites and services available to consumers and other stakeholders. Figure 11.5 and the remainder of this section examine some of the more popular outlets and examples of how companies are making effective use of them.

Mountain Dew literally turned over its brand to its customers, and even let them choose their marketing communications agency.

Facebook	Jacob uses Facebook to do everything from running traditional contests to allowing users to customize their own Facebook photos in Jacob style.
LinkedIn	Price Waterhouse Coopers created a career explorer tool on LinkedIn that allows college students to find jobs that suit them.
Twitter	The dating service Lavalife tweets as part of peak period promotions such as Valentine's Day.
YouTube	Bank of Montreal creates content that allows viewers to learn more about economic forecasts and plan their investments.
Flickr	The Canadian Tourism Commission used Flickr to help users discover new vacation spots in Canada.

FIGURE 11.5
Online Social Networks

Facebook

The primary appeal of Facebook is its size. The site now boasts a membership that is third in size to the populations of China and India. In addition to using the site as a media outlet, many successful marketers have developed a presence on the site. The CEO of Facebook in Canada states that the site has been able to "change the paradigm around what an ad actually is."[27] By engaging customers in a conversation and providing value in return for customers connecting with the brand, companies use Facebook to cost-effectively reach audiences in a way that is typically much more involved and meaningful than is possible through advertising alone.

Montreal-based retailer Jacob uses Facebook as part of its marketing communications, with great success. In fact, apart from in-store advertising, all of its marketing communications budget has been allocated to Facebook.[28] Successful campaigns include a "give your clothes a new lease on life" charity appeal, and a contest that requires contestants to "like" the Jacob page and choose one of six "I am Jacob" words to add to their profile photos. Those photos then get converted to black and white to look like one of the Jacob ads.

In an example of how social networks like Facebook are used in conjunction with other digital media, such as mobile phones, as well as more traditional media, such as print and in-store displays, the retailer Dynamite used QR codes in a recent campaign. The codes, which resemble barcodes, appeared in print material and can be scanned by smart phones. The scan then links the consumer to a behind-the-scenes video of the photo shoot for the posters and the company's Facebook page.[29]

The cost effectiveness of Facebook also has appeal for governments who seek to communicate with stakeholders. A study by the Human Capital Institute detailed the use of social networking within various levels of government and found that 66 percent of all government agencies currently use some form of social networking—from blogs and wikis to instant messaging and discussion boards. Even the CIA has used Facebook to invite students to apply to work at the agency.[30]

LinkedIn

LinkedIn is a business-oriented social networking website. Some describe it as the professional version of Facebook. Its objective is to enable its users to reconnect with past and present colleagues and classmates. It also allows users to discover common connections when they are seeking a job or other business contacts. The

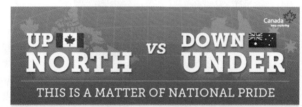

The Canadian Tourism Commission developed an online contest using Facebook, the "Up North vs. Down Under Challenge," and encouraged users to vote on their favorite national icons.

Marketers are using print media as the start of a conversation which continues via QR codes.

The dating site Lavalife tweeted to customers during peak periods like Valentine's Day.

benefits of LinkedIn are the same as those of Facebook, but the way marketers have used the site has been less overtly commercial for traditional marketing purposes. For example, Price Waterhouse Coopers sponsored a new tool on LinkedIn called Career Explorer. College students at 60 campuses chosen by the company were prompted to enter some basic information about themselves and their career aspirations when logging on to the site. They were then shown a list of jobs relevant to their answers.

Twitter

Twitter allows people to follow anyone who cares to share his or her life online. In the user's home page, there is a column that lists all pages that user follows, and connections can check out each other's connections and share common interests. Although less popular than Facebook, Twitter has become almost ubiquitous in marketing communications. Twitter is a hotbed of discussion about many well-known brands because it is used to communicate consumers' thoughts easily and as they occur. In a sense, the site is merely capturing the word-of-mouth that has always been present among consumers and documenting it for others (including the marketers themselves) to see.[31]

Rather than a standalone medium, most marketers use Twitter as part of an overall campaign to take advantage of the opportunity to communicate directly with consumers. For example, the dating site Lavalife uses Twitter as part of ongoing campaigns, including the peak periods around Valentine's Day.[32]

YouTube

Driven by the advent of near-ubiquitous broadband Internet access, online delivery of video content has surged to an unprecedented level. Online Publisher Association reports that 80 percent of users have watched a video ad online and 52 percent of them have taken some sort of action (e.g., visiting the related website). *E-Marketer* reported that the spending on Web video advertising was $511 million in 2009 and reached almost $600 million in 2010.[33]

The clear leader in video content is YouTube. Anyone can post videos to the site, and users can share and comment on the videos with friends. Some firms, such as the Bank of Montreal, have launched their own "channels" within YouTube that allow consumers to follow the company online. The channel was launched as a destination for those seeking commentary on economic issues, and features a series of three-minute videos covering relevant news and trends. "We see new media as an area that can provide us with potential new access to our customer and potential customers," said Peter Scott, a spokesperson for the bank. The channel also performs a PR function through the posting of videos, such as one featuring bank employees at a United Way charity event.[34]

A video created by UVic students to showcase their university went viral, with hundreds of thousands of views in only months.

Another excellent example of how video content allows marketers to try innovative and ground-breaking ideas comes from a recent campaign for Stayfree feminine hygiene products of Johnson and Johnson (J&J). The campaign used men, for perhaps the first time ever, in messages for the category. The campaign included three videos that were distributed via YouTube and other social networks. The videos offered "virtual dates" with three men—Trevor, Brad, and Ryan. In the videos, each a few minutes long, the men talk to the viewer about the differences between Stayfree pads versus the competitors' pads. But because the message is embedded in a

UVicLipDub 1 video Subscribe

7:53 / 9:53   360p

virtual date, the entire video is entertaining and provides value to the viewer who spends time to watch it. As evidence of this, the campaign was a viral hit, with viewers passing the link on the friends.

Flickr
Another popular video and photo content site, similar to YouTube, is Flickr. And just like YouTube, Canadian marketers have tuned into the possibilities of using this online interaction platform. A recent campaign by the Canadian Tourism Commission used Flickr to help Canadians discover new and interesting vacation spots in Canada. Flickr members were invited to share their favourite photos and videos of Canada as part of the CTC's "Locals Know" campaign. Users were able to post and browse through a large selection of favourite travel spots across Canada and get inspired to visit different areas of the country.

LOCALS KNOW.ca
Get great Canadian travel deals.

explorez sans fin
Canada
keep exploring

Users were able to browse through a large selection of favourite travel spots across Canada and get inspired to visit different areas of the country.

Consumer-Generated Advertising
Most of the commercials, videos, and marketing information placed on social network sites have been generated by the company or a professional advertising agency. Now a new method is being used to develop marketing messages. For the 2007 Super Bowl, Doritos featured a commercial that was the result of an ad-making contest for consumers. Converse, Firefox, and Diet Coke have also used materials generated by consumers. Encouraging consumers to create advertisements is a creative version of interactive marketing. The idea is that the viewers of the ad tend to accept a consumer-generated advertisement as being more genuine than a company-produced commercial. Some marketing and advertising experts believe that the future of advertising is in user-generated content rather than agency-produced ads.

To illustrate the power of consumer-generated advertising, consider Nick Haley, an 18-year-old student. Haley is an Apple computer loyalist who received his first Macintosh at the age of three. A few years ago, he was inspired to make a commercial about the Apple iPod Touch upon hearing the song "Music Is My Hot, Hot Sex" and a lyric in the song that said "My music is where I'd like to touch." Using the song as a background, Haley created a fast-paced tour of the abilities of the iPod Touch. He uploaded the video to YouTube. He received four stars out of a possible five and comments such as "That's awesome" and "Makes me want to buy one." Among the viewers of the commercial was an employee at Apple, who asked staff to contact the company's advertising agency TBWA/Chiat/Day. The agency liked the commercial, contacted Haley, and invited him to their office to make a high-definition version of his commercial.[35]

Nick Haley's story is beginning to be repeated as companies and advertising agencies realize the power of consumer-generated advertising. In the words of Haley, "That's the whole point of advertising; it needs to get to the user. If you get the user to make ads, who better?" According to Lee Clow, chairman and chief creative at TBWA Worldwide, consumer-generated ads are part of the new world in which we live: "It's an exciting new format for brands to communicate with their audiences. People's relationship with a brand is becoming a dialog, not a monologue."[36]

Developing a Social Network Presence
The initial steps most marketers take in developing a social network presence for a company are starting a profile page and then accepting "friend requests" from people logging on to the network. Other companies have specific product pages. Coca-Cola, for example, has a page for Sprite, called "Sprite Sips," where people can play with an animated character. Facebook and other social networks treat these brand pages just like other pages; the company can add photos, videos, reviews, and comments, just like individual users.[37]

Nike regularly posts new commercials on YouTube and other sites through either the company's own brand page or a profile page. In addition to commercials, Nike posts videos that typically are generated behind the scenes. These postings provide Nike with additional exposure and allow Nike's marketing department to monitor feedback and get a feel for what the public thinks. The feedback is immediate. The marketing department quickly knows what connects with consumers and what does not. If viewers like the video, it will often generate word-of-mouth buzz. Visitors to the site tell their friends about the video or send them the link. Nike is at the forefront in featuring this type of interactive marketing, and the company's commercials and videos normally generate a huge demand.

Critical Thinking Exercise

It has been argued that using social networks successfully involves going beyond simply "pushing out" messages to users and moving toward more meaningful social engagement. But what does this mean in context? What brands have you encountered on social networks? Which ones have done a good job and which ones have failed? Why have the successful ones been able to gain your attention, friend status, or whatever?

Blogs

Similar to discussions taking place on social media, blogs are now being hosted by some marketers. And certainly many consumers host their own blogs and discuss brands as part of the log content. **Blogs** have been created on a wide range of topics. Some blogs permit visitors to post comments; others are just the ramblings of an individual. What makes blogs powerful is that one consumer dissatisfied with a particular brand can now tell thousands, and in some cases millions, of others. Previously, a bad shopping experience meant that 12 to 15 people would be told about it. Now, however, an individual's complaint can be sent to more than just friends and family. A discontented consumer can speak to anyone who is willing to listen (read) via the Internet.

Reactions to Negative Comments

How should the marketing team react to negative blogs? Some companies hire people to search the Internet for blogs about a company's products. The next issue is what to do when a negative blog is located. Some believe the best approach is to join in the discussion. When they do, some will identify themselves as working for the company. Others try to remain anonymous and try to point out the good things about the brand.

Company-Sponsored Blogging

Some marketing managers have tried to turn the situation around by looking for ways to use blogs to promote products. They try to find methods of blogging that spread positive word-of-mouth communications about the company's brand, including setting up company-sponsored blogs. The goal is to realize the potential marketing power of blogs and how they emulate word-of-mouth communication.

Retailer Lululemon regularly updates customers with yoga and lifestyle-related news through its blog (**http://www.lululemon.com/community/blog/**). The blog encourages customers to visit the site often

Lululemon includes a wide variety of lifestyle-related information on its blog, including information that mixes bicycle safety with fashion.

Source: Source: © Brand X/Thinkstock.

for postings on new styles, yoga tips, and other relevant information. In the past retailers such as Lululemon would have relied on magazines or other media to disseminate this type of information. Now they can connect with customers quicker, and more importantly, interactively. This allows the marketing team to develop a two-way channel of communication with customers.

Do company-sponsored blogs work? Research conducted by ComScore Networks revealed that shoppers who visit blogs spend more than the average shopper. In addition to spending more money, the ComScore study indicated, the average visitor to a blog spends nearly 23 hours per week online, compared with 13 hours per week for the average Internet user.[38]

A company-sponsored blog can provide a number of benefits. It may ease shopper fears about purchasing from a particular company, especially an unknown e-retailer or less well-known brand. The postings and responses from customers give individuals reading the blog a glimpse of how the company deals with customers and the relative level of customer satisfaction of those who have purchased products. A blog can provide the company with an avenue to release information about its products. It also can provide an avenue for customers to voice their opinions. The biggest advantage is that all of this remains under the control of the company.

The company's marketing team must be extremely careful to be honest with the blog and not censor everything that is negative. If it does, consumers will quickly see it as a sham. When a negative comment appears, the marketing department has the opportunity to respond. This provides an avenue for other customers to join in on the discussion, pro and con. Such a dialogue can be very rewarding for a company if it is conducted in an honest and open way. It also provides valuable insights into how customers view the company, its brands, and its products.

Viral Marketing

Technology has created another possibility for digital marketing—**viral marketing**. Viral marketing is preparing a marketing message that in some way is passed from one consumer to another. A viral campaign can take the form of an email or it can be a video that is posted to a personal blog and passed through to other blogs or site visitors. It is a form of advocacy or word-of-mouth endorsement marketing. Viral marketing takes place as one customer passes along a message to other potential buyers. The term "viral" is derived from the image of a person being infected with the marketing message and then spreading it to friends, like a virus. The major difference, however, is that the customer voluntarily sends the message to others.

Viral marketing messages may include advertisements, hyperlinked promotions, online newsletters, streaming videos, and various games. For instance, Blue Marble created a viral marketing program for Scope mouthwash. Consumers were able to send a customized, animated email "kiss" to their friends. The attached marketing message reinforced the brand message that Scope brings people "kissably close." People who received the email kiss could then forward the message to someone else. Scope's tracking technology indicated that most people who received an email kiss forwarded the message. Mazda created a viral marketing campaign that included a video clip attachment about parking

The digital agency Noise uses a blog to communicate with various stakeholders, including clients and potential employees.

Canada Post took viral campaigns to a whole new level with its Holiday Sweater Re-Gift campaign.

cars—a Mazda, of course—and the differences between males and females. The clip and link were passed on to thousands and sparked an international debate on blogs and in other forums about male and female parking capabilities. Globally, the viral marketing campaign generated over a million views in less than a month.[39]

The viral message must *focus on the product or business* so it is not lost. Mazda's campaign focused on parking cars; Scope's campaign focused on the importance of good breath for a kiss. The marketing team must determine *why an individual would want to pass the message along* or tell friends about it. Canada Post created an online campaign to encourage consumers to re-gift—perhaps the ultimate in viral marketing.

Individuals must have an *incentive* to pass the message along. One incentive is to create a message with entertainment value. Or, the incentive can be financial, such as free merchandise or a discount if the message is passed along to friends who make a purchase, log on to a website, or register for an e-newsletter. The incentive could also just be the campaign's uniqueness. A message that can be *personalized* has a great chance of being sent on.

With the many forms of interactive marketing available to companies, some believe viral marketing campaigns have lost some of their lustre. Consumers may also have lost their enthusiasm and are less willing to pass along messages. It is important, therefore, to track the results of a viral campaign and to analyze the resulting data to determine what works and what does not.[40]

Virtual Worlds

Online virtual worlds have become heralded as a technology of substantial future importance for marketers. A **virtual world** is defined as a three-dimensional, computer-generated environment that appears similar to our "real" world, often with a massive number of users all connected to the Internet, and developed to supply online entertainment and social networking for users. The best-known virtual world is Second Life, which now boasts over 130 million users. In total, users around the world have spent more than one billion hours in Second Life. Second Life residents spend an average of about 100 minutes in-world per visit. The equivalent of more than $1 billion has been transacted between Residents in Second Life, who purchase virtual goods and services from one another. Virtual worlds provide extraordinary flexibility and potential for brand building. Tools for promotion include, for example, product placement of 3-D objects (similar to product brands, like beverages, as seen in films), real-world analogs (such as billboards and radio), advergames (mini-games or mini-worlds, with some element of advertising), and cross-promotion.[41]

The significance of brands in virtual worlds, such as Second Life, is already apparent. This virtual world creates more than 250,000 new virtual goods every day, including those in such sectors as auto (e.g., Mercedes, Mazda, and Pontiac), media (e.g., AOL, Reuters, and Sony BMG), travel (e.g., STA Travel), consumer electronics (e.g., Intel, Dell, Nokia, and Sony Ericsson), consumer goods (e.g., Reebok and American Apparel), telecommunications (e.g., TELUS), finance (e.g., ABN Amro and ING), and professional services (e.g., IBM).

Figure 11.6 demonstrates an instance of marketing and brands in Second Life. This form of advertisement helps to build brand awareness and enables users to experience facets of the virtual or real-life product in 3-D. In these examples, the polygonal representations of a real-life car can be examined and even driven (albeit in a limited, computer-controlled fashion), and a mobile phone can be examined and carried on the

avatar. Second Life can also utlilize multimedia to help to promote digital content and products. Typically, such products are in the media
industry, including music, movies, television,
and so on. For example, an album can be promoted and purchased at the same location.

STRENGTHS AND WEAKNESSES OF DIGITAL MEDIA

As with other marketing communications tools,
the wide variety of forms of digital marketing make universal statements about strengths
and weaknesses challenging. Still, a number of
observations can be made.

Source: Reprint Courtesy of International Business Machines Corporation. © International Business Machines Corporation.

FIGURE 11.6
Example of Second Life Marketing
Communication

Strengths of Digital Marketing

Targetability. As mentioned in the introduction, even the advertising media that is executed online shares as much with direct marketing as it does with media. Banner ads can
be highly targeted, based on profiles of web browsers. Search engines offer perhaps the
ultimate in targetability, given that users actively identify their interests, and marketers
can respond directly to those interests through search optimization. Other digital marketing tactics, such as social networks and mobile media, are similarly highly targeted and
customizable to individuals.

Format Flexibility. Unlike other marketing communications tools, such as advertising which is, for the most part, boxed into formats such as the linear 30-second television
advertisement, digital marketing offers virtually unlimited formats, allowing for a high
degree of creativity. The example mentioned earlier of the advertisement coming in the
form of a video game is perhaps the most extreme case of flexibility.

Involvement. A video game or mobile phone app as a form of advertising not only
provides flexibility, it creates an environment where the audience is likely to be more
highly involved with the message than is the case with other marketing communications tools. Consumers who venture to a content-rich website are likely to be much more
highly involved and attuned to a marketing message than consumers who are listening to
the radio in their car, for example. This means that some digital media, such as websites,
can be used to deliver highly complex information or support high-involvement product
marketing.

Relatively Low Cost. Of course not all digital media are low cost. But a number
of digital options available to marketers are extremely low cost. A Facebook page (as
opposed to ads), for example, can be maintained by employees and integrated into existing functions such as PR. The posting of news or other information online can be easily
incorporated into existing routines and done at very little cost. Even search engines such
as Google essentially democratize the search by allowing advertisers to bid for optimization (essentially naming their price), and only paying for clicks or other purchase-related
behaviours.

Weaknesses of Digital Marketing

Limited Reach. Although it may be surprising to some students, digital media are not
as widespread as other media, such as traditional television or newspapers. They are
certainly growing, but while televisions are found in over 95 percent of Canadian

households, Internet penetration is closer to 80 percent. Of those households that do have an Internet connection, many are still on older services and therefore not able to be reached effectively with services such as YouTube. Similarly, mobile phone penetration rates hover around 80 percent, with less than 50 percent of cell phone users carrying smart phones that enable sophisticated mobile marketing or even mobile Web browsing.[42]

Clutter. With so many benefits for marketing communications, digital marketing is becoming crowded. As with any form of marketing communications, the less novel the marketing message, the less likely it will be noticed among so many others. Webpages are often filled with banner ads and often come with pop-ups, the number of phone apps continues to skyrocket, and as brands flock to sites like Facebook and Twitter, marketers will need to work even harder to create value for audiences and stay relevant.

COMMUNICATING ACROSS CULTURES

One of the major advantages digital marketing has over other marketing communications tools is the ability to reach consumers and other stakeholders virtually anywhere in the world. Although some media allow geographic targeting based on IP, others, such as company websites and YouTube, are open to virtually the entire planet. This makes cultural issues particularly salient for marketers. Many obstacles to communicating digitally exist.

One particular problem exists with websites that are intended to span cultural boundaries. Although some companies use local websites to serve local markets (e.g., **Amazon .com** versus **Amazon.ca**), not all marketers can afford to customize local sites to each culture. Further, within Canada it is not possible to accommodate the cultural differences between regions with a national website. Issues include adding information that someone in another region or country would need, such as the country code for telephone numbers. It also requires removing or changing any colours, words, or images that might be offensive to a particular group of people in another culture.

New globalization software has been developed for companies expanding into other countries. One software package translates an English-language website into a large number of foreign languages. Another valuable feature that the software offers is "cultural adaptation," which adjusts a website's terminology, look, and feel to suit local norms. The software also has a feature in which the content that is developed in one location can easily be deployed to all sites around the world. This provides a more consistent look to the websites, without someone spending time modifying every foreign site. Such software makes it easier to create a website prepared in the appropriate native language that also conforms to local customs.[43]

Moving beyond websites, the same cultural concerns present for other marketing communications tools exist with digital marketing. For example, a coherent IMC plan that matches digital media with other marketing communications still provides benefits to the brand through consistency and repetition of visual and verbal cues and messages. Consistency of some elements simply might not be possible across different regions. Bandwidth, for instance, is highly inconsistent not only across nations but also across regions within Canada. For global brands such as IBM, this means using local companies in each country to design individual websites and providing the information used on each site. To ensure consistency, IBM designs the main marketing messages at its central office, but then local companies translate the messages and add reseller contact and pricing information.

"Online communications are continually growing as part of our overall marketing communications toolkit," says Kate Baillie. "We took our time getting into social media. Although we have recently made a concerted effort to grow our capabilities in this area, early on we sat and watched to see which media were for real and which were not worth investing in."

Waiting has paid off for TELUS. "Having the luxury of sufficient resources to run large-scale mass campaigns, we didn't necessarily need the benefits that online programs provide, and now that we see how this media has evolved, we can do a better job of integrating it into our overall plan. So we don't have a 'digital marketing strategy' any more than we have a 'billboard strategy' or a 'direct mail strategy.' Obviously we try to be strategic about how we use this media, as we do any of our communications tools, but we see it as just one part of our overall marketing communications, not as a standalone component. It's not a silver bullet, just as no other media or promotional tool is.

"A lot of companies made mistakes using online media early on, and not really understanding how to use it effectively as part of a campaign. So when Twitter was adopted by many businesses, they just started bombarding people with messages because it's easy and virtually free. Companies then started to realize that if they are going to communicate with someone, it should always add value for the audience. Everyone wants their communication to 'go viral.' But how do we ensure that? There is no way to guarantee that your creative execution, contest, or promo will go viral. So we need to make sure that instead of looking for that one home run, this media is working hard for us on a day-to-day basis just like every other part of our marketing communications plan."

Lara Johnson, Director of Marketing Communications, also explains how TELUS is using digital media. "We recently ran a contest on Facebook where we placed a hippo in a secret spot somewhere in Canada. People were invited to guess where it was. We had more traditional banner ads online driving people to the contest, and had amazing results in both page hits and contest entries. Of course, the contest also played into our core campaign message which is that it doesn't matter where you are in Canada, you'll get great coverage with TELUS' 4G high-speed network."

Online communications are integrated into the overall IMC plan for TELUS.

Lara also sees great potential to engage in the dialogue taking place online. "We know people are talking about us all the time, in various chat rooms and forums. The big ones for us are Facebook, Twitter, and YouTube. So we now monitor what's going on in those media and proactively engage with people online to address their questions or concerns. It's a great way to augment what we are already doing in our customer service function."

Source: Used with permission of Kate Baillie, TELUS Communications.

For help developing your IMC Plan, go to **www.pearsoncanada.ca/clow**.

SUMMARY

Media is converging within a broad digital platform. The proliferation of technology into virtually all corners of our lives means that digital marketing is central to the future of marketing communications. For example, the SNYC feature on Ford cars allows for drivers to access the Web for everything from driving directions to Facebook updates. Digital media has even made our cars an opportunity for dialogue between marketers and customers.

Digital media, broadly speaking, can be characterized as either display or space advertising, or as digital content. The former is roughly similar to other marketing communications tool, such as advertising media, where messages are pushed out to consumers through various forms. Although technology has advanced to the point that these messages can be quite sophisticated and targeted, they still require a consumer to respond in the same way traditional marketing communications always have.

The second form—digital content—is where digital marketing most diverges from other marketing communications tools. The use of the Internet to move beyond pushing messages towards collaboration and dialogue with stakeholders is the most striking difference. There are many examples discussed in this chapter where social networks allow brands to intertwine themselves with people's lives.

The Internet in particular, has essentially democratized marketing communications. Even the smallest budget can accommodate participation in media such as Facebook and Twitter. Customer engagement like that demonstrated by the Mountain Dew example in this chapter is possible for any brand. This is in sharp contrast to some other forms of marketing communications, such as television advertising, which is out of reach for many budgets. The possibilities for messages and content produced at virtually zero cost through media such as YouTube mean that good marketing communications ideas can reach literally millions of people overnight. This reason, along with targetability and the ability to create involvement and dialogue with stakeholders, means that digital marketing—in whatever form the future holds—will continue to move toward the centre of many IMC plans.

KEY TERMS

blogs Online musings by an individual or group; the term is derived from *Web logs*.

impressions The number of times a unique webpage is viewed by someone

in-game advertising The use of a video game environment to deliver advertising messages.

Internet protocol (IP) A unique address consisting of a series of numbers that identifies a device connected to the Internet.

microsite A website that is dedicated to one marketing purpose, separate but linked to a company's website.

pay-per-click A media pricing model that charges advertisers only when a user clicks on an ad.

pay-per-impression A media pricing model that charges advertisers every time an ad is viewed by a user.

search engine optimization (SEO) The process of increasing the probability of a particular company's website emerging from a search.

viral marketing An advertisement that is tied to an email or other form of online communication in which one person passes on the advertisement or email to other consumers.

virtual world A three-dimensional, computer-generated environment that appears similar to our real world.

Web analytics The process of analyzing where someone goes on a website, where they came from, and where they go when they leave.

REVIEW QUESTIONS

1. Define digital marketing.
2. How does an Internet protocol address allow a marketer to identify an audience?
3. What are the four categories of display/space digital advertising described in this chapter?
4. How is banner advertising similar to the media described in Chapter 7? How is it different?
5. What is meant by the term search engine optimization (SEO)? How can it be accomplished?
6. What are the two forms of pricing for advertising online?
7. What are the three forms that mobile media messages can take?
8. How is digital content different than display/space advertising?
9. How can Web analytics be used to measure the success of both display/space advertising and website design?
10. How are consumer reviews, products, and advertising similar? How are they different?
11. What are the five popular social network sites described in this chapter and why do they represent an opportunity for marketing communications?
12. What is a blog? How can blogs be used in marketing communications programs?
13. What is viral marketing? What is the goal of a viral marketing program?
14. What is a virtual world? How can marketers integrate them into both their marketing and their marketing communications plans?

INTEGRATED LEARNING EXERCISES

1. Access each of the following search engines. For each one, discuss how it handles paid search advertising when you type in a search, such as "running shoes." What ads do you see as display ads and what ads are part of the search results? Discuss the differences among the four search engines. Which one do you like the best? Why?

   a. Google (**www.google.ca**)

   b. Yahoo (**www.yahoo.ca**)

   c. Bing (**www.bing.com**)

2. Websites serve a number of different functions. Some are driven primarily by e-commerce, while others are meant to provide an engaging experience with a brand that can't be purchased online (e.g., soft drinks). Access the following sites. What is the primary function of each? For each site, list other functions it offers.

   a. Travelocity (**www.travelocity.ca**)

   b. RBC (**www.rbc.ca**)

   c. Lululemon (**www.lululemon.com**)

   d. Tim Hortons (**www.timhortons.ca**)

3. Blogs provide opportunities for both individuals and businesses to share information, thoughts, and opinions. Go to Google Blog Search at **http://blogsearch.google.com**. Type in a topic that you are interested in exploring that is related to advertising and marketing communications, such as "advertising to children." Locate three blogs on the topic you chose. Discuss who initiated the blog and the value of the information on the blog.

4. Search your inbox. Find the last 10 times someone sent you something "viral" that was sponsored by a marketer (i.e., not a video of someone being hit by accident with a baseball bat)? Make a list of each of these items, whether or not you viewed the item, your reaction, and whether or not you forwarded it on to someone else. What is the difference between the ones that are "more viral" than others? What motivations do you have when you forward things to other people? What could the marketers behind each of the 10 items on your list have done better to help ensure their campaigns are successful virally?

STUDENT PROJECT

Creative Corner

Some print-based ads presented in this chapter used QR codes to integrate with other marketing communications tools. Specifically, the use of the QR code makes the integration with print-based media much more than just a similar look and feel, logo, etc. It actually creates a link between the print and digital media that allows the marketer to engage the consumer in a meaningful way that is not possible with traditional posters, prints, billboards, or other forms of print media.

Assume you are the person in charge of marketing your school. You have decided that QR codes are a great way to integrate the traditional print material you have with some of your digital content. Outline a campaign that will include at least one of the traditional printed materials of your school and your plan to link it through QR codes with digital marketing.

1. What will be the "hook" that will lead potential students to link using the QR code? Provide a layout or description of what they will see then they link online using the QR code.

2. Describe how you will build the various elements of the digital marketing portfolio, such as social networks and your website, to engage potential students.

3. What marketing communications objective(s) do you think the digital marketing portfolio, and the specific items related to the QR code, can achieve?

 # ETHICS IN ACTION

Before reading this short case study, go to YouTube and watch the "United Breaks Guitars" video.

You probably noticed that the video—depending on which version you saw, because there are many versions and even parodies of the video—has many millions of page views. A lot of people have seen this video, much to the chagrin of United Airlines' marketers. The story, as told in the video, is essentially this. Musician Dave Carroll notices baggage handlers abusing his luggage and finds that one of his expensive guitars was damaged. When he asked United for compensation, they told him what many of you have probably also heard when you

complain: no. Frustrated, Dave told the company he would make a video and post it on YouTube. The result was that the video, obviously, went "viral," and at one point, after being featured on a talk show on a major American network, the market capitalization of United dropped by 10 percent. Not surprisingly, United approached Dave and wanted to make it up to him. Because Taylor, the company who made the broken guitar, had already replaced it (as a gesture of goodwill in response to the popularity of the video), he was able to rebuff United.

In hindsight, United should have reimbursed Dave for his guitar and apologized. But the fact remains that for every Dave

Carroll, there are another 100 people who take the time to post a rant online and never get noticed. Hindsight is perfect, but companies cannot simply give in to everyone with a complaint or who wants a refund. Imagine you are a marketer working with Nike. How would you handle responses to people who post, or threaten to post, rants online?

1. What duty of care do you owe people when you sell them shoes or other apparel? Write a one-page "promise" to customers that outlines your commitment to take care of and meet customers' expectations. How will you use digital marketing to convey this message to current and potential customers?

2. How will you monitor what people say about you online? How will you respond to "rants" of disgruntled customers? Write a one-page memo to the Director of Marketing that provides a set of decision criteria or rules you can follow that will tell you whether or not, or how, you should respond to criticisms.

3. Assume one of your highest volume retailers has told you that one customer has asked repeatedly for a refund for a shirt that he claims came apart after only one wash. Based on your promise from point #1 above, they tell him that they will ask you to contact him. They also tell you that he has threatened to follow Dave Carroll's lead and go viral. Write a one-page email to him in response. ●

CASE STUDY | Introducing Credit Unions to the Next Generation

"What a lousy way to start the weekend," Michelle Chan told her friend Kimberly. It was Friday afternoon and the two had just met at Bridges, a local bar, for drinks after work. "Martin wants me to come up with some ideas for Monday morning on how we can use digital marketing to address the demographic problems in our customer base."

Kimberly sensed her friend wanted to vent. Plus, Kimberly had some expertise working with digital media in a previous job, so she thought maybe she could help. "OK, I'm here for you. Tell me all about it."

Michelle is the campaign coordinator for Central 1, which is the organization that represents credit unions in British Columbia and Ontario. The organization serves many back office functions for their members, but one of the more public roles they play is to promote credit unions in general. And one of the most critical roles within this promotion is the activation of new customers. Each individual credit union maintains relationships with their own individual customers, but the job of promoting the category of credit unions (as opposed to banks) falls to Michelle and her team. Although some of the larger credit unions (e.g., **www.vancity.com**) do their own marketing communications to attract new customers, most of the member credit unions are small and rely heavily on the Central 1 organization. The organization creates and executes campaigns under the banners of Credit Unions of BC and Ontario Credit Unions.

"The problem is," began Michelle, "that the younger demographic doesn't work with credit unions, and they don't even know much about them. What they do is usually some misconception, like they are less safe than banks."

Kimberly didn't see the problem. "So, don't older people have more money anyway? Why would you want some 21-year-old when they don't have any money? Just look at us. We both graduated two years ago and it was only last year that I opened an RRSP."

Michelle responded, "There are two problems. First, although young people might not be very profitable customers now, they will be over the next decades. As they buy houses they will need mortgages, or save money for their kids' education, and all of this will almost certainly be done with the financial institution they are with today. But the second reason is that because our customer base skews very old, we know they will stop being customers in the coming years. Unless we can find more young people to choose credit unions over banks, our members will simply run out of customers in the next 20 to 30 years."

Michelle then went back to her earlier point about low awareness among young people. "It's a long-term problem, but one that we need to start working on now because it just takes a long time to change perceptions—or in our case, build perceptions." To highlight her point, Michelle brought one of the pages from her meeting that afternoon. "Just look at these projections. With the normal attrition from older customers over time, and our current rate of acquiring new customers in younger demographics, we will literally lose more than half of our customers over the next 30 years."

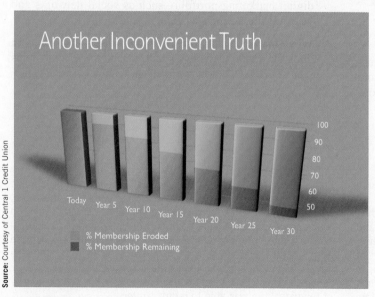

FIGURE 11.7
Membership Loss Over Time for Credit Unions

"Although 18- to 29-year-olds today make up 27 percent of the population, they make up only 8 percent of the base in our membership."

Martin, the VP of Marketing for Central 1 had assigned the task to Michelle because he felt she could get into the headspace of the target audience since she was part of it herself, at 25 years of age. "I'm convinced that digital marketing will play a big role in this campaign," said Michelle. "When I think about my own media habits, and what the research tells us, the 18-to-29 crowd just isn't engaged in media like television and newspaper. Besides, I think some of the digital media opportunities give us a much better chance to have a meaningful dialogue with consumers and make the perception change we need to make."

The 18-to-29 demographic and credit unions do indeed have a lot in common. Michelle's research showed that the target audience demographic value relationships and volunteerism and are loyal to friends and family. They also believe they can make a positive difference, and look for trusted, long-term relationships. "When I think about what credit unions offer, it's a no-brainer," said Michelle. "We are member-based and democratic, and we are not just about profits because we are member-owned. We are as reliable and secure as the banks, but offer so much more." Michelle's notes from the meeting laid out the words "Honesty, Community, Caring, and Trust" as key pillars upon which she felt a campaign could be based.

"The problem is," said Michelle as she looked around the room filled with other people in the same 18-to-29 demographic as her and Kimberly, "if I ask any one of these people what they know about credit unions, I know most of them wouldn't know very much, if anything at all. Most of them probably use the same banks that their parents do. Am I nuts for thinking we can break that cycle and make a meaningful inroad with this audience?"

1. Research credit unions. In a one-page ledger, compare the benefits and weaknesses of credit unions and banks relative to one another. What do credit unions offer that banks don't? What do banks offer that credit unions don't?

2. Michelle feels digital marketing should play a central role in the campaign to attract the 18- to 29-year-old target audience. Do you agree? Develop a five-minute PowerPoint presentation that outlines why digital media—and which forms specifically—lend themselves to the financial services product category.

3. If you were Michelle, what objective(s) would you recommend she set for the campaign she is working on? What are the specific roles that digital media can play in an overall campaign? Write her an email stating your recommended objectives in bullet points.

4. What would be your suggested starting point for the campaign? What forms of digital media would you recommend be used for the campaign and why? Design a layout or proposal for one of the media (e.g., Facebook campaign, YouTube video, etc.) and present it, along with your media recommendations, to the class.

ENDNOTES

1. Matt Hartley, "Going Off the Internet Map," *National Post* (January 27, 2011), p. FP6.

2. 2009 U.S. Digital Year in Review," *comScore.com* (**http://www.comscore.com/Press_Events/Presentations_Whitepapers/2010/The_2009_U.S._Digital_Year_in_Review**, accessed February 18, 2011).

3. Catherine Holahan and Robert D. Hof, "So Many Ads, So Few Clicks," *Businessweek*, no. 4058 (November 12, 2007), p. 38.

4. Ibid.

5. "Social Networking Sites Account for More Than 20 percent of All U.S. Online Display Ad Impressions, According to comScore AD Metrix," *comScore.com* (**http://www.comscore.com/Press_Events/Press_Releases/2009/9/Social_Networking_Sites_Account_for_More_than_20_Percent_of_All_U.S._Online_Display_Ad_Impressions_According_to_comScore_Ad_Metrix**, accessed September 1, 2009).

6. Ibid.

7. I.Nat, "US Weekly Sells Sponsorship of Its Facebook Profile Page," *Advertising Age* (April 27, 2009), p. 28.

8. "Alta Goes Graphic to Reduce Injuries for Young Workers," *Marketing Magazine* online (**http://www.marketingmag.ca/news/marketer-news/alta-goes-graphic-to-reduce-injuries-for-young-workers-18273**, accessed February 19, 2011).

9. Kristin Laird, "Wal-Mart Touts Green Efforts," *Marketing Magazine* online (January 29, 2008) (**http://www.marketingmag.ca/news/marketer-news/wal-mart-touts-green-efforts-13035**, accessed February 19, 2011).

10. "Problem Solved," *BtoB* 92, no. 15 (November 12, 2007), p. 21.

11. Ibid.

12. Josh Quittner, Jessi Hempel, and Lindsay Blakely, "The Battle for Your Social Circle," *Fortune* 156, no. 10 (November 26, 2007), pp. 11–13.

13. "AdWords Beginner's Guide" (**http://adwords.google.com/support/aw/bin/static.py?hl=en&topic=22356&guide=21899&page=guide.cs**, accessed March 31, 2010).

14. RichardWestlund, "Mobile on Fast Forward," *Adweek* 51, no. 11 (March 15, 2010), pp. M1–M5.

15. A. Penev and R-K. Wong, "Framework for Timely and Accurate Ads on Mobile Devices" (doi: 10.1145/1645953.1646089, November 2009).

16. Westlund, "Mobile on Fast Forward."

17. Ibid.

18. "Video Game Advertising," *eMarketer.com* (n.d.) (**http://www.emarketer.com/Reports/All/Emarketer_2000485.aspx**, accessed March 30, 2010).

19. S.Brierley, *The Advertising Handbook* (London: Routledge, 2002).

20. Emily Bryson York, "Starbucks Gets Its Business Brewing Again With Social Media," *Advertising Age* (February 22, 2010) (**http://adage.com/digitalalist10/article?article_id=142202**, accessed May 10, 2010).

21. "Re-Marketing Helps Boost Online Shoppers' Baskets," *Data Strategy* 3, no. 7 (May 2007), p. 9.

22. Donna L. Hoffman and Thomas P. Novak, "How to Acquire Customers on the Web," *Harvard Business Review* 78, no. 3 (May–June 2000), pp. 179–85.

23. Jeff Sweat and Rick Whiting, "Instant Marketing," *InformationWeek,* no. 746 (August 2, 1999), pp. 18–20.

24. Brian Quinton, "Beyond Page Reviews," *Direct* 19, no. 6 (June 1, 2007), pp. 28–30.

25. "Questex Media Launches All Things HiDef.com," *Response* 15, no. 3, p. 10.

26. Natalie Zmuda, "Why Mtn Dew Let Skater Dudes Take Control of Its Marketing," *Advertising Age* (February 22, 2010) (**http://adage.com/digitalalist10/article?article_id=142201**, accessed May 10, 2010).

27. Matt Hartley, "Facebook Changes Paradigm of What an Ad Actually Is," *National Post* (August 11, 2010), p. FP3.

28. Craig MacBride, "Jacob Focuses on Facebook," *Strategy* (February 9, 2011) (**http://www.strategyonline.ca/articles/news/20110209/jacob.html**, accessed February 19, 2011).

29. "Cossette Gets Interactive with Dynamite," *National Post* (February 12, 2011), p. FP12.

30. B.Godwin, "Social Networks and Government" (**http://www.usa.gov/webcontent/technology/social_networks.shtml**, accessed February 20, 2011).

31. Michael Learmonth, "Marketers May Be on Twitter But Not in the Conversation: Study," *Marketing Magazine* (July 28, 2010) (**http://www.marketingmag.ca/news/media-news/marketers-may-be-on-twitter-but-not-in-the-conversation-study-4170**, accessed February 19, 2011).

32. Craig MacBride, "Lavalife Looks to Heat Up February," *Strategy* (February 2, 2011) (**http://www.mediaincanada.com/articles/mic/20110202/lavalife.html**, accessed February 19, 2011).

33. Liao Wei-Shing, Kuan-Ting Chen, and Winston H. Hsu, "AdImage: Video Advertising by Image Matching and Ad Scheduling Optimization," ACM, New York, NY, 2008; "Video Game Advertising," *eMarketer.com* (to come Piblisher details)

34. Jeromy Lloyd, "BMO Talks Shop on YouTube," *Marketing Magazine* (November 16, 2009) (**http://www.marketingmag.ca/news/marketer-news/bmo-talks-shop-on-youtube-11992**, accessed February 19, 2011).

35. Stuart Elliott, "Student's Ad Gets a Remake, and Makes the Big Time," *New York Times* (**www.nytimes.com/2007/10/26/business/media/26appleweb.html**, accessed October 26, 2007).

36. Ibid.

37. "Word of Mouse," *Economist* 385, no. 8554 (November 10, 2007), pp. 77–78.

38. Lorrie Grant, "Retailers Hope Shoppers Buy Blogs as the Place to Go," *USA Today* (August 25, 2005, Money Section), p. 5b.

39. Brian Morrissey, "The Rules of Viral Web Success, At Least for Now," *Adweek* 49, no. 1 (January 7, 2008), p. 13.

40. Ibid.

41. S.Barnes and J. Mattsson, "Brand Value in Virtual Worlds: An Axiological Approach," *Journal of Electronic Commerce Research* 9, no. 3 (2008).

42. "Canadian Mobile Subscriptions to Climb 20% by 2014," *eMarketer.com* (June 10, 2010) (**http://www1.emarketer.com/Article.aspx?R=1007747&AspxAutoDetectCookieSupport=1**, accessed February 19, 2011).

43. "The Worldly Web," *CFO* 19, no. 7 (June 2003), p. 30.

Message Feedback

If you have done a good job in the development, coding, and delivery of the message, the decoding and subsequent outcomes should occur as laid out in the IMC plan objectives. The feedback loop from the audience back to the marketer provides this evidence.

In this final section, we examine the feedback and measurement of the IMC plan. There are two types of feedback from any marketing communications activity. The first type is examined by assessing the objectives of the IMC plan—sales, awareness, brand perceptions, etc. Those will be discussed in Chapter 13. The second type of feedback, which comes from both customers and other stakeholders of the firm, results from marketing communications activities. You might, for example, hear from a regulator with a concern about one of your ads. You might hear from a consumer activist group with a concern about your campaign, or an individual consumer with a complaint about a piece of direct mail. We begin our examination of feedback in Chapter 12 with an examination of the ethical and legal environment of marketing communications.

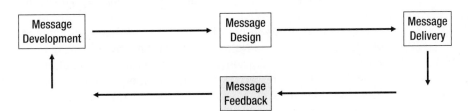

Step 4 in the Communications Process

CHAPTER OBJECTIVES

After reading this chapter, you should be able to answer the following questions:

- **What** legal restrictions apply to marketing communications?
- **Which** governmental agencies are most responsible for enforcing laws regarding IMC programs?
- **What** does the marketing communications industry do to police itself?
- **What** are the major ethical concerns about marketing communications?
- **How** can managers use ethical frameworks to help guide their actions on sensitive ethical issues?

INDUSTRY PROFILE

So You Want to Work in Marketing Communications?

Anthea Rowe, Communications Manager, Network for Business Sustainability, London, Ontario

Anthea Rowe stands at the intersection of two worlds that most people think never meet. As the Communications Manager for the Network for Business Sustainability (**www.nbs.net**) she is responsible for making academic research relevant to managers and helping managers convey their research needs to academics. "It takes more than 10 seconds to describe my job to people at parties," jokes Anthea.

Telling a compelling story is at the heart of Anthea's success. "My job is basically storytelling. I see my job as translating the value of what the organization can bring—rigorous academic research—to practicing managers. To do that, I need to make sure there is something inherently interesting to my audience. For example, if I'm speaking with a journalist I hope will cover a new research report on the environment, I need to understand why the story will be interesting to someone reading the paper with a cup of coffee in the morning—and make that point clearly and convincingly."

Anthea also needs to help researchers and managers understand why they should participate in the Network. "I might find myself talking to a manager, convincing him or her to provide a testimonial or attend one of our conferences. Or I might be asking a researcher to take part in one of our studies. When I'm competing with dozens of other organizations working in the field of sustainability, as well as the normal day-to-day demands confronting every senior businessperson or researcher, I need to have a compelling message. It all comes down to understanding what the audience needs and helping them see how the Network can meet those needs."

Storytelling comes naturally to Anthea, who has a BA and MA in English. Recalling her path to NBS, she says it all began with informational interviews. "People always say that informational interviews are something every student should do to help them figure out their career path. In my case, they actually did clarify where I saw myself being happy." Drawn to corporate communications, Anthea says

Marketing Communications Ethics and Regulations

it was the blend of writing along with technologies like graphic design and the Web that made the career choice particularly attractive.

"After deciding that communications was going to be my field, I did a post-grad diploma in corporate communications and PR to help round out my résumé and landed my first job in marketing. It was just about the most junior position possible, but it was a start."

Working in the business-to-business sector helping a sales team promote software provided Anthea the opportunity to learn on the front lines of selling. But it was also where she had her first experience with doubt about some of the tactics available to marketers. "Like all companies, we were looking to grow our markets. We rented lists to help build our prospect pool, and I had some reservations with that process," says Anthea. "First, because our product was designed specifically for retailers who sold lumber products, it wasn't a perfect fit for other types of companies. But in an effort to grow we would target related companies—ones that sold forklifts, or construction materials, or products in somewhat related fields. We knew our product wasn't perfect for them, and that we needed to learn their business before we could make it perfect. But the pressure to expand meant we had to sell and learn at the same time, and I'm sure that meant more than one customer didn't get the best product for their needs."

Anthea Rowe, Communications Manager, Network for Business Sustainability.

The other concern for Anthea about renting prospect lists was the intrusion it meant for those on the list. "If a contact asks for information, that's one thing, but I never felt comfortable approaching people who hadn't asked to be contacted. We were sending unsolicited ad mail (a.k.a. 'junk mail') to qualified—but unknown—leads. But that's what it took to grow the business, so we did it. Our competitors were doing it, too."

Landing the job at NBS was a great opportunity for Anthea to move into a field where she felt more kinship with her work on a philosophical level. "I've always had a personal interest in environmental sustainability, and now I get to match my personal passion with the mission of the organization."

But working in an organization that promotes sustainability doesn't mean ethical dilemmas don't come up. "The cornerstone of NBS is systematic and rigorous research. It's critical that managers know our research represents the most credible, unbiased perspective available. But some of the things we need to do to make the research meaningful run counter to that promise of objectivity. For instance, if I use a case study to supplement content in one of our reports, have I objectively chosen the best example to go with the research? Or, by providing only a summary of a report, have I been true to the full academic study? It's always a challenge to balance the rigour and objectivity of our brand promise with the need for succinct and compelling communications."

One of the ways Anthea achieves this balance is through the structure of the Network's website. "I'm always mindful of protecting the brand promise of research rigour. So if there is something less rigorous, more anecdotal or representative of one person's subjective point of view, we separate that physically from the rigorous research and make sure the reader clearly knows the difference."

When asked to advise aspiring communications professionals, Anthea suggests three areas of skill development. "First, interpersonal skills are key. At the end of the day I work with people, and I have to understand their needs and respond to those needs. That requires the ability—and desire—to get to know and engage people."

The second skill, building on the first, relates to language. "It's not enough to simply understand what someone needs. You need to be able to communicate how you can help them solve their problem or meet their needs. Superior language skills involve more than just being good at grammar—more than just reciting product features or spec sheets. It's about zeroing in on the issues that matter to your audience and speaking to them in their own language."

The third skill involves research and analysis. "If you can't conduct research and extract meaning from it, you will not be successful in marketing. At its simplest, analysis includes things like tracking responses to marketing campaigns or analyzing trends from your website and other online media. Research involves asking the right questions that get to the heart of a business problem—"Do we truly know who our audience is? Have we identified their core values?"—and conducting research that answers those questions. Only then can you be confident you have a sound marketing strategy."

OVERVIEW

Marketing communications have long been the subject of scrutiny from the general public, special interest groups, and by the government. Those who work in the marketing communications field are often perceived to be much less trustworthy than members of other professions, such as nurses or medical doctors. Indeed, research suggests that the moral development of the marketing communications agency business is somewhat "underdeveloped," with many agency practitioners preferring to either not think about ethical issues, or explain them away as simply part of their jobs.[1]

Perhaps most surprising is that about 70 percent of the public thinks that although marketing communications can provide useful information, it is often untruthful, it attempts to persuade people into buying things they do not need, and it should be more tightly regulated.[2] This chapter examines two interrelated topics covering these areas. First, we will examine the legal environment surrounding marketing communications. Second, we will examine self-regulatory bodies within the marketing communications field designed to police the industry from within. Third, we will examine ethical concerns of marketing communications.

Each of these three areas is essential for any marketing communications professional to understand. The objectives laid out in the IMC plan cannot be fully met if any of them are ignored. A lack of understanding can lead to serious repercussions from regulatory bodies, activist groups, or consumers that can seriously harm the reputation of the company.

MARKETING COMMUNICATIONS REGULATIONS

The two primary marketing communications regulatory agencies in Canada are the Canadian Radio-Television and Telecommunications Commission (CRTC) and the Competition Bureau. Both of these operate at a federal level and mandate who can be targeted with marketing communications, what can be shown in many forms of marketing communications, what support must be offered, and where and when it can be placed in front of specific audiences. Note that virtually every aspect of the creative brief introduced in Chapter 5 is implicated by one or more of these regulations.

The Canadian Radio-Television and Telecommunications Commission (CRTC)

As the name suggests, the CRTC is mainly concerned with broadcast media, including television and radio. Burgeoning rules are in development for regulation of marketing communications practices online and on mobile devices. However, the challenges related to policing these media are extreme, and the CRTC has yet to find a meaningful way to control their marketing communications content. However, the reach of the CRTC in Canadian marketing communications is still significant.

The CRTC regulates how much advertising can appear on Canadian television.

One of the primary ways that the CRTC controls Canadian marketing communications is through the enforcement of limits on the amount of advertising that broadcasters can include with programming. Television broadcasters and networks are prohibited from airing more than 12 minutes of advertising per hour during the broadcast day (beginning at 6 a.m. and ending at midnight).

Other regulatory elements related to the CRTC are the promotion of alcohol. The CRTC expects broadcasters to annually report the amount of alcohol education messages they broadcast, with the idea that this will counter the potential negative effects of one-sided promotions of alcohol. Tobacco products are banned outright from broadcast media in Canada, and Health Canada has a number of additional regulations on the promotion of tobacco products. Finally, the CRTC is required to approve all infomercials aired in Canada. These commercials, defined as being over 12 minutes in length, must clearly state to the viewer that they are paid advertising (versus programming). Similarly, radio broadcasters must do the same for any paid message lasting over three minutes.

The Competition Bureau

The single largest agency charged with regulating Canadian marketing communications practices is the Competition Bureau. A number of regulations play a meaningful role in shaping communications messages to Canadian customers, including regulations on false representations, bait, and switch selling, and the use of prizes and pricing tactics in promotions.

False Representations

Marketers must take care to make accurate representations across a number of areas in their communications messages.

1. Representations Related to the Company Itself
   Marketers can violate this regulation when they misrepresent the nature or size of their business. For example, the words "only" or "similar" can be misleading (e.g., The *only* full-time swimming pool company in the area).

   Misleading company associations are another form of misrepresentation. Companies cannot imply or suggest that they are affiliated with other companies or act on behalf of other companies when there is no formal relationship.

   When advertising a bankruptcy or liquidation, the pending bankruptcy and specific messages related to it must be true. For example, a company cannot advertise a bankruptcy sale indefinitely, since the term *bankruptcy* suggests a short-term event where customers may possess an advantage.

2. Representations Related to Products
   The *Competition Act* states that any representation relating to a product must contain all the information necessary to enable a reasonable purchaser to make a sound purchasing decision. This relates to any number of potential claims made in marketing

This ad for Crest toothpaste contains a claim about reversing gingivitis that must be verified according to the *Competition Act*

INTRODUCING A TOOTHPASTE THAT HAS GINGIVITIS SHAKING IN ITS GUMS.

Crest PRO·HEALTH

CLINICAL GUM PROTECTION

Introducing a toothpaste clinically proven to help reverse gingivitis in just four weeks, putting you on your way to a healthier mouth.

New Crest Pro-Health Clinical Gum Protection. Unlike ordinary toothpaste, it helps eliminate plaque at the gumline, helping prevent gingivitis. It protects these areas dentists check most: cavities, gingivitis, plaque, sensitivity, tartar, whitening, and fresh breath.

life opens up when you do *Crest*

Many food products cleverly suggest taste preference without actually stating it, which avoids the need for legal substantiation.

communications. For example, testimonials in marketing communications must not mislead consumers. If a testimonial is given by someone who is implied to be an expert in a given field (e.g., a mechanic talking about motor oil) the person must actually possess expertise or an actor portrayal should be disclosed. Similarly, any conflicts of interest or misrepresentations (e.g., where a person is implied to have made an endorsement when, in fact, they did not) should be fully disclosed. An example of this type of misrepresentation is when people interviewed on camera are portrayed as customers or users of a product when they are not.

Comparative advertising is another area related to a company's product where misrepresentations can occur. The company must have credible evidence that their product meets any claims made in marketing communications. Further, if there are limitations to such claims they must also be stated. For example, if a brand of gasoline were to be advertised as producing better mileage than several competing brands, and the claim would be accurate under highway driving conditions but inaccurate under city conditions, this limitation should be clearly expressed. Finally, any demonstrations of a product should be shown under equivalent conditions, and demonstrations should not attempt to compare products in uses or methods for which they have not been designed or recommended.

Performance claims about products are also open to scrutiny under the *Competition Act,* in two ways. First, any claim of an adequate test must indicate the only proportion for which it was intended. For example, a national representation of energy savings offered by a product must show that the test a test performed is indicative of broad climate conditions and not only under one particular geography such as southern Ontario.

3. Representations Related to Price
   Many marketing communications include pricing information, which is one of the areas most prone to misrepresentation.

   A baseline is what is referred to as the "ordinary selling price." A product cannot be considered discounted if its ordinary selling price is artificially inflated. The ordinary selling price is determined by using one of two tests: either a substantial volume of the product was sold at that price or a higher price, within a reasonable period of time (volume test); or the product was offered for sale, in good faith, for a substantial period of time at that price or a higher price (time test). Price misrepresentations can manifest themselves in any number of forms:

   - "Reductions of 40 percent to 70 percent on all merchandise," although some items are not reduced as represented.
   - "Discount of 50 percent off all prices shown in a catalogue," where the discount price is in fact the ordinary selling price.
   - "Sale prices in effect" during a specified sale period, although the prices remained unchanged before, during, and after the period.

Ads with discounts must take care to not contravene regulations on pricing.

The word *free*, although technically meaning there is no price, is an area where misrepresentations can occur. For example, when article A is promoted as being free with the purchase of article B, but article B is available at a discount or lesser price, then article A is not free, in fact.

Bait and Switch Selling

Section 74 of the *Competition Act* prohibits **bait and switch selling**, defined as promoting a product at a bargain price and not making the product available for sale in reasonable quantities. The intent, or the "switch" is then to offer another, more expensive option once the customer has shown an interest.

There are, however, areas where this problem can be avoided by marketers who genuinely face inventory shortages:

- It is acceptable that an advertiser clears out old stock in reasonable quantities, but the marketing communications must specify the number of available items.
- If a discontinued line or clearance sale is being promoted, the total quantity of the product available nationally or regionally, if known, could be stated, noting that some stores may not have access to any supply.
- If items listed in a sale flyer become unavailable before the commencement of the sale due to events beyond the retailer's control, a correction notice should be placed on the front of the flyer.

FAMILIPRIX
FÉLICITE
MARIE-HÉLÈNE PRÉMONT
POUR SA
PERFORMANCE
DE MALADE.

Il y a deux jours, la cycliste Marie-Hélène Prémont remportait la médaille d'or
aux Jeux du Commonwealth. Une semaine auparavant,
Familiprix s'associait fièrement à la carrière sportive de cette brillante étudiante
en pharmacie. Quel excellent départ pour un partenariat gagnant!

Familiprix

Marketers from English Canada communicating in Quebec are well advised to seek local guidance on regulations.

- If items will be only available in some stores; the portion of the advertisement relating to those items should be clearly distinguished from the advertising of the products generally available. The phone numbers and retail store addresses should be provided, with an indication that customers should make a call to check for supply availability of any items distinguished in the flyer.
- Although there is no legal requirement that a rain check policy be displayed, it has been found that many complaints, and subsequent preliminary investigations, could have been avoided if the customer had known of the existence of a rain check policy and of its terms and conditions.

Sales Promotions

The Competition Act prohibits the sending of a notice that gives the recipient the general impression that he or she has won a prize or other benefit and asks or gives the option to pay money in order to obtain the prize or benefit. These notices often appear in direct marketing campaigns. This is not an offence if the recipient actually won the prize or the person who sent the notice provides fair and adequate disclosure of the number and value of the prize, the area where it is allocated, and any fact that affects the chances of winning.

Telemarketing carries with it some particular disclosure requirements. Telemarketers must disclose:

- The name of the company or person they are working on behalf of.
- The type of product or business they are promoting.
- The purpose of the call.
- Any condition or restriction related to the product or business they are promoting (e.g., promotional prizes).

Provincial Regulations

Of course, each province also legislates its own jurisdiction, and any marketer must be aware of any local restrictions on marketing communications. In Canada, this can create considerable challenges for marketers with national programs. The province where national marketers require the greatest local consideration is Quebec. If products are to be sold in Quebec, marketing communications are effectively required to be fully bilingual because the Quebec Charter of the French Language requires that most product labelling and accompanying materials, such as warranties, be in French. Labelling in Quebec can also be in another language or languages, provided the French text has equal prominence compared with any other language. Also, in Quebec, commercial advertising aimed at persons younger than 13 is completely prohibited under the *Quebec Consumer Protection Act*. Dairy company Saputo was fined $44,000 for targeting children through a campaign that featured a character named Igor (also the brand name) in CDs and DVDs.[3] Although marketers in other provinces follow specific guidelines (set out in the Broadcast Code for Advertising to Children mentioned below), they are still allowed to target children 12 and under with commercial messages.

MARKETING COMMUNICATIONS INDUSTRY SELF-REGULATION

The primary body responsible for industry self-regulation in Canada is Advertising Standards Canada (ASC) (**www.adstandards.com**). This non-profit organization began in 1957 with the intent of ensuring the viability and integrity of marketing communications in Canada. Membership in the organization includes most of the major marketers in Canada, and many smaller ones as well.

Companies should use the Canadian Code of Advertising Standards as they develop and deliver marketing communications messages to ensure they adhere to the principles laid out in the Code. The Code contains 14 specific clauses that deal with a variety of ethical issues in marketing communications. Below is a synopsis of the clauses. Complete descriptions are found on the Advertising Standards website.

Canadian Code of Advertising Standards Clauses

1. *Accuracy and Clarity.* All pertinent details should be clearly stated in marketing communications, and relevant information should not be omitted. Claims should be reasonably supported and identification of the marketer should be given.

2. *Disguised Advertising Techniques.* Marketers should not create messages made to appear as something other than paid commercial messages.

3. *Price Claims.* Similar to the *Competition Act*, misleading information about normal sale prices is applicable under this clause. Also, qualifying statements such as "UP TO XX % OFF" should be clearly made.

4. *Bait and Switch.* This clause mirrors the regulation under the *Competition Act.*

5. *Guarantees.* Any guarantees should be clearly made, with any conditions or restrictions stated.

6. *Comparative Advertising.* Messages must not exaggerate the importance of differences, and, of course, claims should be substantiated. Messages should not disparage competitors.

7. *Testimonials.* All testimonials should be based on actual experiences with products and represent honest opinions.

8. *Professional or Scientific Claims.* All claims should be applicable in the Canadian context, and any claims by other organizations should not be distorted.

9. *Imitation.* Messages should not contain logos or materials from competitors that may mislead or confuse consumers.

10. *Safety.* Messages should not display acts on unsafe use of products or situations.

11. *Superstition and Fears.* Messages should not exploit superstitions or fears of consumers.

12. *Advertising to Children.* Marketers should not take advantage of children's lack of credulity and experience, nor present information that might lead to emotional, physical, or moral harm to children.

13. *Advertising to Minors.* Messages for products that are illegal for minors should not be delivered in way that is meant to appeal to minors, or depict minors consuming the product in the message itself.

14. *Unacceptable Depictions and Portrayals.* This refers to messages that promote or depict discrimination, violence, unlawful behaviour, or otherwise undermine human dignity.

Adapted from Advertising Standards Canada, *The Canadian Code of Advertising Standards,* 2010, **www.adstandards.com**.

Source: Used with permission of General Mills Marketing Inc.

This ad for Progresso Soups could be scrutinized under multiple clauses of the ASC code, including accuracy and clarity.

Critical Thinking Exercise

What is the difference between a fear appeal and the exploitation of fear or superstitions as laid out in clause #11 of the Canadian Code of Advertising Standards? How can a marketer go too far in using fear appeals? Think of examples of fear appeals you've seen in the past. Were any of them going too far in your opinion? If not, what might the marketer have included that would have pushed the message beyond the limits of clause #11?

This ad for McDonald's clearly states the promotional discount, along with the associated terms of redemption that consumers will need to understand the message.

The Broadcast Code for Advertising to Children

Further to clause #12 in the Canadian Code of Advertising Standards, Ad Standards Canada administers an additional code designed to protect children from marketing communications. The code contains a number of additional items:

Factual Presentation. Marketers must not use subliminal forms of marketing communications, misrepresent things like package size or other performance characteristics of products, and avoid using terms like "new" or "improved" for a period of longer than one year.

Product Prohibitions. Products that are not intended for use by children should not be promoted through child-oriented promotions, and all drugs (with the exception of fluoride toothpaste) should not be promoted to children.

Avoiding Undue Pressure. Messages should not directly urge children to ask their parents to purchase an item, provide a means for direct response, or give more than 50 percent of allocation in a message to a promotion for items such as prizes.

Scheduling. The same commercial or product in the commercial cannot be used more than once every 30 minutes in children's programming, and advertising must be limited to 4 minutes per half hour of children's programming (versus the 12 minutes allowed generally by the CRTC).

Promotion by Characters or Endorsements. Although puppets, characters, or individuals who are well known to children may appear in messages, they must not endorse

The Internet has made enforcement of regulations protecting children much more difficult.

the product itself. This means they can't handle, consume, mention, or otherwise endorse the product. However, characters created by the marketers themselves are acceptable, and characters that are well known to children may be used to provide generic statements about nutrition, safety, and education in children's advertising.

Price and Purchase Terms. Price, including all components of the price and any separate accessories, should be clearly stated. Price can't be downplayed by using words like "only" or "just." Any need for assembly must be clearly stated, and any items used in the messages that are not part of the purchase price should also be clearly stated as such.

Comparison Claims. Comparisons with competitors' products should not diminish the value of those products, and no reference can be made to any previous years' model of the item being promoted.

Safety. Messages should not portray individuals in unsafe situations or products being used in an unsafe manner.

Social Values. Messages should adhere to values that are consistent with social and ethical standards of contemporary Canadian society. Messages cannot imply that products make their owner superior, or that without it one will be open to ridicule.

Adapted from Advertising Standards Canada, *The Broadcast Code for Advertising to Children*, 2010, **www.adstandards.com.**

Critical Thinking Exercise

The Broadcast Code for Advertising to Children was created before the Internet made marketing communications much less controllable. Some critics argue that companies are technically adhering to the elements of the code, while blatantly violating them online. For example, many websites promote games for children with links to product information or even online purchase opportunities. If you were in charge of administering this code, how would you update it to include online media? If you were an advertiser, how would you try to integrate the "spirit" of the code into your online strategy?

The Complaint Process

Anyone is free to lodge a complaint about marketing communications that he or she feels violate one or more of the clauses within the Canadian Code of Advertising Standards. Complaints may be made online or through the mail and are reviewed by staff. Marketing communications that are found to be potentially in violation are analyzed by a council comprised of people from within the industry as well as ordinary citizens who volunteer their time to the process.

The number of complaints is fairly low considering the number of marketing communications messages delivered in Canada. Between the years 2006 and 2009, an average of just over 1,200 complaints were received. These complaints were based on an average of 810 individual ads each year (since many ads received more than one complaint, the number of complaints is higher than the number of ads receiving complaints). Following the complaints review process for those 4 years, an average of 123 complaints were upheld each year. These upheld complaints represented an average of only 55 ads per year. This suggests that the vast majority of marketing communications messages each year in Canada adhere to the standards that are used to self-regulate the industry.

However, complaints to Advertising Standards Canada do not tell the whole story. Obviously, many complaints go to other bodies, such as the Competition Bureau, or directly to the marketers themselves. Many messages that receive complaints might be offensive to some people but not contravene any regulations, legal or otherwise. Still many more messages likely cross ethical boundaries for some consumers who never complain. This is an important group of people, since they may represent a "silent majority." If a marketer crosses an ethical line with consumers, it may result in reputation harm, reduced loyalty, or even immediate brand-switching. Therefore, it is in marketers' best interests to consider ethics as they develop and deliver marketing communications. The third section of this chapter examines a number of ethical issues faced by marketing communications professionals.

ETHICAL ISSUES IN MARKETING COMMUNICATIONS

There are many instances in which marketing communications may be deemed in adherence with legal and self-regulatory guidelines but be ethically suspect. In this section, various ethical issues related to marketing communications are discussed. Ethical frameworks and marketer responses to ethical challenges are also presented.

Ethics and morals are key principles that can be used to guide a person's activities in the world of commerce. **Morals** are beliefs or principles that individuals hold concerning what is right and what is wrong. **Ethics** are moral principles that serve as guidelines for both individuals and organizations. Marketing communications activities are affected by ethical and moral concerns. At the most general level, several major ethical concerns and criticisms have arisen. They include the issues shown in Figure 12.1. Some of the issues relate to aspects of the marketing communications itself, while others are concerns about the effects of marketing communications when they work as intended in the market.

FIGURE 12.1
Ethical Issues in Marketing Communications.

Issues Related to the Content of Marketing Communications Campaigns	Issues Related to the Outcomes from Marketing Communications Campaigns
1. Misleads people or exaggerates the truth	1. Promotes unsafe or unhealthy products
2. Offends people	2. Increases the cost of goods for all consumers
3. Perpetuates stereotypes	3. Encourages people to buy things they can't afford
4. Targets children	4. Emphasizes materialism
5. Infringes on competitors' brands	
6. Encourages gifts and bribes	
7. Undermines privacy	

Content of Marketing Communications Campaigns

The first category of ethical issues includes the elements of the marketing communications mix itself—the messages and target audiences selected by the marketer.

Misleads People or Exaggerates the Truth

As mentioned earlier, about 70 percent of consumers believe that marketing communications can be deceptive or untruthful. But is this just an enduring myth among consumers, or do some marketing communications deceive people? The line between truth and deception can be fuzzy in practice. **Puffery** is the practice of using exaggerated statements in order to subjectively make a product or offer look more appealing. But inherently it is the job of the marketing communications professional to position his or her product more favourably in the marketplace.

Going too far will alienate consumers, but not going far enough might not get the message across. Consider the following simple example. A sales promotion plan calls for discounts of either 10 or 50 percent off a number of selected items in a retail store. The sales promotion only covers 25 percent of the total inventory of the store, and of that 5 percent, only 20 percent will be marked down to the 50 percent level. The remainder will be marked down by 10 percent. The marketing communications message for the sales promotion might contain the following headlines:

- Five percent of all inventory on sale for 50 percent off. An additional 20 percent of inventory on sale for 10 percent off. 75 percent of our items are not on sale at all.
- Twenty-five percent of the items in our store are on sale for either 10 percent or 50 percent off.
- Save up to 50 percent on selected items.
- Save up to 50 percent.

Arguably, the first headline is the most "truthful." But all of the headlines are truthful; some merely exaggerate the sale more than others. If you were the person in charge of this campaign, which headline would you choose? If you were a consumer, would you respond differently to each headline?

Offends People

Many adult products require tasteful marketing communications, even when they are free to be shown through any medium. Feminine hygiene products, condoms, and other personal adult products may be featured in practically any medium. It is the responsibility of the marketing professional to select media that are appropriate as well as create ads that will not be offensive.

In the international arena, this responsibility becomes even greater. In many Islamic countries, advertisements for personal hygiene or sex-related products would be highly offensive. It is important for company leaders to explore these cultural differences before undertaking any kind of marketing campaign.

Another ethical issue that has arisen concerns the use of nudity and sexuality featuring children. For many years, critics disparaged Calvin Klein for pushing the envelope. The original objections arose in the 1980s, when 14-year-old Brooke Shields appeared in an advertisement saying, "Nothing comes between me and my Calvins."

Later, in an attempt to sell children's underwear, the same company decided to prepare a large billboard in Times Square to accompany a series of magazine advertisements. The photo in the ads showed two six-year-old boys arm wrestling, while two girls about the same age were jumping on a sofa. All were only wearing underwear. The ads were pulled after strong objections from numerous groups.

In their attempts to break through clutter, marketers often push the boundaries creatively and this can result in shocking or otherwise offensive campaigns that perhaps weren't even intended to

Some messages from organizations such as Greenpeace often aggressively address issues that many consumers would prefer not to think about.

shock. Nike developed a television commercial that featured a woman being chased through the woods by a man with a chainsaw. She escaped, in theory, because of her Nike shoes and her level of fitness. The ad finished with the statement "You'll Live Longer" linking it to the reason why one should exercise. The ad ran on both NBC and ESPN during the 2000 Olympics broadcast, and although the ESPN broadcast didn't register any complaints, NBC received many complaints and pulled the ad from their broadcasts.[4] What made this ad offensive to one set of viewers and not another?

Perpetuates Stereotypes

Many social commentators have suggested that advertising and other forms of media perpetuate stereotyping of males, females, and minority groups. This leads to several questions. For instance, is segmentation the same as stereotyping? In an era in which the term *political correctness* is routinely used, there is debate regarding what is acceptable. In marketing, some of the categories in which market segments are identified include age, race, gender, social status, and income. When marketing to or portraying individuals from these categories, do advertisers use clichés that are no longer appropriate?

Advertisements often depict teenagers in one-dimensional ways rather than reflecting the complexities of young adulthood. Teens are often depicted as rebellious, carefree, and sexually starved. For baby boomers, the image presented is of a white, well-educated, well-off person with a spacious home and expensive cars and toys instead of the complex makeup of multiple nationalities of all income levels. From a marketing perspective, it is much easier to group people into smaller subgroups with common interests. Is it unethical, bad business, or simply a practical matter to represent or misrepresent consumers in these ways?

Source: Patrick Watson; Pearson Education/PH College.

Elderly people are often stereotyped in advertising.

Once again, the discussion is easier in theory than in practice. Assume you are in charge of selling walk-in baths for Premier Bathrooms (**www.premierbathrooms.ca**). You know that the majority of your customers are elderly and purchase the tubs because they have mobility limitations. When developing your marketing communications, you could feature any of the following people as models:

- an elderly woman with mobility issues who no longer worries about falling now that she has a walk-in bath
- an elderly man who enjoys the tub after playing a light game of tennis
- a young man with no apparent mobility issues who enjoys taking baths in an upright bathtub

As with the sales promotion example, all scenarios are plausible. But given that your market is primarily the elderly, and that females are far more likely to buy your product than males, and that they buy your product to overcome mobility issues, is it smart from a business perspective to use a young man in your marketing communications? How much does your small campaign contribute to, or reflect, the current way that society views the elderly?

Targets Children

Children represent a tremendous level of spending and buying power, over $20 billion annually. The question is what are the appropriate tactics used to reach them?

Mary Pipher, clinical psychologist and author of *The Shelter of Each Other*, suggests that "No one ad is bad, but the combination of 400 ads per day creates in children a combination of narcissism, entitlement, and dissatisfaction."[5] Ads targeted to children employ multiple tactics, including building brand awareness through images and logos, featuring toys and collectibles, and developing tie-ins with television programs and movies, including the recent *Hannah Montana* phenomenon. Characters such as Barney, Ronald McDonald, and Harry Potter vend everything from food to toys to clothes.

With so many potential venues to sell directly to children and to put pressure on their parents, many company leaders believe it is best to "get them while they're young." From a societal perspective, however, the question remains whether such impressionable young minds should be subjected to so many messages. This is because children's ability to differentiate between a paid commercial message and information is not developed until they are at least eight years old. Particularly troubling is the inclusion of marketing messages in schools, where the line between facts and persuasion is particularly vulnerable. Brands from Coke and Pepsi to McDonald's have placed marketing communications messages in school, often through sponsorships.[6]

Infringes on Competitors' Brands

There have always been ethical challenges associated with brand management. One continuing problem is brand infringement. **Brand infringement** occurs when a company creates a brand name that closely resembles a popular or successful brand, such as when the Korrs beer company was formed. In that case, the courts deemed the brand an intentional infringement, and the name was abandoned. Another brand-infringing company that was forced by the courts to give up its name was Victor's Secret.

The brand infringement issue becomes more complex when a brand is so well established that it may be considered a generic term, such as a Kleenex tissue or a Xerox copy. Band-Aid encountered the problem in the 1970s, forcing the marketing team to make sure the product was identified as "Band-Aid Brand Strips" rather than simply "band aids," to keep the competition from being able to use the name.

The newest form of unethical behaviour, at least according to some sources, is called *domain squatting* or *cyber squatting* on the Internet. This is the controversial practice of buying domain names (barnesandnoble.com, kohls.com, labronjames.com, etc.) that are valuable to specific people or businesses in the hope of making a profit by reselling the name. At the extreme, whitehouse.com was a pornographic website. Any new company trying to build a presence in the marketplace may find itself stifled by domain squatters. Names matter, and cyber squatters are willing to take advantage of these activities to make profits at someone else's expense.[7]

Encourages Gifts and Bribes

When marketing to other businesses, close personal contacts are often common, both in personal sales calls and in other venues, such as trade shows. Among the more serious ethical issues are gifts and bribery.

To influence sales, purchasing agents and other members of the buying company are often the recipients of gifts, meals, entertainment, and even free trips. From a personal ethics standpoint, many concerned leaders question accepting personal gifts that are designed to influence business decisions. The International Olympics Committee wrestled with this problem when Salt Lake City was chosen to host the 2002 Winter Olympics. Exorbitant gifts may have swayed the selection process.

Undermines Privacy

Technology is a two-edged sword in the area of marketing communications. On the one hand, it creates marvellous new ways to quickly reach a set of consumers with a key message and to keep in continuous contact with those customers. On the other hand, it can be invasive and intrusive and presents ethical dilemmas for those working on the Web.

The more obvious aspects of privacy, such as what information marketers are allowed to request and requirements for disclosure of how they use personal information, are covered under legal regulation in Canada through the *Personal Information Protection and Electronic Documents Act*. However, a more serious concern with privacy occurs online when consumers may not even know that companies have access to personal information that consumers assume is private.[8]

Canada Direct Insurance created an online golf game in order to get consumers to spend more time with the brand online.

Consumers are typically aware when data such as name, address, and phone number are disclosed because they explicitly offer that information to marketers. Additional information, however, is often extracted, and this process is usually hidden from consumers. The Interactive Advertising Bureau estimates that 80 percent of online campaigns involved some form of tracking that is unknown to the consumer. Much of this data is collected by third parties who track and aggregate consumers' habits, typically through cookies.

Through an aggregation of what consumers view and their interests tracked through online behaviour, companies can piece together a much clearer view of what will likely motivate a consumer to respond to marketing communications. On the one hand, this allows for more targeted marketing communications. But on the other hand, if the consumer doesn't consent to the tracking of information, or even know it is going on, should companies be allowed to track and use personal behaviour data? Further, should they be allowed to share that information, even in aggregate, to third parties who can then also target marketing communications? This coordination between companies is becoming even more seamless as many websites now have central logins, such as TripAdvisor and Facebook. Facebook can now collect information on a consumer's travel experiences and preferences, even when that consumer is not physically using Facebook.

Critical Thinking Exercise

What does Facebook know about you? Have you linked any other websites, such as TripAdvisor, to your Facebook account? What benefits does such a link provide the consumer? What are the potential costs or risks for consumers who make such links?

Outcomes of Marketing Communications Campaigns

The second category of ethical issues concerns those associated with outcomes of marketing communications campaigns. In other words, concerns associated with objectives (or side effects) of marketing communications.

Promotes Unsafe or Unhealthy Products

Although the marketing of specific products, such as tobacco and alcohol, has limitations imposed on it, marketing is often associated with unsafe or unhealthy products. The practice of restricting some products and not others raises questions about free enterprise and why some product categories are banned from using specific media when other product categories do not face this restriction. The argument is a slippery slope given that virtually any product can be shown to be harmful. Indeed, it is possible to die from the consumption of too much water.

Other concerns remain. For example, by the age of 18 the average North American teen has viewed more than 100,000 beer commercials. Critics of the brewing and marketing industries agree: too many beer commercials are designed to encourage underage drinking and build brand loyalty or brand switching in a population that is not even supposed to use the product. Occasional underage drinking can lead to an addiction in a few months, because underage drinkers are less developed mentally, physically, and emotionally.

The questions becomes: Do a few public relations messages, such as the "Know When to Say When" campaign authorized by Budweiser, represent a real attempt to reduce underage drinking, or are they designed to placate the government and critics?

The promotion of prescription drugs is another ethical grey area in marketing communications. Promotion of prescription drugs to Canadian consumers is subject to several restrictions, including the exclusion of any message that promotes a specific drug name with a specific condition or disease. However, proponents of direct-to-consumer promotion of prescription drugs contend that medical practices and drug companies have the right to market services or goods as much as Nike or Wal-Mart has the right to promote their products. In the meantime, advertising companies and marketing teams are continually being asked to convince consumers to purchase new drugs.[9] To ensure consumer protection in Canada, the Pharmaceutical Advertising Advisory Board (**www.paab.ca**) is highly active in reviewing messages directed at consumers. The organization ensures, for example, that all claims and data can be verified and are accurate.

Restrictions that limit direct-to-consumer communications from pharmaceutical companies are designed to protect patient health.

Increases the Cost of Goods Another criticism is that marketing communications increases the costs of goods and services. This debate has been waged for many years. Those critics charge that investments in marketing communications point to the billions of dollars spent between companies that trade share points between each other. Also, by creating some artificial means of differentiation between similar products (e.g., positioning a product based on lifestyle when it is physically very close to a competitors' products) can lead consumes to "over-value" a brand and pay more for it. Certainly there is evidence that consumers are willing to pay more for so-called brand name items than they are for most retail store private label brands. This seems to suggest that investments in marketing communications are responsible for higher prices.

However, those who argue in favour of marketing communications' value point out that by widening the market for some products, lower prices are in fact achieved through economies of scale. They also argue that marketing communications is one means by which consumers learn of products and companies are able to inform consumers.

Critical Thinking Exercise

One argument against marketing communications suggests that companies merely compete with each other for the same customers. If all companies spent less, then they could charge less for their products and still have the same number of customers and profit. But does marketing communications only work to make people switch from one product to another? Think of a case when marketing communications led you to switch your behaviour with a product category that you would have consumed anyway. Then, think of a case where marketing communications led you to buy a product for the first time. Was there a difference in the message in the marketing communications between the two?

Encourages People to Buy Things They Can't Afford

An argument related to higher costs due to investments in marketing communications is that marketing communications encourages people to buy things they either don't need or can't afford. Indeed, if one of the arguments against marketing communications leading

Source: Courtesy of Noise Digital.

IKEA created a wish list online to help consumers plan purchases. Does this create more demand for IKEA products, more preference, or both?

to higher prices is that lower prices come from economies of scale, then it must lead more people to buy. The question is whether it encourages people to buy things they can't afford or don't need, or whether it informs them of products that can help them solve problems and of which they were not aware.

Emphasizes Materialism

A related criticism to the above is that marketing communications more broadly results in a culture of materialism. Given the pervasiveness of marketing communications in our culture, we can't help but be exposed to constant messages about products that can fulfill our every want and desire. We see images of people who are living well because of the goods and services they buy, and critics argue that the result is the upward spiral of materialism. Essentially, we come to believe that possessions are the source of satisfaction, and that we can't be happy unless we are consuming products.

Proponents of marketing communications point out that most marketing communications attempts to mirror existing morals in society. They remind us that people wanted things long before marketing communications were able to inform them of products and services.

Obviously, one campaign cannot meaningfully sway society towards a more materialistic norm. However, each individual ad, when viewed alongside other ads, day after day, year after year may indeed help shape what society considers "normal." This issue becomes a challenge for marketers who seek to avoid contributing to what they see as an increasingly materialistic society. In fact, some marketers have used the argument against materialism as a main message in their marketing communications. A campaign for the recreational vehicle industry (**www.gorving.ca**) takes aim at technology and possessions that inundate our lives. Their message? Go buy an RV and get away from it all. Except you need an RV to do that, of course.

MARKETERS' RESPONSES TO ETHICAL CHALLENGES

The foundation and frameworks for ethical guidelines are derived from several sources. These include philosophy, law, religion, and common sense.

One *philosophy of life* involves maximizing pleasure and minimizing pain. This idea represents **hedonism**. Critics note that life is often more than the simple pursuit of pleasure and avoidance of pain. **Homeostasis** is the natural craving for balance. People balance a variety of urges throughout life.

The **law** offers guidelines regarding right and wrong as well as what is acceptable and what is not within a geographic area. Legal systems are designed to tell people what they can and cannot do. Remember, however, that not all legal systems are the same.

Many **religions**, or belief systems, profess a version of the philosophy that is summarized by the *Golden Rule*: Do unto others as you would have them do unto you. Acting in a morally acceptable manner starts with treating others well. Still, specific religious ideologies vary widely. Many disagreements about what is right or wrong exist. Respect, tolerance, discussion, compromise, and accommodation should become ethical guidelines when the religious views of others contradict your own.

At the end of the day, one overriding constant may be that ethical actions, moral correctness, and social responsibility all boil down to *common sense*. Two processes can be used to analyze an ethical concept. The first is logic and reasoning, which leads to common-sense conclusions. One's conscience may become muted over time if it is continually ignored; however, most people know when they are doing something right or wrong. The second element of common sense is gut instinct. Deep down inside, most people know when something is appropriate or inappropriate. A person's thoughts and gut reaction should never be ignored in an ethical reasoning process.

| ◆ Utilitarianism | ◆ Rights approach |
| ◆ Individualism | ◆ Justice approach |

FIGURE 12.2
Ethical Frameworks

ETHICAL FRAMEWORKS

The building blocks and personal ethical systems noted in the previous sections help to define various approaches to ethical reasoning. As shown in Figure 12.2, there are several ideas about what constitutes the best framework for the analysis of ethical issues, including utilitarianism, individualism, the rights approach, and the justice approach. Marketers can use these frameworks as helpful guidelines when thinking about ethical issues in marketing communications.

Utilitarianism is a means of making decisions based on what is the greatest good for the greatest number of people. Utilitarianism is referred to as the "calculus of pain," because it tries to minimize pain and maximize pleasure for the greatest number of people, relying a great deal on the concept of homeostasis.

Unfortunately, utilitarianism perspectives may overlook the rights or needs of the minority. As an extreme example, the use of slaves may create greater well-being for a vast majority of slaveholders, but at the same time the rights of the few, the slaves, are being destroyed. It is impossible to argue that slavery is ethical.

Ethicists may conclude that utilitarianism involves a judgment call as to what is "good" as well as considering that "good" in light of its effects on both the majority and the minority. Care should be given in deciding how much "pain" to others is acceptable.

Individualism is the degree to which society values personal goals, personal autonomy, privacy over group loyalty, commitments to group norms, involvements in collective activities, social cohesiveness, and intense socialization. Therefore, ethical decisions are based on personal self-interests, so long as one's actions do not harm others.

The individualism approach may cause the weakest members of society to suffer the most. In health care, individualists favour systems in which those with money are able to retain the best medical professionals. The individualist position is consistently used to criticize programs such as socialized medicine. It suggests that those who do not contribute to society's well-being, by being employed and paying taxes, should not have the same access as those who work hard and pay the bills.

The **rights approach** is a means of making decisions based on the belief that each person has fundamental rights that should be respected and protected. These rights include freedom of speech, privacy, and access to due process, plus the right to a safe and healthy environment at work and at home. Rights to free speech include the rights of companies to advertise any kind of product, even those that make people uncomfortable or ones they object to.

The difficulty with the rights approach is that many times the rights of one group, or a certain type of right, may impede on others. For example, there is a conflict between rights to privacy versus freedom of speech, when the issue is a job reference. Someone who has been fired for being incompetent, unreliable, or unethical may wish to keep that information confidential. Freedom of speech, however, should protect the rights of a former employer who simply tells the truth about why the person was terminated. As an ethical framework, the balancing act is present in defining which rights apply to a situation, and which rights take precedent.

The **justice approach** is a method of decision making based on treating all people fairly and consistently. *Distributive justice* concentrates on the fairness of rewards, punishments, and outcomes. *Procedural justice* focuses on fair and consistent application of rules and protocols.

The justice approach suggests that when someone is hurt by another's actions, as an individual or in a collective, there should be consequences. These consequences are supposed to punish the perpetrator for the misdeed and serve as a deterrent to others. Also, when one's actions help others or lead to a greater good, the consequences should be in the form of a reward. In both circumstances (harm or good), the methods by which rewards are granted or negative sanctions are imposed should be based on an impartial, reasonable, and constant program of judgment and justice.

One problem with the justice approach is that what one person considers to be a proper reward or punishment may not seem fair to another. Many people believe capital punishment is a just outcome. Others believe it is never justified. The same is true regarding those who make the judgments. What may seem like a fair procedure to one could appear to be totally biased to another.

Critical Thinking Exercise

Figure 12.2 identifies four ethical frameworks. Each framework has its merits, but which one do you lean toward or believe in the most? Why? Discuss the other three frameworks in terms of your own personal philosophical view of life. Why would you expect your preferred approach to be the one that would be in the best interests of the company that will hire you after graduation?

CODE OF ETHICS

Various individuals and groups have responded to the need for a more ethical environment by creating ethics training programs, codes of ethics, and ethics consulting systems. These attempts are designed to assist individual employees, managers or supervisors, and others within a company facing ethical challenges or dilemmas.

Ethics Training Programs

Ethics training can take place at several points. Early moral training occurs in many families as part of growing up, both in secular settings and in religious organizations. Those attending college receive further instruction. The Association to Advance Collegiate Schools of Business (AACSB), which is a major accrediting body for schools of business, has placed a strong emphasis on ethics instruction for over a decade.

Many corporations now add ethics topics into new employee training programs as well as manager training systems. Some are self-created; others are developed in conjunction with professional organizations and nearby colleges and universities.

Companies that invest in ethical training and codes can find them very rewarding financially.

Codes of Ethics

Many organizations have adopted formal codes of ethics intended to guide behaviour. These codes are developed at one of two levels. First, at the company level, the firm can adopt a specific set of guidelines that employees can use to help make decisions that are aligned with the desired ethical approach of the company. Many firms have written and revised ethical codes. Some of the more common components of codes of ethics are displayed in Figure 12.3.

The second way codes of ethics are developed is within a profession. The marketing profession, through the American Marketing Association (AMA) (**www.marketingpower. com**), offers a code of ethics to its members. The code is comprehensive across all marketing

FIGURE 12.3
Components of Codes of Ethics

- The purpose of the code, including (1) regulation of behavior and (2) inspiration to employees.

- A statement of aspirations often included in a preamble that outlines the ideals a company aspires to for its employees. The statement should include the values and principles of the organization.

- A list of principles.

- A list of rules, if needed.

- A statement regarding how the code was created.

- How the code will be implemented.

- How the code will be publicized internally to employees.

- How the code will be publicized externally to constituents and publics.

- How the code will be enforced.

- A statement regarding how and when the code will be revised.

- Most of the time, values, principles, and rules are listed in order of importance.

activities, including marketing communications. For example, one element of the "fairness" principle is: "Represent products in a clear way in selling, advertising, and other forms of communication; this includes the avoidance of false, misleading, and deceptive promotion."

Critical Thinking Exercise

Find the AMA Code of Ethics on their website (**www.marketingpower.com**). Do you find the code helpful? From the point of view of a manager, consider the examples provided in ethical issues discussed earlier in the chapter: the headline used to promote discounts at a retail store and the selection of models for the promotion of walk-in bathtubs. How would this code suggest the marketer resolve these ethical dilemmas?

COMMUNICATING ACROSS CULTURES

Each individual country has its own set of laws regarding what is legal and what is not in marketing communications. The role of the marketing communications team is to make sure these laws and regulations are clearly understood. The company should make every effort to comply with them.

Remember that legal systems vary. In the United States and many Western countries, the form of law is known as common law. *Common law* is based on local customs, traditions, and precedents. Legal history, previous cases, and national customs serve as guides, and judges typically have more discretion in making legal decisions.

Civil law, which is present in many European countries, is based on a broad set of legal principles, and decisions are made based on legal codes that have been written over time. This gives judges less flexibility.

Theocratic law is based on religious teachings. The most common form of theocratic law is Islamic law, which is based on the *Koran* and *Sunnah*. In many Islamic countries, transactions are regulated in different ways. For instance, charging interest is not permitted in the Islamic system.

Moral reasoning follows a similar pattern in international marketing. One cannot assume that a given system of ethics and morals is completely acceptable in another country. For example, views on the roles of men and women in society vary widely. Any marketing communications activity with an international outreach should employ a cultural assimilator to help individuals understand the different ethical principles present in other nations.

IMC IN PRACTICE

Kate Baillie explains one of her concerns related to both ethics and regulation as follows: "We always need to consider the regulatory framework in which we operate when advertising our single line Home Phone products. Regulation governs our ability to compete on price: we can't sell our service for less than it costs us to deliver. This is considered 'predatory,' when, in fact, our desire may simply be to compete head-to-head in a market that has become very competitive and very sensitive to price."

Although TELUS does use pricing to compete, it relies more on providing value than on a low price.

"Once we hit certain metrics in any given geographical region, we are mostly freed from regulation (we gain 'forbearance'), so that we can compete normally and offer customers in these regions the same pricing that we offer customers in other, already forborne regions. However, the process of proving that a region is fully competitive can be slow, to the point that we actually gain freedom months after we meet the criteria. Not only are two separate pricing structures very inefficient from an advertising perspective (not to mention sales, support, billing, etc.), it means we're not living up to our brand promise of *the future is friendly*— a promise that is crucial for us to uphold. Many mass media vehicles in which we advertise our forborne prices make their way to non-forborne regions (think of how well read the *Vancouver Sun* is in some of our more rural areas). It does not sit well with me that clients see us advertise one price, only to call and find that we are prevented from giving it to them."

Kate aligns her approach to one of the key elements of the brand. "The intelligence attribute of our brand dictates that we treat people with respect and don't insult their intelligence. It can be frustrating to be prevented from offering the same rates as the competition, but we don't try to hide our pricing. Instead, we do our best to differentiate our Home Phone product through quality and reliability, and we work even harder in the community to build goodwill for TELUS.

As for legal issues, Kate's team has to be aware of any changes in communications law to ensure that TELUS is compliant. "An obvious issue for us is the application of language laws in Quebec. That's a very important market for us, so we need to make sure that all of our communications adhere to the guidelines." Other issues range from the use of product performance claims—which need to be backed up by extensive testing—to competitive claims in advertising. In some cases, it's not enough for Kate's team to be aware of how the laws governing telecommunications services affect their advertising. They also need to be aware when competitors are not following the guidelines, or when changes in the competitive environment alter competitive claims. "Some time ago we launched a new wireless network, which enabled us to file a complaint in court over some ads a competitor was running that laid claim to Canada's most reliable network. We were able to gain an injunction against this advertising on the basis that the competitive environment had changed and our competitor's claim was no longer relevant to consumers. Being on top of cases like that means our customers get accurate and relevant information to make their choices. Luckily at TELUS we partner with our legal counsel, who guide us in all of our communication activities."

Source: Used with permission of Kate Baillie, TELUS Communications.

For help developing your IMC Plan, go to **www.pearsoncanada.ca/clow**.

SUMMARY

Feedback from marketing communications campaigns comes from many stakeholders in our society. Governments and activist groups regularly monitor marketing communications, and even individual consumers can take action against a company if they find that their marketing communications crosses a legal or ethical boundary.

In Canada, the CRTC and Competition Bureau are the primary legal regulators of marketing communications. They create and enforce regulations ranging from the amount of marketing communications that can be contained within a given media, who can be targeted through those media, and what can (and cannot) be said within the message.

Obviously, no firm wants to run afoul of legal regulations, so the self-regulating industry body Advertising Standards Canada was created to help the industry police itself and ensure that Canadian marketing communications are viable. This nonprofit organization provides services that let marketers ensure that their communications conform not only to legal requirements but also to softer standards that the industry itself has agreed to follow. The organization also provides an avenue for consumers who wish to make a complaint about any marketing communications message they feel contravenes the industry code. Finally, through a code specific to marketing communications and children, the organization works to provide extra protection for this vulnerable audience that is highly sought after by many marketing communications programs.

Ethics and morals are key principles that can be used to guide a person's activities in the world of commerce. Morals are beliefs or principles that individuals hold concerning what is right and what is wrong. Ethics are moral principles that serve as guidelines for both individuals and organizations. Marketing and marketing communications activities are affected by ethical and moral concerns.

Some of the more common concerns about marketing communications relate to the content of the messages themselves. Some argue that marketing communications misleads people or exaggerates the truth, offends people, perpetuates stereotypes, targets children, infringes on competitors' brands, encourages gifts and bribes, and undermines privacy. Other concerns relate to the outcomes that are part of many IMC plans, with critics charging that marketing communications promote unsafe or unhealthy products, increase the cost of goods for all consumers, encourage people to buy things they can't afford, and emphasize and encourage materialism.

To help marketers navigate the ethical minefield of marketing communications, a number of ethical frameworks and guidelines are available, at both at the company level and the professional level through codes of ethics.

The issues of legality and morality are present in the international arena as well. Each is complicated by different bodies of law and views of ethics in various nations. Companies seeking to expand internationally should be aware of these differences in order to find ways to respond to them.

KEY TERMS

bait and switch selling Promoting a product at a bargain price and not making the product available for sale in reasonable quantities.

brand infringement Occurs when a company creates a brand name that closely resembles a popular or successful brand.

ethics Moral principles that serve as guidelines for both individuals and organizations.

hedonism Maximizing pleasure and minimizing pain.

homeostasis The natural craving for balance.

individualism The degree to which society values personal goals, personal autonomy, privacy over group loyalty, commitments to group norms, involvements in collective activities, social cohesiveness, and intense socialization.

justice approach A method of decision making based on treating all people fairly and consistently.

law Governmental guidelines for what is right and wrong as well as what is acceptable and what is not within a geographic area.

morals Beliefs or principles that individuals hold concerning what is right and what is wrong.

puffery When a firm makes an exaggerated claim about its products or services without making an overt attempt to deceive or mislead.

religions Belief systems.

rights approach A means of making decisions based on the belief that each person has fundamental rights that should be respected and protected.

utilitarianism A means of making decisions based on what is the greatest good for the greatest number of people.

REVIEW QUESTIONS

1. Name the governmental agencies that oversee marketing communications programs.
2. What are the primary areas of marketing communications regulation by the CRTC?
3. What are the primary areas of marketing communications regulation by the Competition Bureau?
4. What is the marketing communications industry's self-regulatory organization called?
5. What two codes does the industry use as self-regulation?
6. Identify the types of ethical complaints that are raised regarding marketing communications.
7. What is puffery? Should a company use a great deal of puffery in its ads? Why or why not?
8. What is brand infringement?
9. Define ethics and morals.
10. Describe four ethical frameworks noted in this chapter.
11. What two types of guidelines can marketers use to help make decisions about ethical concerns?

INTEGRATED LEARNING EXERCISES

1. The Competition Bureau is a major player in the regulation of marketing communications in Canada. But some critics argue that the organization is simply too large and covers too many aspects of business in general to be user-friendly as a marketing communications regulator. See if you agree. Visit their website (**www.competitionbureau.gc.ca**). Imagine that you have just been hired and asked to review the complete marketing communications policies of the firm to ensure they are in compliance with the regulations at the Competition Bureau. Is the information easy to find? What main areas will you cover in the report to your manager?

2. Advertising Standards Canada administers two codes that are designed to self-regulate the marketing communications industry in Canada. But the code is only enforced when someone lodges a complaint. Get today's copy of either the national or local newspaper in your city. Examine the ads and see if you can find any that you feel contravene one or more of the clauses in these two codes. What could the marketers have done differently in their ads to be in compliance with the codes?

3. Imagine you are the VP of Marketing in Canada for toymaker Mattel. As a member of Advertising Standards Canada and an interested stakeholder you have been asked to provide input on the Broadcast Code for Advertising to Children. Find the complete code on the Advertising Standards Canada website. Imagine you are in front of the advisory board that is considering revisions to the content of the code. What changes would you recommend and why? Would your proposed changes allow more marketing communications targeting children, or do you feel the current code doesn't go far enough in restricting marketing communications to children?

4. We know from earlier chapters that sex doesn't always sell. One of the reasons sex appeals may not work is that they may offend some audiences, who tune out the message completely. But we also know that what offends one person might not offend another. Find two print ads that use sex appeals, one that you think is acceptable, and one that you think pushed the boundaries a bit too far (or way too far). What makes the difference? Is it the content of the ad, or the target audience of the specific media, or both?

STUDENT PROJECT

Creative Corner

Most people can point to many ads that they think are at least a little bit offensive, misleading, or otherwise unethical. But most people don't complain about them. One common reason give for remaining silent is that they don't think a complaint will do any good. People also say that they are unsure where complaints should be directed, since ads usually don't come with a complaint hotline. But the people at Advertising Standards Canada spend a great deal of time and effort trying to tell Canadians that they provide one easy avenue to lodge complaints, and if complaints are upheld, they are effective at removing marketing communications from the marketplace.

1. Find an ad or other piece of marketing communications that you feel contravenes the ASC code. Write a letter to ASC with your complaint. You can file the complaint online through their website. Be sure to outline which clause(s) of the code you feel are being contravened.

2. Develop a program that will encourage others to complain about the same ad. Think of your message as a traditional marketing communications challenge. You want people to do something (complain) and your task is to encourage them to do so. You have no budget, so it will likely be done online. But you can also talk to people, hold an event, etc. Which activities will you pursue and why? What will your main message be, and how will you encourage other people that their complaints will actually be heard and acted on? Develop a 10-minute presentation in which you outline your plan for the class.

→ ETHICS IN ACTION

Congratulations! You have just landed a job managing the Molson Canadian beer brand. Because it is one of the most popular brands in Canada, especially with younger demographics, this a dream job for someone in marketing communications. One of your first tasks is to meet with the marketing communications agency to view the rough edit of a television commercial that is in production. The agency executive explains that your predecessor wanted to bring an "edge" to the brand and that therefore the spot is little bit more risqué than previous campaigns.

As you sit down to watch the commercial in the editing suite, here is what you see. The spot opens with what appears to be a college dorm room. A wild party with people dressed only in their underwear is taking place. Everyone has a bottle of Canadian in their hands. Cut to the next morning, and a young man slowly stumbles into the women's bathroom on the floor. He bumps into a young woman who gives him a smile and says "last night was great, thanks." Then he turns the corner and meets another young woman, again wearing only underwear who says "you were fantastic, call me."

As you head back to the office you wonder what to do. Beer advertising has always pushed limits, and used sex appeals. But does this one go too far? To make matters worse, the CBC's *The Fifth Estate* ran a story just last week on how unprotected sex among college students is beginning to create some real social problems, including unplanned pregnancy and sexually transmitted diseases. They pointed a finger at the beer industry and

its promotion of a carefree partying lifestyle as one of the factors contributing to the problem. But before you left, an agency executive explained that the shoot is already done; $275,000 has already been invested into the ad, and to start over basically means spending another $275,000 and at least another 4 weeks. It is early May and you know that if you don't put a spot on air you'll fall behind rival Molson at the start of the busiest beer drinking period all year. Summer represents half the profits for the brand.

1. List the pros and cons of approving the spot as is.

2. What is your decision? Write a one-page memo to the VP of marketing that outlines your rationale and your plan to either make up for lost revenues (if you trash the spot) or perform damage control (if you approve it).

3. To what extent is your decision influenced by the extra media attention given to the beer industry by the media? Do you accept the argument that the beer industry, through the use of marketing communications, creates an atmosphere that encourages excessive partying and perhaps sex through the use of sex appeals?

4. Assume the VP of marketing, who also saw the episode of The Fifth Estate, forces you to trash the spot and to avoid any possibility that the brand can be accused of encouraging partying. Develop a new script/storyboard for a commercial that you think will be effective and steer clear of the issue. ●

CASE STUDY | What Is Unilever Trying to Say?

Dutch consumer goods giant Unilever has many brands that are household names: Lipton, Hellman's, Vaseline, Snuggles, Ragu, and Ben and Jerry's, to name a few. But one of their most popular brands is Dove.

As part of a brand rationalization process, where the company sought to reduce the number of brands in its portfolio, Dove was designated a "master brand" whose name would appear on a number of products in related categories, such as soaps, shampoos, and the like. But this meant that the brand had to move from a positioning that focused primarily on the functional benefits of the product to something that could accommodate a wider variety of products. The original Dove bar was, for decades, positioned as a "beauty bar." Something other than soap. In fact, television ads always included a distinct claim that Dove was not soap. Soap dried out skin, whereas Dove provided skin with moisture.

But for other products, like shampoo, this moisture positioning no longer made sense. The marketing communications had to change. The direction the brand took was the now famous "Campaign for Real Beauty." Launched in 2002, the campaign was designed to give the brand a point of view about women and issues they cared about. Research demonstrated that very few women described themselves as beautiful. The

brand capitalized on this by positioning itself as a brand that allowed women to feel beautiful, and essentially chastised the industry to which it belonged for causing unrealistic stereotypes through marketing communications.

The campaign for real beauty was a huge success. It featured a number of memorable advertising executions, including one that aired during the Super Bowl in 2008. In that ad, the actual children of Dove employees were featured along with the appearance-related problems they encounter, all under the song "True Colours." For example, one Asian girl with black hair was featured with the words "Wishes she was blond" accompanying her image on the screen. In another image, a young girl with freckles appeared with the line "Hates her freckles" under her face. The ad was a resounding success, even with the predominantly male Super Bowl viewership. All of these men have daughters, sisters, nieces who they can imagine being similarly troubled by the unrealistic expectations set by the "beauty industry."

In another ad, which was created as a YouTube video, the shot opens with a young girl. As the camera holds on her face, an "onslaught" of images from the beauty industry flashes on the screen. In each image, shown for fractions of a second, the viewer understands that over the years the little girl

Unilever argues against stereotypical beauty through its Dove brand but celebrates it through the Axe brand.

in the ad will be exposed to literally thousands of messages that will lead her to feel inadequate. The advertisement highlights the Dove Self-Esteem Fund. which is designed to help young girls feel comfortable with their beauty and to reject beauty industry stereotypes. The ad closes with the line, "Talk to your daughter before the beauty industry does." The ad can be found on YouTube by searching the terms Dove and Onslaught.

However, by putting the brand's point of view so strongly at the forefront of the marketing communications message and using online media such as YouTube to deliver the message, the campaign was sure to evoke response. Much of the response questioned the wisdom behind the campaign. If the product category is aspirational, does it make sense to send a message encouraging people not to aspire? But some of the other feedback involved deeper criticism of the motives of the parent company, Unilever.

The heart of this criticism—ironically also found on YouTube—features a parody video of the Onslaught video by Dove. In this video, instead of being from the "beauty industry," the images flashing are from actual Axe commercials. The images feature scantily clad women swooning over men or pole dancing, and other behaviours. The images from the Axe commercials clearly portray women as thin and large-breasted, with unusually high sex drives. Hardly the stuff that builds self-esteem in little freckled girls. The line at the end of the parody video is, "Talk to your daughter before Unilever does." Although not as popular as the original Dove YouTube video, the parody had hundreds of thousands of viewers, with many commenting that they were upset with parent company Unilever for playing both sides of this issue under different brand names.

By taking the Dove message into online media, and indeed by taking the point of view against traditional female stereotypes, the brand managers must have known the corporate connection to the Axe brand would emerge. But the brand portfolio approach taken by Unilever, similar to that of other consumer goods conglomerates like Procter & Gamble, means that each brand has autonomous management.

1. Did you know that Unilever was the company behind both the Dove and Axe brands? If you were the CEO responsible for the entire portfolio of brands, what would be your response to criticisms such as the parody video? Write a memo to the brand managers for each brand outlining the steps you want them to take.

2. Find three ads for the Axe brand. Based on your reading of the Canadian Code of Advertising Standards, do you feel the ads contravene any of the clauses?

3. Utilitarianism is a very popular ethical framework in boardrooms around the world. Most managers won't reject an idea because it might treat someone as a means to an end, for example, but they will reject treating people as a means to an end if it is unprofitable to do so. Using the utilitarian framework of costs and benefits, develop a ledger sheet for the Unilever CEO that outlines what is gained, and at what cost, from running both campaigns simultaneously.

4. Imagine you have a nine-year-old daughter. Taking the advice of the parody ad, you plan to talk to your daughter before Unilever does. You know she will soon, if she hasn't already, be exposed to marketing communications from the Axe brand. You know she has already seen elements of the Dove campaign. You are nervous to talk to her about how both brands send different messages, so you decide to write down your thoughts first. Draft a one-page list of the points you want to make to your daughter and explain how these two brands can be supported by the same company.

ENDNOTES

1. Minette E. Drumwright and Patrick Murphy, "How Advertising Practitioners View Ethics," *Journal of Advertising* 33, no. 2 (Summer 2004), pp. 7–24.

2. John E. Calfee and Debra Jones Ringold, "The 70% Majority: Enduring Consumer Beliefs About Advertising," *Journal of Public Policy & Marketing* 13, no. 2 (Fall 1994), pp. 228–238.

3. Quellet, "How Not to Market to Children in Quebec," National Post (March 10, 2009), p. F12.

4. George G. Brenkert, *Marketing Ethics* (Blackwell Publishing, Malden, MA, 2008).

5. Mary Pipher, *The Shelter of Each Other* (New York: Ballentine Books, 1996).

6. Susan Linn, *Consuming Kids: The Hostile Takeover of Childhood* (The New Press, New York, NY, 2004).

7. Internet Marketing Register (**www.marketing-register.com**, accessed February 28, 2005).

8. Nehf, "Shopping for Privacy on the Internet," *Journal of Consumer Affairs* 41, no. 2 (2007), pp. 351–375.

9. *ABC Nightly News* (May 30, 2002).

CHAPTER OBJECTIVES

After reading this chapter, you should be able to answer the following questions:

- **Which** items should be assessed when evaluating an IMC program?
- **How** are evaluations of messages different from measures of behavioural responses?
- **When** are marketing communications evaluated?
- **What** are some of the commonly used measures for marketing communications?
- **How** can marketers ensure their measures are appropriate?
- **Why** do some marketers fail to test or measure marketing communications?

INDUSTRY PROFILE
So You Want to Work in Marketing Communications?

Anita Kapadia, Marketing Manager, ResponseTek, Vancouver, British Columbia/Toronto, Ontario

ResponseTek provides customer experience management software for businesses that want to ensure their customers have the best experience possible. "Customer experience management is different from customer relationship management software," explains Marketing Manager Anita Kapadia. "CRM is based on allowing a company to manage relationships with individual customers, to optimize their revenue, loyalty, or some other specific customer outcome. What we provide is software that lets companies manage the overall customer experience at an aggregate level. For example, WestJet uses our software to manage and act on customer feedback from all sorts of sources such as their website and emails, so they can continually improve satisfaction and loyalty based directly on what customers are telling them."

Because all of ResponseTek's clients require a unique solution, one of the company's strengths is that the software can easily be tailored to meet specific client needs. And it also means that the marketing communications and sales cycle is quite different from consumer segments. "It's much more targeted than most consumer-based marketing communications," explains Anita. "We rely heavily on direct marketing, using things like email because we have a fairly limited universe of potential clients that we can work with.

"A typical campaign for us might include a series of emails that we would send to a targeted database of leads—people who are responsible for the customer experience within their firm. We will send them three or four emails that offer educational information about customer experience management and trends within the industry. They would click through from that white paper or case study to our website, where we would provide more information about the industry and our company specifically."

One of the key benefits of relying on such a targeted approach is that it is relatively easy to see how the marketing communications are working in the market.

Evaluating an Integrated Marketing Program

"In the email campaigns, for example, we measure responses at each point along the customer sales cycle, beginning with the first click from that email. We know how many people opened the email and how many people read it. From there we track how many clicked through to the prospect registration page, which is where we ask them to identify themselves. The next step we track is how many proceed to download any of the documents we make available on our website. And we get all of this data in real time, down to the very second at which it is happening." The results from these stages tell Anita how the campaign is working, and how she might tailor future campaigns.

A big part of these campaigns involves testing various elements of the message. For example, Anita recently tested the effect of changing the days of the week that the email is sent to prospects. "Our emails are usually timed to go out at 4 a.m. so they are among the first things in the inbox when people check their email in the morning. We tested to see if there is a difference between emails that go out on a Monday versus a Thursday, for example. Although we're not yet sure why, we found that emails sent on Monday and Wednesday were winners over the other days of the week. We're working on future research to see if we can figure out what is behind this effect, so we can make sure all future campaigns are more effective.

Another element of testing and measurement for Anita concerns the creative elements of the communications. In one recent campaign, a salesperson felt that a more personal email from him directly would outperform the generic marketing email. So Anita

Anita Kapadia, Marketing Manager, ResponseTek.

tested the two approaches alongside each other to see if the more personalized approach worked better than the traditional method of one email from the corporate office sent to everyone.

These tests and measures are critical to the success of the firm, given that the average purchase for any one customer is in the hundreds of thousands of dollars. "Even an improvement on 1 percent on response to our campaigns can mean the difference of millions of dollars of revenue each year."

Anita links her career success to three things: ambition, attitude, and aptitude. "I have been ambitious in my career so far. I haven't been afraid to chase jobs that were a bit outside my comfort level, or maybe focused on aspects of marketing that I have yet to master."

For attitude, it begins with Anita's smile. "I'm just a positive person at heart, and that has helped me a lot. Every job, especially those at the entry level, includes tasks that are more mundane and less glamorous than most people would like. It's important to take on those tasks with positive energy because employers want to know that you can be flexible and adapt."

The third element—aptitude—has been especially important in Anita's job at ResponseTek. "Because we are a relatively small company, my role involves continually learning new things. I am 'the' marketing person at the company; there is no department per se. So I've had to be willing to learn as I go. One of the biggest challenges in this job has been the need for me to have some basic design skills. When we publish documents on our website, it helps if I can make them aesthetically appealing. This is a big shift from my experience working in advertising agencies where people in my role were discouraged from getting involved in design. At small firms, there isn't always the luxury of specialized roles. So I'm a bit of a jack-of-all-trades, but that is great because I feel totally valued and appreciated."

Anita offers two pieces of advice for students interested in working in positions like hers. The first concerns aptitude and the ability to learn. "Look for learning wherever you can find it. When I started at ResponseTek I knew I was going to need to brush up my skills in design programs like Adobe Creative Suite. So I took my friend who works with this program out to dinner and asked her to show me what she knew. Friends can be a great resource for learning new skills."

The second piece of advice concerns knowing your limits, and asking questions when you need more information. "In any marketing role you can expect to have your plate full. So it's important to ask questions if you don't understand something. If you don't, the work just gets backed up, and piled higher, and you run the risk of not being able to get out from under it. Try to always stay one step ahead of your job."

OVERVIEW

John Wanamaker, a well-known nineteenth-century department store owner, once remarked, "I know half the money I spend on advertising is wasted, but I can never find out which half." Given the explosion of marketing communications media over the past hundred years, evaluating the effectiveness of marketing communications has become increasingly difficult. In an environment in which company leaders demand measurable results, the challenge for marketers is to offer evidence that a campaign will be successful *before* it is even launched, along with additional proof *after* the campaign. This is understandable, because company leaders are trying to allocate marketing funds wisely.

To meet this growing insistence upon accountability, marketing researchers spend more time and energy seeking to develop new and more accurate measures of success. These measures, known as **metrics**, should accurately portray the effectiveness of a marketing communications plan, which is not an easy task.

This final chapter is devoted to the various methods available for evaluating the overall success of an IMC program as well as the success of individual components of the plan. Evaluations can be based on either message evaluations or respondent behaviour evaluations. Essentially, message evaluation seeks to understand what an audience thinks or feels in response to a message, while respondent behaviour evaluation measures what the audience actually does in response to a message.

Message evaluation techniques examine the message and the physical design of the advertisement, coupon, direct marketing piece, or whatever the form of marketing communications. Message evaluation procedures include such things as the study of actors in advertisements individuals who speak in radio ads. A message evaluation program considers the cognitive components associated with an ad, such as recall and recognition, as well as emotional and attitudinal responses.

Respondent behaviour evaluations address visible customer actions, including store visits, inquiries, or actual purchases. This category contains evaluation techniques that are measured using numbers, such as the number of coupons that are redeemed, the number of hits on a website, and changes in sales.

The emphasis on providing compelling proof that advertising actually works has led to a greater emphasis on respondent behaviours. Higher sales, increases in store traffic, a greater number of daily Internet hits on a website, and other numbers-based outcomes appeal to many managers. At the same time, both message evaluations and behavioural responses should be used to help the marketing communications team build short-term results and achieve long-term success. Remember, an audience may need to go through many stages in the purchase process before actual sale is made. Therefore, it is important that the measurement of the IMC plan be related to the specific objectives set for the overall IMC plan and be specifically designed to measure outcomes subsumed under the broader objective (i.e., measures of brand awareness are part of a larger objective of sales).

Many ads that appear in media such as transit advertising are focused on brand awareness and notoriety given their limited content.

MATCHING METHODS WITH IMC OBJECTIVES

Methods of evaluation should be chosen that match the objectives being measured.[1] When the objective of a marketing communications campaign is to increase customer awareness and recall of a brand, then the level of customer awareness should be measured. If the objective is to create sales, and specific levels of awareness and recall are needed before sales can be generated, then awareness, recall, and sales levels should all be measured to understand how awareness and recall led (or did not lead) to sales. It is critical that marketers don't only focus on short-term outcomes such as sales. Brand awareness and loyalty are built over many years, and these are often the foundation required for successful short-term objectives associated with outcomes like sales.

Individual elements of the marketing communications mix—advertising media, direct marketing, sales promotion, public relations, and digital marketing—can all serve multiple objectives within an IMC plan. However, as discussed in Chapters 7 through 11, some elements of the mix are more disposed to specific stages of customer decision making. For example, advertising media and public relations tend to be very effective at generating awareness and creating brand perceptions. Sales promotion and direct marketing, on the other hand, are particularly well suited to later stages in the process, including the actual purchase and post-purchase behaviours. Given the particular diversity within digital media, objectives for it span across any number of these stages, including the evaluation criteria stage through avenues such as company websites, online forums, and social networks.

Broadly speaking, each of these elements of the marketing communications mix can be measured using inputs, outputs, and outcomes.

Advertising Media. Inputs include the expected reach and frequency of a media buy, or the amount of GRPs in a media plan. Outputs include the effective reach and frequency, or the number of people who were actually exposed to the message. Outcomes include the result of the outputs. In the case of media, it can be anything

Many public service messages are designed to primarily generate web site traffic.

Promotions are often tied to sales-related objectives.

from increased levels of awareness and recall of a brand to visiting a company website, depending on the specific objectives set for media in the IMC plan.

Direct Marketing. Inputs include the number of direct mail packages or emails delivered, and outputs can be the number of packages that were effectively delivered or emails that didn't bounce back. Outcomes can be specific actions taken by the audience in response to the message, such as click-throughs to a company website or retail visits.

Sales Promotion. Inputs in sales promotion include things such as the number of coupons delivered or the size of rebates offered. Outputs include metrics such as the number of contest entries or rebates claimed. Outcomes of sales promotions are usually tied to sales or are sales-related, such as purchases or sales presentations that are delivered in exchange for a free gift.

Public Relations. Similar to other elements of the marketing communications mix, inputs in public relations include the efforts of the firm to communicate with various audiences, such as the number of press releases issued or CSR reports delivered. Outputs include things such as "impressions," which refers to the number of people who were exposed to the message. Impressions are determined by calculating the circulation of media that carried a story. Outcomes include measures that capture the intended objectives of PR, such as brand perceptions or likeability.

Digital Marketing. Because of the similarity of digital marketing across various dimensions to other elements of the marketing communications mix, inputs, outputs, and outcomes share similarities. Inputs can include the number of banner ads delivered or the number of discussion forums in which the company engages. Outputs might include click-throughs to websites or other online resources. Outcomes can vary from actual sales (in the case of clicking through to an online store) to brand awareness or recall, depending on the role digital media is expected to play in the IMC plan.

In general, inputs are easy to measure. They are simply an accounting of the communications activity of the firm. Outputs and outcomes require more proactive measurement of the part of the firm. Regardless of the specific element of the marketing communications mix that requires measurement, the metrics available to track various outputs and outcomes are the same. And as mentioned earlier, research can uncover these outcomes and/or outputs at various stages of the IMC development process. They can occur before the message is delivered, or after the message is delivered. Each of these is discussed next.

Critical Thinking Exercise

Given that the IMC plan is ultimately in pursuit of an overall goal, what is the value of mapping input, outputs, and outcomes for each individual component? What value is there in knowing how many emails went out, how many were read, and what the audience did in response to those emails? Why wouldn't a marketer just focus on the outcomes, since that's the only thing that delivers results?

MEASUREMENT TIMING

Examination of outputs and/or outcomes from marketing communications such as television advertising or a Web banner can be performed using metrics taken in *pre-tests* before the message is delivered, or in *post-tests* after the message is delivered.

Pre-Test Measurement Options

Concept Testing

Concept testing examines the proposed content of marketing communications and the impact that content may have on a potential target audience. Many agencies conduct concept tests when developing an advertisement or promotional piece. It can cost hundreds of thousands of dollars to produce just one television commercial. Therefore, it is clearly more cost-effective to test a concept in the early stages of development rather than after production of the message.[2] When testing potential television advertising, researchers will often use a **storyboard**, which is a series of still photographs or sketches outlining the structure of the commercial. If changes must be made, it is less costly to complete them during the planning stage than after the marketing piece has been completed. Also, once the marketing communications item is finished, those who worked on the piece tend to feel a sense of ownership and become resistant to making changes.

The most common concept testing procedure is a focus group. *Focus groups* normally consist of 8 to 10 people who are representative of the target market. These individuals are paid money or given financial incentives, such as gift certificates, to entice them to participate. In most cases, it is wise to use independent marketing research firms to conduct focus groups. The goal is to prevent biased results. An independent company is more likely to report that a certain advertising approach did not work than is someone who developed the approach and has a vested interest in it.

The number of focus groups used to study an issue varies greatly. It can be as many as 50 or as few as one. Focus group reactions can be quite different. Results are affected by the makeup of the group and the ways the session is conducted. As a result, it is risky to base a decision on just a single focus group's opinion. A humorous ad may have a great deal of appeal to one group, yet another might disagree or even find it offensive. It is a good idea to study the responses of several groups to study the impact of the humour on a series of individuals. Even trained focus group leaders experience varying results due to the composition of the group, the question being asked, and the degree of formality in the session. Further, one person's opinions may strongly influence the rest of the group. Therefore, most agencies use more than one group in order to ensure more reliable results. When several different focus groups arrive at the same conclusion, the finding is more reliable.

As highlighted in Figure 13.1, several components of a marketing communications plan can be evaluated with concept tests. Evaluations are typically performed using either comprehension or reaction tests, or both. *Comprehension tests* are used when participants in a study are asked the meaning of a proposed marketing communications piece. The idea is to make sure viewers correctly understand the message. The moderator can also explore the reasons why the intended message was misinterpreted.

Reaction tests are used to determine overall feelings about a proposed marketing piece, most notably whether the response is negative or positive. If the focus group reacts negatively to an ad concept or proposed copy, the agency can make the changes before the ad is developed. It is possible for an advertising concept to be correctly comprehended but elicit negative emotions. Therefore, exploring any negative feelings provides marketers with inputs to modify the marketing piece.

Copytesting

The second form of message evaluation, copytests, is used when the marketing piece is finished or in its final stages of development. **Copytests** are designed to elicit responses to the main message as well as the format used to present the message. For many television

---

- Copy or verbal component of an advertisement
- Message and its meaning
- Translation of copy in an international ad
- Effectiveness of peripheral cues, such as product placement in the ad and props used
- Value associated with an offer or prize in a contest

FIGURE 13.1
Examples of Components of a Marketing Communications Plan that Can Be Evaluated with Concept Tests

ads, copytests are conducted using a version that is filmed by agency members rather than professional actors.

Two common copytesting techniques are portfolio and theatre tests. Both place the marketing piece with various other samples. A **portfolio test** is a display of a set of printed marketing communications, one of which is the message being evaluated. A **theatre test** is a display of a set of television ads, including the one being evaluated. The individuals who participate do not know which piece is under scrutiny. Both techniques mimic reality in the sense that consumers normally are exposed to multiple messages, such as when a radio or television station plays a series of commercials in a row, when a set of newspaper ads appears on a single page, or when a consumer picks up a stack of mail from the mailbox. The tests also allow researchers the opportunity to compare the target piece with other marketing messages. For these approaches to yield the optimal findings, it is essential that all of the marketing pieces shown be in the same stage of development (e.g., a set of storyboards or a series of nearly completed coupon offers).

Copytesting can utilize focus groups as well as other measurement devices. An ad or coupon that is in the final stage of design can be tested with a **mall intercept technique**. The approach involves stopping shoppers. They are asked to evaluate the item. The mall intercept technique can incorporate a portfolio approach. To do so, subjects are asked to examine the marketing piece, which is mixed in with 6 to 10 other ads, coupons, or other marketing communications pieces. This is a better approach than showing an item by itself. The disadvantage of displaying only one item is that people tend to give it a more positive evaluation than when it is mixed with others. Comprehension and reaction tests are commonly utilized in a mall intercept setting.

Theatre tests are often used to evaluate television commercials. The test ad is placed among other ads within a television documentary or a new show, such as a pilot episode of a new comedy or drama. The advantage of using a new show is that it is better able to hold the subject's interest. At the end of the program, the individuals participating in the study are asked for reactions to the ads. For more valid results, those participating in the study should not know which ad is being tested.

Roper Starch Worldwide developed a copytesting system called ADD+IMPACT. The goal of the program is to study consumer reactions to communications before they are launched. As part of the testing process, Roper conducts one-on-one interviews with 60 or more consumers. Each participant responds to open-ended questions as well as more standardized, closed-ended attitudinal questions. The results of the test, the transcripts, and a quantitative analysis of the numbers-based responses are provided to clients within two weeks of the test. By testing the message prior to a launch, marketers are more likely to know what people think about the message and what type of reaction to expect.[3]

There is some controversy regarding copytesting. First, a number of marketers strongly believe that copytesting favours rational approaches over affective or even conative methods. Second, some individuals believe copytests stifle the creativity that is needed to produce ads that will stand out in the clutter. Recently, teams working for brands such as Nike, Volkswagen, Budweiser, and Target have been allowed to skip the copytesting phase of advertising design and move straight into production. The last reason given is that some agency leaders believe that copytests are likely to lead to ad messages about product benefits that are believable and understandable to members of a focus group. Most consumers know little, if anything, about how to create an effective ad. It may not make sense to have them serving as final judges of an ad's quality.

Although a number of marketing professionals do not favour using copytests, the majority believe they are necessary, primarily due to accountability issues. When it is time to make a decision to go

A mall intercept technique is often used for copytesting advertisements and other communications pieces.

forward on a high-dollar campaign, marketers want evidence that supports the decision. A creative's "gut feeling" is difficult to justify in a corporate boardroom when millions of dollars are at stake. Some members of a marketing communications team may feel that an idea is good and that copytesting wastes time and money, but they still recognize that top management approval needs evidence the campaign will succeed. The copytesting techniques that are currently available may not be perfect, but it seems likely they will continue to be used.[4]

Persuasion Analysis

Closely related to copytesting, persuasion analysis takes the process one step further by requiring the audience to not only state preferences or attitudes to specific messages, but also make more subtle evaluations based on their exposure to communications messages.

A researcher analyzing the persuasiveness of a television ad may start by gathering a group of consumers in a theatre. Measures of brand attitudes and purchase intentions are then gathered for the test brand and other brands put in the study. A series of commercials is shown as part of a program. Next, measures are taken to see if any changes in attitude or purchase intentions resulted from exposure to the ads. The amount of change indicates how well the persuasion in the ad worked.

One company that conducts persuasion analysis programs is ASI Market Research. Typically, a sample of 250 consumers is recruited to attend a new television program. Once they are in the theatre, the consumers are informed that prizes will be given away through a draw. These individuals are asked to identify the specific brand they prefer in each product category. The subjects are then shown two new TV programs, complete with commercials. At the end, the subjects are told that a product was inadvertently left off the initial survey, and they are asked to fill the form out again in order to enter the draw. ASI compares before and after responses to the same questions in order to see if there were any changes in attitudes; the subjects are not aware of the intention of the study.[5]

Knowing that the message actually has persuasive power is a major advantage for the marketer. Attempts to assess the impact of such messages before they are released to a wider audience are a solid investment of marketing communications dollars.

Emotional Reaction Tests

Some pre-testing techniques have gone further—to examine more deeply an audience's emotional reaction to proposed marketing communications. This is useful, since many messages are designed to elicit emotional responses from the audience and appealing to emotions can be helpful in achieving objectives such as increased purchases.[6]

A **warmth monitor** is one method developed to measure emotions. The concept behind the warmth monitor is that feelings of warmth are positive when they are directed toward an ad or a product. To measure warmth, subjects are asked to manipulate a joystick while watching a commercial. The movements track reactions to a commercial by making marks on a sheet of paper containing four lines. The four lines are labelled:

1. Absence of warmth
2. Neutral
3. Warmhearted or tender
4. Emotional

The warmth metre was developed to evaluate TV ads. It can be adapted to radio ads.[7]

A more sophisticated warmth meter was developed at the University of Hawaii. Individuals view advertisements in a theatre-type lab featuring a big-screen television. Those who feel negatively about what they are watching pull a joystick downward. Those who feel more positively push the joystick in the opposite direction. Thus, as they are watching the commercial, the subjects constantly move the joystick, thereby conveying their feelings during every moment of the ad. The results of the 20 participants are tallied into one graph and then superimposed on the footage of the commercial. This technology allows an advertiser to see which parts of the ad elicit positive emotions and which parts elicit negative emotions. After graphing the test results, the group can then

Messages for charities such as the Ottawa Humane Society often rely on a high degree of emotional connection to reach their objectives.

Source: Courtesy of the Ottawa Humane Society.

be used as a focus group to discuss the ad and to explain why group members felt the way they did at various moments of the ad.[8] The same technique has been adapted to political debates on television.

A similar technology has been developed by Reactions & Opinions, Inc. for use on the Internet. Reactions & Opinions can poll 1,000 or more people who view an advertisement online. As they watch the ad on streaming video, participants use a mouse to move a tab on a sliding scale from 1 to 10. If they like what they see, they slide the scale toward the 10. Those who don't like what they see slide the scale toward the 1. After the data have been collected, a graph can be superimposed on the advertisement. This shows the advertiser the likable and unlikable parts of the commercial. A major advantage of using the Internet is that subjects selected for the study can provide ratings at their convenience. If the agency needs a focus group to discuss the ad, subjects can be selected from the participants. The focus group session can even be held online.[9]

Most of the time, emotions are associated with shorter-term events, such as the reaction toward a given message. At the same time, emotions are strongly held in the memories of most people. An ad that made a viewer angry may be retrieved, along with the accompanying anger, every time the individual remembers either the ad or the company. It is wise to attempt to discover emotional responses to ads before they are released.

Physiological Arousal Tests

Emotional reaction tests are *self-report* instruments. In other words, individuals report their feelings as they see fit. Although this may not be a flawed instrument, many marketing researchers are interested in finding ways to measure emotions and feelings without relying on people to self-report how they feel.

Physiological arousal tests measure fluctuations in a person's body functions that are associated with changing emotions. The primary physiological arousal tests are shown in Figure 13.2.

FIGURE 13.2
The Primary Psychological Arousal Tests

◆ **Psychogalvanometer**

◆ **Pupillometric meter**

◆ **Psychophysiology**

A **psychogalvanometer** measures a person's perspiration levels. It works by evaluating the amount of perspiration in the palm and fingers. As an individual reacts emotionally to a situation (in this case, a marketing communications message), the amount of perspiration generated changes. Perhaps you have noticed that you sweat when watching an exciting movie or sports event. This arousal indicates interest and emotional involvement. A message producing these effects may be more memorable and powerful than something boring.

Emotional reactions can be negative or positive. The psychogalvanometer simply measures the individual's physiological reaction. One benefit of the psychogalvanometer is that it can be used to assess emotional reactions to many different types of marketing communications pieces, including television commercials, consumer promotions, and trade promotions.

A **pupillometric meter** measures the dilation of a person's pupil. Dilation levels also change with emotional arousal. A person who is frightened has wider pupils, as does someone who is excited. Pupil dilation can be studied as the subject views a television or print advertisement. Pupils dilate more when the person reacts positively to the marketing communication. Pupils become smaller when the subject reacts negatively.

When conducting a test, the subject's head can be set in a fixed position. The dilation of the pupil can then be measured while viewing the ad. In this way, each aspect of the message can be evaluated for positive or negative responses. A graph can be superimposed on the commercial to show evaluators how each person responded to the advertisement.

In recent years, significant advances have occurred in **psychophysiology,** which is a brain-image measurement process. It tracks the flow and movement of electrical currents in the brain. One study demonstrated that the currents in a subject's brain indicate a preference for Coke or Pepsi that is the same as the product the person chooses in a blind taste test. According to neuroscientist Justin Meaux, "Preference has measurable correlates in the brain; you can see it." Richard Siberstein, an Australian neuroscientist, used physiological measurements of the brain to show that successful ads tend to generate higher levels of emotional engagement and long-term memory coding.[10]

To demonstrate how physiological tests work, consider an advertisement that is sexually provocative. In a focus group, respondents may enjoy the ad but cover up these feelings, stating that the ad is sexist and inappropriate. These reactions may be due to social pressure; they may also occur because the subjects want to be accepted by those around them. The same individual may not move the joystick to report his or her true feelings when participating in a study using the warmth monitor. The stigma attached to sex in advertising often affects self-reported reactions. Thus, a physiological arousal test may be a better indicator of a person's true response.

The most recent research in this area has been by companies such as EmSense, Neuro-Focus, and OTX Research. These companies are experimenting with portable devices that measure both brain waves and biological data. Coca-Cola used this methodology to evaluate which ads to use during the 2008 Super Bowl. Coke produced a dozen ads, which were evaluated by the EmSense device, which is shaped like a thin, plastic headband. The EmSense measures brain waves and monitors breathing, heart rate, blinking

Source: © iStockphoto/Thinkstock.

Physiological arousal tests could be used to study the impact of sexual appeals in communications.

of the eyes, and skin temperature of consumers as they watch ads. Through these physiological measurements, Coca-Cola researchers were able to determine which ads to use during the Super Bowl. Some Super Bowl ads were modified to produce higher levels of emotion.[11]

Many advertising researchers believe physiological arousal tests are more accurate than emotional reaction tests, because physiological arousal cannot easily be faked. As scientists gain a better understanding of physiological responses, the brain, and the electrical currents that move through the brain, the use of these methods of evaluation is likely to increase.[12]

Purchase Simulation Tests

One additional way of avoiding self-reported attitudes or intentions from a test audience is to use a *simulated purchase test*. Research Systems Corporation (RSC) is a leading marketing research firm that specializes in purchase simulation studies. RSC tests the impact of commercials by studying consumer behaviours in a controlled laboratory environment.

RSC does not ask consumers to render opinions, to describe their attitudes, or even whether they plan to purchase the product. Instead, RSC creates a simulated shopping experience. Subjects are able to choose from a variety of products they would see on a normal store shelf. After completing a simulated shopping exercise, the subjects are seated and watch a television preview containing various commercials. The participants are asked to watch the TV preview as they would watch any TV show at home. The test ad is placed in with other ads, and the subjects do not know which ad is being tested.

When the preview is completed, the subjects are asked to participate in a second shopping exercise. Researchers then compare the products chosen in the first shopping trip to those selected in the second. Shifts in brand choices are at least partly due to the effectiveness of the advertisement, because it is the only variable that has changed.

A major advantage of this methodology is that the test procedures do not rely on opinions and attitudes. Among other things, this means that RSC's procedure can be used in international markets as well as domestic markets.[13] In some cultures, subjects tend to seek to please the interviewer who asks questions about opinions and attitudes. As a result, the answers are polite and socially acceptable. The same subjects may also seek to provide answers they think the interviewer wants to hear. By studying purchases instead of soliciting opinions, researchers leave subjects free to respond in a more accurate fashion.

Any methodology designed to tap into behaviours rather than emotions and feelings has a built-in advantage. Opinions and attitudes change and can be quickly affected by other variables in a situation. Observing behaviours and changes in behaviours gets more quickly to the point of the experiment, which is whether the buyer can be influenced in a tangible way by a marketing communications tool.

Critical Thinking Exercise

Opponents of concept and copytesting argue that the lab environments in which they are conducted render them virtually useless, since people process messages differently in the "real world." Do you agree with this idea? Which of the pre-test techniques discussed above do you think most closely resembles the real-world experience of the audience? Do you think those who say that audiences simply cannot design effective messages are right, and that this type of testing should be discouraged? Why or why not?

- ◆ Product name or brand
- ◆ Firm name
- ◆ Company location
- ◆ Theme music
- ◆ Spokesperson

- ◆ Tagline
- ◆ Incentive being offered
- ◆ Product attributes
- ◆ Primary selling point of communication piece

FIGURE 13.3
Items Tested for Recall

Post-Test Measurement Options

Recall Tests

One popular method used to evaluate the effectiveness of marketing communications is a **recall test** which involves asking an individual to recall what communications messages he or she viewed in a given setting or time period. Then, in progressive steps, the subject is asked to identify information about the message. Figure 13.3 lists some of the parts of marketing communications messages that can be tested for recall.

The most common form of recall test is the **day-after recall (DAR)** test. The DAR method is often used to evaluate TV advertisements. Individuals participating in the study are contacted by phone the day after the advertisement first appears. Normally, they are tested using an approach called **unaided recall** , in which the subjects are asked to name, or recall, the ads they saw or heard the previous evening, without being given any prompts or memory jogs. For magazines and newspaper ads, there are two approaches. In the first, consumers are contacted the day after the ad appeared or they received the magazine. The individuals name the ads they recall and then are asked a series of questions to discover the features of the advertisements they remember. In the second, an individual is given a magazine for a certain period of time (normally one week) and instructed to read it as he or she normally would during leisure time. Then, the researcher returns and asks a series of questions about which ads became memorable and what features the individual could remember. In the business-to-business sector, the second method is a popular way to test ads for trade journals.

The day-after recall method works best when the objective is to measure the extent to which consumers have learned or remembered the content of an ad. DAR is a valuable test, because marketers know that increased recall enhances the probability that the brand is becoming a part of the consumer's evoked set, or the primary choices remembered when purchase alternatives are considered. An evoked-set brand is much more likely to be purchased.[14]

The second type of recall test is the **aided recall** method. With this method, consumers are prompted by being told the product category and, if necessary, names of specific brands in the category. The respondent does not know which brand or ad is being tested. When the consumer states that he or she does recall seeing a specific brand being advertised, the person then is asked to provide as many details as possible about the ad. At that point, no further clues are given regarding the ad's content.

Most researchers believe the unaided recall approach is superior to other evaluative tests because it indicates an advertisement has become lodged in the person's memory. Unaided recall is also better than aided recall because some people may respond to a prompt by saying they do indeed remember an ad, even when they are uncertain. Recall scores are

This 3M advertisement could be tested using either aided or unaided recall to see if viewers noticed the Spanish wording.

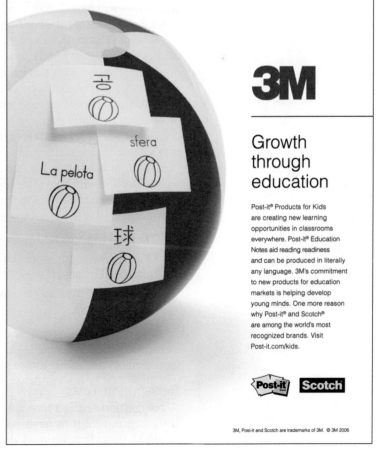

Source: Courtesy of 3M.

FIGURE 13.4
Factors Researchers Must Keep in Mind
When Evaluating Recall Tests

◆ The respondent's attitude towards advertising in general

◆ Prominence of the brand name in the ad

◆ Use or familiarity of the brand to the respondent

◆ Age of the respondent

almost always higher when the aided recall method is used. Some ad agencies use both methods. First, they use unaided recall to gather basic information. Then, the researcher follows up with prompts to delve deeper into the memories that are present, even if it takes a little help to dig them out.

In both aided and unaided recall tests, if incorrect information is provided, the researcher continues the questioning. Individuals are not told they have given inaccurate answers. Incorrect responses are important data to record. Memory is not always accurate in both aided and unaided recall situations. Consequently, people give incorrect answers. In other words, they may mention commercials that did not actually appear during the test period, but rather were viewed at some other time. Although this may seem strange, bear in mind that the average person sees between 50 and 100 ads on a typical night of television viewing. It is easy to become confused.

An incorrect response is often triggered by exposure to a similar ad. For example, a person may remember seeing a commercial for Firestone tires when it was actually presented by Uniroyal. Seeing the Uniroyal ad triggered the recall of the Firestone brand because the individual is more familiar with Firestone or holds the brand in higher esteem. This type of error is more common in aided recall tests. In that situation, the individual is being provided with clues from a particular product category, which increases the odds of remembering the wrong brand.

Marketers consider four factors when evaluating recall tests (see Figure 13.4). The first is a person's general attitude toward advertising. Individuals who regularly watch ads, believe advertising helps them stay informed, and have positive attitudes toward advertising will have higher recall scores. It is important, therefore, to measure a person's general attitude toward advertising in evaluating recall scores.[15]

A second factor that impacts recall scores is the prominence of the brand name in the ad. Recall scores are highly sensitive to the presence of a brand name and its visibility or prominence in the ad. Television ad copy that mentions the brand name 7 times during the 30 seconds is likely to receive higher recall scores than an ad that states the name only once. A third factor is that an individual is more likely to remember a brand name that he or she uses regularly, especially if it is featured prominently in the ad. Institutional ads normally have lower recall scores because of the difficulty in remembering the organization's name.[16]

The fourth factor is the age of the respondent used in the recall tests. Recall scores tend to decline with age. Older people do not remember things as well. Figure 13.5 displays average recall scores for different age segments using both DAR and brand recall instruments.[17] There are several explanations for lower recall scores in older people:

- They have reduced short-term recall capacity.
- Older persons are more fixed in terms of brand choices, making them less easily influenced by advertisements.
- The TV ads used to develop Figure 13.5 may have been targeted more toward younger people.

For whatever reason, age does affect recall scores. Still, recall tests are valuable instruments used in testing to see if the ad has the potential to move into a person's long-term memory and affect future purchase decisions.

Recognition Tests

A **recognition test** is a format in which individuals are given copies of an ad and asked if they recognize it or have seen it before. Those who say they have seen the ad are asked to provide additional details about when and where the ad was encountered

Day-After Recall		Brand Recall	
Age Segment	AverageRecall	AgeSegment	Average Recall
12–17	34%	13–17	70%
18–34	29%	18–34	53%
35–49	24%	35+	36%
50–65	22%		

Source: Based on Joel S. Debow, "Advertising Recognition and Recall by Age—Including Teens,"*Journal of Advertising Research* 35, no. 5 (September–October 1995), pp. 55–60.

FIGURE 13.5
Impact of Age on DAR and Brand Recall

(e.g., specific television program, the name of the magazine, the location of the billboard). This information is collected to validate that it was indeed seen. Next, the individual is asked a series of questions about the ad itself. This helps the researcher gather information and insights into consumer attitudes and reactions to the ad. Recognition tests are best suited to testing for comprehension of and reactions to ads. In contrast, recall tests tend to work well when testing brand and ad awareness. Recognition tests help when the advertiser is more concerned about how the ad is received and what information is being comprehended. This is especially important for ads using a cognitive message strategy, in which some type of reasoning process is invoked in persuading the consumer about the value of a product.

Unlike a recall test, a recognition test is not a memory test. Recognition measures a person's interest in a particular advertisement.[18] Ads that are of no interest do not register and are not remembered. In a recognition test, it is as if the respondent is saying, "Yes, advertisements of that kind usually attract my attention, so I did pause and look at it when I went through the magazine." An ad that a person likes is about 75 percent more likely to be recognized than an ad the individual did not like. This is one reason celebrities are selected for ads, such as the milk ad featuring Spike Lee in this section. If an individual likes the celebrity in the advertisement, then he or she will be more likely to recognize the ad. For ads the respondent thought were interesting, the odds of recognition were about 50 percent higher than for ads that were deemed not interesting.[19]

Further, when the consumer uses the brand being displayed in the ad, the likelihood of recognizing the ad rises. A person who uses a brand is about 50 percent more likely to recognize the ad than an individual who does not. Researchers look beyond the number of respondents who recognize a particular ad. Researchers then ask the subjects about the brands that they normally buy in the product category, if they liked the ad, and if they found the ad to be interesting.

A recognition score is also affected by factors such as the colour and size of the ad. Larger ads are more easily noticed, as are colour ads (as compared with black and white).[20] As a result, when studying ad recognition the research team should also account for the size of the print ad, whether the ad is in colour, and the length of the broadcast ad.

One difference between recognition scores and recall scores is that recognition scores do not decline over time, primarily because consumer interests remain relatively stable. If a person liked the milk ad with Spike Lee when he or

Using celebrities such as the Dixie Chicks increases recall and recognition through greater interest in and liking of the ad.

Source: Used with permission of Deutche Inc. on behalf of the Milk Processors Education Program.

she first viewed the ad, it is likely he or she will like the ad and recognize it in the future, even months after it first appeared.

Recognition and recall tests measure different things. Consequently, many research teams perform both tests on the same subjects. First, recall measures are used at the start of the interview and then recognition tests are given later. A subject may have viewed an ad during a particular TV show but not mention the ad when undergoing a recall test. The respondent can then be given a recognition test to see if he or she remembers seeing the ad.

Recall and recognition do have things in common. For one, both help to establish the brand in the consumer's mind.[21] Loyalty and brand equity are more likely to result. Therefore, even though recall and recognition are more oriented toward the short-term impact of a given ad or campaign, the long-term consequences of a series of successful and memorable ads should be considered.

Critical Thinking Exercise

Obviously, for a marketing communications to be effective, the audience must first be exposed to that message. But given the high number of marketing communications messages most consumers encounter every day, most simply can't keep track and are therefore not consciously aware of their exposure. This suggests that recall tests are not a particularly effective means of tracking marketing communications. Do you agree or disagree? What value can a recall test offer a marketing communications team?

Sales and Response Rates

Measuring changes in sales following a marketing campaign is relatively simple. Universal product codes and scanner data are available from many retail outlets. These data are available on a weekly and, in some situations, daily basis. It is available by store. Many retail outlets even have access to sales information on a real-time basis, and the information can be accessed at any point during the day.

Scanner data make it possible for companies to monitor sales and help both the retailer and the manufacturer discover the impact of a particular marketing communications program. Remember that extraneous factors can affect sales. Under an IMC plan, it would be difficult to know which specific element moved the customer to action. A company featuring a fall line of jackets may be affected by a cold snap. If so, what caused the customer to buy—the IMC or the weather? Firms utilizing trade and consumer promotion programs must account for the impact of both the promotion and the advertising when studying sales figures. Sales are one indicator of effectiveness; however, they may be influenced by additional factors.

First, as just discussed, it is difficult to distinguish *the effects of marketing communications from other factors*. This is because IMC messages have short- and long-term effects, and consumers and businesses see them in so many different contexts. Thus, the direct impact of one message or one campaign on sales is difficult to decipher.

Second, *marketing communications often have delayed impacts*. Many times consumers encounter messages and are persuaded to purchase the product, but will not actually make the buy until later, when they actually need the item. A woman may be convinced that she wants to buy a piece of jewellery from Tiffany. Still, rather than buying it herself, she leaves several well-placed hints for her husband before her next birthday, which could be several months later. The problem is that her husband may have purchased another brand of jewellery or a different gift entirely. So, she either waits for another special occasion for her husband to purchase the jewellery or she makes the purchase herself at a later time.

Third, many times consumers may decide to make purchases based on one element of IMC but *change their minds when they arrive at the retail store*. A competing brand may be on sale, the store could be out of the desired brand, or the salesperson could persuade the customer that another brand is better. In each case, the communications portion of the marketing mix was successful on one level but another factor interfered before the purchase was made.

Fourth, marketing communications is an essential component of building brand awareness and brand equity. Although sales may not be the result immediately, *the campaign may build brand equity,* which in turn will influence future purchases.

Still, some of those elements of the IMC plan that are specifically designed to focus on sales as their objective— such as trade and consumer promotions and direct marketing—are easier to link to actual sales. Manufacturers can study the impact of trade promotions by observing changes in sales to the retailers at the time the promotions are being offered.

POP display effectiveness is measured primarily through sales data.

The same is true for consumer promotions, such as coupons, contests, and point-of-purchase displays. Many manufacturers' representatives push hard to get retailers to use the company's POP displays. At the same time, the retailer is more interested in the effects of the display on sales. Using scanner data, both the retailer and the manufacturer can measure the impact of a POP display. Retailers normally use POPs that have demonstrated the ability to boost sales.

To track the impact of POP displays, a number of firms, including Frito-Lay, Procter & Gamble, and Warner-Lambert joined together as initial sponsors of a program developed by Point-of-Purchase Advertising International (POPAI). In the initial study, POPAI tracked 25 different product categories in 250 supermarkets nationwide. Sponsors paid between $50,000 and $75,000 to receive customized data about the POP displays featuring particular brands. One advantage of using POPAI data is that each firm can not only see the impact of the POP for its brand, but also receive comparative data showing how well the display fared against other displays. The major advantage of the POPAI program is its low cost. Sponsors of the POPAI program obtained valuable data at a much lower cost than if they had sought the information on their own.[22]

A wide variety of responses to marketing communications programs are available besides sales. Figure 13.6 lists some of the responses that can be tracked. These are typically actions taken by the audience that are meant to move them along the purchase decision-making process. These items are described in the remainder of this section.

One method of measuring the impact of marketing communications is to assign a *toll-free number* to each marketing piece. A great deal of information can be collected during an inbound call. Sales data can be recorded and demographic information gathered. Psychographic information then can be added by contacting various commercial services.

In business-to-business situations, a toll-free number provides contact names to help the vendor discover who is performing the various functions in the buying centre. As a result, a toll-free number can be used to generate valuable customer information that can be tied to the sales data. Knowing who is responding to each offer helps a firm better understand its customers and the approach that should be used for each target group.

Online responses are increasingly common measures. It is possible to track responses to marketing communications through page views. For instance, the Canadian Tourism Commission tested the effectiveness of television, radio, direct mail, and online marketing communications. Each ad used a different URL for viewers to access additional

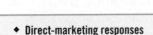

◆ Changes in sales	◆ Direct-marketing responses
◆ Telephone inquiries	◆ Redemption rate of sales promotion offers—Coupons, premiums, contests, sweepstakes
◆ Response cards	
◆ Internet responses	

FIGURE 13.6
Responses to Marketing Messages That Can Be Tracked

Source: © Sam Dao/Alamy Images/Getstock.com

This campaign for the City of Regina featured a website, using click-throughs as a vital measure of success.

information. To the tourist, there was no perceivable difference, because each URL took the person to the designated Canadian Tourism Commission site. The Tourism Commission could easily track which ad the person viewed by which URL the person used. This made it possible to count the number of visitors from each form of marketing communications.[23]

When the media is online, click-throughs are still the number one way companies measure the impact of marketing communications. They provide companies with an idea of how many people who see an online ad click on it and go to the new website. Once there, other metrics that are used include length of engagement, redemption and response rates, and sales. Redemption rates and response rates occur when visitors to the site take some action, and of course sales occur when the individual makes an actual purchase. A newer metric that is being used is length of engagement, which measures how long the person stays on the site. It is a surrogate measure of a person's interest in the product and site being visited.

AdKnowledge introduced an online management tool called MarketingMatch Planner to evaluate Internet advertising campaigns. MarketMatch Planner software includes two components: Campaign Manager and Administrator. Campaign Manager records traffic to a site and performs post-buy analysis. Administrator integrates Web ad-buy data and performance analysis with the firm's accounting and billing systems. In addition, MarketMatch Planner has the capability of integrating third-party data, including audience demographics, from the following sources:

- MediaMetrix for basic demographics
- NetRatings for GRP and other ratings instruments
- Psychographic data from SRI Consulting
- Website ratings and descriptions from NetGuide
- Web traffic audit data from BPA Interactive

Data from online campaigns should be evaluated carefully. Results should be viewed in light of the company's IMC objectives. An IMC objective of building brand awareness requires something other than Internet sales data to be assessed. An Internet ad can bring awareness to a brand but not lead to an online purchase. This might occur, for example, when a consumer or business uses the Internet to gather information but then makes the actual purchase at a retail store, or by telephone. When that happens, the impact of an Internet advertising campaign may not be able to reflect all of the brand awareness or sales that the campaign generated.

Critical Thinking Exercise

Assume you are the owner of a small company that operates in a product category that has a relatively lengthy consumer decision-making process: kitchen cabinets. As a small business, you can't afford to take years to build brand recognition and loyalty. You need your marketing communications to deliver sales right away. But with so many factors influencing sales, you need to turn to other measures to determine if your marketing communications are effective. Since you have started advertising in a local newspaper, you find that visits to your website have increased dramatically. However, the consumers who visit the website do not subsequently request an estimate. What is your next step? How will you recalibrate your campaign, and what tests will you use to solve this problem?

Test Markets

Another form of measuring responses to marketing communications is through the use of test markets. Test markets are used when company leaders examine the effects of a marketing communications effort on a small scale before launching a national or international campaign. The primary advantage of test markets is that an organization can examine several elements of a marketing communications program. If the test market is successful, then it is likely that the national campaign also will be effective. It is also an excellent method of testing a campaign in a new country before launching a full-scale international campaign. In addition to marketing communications, test market programs can be used to assess marketing mix elements such as price and product introductions.

Test markets are cost-effective methods to analyze and make changes in marketing efforts before millions of dollars are spent on something that will not accomplish the intended objectives. Ads can be modified, promotions revised, and pricing policies revisited before a more widespread program is undertaken. For example, McDonald's tested new ads that touted cleaner restaurants and friendlier service. The goal of the ads was to test a campaign emphasizing McDonald's effort to improve in-store and drive-through service. Two television spots and one radio spot were produced and aired in two test cities. Reactions from the test markets provided McDonald's marketing team and the advertising agency with information about the impact of ad campaign, the parts of the ad that should be modified, and whether the campaign should be launched nationally.[24]

One major advantage of a test market is that it resembles an actual situation more than any of the other tests discussed thus far. The key is to make sure that the site selected for the test market strongly resembles the target population. A product targeted toward senior citizens should be studied in an area with a high concentration of senior citizens.

It is also important to design the test marketing campaign as close to the national or full marketing plan as possible. A lengthy time lapse may cause a company to experience differing results. The goal is to make sure the test market is a mirror image of the actual marketing program.

A test market can be as short as a few days or as long as two to three years. The longer the test market program runs, the more accurate the results. A test that is too short may yield less reliable results. But if the test market is too long, the national market situation may change and the test market may no longer be a representative sample. The greater fear, however, is that the competition is able to study what is going on. This gives competitors time to react to the proposed marketing campaign.

Competing companies can respond to a test market program in one of two ways. First, some firms may introduce a special promotion in the test market area in order to confound the results. This may reduce the sales for the product or campaign, making it appear less attractive than it actually is. The second approach is not to intervene in the test market, but to use the time to prepare a counter-marketing campaign. Firms that use this tactic are ready when the national launch occurs, and the impact may be that the test market results are not as predictive of what will happen.

Scanner data make it possible for results from test market campaigns to be quickly available. The

Many restaurants use test markets before launching promotions or products nationally.

Really, really, good chicken.

Grab a whole chicken with 2 regular sides for just 19.99!

Nando's
flame-grilled chicken
www.nandoscanada.com

Nando's Strawberry Hill
12101 72nd Ave, Surrey
604-502-8010

Nando's Guildford
15190 101st Ave, Surrey
604-587-3210

This voucher is valid only at Nando's Strawberry Hill and Nando's Guildford. Cannot be combined with any other offer. Expires October 15th, 2011.

Source: Courtesy of Nando's Flame-Grilled Chicken Canada.

figures can be studied to determine if test market results are acceptable. A firm also can design several versions of a marketing campaign in different test markets. Through scanner data, the firm can compare the sales from each test market to determine which version is the best. For example, in one test market the firm may present an advertising campaign only. In the second test market coupons may be added to the ad program. In test market three, a premium can be combined with advertising. The results from each area help the marketing team understand which type of marketing communications tactic to use.

Other test markets can study different prices in different regions in order to determine the price to charge and the elasticity associated with that price. It is also possible to vary the size of the coupon or premium to discover the impact. Rather than making a change at the national level, company leaders can modify the consumer promotion in selected markets to see what happens.

Test marketing offers the opportunity to test communications ideas in more true-to-life settings. They can be used for trade and consumer promotions, direct marketing, and other marketing communications tools. They are not quite as accurate when assessing advertising because changes in sales take longer, and the test market program may not be long enough to measure the full impact. In any case, test markets are valuable instruments to use when examining specific marketing features and more general communications campaigns.

EVALUATION CRITERIA

For all of the measurement and research programs mentioned thus far, it is important to establish quality evaluation criteria. One helpful program is **positioning advertising copytesting (PACT)**, which was created to evaluate television ads. It was formulated by 21 leading advertising agencies.[25] Even though PACT examines the issues involved in copytesting television ads, the principles can be applied to any type of message evaluation system and all types of media. Figure 13.7 lists the nine main principles. These should be followed when a written or verbal marketing communications piece is being tested.

First, no matter which procedure is used, it should be *relevant to the marketing communications objective being tested.* If the objective of a coupon promotion is to stimulate trial purchases, then the test should evaluate the coupon's copy in order to determine its ability to stimulate trial purchases. On the other hand, an evaluation of attitudes toward a brand would require a different instrument.

Researchers should agree on how the results are going to be used when selecting test instruments. They should also agree on the design of the test in order to obtain the desired results. This is especially true for the preparation stage in message development, because many tests are used to determine whether the marketing communications piece eventually will be created.

The research team should also decide on a *cutoff score* to be used following the test. This will prevent biases from entering into the findings about the ad's potential effectiveness. Many ad agencies use test markets for new advertisements before they are launched

FIGURE 13.7
Copytesting Principles of PACT

- Testing procedure should be relevant to the advertising objectives.
- In advance of each test, researchers should agree on how the results will be used.
- Multiple measures should be used.
- The test should be based on some theory or model of human response to communication.
- The testing procedure should allow for more than one exposure to the advertisement, if necessary.
- In selecting alternate advertisements to include in the test, each should be at the same stage in the process as the test ad.
- The test should provide controls to avoid biases.
- The sample used for the test should be representative of the target sample.
- The testing procedure should demonstrate reliability and validity.

Source: Adapted from *PACT-Positioning Advertising Copy Testing, A Consensus Credo Representing the Views of Leading American Advertising Agencies* (1982), PACT Chairwoman, Sonia Yuspeh, New York: J. Walter Thompson Co., (January), 28pp.

in a larger area. A recall method used to determine if people in the target market remember seeing the ad should have a prearranged cutoff score. In other words, the acceptable percentage may be established so that 25 percent of the sample should remember the ad in order to move forward with the campaign. If the percentage is not reached, the ad has failed the test.

Using multiple measures allows for more precise evaluations of ads and campaigns. It is possible for a well-designed message to fail one particular testing procedure yet score higher on others. Consumers and business buyers who are the targets of marketing communications are complex human beings. Various people may perceive individual messages differently. As a result, marketers usually try to develop more than one measure so that there is greater agreement on whether the ad or campaign will succeed and reach its desired goals.

The test to be used should be *based on some theory or model of human response to communication*. This makes it more likely that the test will be a predictive tool of human behaviour. The objective is to enhance the odds that the communication will actually produce the desired results (going to the website, visiting the store, or making a purchase) when the campaign is launched. Possibilities include the purchase decision-making process, the mutliattribute model, or any other basis used to explain how individuals make decisions based on marketing communications.

Many testing procedures are based on a single exposure. Although in many cases this is sufficient for research purposes, there are times when *multiple exposures* are necessary to obtain reliable test results. For complex messages, more than one exposure may be needed. The human mind can comprehend only so much information in one exposure. It is vital to make sure the person can and does comprehend the message in order to determine whether it can achieve its desired effects.

Often messages are tested in combination with others to disguise the one being examined. Placing the test marketing piece in with others means the test subjects do not know which one is being evaluated. This prevents personal biases from affecting judgments. To ensure valid results, *the alternative messages should be in the same stage of process development*. Thus, if ad copy is being tested prior to ad development, then the alternative ads should also be in the ad copy development stage rather than established ads.

Next, adequate controls must be in place to *prevent biases and external factors from affecting results*. To help control external factors, experimental designs are often used.

Tests for messages like this one from an east coast company should be conducted within the relevant target geographies.

When conducting experiments, researchers try to keep as many things as constant as possible and manipulate only one variable at a time. For instance, in a theatre test the temperature, time of day, room lighting, television program, and ads shown can all be the same. Then, the researcher may display the program and ads to an all-male audience, followed by an all-female audience. Changing only one variable (gender) makes it possible to see if the ad, in a controlled environment, is perceived differently by men than by women.

This does not mean that field tests are ineffective. Testing marketing communications in real-world situations is extremely valuable because they approximate reality. Still, when conducting field tests, such as mall intercepts, those performing the testing must try to control as many variables as possible. Thus, the same mall, same questions, and same ads are shown. Then, age, gender, or other variables can be manipulated one at a time.

As with any research procedure, sampling procedures are important. It is crucial for the *sample being used to be representative of the target population*. For example, if a print ad designed for bilingual Montrealers is to be tested, the sample used in the test should be from the same population.

AtlanticCirque.com   SCHOOL OF CIRCUS ARTS

Source: Courtesy of Cossette East.

Finally, researchers must continually try to make tests *reliable and valid*. Reliable means repeatable. In other words, if the same test is given five times to the same person, the individual should respond in the same way each time. If a respondent is "emotional" on one iteration of a warmth test and "neutral" when the message is shown a second time, the research team will wonder if the test is reliable.

Valid means generalizable. Valid research findings can be generalized to other groups. For instance, when a focus group of women finds an ad to be funny, and then a group of men reacts in the same way, the finding that the humour is effective is more valid. This would be an increasingly valuable outcome if the results were generalizable to people of various ages and races. Many times an ad may be reliable, or repeatable, in the same group, but not valid or generalizable to other groups of consumers or business buyers.

Critical Thinking Exercise

Pick up most academic journals and you will find that researchers use student samples in order to test their hypotheses. Studies range from attitudes toward different media and products to purchase intentions based on different pricing strategies. Critics argue that the use of students occurs simply because most researchers working at universities and colleges have easy access to students in their classrooms. They charge that the student population does not reflect the real world and therefore most of these tests are invalid. Do you agree? Name three products for which a student sample would not be appropriate to use in a pre-test for marketing communications.

When testing different concepts for marketing communications, it is important the evaluation be reliable and valid.

Source: © STOCK4B-RF/Jupiter Images.

The PACT principles are helpful when designing tests of both short-term and long-term effects from marketing communications. The goal is to generate data that document what a company is doing works. When this occurs, the company and its marketing communications team have access to invaluable information.

WHY SOME MARKETERS DON'T MEASURE

Many marketers invest millions of dollars into marketing communications that are simply ineffective. But without proper measurement this waste of valuable firm resources will never be corrected. Indeed, research suggests that the majority of marketers do not perform adequate tests of their marketing communications, either in pre- or post-test phases. One study found that only 25 percent of marketers evaluate ongoing campaigns to measure effectiveness.[26] Gerard Tellis points out three reasons why this is the case. First, most campaigns go through several rounds of evaluation with various internal audiences and are subject to high degrees of scrutiny. Therefore, some argue that further research is not necessary. Second, he suggests that marketers view the costs of testing as taking away from the "working dollars" that are invested in executing the campaign itself. Each dollar spent on testing, for example, is a dollar taken away from media, public relations, or other activities within the IMC plan. Third, he points out that many managers misunderstand the time and expense required to measure and test.[27]

This lack of testing and measurement is sustained by three factors.[28]

1. *Conflicts of Interests between Clients and Agencies.* Most agencies are compensated relative to the size of the overall

campaign, not the effectiveness of the campaign. Also, those involved in the creative process worry that excessive introspection through research will dampen creativity and original thought. Remember, those working in creative development gain currency in their careers by pushing the envelope creatively more than they do by creating unremarkable campaigns that drive sales.

2. *Competitive Pressures.* Many marketers feel that the only reason to invest in marketing communications is to blunt the effectiveness of a competitors' marketing communications. Therefore, testing is not required since presence in the market is not an option, and mere presence delivers the desired result.

3. *Rewards Based on Revenues.* Most managers are rewarded based on sales, not profits. So the incentive is to gain as large of a marketing communications budget as possible to drive sales, even if they are delivered at less than optimal profit levels.

EVALUATING THE OVERALL IMC PROGRAM

As has been noted throughout this textbook, the huge expenditures companies make on marketing communications have led CEOs and other executives to continue to push for greater accountability. These individuals, as well as stockholders and boards of directors, want to know what type of return results when a firm spends a large sum of money on marketing communications. The idea is to try to discover the *return on investment (ROI)* of a marketing communications campaign.

The problem is that there is no agreement about what the ROI means when it is applied to marketing communications. There is also no consensus on how to measure marketing ROI. In one study, more than 70 percent of marketers said it would be difficult to measure the impact of marketing communications on sales. The same number predicted that it would be extremely difficult for the marketing industry to reach any agreement on what constitutes ROI for marketing communications. Figure 13.8 lists some of the potential definitions of marketing ROI. The most commonly used descriptions of ROI are outcome responses, such as incremental sales, total sales, and market share. Notice that the measures used to set prices for media, such as gross rating points delivered and reach/frequency achieved, are not often considered the best definition of ROI.[29]

This confusion is likely to continue. This means those in the marketing profession should keep trying to identify some way to measure the impact of marketing communications, ultimately in dollars and cents.

Many years ago, Peter Drucker outlined a series of goal areas that are indicative of organizational health. These goals match very well with the objectives of an IMC program and are listed in Figure 13.9.[30] As marketers struggle to find a way to measure ROI of marketing communications expenditures, understanding the various measures of overall health of an organization can provide valuable insight into how marketing communications contributes.

Market share has long been linked to profitability. It demonstrates consumer acceptance, brand loyalty, and a strong competitive position. A promotions opportunity analysis should help the marketing team understand both market share and the relative strengths and weaknesses of the competition. IMC programs are designed to hold and build market share.

Definition of ROI	Percent Using
Incremental sales from marketing	66%
Changes in brand awareness	57
Total sales revenue from marketing	55
Changes in purchase intentions	55
Changes in market share	49
Ratio of advertising costs to sales	34
Reach/frequency achieved	30
Gross rating points delivered	25

FIGURE 13.8
Definitions of ROI for Marketing

Source: Paul J. Gough, "Study: Marketers Struggle to Measure Effectiveness," *SHOOT Magazine*, Vol. 45, No. 29 (August 20, 2004), pp. 7–8.

FIGURE 13.9
Measures of Overall Health of a Company

- ◆ Market share
- ◆ Level of innovation
- ◆ Productivity
- ◆ Physical and financial resources

- ◆ Profitability
- ◆ Manager performance and development
- ◆ Employee performance and attitudes
- ◆ Social responsibility

Source: Based on Peter Drucker, *Management: Tasks, Responsibilities,* Practices (New York: Harper and Row, 1974).

Innovation is finding new and different ways to achieve objectives. This applies to many marketing activities, including new and unusual trade and consumer promotions, public relations events and sponsorships, e-commerce and e-active programs, and the firm's advertising efforts.

Productivity is reflective of the industry's increasing emphasis on results. IMC experts are being asked to demonstrate tangible results from IMC campaigns. Both short- and long-term measures of the effects of advertisements and promotions demonstrate the "productivity" of the organization in terms of gaining new customers, building recognition in the marketplace, determining sales per customer, and other measures.

Physical and financial resources are also important to an IMC program. Physical resources include the most up-to-date computer and Internet capabilities. The firm must provide sufficient financial resources to reach this goal. Scanner technologies and other devices that keep the firm in contact with consumers are vital elements in the long-term success of an IMC plan.

Communications for the Paralympics also helped create enthusiasm among volunteers for the games.

Source: Courtesy of Canadian Paralympic Committee.

Profitability is vital for the marketing department and the overall organization. Many IMC managers know that more than sales are at issue when assessing success. Sales must generate profits in order for the company to survive and thrive.

Manager performance and development is possibly an overlooked part of an IMC program. Effective marketing communications teams must develop pipelines of new, talented individuals across all roles within the field in order to succeed in the long term. Also, new people must be trained and prepared for promotion to more important roles.

Employee performance and attitudes reflect not only morale within the marketing department, but also relations with other departments and groups. An effective IMC plan consists of building bridges with other internal departments so that everyone is aware of the thrust and theme of the program. Satisfied and positive employees are more likely to help the firm promote its image.

Social responsibility is linked to the long-term well-being of an organization. Brand equity and loyalty are hurt when the firm is known for illegal or unethical actions. Therefore, marketing leaders should encourage all of the members of an organization to act in ethical and socially responsible ways.

When these goals are being reached, it is likely that the firm's IMC program is working well. Beyond these targets, IMC plans should continually emphasize the evolving nature of relationships with customers and other stakeholders. Simply stated, every chapter in this book implies a series of key performance targets for IMC programs that should guide the actions of the marketing communications team both in the short term and for the long haul. Firms that are able to maintain one clear voice in a cluttered marketplace stand the best chance of gaining customer interest and attention as well as developing long-term bonds with all key publics and stakeholders. An effective IMC program helps set the standards and measure performance and, in the end, becomes the model for marketing success for the entire organization.

COMMUNICATING ACROSS CULTURES

Many of the techniques described in this chapter are available worldwide. IMC programs should be assessed in several ways, including: (1) domestic results, (2) results in other countries, and (3) results as an overall organization.

Individual marketing communications mix elements are examined within the countries in which they appear. Due to differing standards regarding message content, they must be evaluated in light of local cultures and purchasing habits.

Many times, marketing communications programs must be assessed across regional or national boundaries. For example, a campaign launched in Europe leads to evaluations in individual countries such as France, Spain, and Italy, but also as a collective, such as the European Union. Measures of attitudes are difficult to collect. Sales are easier to assess due to the use of the Euro in all of these nations; however, inflation rates and other statistics are affected by local conditions.

It may be advisable to contract with local marketing communications agencies to discover which techniques are most viable in other countries. For example, in some nations the use of coupons is seen as a sign of poverty, and users are either secretive or embarrassed about redeeming them. In those situations it is helpful to study results in light of the cultural norms that are present.

Numerous multinational conglomerates assess advertising and promotional efforts through regional offices. For instance, Pacific Rim information will be combined with information from Europe, Africa, and other places. The goal is to make sure an overall image and theme is projected worldwide.

IMC IN PRACTICE

"Years ago we were followers of the philosophy that half of our marketing communications worked, we just didn't know which half," quips Kate Baillie. "We tracked solely on the basis of sales. If we were winning the war for market share, everything was fine. If we weren't, we'd spend more money.

"Now we have a completely different approach. We are still learning which things are important to measure, but we measure most aspects of our marketing communications. At the end of the day, the advertising results that really matter are those related to sales, but we know there are a lot of things that have to happen before we make a sale. So we look to track those things, and understand how our marketing communications can play a role in that process."

Tracking involves aspects related to the overall brand, as well as specific campaigns or executions. "On the brand side we measure things like overall perception of the brand. Do people rate us positively or negatively? Are they aware of our brand, what kind of recall does our brand have, etc.? Then, on the campaign side, we also track to see if individual ads are creating an impact."

Lara Johnson, Director of Marketing Communications, adds a third level of tracking for TELUS marketing communications. "The million dollar question is 'How do you know that a dollar spent in one media wouldn't be better spent in another, or spent in another part of the country, or for another product or service?' We've started working with a company to model this for us. Based on unaided recall surveys taken weekly, we match our media and our competitors to how aware consumers are about the industry's communications."

Television advertising for TELUS creates awareness and brand recall.

Source: Courtesy of TELUS.

Of course, part of the evaluation involves work before marketing communications even get in front of an audience. "We do a lot of pretesting to make sure our marketing communications, once created, will resonate with audiences," says Kate. But the pretesting involves a blend of audience with expertise of the marketing team. "We don't test creative executions—it's a poor use of a focus group to ask them to tell you if they think the font is too big. But we do want people to tell us what the important aspects of our message should be. For example, if we are creating a message for a device, is the operating system more important than some other product attributes? We take measures to evaluate our campaigns even before they are developed, and this helps ensure success throughout the creative and media development. And we do test the attributes of our critters to ensure they are consistent with the message we want to deliver during the campaign."

Source: Used with permission of Kate Baillie, TELUS Communications.

For help developing your IMC Plan, go to **www.pearsoncanada.ca/clow**.

SUMMARY

Assessing an IMC program involves examining the effects of individual marketing communications mix components, such as public relations or media, as well as the overall program. The effectiveness of each individual component can be measured based on the specific objectives of that single component. For example, media advertising can be measured to ensure it is delivering the brand awareness and positioning as intended. The overall IMC program should also be measured to ensure that all the individual components are achieving the overall IMC plan objectives. These measurements are based on both message evaluations and target audience behaviours, depending on the objectives. A wide variety of techniques can be used. Most of the time, marketing managers and advertisement agencies use several different methods in order to get the best picture of a marketing communication's potential for success.

Messages are evaluated both before and after their execution, known as either pre-tests or post-tests. Pre-test evaluations try to understand how a target audience will receive and comprehend the message, and whether the desired outcome is likely to occur. Post-tests seek to measure the actual effectiveness of marketing communications once they are placed in the market.

The guiding principles for any marketing tool include agreement on how test results will be used, pre-establishing a cutoff score for a test's results, using multiple measures, basing studies on models of human behaviours, using multiple exposures, testing marketing instruments that are in the same stage of development, and preventing as many biases as possible while conducting the test. Many times it is difficult for certain members of the marketing team to be objective, especially when they had the idea for the ad or campaign. In these instances, it is better to retain an outside research agency to study the project.

IMC plans are general, overall plans for the entire company. Therefore, more general and long-term criteria should be included in any evaluation of an IMC program. When the IMC theme and voice are clear, the company is achieving its long-range objectives, the principles stated in this book are being applied efficiently and effectively, and the company is in the best position to succeed at all levels, including in all international operations.

KEY TERMS

aided recall A test in which consumers are prompted by being told information such as the product category and, if necessary, names of specific brands to see if they recall an ad.

concept testing An evaluation of the content or concept of the ad and the impact that concept will have on potential customers.

copytests Tests that are used to evaluate a marketing piece that is finished or is in its final stages prior to production.

day-after recall (DAR) Individuals participating in a study are contacted the day after an advertisement appears to see if they remember encountering the ad.

mall intercept technique A test whereby people are stopped in a shopping mall and asked to evaluate a marketing item.

message evaluation techniques Methods used to examine the creative message and the physical design of an advertisement, coupon, or direct marketing piece.

metrics Measures that are designed to accurately portray the effectiveness of a marketing communications plan.

portfolio test A test of an advertisement using a set of print ads, one of which is the ad being evaluated.

positioning advertising copytesting (PACT) Principles to use when assessing the effectiveness of various messages.

psychogalvanometer A device that measures perspiration levels.

psychophysiology A brain-image measurement process.

pupillometric meter A device that measures the dilation of a person's pupils.

recall tests An approach in which an individual is asked to recall ads he or she has viewed in a given time period or setting.

recognition tests A test format in which individuals are given copies of an ad and asked if they recognize it.

respondent behaviour evaluations Methods used to examine visible customer actions, including making store visits, inquiries, or actual purchases.

storyboard A series of still photographs or sketches that outlines the structure of a television ad.

theatre test A test of an advertisement using a set of television ads, including the one being evaluated.

unaided recall A test in which subjects are asked to name, or recall, the ad without any prompts or memory jogs.

warmth monitor A method to measure emotional responses to advertisements.

REVIEW QUESTIONS

1. What is the difference between a message evaluation and respondent behaviours when assessing the effectiveness of marketing communications?

2. What are some typical objectives and related measures for each of the five elements of the marketing communications mix?

3. Name the different types of pre-tests outlined in this chapter.

4. What does a concept test evaluate? How are storyboards and focus groups used in concept tests?

5. Describe the use of portfolio tests and theatre tests in copytesting programs.

6. What is a warmth monitor? What does it measure?

7. Describe how psychogalvanometers, pupillometric meters, and psychophysiology analysis techniques are used in evaluating advertisements.

8. Describe a purchase simulation test.

9. What is DAR? How are aided and unaided recall tests used in conjunction with DAR evaluations? What problems are associated with both types of tests?

10. What is a recognition test? How does it differ from a recall test?

11. Name the different types of post-tests outlined in this chapter.

12. What items can be evaluated using test markets?

13. Name and describe the criteria that can be used to assess the impact of the overall IMC program, as noted in this chapter.

14. What are three reasons why marketing communications are rarely measured, and what are three reasons why this lack of measurement is sustained?

INTEGRATED LEARNING EXERCISES

1. Pick five print or television advertisements that provide website URLs. Visit each site. Was the website a natural extension of the advertisement? What connection or similarities did you see between the website and the advertisement? Do you think your response was tracked? How can you tell?

2. Ipsos Canada (**www.ipsos.ca**) is a research firm specializing in marketing communications. Access the company's products and services. Within the pre-test and post-test phases of marketing communications measurement, what services are offered? How would each be used?

3. Pick out five print advertisements you like. Conduct an aided recall test of these five ads. Ask five individuals, independently, if they saw the ad. Mention only the brand name. If so, ask them to recall, in an unaided fashion, as much about the ad as they can. If they do not remember the ad immediately, give them cues. Be sure to record how much each person

remembers unaided and how much each person remembers with additional information. Report your results. Based on the results of your recall test, do you think the investment behind the print ad was wise? Why or why not?

4. Assume you are the marketing manager for McDonald's. The CEO has asked what the return is from McDonald's yearly Monopoly promotion. Each year the company invests millions of dollars in it, and sales do increase each year during that period. Still, the CEO wonders if the increase is due to seasonality, or if the campaign can achieve the same level of sales increase with a lower investment. As you begin to plan for next year's annual promotion, review the pre-test and post-test options available to you. Pick the priority test for both, before and after the launch. Why did you prioritize those measures? Write a one-page memo to the CEO outlining how your proposed measurement plans will help address her concern.

CREATIVE CORNER

Student Project

After leaders at PepsiCo and Starbucks became concerned about the diminishing supply of fresh, clean water, they teamed together to sell Ethos Water. The product's distribution has expanded and it is now sold in major grocery stores, convenience stores, and drug stores. The goal of Ethos Water is to ensure that children throughout the world have clean water.

Access the Ethos Water website at **www.ethoswater.com**. After reviewing the site, design a print ad for a magazine aimed at college students in your area. When you have finished designing the ad, trade your ad with another student or ask him or her to show it to 10 students not enrolled in a class that is using this textbook. Explain to the student how to conduct a copytest to gather attitudes and opinions about the ad. Before conducting the copytest, make a list of questions that you want to ask. Some suggestions are:

1. Have you ever heard of Ethos Water?

2. What do you think is the primary message of this advertisement?

3. Does the copy make sense? Is it understandable?

4. Does the visual attract your attention?

5. What types of feelings does the ad elicit?

6. How likely would you be to access the Ethos Water website for more information?

7. What is your overall evaluation of the advertisement?

It is important that someone else conduct the copytest for you to gain honest answers. Respondents are less likely to be honest, especially about any negative feedback, if you show them the ad and they know you designed it.

→ ETHICS IN ACTION

What do marketers do when they find that investments in a medium are not producing results? They will withdraw investments from the medium, of course. Many commentators suggest that this is exactly what is happening with television advertising today. The popularity of personal video

recorders (PVRs) and other technologies that allow viewers to skip commercials means that advertisers aren't getting what they paid for—the eyes of viewers. Distractions have always been present—people leave the room when commercials come on, change the channel, or simply ignore the television during commercial breaks.

But skipping the ads completely seems different to some people since it creates selective exposure at a much wider scale than previous consumer behaviours. Indeed, the ability to skip ads is listed as a feature in many campaigns designed to sell PVRs.

One of the tactics used by marketers to avoid the problem, as discussed earlier in this book, is to use product placement to inject brand messages directly into content that cannot be skipped. But when advertisers find that traditional 30-second commercials are no longer being watched, what will they do? The answer, of course, is to stop using television advertising as a medium. The problem is that the advertising they pay for greatly reduces the cost of the entertainment we all enjoy on television. In essence, by completely eliminating the exposure to all television advertising, we are "stealing" the television programming. Although some might be uncomfortable with the harsh term, consider the result of programming theft on a wide scale. One of three results is possible:

a) Increased product placement, to the point that the entertainment largely is there to promote products. If the commercials aired under the CRTC limit were all translated into product placements, the television show would have very few minutes without commercial placements.

b) The cost to view the shows will increase to compensate for the loss of advertising revenue.

c) The content ceases to exist, and the viewer-created entertainment found for free on sites such as YouTube becomes the television programming of the future.

1. Do you feel that skipping advertising using PVRs is unethical? If you see nothing wrong with it, write a letter to the CEO of a television network to convince him or her that the practice is completely ethical. If you do think it is unethical, write a letter to your friends who see nothing wrong with it, explaining your difference in opinion.

2. In what other ways can technology muddy the waters for marketers seeking to measure the performance of marketing communications? As discussed in an earlier chapter, the problem of selective exposure is not limited to television. If you found that your television advertising (or any other form of marketing communications) wasn't meeting its objectives, how would you determine if it's a problem with the message or an exposure problem? ●

CASE STUDY | Measuring Return from Corporate Social Responsibility

Isaac Johnston wasn't sure where to start. Isaac, the Director of Corporate Social Responsibility (CSR) with Vancouver-based mining company MiningCo, had just met with CEO Gloria DePacqueville. Gloria explained that the board of directors, while supportive of the CSR efforts of the firm, was starting to question what the return was from the $5.5 million budget in Isaac's department. "We are looking for budget cuts, and, let's face it, some donations to charities and some ads talking about what a great job we do conserving energy are easy targets for the chopping block," explained Gloria. "What I need from you is a plan to figure out how we can respond. I am behind the CSR effort of this firm, but I need data. I need to report back to the board next month with a solid plan of how we will measure what that $5.5 million is getting us."

CSR at MiningCo had been increasingly funded as a specific department for the past five years. MiningCo began the department in recognition of the significant impacts the company has on the environment and communities in which it operates. The company operates five mines across the Northwest Territories, northern British Columbia, Yukon, and Quebec. All of the mines are in remote parts of these regions, and the local residents are primarily Aboriginal peoples. The company employs 2,500 people across its mining operations and another 275 at the head office in Vancouver. The mines produce mainly copper, which is sold almost exclusively to large industrial buyers in Asia. Revenues last year were $341 million. The budget for the department had grown from only $1 million five years ago to the present $5.5 million.

Isaac had always enjoyed the job because he felt like he got to do some "good" things with his career. He personally saw young aboriginal students being given a chance to attend university through company scholarships. He knew that positive environmental impacts came out of programs he implemented, such as the workplace recycling program at the head office in Vancouver, and he was proud of the work done on the operations side to reduce the environmental footprint of the mining process.

Although he had never sought to measure the effects of these initiatives, Isaac had always built the CSR program with an eye toward impacting various stakeholders of the company—everyone from customers to governments to community groups in the areas where the company mines are located. The logical place for Isaac to start was with a review of the various CSR activities of the company and the potential effects they might have on stakeholders.

The CSR activities in the $5.5 million budget were basically split down the middle. One half included the actual things the company did in its CSR portfolio, such as charity donations and recycling programs. The other half included money allocated to various forms of communicating these initiatives to various key audiences. The money for the donations came out of Isaac's budget, but the cost of the other programs (e.g., recycling program) did not. He developed the following table as a starting point.

For each stakeholder identified, Isaac saw a potential business benefit to the company:

- Governments—issue permits, provide regulation for operations, conduct inspections

- Community groups and activists—lobby governments, encourage protests/provide statements of support

- Employees— boost morale, increase company pride, recruit new employees

Now that Isaac had organized his department, he started to feel better about his task. He was convinced that the CSR activities added value and would be justified through the use of measurement. Still, moving from this starting point to a place where he could articulate why the $5.5 million should be maintained was going to be tough. Taking a break, he walked down to the Starbuck's in the lobby of the building and told himself that he wasn't leaving that night until he figured this thing out.

Source: © Larry Macdougal/MaXximages.com.

MiningCo donates to charities in the local communities where mines are operated.

1. Based on the table above, set precise objectives for each CSR activity. Identify the key stakeholder audience, and what specific things you expect that CSR can change with those audiences.

2. For each objective, lay out a measurement plan to determine if the objectives are being met. Who will be your sample, what will be your key measures, and how will you transform these metrics into financial business performance for the board?

3. Examine the stakeholders identified in the table. Do you think Isaac has forgotten any key stakeholders who should be included?

4. Prepare a 15-minute PowerPoint presentation for the board of directors in which you outline your plan to measure the effects of the CSR activities. Will you recommend keeping all of them going forward, or do you expect some to be "unprofitable"?

CSR Budget Allocation

Activity	Related Communications	Intended Stakeholders
Charity Donations:		
$500,000 to various community groups in each of the five mining areas across four provinces. Total: $2.5 million.	Local newspapers in each community: $100,000 in total *Vancouver Sun* and *The Globe and Mail* print ads: $150,000 Public relations consulting fees (to help gain media coverage): $25,000	Community governments, activist groups, citizens Provincial and national governments, activist groups, citizens
$1 million to fund a yearly scholarship program (in the areas of geology and business) at four colleges and universities in the Vancouver area.	*Vancouver Sun* print ads: $100,000 Campus newspaper print ads: $40,000 Online banner ads—various sites, geo-targeted at Vancouver: $100,000 Public relations consulting fees (to help gain media coverage): $25,000	Potential employees Provincial governments, activist groups
Business Practices:		
Environmental Impact Reduction programs at mines—reduce emissions and waste by 15%	Radio ads on local radio stations near mines: $250,000 total Newspaper ads in local papers: $100,000 total Ads in *Vancouver Sun*: $100,000 Ads in *The Globe and Mail*: $200,000	Governments at all levels, community and activist groups both nationally and internationally (e.g., Greenpeace). Employees
Head Office Recycling Program	Company intranet: $15,000 Newspaper ads in *Vancouver Sun*: $40,000	Employees Activist groups locally
Health and Safety Programs in Mine Operations—designed to reduce workplace injury	Local newspaper and radio ads: $100,000 *Vancouver Sun* and *The Globe and Mail* ads: $200,000	Employees Governments at all levels Activist groups
Overall:		
Annual CSR Report and website	$500,000	All stakeholders mentioned earlier and shareholders

Note: This case study is fictional and any resemblance to real businesses is coincidental. The events of the case study are real; many businesses have gone through similar circumstances.

ENDNOTES

1 Gordon A. Wyner, "Narrowing the Gap," *Marketing Research* 16, no. 1 (Spring 2004), pp. 6–7.

2 Christina Merrill, "Roper Expands Testing," *Adweek Eastern Edition* 37, no. 45 (November 4, 1996), p. 6.

3 Ibid.

4 Stefano Hatfield, "Testing on Trial," *Creativity* 11, no. 9 (October 2003), pp. 18–21.

5 David W. Stewart, David H. Furse, and Randall P. Kozak, "A Guide to Commercial Copytesting Services," in James Leigh and Claude Martin, Jr., eds. *Current Issues and Research in Advertising* (Ann Arbor: Division of Research, Graduate School of Business, University of Michigan, 1983), pp. 1–44.

6 Steven P. Brown and Douglas M. Stayman, "Antecedents and Consequences of Attitude Toward the Ad: A Meta-Analysis," *Journal of Consumer Research* 19 (June 1992), pp. 34–51.

7 Douglas M. Stayman and David A. Aaker, "Continuous Measurement of Self-Report or Emotional Response," *Psychology and Marketing* 10 (May–June 1993), pp. 199–214.

8 Freddie Campos, "UH Facility Test Ads for $500," *Pacific Business News* 35, no. 23 (August 18, 1997), pp. A1–A2.

9 Patricia Riedman, "DiscoverWhy Tests TV Commercials Online," *Advertising Age* 71, no. 13 (March 27, 2000), pp. 46–47.

10 Bruce F. Hall, "On Measuring the Power of Communications," *Journal of Advertising Research* 44, no. 2 (June 2004), pp. 181–88.

11 Steve Mclellan, "Mind Over Matter: New Tools Put Brands in Touch with Feelings," *Adweek* (**www.adweek.com**, February 18, 2008).

12 Hall, "On Measuring the Power of Communications."

13 Tim Triplett, "Researchers Probe Ad Effectiveness Globally," *Marketing News* 28, no. 18 (August 29, 1994), pp. 6–7.

14 David W. Stewart, "Measures, Methods, and Models in Advertising Research," *Journal of Advertising* 29, no. 3 (1989), pp. 54–60.

15 Abhilasha Mehta, "Advertising Attitudes and Advertising Effectiveness," *Journal of Advertising Research* 40, no. 3 (May–June 2000), pp. 67–72.

16 William D. Wells, "Recognition, Recall, and Rating Scales," *Journal of Advertising Research* 40, no. 6 (November–December 2000), pp. 14–20.

17 Joel S. Debow, "Advertising Recognition and Recall by Age—Including Teens," *Journal of Advertising Research* 35, no. 5 (September–October 1995), pp. 55–60.

18 William D. Wells, "Recognition, Recall, and Rating Scales," *Journal of Advertising Research* 40, no. 6 (November–December 2000), pp. 14–20.

19 Jan Stapel, "Recall and Recognition: A Very Close Relationship," *Journal of Advertising Research* 38, no. 4 (July–August 1998), pp. 41–45.

20 William D. Wells, "Recognition, Recall, and Rating Scales," *Journal of Advertising Research* 40, no. 6 (November–December 2000), pp. 14–20.

21 Stapel, "Recall and Recognition."

22 Amanda Beeler, "POPAI Initiates Study Tracking Effectiveness of Displays," *Advertising Age* 71, no. 15 (April 10, 2000), p. 54.

23 Chris Dillabough, "Web Lets Canadian Tourism Test Media Effectiveness," *New Media Age* (October 31, 2002), p. 12.

24 Kate MacArthur, "McDonald's Tests Ads That Focus on Service," *Advertising Age* 74, no. 1 (January 6, 2003), p. 3.

25 Based on PACT document published in *Journal of Marketing* 11, no. 4 (1982), pp. 4–29.

26 Benjamin Lipstein and James P. Neelankavil, "Television Advertising Copy Research: A Critical Review of the State of the Art," *Journal of Advertising Research* 24 (no. 2, 1984), pp. 19–25.

27 Gerard J. Tellis, *Effective Advertising*, 2004, Sage Publishing, Thousand Oaks.

28 Ibid.

29 Paul J. Cough, "Study: Marketers Struggle to Measure Effectiveness," *Shoot* 45, no. 29 (August 20, 2004), pp. 7–8.

30 Peter Drucker, *Management: Tasks, Responsibilities, Practices* (New York: Harper & Row, 1974).

Name/Organization Index